The Lambeth Conference

The Lambeth Conference

Theology, History, Polity and Purpose

Edited by Paul Avis and Benjamin M. Guyer

t&tclark

LONDON · NEW YORK · OXFORD · NEW DELHI · SYDNEY

T&T CLARK
Bloomsbury Publishing Plc
50 Bedford Square, London, WC1B 3DP, UK
1385 Broadway, New York, NY 10018, USA

BLOOMSBURY, T&T CLARK and the T&T Clark logo
are trademarks of Bloomsbury Publishing Plc

First published 2017
Paperback edition first published in 2019

A catalogue record for this book is available from the British Library.

Library of Congress Cataloging-in-Publication Data
Names: Avis, Paul D. L., editor. | Guyer, Benjamin, editor.
Title: The Lambeth Conference: theology, history, polity and purpose /
edited by Paul Avis and Benjamin M. Guyer.
Description: New York: Bloomsbury T&T Clark, An imprint of Bloomsbury
Publishing Plc, 2017. | Includes bibliographical references and index.
Identifiers: LCCN 2017032159| ISBN 9780567662316 (hb) |
ISBN 9780567662330 (epdf)
Subjects: LCSH: Lambeth Conference. | Anglican Communion.
Classification: LCC BX5021.L5 L36 2017 | DDC 262/.53–dc23

ISBN: HB: 978-0-5676-6231-6
PB: 978-0-5676-8917-7
ePDF: 978-0-5676-6233-0
ePub: 978-0-5676-6232-3

Typeset by Deanta Global Publishing Services, Chennai, India

To find out more about our authors and books visit
www.bloomsbury.com and sign up for our newsletters.

Contents

Foreword: The Archbishop of Canterbury

I am very grateful to Paul Avis and Ben Guyer for bringing together this important collection of essays. It is of course timely as we approach the next Lambeth Conference.

I was struck by this sentence in the editors' preface to the book: 'We hope and pray that these chapters will communicate – and, more importantly, re-inspire – some of the faith, dedication and utterly infectious joy that the Lambeth Conference has generated over the last 150 years.'

I pray that the Lambeth Conference in 2020 will indeed be an opportunity for expressing faith, dedication and utterly infectious joy. It is of course only with the crucial aid of reflecting back on what has happened that we can begin to move forward and make sense of what is happening in the present.

I therefore commend this book of essays and hope that others will read them carefully as a preparation for further reflection on the Lambeth Conference and its part in the complex web of relationship in the Anglican Communion.

$+$ Justin

The Most Reverend and Right Honourable Justin Welby

Editorial Preface

This volume of scholarly studies is being published 150 years after the first Lambeth Conference of Anglican bishops in 1867. The Conference that will convene in 2020 will be the fifteenth in the series. The last major study of the Lambeth Conference, Alan M. G. Stephenson's *Anglicanism and the Lambeth Conferences*, was published forty years ago.[1] Much has happened in Anglicanism since then; a fresh, thorough and comprehensive account is overdue. Surveying a range of historical, theological and constitutional topics, these essays collectively lay the foundations for future scholarship on the Lambeth Conference as a major institution of the Anglican Communion.

The first Lambeth Conference was a new departure for the world's Anglicans. That conference was not intended as the first Lambeth Conference – no sequel was envisaged at the time. However, bishops and laity found the 1867 meeting both electrifying and inspiring, and within a few years of its conclusion, there were calls for another such conference. From 1878 until 2008, the Lambeth Conference took place every ten years. There were only three exceptions during this 130-year period. The fourth Lambeth Conference was held in 1897 rather than 1898 so that all Anglican bishops might gather together in commemoration of the 1,300th anniversary of St. Augustine's missionary venture into England.[2] The two world wars inevitably brought about considerable disruption: the 1918 Conference was pushed back to 1920, and the 1940 Conference was delayed until 1948. But with the practice of decennial gatherings already set, in the post-war period the Conferences met without fail each decade for the next sixty years.

Given this pattern, the next Conference should have taken place in 2018. But the Anglican Communion is not what it once was. Bonds of affection have, in some places, been replaced with fetters of discord; matters of long-standing consensus have become topics of acrimonious debate. Nonetheless, as the

---

[1] Alan M. G. Stephenson, *Anglicanism and the Lambeth Conferences* (London: SPCK, 1978). See also id., *The First Lambeth Conference, 1867* (London: SPCK, 1967).

[2] Stephenson, *Anglicanism and the Lambeth Conferences*, p. 94.

chapters in this book show, with 150 years of history and attendant influence, the Lambeth Conference is a defining feature of modern Anglicanism. Because of its institutional nature, the Lambeth Conference is best spoken of in the singular, as an enduring reality. Anglicans refer not to 'the Lambeth Conferences' (plural), but to 'the Lambeth Conference' (singular), specifying only the year in which it took place (e.g. 'the Lambeth Conference 1920' or 'the 1920 Lambeth Conference'). As with every institution, the membership changes from one meeting to another, but as with a Parliament or Congress, the meetings of the Lambeth Conference are not one-off events. The whole is greater than the sum of its parts.

The Lambeth Conference is often described as one of the Anglican Communion's four Instruments of Communion. The other three are the office and ministry of the Archbishop of Canterbury, the incumbent for the time being of the oldest Primatial See of the English Church; the Primates' Meeting, which consists of the senior archbishop or metropolitan of each member church of the Communion and the Anglican Consultative Council (ACC), the only body that is both governed by a constitution and made up of representatives who are not ex officio, but elected or appointed by each member church. It is no exaggeration to claim that the Lambeth Conference has done more than any other Anglican 'Instrument' to create and facilitate the modern Anglican Communion. In the light of current debate and dissension, it is especially important that Anglicans and their ecumenical partners have a clear understanding of the role played by the Lambeth Conference in this regard. False memories die the slowest of deaths; partisan historical narratives are often the handmaidens of long-lasting ecclesial division. Discord must not be allowed to occlude the deep historical and theological roots that all Anglicans share.

The Lambeth Conference has played a decisive role in shaping and even creating the other three Instruments of Communion. The ACC came into existence in 1968, when the Lambeth Conference of that same year passed Resolution 69. The wording of that resolution is important; the ACC was not created by fiat, but by mediating a request to the provinces of the Anglican Communion: 'The Conference accepts and endorses the appended proposals concerning the Anglican Consultative Council and its Constitution and submits them to the member Churches of the Anglican Communion for approval.' The

resolution specified that approval would come 'by a two-thirds majority' sent
to the Lambeth Consultative Body (LCB), and further specified the contents
of the ACC's constitution and its schedule of membership. Resolution 69
indicated no possibility that non-approval by a province necessarily excluded
that province from continued membership; rather, the minority would be
bound by the decision of the majority. Spurred by the Lambeth Conference,
the Anglican Communion's provinces approved the creation of the ACC,
which held its first meeting in Limuru, Kenya, in 1971.

The ACC is not the only body that the Lambeth Conference has helped
bring to birth. The LCB was created by the 1897 Lambeth Conference and
formed so that 'resort may be had, if desired, by the national Churches,
provinces, and extra-provincial dioceses of the Anglican Communion either
for information or for advice, and that the Archbishop of Canterbury be
requested to take such steps as he may think most desirable for the creation
of this consultative body'.[3] The 1930 Lambeth Conference further specified
that the LCB should 'be prepared to advise on questions of faith, order, policy
or administration', and, more importantly, begin the work of normalizing its
membership, requiring that it 'should consist of not less than 18 members'.[4]
The LCB continues to exist as an ad hoc group, advising the Archbishop
of Canterbury on matters pertaining to the Lambeth Conference, but the
ACC has taken over duties pertaining to policy and administration, and
to a lesser extent, faith and order. The creation of both the LCB and the
ACC are abiding testaments to the importance of the Lambeth Conference,
and to its capacity for authoritative suasion in leading the wider Anglican
Communion.

Although the Lambeth Conference did not create the other two
Instruments of Communion, it shaped them decisively. The Lambeth
Conference very much recreated the Archbishopric of Canterbury as an
episcopal see of international import. By the late nineteenth century, a
synergistic relationship had developed between the Lambeth Conference and
the Archbishop of Canterbury. When Archbishop Charles Thomas Longley
endorsed the 1865 Canadian proposal for convening an international synod
of Anglican bishops, he took on the responsibility of issuing personal

³ LC 1897, Res. 5.
⁴ LC 1930, Res. 50.

invitations to each Anglican bishop. All later Archbishops of Canterbury have followed Longley in this regard. This gives Canterbury a position of unparalleled influence in shaping global Anglicanism. Importantly, Archbishop Longley set a precedent in a second way by not inviting the South African Bishop John Colenso, whose theology had been condemned as heterodox by every provincial Anglican body then in existence. Invitations to the Lambeth Conference are not a foregone conclusion. The prestige accorded through the Lambeth Conference to the Archbishop of Canterbury enabled Archbishop Donald Coggan to create the Primates' Meeting, the fourth Instrument of Communion, in 1978.

The nomenclature 'Instruments of Communion' points to an imperative and priority for the Anglican Communion in recent times – to hold together. The Anglican Communion will not last if it settles for merely pragmatic political ties and props in order to avoid falling apart. If it is to have a meaningful quality of communion, the Anglican Communion must cultivate an ecclesial character and quality expressible in a globally interchangeable ordained ministry, the exercise of episcopal collegiality, a common sacramental life and structures for consultation and discernment, arriving at a common mind on all essential matters. This includes, but is not limited to, recognizing in one another biblical fidelity and creedal orthodoxy. Our communion as Anglicans must instantiate the biblical notion of *koinonia*, sharing and participating together in a reality greater than ourselves. That reality is the realm of the grace of God, mediated to us through the saving work of the Lord Jesus Christ and energized by the power of the Holy Spirit. The whole is greater than the sum of its parts.

The Anglican Communion is a communion of churches. It is not constituted as a global church with a common set of liturgies or a unified canon law. The Anglican Communion does have shared, international structures of governance and guidance – the Instruments of Communion – but liturgies, disciplinary procedures and official policies on many matters are administered at the provincial or local level. Because of shared historical roots in the Church of England, there are strong family resemblances between the liturgies, laws and structures of governance of member churches. The ideal balance between local autonomy and international communion is best encapsulated by the phrase 'Mutual Responsibility and Interdependence'

(MRI), which dates from the 1963 Anglican Congress in Toronto, Canada. The Lambeth Conference is nothing if not a collective episcopal commitment to this very principle.

We hope and pray that these chapters will communicate – and, more importantly, re-inspire – some of the faith, dedication and utterly infectious joy that the Lambeth Conference has generated over the last 150 years. More specifically, as we told contributors, the purpose of our book is fourfold:

1. to affirm the strategic importance of the Lambeth Conference as an enduring institution of the Anglican Communion, marking its first 150 years of existence, while also attempting to raise its public profile both within the Communion and ecumenically;
2. to provide a range of scholarly in-depth resources – historical, ecclesiological, ecumenical and constitutional – to serve as background preparatory material for the next Lambeth Conference and those that will follow, by informing and resourcing the participants – the bishops of the Anglican Communion and the many ecumenical observers – and all others who will follow the course of the Conference closely and be affected by its outcomes;
3. to provide scholarly resources and tools for any and all persons who are or will be engaged in academic research into the history, theology, polity and influence of Anglicanism, such as journalists, scholars, teachers of Anglican studies, clergy and church commentators;
4. to promote and assist the revival of Anglican theology, ecclesiology, polity and historical self-understanding more broadly, setting contemporary Anglican theology and practice upon the firm foundation of the Anglican inheritance of faith, in subordination to Holy Scripture and the ecumenical creeds, as 'our inspiration and guidance under God'.

Accordingly, this book falls into two parts. The first consists of studies that deal with the history, theology, constitution and purpose of the Lambeth Conference. The second, shorter, part consists of more individual, personal and pastoral perspectives concerning the Lambeth Conference and Anglicanism more generally. History studies the past, but tradition strives to preserve something of it. Tradition is a value judgement; it is not the fullness of the past, but a consciously cultivated continuity that links select elements from prior ages with our own time. The Lambeth Conference has bequeathed a legacy in which there is much to celebrate and give thanks for. Its tradition is worth cultivating.

We are most grateful to all of the contributors, who have given of their time and talents and shared their scholarship and insights. We also thank the Archbishop of Canterbury, the Most Reverend and Right Honourable Justin Welby, for agreeing to contribute a foreword to this book.

Paul Avis
Church of England

Benjamin M. Guyer
The Episcopal Church (USA)

Contributors

Paul Avis spent twenty-three years in parish ministry and was then General Secretary of the Council for Christian Unity of the Church of England, 1998–2011, and Theological Consultant to the Anglican Communion Office, 2011–12 where he produced *Becoming a Bishop: A Theological Handbook of Episcopal Ministry* (Bloomsbury T&T Clark) for the bishops of the Anglican Communion. Paul has been a Chaplain to HM Queen Elizabeth II, honorary professor in the Department of Theology and Religion, University of Exeter, and consecutively Prebendary, Sub Dean and Canon Theologian of Exeter Cathedral. He has been a senior inspector of theological colleges and courses since 1998 and serves on the Inter-Anglican Standing Commission on Unity, Faith and Order. He is currently an honorary research Fellow, Department of Theology and Religion, University of Exeter, and honorary professor in the Department of Theology and Religion, University of Durham; editor-in-chief of *Ecclesiology* and editor of the *Anglican-Episcopal Theology and History* series published by Brill. Among his books are several on Anglicanism: *Anglicanism and the Christian Church: Historical Resources in Theological Perspective* (revised edition 2002), *The Identity of Anglicanism: Essentials of Anglican Identity* (2008), *The Vocation of Anglicanism* (2016), all published by Bloomsbury T&T Clark, and *The Anglican Understanding of the Church: An Introduction*, published by SPCK. He has written on conciliarity in *Beyond the Reformation: Authority, Primacy and Unity in the Conciliar Tradition* (T&T Clark, 2006). He is also the editor of the *Oxford Handbook of Ecclesiology* (Oxford University Press, 2017). Paul serves as an honorary assistant priest in the Axminster group of parishes, Diocese of Exeter.

Alyson Barnett-Cowan is the President of the Canadian Council of Churches. A priest in the Anglican Church of Canada, she served as Director for Faith, Worship and Ministry and as Ecumenical Officer for the Anglican Church of Canada and then as Director for Unity Faith and Order for the Anglican Communion and was Interim Secretary General in 2015. Alyson is a canon of St Matteo's Cathedral in the Diocese of Brandon (Canada) and holds four honorary doctorates. She served as coopted staff for the ecumenical work of both the 1998 and 2008 Lambeth Conferences.

Donald Bolen is currently the Roman Catholic Archbishop of Regina in Saskatchewan, Canada. He had formerly served as Bishop of the Diocese of Saskatoon, from 2010 to 2016. Ordained a priest for the Archdiocese of Regina in October, 1991, he was assigned to pastoral ministry, taught Religious Studies at Campion College at the University of Regina, and began doctoral work on the Anglican-Roman Catholic International Commission (ARCIC). In 2001, he was asked to work at the Pontifical Council for Promoting Christian Unity in Rome, serving as the staff person for the Catholic Church's relations with the Anglican Communion and World Methodist Council. From 2001 to 2008 he served as co-secretary for ARCIC, and for the International Anglican-Roman Catholic Commission for Unity and Mission (IARCCUM). Archbishop Bolen is currently a Member of the Pontifical Council for the Promotion of Christian Unity, Co-Chair of IARCCUM, and Co-Chair of the Canadian Anglican-Roman Catholic Theological Dialogue. He served as the Co-Chair of the Joint International Commission for Dialogue between the World Methodist Council and the Catholic Church (2013–16) and as a member of the International Consultation between the Catholic Church and the World Evangelical Alliance (2009–16). Don has written and lectured extensively in the field of ecumenism.

Gregory Kenneth Cameron is the Bishop of St Asaph in the Church in Wales. He holds degrees in Theology and Christian Doctrine from the Universities of Cambridge and Wales, and a degree in Canon Law from the University of Wales. Prior to his election as Bishop, he worked from 2003 to 2009 as the Deputy Secretary General of the Anglican Communion and Director of Ecumenical Affairs, in which role he served the ecumenical conversations of the Communion, and was Secretary to many of the Anglican Communion Commissions set up during his period of office. He participated in all of the bilateral dialogues of the Communion, and was also appointed as Secretary successively to the Lambeth Commission on Communion, which produced *the Windsor Report*, the Reception Reference Group, the Covenant Design Group and the Windsor Continuation Group. Gregory is currently Anglican Co-Chair of the Anglican Oriental Orthodox Dialogue.

Mark Chapman is Vice-Principal and Academic Dean of Ripon College Cuddesdon, Oxford, Professor of the History of Modern Theology in the University of Oxford, and Canon Theologian of Truro Cathedral, as well as assistant priest in three rural churches in Oxfordshire. He is currently a member of the General Synod of the Church of England and is vice chair of the Ecclesiological Investigations International Research Network. He has published widely in many different areas of theology and church history. His most recent books are *Theology and Society in Three Cities: Berlin, Oxford and Chicago, 1800-1914* (Cambridge: James Clarke, 2014), *The Fantasy of Reunion: Anglicans, Catholics, and Ecumenism, 1833-1880* (Oxford University Press, 2014) and *Anglican Theology* (T&T Clark, 2012). Mark's other books include *Anglicanism: A Very Short Introduction* (Oxford University Press, 2006). He is the editor or co-editor of several works, including the *Oxford Handbook of Anglican Studies* (Oxford University Press, 2015).

Richard Deadman read Theology at the University of Exeter and Canon Law (LLM) at the Cardiff Law School. He has served as an assistant and collaborator to Professor Norman Doe. Richard is currently the Vicar of Saint Matthew's, Newcastle.

Norman Doe, DCL (Lambeth) and LLD (Cambridge), is a professor of law at Cardiff University and Director there of the Centre for Law and Religion. His books include *Fundamental Authority in Late Medieval English Law* (1990) and *Christian Law* (2013), both published by Cambridge University Press; *The Legal Framework of the Church of England* (1996), *Canon Law in the Anglican Communion* (1998) and *Law and Religion in Europe* (2011), published by Oxford University Press. He contributed to 'A Statement of Principles of Christian Law', issued by the Christian Law Panel of Experts (Rome 2013–16). He has also written *An Anglican Covenant* (Canterbury Press, 2008). A visiting professor at Paris University and KU Leuven, Norman was visiting fellow at Trinity College Oxford (2011) and visiting scholar at Corpus Christi College Oxford (2015), founding member of the Colloquium of Anglican and Roman Catholic Canon Lawyers (1999), and acted as a consultant on canon law to the Anglican Communion, including the project which led to *The Principles of Canon Law Common to the Churches of the Anglican Communion* (2008), served on the Lambeth Commission (2003–4), and is Chancellor of the

Diocese of Bangor. He is director of the LLM in Canon Law at Cardiff Law School which he set up in 1991.

Andrew Goddard is a Senior Research Fellow at the Kirby Laing Institute for Christian Ethics, an ordained Anglican based at St James the Less, Pimlico and the Lancelot Andrewes Honorary Canon of Winchester Cathedral. He is also Adjunct Assistant Professor of Anglican Studies, Fuller Theological Seminary where he teaches Anglican History and Polity. Andrew has written on Anglican discussions on sexuality, the Anglican Communion and the Anglican Covenant online for the Anglican Communion Institute and Fulcrum, and as a contributor to *The Wiley-Blackwell Companion to the Anglican Communion*, *The Oxford Handbook of Anglican Studies, Pro Communione: Theological Essays on the Anglican Covenant*, and *The Anglican Covenant*.

Benjamin M. Guyer is Lecturer in the Department of History and Philosophy at the University of Tennessee Martin. He gained his doctorate from the University of Kansas. He has published in *The Sixteenth Century Journal* and *The Living Church*, and is the editor of *The Beauty of Holiness: The Caroline Divines and Their Writings* (Canterbury Press, 2012) and *Pro Communione: Theological Essays on the Anglican Covenant* (Wipf and Stock, 2012).

Victoria Matthews was ordained to each of the three orders of ministry in the Diocese of Toronto in the Anglican Church of Canada. She has served as Bishop Suffragan of Toronto (1994–7), Diocesan Bishop of the Diocese of Edmonton, Canada (1997-2007) and Bishop in Residence of Wycliffe College, Toronto (2008). Since 2008 she has been Bishop of Christchurch in the Anglican Church in Aotearoa, New Zealand and Polynesia. She was a member of the Communications Committee of Lambeth 1998 as well as serving on the Planning Group for that Lambeth Conference. During the 2008 Lambeth Conference she was a member of the Windsor Report Continuation Group which addressed the Lambeth Conference on three occasions. Victoria is a member of the Inter-Anglican Standing Commission on Unity, Faith and Order. Her academic degrees in theology and divinity are from Trinity College at the University of Toronto and Yale University.

Charlotte Methuen is Professor of Church History at the University of Glasgow and an Anglican priest. Her research focuses in three main areas: the Reformation, the Ecumenical Movement, and the history of women's ministry.

She has published a number of articles exploring the Church of England's ecumenical relationships in the aftermath of the First World War, and is preparing a monograph on George Bell and the Ecumenical Movement, 1918–1937. Before moving to Glasgow, Charlotte taught Liturgy and Church History at Ripon College Cuddesdon, and Church History at Oxford University. She has also taught Church History at the Universities of Bochum and Hamburg, in Germany. Her study of the history of ecumenism is rooted in her experience of living and teaching in Germany as well as England and Scotland. She is a member of the Inter-Church Relations Committee of the Scottish Episcopal Church and of the Inter-Anglican Standing Commission on Unity, Faith and Order of the Anglican Communion. She has also served on the Church of England's Faith and Order Commission; the Meissen Commission, which oversees relations between the Church of England and the German Protestant Church; and the Anglican Lutheran International Commission.

Jeremy Morris is Master of Trinity Hall, Cambridge, and an Affiliated Lecturer in the Faculty of Divinity. An Anglican priest, he was previously Dean of Chapel of King's College, Cambridge, Dean of Trinity Hall, and Vice-Principal of Westcott House, Cambridge. For many years he was a member of the Faith and Order Group, and then of the Faith and Order Commission, of the Church of England. He is Director of the Archbishop's Examination in Theology. Jeremy is a specialist in modern religious history, including the Anglican tradition, the Ecumenical Movement and arguments about secularization. His books include *F. D. Maurice and the Crisis of Christian Authority* (Oxford University Press, 2005), *The Church in the Modern Age* (I. B. Tauris, 2007), *The High Church Revival in the Church of England: Arguments and Identities* (Brill, 2016), and, as editor, *The Oxford History of Anglicanism, Vol. 4: Global Western Anglicanism c.1910-2000* (Oxford University Press, 2017). His current research project is a history of the Eucharist in Western Europe since 1800.

Martyn Percy is Dean of Christ Church, Oxford, one of Oxford's largest colleges. Christ Church is also the Cathedral Church of the Diocese of Oxford. From 2004 to 2014 he was Principal of Ripon College Cuddesdon. Martyn is a member of the Faculty of Theology at the University of Oxford, and tutors in the Social Sciences Division and the Saïd Business School of the University of Oxford. He is also Professor of Theological Education at King's College

London and Professorial Research Fellow at Heythrop College, University of London. Since 2017 he has been a visiting professor at the Centre for the Study of Values, University of Winchester. Martyn writes and teaches on Christianity and contemporary culture, modern ecclesiology and contextual and pastoral theology. His recent books include *Anglicanism: Confidence, Commitment and Communion* (Ashgate, 2013), *The Futures of Anglicanism: Currents, Contours, Charts* (Routledge, 2017) and *Thirty-Nine New Articles: An Anglican Landscape of Faith* (Canterbury Press, 2014). He is a co-editor of the *Oxford Handbook of Anglican Studies* (Oxford University Press, 2015).

Stephen Pickard is Executive Director of the Australian Centre for Christianity and Culture; Director of the Strategic Research Centre in Public and Contextual Theology and Professor of Theology, Charles Sturt University, Canberra, Australia. He has served as a Bishop for the past decade and is currently an Assistant Bishop in the Anglican Diocese of Canberra and Gouburn. He has undertaken a range of ministerial and academic appointments over three decades in Australia and the United Kingdom. Stephen is deputy chair of the Inter-Anglican Standing Commission on Unity, Faith and Order; Chair of the Ministry and Mission Commission of the Anglican Church of Australia, and a Six Preacher at Canterbury Cathedral. His teaching, writing and research is in the area of ecclesiology, ministry and mission and his publications include *Theological Foundations for Collaborative Ministry* (Ashgate 2009); *In-Between God: Theology, Community and Discipleship* (AFT 2011); and *Seeking the Church: An Introduction to Ecclesiology* (SCM, 2012).

Ephraim Radner is Professor of Historical Theology at Wycliffe College at the University of Toronto. An Anglican priest and former missionary in Burundi, he has also served in several parishes of the Episcopal Church. He is the author of several books on ecclesiology: *The End of the Church* (Eerdmans, 1998), *A Brutal Unity: The Spiritual Politics of the Christian Church* (Baylor University Press, 2012); Anglicanism: *The Fate of Communion: The Agony of Anglicanism and the Future of a Global Church* (with Philip Turner; Eerdmans, 2006); hermeneutics: *Time and the Word: Figural Reading of the Christian Scriptures* (Eerdmans, 2016); and Christian anthropology: *A Time to Keep: Theology, Mortality, and the Shape of a Human Life* (Baylor 2016).

Cathy Ross is Tutor in Contextual Theology at Ripon College Cuddesdon, MA Coordinator for Pioneer Leadership Training at CMS (Church Mission Society) and Lecturer in Mission at Regent's Park College, Oxford. She comes from Aotearoa/NZ. Until mid-2010 she managed the Crowther Centre for Mission Education at CMS, and was the J. V. Taylor Fellow in Missiology at Regent's Park College, Oxford. She is also the General Secretary of the International Association for Mission Studies. She has previously worked in Rwanda, Congo and Uganda with NZCMS. Her recent publications include: *Women with a Mission: Rediscovering Missionary Wives in Early New Zealand* (Auckland: Penguin, 2006); *Mission in the 21st Century: Exploring the Five Marks of Global Mission* (ed. with Andrew Walls; London: Darton, Longman and Todd, 2008); *Life-Widening Mission: Global Anglican Perspectives* (Oxford: Regnum, 2012); *Mission in Context* (with John Corrie; Ashgate, 2012); *The Pioneer Gift* (with Jonny Baker; London: SCM, 2014); *Mission on the Road to Emmaus,* (with Steve Bevans; London: SCM, 2015) and *Pioneering Spirituality* (with Jonny Baker; London: SCM, 2015). Her research interests are in the areas of contextual theologies, World Christianity, feminist theologies and hospitality.

Mary Tanner taught Old Testament at Hull and Bristol Universities and Westcott House, Cambridge. She served as the General Secretary of the Church of England's Council for Christian Unity 1991–8. She was a member of the Faith and Order Commission of the World Council of Churches from 1973 and its Moderator 1991–8. From 2007 to 2013 she was President for Europe of the World Council of Churches. She has also been a member of the Anglican-Roman Catholic International Commission (ARCIC) and of a number of European conversations. Within the Anglican Communion Mary was a member of the Archbishop of Canterbury's Commission on Women and the Episcopate, the International Theological and Doctrinal Commission and the Windsor Continuation Group. She was a consultant to the ecumenical sections of the 1988 and 1998 Lambeth Conferences and acted as Ecumenical Dean for the Archbishop of Canterbury at the 2008 Conference. She has been a visiting professor at the General Seminary, New York, the Tantur Ecumenical Institute, Jerusalem, and the Pontifical University of St Thomas Aquinas in Rome. She has published extensively on Anglican and ecumenical matters. She is a Lay Canon Emeritus of Guildford Cathedral and was made a Dame of the British Empire by HM Queen Elizabeth II.

Mark D. Thompson is the Principal of Moore Theological College in Sydney, Australia, and the head of its Theology, Philosophy and Ethics department. He is an ordained Anglican in the Diocese of Sydney, a member of its synod and Standing Committee, a canon of St Andrew's Cathedral and the chair of the Sydney Diocesan Doctrine Commission. He is also a member of the General Synod of the Anglican Church of Australia and a member of its Doctrine Commission. He has been from its foundation a member of the GAFCON Theological Resource Group and attended both GAFCON I (Jerusalem, 2008) and GAFCON II (Nairobi, 2013). He holds degrees from Macquarie University, the Australian College of Theology and Oxford University. His DPhil was awarded for a thesis on the relationship between authority and interpretation in Martin Luther's approach to Scripture. He is the author of numerous books and articles on the doctrines of Scripture, the Trinity, Christology, and justification by faith, including *A Clear and Present Word: The Clarity of Scripture* (Leicester: IVP, 2006).

Part One

Theological, Historical and Constitutional Studies

The Lambeth Conference Among the Instruments of Communion

Stephen Pickard

'For peace and charity': Anglican episcopal collegiality

In Archbishop Charles Longley's opening address to the first Lambeth Conference in 1867 he said: 'It has never been contemplated that we should assume the functions of a general synod of all the churches in full communion with the Church of England, and take upon ourselves to enact canons that should be binding.' Similarly, in connection with the 1878 Conference, Archbishop Tait ruled out any attempt to define doctrine.[1] What Longley and Tait were seeking to guard against was any suggestion that the Conference might assume the role of a *magisterium* that would issue decrees of a doctrinal nature, which Anglicans throughout the world would be required to accept.[2]

The invitation extended in 1867 to those bishops in visible communion with the United Church of England and Ireland was for the purpose of communion, conference and consultation. Longley's hope was that this 'would greatly tend to maintain practically the Unity of the Faith, while they would bind us in straighter [= straiter] bonds of peace and brotherly charity'.[3] For 'peace and charity' the bishops of the emerging communion of churches in fellowship

---

[1] R. T. Davidson, *The Origin and History of the Lambeth Conferences of 1867 and 1878* (London: SPCK, 1888), p. 18.

[2] *Towards a Symphony of Instruments: An Historical and Theological Consideration of the Instruments of Communion of the Anglican Communion*, A Working Paper of the Inter-Anglican Standing Commission on Unity, Faith and Order (IASCUFO); Unity Faith and Order Paper No. 1, for the Anglican Consultative Council, Auckland, 2013 (ACC15), para. 2.3.1. Hereinafter, *Symphony of Instruments*, IASCUFO. *http://www.anglicancommunion.org/media/209979/Towards-a-Symphony-of-Instruments-Web-Version.pdf*

[3] A. M. G. Stephenson, *The First Lambeth Conference 1867* (London: SPCK, 1967), pp. 187–8.

with the ancient See of Canterbury, presided over by the Archbishop of Canterbury, would seek common counsel on matters of faith, order and life in the context of prayer and worship.

The idea that such a gathering might constitute an 'instrument of unity' would no doubt have seemed odd for an Anglican Communion in its infancy.[4] The express desire was to share a deeper episcopal collegiality occasioned by a number of tensions and controversies in the churches.[5] It took well over a century after the first Lambeth Conference for the invention of the concept 'instruments of unity'. And in the past thirty years a further two 'instruments of unity' have been added to complement the Lambeth Conference. The status of the See of Canterbury as an instrument of unity is a subject of discussion though the weight of opinion seems to regard it as one of the instruments.[6]

Since the first Lambeth Conference there has been a remarkable expansion of the fellowship of churches in communion with the See of Canterbury. In response to the increasing complexity of the Anglican Communion, additional structures and mechanisms have been created to facilitate conversation, counsel and communion. The relationships between these different but related instruments have been at times tense and on other occasions remarkably life-giving to the Communion and its mission. After 150 years of Lambeth Conferences a number of questions arise. How might we understand the Lambeth Conference among the Instruments of Communion? How might the 'peace and charity' of the Anglican Communion be advanced by Anglican Bishops meeting together at the Lambeth Conference? How might this gathering serve the Gospel of God and the whole church?

The invention of the instruments of unity

The appeal to 'instruments of unity' is a relatively recent invention in response to a complex political ecclesiastical reality. It is true that Archbishop Longley envisaged the Lambeth Conference as a means to unity and communion; a

---

4   It seems that the term 'Anglican Communion' was first used in 1847. See C. J. Podmore, *Aspects of Anglican Identity* (London: Church House Publishing, 2005), chapter 3.

5   *Symphony of Instruments*, IASCUFO, para. 16–17.

6   *Symphony of Instruments*, IASCUFO; see discussion in paras. 3.3.3–3.3.7.

role that was also envisaged for the Archbishop of Canterbury. In this sense both the Lambeth Conference and the See of Canterbury are not 'inventions'. However, the modern deployment of the language of 'instrument' for both these 'means' of unity and communion, and the subsequent application of instrument language to the Anglican Consultative Council (ACC) and Primates has significantly changed the way in which these particular four structures of Anglicanism are perceived and function in the life of the Anglican Communion. Instrument-type language is a peculiarly modern feature of institutional life associated with a mechanical and transactional temper that runs counter to more organic and relational forms of ecclesial life. The phrase 'instruments of unity' is a creature of this modern development. In this sense it is truly a recent invention which is not unimportant for the ethos and culture of Anglicanism.

The concept of instruments of unity had its origins in the Ecumenical Movement in the 1970s. It appears that the term 'instrument of unity' was used in discussions on the ecclesiological significance of the varieties of Christian councils that emerged in the post-war years. Lukas Vischer insisted that Christian Councils should be 'instruments of unity'. By this he meant that the ecclesial reality should not be sought in Christian Councils but in the communion among the churches. He argued that 'as structures, Christian Councils have only *an instrumental ecclesiological significance* in the promotion of this communion'.[7] This instrumental and provisional role was underscored in the 1982 *Consultation on the Significance and Contribution of Councils of Churches in the Ecumenical Movement* in Venice and the 1986 Second Consultation on Councils of Churches as 'Instruments of Unity within the One Ecumenical Movement' in Geneva. The adoption by Anglicans of such language can be traced to the seventh meeting of the ACC in 1987 where the phrase 'instruments of unity' appeared in the report 'Unity and Diversity within the Anglican Communion: A way forward'. It was used as a collective name for the Archbishop of Canterbury, the Lambeth Conference, the ACC and the Primates' Meeting. Before this, Lambeth 1978 used the term 'structures

---

[7] For the historical context, see *Symphony of Instruments*, IASCUFO, para. 6.2.1 footnote 86. This note quotes from Rev'd Dr Michael Poon's paper, 'The Anglican Communion as Communion of Churches: On the historic significance of the Anglican Covenant'; a paper prepared for the South-South Encounter, 2010 and made available by Dr Poon to IASCUFO.

in the Anglican Communion' and in 1984 the Secretary General used the term 'inter-Anglican organization' in his ACC-6 opening speech.[8]

As early as the 1968 Lambeth Conference, the ACC was referred to as 'an instrument of common action'.[9] The concept of 'instrument' was invoked in the *Virginia Report* of 1997.[10] However it is attached in a rather loose manner to a range of phrases: for example, 'Instruments of Communion'; 'instruments of Anglican belonging at the world level' (5.28); 'international Anglican instruments of unity' (6.23); 'worldwide instruments of communion' and 'instruments of interdependence' (6.34); 'instruments of the Anglican Communion' (6.32). Furthermore the report states that the episcopate is 'the primary instrument of Anglican unity' (3.51) and it recognizes the need in the Anglican Communion for 'appropriate instruments' (5.20). The ACC is identified as 'unique among the international Anglican instruments of unity' by virtue of the inclusion of laity among its members (6.23). While not specifically noted in the *Virginia Report*, the ACC, as a consultative body, has a constitution to govern its functioning. Its creation required the agreement of two-thirds of the churches in the Anglican Communion. Neither the Lambeth Conference nor the Primates' Meeting required any approval from member churches. Three things are to be noted in the *Virginia Report*. First, an uncritical acceptance of the language of 'instrument'; second, a loose association of 'instrument' with a range of phrases relating to matters of ecclesial structure; and third, 'Instruments of Communion' was evidently the preferred general identifier regarding 'instruments'.

Certainly since the *Virginia Report* the language of instruments has become part of the stock-in-trade of international Anglican discourse. In Michael Poon's view the 'uncritical use of concepts from the ecumenical movement', such as the concept of 'instruments of unity', aggravates what has been referred to by some as an 'ecclesial deficit' in Anglicanism. The idea of an ecclesial deficit was discussed in the *Windsor Continuation Group Report to the Archbishop of Canterbury* in December 2008. The report noted that 'a central deficit in the

---

[8] *Symphony of Instruments*, IASCUFO, para. 6.2.1, footnote 87, quoting Poon, 'The Anglican Communion as Communion of Churches', para. 38.

[9] See 1968 Lambeth Conference resolution 69.

[10] *The Virginia Report: The Report of the Inter-Anglican Theological and Doctrinal Commission*, Anglican Consultative Council (London: Anglican Communion Office, 1997). Paragraph references in text.

life of the Communion is its inability to uphold structures which can make decisions which carry force in the life of the Churches of the Communion, or even give any definitive guidance to them'.[11] The report then noted that 'other commentators will argue that such mechanisms are entirely unnecessary, but this touches upon the heart of what it is to live as a Communion of Churches'. The ecclesial deficit concerns both the determination of the limits of diversity in the fellowship of Anglican churches and capacity to exercise authority to discipline churches that disregard such limits. What this means is that the notion of an 'ecclesial deficit' is an essentially contested ecclesiological concept. On the general issue of new terminology, specifically 'instruments' language, Michael Poon's comments are apposite:

> The last decade saw the creation of concepts and structures to uphold the Communion at international level, without thinking through their ecclesial implications and their connection to the ecclesial realities of the particular Churches. So the Communion structures unwittingly set Anglican Churches worldwide on a collision course with one another. These terminologies came from specific Protestant denominational settings; but there was little discussion and explanation of what they mean in Anglican terms ecclesiologically.[12]

There is little to suggest that the concept of 'instruments' has been subject to any critical assessment as to its appropriateness or what it might signify. Instruments are things that you use to achieve certain ends. A hammer is an instrument for striking a nail in order to build or repair some structure; a dentist's drill is an instrument. This tool-like quality is reflected in the etymology of 'instrument', meaning a 'tool or apparatus'. It was originally connected with a musical instrument. Interestingly it also included the sense of 'arrange and furnish'. The adjective 'instrumental' points to something that is 'serviceable' or 'useful'.[13] But how serviceable and useful are the Instruments of Communion?

---

[11] *Windsor Continuation Group Report to the Archbishop of Canterbury* 2008, section D, para. 51. http://www.anglicancommunion.org/media/100354/The-Windsor-Continuation-Group.pdf
[12] Poon, 'Anglican Communion as Communion of Churches', para. 38.
[13] For further information, see 'instrument' in *The Shorter Oxford English Dictionary* (London: Guild Publishing, 1988).

A sympathetic imagination for the instruments

In times of tension and conflict in the Anglican Communion it is common to find fault with those structures and processes of consultation (commonly referred to as 'instruments') that are designed to sustain and enhance common life and unity. For some, the instruments have been rendered impotent to assist in the repair and mission of the Anglican fellowship of churches. As such they are pronounced useless; to be cast aside in favour of alternative mechanisms for ordering the unwieldy Body of Christ.[14] It seems that the Instruments of Communion are no longer the subject of a sympathetic ecclesial imagination that 'bears all things, believes all things, hopes all things, endures all things' (1 Cor. 13.7). A certain ecclesiological amnesia prevails. It is too easily forgotten that structures and processes for 'peace and charity' only work if they are informed and directed by a spiritual sensibility alive to the movement of the Holy Spirit. This is the Spirit of God that weaves wisdom through the forms and structures of ecclesial life and justifies the depiction of the Lambeth Conference as a fellowship in the Spirit.[15]

Ecclesial structures and processes ought to function as conduits for the flow of divine energy. Indeed structures have to be Spirit directed to be fruitful. Conversely energies of the divine Spirit require a christomorphic patterning to remain faithful to the Gospel of God. The absence of a spiritually attuned sympathetic imagination in relation to ecclesial ordering is at heart a theological matter. And the absence of this quality represents a genuine 'ecclesial deficit'. At its deepest level it arises from a failure to attend to the dynamic way in which the Holy Spirit brings to light and action the form of Christ in the church and the world. As soon as Instruments of Communion are evacuated of a sympathetic ecclesial imagination it is inevitable that they will become subject to sectional or personal interests. The Lambeth Conference, in a unique way among the instruments (to be developed later in this chapter), provides the optimal conditions for the recovery and nurture of just such a sympathetic ecclesial imagination informed by the Spirit of Christ.

---

[14] See the assessment of Ephraim Radner, 'Can the Instruments of Unity be Repaired?', www.anglicancommunioninstitute.com, October 5, 2010.
[15] The 1920 Lambeth Conference described itself as such: 'The Conference is a fellowship in the Spirit.'

The gift-like character of Instruments of Communion

The appeal for a sympathetic imagination with regard to the instruments is counter-intuitive to the general way in which structures and processes are treated in the Church and more generally in society today. It is commonplace to regard social structures and processes as debased forms of ecclesial life operating at some remove from the purity of the Gospel and discipleship, at best necessary practical means to achieve certain ends. This utilitarian approach to the Instruments of Communion means they become mere artefacts to be manoeuvred and used as the will dictates. That will might be an individual, interest group, party or sectional church interest. The Anglican Communion urgently requires a positive theological appreciation of the Instruments of Communion. This needs to be allied with a corresponding spiritual discernment and energy to dwell in the instruments in a manner that honours the Gospel. This is important for all of the Instruments of Communion and, as I will argue later in this chapter, in a quite particular sense for the Lambeth Conference.

Developing a richer theological understanding of the instruments has been part of the challenge of the work of the Archbishop of Canterbury's *Inter-Anglican Standing Commission on Unity, Faith and Order* (IASCUFO). In a series of reports prepared for ACC15 (2013 Auckland) and ACC16 (2016 Lusaka), IASCUFO proposed a theological approach to the Instruments of Communion developed (a) in terms of instruments as gifts for deepening the life of the Anglican Communion and (b) as signs of God's grace for the building up the fellowship of Anglican Churches as part of the worldwide Body of Christ.[16] These reports emphasized that the Instruments of Communion were made up of people with their gifts, graces and frailties. Because of this, the instruments require the care and attention of trusted servants who act as stewards of the Instruments of Communion. Extending this line of reasoning we note a number of things.

The Instruments of Communion are designed to facilitate communication, conversation and consensus building among the fellowship of Anglican

---

[16] See footnote 2 above re: ACC15; and Resolution 16.21 of ACC16 on the Instruments of Communion, http://www.anglicancommunion.org/media/234449/acc-16-resolutions-2016.pdf.

Churches. In short, the instruments provide ways by which the Anglican Communion seeks the wisdom of the Spirit of God for a deeper communion and faithful witness to Christ in the world. This suggests that the instruments may be more appropriately considered as gifts for deepening communion.[17] The deepening of communion serves the Anglican Churches' mission in the world (Jon. 17.21). The history of the Lambeth Conferences bears witness to the importance of the Church's engagement with the world and a deep concern for the common good as a fundamental element of the episcopal vocation.[18] Consequently the Lambeth Conference ought never be regarded as a self-serving instrument but one orientated towards mission.

The instruments are not states of affairs, nor static entities. Rather – because the people of God, in different and complementary ways, constitute the instruments – they belong to the rich communicative networks of Anglican life in the world. Their function and impact will inevitably become the focal point for change, controversy and new possibilities. This is all part of a dynamic catholicity.[19] The vulnerability of the instruments to change and development does not diminish their gift-like character but simply witnesses to the way in which true gifts actually work in the world.

Concerns have often been expressed that the use of the word 'instruments' ignores the human and relational dimensions of the instruments. Certainly instrumental language can make it difficult to appreciate the instruments as gifts for an enhanced and dynamic Body of Christ. Accordingly it is vital to remember that the instruments are living gifts for communion. The gift-like character of the instruments can be more sympathetically received by the consistent use of the language of 'communion' rather than 'unity'. In contemporary usage 'communion' has a broader and richer connotation than the term 'unity'. Unfortunately, unity has been too easily associated with structural and legal aspects of the Church. Such things are important but they are not

---

[17] For a more developed examination of the Instruments of Communion in terms of a theology of gift, see Stephen Pickard, 'Gifts of Communion: Recovering an Anglican Approach to the "Instruments of Unity"', *Journal of Anglican Studies*, vol. 11.2 (November 2013), pp. 233–55. The *Virginia Report* 1997, 1.14, referred to the 'instruments of communion which are a gift of God to the Church help to hold us in the life of the triune God'. However this brief reference remained undeveloped in the report.

[18] For example, George Victor Browning, *Sabbath and the Common Good: Prospects for a New Humanity* (Echo Books, 2016).

[19] *Communion, Conflict and Hope*, The Kuala Lumpur Report of the Third Inter-Anglican Theological and Doctrinal Commission (London: Anglican Communion Office, 2008), paras 45–49.

the only or the most significant aspects of union with God and each other. The language of 'communion' offers a needed relational balance to the language of 'instruments'. The emphasis on communion terminology is more resonant with the role of human agency and theological focus on God that actually underlies the purpose of the Instruments of Communion. Language, as is well known, has a significant part to play in changing expectations and attitudes.

The real challenge is to recover the priority of a gift-centred approach to the Instruments of Communion. The instruments always remain vulnerable to distortion and misuse. For example, the objectification of instruments leaves them vulnerable to sectional interests to prosecute their own ideas of communion, its repair and/or progress. It also promotes false expectations of what is possible. A gift-centred approach to the structures of Anglican polity is more resistant to the instruments being deployed to patch up or fix problems. A gift-centred approach belongs to an environment that fosters consensus-building, good quality communication and responsible and accountable engagement. The Anglican Communion is called to bear witness through common practice to the incarnate Lord and the power of the Holy Spirit. A gift-centred approach will encourage a reconceiving of the instruments as structures and forms of embodied wisdom for the Anglican fellowship of churches, for the purpose of strengthening witness to Christ in the world. The instruments have to be reassessed, reshaped and reinvigorated against this wider horizon.

I have argued that the instruments are God's gift for deepening the life of the Anglican Communion. But this is not an end in itself. Fostering communion draws people closer to one another and to God the Holy Trinity. This suggests that the instruments belong to the mission of the Church of God. Indeed nurturing communion for the inner life of the churches of the Anglican Communion would cease to be communion in the Gospel of God if it was an introverted or self-serving communion. The wider horizon for the operation of the Instruments of Communion is the mission of the Church. Moreover as gifts, the instruments have a sacramental character. It is in and through such relational church structures that the people of God may hear the voice of the living God and discern signs of God's presence and work in the world. As the Church is a sign of the coming kingdom,[20] so too the Instruments of

---

[20] The Church as sign of the kingdom is developed in *The Church: Towards a Common Vision,* Faith and Order Paper no. 214 (Geneva: World Council of Churches, 2013), paras. 25–7.

Communion can be understood as ecclesial signs enabling the Church to be a sign of God's grace and goodness. This sign-like character of the instruments orientates them towards the future and draws attention to their contingent and provisional nature. As a consequence they are signs that require the care and attention of trusted servants who act as stewards of communion.

Stewards of the instruments

This consideration raises an important question: What responsibility do human agents have for the Instruments of Communion? If the instruments are received as gifts and signs of communion, then clearly they have to be treated with respect and care. In this context those responsible for the exercise of the gifts do so as stewards and servants of the instruments. When this is undertaken well the Church's witness to the Gospel of God in the world is enriched. In this sense stewardship is a broad-ranging vocation set against the horizon of the mission of God in the world.

The concept of stewardship has been important when considering human responsibility for creation. The early chapters of the Book of Genesis point to creation as the gift of a good and caring God. The God of this remarkable and interdependent creation has the character of the benevolent care and kindly oversight in the ancient tradition of the shepherd King. Human beings, created in the image of such a God, are given responsibility to care for the earth and its creatures. As such the human vocation is to follow the pattern of care and delight in creation of the God whose image they bear. The human vocation as a steward of the garden of creation is a delegated responsibility from a good and kind God. Stewardship is an activity and calling that requires a close, respectful and responsible relationship with the earth and all living things.

This background of the stewardship of creation may be helpful when we deploy the idea of stewardship in relation to the Church. This involves a move from stewardship of creation to stewardship of the community of the new creation; the Body of Christ. Christ is Head of the Body and bestows gifts on the people of the Church in order that through the Church the many riches of the wisdom of God might be shown to the world (Eph. 3.10). Disciples of Christ, and in particular those called to care and exercise oversight of the Body of Christ, are called to tend the garden of the new creation, the household (*oikos*) of the Lord. And they are called to undertake this vocation after the manner of Christ in humble obedience to the Gospel. In this vein the Apostle Paul refers to himself and his fellow apostolic leaders as 'servants of Christ and stewards of God's mysteries' (1 Cor. 4.1). The new household is the fellowship in the Spirit, the communion of the faithful in Christ. This household is the result of the revealing of God's mysteries, that is, 'the secret knowledge of God's purposes, disclosed in the Gospel'.[21] Stewards have responsibility for the good ordering and common good of the household of faith. As in the first creation, so in the new creation, stewardship is a delegated and representative responsibility. Moreover, it is a delegation of trust (1 Cor. 4.2). And this vocation mirrors the original creation, that is, it requires a stewardship of the communion of the faithful after the pattern of Christ the Good Shepherd (Jon. 10). Stewards of the mysteries of God, as is abundantly clear from Paul's letters, exercise their calling on many fronts as ambassadors of Christ, pastoral carers of the churches, and as teachers of the spiritual truths of the Gospel.

This move from stewardship of creation to stewardship of communion provides a fresh way to reconsider the purpose of the Instruments of Communion. The instruments are intended to strengthen and enhance the Anglican Communion. But to fulfil this the instruments require the exercise of good stewardship. This provides a rich theological and missional horizon for the Instruments of Communion. It also draws attention to the great responsibility entrusted to the servants of God for the good functioning of the instruments. It also calls attention to the moral claim upon those called to fulfil this ministry of stewardship in the life of the Anglican Communion. The exercise of stewardship is undertaken by frail human beings, called to repentance and prayerfulness, subject to wilful blindness of many kinds; especially when it comes to the exercise of power and authority. The servants and stewards of the Instruments of Communion are called to exercise this particular vocation under the guidance of the Holy Spirit and with openness to correction and challenge.

Consideration of personal agency and responsibility for the good operation of the instruments highlights the importance of the careful appointment and

---

[21] See C. K. Barrett, *A Commentary on the First Epistle of the Corinthians* (2nd edn, London: Adam & Charles Black, 1971), p. 100.

ongoing education of all those called to high office in the Church of God. It also calls attention to the need for robust synodical processes for the election and appointment of bishops. This in turn puts a spotlight on those qualities that are particularly needful for bishops today. Relevant here are not only matters of personal character but also of ecclesial intelligence. This latter quality requires an appreciation of the particular contribution of the Anglican Communion to the vitality of the Body of Christ. Moreover, in a time of significant transitions in society and church, a bishop's capacity to listen, collaborate, harness conflict and embody spiritual and theological wisdom becomes critical. Such capabilities are especially important in appointments to episcopal leadership in order to balance the emphasis on management and provide a check on political and partisan interests that infect the churches and mimic their host cultures across the globe.[22] Such considerations go to the heart of the capacity of the Instruments of Communion to function in the life of the Anglican fellowship of churches as genuine gifts, signs and witnesses to the coming Kingdom of God.

The Lambeth Conference: What kind of gift?

How might an approach to the Instruments of Communion in terms of gift and sign contribute to the renewal of the Lambeth Conference in the Anglican Communion? In this respect, I note that the very language of gift transforms the Lambeth Conference from *mere* instrument to achieve an end – in this case enhancement of the fellowship of Anglican churches – into something that is fundamentally relational. When the bishops of the Anglican Communion meet they are already saying something important about the life of the Body of Christ and their shared care for the churches. Their meeting is an embodiment of what it means to share in the gift of the Gospel that creates and sustains the Body of Christ.[23] The giving and receiving of the gift of God in Christ is unfolded, ordered and released through the episcopal body. Through face-to-face encounter,

---

[22] See Martin Percy, 'Emergent Archiepiscopal Leadership within the Anglican Communion', *Journal of Anglican Studies*, 14.1 (May 2016), pp. 46–70.

[23] For example, see *Communion, Conflict and Hope*, The Kuala Lumpur Report, Appendix 2, 'The Anglican Way: The Significance of the Episcopal Office for the Communion of the Church', Thesis Nine: 'The bishop serves the collegial life of the Church through the nurture of strong bonds with bishops of the Anglican Communion and those who share episcope in other Christian churches', p. 64.

listening and common prayer, God's gift of Communion is honoured. And this dynamic quality of God's gift is magnified as the bishops of the church recognize the gift of God in each other and in the churches that they bring to Lambeth. From this point of view, the Lambeth Conference is not first of all an instrument to achieve an end. Rather gathering and being bishops together is itself a sign of the gift of God for communion with the world and its peoples. The gift-like character of the Lambeth Conference is a check on the natural human default of misusing the gathering for political ends that tends to undermine the unity of the Body of Christ.

The remarkable thing about the gift-like character of the Lambeth Conference is that it is recognized and overflows through a rich and attractive diversity of episcopal life. Bishops from the Communion display the marks of different cultural, ethnic, linguistic and Christian ways of being in the world. The Lambeth gift is a gift of colour and life: a sign of the colour and life of the Spirit of life and love.

Of course the gift, like all gifts, has to be appropriated. God's gift of togetherness remains a task to be undertaken. This requires spiritual maturity, attention to the virtues and the discipline of the Holy Spirit. This will inevitably draw bishops into the costly dimension of God's gift. Sharing in life together, meeting for prayer and counsel, and learning to behold the face of Christ in worship: all such activities are a cause for great joy and humble recognition of the fragile character of the gift of common life. The Lambeth Conference is that time and place where these dimensions of the gift of communion with God and one another are tested, wrestled with and patiently endured. This is why the discipline and steadfastness of the Holy Spirit embodied in common prayer and Eucharist is the vital energy of the Lambeth Conference.

If the Lambeth Conference is an instrument of communion, it is an instrument in a very particular way patterned after the gift of God in Christ. In this sense, first and foremost – and prior to being an Instrument of Communion – the Lambeth Conference is a sign of the work of God breathing life and purpose into the Body of Christ. The bishops of the Lambeth Conference belong to a rich ecclesial ecology nurtured by the infinite identity of God in Christ. In this sense, the Lambeth Conference is caught up in the greater mystery of the Church in God's world. In short it is a participant in this mystery in micro as it were – having a sign-like character that is future orientated with an unfinished dynamic quality. There is an analogy here with the

ancient fourfold marks of the Church. Such marks represent both a gift to the
church and an emergent property of the Church; marks that have to be received
as a gift and a task that remains on the agenda. In a similar manner the Lambeth
Conference is not simply something established and secure. Rather it is a mode
of togetherness that requires reconstitution and repetition in order for it to be
a living gift of communion for the churches. The Lambeth Conference is thus
an emergent property of *koinonia* and as such requires responsible stewardship.

The Lambeth Bishops: What kind of stewards?

This leads to consideration of that other dimension of the instruments previously
discussed, that is, stewardship. Specifically what kind of stewardship is required
of the bishops of the Lambeth Conference? How might the Lambeth Conference
exercise an appropriate episcopal stewardship in the Anglican Communion?
These questions go to the heart of the importance of the Instruments of
Communion. When the bishops of the Anglican Communion meet at the
Lambeth Conference for counsel and prayer, they are gathered as seekers of
a common wisdom in their 'care of the churches'. How is such wisdom to be
found and lived? Good stewardship of the Anglican Communion occurs when
wisdom emerges through open, generous, truthful and sustained exchanges.
This will inevitably be costly and require great humility. Being stewards of God's
wisdom may seem too lofty an ideal for the Lambeth gathering. One reason
for this is that wisdom is multifaceted and too often it becomes ensnared in
ecclesial brambles of the party or sectional interest variety. When this occurs,
wisdom quickly evaporates. This requires further explanation.

   In the nineteenth century, the famous ex-Anglican, John Henry Newman
republished his essays on the Via Media of the Anglican Church (1879) – first
published as the *Prophetical Office of the Church* in 1837. Newman identified
theology as one of the three fundamental powers of the Church.[24] Theology
(Newman's system of philosophy) offered a critical stance in relation to
the other two powers, the sacramental and worship tradition (ritual) and
ecclesiastical rule (political power). Liturgy and polity required this third

---

[24] John Henry Newman, *The Via Media of the Anglican Church,* 2 vols (3rd edn, London: Basil
   Montagu Pickering, 1877), vol. 1, *Lectures on the Prophetical Office of the Church Viewed Relatively
   to Romanism and Popular Protestantism,* Preface, pp. 40 ff.

power (theology) as an essential hermeneutic for the ongoing faithfulness of the Church to the Gospel. Without this third power the Church was easily directed into an unhealthy sacramentalism and/or an unfettered abuse of ecclesiastical power. Church history bore testimony to the conflict that often occurred between these three indispensable elements of the life of the Church. Newman considered that the theological vocation was essential to preserve and foster a critical and reforming spirit.

Newman's approach to the powers of the Church (theological/critical; sacramental/worship and ecclesiastical/political) offers a fuller understanding of how wisdom is constituted and manifests itself. The history of the Lambeth Conferences indicates that it embodies all three dimensions of wisdom as it seeks common counsel, prays and breaks bread and engages in thoughtful dialogue. Moreover, a wise stewardship will seek a balance between these three dimensions of ecclesial wisdom. The great danger for the Lambeth Conference is that one element will dominate the others. In times of tension and controversy the temptation is to resort to ecclesiastical/political solutions. The sacramental/worship life can become somewhat perfunctory and its transformative power can be nullified when the overarching concern is for political/sectional outcomes. Similarly, genuine theological engagement can be too quickly set aside or dismissed as irrelevant to pressing practical concerns. The Lambeth Conference works best and fulfils its deepest aspirations when the delicate balance between theology, worship and polity is pursued for the sake of the well-being of the whole body.

The foregoing discussion suggests that the Lambeth Conference can exercise a stewardship of *koinonia* in the Gospel as it intentionally pursues a wisdom that draws upon the rich heritage of Anglican faith and order. This leads to a reconception of the Lambeth Conference in terms of stewardship of God's wisdom for the world.

The Lambeth Conference within the symphony of instruments

The present inquiry into the Lambeth Conference in relation to the Instruments of Communion points to the significance of the episcopate in the life of the Anglican Communion. In the normal course of ecclesial life, a bishop in his or her diocese is the fundamental unit of the *ecclesia*. The fellowship of Anglican churches has approximately 1,000 bishops worldwide, exercising episcopal oversight over 80 million Anglican Christians in 164 countries. We might say that this phenomenon represents the Anglican part of the Body of Christ in its spread-out form; in *extensity*.[25] This dispersed body is called to be faithful to the good news of God in myriad local contexts. Being the Church in extensity mode is the way in which mission takes place.

When those whose charism is the 'care of the churches' are called together to pray, seek mutual counsel and work for the peace and charity of the churches, they bring with them the people they serve. They bring them in their hearts and minds, and by virtue of the office they occupy. The Lambeth Conference represents the episcopally ordered Body of Christ in *intensity* mode. The form of the Church concentrated in the gathered episcopal body is, in an important ecclesiological sense, the church 'in micro'. An interesting analogy is provided by Anthony Hanson who argued that the pioneer ministry of the early apostles did not create the Church; rather 'the ministry is originally the Church *in nucleo*'.[26] Accordingly, the 'ministry shows in miniature what the Church should be'.[27] In like manner, the bishops of the Lambeth Conference represent the Church *in nucleo* and witness to the character and form of the Body of Christ. This makes sense within an Anglican polity where the Lambeth Conference can be regarded as embodying a particular intensification of the Anglican Communion.

This consideration also means that the Lambeth Conference does not live to itself but is accountable to the whole body from which it emerges and in relation to which it exercises episcopal oversight and care. Indeed without the whole ecclesial body and its ministries the episcopate would not have emerged. In this sense it is the Body of Christ that brings forth the episcopal body. Yet the episcopate is a genuinely new entity within the complex institutional nature of the *ecclesia* of God. In this sense, the episcopate cannot be reduced to its constituent parts. There is genuine novelty in the ecclesial system.[28]

---

[25] For discussion of the relationship between extensity and intensity in ecclesiology, see Daniel W. Hardy, *Finding the Church: The Dynamic Truth of Anglicanism* (London: SCM, 2001), pp. 109ff.

[26] Anthony Hanson, *The Pioneer Ministry* (London: SPCK, 1975 [1961]), pp. 86, 94, 155.

[27] Hanson, *The Pioneer Ministry*, p. 60.

[28] On the novelty of the episcopate, see Robin Lane Fox, *Pagans and Christians* (London: Penguin, 1991), chap. 10, 'Bishops and Authority'.

The episcopal order and the whole body of the Church release each other to be the Church. The episcopal body acts in such a way that the energy of the various ministries is released and directed for the purposes of the whole Church. Yet even as this occurs, the episcopal body is confirmed in its purpose and significance as the whole Church lives and ministers faithfully in accordance with God's purposes. In this way, the orders of ministry establish each other and foster each other's work and purpose. Thus it can truly be said that the ministry of the episcopate and the ministries of the whole people of God bring each other into being.[29] This fundamental interrelatedness of the whole body with the episcopate is the reason that the whole body of the Anglican Communion that comes to the Lambeth Conference, embodied in the bishops.

This discussion, about the relationship between the episcopal body gathered at the Lambeth Conference and the wider body, may seem somewhat of a diversion. However, I want to argue that it is straight to the point of the significance of the Lambeth Conference. In fact this relationship between the Lambeth Conference and the wider Communion gives to this instrument of communion a unique significance in relation to the other instruments. How so? In the first and most obvious sense, the Lambeth Conference

> 'mbodies the collective pastorate of the bishops. As the corporate gathering of the most representative ministers of the Anglican Communion, it has considerable spiritual, moral and pastoral authority. It includes within itself the greater part of the other Instruments of Communion – there is some useful overlapping that points to the communion or harmony of instruments: the Archbishop of Canterbury belongs among his fellow bishops as first among equals, and the Primates take their place among the bishops too; the episcopal members of the Anglican Consultative Council are also members of the Lambeth Conference.'[30]

This suggests that, from an *ecclesial* point of view, the Lambeth Conference has a particular primacy among the Instruments of Communion. It is the primary body in which the whole Communion is gathered in its episcopal form. While the See of Canterbury has historical precedence, nonetheless unlike Rome, this does not translate into a certain ecclesial and legal priority. Rather, the

---

[29] Stephen Pickard, *Theological Foundations for Collaborative Ministry* (Aldershot: Ashgate, 2009), chap. 9.
[30] *Symphony of Instruments*, IASCUFO, 2.5.1.

Archbishop who occupies the See of Canterbury is *of* the episcopal body in the same way as all other bishops. The Primates, while a further executive-type elevation of the bishops and archbishops of national churches, do not constitute another fourth-order 'extra episcopal', but are *of* the order of bishops. The Primates and the Archbishop of Canterbury may contribute to the achievement of common counsel among the bishops, yet these more organisationally focused episcopal levels are always being drawn into the larger episcopal body and the whole Church which brought them forth. Although such bodies may behave at times in an executive manner, in fact their authority does not extend that far.

A recent example of the tensions that can arise between the instruments became apparent in the discussions and subsequent communications arising from the ACC meeting (ACC-16) in April 2016 in Luska, Zambia. The issue focused on the status of the January 2016 Primates' deliberations and their admonition of the Episcopal Church of the USA (TEC). The Secretary General of the Anglican Communion, Archbishop Josiah Idowu-Fearon, rejected criticism from six former members of the ACC's standing committee of statements they made during and after ACC-16. The comments centred on Resolution 16.24, 'Walking Together', which dealt with how the ACC responded to the Primates' Gathering and Meeting in January.[31]

What then of the Lambeth Conference in relation to the ACC? The ACC reminds us that the body of Christ is only fully itself when it is seen to consist of laity as well as clergy. For practical purposes and precisely because Anglican polity recognizes the dynamic and symbiotic relationship that obtains between the people and their bishops, the ACC has emerged in time and space to bring to focus the breadth and depth of all the baptized of the Anglican Communion. It makes sense within an Anglican polity. It does not usurp episcopal authority, but it does remind everyone how the Body of Christ is constituted and the rich and complex pattern of mutual accountability in the Body of Christ.

The uniqueness of the Lambeth Conference as an instrument of communion derives from the fundamental relationship between the episcopal body and the wider Body of Christ. Theologically they inhere in each other and when the episcopal body meets as the Lambeth Conference then the whole of the

---

[31] For further information, see http://www.anglicannews.org/news/2016/05/secretary-general-rejects-criticism-over-walking-together-resolution.aspx.

Communion is gathered under the form of the episcopate. This is not simply a high doctrine of the episcopate; it is a high doctrine of the Church. It also makes it abundantly clear, at least from an ecclesiological point of view, that the Lambeth Conference is accountable to the whole body to which it is yoked. It also means that withdrawing from the episcopal body represents a serious fracture of the ecclesial body.

It is probably not too much of an exaggeration to state that currently our ecclesial consciousness is somewhat brittle. This shows itself by the fact that as a fellowship of churches we struggle to appreciate that Anglican polity and life is premised on diversity and mutual discernment. When we lack this understanding it is exceedingly difficult to recover a truly sympathetic imagination for the possibilities for peace and charity offered to the Anglican Communion through its instruments. The danger is that we might fail to recognize that it is only when there emerges a deeper sense of the unity and/or integration between the Instruments of Communion that the true gift-like character of the instruments can be properly displayed. It is easily forgotten that the instruments are interrelated, that they form a true symphony of instruments. By treating each instrument separately, or by failing to recognize their interconnectedness, we lose sight of our own essential connectedness and accountability to each other, and the value of the instruments to deepen Anglican life. When this occurs the Anglican Communion suffers increasing fragmentation and disconnection. This in turn breeds greater dissatisfaction with, and rejection of, those means by which Anglicans maintain the 'bonds of affection' so essential for our common life.

Recovering a sense of the symphony of instruments for the common good and well-being of the Communion is vital. For example, the Archbishop of Canterbury and the Lambeth Conference have a natural reciprocity, as do the Primates and the ACC. Closer intentional cooperation between these different instruments nurtures the Anglican ideal of an organic, conversational and conciliar ethos. The fact that there may be tensions between these different bodies is natural and to be expected, but this is not a reason for jettisoning one or other of the bodies or diminishing one and exalting another. This is not the way of communion in the instruments. In truth, the instruments together exercise a collaborative ministry in and for the Anglican Communion and indeed beyond. As such, the instruments are orientated to or 'lean' towards one another, they receive their life from each other and are best able to make their particular and unique contributions to the whole as they recognize their indebtedness to each other. In this way, they become living parts of the Body of Christ intended for God's glory.

Lambeth Conference: Unfinished gift for the unfinished church

The fact that the instruments have emerged in history – often in times of conflict and uncertainty in the Church – points to the fact that the instruments are contingent and therefore provisional and unfinished. The instruments will probably undergo change and modification as the contexts and circumstances of being the Church also change and evolve. So too we can and should expect the Lambeth Conference to undergo change with respect to its form and content over time and in response to new circumstances.

The contingent nature of the instruments goes hand in hand with their gift-like character. The instruments are gifts of the Spirit that have emerged through a process and within specific historical contexts. This means that, as stated earlier, the instruments represent both a gift and a task for the Anglican Communion. Their operation and ongoing value for the Communion requires active human participation and an imaginative effort to follow what the Spirit is saying to the Church as the future unfolds. For the reasons outlined in this chapter, this is a particular vocation and critical challenge for the Lambeth Conference.

The fact that the instruments are contingent and subject to change also means that there will be an inevitable messiness about the way the instruments function as God-given gifts. These considerations reveal the instruments to be not signs of a steady-state church, but of an unfinished ecclesial body 'on the way'. As such, the instruments are signs of work to be done for the sake of the Church's mission in the world. The Lambeth Conference participates in this ongoing work of the Body of Christ. As such, it too can be a means whereby the multifaceted riches of God's wisdom in Christ might be manifest in heaven and upon earth (Eph. 3.10).

2

The Archbishop of Canterbury and the Lambeth Conference

Paul Avis

Evolution of the See of Canterbury

The ministry of the Archbishop of Canterbury goes back to the mission of Augustine (AD 534–604), who was sent by Pope Gregory I ('Gregory the Great'; Pope AD 590–604) in AD 596 to convert the Anglo-Saxons in England. Augustine, named after an even more famous earlier bishop, St Augustine of Hippo, was a monk and was soon made an abbot to strengthen his authority over his companion monks, but was not yet a bishop. Most of what we know about Augustine's mission comes from *The Ecclesiastical History of the English Nation* by the Venerable Bede, which was completed by Bede in the monastery of Jarrow in the north-east of England in 731.[1] To compile his work, which necessarily he had to do on the basis of selective sources, Bede had access to documents that had been preserved at Canterbury since the days of Augustine himself. Bede describes the origin of Augustine's mission like this: 'Moved by divine inspiration … [Gregory] sent the servant of God, Augustine, and with him several other monks, who feared the Lord, to preach the word of God to the English nation.'[2] The monks sensed that they were venturing into the unknown, to a land of pagan darkness and violence; they did not expect

---

[1] J. M. Wallace-Hadrill et al. (ed.), *Bede's Ecclesiastical History of the English People: A Historical Commentary* (Oxford: The Clarendon Press, 1988); J. Robert Wright, *A Companion to Bede: A Reader's Commentary on* The Ecclesiastical History of the English People (Grand Rapids, MI: Eerdmans, 2008); Gerald Bonner, 'Some Factors in the Conversion of the English: The Men and the Churches', *Tufton Review* 1.1 (1997), pp. 14–29.

[2] Bede, *The Ecclesiastical History of the English Nation and the Lives of St Cuthbert and the Abbots* (London: Dent (Everyman Library), 1910), p. 33 (chapter xxiii). For Gregory, see R. A. Markus, *Gregory the Great and his World* (Cambridge: Cambridge University Press, 1997).

to return home. On their way to England they lost their nerve – Augustine himself seems to have vacillated – and proposed to turn back. Augustine's commission needed to be reinforced by Pope Gregory with words of authority and encouragement.

In fact Augustine was not coming to an entirely pagan country. Although Pope Gregory probably thought that he was sending Augustine to a completely non-Christian land, England had been partly Christianized in the past.[3] The Christian faith had arrived with the Roman armies and their camp followers half a millennium before, from AD 43. The Celtic expression of Christianity continued to flourish in western Britain. St Patrick had evangelized Ireland in the second half of the fifth century and, according to tradition, had founded the See of Armagh, which predates the See of Canterbury. St David, who died around 601, consolidated Christianity in Wales. A generation before Augustine's mission, Columba had set sail across the Irish Sea in 563, landing on Iona, off the coast of the Isle of Mull in North-West Scotland, where he founded the first of his many monasteries. Columba died in the year that Augustine reached England, 597. In England itself the Anglo-Saxon invasions had driven Celtic Christianity back to the margins of the land and had replaced it with pagan rites.[4] England needed to be re-evangelized.

Augustine and his band of missionary monks approached the town of Durovernum Cantiacorum (the modern Canterbury), reportedly holding up a silver cross and a painting of Christ crucified. They requested a meeting with Ethelberht, at the time the *Bretwalda* or 'over-king' among the Saxon kingdoms (England was not yet a unified nation). Ethelberht had a Christian wife Bertha (who had come from Paris in 560), and was not himself antagonistic to Christianity, but it was several years before he was converted and underwent baptism himself, probably in the spring of 601 (though his son, Eadbald, remained a pagan when he succeeded his father in 616). Meanwhile, Augustine had been invested with additional authority by his consecration as 'Bishop of the English', probably at Arles in Gaul (modern France) in 597–8.[5] In 601

---

[3] Robin Fleming, *Britain After Rome* (Harmondsworth: Penguin, 2011), p. 131.
[4] See H. Meyr-Harting, *The Coming of Christianity to Anglo-Saxon England* (Batsford: Book Club Associates, 1977); Barbara Yorke, *The Conversion of Britain 600-800* (Harlow: Pearson, 2006); Malcolm Lambert, *Christians and Pagans: The Conversion of Britain from Alban to Bede* (New Haven: Yale, 2010).
[5] Margaret Deanesly, *Augustine of Canterbury* (London: Nelson, 1964), pp. 39–40.

Augustine received reinforcements from Rome and a mandate from Gregory to consecrate some of the recent arrivals as bishops. The party included Mellitus, who became Bishop of London, and Paulinus who evangelized the North of England. Paulinus became Bishop of York in 625 (the Bishop of that see being first mentioned as early as 314) and baptized Edwin, King of Northumbria, two years later.[6] (In 735 the then Bishop of York, Egbert, was elevated to Archbishop.) Shortly before his death in 604 Augustine consecrated Laurentius, who had travelled with him from Rome in 596, as his successor. It was uncanonical to act without the pope's authority, but Augustine's initiative secured unbroken continuity for the Roman Church in England. England was not fully converted to Christianity until the end of the seventh century, under Theodore of Tarsus, Archbishop of Canterbury 668–690. Though he was the eighth incumbent of the See of Canterbury, Theodore was the first Archbishop to preside over the whole English church.

It was either Augustine himself or the second expedition that brought the St Augustine Gospels (otherwise known as the Canterbury Gospels) to England – the oldest surviving illuminated Gospels in Latin and one of the oldest European books of any kind. In the Middle Ages they rested on the altar of the Abbey of Canterbury and after the Dissolution of the Monasteries by King Henry VIII in 1538 they were transferred to the custody of the Cathedral. In 1585 Archbishop Matthew Parker gave them, with many other valuable works, to Corpus Christi College, Cambridge, where they have resided to this day. In times past Archbishops of Canterbury swore the oaths on these Gospels at their enthronement and this practice was restored in 1945 for the enthronement of Geoffrey Fisher. Every new Archbishop of Canterbury promises to preserve the rights of 'this Cathedral and Metropolitical Church of Christ'. When this ancient oath is sworn in this ancient church the centuries roll back and yesterday becomes today.[7] The Gospels are conveyed, in the custody of the librarian of Corpus Christi College, to Canterbury or Westminster Abbey for major celebrations. Archbishop Robert Runcie and Pope John Paul II kissed

---

[6] Other sources claim that Edwin was baptized not by the Roman Paulinus, but by the British or Celtic Rhun, son of King Urien of Rheged and possibly a cleric or even a Bishop himself. It is possible that Rhun acted as sponsor or godfather to Edwin – terminology was inexact and ambiguous; see Caitlin Corning, 'The Baptism of Edwin, King of Northumbria: A New Analysis of the British Tradition', *Northern History* 36 (2000), pp. 5–15.

[7] Cf. Edward Carpenter, *Cantuar: The Archbishops in Their Office* (London: Cassell, 1971 (3rd edn, co-author Adrian Hastings, 1997)), p. 2.

the Gospels, which were placed on St Augustine's chair, during that pope's visit to England in 1982.[8] Archbishop Rowan Williams and Pope Benedict XVI together reverenced the Gospels after the book had been carried in a solemn but joyous procession, with banners, in Westminster Abbey in 2010 during that pope's state visit to the United Kingdom. In January 2016 the Gospels were exhibited in Canterbury Cathedral, together with the head of a crozier belonging to Pope Gregory, brought from Italy for the purpose, for the final service of the meeting of the Primates of the Anglican Communion.

Augustine did not carry out Pope Gregory's instructions to make Londinium (London) his seat, choosing Canterbury instead. Shortly after his arrival, he consecrated an existing Roman church in Canterbury as his Cathedral Church of Christ. This first cathedral was destroyed by fire in 1067, the year after the Norman invasion of England. Rebuilt by Archbishop Lanfranc, the new cathedral was extended by Archbishop Anselm and consecrated in 1130. The crypt contains Roman and Saxon fragments, though it is mainly Norman. In the second half of the fourteenth century Archbishop Sudbury remodelled the choir and nave. St Augustine's Chair, made of Purbeck marble, probably dates from the thirteenth century. Canterbury Cathedral is still, of course, the 'seat' of the Archbishop of Canterbury and for that reason it has a special significance for Anglicans throughout the world and is regarded as the mother church of the Anglican Communion.

The Archbishop of Canterbury is the Primate of the first metropolitical see of the English Church (and thus of the Anglican Communion) to be founded after the mission of St Augustine. Until the early 1530s, when Henry VIII repudiated papal authority, the See of Canterbury and with it the whole of the English Church was part of the Western or Latin Church and under the Roman jurisdiction. To date there have been 105 Archbishops of Canterbury. In the medieval period a succession of popes re-affirmed the primacy of the See of Canterbury over that of York.[9] In the mid-fourteenth century the pope settled the competing claims of the Archbishops of Canterbury and York with the wisdom of Solomon by decreeing that the former was Primate of All England, while the latter was Primate of England.

---

[8] Humphrey Carpenter, *Robert Runcie* (London: Hodder and Stoughton, 1996), p. 251.
[9] This is documented in (Lambert Beauduin), 'The Church of England United not Absorbed', a paper contributed to the Malines Conversations in 1925: A. Denaux and J. Dick (eds), *From Malines to ARCIC: The Malines Conversations Commemorated* (Leuven: Leuven University Press, 1997), pp. 35–46.

Several Archbishops of Canterbury have undergone martyrdom, beginning with Alphege in 1012, who was hacked to death in Danish captivity because he refused to allow the money of the poor to be used for his ransom. Thomas Becket was killed in his cathedral in 1170 by knights who believed that they were carrying out the wishes of King Henry II. Archbishop Sudbury was killed in the Peasants' Revolt in 1381 (perhaps more a political victim than a martyr). Thomas Cranmer was burned at the stake under the Roman Catholic Queen Mary in 1556. In 1645 William Laud was sent to the executioner's block by Parliament; his King, Charles I, followed in 1649.

How have Archbishops of Canterbury shaped the Lambeth Conference?

Archbishops of Canterbury convene the Lambeth Conference and preside at it.[10] How have the Archbishops personally shaped the conferences that they have initiated and chaired? What role have they played in their proceedings and with what particular emphases? How have they coped in the chair? In this section I will sketch some impressions, based on the available literature, up to the conference of 1988, in other words excluding those Archbishops of Canterbury who are still living (George Carey, 1998, and Rowan Williams, 2008).

What we know as the first Lambeth Conference – at the time probably no one thought that such a conference would become a regular event and certainly not a major institution of Anglicanism – was called by Archbishop Charles Thomas Longley in response to requests for fraternal consultation and authoritative action from the Anglican bishops of Canada and the United States.[11] The bishops were concerned about threats to Anglican integrity and

---

[10] For the Lambeth Conference as an Instrument of Communion, see the chapter by Stephen Pickard in this book.

[11] See Alan M. G. Stephenson, *The First Lambeth Conference 1867* (London: SPCK, 1967); id., *Anglicanism and the Lambeth Conferences* (London: SPCK, 1978); R. T. Davidson, *The Origin and History of the Lambeth Conferences of 1867 and 1878* (London: SPCK, 1888); Robert W. Prichard, 'The Lambeth Conferences', in Ian S. Markham, J. Barney Hawkins IV, Justyn Terry and Leslie Nuñez Steffensen (eds), *The Wiley-Blackwell Companion to the Anglican Communion* (Malden, MA; Oxford; Chichester: Wiley-Blackwell, 2013), chapter 7; Norman Doe, 'The Instruments of Unity and Communion in Global Anglicanism', in Markham, Hawkins, Terry and Steffensen (eds), *The Wiley-Blackwell Companion to the Anglican Communion*, chapter 4; Roger Coleman (ed.), *Resolutions of the Twelve Lambeth Conferences 1867-1988* (Toronto: Anglican Book Centre, 1992); Paul Avis, 'Anglican

cohesion arising from various quarters: (1) Bishop Colenso's rationalistic biblical interpretation and his acceptance of polygamy in the diocese of Natal that had led to his irregular excommunication and deposition and replacement by his militantly conservative metropolitan Bishop Gray of Capetown, and the consequent bitter ecclesiological and legal controversy; (2) critical and speculative theology in the collection *Essays and Reviews* (1860) that caused a storm of protest in the Church of England that has never been equalled, before or since; (3) the restoration of the Roman Catholic territorial hierarchy in England and Wales in 1850 (the so-called papal aggression), and the definition of the dogma of the Immaculate Conception of the Blessed Virgin Mary by Pope Pius IX in 1854. In the face of opposition and refusals (York, Carlisle, Durham, Ripon, Peterborough, Manchester), Longley tried to calm fears and suspicions. He insisted that the gathering of bishops would be a 'conference', not a synod or council; it would be for 'brotherly consultation' and take place in the context of Holy Communion. Longley specifically described the gathering as an expression of 'communion'. It would not lay down definitions of doctrine, but would facilitate common counsel and strengthen the bonds of charity. It would meet, he said, 'under my presidency'.[12]

The sermon at the opening service of Holy Communion in Lambeth Palace chapel was preached at length by the Bishop of Illinois. The bishops, who were living in comfort and dining in state, were afraid of becoming objects of ridicule if his address became public – his text was 'We fill up what is behind in the sufferings of Christ.' It seems that the agenda had not been settled in advance, so there was all to play for. Vigorous attempts were made to get the Colenso–Gray issue debated, involving heated, emotional and passionate exchanges. In these circumstances Archbishop Longley's grip on the proceedings occasionally faltered. The aged Bishop of St David's, the eminent historian and liberal thinker Connop Thirlwall, had agreed to be present only because he had received an assurance from Archbishop Longley that the matter would not be debated. When Thirlwall was attacked by the Bishop of New Zealand, he was defended by the Bishop of Ely (Harold Browne) as not only the most

Conciliarism: The Lambeth Conference as an Instrument of Communion'; in Mark D. Chapman, Sathianathan Clarke and Martyn Percy (eds), *The Oxford Handbook of Anglican Studies* (Oxford: Oxford University Press, 2015), chapter 3. The Lambeth Conference resolutions are available online at www.lambethconference.org (accessed 11 May 2016)

[12] On the hopes and intentions behind the 1867 Lambeth Conference, see the chapter by Benjamin Guyer in this book.

learned prelate in Europe, but probably the most learned bishop in the history of the Church![13] The intransigent Bishop Gray went on to provoke further trouble during and after the conference, vaunting his metropolitical authority. So heated were these debates that many bishops were not keen to repeat the experiment.[14]

The second conference, in 1878, was called by Archbishop Tait who was one of those who (as Bishop of London) had insisted to Longley that the first conference should not debate the Colenso affair (bound up as it was with matters of English law and the church–state connection) in the presence of bishops, such as the Americans, who were not concerned with it. Tait consulted all the bishops of the Communion asking their opinion about a second conference. The response was overwhelmingly affirmative, provided that it were to be longer than the first.[15] In 1878 there was pressure for some definitive doctrinal statements, for example on biblical inspiration, but Tait, like Longley before him, insisted that questions of doctrinal interpretation (and of church discipline) would be excluded from the agenda.[16] Why then bring all the bishops together from the far corners of the earth? Tait's correspondence with the American church clarified this issue. Working for the Kingdom of God was to be at the centre of their concerns; various practical avenues for that work were identified, including the unity of the Anglican Communion and how to respond to modern unbelief.[17] In his opening address Tait tactfully gave recognition to the diversity of constitutions in the churches of the Communion, while explaining and defending the polity of the Church of England and its connection with the Crown. He was careful not to tread on the American bishops' toes. In conclusion he brought the bishops back to the centrality of the Gospel and the catholicity of the Church.[18] Whereas the first conference deliberated for four days, the second worked for a month: a week in plenary, two weeks in committee and the final week together again to consider the committees' submissions and to finalize the resolutions. Under

---

[13] Randall Thomas Davidson and William Benham, *Life of Archibald Campbell Tait: Archbishop of Canterbury* (3rd edn, London: Macmillan, 1891), vol. 1, pp. 378–9.
[14] Davidson and Benham, *Life of Tait*, vol. 2, p. 362.
[15] Ibid., p. 368.
[16] Ibid., pp. 363–7.
[17] Ibid., pp. 268–9.
[18] Ibid., pp. 371–5.

Tait's wise and firm guidance the Lambeth Conference had now become a valued institution of the Anglican Communion, one with a future.

The archbishop who in 1888 called the third Lambeth Conference, Edward White Benson, recorded in his diary his own similar words from the opening of the conference: 'The Conference was in no sense a Synod and not adapted, or competent, or within its powers, if it should attempt to make binding decisions on doctrines or discipline.'[19] Benson prepared meticulously for – but did not live to preside at – the conference of 1897. Brooke Foss Westcott, Bishop of Durham, described how Benson envisaged the next conference: 'Here he saw an occasion not for the decision of matters of debate, but for setting before the whole Anglican Communion the lesson of brotherly love, for realising its unity and growth, for laying the foundation of a stronger life in … the power of the indwelling Spirit.'[20] A. H. Baynes, the Bishop of Natal, observed that, given the potentiality but also the fragility of the conference, Benson (who was a patristic scholar and a dyed-in-the-wool churchman) 'spoke with the authority of one who had all ecclesiastical history behind him spread out for reference and guidance.'[21]

Benson's sudden, untimely death meant that it was his successor Frederick Temple, previously Bishop of Exeter and then of London, who presided at the 1897 Lambeth Conference. It was Temple's third conference. He had been present in 1878 and also in 1888, when his contribution, in the form of a report on the Bible, had been rebuffed (his contribution to *Essays and Reviews* still dogged his footsteps). Following Benson's death the bishops convened in a subdued and not particularly expectant spirit. But Temple galvanized the Conference, winning the hearts of all, especially the American bishops, who had found his uncompromising style at first difficult to stomach. But Temple was not described as 'granite on fire' for nothing. With headmasterly discipline and brusque but amusing interventions from the chair, he steered the discussions safely to port. Temple wrote the conference encyclical himself, overnight. The bishops marked the 1,300th anniversary of Augustine's landing by a pilgrimage to Glastonbury as 'the cradle of British Christianity', where a

---

[19] A. C. Benson (ed.), *The Life of Edward White Benson, Sometime Archbishop of Canterbury*, 2 vols (London: Macmillan, 1900), vol. 2, p. 214; also Stephenson, *Anglicanism and the Lambeth Conferences*, p. 79.

[20] Benson, *Benson*, vol. 2, p. 695.

[21] Ibid., pp. 751–2.

hugely impressive procession, augmented by hundreds of local clergy, took place.[22] A committee report on 'The Organization of the Anglican Communion' proposed that the Lambeth Conference should be held every ten years and that a 'Tribunal of Reference' should be established, chaired by the Archbishop of Canterbury and with episcopal representation from those colonial and missionary churches that would determine to accept its decisions. It would be 'a court of arbitration on judicial matters', said Bishop John Wordsworth, the chairman of the committee. The idea was viewed with grave suspicion by the American bishops in particular and was not taken up. However, the conference resolved (Resolution 5) that the Archbishop of Canterbury should constitute a 'consultative body' to offer information and advice to those member churches that requested it. It began its work, but its proceedings were not made public.[23]

When Randall Davidson became Archbishop of Canterbury in 1903 he had already attended three Lambeth Conferences. He had edited the proceedings of the 1867, 1878 and 1897 conferences.[24] He had made himself indispensable. He would convene and preside at two more: 1908 and 1920. Sagacious, prudent and cautious, Davidson was the consummate 'safe pair of hands'. But he was also an ecclesiastical statesman, above the fray, and had been an adviser to the sovereign (Queen Victoria, who had died in 1901). Before the Lambeth Conference 1908, Davidson was invited by the Presiding Bishop, Thomas March Clark, who had been at the 1867 Conference, to address the General Convention of the Protestant Episcopal Church of the United States (PECUSA) in 1904. By the time of the 1908 Lambeth Conference Davidson had a vast knowledge of the churches of the Communion.[25]

The 1908 Conference is the only one to have virtually coincided with a Pan-Anglican Congress (other Congresses were held in 1954 and 1963). A great gathering of Anglican clergy and laity (men and women) was proposed by Bishop Montgomery (Secretary of the Society for the Propagation of the Gospel (SPG), the father of Field Marshall Bernard Montgomery). In preparation for

---

[22] E. G. Sandford (ed.), *Memoirs of Archbishop Temple by Seven Friends*, 2 vols (London: Macmillan, 1906), vol. 2, pp. 268–80; see also Peter Hinchliff, *Frederick Temple: Archbishop of Canterbury* (Oxford: Clarendon Press, 1998).

[23] Stephenson, *Anglicanism and the Lambeth Conferences*, pp. 101–4.

[24] Davidson, *The Origin and History of the Lambeth Conferences of 1867 and 1878*.

[25] G. K. A. Bell, *Randall Davidson: Archbishop of Canterbury* (3rd edn, London: Oxford University Press, 1952). Davidson's Anglican ecclesiology can be seen in his second visitation charge, *The Character and Call of the Church of England* (London: Macmillan, 1912).

the Congress, all Anglican bishops were asked about the questions that they faced in their own region and what problems they thought others faced. But to the third question, 'What is the chief corporate duty of the whole Anglican Communion at this time?', 'no confident answers were forthcoming'.[26] The purpose of the Congress was primarily educational: divided into sections, the participants heard papers and responses on a range of topical theological and missiological issues from a galaxy of scholars and experts. As George Bell put it, the Congress was 'intended to stir the imagination of the Anglican Communion'.[27] Proposals by E. J. Palmer to give the Lambeth Conference synodical status as 'a General Council of the Anglican Communion', and to create an Executive Council of 'Patriarchs' of the Communion were given short shrift. No resolutions were tabled, but the proceedings of the Congress filled half a dozen volumes. The strain and stress was great and Davidson vowed that never again should an Anglican Congress and a Lambeth Conference be held in the same year.[28]

Davidson chaired all sessions of the 1908 Conference. His handling of tricky issues was masterly and his presidency was marked by a characteristic judiciousness. If anything, he was a little too patient and tolerant in the face of long-winded or irrelevant interventions. All the chairs of committees were diocesan bishops of the Church of England, but the sermon at the final service of Holy Communion in St Paul's Cathedral was preached by the Presiding Bishop of the American church, Daniel S. Tuttle. The conference pilgrimage was to Lindisfarne (Holy Island), off the coast of Northumberland where, by a miscalculation of the tide over the causeway, many bishops and their ladies found themselves waist-deep in the sea. Davidson was a great Archbishop, but he was not Moses.

Davidson needed all his wisdom and skill to steer the Lambeth Conference 1920. Elements of the Church of England were polarized between militant modernists like Henry Major and intransigent traditionalists like Charles Gore, recently retired as Bishop of Oxford. (Gore and a few other eminent, retired bishops were invited, but they declined to attend on the grounds that they no longer held office.) Gore and Bishop Gibson of Gloucester wanted the

[26] Stephenson, *Anglicanism and the Lambeth Conferences*, pp. 112–13.
[27] Bell, *Randall Davidson*, p. 569.
[28] Ibid., p. 569.

conference to affirm the literal interpretation of the creeds. Gore hinted at a schism of Anglican Catholics. The canny Davidson was determined to avoid a debate that would split the Conference and therefore to keep the interpretation of the creeds off the agenda. He astutely steered between the extremes. He wrote to Gibson of his fears of alienating some of the most thoughtful and devout of the younger generation of Anglicans who were feeling their way to faith and would, he believed, be greatly deterred by a conference resolution insisting on the strict letter of the creeds and, moreover, the encouragement that such a statement would give to hot-headed clergymen to denounce from the pulpit more symbolic, metaphorical interpretations. On the other hand, in his opening address from the chair of St Augustine in Canterbury Cathedral, Davidson astutely praised the enduring power and validity of the creeds, while recalling that his great predecessors had found ways to commend the faith to their own generation.[29]

Cosmo Gordon Lang made his Lambeth Conference reputation before he became Archbishop of Canterbury. It was largely thanks to Lang (then Archbishop of York) that the Lambeth Conference 1920 was the most influential of all the conferences up to the present day, and that its influence was felt above all in the sphere of Christian unity.[30] In the aftermath of the First World War, 1914–18, it was inevitable that the conference should take the themes of reconciliation, fellowship and unity. Although reconciliation was in the air, for various reasons the conference did not augur well. As its success hung in the balance, Lang, assisted by George Bell (then chaplain and secretary to Archbishop Davidson; later Bishop of Chichester) pulled a rabbit out of the hat with the idea of an appeal for unity to the whole Christian world. The secret of the approach was to invite and persuade, not to argue; to concentrate on what was positive, not to highlight the difficulties. A committee of all the talents crafted a text that has stood the test of time: the *Appeal to All Christian People*. It was addressed to all the faithful – all baptized persons – within the universal Church and struck a winning note of penitence and hope. It restated the 'Lambeth Quadrilateral' of 1888, which was derived from the 'Chicago

---

[29]   Bell, *Randall Davidson*, pp. 1004–7.
[30]   Stephenson, *Anglicanism and the Lambeth Conferences*, pp. 128–54; Roger Lloyd, *The Church of England 1900-1965* (London: SCM Press, 1966), pp. 403–12; Bell, *Randall Davidson*, pp. 1003–15; J. G. Lockhart, *Cosmo Gordon Lang* (London: Hodder & Stoughton, 1949), pp. 264–84; H. Hensley Henson, *Retrospect of an Unimportant Life, vol. 2, 1920-1939* (Oxford, 1943), pp. 1–23.

Quadrilateral' (1886) of the Protestant Episcopal Church of the United States, a formula shaped by the writings of William Reed Huntington.[31] Lang 'led and guided the committee with a skill, a tact and a vision which was quite incomparable'.[32] Looking back, Bell paid tribute to Lang's work for unity: 'There is no man in the whole Anglican Communion who has left a deeper impression on the whole Unity movement in that Communion between 1920 and 1947 than Lang' – not even William Temple, he wrote.[33] Under Lang's leadership, the committee had found the Holy Grail of ecumenical rhetoric.[34]

When Davidson retired, after twenty-five years as Archbishop of Canterbury, he compiled the proceedings of all the conferences to date.[35] Probably he is the Archbishop who has given most unstinting service to the Lambeth Conference, as secretary (or assistant) to three conferences, as convener and president of two further conferences, and as the annalist of all to date.

Lang returned in 1930 to preside as Archbishop of Canterbury (1928–42).[36] The conference took as its theme the perennial challenge, 'The Faith and Witness of the Church in this Generation'. The momentum of Christian unity created by the Conference (of 1920) was continued, the Conference noting progress with the Orthodox, the Old Catholics and the Church of Sweden. Lang acknowledged his debt to expert advice on the byzantine ways of the Eastern churches. The conference ran into choppy waters on the subjects of birth control and Anglicans accepting ecumenical eucharistic hospitality and at least two bishops walked out. Lang felt that the encyclical letter had turned out to be too long and wordy, that there was too much exhortation and not enough information. As with Frederick Temple's handling of 1897, the American and many Canadian bishops had reservations about Lang's patrician style of chairing the proceedings in 1930. Lang invited the Presiding Bishop of the Protestant Episcopal Church of the United States, James DeWolf Perry,

---

[31] See further the chapter by Mark D. Chapman in this book.
[32] Lloyd, *Church of England*, p. 406. See further the chapter by Charlotte Methuen in this book.
[33] Lockhart, *Cosmo Gordon Lang*, p. 273.
[34] See further Paul Avis, 'Anglicanism and Christian Unity in the Twentieth Century', in Jeremy Morris (ed.), *The Oxford History of Anglicanism, Volume IV: Global Western Anglicanism, c. 1910–present* (Oxford: Oxford University Press, 2017), chapter 9.
[35] Randall Davidson (ed.), *The Six Lambeth Conferences 1867-1920: Compiled under the direction of the Most Reverend Lord Davidson of Lambeth, Archbishop of Canterbury 1903-1928* (London: SPCK, 1929).
[36] Lockhart, *Cosmo Gordon Lang*, chapter XXVIII. Robert Beaken's excellent study, *Cosmo Lang: Archbishop in War and Crisis* (London and New York: I. B. Tauris, 2012) does not include discussion of Lang's role in the 1920 and 1930 Lambeth Conferences.

to preach at the final service of Holy Communion in Westminster Abbey. T. S. Eliot commented that the conference had affirmed, more clearly than previous ones, the catholicity of Anglicanism.

At the 1930 Conference William Temple, now Archbishop of York, made his mark, preaching at the inaugural service in St Paul's and chairing the Committee on Unity, composed of seventy-three bishops. Temple had attended the 1908 Anglican Congress as a lay person and the 1910 Edinburgh International Missionary Conference as a young priest, and in 1920, not yet a bishop, he had addressed Lang's committee on reunion. Large gatherings were his *forte*, or one of the many. Public speaking was in his blood and his chairmanship was superb. But Temple did not live to preside at a post-war conference, though by his writings and personal ministry he had paved the way for it. He died at a most untimely moment in 1944 after only two and a half years at Canterbury, and was succeeded by Geoffrey Fisher. William Temple had his shortcomings, but Archbishops of Canterbury who have attained the combined spiritual, pastoral, intellectual, theological and strategic stature of Temple have been very rare.[37]

Geoffrey Fisher's first Lambeth Conference was the one at which he presided, 1948 (he had been a bishop since 1932). To jog the corporate memory of the Communion and to resource the first conference for eighteen years, with a world war intervening, a volume of texts was produced, containing the full reports from 1920 and 1930, together with selected resolutions of the conferences from 1867 to 1908.[38] Fisher was determined not to repeat the shortcomings of Lang's *de haut en bas* method of chairing in 1930. He built on his warm friendship with Henry Knox Sherrill, Presiding Bishop of the American church, showing him much courtesy in the conference and inviting him to preach at the inaugural service in St Paul's Cathedral on 4 July, Independence Day. One of the American bishops commented on 'the masterly blend of geniality, resource and firmness with which he [Fisher] guided the Conference through all its phases'. Though a confident, buoyant and supremely capable leader, Fisher was also a friendly, kind and thoughtful person, with a warm sense of humour. He

---

[37] On William Temple, see F. A. Iremonger, *William Temple, Archbishop of Canterbury: His Life and Letters* (London: Oxford University Press, 1948); Alan Suggate, *William Temple and Christian Social Ethics Today* (Edinburgh: T&T Clark, 1987); John Kent, *William Temple: Church, State and Society in Britain* (Cambridge: Cambridge University Press, 1992). An excellent introduction and anthology is Stephen Spencer, *Christ in all Things: William Temple and his Writings* (London: Canterbury Press, 1915).

[38] *The Lambeth Conferences (1867-1930)* (London: SPCK, 1948).

had the necessary touch. The Anglican Communion began to feel like a real family. Sherrill wrote to Fisher afterwards: 'It is impossible to over-state what the Conference meant to all of us Americans.'[39]

Fisher resisted, both in 1948 and in 1958, suggestions that theologians should be present to advise the bishops. They needed no help in reflecting on their extensive experience, he said. This policy – and attitude – changed in 1968 under Michael Ramsey, himself of course a mighty theologian.

The 1948 Conference received a subtle statement on authority in Anglicanism, produced by a committee chaired by Philip Carrington, Archbishop of Quebec. The report, while not solving all questions, has remained a benchmark of Anglican theological identity. Previous Lambeth Conferences, it noted, 'have wisely rejected proposals for a formal primacy of Canterbury, for an Appellate Tribunal, and for giving the Conference the status of a legislative synod'; the Conference 'remains advisory'. Then came the constructive formula: 'The positive nature of the authority which binds the Anglican Communion together is therefore seen to be moral and spiritual, resting on the truth of the Gospel, and on a charity which is patient and willing to defer to the common mind.' The authority that the Anglican Communion has inherited from the undivided Church is 'distributed among Scripture, Tradition, Creeds, the Ministry of the Word and Sacraments, the witness of saints, and the *consensus fidelium*, which is the continuing experience of the Holy Spirit through His faithful people in the Church.' It is thus 'a dispersed rather than a centralized authority', in a way that reflects 'God's loving provision against the temptations to tyranny and the dangers of unchecked power'.[40]

Fisher and Davidson are the only Archbishops to have presided over two Lambeth Conferences. By 1958 Fisher knew many Anglican churches at first-hand and had successfully courted the American church. But Lambeth 1958 was no mere re-run for him. The sense of fellowship was, if anything, stronger and more fervent than in 1948. Once again Fisher gave Sherrill a notable place in the proceedings, inviting him to preach at the farewell service in Westminster Abbey. Fisher commented emotionally as he bade Godspeed to

---

[39] On Fisher, see Edward Carpenter, *Archbishop Fisher: His Life and Times* (Norwich: The Canterbury Press. 1991); Andrew Chandler and David Hein, *Archbishop Fisher, 1945-1961: Church, State and World* (Farnham, Surrey and Burlington, VT: Ashgate, 2012).

[40] *Lambeth Conference 1948: Encyclical Letter from the Bishops Together with the Resolutions and Reports* (London: SPCK, 1948), Part II, pp. 84–5.

the departing bishops: 'We have in the last five weeks been living close to the kingdom of heaven.' He could not go on and gave way to tears.[41]

Following the template of earlier conferences, the 1958 Conference's encyclical letter was addressed 'to the faithful in Jesus Christ', not merely to Anglicans. The opening greeting slightly nuanced earlier forms in a more ecclesiologically correct direction: 'We, Archbishops and Bishops of the Holy Catholic and Apostolic Church in communion with the See of Canterbury [rather than in communion with "the Church of England" (1920, 1930) or with "the Archbishop of Canterbury" (1948)] ... under the presidency of Geoffrey, Archbishop of Canterbury, in the year of our Lord one thousand nine hundred and fifty-eight, send you greeting in the name of our Lord and Saviour Jesus Christ.'[42] The conference was notable for its work on the family in contemporary society and for the report on the authority and message of the Bible, of which Michael Ramsey, then Archbishop of York, was the leading light.[43] The encyclical pointed out that one of the 'distinguishing marks' of the Anglican Communion was 'the supreme importance which is attached to the authority of the Bible in the formulation of doctrine'.[44]

George Bell, though retired and soon to die, was present; it was his fourth conference. Bell felt that the agenda was overloaded and that the bishops were being hustled through it by an excess of administrative efficiency. The 1958 Conference also authorized the Archbishop, with the consent of others, to appoint for the first time an Executive Officer of the Anglican Communion. It was to be Stephen Bayne, Bishop of Olympia, Seattle, whose admirable discharge of the office ensured that the role would be perpetuated. Both before and after the conference and during it Fisher gave patient, detailed attention to setting the newly independent churches of the Anglican Communion on a sound constitutional footing.[45]

---

[41] Carpenter, *Archbishop Fisher*, pp. 475–6. The antidote to sentimentality was provided by the sardonic Bishop of London, H. C. Montgomery Campbell, who commented that if one attended the Lambeth Conference there was no need to go to the zoo, 'for here we have asses that bray, monkeys that play and elephants that never forget' (oral tradition).

[42] *The Lambeth Conference 1958: The Encyclical Letter from the Bishops Together with the Resolutions and Reports* (London: SPCK; Greenwich, CT: Seabury Press, 1958), Part 1, p. 17.

[43] *The Lambeth Conference 1958*, Part 2, pp. 1–18.

[44] *The Lambeth Conference 1958*, Part 1, p. 18.

[45] Edward Carpenter, *Archbishop Fisher: His Life and Times*, chapter 35. For an insightful, revisionist study of Fisher, see Andrew Chandler and David Hein, *Archbishop Fisher, 1945-1961: Church, State and World*.

Michael Ramsey attended his first Lambeth Conference in 1958 as Archbishop of York, receiving acclaim from most but opprobrium from others for his report on the authority and use of the Bible in the modern world. In the period between his enthronement at Canterbury in 1961 and the Lambeth Conference of 1968 Ramsey travelled to address a number of large conventions – not his favourite venues – including the World Council of Churches (WCC) Third Assembly in New Delhi in 1961 (where he spoke passionately about the imperative of church unity), and immediately before the Lambeth Conference of 1968 the WCC Fourth Assembly in Uppsala. (He had previously attended the inaugural Assembly of the WCC in Amsterdam in 1948 and the Second Assembly, at Evanston, Illinois, in 1954, but felt uncomfortable, perhaps even distressed, by the huge scale and rather triumphalist tone of the Evanston Assembly which, he believed, militated against humble, prayerful reflection and consultation.) He was at the notable Anglican Congress in Toronto (1963) with its theme, 'Mutual Responsibility and Interdependence in the Body of Christ'. Following the Second Vatican Council (1962–65) Ramsey visited Pope Paul VI (1966) and they initiated a still ongoing theological dialogue (now the Anglican – Roman Catholic International Commission: ARCIC).

There was a marked change of style for the 1968 Conference. Ramsey had encouraged the forming of numerous small committees of about fifteen bishops each, so that all bishops who had something to say could contribute to the discussion. Ramsey wanted theologians and other advisers to be present and a rich crop (26) from around the Communion participated, contributing to plenary debates and raising the intellectual tone. The agenda was heavily theological and issues of social justice were also more prominent than in 1958. Ecumenical observers – seventy-six of them – were present for the first time. The press and public were allowed into certain plenaries. It was the first 'gaiterless' conference. Pope Paul VI sent greetings by the hand of (the then) Bishop Willebrands, and Archbishop Athenagoras of Thyateira brought a message of goodwill from the Ecumenical Patriarch. Instead of an encyclical, the conference issued a rather terse, heavily prescriptive and therefore not very persuasive or winsome 'message'.[46] Ramsey kept debates to time but often allowed the discussion to drift. At one point there was confusion and

---

[46] *The Lambeth Conference 1968: Resolutions and Reports* (London: SPCK; New York: Seabury Press, 1968).

uproar. Chairing debates was not his strong point. He was infinitely bored by poor-quality speeches and took the opportunity to catch up with his letter writing. He sought to facilitate a prayerful, spiritual, reflective gathering of the bishops and partly succeeded.[47] It was this conference that recommended that a representative Anglican Consultative Council (ACC) be created to replace the Lambeth Consultative Body. Importantly, Lambeth 1968 has a claim to be considered the first post-colonial conference, where paternalism gave way to equal brotherhood.[48]

The 1978 Conference was called and presided over by Archbishop Donald Coggan, a 'caretaker' Archbishop of Canterbury in the eyes of many, but an efficient administrator, a student of the Scriptures and an evangelist at heart. Coggan was, however, no ecclesiologist. The conference wrestled, without acrimony and with the assistance of the learning and wisdom of Professor John Macquarrie, with the question of the ordination of women as priests, which had begun to happen in some member churches. Other theological consultants included Professors Henry Chadwick, David Jenkins and Stephen Sykes. Consultants and ecumenical observers were free to contribute to debates. The resolutions tended to be discursive, some being mini-essays; the drafting was rather out of control. The conference resolved (Resolution 13) that the calling of future conferences should fall to the Archbishop of Canterbury, in consultation with 'the other primates', but that it need not necessarily be held in the Archbishop's Province. The Section 3 report, on 'The Anglican Communion in the world-wide Church', suggested (I think I detect the hand of Stephen Sykes here) that the 'distinctive doctrinal basis' of the churches of the Communion was chiefly to be found in 'the patterning of elements shared in common with other Churches'. The Anglican 'doctrinal fundamentals' were to be found in the constitutions, canons and prayer books of the churches, together with the statements of Lambeth Conferences. It was held together by the threefold ministry and the historic episcopate; and 'personally grounded in the loyal relationship of each of the Churches to the Archbishop of Canterbury who is freely recognized as a focus of unity'.[49] The

[47] Owen Chadwick, *Michael Ramsey: A Life* (Oxford: Clarendon Press, 1990), pp. 98–9, 273–6.

[48] Peter Webster, *Archbishop Ramsey: The Shape of the Church* (Farnham, Surrey and Burlington, VT: Ashgate, 2015), pp. 23–4.

[49] *The Report of the Lambeth Conference 1978* (London: CIO Publishing, 1978), pp. 98ff.

'dispersed' character of authority for Anglicans, classically stated in 1948, was reaffirmed. Regular meetings of the Primates were encouraged and Dr Coggan spoke of his intention to gather the Primates 'for leisurely thought, prayer, and deep consultation', and in close liaison with the ACC, perhaps every two years.[50] This is, of course, the origin of the Primates' Meeting, now one of the four Instruments of Communion.

Archbishop Robert Runcie welcomed the bishops of the Anglican Communion to the 1988 Lambeth Conference with his characteristic warmth, charm and humour. He had learnt from his experience of Anglican–Orthodox dialogue the dictum, 'A bishop brings his diocese with him' and made this a mantra of his conference presidency (he had been a member of the Anglican–Orthodox dialogue since 1973 and became its chairman the following year).[51] He had attended the 1978 Conference as Bishop of St Albans and had warned the Conference against antagonizing the Orthodox by ordaining women.[52] It is well known that Runcie relied on proven advisers to draft his addresses, which were then 'Runcified', given his personal stamp. On the whole, this process made the archbishop a good theologian. In this case, he and the conference embraced the ecumenical theology of *koinonia*. The conference was all the stronger for the input of ecumenical theologians, both Anglican and other (the Orthodox John Zizioulas among them). In Archbishop Runcie's opening address on 'The Nature of the Unity We Seek' he brought together unity within the Anglican Communion, ecumenical unity between the churches, and the unity of God's creation.[53] He stressed the provisionality of Anglicanism (which perhaps made better sense in that ecumenical spring than it does now), hoped for the reform of the Roman papacy, rejected 'denominational federalism' in favour of 'visible organic unity' and affirmed that diversity should be celebrated. The conference resolved that the new Inter-Anglican Theological and Doctrinal Commission should study the nature of communion (this eventually resulted in the *Virginia Report*, 1997), that the Primates' Meeting should have 'an enhanced responsibility' in 'offering guidance on doctrinal,

[50] *The Report of the Lambeth Conference 1978*, pp. 103, 123.

[51] Carpenter, *Robert Runcie*, p. 366.

[52] Margaret Duggan, *Runcie: The Making of an Archbishop* (London: Hodder and Stoughton, 1983), pp. 165–7, 180–1.

[53] *The Truth Shall Make You Free: The Lambeth Conference 1988; The Reports, Resolutions and Pastoral Letters from the Bishops* (London: Anglican Consultative Council, 1988), pp. 11–24.

moral and pastoral matters', and that the other churches of the Anglican Communion should have some input into the appointment of future Archbishops of Canterbury (Resolution 18).[54] Lambeth 1988 was, Runcie claimed, the most skilfully planned of all Lambeth Conferences and the one with the most 'molecular structure'.[55] It had a substantial theological agenda and broad ecumenical horizons, suitably resourced, because Robert Runcie knew where to turn for advice.

The Lambeth Conference – I prefer to speak of it as a single enduring institution, rather than as a series of sporadic events – has been convened since 1867 by the Archbishop of Canterbury in office at the time. It meets within the Archbishop's diocese and worships in the cathedral that is the seat of his (or, in the future, her) episcopal ministry. It forms the collective pastorate of the Anglican Communion. The gathered bishops represent and symbolically embody their dioceses. Although from first to last the conference has declined to claim juridical authority and therefore, like the other Instruments of Communion, cannot issue any binding directives to the churches of the Communion, the Lambeth Conference has considerable moral, pastoral and spiritual weight and authority. That kind of authority is fragile as well as precious and needs to be well stewarded by the Archbishops of Canterbury as they convene and preside and by those who advise and assist them, lest it be devalued by poor process leading to rash or unsubtle judgements, particularly ones that are intrinsically and inevitably divisive.

What has the Lambeth Conference said about the Archbishop of Canterbury?

Since Archbishop Longley called the first Lambeth Conference in 1867, various conferences, particularly the more recent ones, have made formal statements about the office, role and ministry of the Archbishop of Canterbury. The Lambeth Conference 1897, in requesting that there should be further Conferences at ten-yearly intervals, acknowledged that it would

---

[54] *The Truth Shall Make You Free*, pp. 216–18.
[55] Carpenter, *Robert Runcie*, p. 368.

be for the Archbishop to gather such Conferences.[56] The 1930 Conference underlined the constitutive role of the Archbishop of Canterbury when it defined the Anglican Communion as 'a fellowship, within the one, holy, catholic and apostolic Church', of dioceses, provinces and regional churches that are 'in communion with the See of Canterbury'.[57] Interestingly, in the proceedings of the 1948 Conference, which is notable for its elaborate statement about authority, the office of Archbishop of Canterbury is virtually invisible.[58] The 1958 Conference recommended that a 'Consultative Body' be established 'to assist the Archbishop of Canterbury in the preparation of the business of the ensuing Conference' and 'to consider matters referred to the Archbishop of Canterbury on which he requests its aid and to advise him' and, furthermore, 'to deal with matters referred to it by the Archbishop of Canterbury or by any bishop or group of bishops'. The resolution recognized that the Archbishop would be 'ex officio Chairman' of this Consultative Body and would 'summon' its members to meet.[59] The 1968 Conference's section report on unity made a quite low-key statement about the place of the Archbishop of Canterbury within the Communion. While emphasizing the collegiality of the episcopate, the report recognized that within the college of bishops there must be a president. It observed that 'this position is at present held by the occupant of the historic See of Canterbury, who enjoys a primacy of honour, not of jurisdiction'. It added that this primacy involves 'in a particular way, that care of all the churches which is shared by all the bishops'.[60]

The 1978 Lambeth Conference section report dealing with the Anglican Communion within the universal Church affirmed (though the text is hardly a model of clarity) that the basis of the Communion 'is personally grounded in the loyal relationship of each of the Churches to the Archbishop of Canterbury who is freely recognised as the focus of unity'.[61] The 1978 resolutions described the Archbishop as the 'President' of the Lambeth Conference and of the ACC

---

[56] LC 1897, Resolution 2: Coleman, p. 16.
[57] LC 1930, Resolutions 48 and 49: Coleman pp. 83–4.
[58] *The Lambeth Conference 1948: The Encyclical Letter from the Bishops; Together with Resolutions and Reports* (London: SPCK, 1948). The classic statement on authority is in section report IV, III (pp. 84–6).
[59] LC 1958, Resolution 61, (a) and (b): Coleman, p. 134.
[60] *The Lambeth Conference 1968* (London: SPCK; New York: Seabury Press, 1968), p. 137.
[61] *The Report of the Lambeth Conference 1978* (London: CIO, 1978), p. 98.

and affirmed that it remained the prerogative of the Archbishop to call a Lambeth Conference, but recommended that he should make his decision in consultation with other Primates.[62]

The conference of 1988, in urging that the Primates should have a strengthened 'collegial role', also recognized that the meetings of the Primates were presided over by the Archbishop of Canterbury. This conference also recommended (as noted above) that, in the appointment of any future Archbishop of Canterbury, the Crown Appointments Commission (now the Crown Nominations Commission) of the General Synod of the Church of England should 'be asked to bring the primates of the Communion into the process of consultation'.[63] Subsequent practice has reflected this concern by providing for the Primates' Meeting to elect one of its number to be a voting member of the Crown Nominations Commission, while the Secretary General of the ACC has a non-voting seat.[64]

In the light of the appalling failure of ecclesial structures in the Rwanda genocide, the conference of 1998 raised the question of in what circumstances the Archbishop of Canterbury should have 'an extra-ordinary [*sic*] ministry of episcopé (pastoral oversight), support and reconciliation with regard to the internal affairs of a Province other than his own for the sake of maintaining communion within the said Province and between the said Province and the rest of the Anglican Communion'.[65] The Lambeth Commission that produced the *Windsor Report* of 2004 had this question as part of its mandate, but did not directly address it in the report. The constitutional position is that the Archbishop of Canterbury visits member churches of the Communion at their invitation. The Lambeth Conference 2008 did not produce any formal resolutions, but the role of the Archbishop, Rowan Williams, was pivotal in holding the conference together and resourcing its prayer and reflection.

---

[62] Ibid., Resolutions 12 and 13 (p. 42).
[63] LC 1988, Resolution 18.2 (a) and (b): *The Truth Shall Make You Free*, p. 216; Coleman, p. 207.
[64] See further *Working with the Spirit: A Review of the Crown Appointments Commission and Related Matters* (London: Church House Publishing, 2001), p. 57 (para. 3.82). *To Lead and to Serve: The Report of the Review of the See of Canterbury* ('the Hurd Report') (London: Church House Publishing, 2001), p. 48. These reports suggested that the chair of the ACC should be a voting member of the Crown Nominations Commission (formerly the Crown Appointments Commission) and that the Secretary General of the ACC should in future have a vote.
[65] LC 1998, IV, 13: http://www.lambethconference.org/resolutions/1998/1998-4-13.cfm.

How have commissions of the Communion described the Archbishop?

In addition to the resolutions and section reports of the Lambeth Conference, various commissions set up by the Anglican Communion in recent times have discussed the role of the Archbishop of Canterbury. The *Virginia Report* (1997) described the Archbishop of Canterbury's ministry in the Communion as that of 'a pastor in the service of unity', offering care and support to the churches (provinces) of the Communion by invitation of the member churches. It went on to say that 'the interdependence of the Anglican Communion becomes most clearly visible when the Archbishop of Canterbury exercises his primatial office as an enabler of mission, pastoral care and healing in those situations of need to which he is called'.[66]

Interestingly, the *Virginia Report* describes the Archbishop of Canterbury as 'Primate of the Anglican Communion'.[67] This title has not been picked up since *the Virginia Report* and it is not difficult to see why. Although the Archbishop does have a degree of primacy – primus inter pares, first among equals – among Anglican bishops by virtue of his (or her in the future) presidency of the Lambeth Conference, the Primates' Meeting and the ACC, it is strange to describe him as 'Primate' of the Communion as such – as though his metropolitical jurisdiction extended throughout the Communion, as a sort of universal archbishop. That would be a quasi-papal role. The Archbishop does not have any primatial jurisdiction outside the Church of England. The term 'Primate of the Anglican Communion' was inept.[68]

The *Windsor Report* (2004) describes the Archbishop of Canterbury, 'both in his person and his office', as 'the pivotal instrument and focus of unity', observing that 'relationship to him became a touchstone of what it was to be Anglican'.[69] It therefore seems rather inconsistent when, a few pages later, the report suggests that the Archbishop of Canterbury should not be counted among the instruments of unity, but should be seen as 'the focus of unity' – but then on the same page again places the Archbishop among the 'Instruments

---

[66] *Virginia Report*, 6.2.
[67] Ibid., 6.6.
[68] On the Archbishop of Canterbury's primatial authority and related questions, see Podmore, *Aspects of Anglican Identity*, chapter 5.
[69] *The Windsor Report* (London: Anglican Communion Office, 2004), para. 99 (p. 55).

of Unity'.[70] This is a little incoherent. It may seem odd to describe a person as an 'instrument', but it is the office and ministry, the responsibility and the authority bestowed upon that individual, that are in mind when the Archbishop of Canterbury is designated as one of the four Instruments of Communion.

The *Windsor Report* seeks to strengthen the role of the Archbishop. He (it was bound to be a 'he' until recently) should not be regarded as a mere 'figurehead', but as 'the central focus of both unity and mission within the Communion'. He has 'a very significant teaching role' and Anglicans should be able to look to him 'to articulate the mind of the Communion especially in areas of controversy'. He should be able 'to speak directly to any provincial situation on behalf of the Communion when this is deemed advisable'. He should have complete discretion about when to call the Lambeth Conference or the Primates' Meeting and sole discretion about whom to invite and on what terms. However, the report goes on to guard against any suggestion that it is giving the Archbishop some kind of arbitrary power, by recommending that he should have the benefit of a Council of Advice in exercising this discretion.[71] Archbishop Justin Welby consulted all of his fellow Primates (except the Primate of Nigeria who would not play ball) in person and on their home wicket in the run up to the Primates' Gathering and Meeting in January 2016.

The report of the Windsor Continuation Group (2009) puts the Archbishop firmly back among the Instruments of Communion. It points out that the pivotal presidential role exercised by Archbishop Rowan Williams at the 2008 Lambeth Conference, evidenced by his three presidential addresses, has 'highlighted the extent to which there is scope for the ministry of a personal primacy at the level of the worldwide Communion'. The report urges, however, that this ministry should be exercised in personal, collegial and communal ways, as the World Council of Churches' Faith and Order report *Baptism, Eucharist and Ministry* (1982) had proposed for all ordained ministry.[72] The collegial mode of the Archbishop's ministry is exercised formally in conjunction with the bishops of the Communion through the Lambeth Conference and the Primates' Meeting; the communal context is provided, rather nominally, at

---

[70] Ibid., paras 105, 108 (p. 58). It is not entirely clear what is implied when, in Appendix 1 (pp. 79–80) the Anglican Communion Office is discussed in the context of the Instruments of Communion.

[71] Ibid., paras 109–12 (pp. 59–60).

[72] *Baptism, Eucharist and Ministry*, M26.

the global level by the ACC. The report of the Windsor Continuation Group makes a couple of tentative suggestions about how the Archbishops might be assisted in carrying out their role.[73]

The text of the proposed Anglican Communion Covenant contains a descriptive statement about the role accorded to the Archbishop within the Communion:

> We accord the Archbishop of Canterbury, as the Bishop of the See of Canterbury with which Anglicans have historically been in communion, a primacy of honour and respect among the college of bishops in the Anglican Communion as first among equals (*primus inter pares*). As a focus and means of unity, the Archbishop gathers and works with the Lambeth Conference and Primates' Meeting, and presides in the Anglican Consultative Council. (3.1.4: I)

It is worth noting that (1) neither this statement nor the proposed arrangements for the outworking of covenant commitments entails any executive role for the Archbishop of Canterbury; but equally (2) the covenant does not envisage a purely symbolic role for the Archbishop; the Archbishop is not only a 'focus' but also a 'means' of unity: this is to echo the language of 'instrument'.

The collegial *Locus* of the Archbishop of Canterbury

In order to understand Anglicanism, we must grasp the unique role of the Archbishop of Canterbury. Canterbury itself is important because it is historically the first metropolitical see (the seat of the archbishop who has primatial authority) of the Church of England and therefore – for originally historical reasons, but Anglicans take history seriously, or used to – of the Anglican Communion.[74] It is significant that the Archbishop of Canterbury is also a diocesan bishop, the 'chief pastor' of a 'local church'. It is significant not only because it earths the Archbishop's work for the Communion in the day-to-day life and practice of the Church, but also because it gives the Archbishop a place and a base that is ecclesiological rather than organizational. As well as

---

[73] The Windsor Continuation Group, 'Report to the Archbishop of Canterbury' (2009), paras 62–4 (p. 13).
[74] Paul Avis, *The Identity of Anglicanism: Essentials of Anglican Ecclesiology* (London and New York: T&T Clark, 2008), pp. 61–2.

situating the Archbishop in a diocese (a 'local church' in the ecclesiological sense), it also places him or her within a college of bishops, that of the Church of England. The College of Bishops of the Church of England includes all serving bishops, suffragans as well as diocesans. The House of Bishops is a synodical entity, alongside the Houses of Clergy and of Laity, and is composed of the diocesan bishops and certain suffragans elected by their peers. Although the Archbishop of Canterbury is a joint President, with the Archbishop of York, of the General Synod and will also chair certain kinds of debates, fundamentally he or she is a diocesan bishop existing in solidarity (as St Cyprian put it in the third century) with other diocesan bishops and therefore called and required to operate collegially.

The diocesan and collegial *loci* of the Archbishop of Canterbury are the foundation of his or her wider role in the Anglican Communion. They also serve to limit the power, prestige and authority of the role. Indeed, those words – power, prestige and authority – ring falsely in this connection. They are inappropriate and inapplicable to the office of the Archbishop. The Archbishop of Canterbury has little or no direct power in any context, as the Archbishops themselves have been the first to acknowledge (or bemoan). If there is prestige, it is not inherent and can only be accorded by others; it can easily be squandered. The authority of the office, beyond the Church of England, is a purely spiritual, moral and pastoral authority – though I in no way underestimate the significance of those attributes. That kind of authority cannot be claimed; it can only be recognized and responded to. If Archbishop Lang presided at Lambeth 1930 in a somewhat prelatical and unwittingly pompous manner, Archbishop Fisher, though second to none in personal power and ability, set things right in 1948 (the times had radically changed of course anyway) by a style that, while supremely competent, was at the same time affable, kindly and self-deprecating. Ecclesiologically, the Archbishop of Canterbury is positioned *alongside* the other bishops of the Communion, in fellowship, solidarity and fraternal solicitude (solicitude was one of Lang's favoured terms for his care of the churches). Those bishops and their churches have traditionally accorded the Archbishop of Canterbury a primacy of honour and a convening and presiding role. It is not the case that all Anglican bishops are equal, but some are more equal than others (to adapt George Orwell in *Animal Farm*). The Archbishop of Canterbury does not have personal rank and the polity of the Communion is not hierarchical.[75] It has been acknowledged since Archbishop Longley obliquely, but firmly, sketched a few ground rules in 1867 – and was explicitly laid down by the Lambeth Conference 1930, Resolution 49 – that member churches ('provinces') need to be in communion with the See of Canterbury as a necessary but not sufficient condition of belonging to the Anglican Communion. They remain in communion with that see regardless of who the current incumbent may be. Archbishops come and go but the see continues in being and has done so since 597.

It is clear from the history of the century and a half that has passed since the first Lambeth Conference, and from the formal statements that the Anglican Communion has produced since then, that the Archbishop of Canterbury has had and continues to have a pivotal role with regard to the identity, unity and coherence of the Anglican Communion – all matters that are currently of great importance and urgency for Anglicans. It puts the Archbishop's Anglican Communion role in the right perspective when we call to mind that the Archbishop is prayed for daily in Anglican celebrations of the liturgy around the world.

It was the Archbishop of Canterbury who, in 1867, initiated the Lambeth Conference in the face of doubts and opposition, and it is the Archbishop of Canterbury who continues to invite the bishops of the Communion to attend it. From time to time the Archbishop may exercise some discretion, no doubt after discreet consultation, in the interests of Anglican unity, harmony and coherence, over whom he invites and whom he chooses not to invite. He presides over the Conference's proceedings and guides its deliberations (Rowan Williams gave unprecedented input of a theological and reflective nature into the 2008 Lambeth Conference). That is to say that the Archbishop is the convener, host and president of the Lambeth Conference, which many would consider the most significant of the Instruments of Communion. There is thus an intimate connection between the ministry of the Archbishop and the Lambeth Conference of all the bishops. The Archbishop also convenes the Primates' Meeting and presides over its business. Constitutionally, the Archbishop is President of the ACC.

---

[75] See further, Paul Avis, 'Polity and Polemics: The Function of Ecclesiastical Polity in Theology and Practice', *Ecclesiastical Law Journal* 18 (2016), pp. 2–13.

The office and ministry of the Archbishop of Canterbury is integral to the way that the Anglican Communion is constituted, as a worldwide fellowship of self-governing but interdependent churches. But a relationship to and connection with the Archbishop of Canterbury is also a criterion of membership of the Communion, for it is not possible for a church to be a member of the Communion without being in communion with the Archbishop as the Bishop of the See of Canterbury. Through communion with the See of Canterbury, Anglican Churches are held in communion with the Church of England and with each other, and this is reflected in the constitutions or canons of a number of member churches, while those non-Anglican Churches that are in communion with the Anglican Communion are also in communion with the See of Canterbury. 'The litmus-test of membership of the Anglican Communion is to be in communion with the See of Canterbury. Of course, this cannot be the only condition for membership of the Communion. A common faith and order; a shared tradition of liturgy, theology and spirituality; and participation in the [other] instruments of the Communion are also involved. But it is the ultimate criterion.'[76]

The communion (*koinonia*; *communio*) that Anglicans thankfully receive as a gift from God in the church is conciliar and sacramental in nature: indeed the two aspects are bound together in Anglican ecclesiology. It is as a eucharistic body that the Anglican bishops come together in the Lambeth Conference to take prayerful counsel with one another as they gather around the open page of Scripture. The intimate connection between the conciliar and the sacramental dimensions of communion are particularly clearly manifested when the Archbishop of Canterbury presides and often preaches at the opening eucharistic celebration of the Lambeth Conference in Canterbury Cathedral, the bishops being, as it were, gathered around the seat of St Augustine. But that opening celebration of the Eucharist also makes it clear that the Archbishop is set in the midst of the community of Anglican bishops and intends to exercise his or her unique responsibilities in consultation and collaboration with his or her fellow bishops. Except at meetings of the ACC, the Archbishop relates to the Anglican clergy and lay faithful around the world indirectly, through their bishops, not immediately (unlike the claims made for and by the papacy

---

[76] Avis, *The Identity of Anglicanism*, p. 62.

in the Roman Catholic Church). But at the ACC the communal nature of the Archbishop's ministry becomes apparent: it is exercised in consultation and collaboration with the bishops, with other clergy and with laypeople of the Communion who are present in a representative capacity in the ACC.

Conclusion

In 1935 the then Archbishop of Canterbury, Cosmo Lang, wrote, 'The job is really impossible for one man, yet only one man can do it.'[77] What Lang thought about the pressures and burdens of the office is even more true today, but the masculine gender is now out of date. In this chapter we have generally used the male pronoun for the Archbishop of Canterbury. That is currently applicable and so it would seem a little artificial to say he or she every time; but it probably will not always be the case that the Archbishop is male. In July 2014 the Church of England's General Synod finally opened the way for women to be ordained to the office of bishop in that church. If bishop, then eventually archbishop, both of York and of Canterbury. Such a step would be of incalculable symbolic significance both for Anglicanism and for the whole Christian Church, given the Church's appalling record on gender equality and the treatment of women. But it has been a constant refrain of this chapter to insist that it is not the individual but the office that matters.

George Bell, Bishop of Chichester until 1958, had been chaplain to Randall Davidson, Archbishop of Canterbury from 1903 to 1928, and wrote his life. It is one of the great ecclesiastical biographies. In the third edition (1952) he added a preface in which he reflected on the changes in the office and work of Archbishop during the past century, and compared the first three primacies of the twentieth century, those of Davidson, Lang and William Temple. Bell's main conclusion was that as the authority and prestige of the office had steadily declined in society and in the councils of state, the personal, spiritual qualities of the incumbents had become more crucial: 'While the prestige of the institution may have waned, the character and gifts of the person count for more and more.' Bell noted that every Archbishop was dependent on his office: 'Every Archbishop derives great potential moral authority from his office, and

---

[77] Lockhart, *Cosmo Gordon Lang*, p. 372.

in the exercise of that moral authority his personal qualities count for more and more.'[78] The ministry of the Archbishop of Canterbury depends hugely on the personal spiritual, moral and theological qualities of the person who exercises it – that is undeniable. But the office is greater than any one occupant of it. The office of Archbishop has been shaped by history, struggle and conflict. It has been moulded by the prayer and the scholarship, the leadership and the witness, even to martyrdom in some cases, of previous incumbents. It is the marriage of the historic office with the personal abilities, gifts and spiritual calibre of the incumbent that is the key to the authority of the Archbishop of Canterbury.

Whoever may be the occupant of the office at any one time, the ministry of the Archbishop of Canterbury commends itself to the Anglican Communion (and to the universal Church too) as a paradigm of episcopal ministry that is personal and pastoral, that gathers, guides, leads and challenges. But not only has the office and ministry of Archbishop of Canterbury given much to the Anglican Communion, especially through the Archbishop's presidency of the Lambeth Conference, but the Lambeth Conference has given much of substance to the office and ministry of the Archbishop. The Lambeth Conference has provided the Archbishop with an enhanced international role and a global platform, a ministry that extends beyond the Church of England. There is a symbiotic relationship between the Archbishop and the Lambeth Conference, one of interdependence and reciprocity. A successful Conference, fruitful in faithful testimony to the Gospel and wise guidance to the Communion, a conference that models constructive conciliar working in the context of communion, is a boon to an Archbishop of Canterbury. But to convene, lead and preside at a Lambeth Conference is possibly the supreme challenge of an archiepiscopate. We have seen how wise Archbishops discarded the colonial mindset, kept inevitably divisive topics off the agenda, sought the help of theologians and other experts, courted the American church as the most significant Anglican church of the time after the Church of England, kept the lid on long-winded speeches and prolix resolution-making and, all in all, won the hearts of the bishops.

---

[78] G. K. A. Bell, *Randall Davidson, Archbishop of Canterbury* (London: Oxford University Press, 1952), pp. v–xxviii at pp. vi and xiii.

The ministry of the Archbishop of Canterbury is manifestly both catholic and reformed. It stretches back beyond the Reformation to the mission of St Augustine of Canterbury in the early European Middle Ages, but was reshaped at the time of the Reformation by the authority of the Gospel and the Reformation imperatives of word, sacrament and pastoral care. It is a ministry that is not hierarchical and unaccountable, but constitutional, accessible, fraternal and challengeable. It is just such an office and ministry that has, on the whole, well served the Lambeth Conference.

3

'This Unprecedented Step': The Royal Supremacy and the 1867 Lambeth Conference[1]

Benjamin M. Guyer

Let us hope that the time is approaching when, as a great witness for Christ and His truth, the Anglican Church in all its branches will make some more real and effectual advance towards manifesting her unity before men, and gathering up the scattered fragments of the great human family in one body in Christ, by bringing together witnesses from every land, for those children, whom the Lord has already given her, and who are now really and actually one with her in their faith and ministry.

Francis Fulford (1866)[2]

On 12 February 1867, Charles Thomas Longley, Archbishop of Canterbury, addressed the Church of England's Upper House of Convocation about holding a global gathering of Anglican bishops under his presidency. Discussing the nature of the meeting, he pointedly stated, 'I repudiate all idea of convening any assembly that can be justly called "a Synod," or that can enact canons or attempt to do acts which be in direct opposition to the authority of the Crown, which forbids the taking any such step.'[3] Many subsequent commentators have treated these words as a constitutional declaration, portraying the Archbishop as having determined by fiat what the Lambeth Conference must forever be: a purely

---

[1] I am grateful to Andrew Atherstone, Paul Avis and Ross N. Hebb for comments on earlier versions of this chapter. Any and all faults remain my own.
[2] Francis Fulford, *A Pan-Anglican Synod: A Sermon Preached at the General Ordination held by the Right Reverend the Lord Bishop of Oxford, in the Cathedral Church of Christ in Oxford, on Sunday Dec. 23, 1866* (Oxford: Rivingtons and Montreal: Dawsons, 1867), p. 13.
[3] *Chronicle of Convocation*, Upper House: Tuesday, February 12, 1867, pp. 646–7.

consultative gathering wholly devoid of corrective or even directive authority. In *The First Lambeth Conference, 1867*, the only monograph-length study of the topic, Alan M. G. Stephenson repeatedly praised Longley and described the Archbishop's refusal of synodical authority as a 'wise decision'.[4] Archbishop Michael Ramsey took a similar view, commenting that in 1867, 'there was inaugurated a series of Conferences of such a character as to prove through a century that there can be no Pan-Anglican authoritative Synod and no Anglican Patriarchate, but a family of Churches able to advise one another collectively on the understanding of the Faith and of the Church's contemporary needs and tasks while possessing no organ of formal authority other than that of the Synods of each Anglican church.'[5] But is this interpretation correct?

In this chapter, I argue that emphasizing the first part of Longley's statement, in which he denied that the Lambeth Conference would be a synod, misses what was, for contemporaries, a far more important matter: his immediately stated deference to the royal supremacy. Scholarship has long recognized that theological debates in the 1860s over *Essays and Reviews* and the theology of Bishop John Colenso helped spur the 1867 episcopal gathering subsequently known as the first Lambeth Conference.[6] The Canadian church named both theological controversies in its 1865 request to Archbishop Longley for an international Anglican synod. However, focusing on the concerns stated in the

---

[4] Alan M. G. Stephenson, *The First Lambeth Conference, 1867* (London: SPCK, 1967), p. 308; see also pp. 278–9, 310, 325, 331.

[5] Michael Ramsey, Foreword to Alan M. G. Stephenson, *The First Lambeth Conference*, p. xiii. The non-synodical nature of the first Lambeth Conference is widely assumed. See, for example, Owen Chadwick, 'The Lambeth Conference: An Historical Perspective', *Anglican and Episcopal History*, Vol. LVIII, No. 3, September 1989, pp. 259–77, at pp. 268–9, 274–5, 277; J. Robert Wright, 'The Authority of Lambeth Conferences, 1867–1988', *Anglican and Episcopal History*, Vol. LVIII, No. 3, September 1989, pp. 278–90, at pp. 278–9, 283–5, 287. Wright concludes his essay by calling for 'critical examination' of the 'vacuum of authority' in contemporary Anglicanism. More recently, Robert W. Prichard has taken a slightly different line, noting that Anglicans currently disagree about the authority of the Lambeth Conference'. See Robert W. Prichard, 'The Lambeth Conferences', in Ian S. Markham, J. Barney Hawkins IV, Justyn Terry and Leslie Nuñez Steffensen (eds.), *The Wiley-Blackwell Companion to the Anglican Communion* (Malden: Wiley-Blackwell, 2013), pp. 91–104. Ross N. Hebb, 'The Canadians at Lambeth: An Examination of the Canadian Bishops at the Lambeth Conferences of 1867, 1878 and 1888', *Journal of the Canadian Church Historical Society*, XLIX (2007), pp. 5–37, emphasizes the same lack of synodical authority while pointing to its inadequacy.

[6] See, for example, Peter Hinchliff, *John William Colenso* (London: Thomas Nelson and Sons, 1964), pp. 184–5; Stephenson, *The First Lambeth Conference*, ch. 7 (on *Essays and Reviews*) and ch. 8 (on Colenso); William L. Sachs, *The Transformation of Anglicanism: From State Church to Global Communion* (Cambridge: Cambridge University Press, 1993), pp. 201–5, at p. 202; Josef L. Altholz, *Anatomy of a Controversy: The Debate Over 'Essays & Reviews'* (Aldershot: Scolar Press, 1994), pp. 130–1; Hebb, 'The Canadians at Lambeth', pp. 7–8; Stewart J. Brown, *Providence and Empire 1815 - 1914* (Harlow: Pearson Longman, 2008), pp. 240–1.

Canadian proposal has resulted in ignorance of other issues that were equally important. Throughout the Anglican world, and especially in England, the horizon of relevant theological controversy extended back to 1850. Studying debates about the royal supremacy will significantly nuance our understanding of the first Lambeth Conference, allowing us to better understand concerns over the authority of the 1867 episcopal gathering, and how those same debates have been used and misused in later Anglican tradition. Simply stated, the first Lambeth Conference was intended to be a synod. The royal supremacy prevented it from being so.

I Defining the royal supremacy

The royal supremacy is a collective term that denotes two variant forms of a sixteenth-century doctrine about royal authority in and over the Church of England. Henry VIII promulgated the first version; his daughter Elizabeth promulgated the second. Although sixteenth-century ecclesiastical history is often subsumed under the soteriological debates spurred by Martin Luther, among both Protestants and Catholics the same period saw a high-water mark in the history of royal involvement in ecclesiastical affairs. A long history lay behind these developments. Sketching it briefly will help us understand not just the history of sixteenth-century England, but how the eventual absence of an active royal supremacy within the Church of England resulted in a significant vacuum of authority within the wider Anglican Communion.

In the eleventh century, the papacy began taking steps to remove the Catholic Church from royal influence and control.[7] These developments, collectively known as the Gregorian reforms, were not wholly successful and had a very different and unintended outcome; Pope Gregory VII and his supporters initiated a recurring struggle between papal and royal authority that animated much of the high politics of Western Christendom for the next five hundred years. Theologically and politically, much was often at stake in these debates. One major reformist concern was the rite of coronation,

---

[7] Helpful overviews of the Gregorian reforms and their aftermath may be found in Uta Renate Blumenthal, *The Investiture Controversy: Church and Monarchy from the Ninth to the Twelfth Century* (Philadelphia: University of Pennsylvania Press, 1988); Kathleen Cushing, *Reform and the Papacy in the Eleventh Century: Spirituality and Social Change* (Manchester: Manchester University Press, 2005).

which centred on the anointing of the monarch. It was widely believed that this granted the monarch an administrative and even sacerdotal role in the Church, but in the mid-eleventh century some reformers began denying this, arguing that the king was only a layman.[8] Their argument carried significant implications for a much larger issue, the role of the king in ecclesiastical affairs. In the dispute between the German Emperor Henry IV and Gregory VII over 'lay' investiture,[9] emperor and pope excommunicated one another. Henry then appointed a pope whom he recognized, while Gregory claimed that Henry's excommunication absolved subjects of their political obligations to the emperor. Germany thus erupted in civil war. Gregory died in exile and Henry eventually secured his throne, but the twelfth century dawned upon a fundamentally altered political and ecclesiastical landscape, even though the issues raised by these events went unresolved. In the twelfth and thirteenth centuries, excommunication, threats of civil war and eventually the papal interdict punctuated the narrative of Western Christendom.

As a working theory of ecclesial order, royal supremacy did not die. Its ascent in popularity began as a response to the unprecedented breakdown of papal authority during the (Western) Great Schism (1378–1417), when the entire Western church split between two and then three rival claimants to the See of Rome. Appeals to royal intervention and even headship were not uncommon in the fifteenth century. Some Anglicans today look back to the fifteenth century as the era of conciliarism – a time when church councils asserted their authority over the pope by declaring the authority of all bishops as equal.[10] It is just as accurate to describe the conciliar era as the birth of modern royal supremacy. In *The Catholic Concordance* (1433), arguably the most developed work of conciliarist theory, Nicholas of Cusa set forth a vision of the relationship between royal and papal authority that gave the Holy Roman Emperor ultimate responsibility for the well-being of both Church and Empire. Quite unlike papal theorists who looked for the pope to secure the relationship

---

[8] Blumenthal, *The Investiture Controversy*, p. 87; for a more general analysis of royal anointing and its meanings, see George H. Williams, *The Norman Anonymous of 1100 A.D.: Toward the Identification and Evaluation of the So-Called Anonymous of York* (Cambridge, MA: Harvard University Press, 1951; reprinted Eugene, OR: Wipf and Stock, 2008), pp. 79–82.

[9] The very term 'lay investiture' presumes the normative validity of the papal claim that monarchs are merely laity, a claim that many monarchs and their supporters denied.

[10] See, for example, Paul Avis, *Beyond the Reformation? Authority, Primacy and Unity in the Conciliar Tradition* (London: T&T Clark, 2006); Paul Valliere, *Conciliarism: A History of Decision-Making in the Church* (Cambridge: Cambridge University Press, 2012).

between these, Cusa exhorted the emperor, 'Act with most eager zeal to do this for your immortal glory, o most kind prince, so that thus the way to peace in the church and eternal fame for you and your subjects may be re-established in our time, in praise of Christ who reigns blessed forever.'[11] By the end of the 1430s, both the king of France and the electors of the Holy Roman Empire drew upon conciliar theory to attain far greater control over the churches in their lands. In France, the Pragmatic Sanction of Bourges extended the king's influence over episcopal elections while limiting the amount of money paid by the kingdom to the papacy. A similar proposal, the *Instrumentum Acceptationis*, was advanced in Germany, although the emperor did not ultimately endorse it.[12] It was with good reason that some seventeenth-century Anglican apologists argued that the Pragmatic Sanction of Bourges laid the groundwork for the royal supremacy advocated by sixteenth-century Tudor sovereigns.[13]

The first version of the royal supremacy was promulgated in 1534, when Henry VIII was declared 'supreme head in earth' of the Church of England. His son Edward VI maintained this title. It has long been debated whether Henry sought to pattern his royal supremacy upon the papal supremacy. In some ways, the answer appears to be positive. For example, during Henry's reign, Archbishops were expected to affirm their loyalty to the king when they received the pallium; under the papacy, they had affirmed their loyalty to the pope when they received the same.[14] Through *The King's Book* of 1543, Henry also played a proactive role in formulating doctrine – a role unusual for a king, but not for a pope. Later monarchs – notably Elizabeth I, James I, Charles I and Charles II – played a decisive role in shaping Anglican doctrine, as well as canon law and liturgy. No less importantly, Henry did not take on all papal roles. He did not conceive of the monarch as a *rex sacerdos* (priest king), who participated in the consecration of the Eucharist. The Henrician model became the norm for later English monarchs, but such a decision was

---

[11] Nicholas of Cusa, *Nicholas of Cusa, The Catholic Concordance*, translated and edited by Paul E. Sigmund (Cambridge: Cambridge University Press, 1991), para. 597, p. 322.

[12] Michiel Decaluwe, *A Successful Defeat: Eugene IV's Struggle with the Council of Basel for Ultimate Authority in the Church, 1431 – 1449* (Brussels: Institut Historique Belge de Rome, 2009), pp. 291–3

[13] John Shaw, *Origo Protestantium* (London, 1677), p. 5; Anonymous [Gilbert Burnet?], *Reflections on the Relation of the English Reformation, Lately Printed at Oxford, Part I* (Amsterdam, 1688), pp. 13–15.

[14] Paul Ayris, 'God's Viceregent and Christ's Vicar: the Relationship between the Crown and the archbishopric of Canterbury, 1533–53', in Paul Ayris and David Selwyn (eds.), *Thomas Cranmer: Churchman and Scholar* (Woodbridge: The Boydell Press, 1993), pp. 115–56, at pp. 134–5.

not a foregone conclusion. In Anglo-Saxon times, kings entered the sanctuary and presented the bread and wine at their coronation.[15] Although this practice died out with the Norman invasion, it remained a topic of live discussion in the writings of the twelfth-century 'Norman Anonymous', whose work was preserved by Matthew Parker, the first Archbishop of Canterbury under Elizabeth I.[16] Sixteenth-century kings of France also took on a priestly role by receiving both the bread and the wine at their coronation. This set them apart from other laity, who received only the bread.[17] But whatever the vestiges of priesthood in the history of Christian monarchy, the papacy always retained its full range of liturgical and theological duties.

The second version of the royal supremacy was promulgated under Elizabeth I, who styled herself 'supreme governor' rather than 'supreme head'. In the Thirty-nine Articles of Religion (1571), the royal supremacy was defined with greater clarity and two broad limitations were placed upon the monarch's authority in religious matters: 'We geve not to our princes the ministring either of gods word, or of the Sacramentes.' Rather, monarchs had 'that only prerogative, whiche we see to have ben geven always to all godly Princes in holy Scriptures by God hym selfe, that is, that they shoulde rule all estates and degrees committed to their charge by GOD, whether they be Ecclesiasticall or Temporall, and restrayne with the civill sworde the stubberne and evyll doers'.[18] The Articles did, however, give monarchs both within and beyond England a key role in calling ecumenical councils. Article 21 stated that 'Generall Counsels may not be gathered together without the commaundement and wyll of princes'.[19] As defined under Elizabeth, royal supremacy gave the monarch neither a priestly nor an episcopal role within the Church of England, but it did nothing to inhibit the monarch's immense influence domestically, and did everything to give the monarch an international, ecumenical role. As we will see, Article 21 played a decisive role in shaping the first Lambeth Conference as well.

---

[15] William A. Chaney, *The Cult of Kingship in Anglo-Saxon England: The Transition from Paganism to Christianity* (Berkeley and Los Angeles: University of California Press, 1970), pp. 69–70; Williams, *The Norman Anonymous*, pp. 169–70. It might be argued that in some churches today, laity also present the bread and wine, but what matters is that in Anglo-Saxon times, laity did not do so – only the king did.

[16] Williams, *The Norman Anonymous*, pp. 167–74; on Archbishop Parker's role in preserving these texts, see ibid., pp. 24–7.

[17] Frederic J. Baumgartner, *France in the Sixteenth Century* (New York: St. Martin's Press, 1995), p. 9.

[18] The Church of England, *Articles of Religion* (London, 1571; STC 10038.11), Art. 37.

[19] Ibid., Art. 21.

The royal supremacy was not merely a question of ecclesiastical polity; it also received canonical, devotional and liturgical expression. When the Church of England crafted a new canon law in 1604, the canons defended the royal supremacy as identical with 'the same authority in causes Ecclesiastical that the godly Kings had amongst the Iewes, and Christian Emperors in the Primitive Church'. More importantly, the canons excommunicated any and all 'Impugners of the Kings Supremacie'.[20] In some British dependencies, notably Canada, canon law revision began in the late 1850s, but in England, the 1604 canons remained in use through the mid-twentieth century. For most Anglican provinces, the canonical vision of the seventeenth century remained wholly familiar in 1867, and in England it remained binding. Royal authority was also attached to popular devotion through the royal touch. Extending back to the time of Edward the Confessor, it was popularly believed that English monarchs could cure the sick of many diseases, particularly scrofula.[21] Henry VII gave the royal touch its first set liturgical expression, and with the exception of William and Mary, every monarch until George I practised the royal touch. Despite Hanoverian reticence, the royal touch continued to be administered by the Stuart descendants of James II, and popular belief in the effectiveness of Stuart relics has been documented to as late as 1901.[22] Although not dependent upon the royal supremacy, the royal touch bestowed an aura of miraculous grace upon the Church of England's supreme governor.

Liturgy similarly expressed a wide range of themes that buttressed the monarch's oversight of church and state. The liturgy for the royal touch was often included in the Book of Common Prayer, and the 1662 Book of Common Prayer contained three new liturgies that endorsed royal authority while simultaneously inveighing against the sinfulness of trying to overthrow it. The first liturgy commemorated the Gunpowder Plot, when Catholic extremists tried but failed to explode Parliament and King James VI and I. The second liturgy observed the martyrdom of Charles I, whom the 1662 liturgical calendar commemorated as King Charles the Martyr; 30 January, the date of

---

[20] The Church of England, *Constitutions and Canons Ecclesiasticall* (London, 1604; STC 10070), Canon II.

[21] The royal touch is now believed to have originated in France. The most recent analysis may be found in Stephen Brogan, *The Royal Touch in Early Modern England: Politics, Medicine and Sin* (Woodbridge: The Boydell Press, 2015), pp. 27–30.

[22] Marc Bloch, *The Royal Touch: Monarchy and Miracles in France and England*, trans. J. E. Anderson (New York: Dorset Press, 1989), pp. 222–3.

his death, was appointed a day of fasting. The third liturgy offered thanksgiving on the 29 May, when the monarchy was restored in 1660, and which led to the subsequent restoration of the Church of England. The Restoration further saw Charles II take on a special role in the liturgy. On Christmas, Easter and Whitsun (Pentecost), he received the alms of the Chapel Royal and placed them directly on the altar, thereby intimating an intercessory and even priestly role.[23] These were not simply 'state services' divorced from broader patterns of Anglican faith and devotion.[24] Rather, all three liturgies were used annually for almost two hundred years; only in 1859 did Parliament render them optional. Insofar as the rule of praying and the rule of believing depend upon one another, these long-used annual observances cannot be treated as merely tangential to Anglican history. To the contrary, they reveal much about the normative memories and ideals that existed for many Anglicans in the years immediately prior to the first Lambeth Conference.

II Debating the royal supremacy

Mid-nineteenth-century debates over the royal supremacy developed out of a seemingly unrelated dispute concerning the sacrament of baptism.[25] In 1847 Queen Victoria requested that Henry Phillpotts, Bishop of Exeter, install the Rev. George Cornelius Gorham at Brampford Speke, of which the Queen was patron. After examining Gorham, the Bishop refused to do so, arguing that Gorham's rejection of baptismal regeneration rendered him unfit for ministry. Gorham sought to have the Bishop's decision reversed by appealing to the Court of Arches, an ecclesiastical court, which subsequently ruled in favour of the Bishop; but in a wholly unprecedented move, Gorham appealed this decision to

---

[23] Anna Keay, *The Magnificent Monarch: Charles II and the Ceremonies of Power* (London: Continuum, 2008), pp. 154, 158.

[24] Charles Hefling, 'The State Services', in Charles Hefling and Cynthia Shattuck (eds), *The Oxford Guide to The Book of Common Prayer: A Worldwide Survey* (Oxford: Oxford University Press), pp. 73–5.

[25] There is regrettably little historical scholarship on nineteenth-century theologies of the monarchy. However, much good material may be found in Peter Nockles, 'Church and King: Tractarian Politics Reappraised', in Paul Vaiss (ed.), *From Oxford to the People: Reconsidering Newman & the Oxford Movement* (Herefordshire: Gracewing, 1996), pp. 93–123; see also David de Giustino, 'Disconnecting Church and State: Richard Whately's Ideas in the 1830s', *Albion: A Quarterly Journal Concerned with British Studies*, Vol. 35, No. 1 (Spring, 2003), pp. 53–70.

a secular court, the Judicial Committee of the Privy Council.[26] Having a secular court rule on an ecclesiastical matter was extremely unusual, and although the Judicial Committee dealt with some ecclesiastical issues, it had never before dealt with theology. Consequently, its membership included neither bishops nor archbishops. Although the Bishop of London and the Archbishops of Canterbury and York attended the trial and were consulted for their opinions, their merely advisory role effectively sidelined the Church of England in reaching the final verdict. When the Judicial Committee ruled in Gorham's favour, and when the Crown then ratified the decision, the initial debate over sacramental theology took an entirely new direction. As one clergyman observed, 'The Royal Supremacy in causes ecclesiastical has by the case of Gorham v. the Bishop of Exeter been brought before the minds of all churchmen as an object of engrossing interest.'[27] The problem was not the royal supremacy as such, but the fact that, having been exercised through a secular court, the decision encroached upon the Church's own autonomy. In the words of another clergyman, 'The decision of the Judicial Committee of the Privy Council in Mr Gorham's case is looked upon by many, as evidencing a design upon the part of the Crown to control the Church in matters which, in an especial manner, lie within her Province as Christian.'[28] In 1850 dispute over the royal supremacy became a defining feature of public debate in England. It remained so for decades.

One response to the Gorham crisis was pastoral. The Diocese of Ripon offers a good window on matters, not least because its Bishop at the time was Charles Thomas Longley. In an appendix to a pastoral letter written to his diocese, the Bishop reprinted six addresses, containing a combined total of 151 clerical signatures, which he had received about the Gorham crisis. Five of the addresses protested the decision of the Judicial Committee of the Privy Council; one address expressed concern with the state of upset, and called for the Church of England to maintain both its principles and its connection with the Crown. Given that Longley later called the first Lambeth Conference, it is tempting to read the fifth appended address in prophetic terms: 'We feel

---

[26] A helpful overview of the Gorham trial may be found in S. M. Waddams, *Law, Politics and the Church of England: The Career of Stephen Lushington 1782 – 1873* (Cambridge: Cambridge University Press, 1992), pp. 271–80.

[27] T. W. Allies, *The Royal Supremacy: Viewed in Reference to the Two Spiritual Powers of Order and Jurisdiction* (London: William Pickering, 1850), p. 5.

[28] W. W. Stoddart, *The Royal Supremacy in the Church of England, Considered Chiefly with Reference to the Appellate Jurisdiction* (London: Francis & John Rivington, 1851), p. 9.

strongly how desirable it is for the integrity of the Church, that measures be forthwith taken to secure to her an effectual mode of giving her authoritative declaration on this, as well as on other spiritual questions; and we, therefore, urgently pray that your Lordship will take such steps as may seem expedient for that purpose.'[29] In fact, Longley did not believe that the Crown had overstepped its legal bounds in appointing the members of the Judicial Committee, but he did hold its membership to be 'a real grievance' and supported petitioning the Queen to change its composition.[30] Thus maintaining the connection with the Crown, Longley rearticulated the Church of England's traditional teaching. He stood quite against Gorham by defending the doctrine of baptismal regeneration. 'I must say that any assertion which empties the Sacrament of Baptism of its grace, is as essentially opposed to the Articles as it is to the Prayer Book.'[31] Longley's 1850 pastoral letter reveals that well before the first Lambeth Conference, he strove to maintain the full scope of the Church of England's doctrine without undermining the royal supremacy.

Another set of responses were made at the national level and consisted of trying to restore a perceived prior equilibrium between the Crown and the Church of England.[32] Distress over the legal implications of Gorham's successful appeal required a clear restatement of the precise relationship between church and state. The most long-lived such analysis was William Gladstone's *Remarks on the Royal Supremacy: As it is Defined by Reason, History, and the Constitution*. Originally written as a letter to Charles Blomfield, Bishop of London, it was printed for the wider public in 1850, and further editions appeared in 1865 and 1877. Gladstone had no kind words for either Gorham or the Judicial Committee of the Privy Council, describing the latter's willingness to even hear the case a matter of 'gross indecency' that had brought forth 'evil fruits'.[33] Noting that the decision had caused some to consider leaving the

---

[29] Charles Thomas Longley, *A Pastoral Letter to the Clergy of the Diocese of Ripon* (London: Francis & John Rivington, 1850), p. 29.

[30] Ibid., p. 10.

[31] Ibid., pp. 14–15.

[32] There were a variety of approaches. A doctrinal framework was advanced by E. B. Pusey, *The Royal Supremacy not an Arbitrary Authority but Limited by the Laws of the Church, of which Kings are Members* (Oxford: John Henry Parker, 1850); F. C. Massingberd, *The Policy of the Church of Rome Promoted by the Abuse of the Royal Supremacy* (London: Francis & John Rivington, 1852) offered a more polemical take on matters.

[33] W. E. Gladstone, *Remarks on the Royal Supremacy: As it is Defined by Reason, History, and the Constitution* (London: John Murray, 1850), pp. 4, 5.

Church of England and that others had actually done so,[34] Gladstone believed that present confusion would benefit from a historically sound analysis and coherent restatement of the law. Although it is now common to describe the Church of England as Erastian,[35] Gladstone and many of his contemporaries denied that this was the case. For Gladstone, Erastianism was an egregious theological error, justifiable only by relying upon 'the authority of Pagan precedent'.[36] He sought to show that the Church did not depend on the state but instead supported it as an independent entity.

Gladstone began his study by challenging a claim made by the Anglican clergyman T. W. Allies, who held that under Henry VIII, the royal supremacy was intended as an exact copy of the papal supremacy. According to Allies, the papacy had not only been 'the source and centre of ecclesiastical jurisdiction', but that 'by a necessary consequence it was Supreme Judge of doctrine: for it is impossible in practice to dissever supremacy of jurisdiction from carrying with it the supreme judgment of doctrine'.[37] Anglican converts to Roman Catholicism sometimes offered a similar perspective, arguing that because the Church of Rome was not tied to the English state, it was free to maintain orthodoxy in a way that the Church of England could not. A good example comes from Robert Isaac Wilberforce, an Anglican clergyman who publicly repudiated the royal supremacy shortly before converting to Roman Catholicism. Citing the Articles of Religion, he held that although the Church of England had 'power to decree rites and ceremonies', the same authority had been 'dissipated by the Gorham Case'.[38] According to Wilberforce, the Church of England was the victim of a political arrangement in which the state no longer honoured the law – a reading of the situation not far removed from Gladstone's own argument.

Revisiting Tudor legislation, Gladstone countered that there was neither a legal nor a historical basis for making the Crown the final arbiter in theological

---

[34] Ibid., pp. 77–8.
[35] The term itself is problematic. Thomas Erastus was barely ten years of age when Henry VIII declared the royal supremacy; under Elizabeth and subsequent monarchs, almost nothing by Erastus was printed in England. The term 'Erastian' is a misnomer when applied to England because the royal supremacy predated Erastus' own writings.
[36] Gladstone, *Remarks on the Royal Supremacy* (1850), p. 24.
[37] Allies, *The Royal Supremacy*, p. 34.
[38] Robert Isaac Wilberforce, *An Inquiry into the Principles of Church-Authority; Or, Reasons for Recalling My Subscription to the Royal Supremacy* (London: Longman, Brown, Green, and Longmans, 1854), pp. 216–17.

disputes. Whatever Henry VIII's intentions might have been, his ecclesiastical legislation had been repealed in the reign of Mary I (1553–1558) and not subsequently revived. Elizabeth, c. 1 (section 17) was the legal basis for the continued exercise of royal supremacy. It directed that

> such jurisdictions, privileges, superiorities, and pre-eminences, spiritual and ecclesiastical, as by any spiritual or ecclesiastical power or authority hath heretofore been or may lawfully be exercised or used for the visitation of the ecclesiastical state and persons, and for reformation, order, and correction of the same, and of all manners of errors, heresies, schisms, abuses, offenses, contempts, and enormities, shall for ever, by authority of this present parliament, be united and annexed to the imperial crown of this realm.[39]

On Gladstone's reading, the Crown did not claim to be 'the source or fountain-head of ecclesiastical jurisdiction'. Rather, it claimed only 'powers for the reparation of defect and the reform of abuse'.[40] He compared the Church with the family; each was regulated but neither was created by the state.[41] Gladstone distinguished between the Church's capacity for self-government, which Tudor legislation had never questioned, and the coercive jurisdiction of the Crown.[42] A law was one thing; the *force* of the law was something else. The Church of England determined the content of its own canon law, and the Crown supplied the force that made the canon law binding upon English subjects. If the Judicial Committee of the Privy Council had allowed the Court of Arches' decision to stand, it would have added force to the ecclesiastical court's determination. In reversing the decision, the Judicial Committee overstepped its bounds.

III Obviating the royal supremacy

Bishop Phillpotts had his own response to the Judicial Committee's decision. He took the unprecedented step of calling a diocesan synod, which met in 1851.[43] In his letter of invitation, the Bishop outlined the synod's aims and schedule.

[39] Cited in Gladstone, *Remarks on the Royal Supremacy*, p. 13.
[40] Ibid., p. 14.
[41] Ibid., p. 15.
[42] Ibid., pp. 34–5.
[43] Much helpful background material may be found in Arthur Burns, *The Diocesan Revival in the Church of England c. 1800 – 1870* (Oxford: Clarendon Press, 1999), pp. 223–44.

It would open with Morning Prayer and the Holy Eucharist; the remainder of the first day would be devoted to discussions on baptism, while the second and third days would turn to other ministerial matters. Fearing that attendance by every clergyman of the diocese would make the synod unworkably large, the Bishop proposed a system of representation in which each deanery elected two participants. He invited clergy 'to transmit to me any questions which they may recommend for the consideration of the Synod',[44] and he in turn sent the clergy a set of draft declarations and proposed fifteen points for discussion.[45] A flurry of academic, pastoral and polemical literature followed. Gorham offered two arguments against the Exeter synod, first protesting *'the illegality of a Diocesan Synod assembled without the permission of the Crown',*[46] and then emphasizing a lack of precedent for the Bishop's allowance of representation.[47] Others defended both the Exeter synod and the revival of diocesan synods more generally.[48] Most importantly, the legality of diocesan synods was debated in Parliament. There was some concern that the Exeter synod would violate the civil law, but it was determined that insofar as Bishop Phillpotts would not propose any canons, then he did not need a royal writ to revive what parliamentary onlookers recognized as an ancient but long-abandoned institution.[49] In this regard, the choice of language used at the Exeter synod is extremely important. Those gathered did not pass canons – the synod had no authority to do so. Instead, they passed twelve 'Resolutions', the content of which was heavily drawn from the fifteen points originally proposed by Bishop Phillpotts. Other advocates of diocesan synods rapidly embraced as normative three elements of the Exeter synod: its opening Eucharist, the exclusively clerical attendance and the circulation of draft resolutions beforehand.[50] In all

---

[44] The letter is reprinted in *Acts of the Diocesan Synod*, second edn (London: John Murray, 1851), p. 1.

[45] Ibid., p. 2.

[46] George Cornelius Gorham, *The Exeter Synod*, second edn (Piccadilly: Hatchard, 1851), p. 22; emphasis in the original.

[47] Ibid., pp. 27–8.

[48] See, for example, George Trevor, *Diocesan Synods* (London: G. Bell, 1851); John Ingle, *The Synod no Treason* (London: J. Masters, 1851).

[49] The substance of the parliamentary debate is reprinted in Gorham, *The Exeter Synod*, second edn, pp. 31–5.

[50] In addition to the example of the 1851 Exeter Synod, for general background on developing approaches to the Eucharist at the time, see Burns, *The Diocesan Revival in the Church of England*, p. 122; see also William Pound, *Synods the Scriptural Remedy against Schism and Division in the Christian Church* (London: Rivington, 1852), which treats the Eucharist and synods as sharing, in an intertwined fashion, apostolic precedent. On membership, see Christopher Wordsworth, 'Diocesan Synods, and Diocesan Conferences', in *Miscellanies: Literary and Religious*, three vols. (London,

of this, the 1867 Lambeth Conference would follow in the footsteps of the 1851 Exeter synod.

With diocesan synods now a reality, provincial synods also seemed a distinct possibility. One of the earliest responses to the Gorham judgement was a protest by the Rev. George Anthony Denison, who pledged 'to use all lawful means within my reach to assist in obtaining, without delay, some further formal declaration, by a lawful Synod of the Church of England, as to what is, and what is not, the doctrine of the Church of England in respect to the Holy Sacrament of Baptism'.[51] Denison went so far as to send his protest to the Prime Minister, Lord John Russell, who read it from the floor of the House of Commons on 18 March 1850. While still pledging allegiance to the royal supremacy, Denison averred, 'I humbly conceive that the Constitution does not attribute to the Crown, without a Synod lawfully assembled, the right of deciding a question of Doctrine'.[52] Later that summer, Denison, Robert Wilberforce and a number of other clergy published a set of Resolutions against the Gorham judgement that included an open call for the revival of Convocation.[53] The last major proposal for restoring Convocation had been made almost a decade earlier. Predating the Gorham debates and thus occurring in a rather different ecclesial context, the Rev. Thomas Lathbury had published a history of Convocation in 1842, the centennial of Convocation's last meeting. He hoped that his work would 'give a succinct and connected history of the proceedings of Anglican Ecclesiastical Councils from the earliest period',[54] and he believed that the Crown would willingly 'submit to the consideration of Convocation such matters as in their judgment might be desirable, if the bishops and clergy were to express an opinion in favour of the revival'.[55] In the preface to the second edition of his work, which appeared in 1853, he named neither Gorham nor the Judicial Committee of the Privy Council, but wryly noted that 'since the previous edition of this work was published, the Convocation question has excited much more attention than

Oxford, and Cambridge: Rivingtons, 1879), Vol. III, pp. 155–65, at p. 164; on the importance of pre-circulated resolutions, see Burns, *The Diocesan Revival in the Church of England*, pp. 234–5.

[51] George Anthony Denison, *Notes of My Life, 1805 – 1878* (Oxford and London: James Parker and Co., 1879), third edn, p. 195.

[52] Ibid., p. 196.

[53] Ibid., pp. 197–9, esp. n. VIII.

[54] Thomas Lathbury, *A History of the Convocation of the Church of England: From the Earliest Period to the Year 1742*, second edn (London: J. Leslie, 1853), p. iv.

[55] Ibid., p. vi.

was formerly bestowed on it'.[56] The Gorham controversy had made the revival of Convocation a matter of renewed but urgent concern.

For other members of the Church of England, the church–state connection was a matter of vital import – and, according to some, the pursuit of ecclesial independence was tantamount to heresy. Weeks after Denison and his colleagues published their Resolutions, an anonymously authored response was published entitled *Convocations and Synods: Are They the Remedies for Existing Evils.*[57] The author claimed that requesting the revival of Convocation was 'hopeless',[58] and that even if the monarch allowed Convocation to assemble, its pronouncements would not be authoritative.[59] Evidently, this approach did not satisfy. In 1850, discussion began in earnest to revive the Convocation of Canterbury, which held its first meeting in 1852. But others continued protesting the rapidly changing relationship between the national church and the royal supremacy. William Peace, a thoroughgoing opponent of the Oxford Movement, published a diatribe against the revival of Convocation in 1860. The cover page of his book bluntly stated: 'An independent Ecclesiastical Association, possessed of deliberative, legislative, judicial, and executive authority, is incompatible with the supremacy of the crown, with the freedom of the subject, and with the welfare and peace of the kingdom.'[60] He repeated the exact same quote at the end of his work.[61] Buying fully into the Oxford Movement's own historiography,[62] he believed that 'the spirit of the Laudian heresy is again in the ascendant' – a spirit that he explicitly identified as 'a vile conspiracy'.[63] Granting the Church of England a greater degree of independence

---

[56] Ibid., p. iii.
[57] Anonymous, *Convocations and Synods: Are They the Remedies for Existing Evils: A Second Letter by an Anglican Layman* (London: William Pickering, 1850).
[58] Ibid., p. 9.
[59] Ibid., pp. 11–12.
[60] William Peace, *Phases of Convocation: Anglicans Synods, A.D. 601 to A.D. 1860* (London: Partridge and Co., 1860).
[61] Ibid., p. 167.
[62] Through its unfinished *Library of Anglo-Catholic Theology* (LACT), the Oxford Movement portrayed itself as the heir of a Caroline-era High Church movement allegedly centred on Archbishop William Laud. For a critique of the Oxford Movement's understanding of the seventeenth century, see Peter B. Nockles, 'Anglicanism "represented" or "misrepresented"? The Oxford Movement, Evangelicalism, and History: The controversial use of the Caroline Divines in the Victorian Church of England', in Sheridan Gilley (ed.), *Victorian Churches and Churchmen: Essays Presented to Vincent Alan McClelland* (Woodbridge: The Catholic Record Society and The Boydell Press, 2005), pp. 308–69. A broad overview of Caroline-era divinity that rejects the influence of the LACT on subsequent historiography may be found in Benjamin M. Guyer, *The Beauty of Holiness: The Caroline Divines and Their Writings* (London: Canterbury Press, 2012), pp. 1–26.
[63] Peace, *Phases of Convocation*, pp. 169, 170.

would only lead to the spread of heresy, which Peace principally identified as similarity to Roman Catholicism. He warned of impending judgement: 'Will not God visit a people for such delinquencies?'[64] This protest against ecclesial independence was but one voice in a growing cacophony of perspectives. It did not prove influential; the Convocation of York was revived in 1861.

The second edition of Gladstone's *Remarks on the Royal Supremacy* was published in 1865. His arguments were echoed in two other pamphlets printed that same year. One of these, *The Royal Supremacy and the Court of Final Appeal*, was authored anonymously, but the Hon. Colin Lindsay wrote *The Royal Supremacy and Church Emancipation*.[65] Like Gladstone, both authors denied that the royal supremacy entailed Erastianism,[66] but Lindsay took matters a step further. Whereas Gladstone offered a conservative argument, encouraging a return to Tudor law, Lindsay argued that the Church of England had to become proactive in developing its own legislation. He proposed a six-point concordat between the Church of England and the English state. Lindsay believed that the Crown should play a role in three areas: by selecting bishops from a list created by the Dean and chapter of the Cathedral (point one), by consenting to bishops for newly created sees upon their election 'by the clergy and lay communicants of the Church' (point two),[67] and by consenting to the division of preexisting sees (point five). In each of these areas, the monarch would thus retain an executive role. In three other areas, he called for ecclesial independence. He wanted bishops alone to appoint 'all Deans and other dignitaries of the Church' (point three),[68] and he called for ecclesiastical appeals made to the Judicial Committee of the Privy Council to 'be remitted to the Archbishops and Bishops of the four provinces' [of the United Church of Britain and Ireland], who would then decide the matters in their respective synods (point six).[69] Lindsay's fourth point was his longest. He

---

[64] Ibid., p. 170.

[65] A Clergyman of the Diocese of Hereford, *The Royal Supremacy and the Court of Final Appeal* (Oxford and London: John Henry and James Parker, 1865); Colin Lindsay, *The Royal Supremacy and Church Emancipation* (London and Oxford: J. H. and J. Parker, 1865).

[66] A Clergyman of the Diocese of Hereford, *The Royal Supremacy and the Court of Final Appeal*, p. 34; Lindsay, *The Royal Supremacy and Church Emancipation*, is concerned with Erastianism throughout, for example, pp. 5, 12, 22, 36–7; on pp. 18–23, he denies that the Church of England's concessions to the state give the monarch power to determine doctrine.

[67] Lindsay, *The Royal Supremacy*, p. 60.

[68] Ibid., p. 61.

[69] Ibid., pp. 61–2.

proposed 'that the Church be allowed without impediment to celebrate her national, provincial, and diocesan Synods or Convocations, and that she be permitted to hold free discussion on any topic of ecclesiastical interest'.[70] In his second and fifth points, Lindsay was clear that the Church's decisions would be made with 'the consent of the Crown', but in the fourth point of his proposed concordat, he used the exact opposite language, arguing that the Church of England should make and revise its own canons '*without* any consent of the Crown being required'.[71] Lindsay did not call for disestablishment, but for a new degree of legislative independence.

IV Rejecting the royal supremacy

The earliest calls for an international gathering of Anglican bishops came from North America. The first came in 1851 from John Henry Hopkins, Bishop of Vermont and later Presiding Bishop of the Episcopal Church; the second came in 1865 from the Provincial Synod of Canada. Both requests expressly named a *synod* under the presidency of the Archbishop of Canterbury as the goal of their petition.[72] However similar, the two requests came in the wake of very different controversies. Hopkins wrote in reference to the Gorham controversy, which he had followed closely,[73] while the Provincial Synod of Canada wrote in reference to the controversies over Colenso and *Essays and Reviews*.

Hopkins broached the topic of an Anglican synod in response to an invitation to the bishops of the Episcopal Church from John Bird Sumner, Archbishop of Canterbury (1848 – 1862). Inviting them to attend the third jubilee of the Society for the Propagation of the Gospel, Archbishop Sumner asked 'whether, in a time of controversy and division, the close communion which binds the

---

[70] Ibid., p. 61.

[71] Ibid.; emphases mine.

[72] The point is often missed but is clearly recognized by Hebb, 'The Canadians at Lambeth', for example, pp. 14–15, 17, 20; idem., 'The Americans at Lambeth', *Anglican and Episcopal History*, Vol. 78, No. 1 (March 2009), pp. 30–66, esp. pp. 33–4, and 37–8.

[73] Hopkins published *The Case of the Rev. Mr. Gorham against the Bishop of Exeter, Considered* (Burlington: E. Smith & Co., 1849), which was originally delivered as a clerical address. A mildly critical but insightful overview of his views can be found in John Henry Hopkins, Jr., *The Life of the Late Right Reverend John Henry Hopkins* (F. J. Huntington and Co., 1873), pp. 280–1.

Churches of America and England in one would not be strikingly manifested to the world.[74] Hopkins responded:

> I fervently hope that the time may come when we shall meet together in the good old fashion of Synodical action. How natural and how reasonable would it seem to be if 'in a time of controversy and division' there should be a Council of all Bishops in communion with your Grace; and would not such an assemblage exhibit the most solemn and, under God, the most influential aspect of strength and unity in maintaining the true Gospel? It is my own firm belief that such a measure would be productive of immense advantage, and would exercise a moral influence far beyond that of any secular legislation.[75]

Sumner did not act on Hopkins' proposal but others rapidly picked it up, sometimes citing the above paragraph in full.[76] This included the popular Anglican press in 1854 and 1855; Hopkins' words were repeated in the English periodical *The Christian Remembrancer* and in the American publication *The Church Journal*.[77] Through popular publications such as these, Hopkins' hope was disseminated on both sides of the Atlantic.

Progress came only after the new controversies of the early 1860s. Of these two debates, the less upsetting concerned Bishop John Colenso. He defended the temporary allowance of polygamy in missionary settings where it was practised, and also argued against contemporary understandings of the atonement, which was taken as an attack on the Book of Common Prayer.[78] By the middle of the decade, the Anglican churches of Canada, England and the United States had all condemned Colenso's theology.[79] Far more upsetting was the 1860 collection *Essays and Reviews*, which used German biblical scholarship to question more traditional understandings of the Bible,

---

[74] Society for the Propagation of the Gospel, *Classified Digest of the Records of the Society for the Propagation of the Gospel in Foreign Parts 1701 – 1892*, fourth edn (London: SPG, 1894), p. 81.

[75] Hopkins, Jr., *The Life of the Late Right Reverend John Henry Hopkins*, p. 392 n. 1.

[76] Henry Caswall, *America, and the American Church*, second edn (London: John and Charles Mozley, 1851), pp. 394–5; Hopkins' full letter is printed in Stephenson, *The First Lambeth Conference*, pp. 43–4.

[77] Anonymous, 'Caswall's America', *The Christian Remembrancer: A Quarterly Review*, Vol. XXIII (1852), pp. 329–63, at pp. 359–60; for *The Church Journal*, see Hopkins, Jr., *The Life of the Late Right Reverend John Henry Hopkins*, p. 392–3. At least one popular Anglican publication disseminated Hopkins, Jr.'s view in the late 1870s; see Hopkins, Jr., 'Pan-Anglican Conferences: How the Idea of Them Arose', *The Churchman*, May 17, 1879, p. 535.

[78] Hinchliff, *John William Colenso*, pp. 81–4.

[79] Stephenson, *The First Lambeth Conference*, pp. 136, 146.

particularly the nature of its inspiration. With 150 pamphlets published against *Essays and Reviews*, it is not unfair to describe it as *The Times* did in 1861: 'The great religious scandal of the day'.[80] More than 148,000 people, including nearly half of the clergy in the Church of England, signed petitions against the work.[81] Two of the contributors, the clergymen Rowland Williams and Henry Bristow Wilson, were brought up on heresy charges; although both were judged guilty in the Court of Arches in early 1862, the decision was reversed two years later upon successful appeal to the Judicial Committee of the Privy Council. This time, the Bishop of London and the Archbishops of Canterbury and York sat on the Judicial Committee, and although all three condemned *Essays and Reviews*, only Archbishops Longley (Canterbury) and Thomson (York) dissented from the majority decision.[82] On 21–22 June 1864, Canterbury Convocation responded to the Judicial Committee's verdict by declaring that *Essays and Reviews* contained 'false and dangerous statements, and reasonings at variance with the teaching of the Church of England, and deserving the condemnation of the Synod'.[83] In September 1865, the Provincial Synod of Canada responded to all of this by drafting a letter to the Archbishop of Canterbury. The Canadians began by noting that because of 'the recent decisions of the Judicial Committee of the Privy Council in the well-known case respecting the *Essays and Reviews*, and also in the case of the Bishop of Natal and the Bishop of Cape-Town', many of the faithful had become 'unsettled or painfully alarmed'. The reason was simple: 'Doctrines hitherto believed to be Scriptural, and undoubtedly held by the members of the Church of England and Ireland' had been undermined.[84] The Canadians proposed a simple solution, requesting that Archbishop Longley 'convene a National Synod of the Bishops of the Anglican Church at home and abroad'.[85]

Behind the Canadian proposal was an important but often ignored political element. By 1865, the two North American churches differed from the Church

[80] Altholz, *Anatomy of a Controversy*, p. 70.
[81] Ibid., pp. 50–1, 117–20.
[82] The Bishop of London, Archibald Campbell Tait, supported the appeal on the technical basis that the specific charges brought against Williams and Wilson could not be sustained; Tait did not accept the theological claims made in *Essays and Reviews*. Detailed analysis of the appeal process may be found in Victor Shea and William Whitla (eds.), *Essays and Reviews: The 1860 Text and its Readings* (Charlottesville and London: University Press of Virginia, 2000), pp. 749–55.
[83] The full text of the condemnation is reprinted in ibid., pp. 672–6.
[84] Francis Fulford, *A Pan-Anglican Synod*, p. 18.
[85] Ibid., pp. 18–19.

of England in their respective approaches to the British Crown. In the United States, this change of affairs followed the American Revolution, and in 1801 the Episcopal Church rewrote portions of the Articles of Religion. Article 21, which had given monarchs a role in calling 'Generall Counsels', was cut entirely. Still more importantly, the American revision of Article 37 redefined the relationship between church and state. In 1571, the Church of England had determined that the monarch 'shoulde rule all estates and degrees committed to their charge by GOD, whether they be Ecclesiasticall or Temporall'.[86] Wholly against this position, the new American version instead claimed, 'The Power of the Civil Magistrate extendeth to all men, as well Clergy as Laity, in all things temporal; *but hath no authority in things purely spiritual*.'[87] In the United States, the newly formed government did not wish to interfere – a situation that newly formed churches were happy to live with. In Canada, different but equally important developments took place in the mid-nineteenth century. The Church of England was disestablished in the diocese of Nova Scotia in 1850. Three years later, state endowment for the church was brought to an end in Canada, and in 1854 the Diocese of Upper Canada was also disestablished. Queen Victoria then gave the Canadian church the right of self-government by assenting to the Canadian Synod Act of 1857.[88] A General Assembly was rapidly formed, and in 1860, Francis Fulford, appointed by the Queen as Bishop of Montreal in 1850, was elevated as metropolitan over the entire Canadian church. He strongly supported disestablishment and opposed the Canadian church claiming political privileges.[89] In 1861, at Fulford's initiative, the first Provincial Synod met and began to steer the Church of Canada in a new and independent direction. Neither the American nor the Canadian requests envisioned that a synod might be hampered by the state.

By the end of 1866, there was little reason to doubt that an Anglican synod was forthcoming. Two other sources indicate that all parties on both sides of the Atlantic agreed upon the need for a *synod*, and they expressly termed it such. First, Archbishop Longley replied to the Canadians in December 1865.

---

[86] The Church of England, *Articles of Religion*, Art. 37.

[87] The Episcopal Church (USA), The Book of Common Prayer (1979), Art. 37 (New York: Oxford University Press, 1979), p. 875; emphasis added.

[88] For a helpful overview, see Alan L. Hayes, *Anglicans in Canada: Controversies and Identity in Historical Perspective* (Urbana and Chicago: University of Illinois Press, 2004), pp. 88–92; The Canadian Synod Act is reprinted on pp. 252–3.

[89] Fennings Taylor, *The Last Three Bishops, Appointed by the Crown, for the Anglican Church of Canada* (Montreal: John Lovell, 1869), pp. 58, 67.

Given his later apparent rejection of the Lambeth Conference as a synod, it is easy to miss the actual wording of his response. He told the Canadians, 'The meeting of such a Synod as you propose is not by any means foreign to my own feelings, and I think it might tend to prevent those inconveniences the possibility of which you anticipate.'[90] The Archbishop only requested the opportunity to consult with other bishops in the British Empire before making any decision on when the synod would meet. Second, on 23 December 1866, Francis Fulford preached at an ordination in the diocese of Oxford. He entitled his sermon *A Pan-Anglican Synod*. He told those gathered that the Provincial Synod of Canada had called for 'a general assembly or great council' and that the Archbishop of Canterbury and the Committee of the Lower House of the Convocation of Canterbury had each expressed their agreement with the Canadian request.[91] Fulford believed that the 'Pan-Anglican Synod' would yield important benefits. One would be 'the restoration of unity with other branches of the Church'. A second benefit pertained directly to the world's Anglicans:

> It will be in such general assemblies, for which the time is surely now fully come, when ecclesiastical principles and practice and catholic ways and usages are so well understood, that by intercourse and connexion with others, we may be encouraged to persevere under pressure of local difficulties, seeing that however our own, in any particular place, may be a day of small things, yet that as a whole, 'we being many are one body in Christ'.[92]

An international gathering – variously termed a synod, a general assembly and a great council – would not only transcend local identity and local struggle, but would remind local Anglican churches that they are part of a larger whole defined by shared principles and practices.

V Obviating the royal supremacy – again!

Things changed quite unexpectedly in mid-February 1867 – or so it has been made to seem. On 12 February, Samuel Wilberforce, Bishop of Oxford,

---

[90] Fulford, *A Pan-Anglican Synod*, pp. 19–20.
[91] Ibid., p. 14.
[92] Ibid.

presented the Canadian request for a synod before the Church of England's
Upper House of Convocation. He commented:

> I only think it necessary to say that I suppose the words 'convention of a
> Synod' to be used loosely, and with a certain latitude of meaning; because, of
> course, your Grace could not undertake to convene 'a Synod of the Bishops
> of all the Churches in communion with the Church of England,' without the
> consent of Imperial authority, our Article clearly showing that such general
> Synods are to be gathered with the consent of the Imperial power.[93]

The Article referenced here was Article 21 of the Articles of Religion, which
the American church had cut in 1801. Originally intended to limit the power
of the pope by making monarchs responsible for the calling of ecumenical
councils, Wilberforce glossed 'our Article' on a much more local basis, arguing
that because Queen Victoria had not called the world's Anglican bishops
together, the Canadian proposal could not be met with a formal, law-making
synod. Archbishop Longley then responded with his oft-quoted promise,
'I repudiate all idea of convening any assembly that can be justly called "a
Synod," or that can enact canons or attempt to do acts which be in direct
opposition to the authority of the Crown, which forbids the taking any such
step.' But as the foregoing discussion shows, and as the immediate context
of Wilberforce's words makes especially clear, it is simply wrong to treat the
first part of Longley's words as a constitutional declaration of what all future
Lambeth Conferences could and could not be. Rather, the reason for Longley's
restriction is found in the second half of his statement, which underscored
the authority of the Crown. This was quite far removed from the content of
discussions since September 1865, all of which agreed upon the need for a
synod because of recent doctrinal disputes, and none of which referenced the
royal supremacy. The first Lambeth Conference lacked synodical authority not
because of Longley's conviction but by way of concession to the Crown.

In his invitation of 22 February to the world's Anglican bishops, Archbishop
Longley did not describe the forthcoming gathering as 'the Lambeth
Conference', but as 'a meeting of the bishops in visible communion with the
United Church of England and Ireland'.[94] Longley did not use the word 'synod'

---

[93] *Chronicle of Convocation*, Upper House: Tuesday, 12 February 1867, p. 646.
[94] Randall Thomas Davidson, *Origin and History of the Lambeth Conferences of 1867 and 1878* (London: Society for Promoting Christian Knowledge, 1888), p. 7.

in his invitation, but he sent clear signs to invitees that the meeting, with its express aims of 'brotherly communion and conference',[95] would be run very much like a synod. This can be seen in three ways. First, Longley proposed beginning the meeting by celebrating Holy Communion, 'the highest act of the Church's worship'.[96] Second, he recognized that some bishops might not be able to attend and thus allowed them to send an episcopal representative.[97] The third example comes not from the February invitation but from July of that same year, when Archbishop Longley circulated a set of proposed resolutions to the invited bishops.[98] By proposing 'resolutions' instead of 'canons', Longley would be able to circumvent any legal arguments against the proceedings. In all of this, the first Lambeth Conference was entirely like the Exeter synod. In his opening address, the Archbishop further drove home the near-synodical nature of this gathering. When he addressed the bishops at the opening session, he described their meeting as 'this unprecedented step'.[99] This phrase did not mean that Longley conceived of the conference as something merely ad hoc. Rather, he explicitly described the resolutions that would be passed by the conference as 'safe guides to future action'.[100] Wholly unprecedented in itself, the conference at Lambeth intentionally set precedents. The 1867 gathering was not a synod, but something very, very close to it.

Samuel Wilberforce may have believed that the Crown forbade taking any sort of synodical step, but Archbishop Longley looked for the Lambeth Conference to take other steps, and he encouraged the bishops in attendance to take their own steps as well. Early on the second day (Wednesday, 25 September), the programme was altered. The original schedule had proposed that the second day of the conference would encompass three discussions of metropolitical authority, while a discussion of Anglican unity, entitled 'Conditions of Union', was slated last. A large number of bishops drafted a new schedule that made 'Conditions of Union' the first order of business.[101] They explained that their

[95] Ibid.

[96] Ibid., p. 8.

[97] Ibid., pp. 8–9.

[98] The resolutions as originally proposed, along with the suggested resolutions of Bishop Gray of Cape Town, may be found in Stephenson, *The First Lambeth Conference*, pp. 335–43.

[99] Davidson, *Origin and History of the Lambeth Conferences of 1867 and 1878*, p. 43.

[100] Ibid., p. 45.

[101] Ibid., pp. 37–42 (the original schedule; the original schedule for day two is on pp. 39–41), and pp. 48–53 (the revised schedule); a very helpful overview may be found in Hebb, 'The Americans at Lambeth', pp. 48–53.

goal was 'the due and Canonical subordination of the Synods of the several Branches to the higher authority of the Synods above them, the Diocesan Synod being recognized as inferior to the Provincial Synod, and the Provincial Synod to some higher Synod or Synods of the Anglican Communion'.[102] Because no 'higher Synod or Synods' existed, it was further specified that time would be spent discussing the creation of such a synod. A small number of English and colonial bishops protested against the proposed change to the second day's programme, but Longley sided with those who advanced the new schedule, arguing that it would aid Anglican unity.[103] The new schedule proposed new resolutions as well. The fourth was entitled 'This Meeting to be followed by other Meetings'. It asserted that 'it is desirable that a General Synod of the Bishops of the Anglican Communion ... should be assembled from time to time under the Presidency of the Primate of all England'.[104] The fifth resolution called for the next meeting to occur in the 1870s, and the ninth resolution, entitled 'Declaration of Submission to Regulations of Synods', proposed 'that all Bishops at their Consecration should be required to make a written Declaration of adhesion and submission to the regulations agreed upon by the General Synod of the Anglican Communion'.[105] Unprecedented steps were indeed being taken, and further such steps were being envisioned.

Eight committees were appointed to discuss the resolutions of the conference after it concluded. The first committee dealt with the as-yet uncreated 'higher Synod'. In *The First Lambeth Conference*, Stephenson discussed this report in the strangest of ways, quoting just two words from it – the phrase 'moral weight',[106] which the report used to describe the decisions and determinations of episcopal gatherings where state law did not give all participating churches free rein to make their own decisions. In Stephenson's words, the authors of the report 'confessed that a Pan-Anglican synod was an impossibility. This verdict – one of the most important conclusions that came out of the First Lambeth Conference – is of great significance.' Turning from the descriptive to the prescriptive and conflating them in the process, Stephenson advised

---

[102] Davidson, *Origin and History of the Lambeth Conferences of 1867 and 1878*, p. 49.
[103] Stephenson, *The First Lambeth Conference*, p. 256.
[104] Davidson, *Origin and History of the Lambeth Conferences of 1867 and 1878*, p. 51.
[105] Ibid., p. 53.
[106] Stephenson, *The First Lambeth Conference*, p. 309; the phrase 'moral weight' may be found in Davidson, *Origin and History of the Lambeth Conferences of 1867 and 1878*, p. 77.

his readers, 'We must be thankful for this wise decision, which the Anglican Communion has never retracted, in spite of demands that it should do so. Longley's original decision has been upheld.'[107] It has already been shown that Longley made no 'original decision' about the Lambeth Conference, whether that of 1867 or those that (he could not have known) would follow after. The same is true of the committee here under discussion; nothing in its report justifies Stephenson's interpretation. The first committee's report left no room for confusion. 'The objections that may be urged against the united action of Churches which are more or less free to act independently, and other Churches whose constitution is fixed not only by ancient ecclesiastical laws and usages, *but by the law of the State*, are obvious.'[108] However, the authors believed that the success of the Lambeth Conference indicated that the difficulties inherent in creating a higher synod were 'not insuperable' and that they 'may be overcome.'[109] The report *never* claimed that a higher synod was, in Stephenson's words, 'an impossibility' – the committee used neither the word 'impossibility' nor any of its synonyms, derivations or cognates. Yes, the royal supremacy created problems for the immediate future; no, these problems were not insurmountable.

The second committee, which discussed the creation of a tribunal for the Anglican Communion, also recognized the problem of state law but did not consider the matter intractable. They wrote, 'Your Committee recommend that such a Tribunal be established.'[110] Like the first committee, they were 'sensible of the great difficulty of forming a Tribunal ... lest it should interfere with the liberties of the Colonial Churches, or should have any appearance of *collision with the Courts established by law*, either here or in Her Majesty's foreign possessions'.[111] This addressed long-standing concerns about the Judicial Committee of the Privy Council, as well as any other secular courts. The report emphasized 'the necessity of proceeding with caution,'[112] and then laid out stipulations for the tribunal's membership and procedures. For example, the report suggested that the tribunal use 'the standards of faith and

---

[107] Stephenson, *The First Lambeth Conference*, p. 308.
[108] Davidson, *Origin and History of the Lambeth Conferences of 1867 and 1878*, p. 77; emphasis mine.
[109] Ibid.
[110] Ibid., p. 79.
[111] Ibid., p. 80; emphasis mine.
[112] Ibid.

doctrine' of the United Church of England and Ireland, that only bishops and archbishops should sit as judges, and that the Archbishop of Canterbury should be President of the tribunal. Recognizing the possibility of future doctrinal dispute, they wrote, 'As to all matters not defined in such formularies, the judgments should be framed on any conclusions which shall be hereafter agreed to at any Council or Congress of the whole Anglican Communion.'[113] Future episcopal meetings were thus a possibility; if and when they happened, their decisions would set precedents for the tribunal's own future judgements. The Lambeth Conference was intended to be a synod. The royal supremacy prevented it from being so – but the 1867 committees flatly denied that this situation was the last word on the subject.

Conclusion

At the beginning of 1867, Walter Bagehot finished *The English Constitution*, his most enduring work. Two of its chapters discussed the monarchy. Bagehot freely conceded that the power of monarchy lay in its religious origins,[114] and that although much had changed since the seventeenth century, when sacramental kingship was at the height of its popularity and influence, mystery remained central to its continued appeal.[115] "'The divinity which doth hedge a king" may have less sanctity than it had, but it still has much sanctity.'[116] In 1867, the monarchy may have remained a mystical symbol and even a moral authority for the English,[117] but it held no analogous position for some churches of the burgeoning Anglican Communion, especially that in the United States, and it played no analogous role at the first Lambeth Conference. In the latter half of Queen Victoria's reign, Crown and Mitre travelled in different directions. Victoria's own religious practice was rather unusual; she cared little for services according to the Book of Common Prayer.[118] More tellingly, it was not until

---

[113] Ibid., p. 81.

[114] Walter Bagehot, *The English Constitution* (Oxford: Oxford University Press, 2009), pp. 41–2.

[115] Ibid., p. 54.

[116] Ibid., p. 66.

[117] Ibid., pp. 44–5.

[118] William M. Kuhn, *Democratic Royalism: The Transformation of the British Monarchy, 1861 – 1914* (London: Macmillan, 1996), pp. 86; see also pp. 43 and 62 for Victoria's general dislike of *any* ceremony and her increased distaste for even public celebration.

the 1897 Lambeth Conference that Victoria first bothered to greet any of the bishops visiting England for a Lambeth Conference,[119] and when they later attended a reception with the Queen, she remarked to one of her attendants that she had little affection for them.[120] Subsequent monarchs were more active and gracious. King Edward VII received the bishops at Buckingham Palace, and later monarchs held receptions for the bishops as well, as Queen Elizabeth II has done regularly. But it is, at most, an open question whether the British Crown retains any import for the wider Anglican Communion.

In place of the Crown, Anglicans today have the Lambeth Conference. In his 1967 study, Stephenson rightly noted that the Lambeth Conference is 'now regarded as the focus of the Anglican Communion'.[121] The Lambeth Conference ascended to this position because it excited attendees and observers. Shortly before the gathering, Presiding Bishop Hopkins expressed his firm belief: 'That such an imposing Council of reformed Bishops will attract the most universal interest, cannot be doubted. Nothing like it has ever been known, since the great Reformation.'[122] Shortly after the Conference, *The Colonial Church Chronicle, Missionary Journal* and *Foreign Ecclesiastical Reporter* summarized the Lambeth Conference for its readers: 'Its success is, of itself, the best and sufficient answer to the many objections and scruples which some had expressed concerning it.'[123] The article noted with satisfaction that 'the conclave thus gathered from a far wider area than any of the Oecumenical Councils of old'.[124] The author had no doubts about the importance of what had just transpired, and predicted not only that 'this Conference will fulfil the same function for the Anglican portion of the Christendom which was fulfilled by the Oecumenic Synods for the whole',[125] but also that 'a synodical character, indeed, can hardly be dissociated from the Lambeth acts themselves; and certainly posterity will regard this Conference as being in effect, in all but name, a General Anglican Council'.[126] Bishops who could not attend often held

---

[119] Chadwick, 'The Lambeth Conference: An Historical Perspective', pp. 269–70.
[120] Ian Bradley, *God Save the Queen: The Spiritual Heart of Monarchy*, second edn (London and New York: Continuum, 2012), p. 159.
[121] Stephenson, *The First Lambeth Conference*, p. 1.
[122] Hopkins, Jr., *The Life of the Late Right Reverend John Henry Hopkins*, p. 395.
[123] 'Results of the Lambeth Conference', *The Colonial Church Chronicle, Missionary Journal, and Foreign Ecclesiastical Reporter*, Vol. 21, December 1867, p. 481.
[124] Ibid.
[125] Ibid., p. 482.
[126] Ibid.

the gathering in equally high regard; John Strachan of Canada believed that the Lambeth Conference was the most important episcopal gathering since the ecumenical councils of the early Church.[127] The synodical language and hopes of the earliest requests had outlived Archbishop Longley's seemingly altered position of 12 February 1867.

In the years immediately following the Lambeth Conference, excitement and hope only grew. At the 1868 Church Congress in Ireland, Samuel Gleason, Archdeacon of Montreal, told his audience that Anglican bishops in the United States and Canada 'have shewn by the active interest they took in that memorable event, the *Episcopal Conference* at Lambeth, that their hope and their effort are so to be united with the Church of England and Ireland, that they together with her and the whole Colonial Church may, through the gift and grace of God the Father, become one organized body'.[128] Others believed that the combined force of Canadian disestablishment and the Lambeth Conference would soon lead to the disestablishment of the Church of England. Canadian author Fennings Taylor surmised that 'the changes through which the Church of England is now passing have in no small degree been hastened by the example which the Anglican Church of Canada has supplied.'[129] Taylor specified that the Lambeth Conference had brought 'advantages', but hinted at 'greater and more lasting blessings which that unprecedented assembly may be expected to inaugurate.'[130] Given this appeal to 'the example' of the Canadian church, Taylor likely meant one thing: disestablishment. Critics of the Lambeth Conference feared precisely this, and the small number of bishops who boycotted the conference all came from the United Church of England and Ireland.[131] Nonetheless, in giving rise to speculation about a shared and united Anglican future, the Lambeth Conference also birthed an international

---

[127] Stephenson, *The First Lambeth Conference*, p. 196.
[128] Samuel Gilson, 'The American and Canadian Churches', in *Authorized Report of the Church Congress, Held in Dublin* (Dublin: Hodges, Smith & Foster, 1868), p. 232.
[129] Taylor, *The Last Three Bishops, Appointed by the Crown*, p. vi.
[130] Ibid., p. 109.
[131] For the Archbishop of York's concerns, see Terrence J. Gerighty, 'Canterbury and York in Disaccord: a Failure at the First Lambeth Conference: The Longley-Thomson Correspondence and the First Lambeth Conference, 1867', *Historical Magazine of the Protestant Episcopal Church*, Vol. 42, No. 4 (December, 1973), pp. 429–35. Stephenson, *The First Lambeth Conference*, pp. 189–200, discusses responses to Longley's invitation. He estimates that about 140 invitations were sent out; 76 bishops attended, 41 bishops outside of England were unable to do so, and 2 American bishops did not respond. Of the English and Irish bishops, 4 did not attend due to either age or infirmity; on non-attendance by 11 of the English and Irish bishops, at least 10 of whom did so in protest of the conference, see Stephenson, *The First Lambeth Conference*, pp. 192–3, 217–19.

Anglican identity more expansive than an identity circumscribed by the Church of England alone.[132]

Given all of this, why is the Lambeth Conference so often seen today in *non*-synodical terms? Several things can be pointed to. First, and as already noted, Archbishop Longley did not describe his 1867 gathering as 'the Lambeth Conference'. This proper noun became normative only in the decade that followed; several of the reports produced by the 1867 meeting used the term 'the Lambeth Conference',[133] and when the Canadians requested 'a second meeting of the Conference' in 1872, they denoted its predecessor 'the Lambeth Conference'.[134] Surviving evidence reveals a considerable amount of terminological diversity among participants in 1867. Some of this predated the Conference; as already noted, Hopkins had requested a 'synod' as early as 1851, and Fulford's 1866 sermon freely equated a 'Pan-Anglican Synod' with 'a general assembly or great council'. Bishops at the conference used a wide range of terms, such as 'the Council'[135] and 'the Pan-Anglican' (itself an abbreviation of Fulford's phrase 'Pan-Anglican Synod').[136] The first and second committee reports that followed the conclusion of the 1867 gathering were similar, proposing that future meetings be held under the title 'Congress' or 'Council'.[137] As late as 1873, Bishop George Augustus Selwyn of New Zealand described the possible follow-up to the 1867 conference as 'A General Council of the Bishops of the Anglican Communion'.[138] One could argue that the first Lambeth Conference was the site of semantic confusion, but it is more accurate to argue the exact opposite: far from confusion, the first Lambeth

---

[132] A contrary view holds that contemporary Anglican identity is a product of the Oxford Movement. This thesis is delineated in Sachs, *The Transformation of Anglicanism*, pp. 2–3, who points specifically to John Henry Newman. It is applied more generally to Anglo-Catholicism by Diarmaid MacCulloch, 'The Myth of the English Reformation', *Journal of British Studies*, Vol. 30, No. 1 (January 1991), pp. 1–19. Some strictures on MacCulloch's viewpoint may be found in Peter Nockles, 'The Reformation Revised? The Contested Reception of the English Reformation in Nineteenth-Century Protestantism', *Bulletin of the John Rylands Library*, Vol. 90, No. 1 (Spring 2014), pp. 231–56. For a general overview of the matter, see Alexander Faludy, 'A son of the Reformation? Walter Frere's historical scholarship reviewed', in Benjamin Gordon-Taylor and Nicholas Stebbing CR (eds), *Walter Frere: Scholar, Monk, Bishop* (London: Canterbury Press, 2011), pp. 119–42. For general background on the meanings of 'Anglican', see Peter B. Nockles, *The Oxford Movement in Context: Anglican High Churchmanship 1760 – 1857* (Cambridge: Cambridge University Press, 1994), pp. 39–43.

[133] Davidson, *Origin and History of the Lambeth Conferences of 1867 and 1878*, pp. 79 (Committee B), 92 (Committee G), 95 (Committee H).

[134] Ibid., pp. 101–2.

[135] Stephenson, *The First Lambeth Conference*, pp. 214–15.

[136] Ibid., p. 239.

[137] Davidson, *Origin and History of the Lambeth Conferences of 1867 and 1878*, pp. 77, 78, 81.

[138] Ibid., p. 17.

Conference was the subject of repeated semantic assertion. Attendees wanted and expected a synod, a council, a general assembly.

Thus, instead of looking at Longley's 1867 meeting, we must turn to later history. A key development came in 1871, when Bishop Christopher Wordsworth published his influential essay 'Diocesan Synods, and Diocesan Conferences'. The late 1860s and early 1870s saw considerable terminological refinement for the wide variety of ecclesial meetings then taking place in the Church of England.[139] As Arthur Burns has noted, 'The distinction between the diocesan "synod" and "conference" developed only slowly; at first "synod" sometimes denoted assemblies that would later be classified as "conferences".'[140] We can see some of this development by comparing Wordsworth's 1871 essay with James Wayland Joyce's 1855 book *England's Sacred Synods*. While noting that diocesan synods had become 'less common since the period of the Reformation', Joyce listed a small number of diocesan synods that had occurred since the sixteenth century, and concluded his list with the Exeter synod of 1851.[141] Sixteen years later, however, Bishop Wordsworth wrote that 'the Synod held at Exeter, on June 25 and 26, 1851, which consisted merely of delegates, could hardly be called a Diocesan Synod in the proper sense of the term, as will hereafter appear'.[142] The shift between Joyce and Wordsworth was due at least in part to developing ideas about the place of canons. Joyce did not define a diocesan synod with reference to its right of passing and enforcing canons; following the legislation of Henry VIII, he located this right with convocations.[143] Wordsworth, however, dissented from this view, and concluded that if a diocesan synod could not pass canons, then it simply was not a diocesan synod.[144] Bishop Wordsworth defined a 'diocesan conference' as an event that contained both laity and clergy, where they together deliberated 'not on controverted questions of Theology, or on the settled Articles of our Faith, but on various topics which arise from time to time, and vitally affect the interests of religion and the Church'.[145] With the exception of the involvement of the laity, Wordsworth's definition of a diocesan conference describes later

---

[139] Burns, *The Diocesan Revival in the Church of England*, ch. 9, esp. pp. 244–50.

[140] Ibid., p. 216 n. 1.

[141] James Wayland Joyce, *England's Sacred Synods: A Constitutional History of the Convocations of the Clergy* (London: Rivingtons, 1855), p. 39.

[142] Wordsworth, 'Diocesan Synods, and Diocesan Conferences', p. 158 n. 8.

[143] Joyce, *England's Sacred Synods*, p. 40.

[144] Wordsworth, 'Diocesan Synods, and Diocesan Conferences', p. 162.

[145] Ibid., p. 164.

Lambeth Conferences quite well. By the time of the 1878 Lambeth Conference, a distinction between 'synod' and 'conference', unknown in the 1860s, was becoming commonplace. At that Conference, 'synod' and 'conference' were firmly distinguished. The report of the first committee described a synod as 'too great to allow of our recommending it for present adoption', and described the second Lambeth Conference as an 'experiment, now twice tried' of 'combining together for consultation'.[146] Ambiguities surrounding the nature of the first Lambeth Conference were thus resolved according to the developing semantic norms of the 1870s, and the aspirations found in the committee reports of 1867 were sidelined by the committee reports of 1878. The first Lambeth Conference has been viewed through this prism ever since.[147]

Even if still a defining facet of the English church, the Crown has become Anglicanism's absent and largely forgotten centre. Like its capacity for theological suasion, its various claims – canonical and liturgical, devotional and doctrinal – have little place and no analogue in the wider Anglican Communion today. No one should be surprised that the Lambeth Conference has, like the Crown before it, also become a source of tension and disagreement; all forms of authority enter such periods of difficulty. It is genuinely remarkable, however, that it took so very long for such contests to arise. Perhaps the problem is less the Lambeth Conference than the conflict-ridden baby boomer generation and its influence, although that is a subject for another essay. When describing the Lambeth Conference, particularly its origins, there is simply no excuse for continuing to rely on a half-cited statement by Archbishop Longley. We should instead turn to the first Lambeth Conference itself:

> That, in the opinion of this Conference, Unity in Faith and Discipline will be best maintained among the several branches of the Anglican Communion by due and canonical subordination of the Synods of the several branches to the higher authority of a Synod or Synods above them.[148]

The origins of a thing always remain in that thing. Steps unprecedented may still be taken.

---

[146] Davidson, *Origin and History of the Lambeth Conferences of 1867 and 1878*, p. 120.

[147] This is not to deny that other, later developments, both within and outside of the Anglican Communion, have also shaped subsequent appraisals of the Lambeth Conference, particularly that which met in 1867.

[148] Ibid., p. 63 (Resolution IV).

4

William Reed Huntington, American Catholicity and the Chicago—Lambeth Quadrilateral[1]

Mark D. Chapman

Despite its name and origins, the Anglican Communion has not always had an easy relationship with England and its established church. From the very beginnings of the Church of England, which was founded on the 'containment' of the church within national boundaries, the problem of the catholicity of the church has repeatedly come to the fore. With the development of forms of Anglicanism outside England and even more crucially outside the British Empire, the problem of international catholicity became increasingly pressing. Many, not least in the Oxford Movement, sought the solution in apostolicity by tracing the authority of the present church back to the primitive church, but this did little to help with the 'spatial catholicity' between those churches across the world which could no longer be held together by the British monarchy. Indeed, outside England from as early as the seventeenth century the understanding of episcopacy was sometimes modified into something more 'primitive' than what could be regarded as the debased and worldly form of episcopacy displayed by English prelates.[2] This meant that when Anglicanism left the imperial Crown behind

---

[1] This chapter began life as two guest lectures on 'The National and International Church' held during the Advanced Degrees Program at the School of Theology at the University of South, Sewanee, Tennessee on 20 and 21 June 2012. I am grateful to Dr Ben King and to the Faculty and students who made my stay so enjoyable.

[2] Samuel Wilberforce, *A History of the Protestant Episcopal Church in America* (London: Rivington, third edition, 1856), pp. 113, 251, 293. Some of these ideas resemble those of James Ussher in the seventeenth century. See J. P. Cunningham, 'The Eirenicon and the "primitive episcopacy" of

– as it did in the United States – serious questions were raised about the nature of both catholicity and sovereignty. This raised a number of important questions: What possibilities were there for an Anglican Church which could expect no privileges from a civil authority? Did this mean that Anglicanism would be rendered impossible? What kind of 'catholic' church was the Protestant Episcopal Church supposed to be in a land created by Protestant dissent, in which – at least arguably – the Baptist ethos won?[3] How was an Anglican Church possible on the basis of a conception of churches as free corporations independent from the state and without the royal supremacy as the guarantor of its authority? Could the model of the primitive church, albeit shorn of its theocratic overtones, prove sufficient for the catholic identity of the Church?[4]

Alongside the traditional English settlement of religion, there developed a distinctive American style of Anglican catholicity which built on the early years of the Protestant Episcopal Church in the United States.[5] Indeed, it would be reasonable to suggest that subsequent Anglican conceptions of catholicity, not least in the so-called Lambeth Quadrilateral which was accepted at the Lambeth Conference of 1888, owe at least as much to America as they do to England. Key to shaping this form of American catholic identity was the indefatigable churchman and campaigner William

---

James Ussher: an Irish Panacea for Britannia's Ailment' in *Reformation and Renaissance Review* 8 (2006), pp. 128–46. On Ussher, see Alan Ford, *James Ussher: Theology, History, and Politics in early-modern Ireland and England* (Oxford: Oxford University Press, 2007), especially chapter 10. On the development of episcopacy in the American church, see Clara O. Loveland, *The Critical Years: The Reconstitution of the Anglican Church in the United States of America* (Greenwich: Connecticut, 1956); Frederick V. Mills, Sr, *Bishops by Ballot: An Eighteenth-Century Ecclesiastical Revolution* (New York: Oxford University Press, 1978); Peter Doll, *Revolution, Religion and National Identity* (Madison: Farleigh Dickinson, 2000). For a comparative account of the English and American churches to 1867, see H. G. G. Herklots, *The Church of England and the American Episcopal Church: From the First Voyages of Discovery to the First Lambeth Conference* (London: Mowbray, 1966).

[3] See J. C. D. Clark, *The Language of Liberty, 1660-1832: Political Discourse and Social Dynamics in the Anglo-American World* (Cambridge: Cambridge University Press, 1994); and J. C. D. Clark, 'Historiographical Reviews: Secularization and modernization: the failure of a "grand narrative"', *The Historical Journal* 55 (2012), pp. 161–94, especially p. 178.

[4] Colin Podmore has analysed the different approaches between the English and American churches in what is principally a historical and constitutional account in 'A Tale of Two Churches: The Ecclesiologies of The Episcopal Church and the Church of England Compared', *International Journal for the Study of the Christian Church* 8 (2008), pp. 124–54. Paul V. Marshall uses the term 'American ecclesiology' in *One, Catholic, and Apostolic: Samuel Seabury and the Early Episcopal Church* (New York: Church Publishing, 2004), chapter 3.

[5] Mills, *Bishops by Ballot*, p. xii, speaks of his study of the early years of the development of episcopacy in the United States as that of 'the substitution and canonization of republican concepts and practices in place of hierarchical ones within one religious denomination'.

Reed Huntington (1838–1909).[6] Not merely did he help direct the Episcopal Church towards home reunion after the divisions of the Civil War, he was also one of the most formative influences on modern Anglican identity. How he came to his ideas of 'American Catholicity' is highly illuminating and reveals something of how the political settlements of England and America affected the development of Anglican concepts of catholicity. During his time at Harvard from 1855, Huntington had turned from the high church Episcopalianism of his childhood to embrace the Unitarianism of his mentor, the chemist Josiah Parsons Cooke. However, under the influence of his distant cousin Frederic Dan Huntington (1819–1904), afterwards Bishop of Central New York, who had similarly made the transition to Unitarianism and back again, he returned to Episcopalianism. In 1861 he sought ordination from the Evangelical Bishop of Massachusetts, Manton Eastburn, but was refused on the grounds of his difficulties in accepting the authority of the Thirty-Nine Articles.[7]

After this disappointment Huntington visited England. Like many others at the time, he made the pilgrimage to the village of Hursley, near Winchester, where, living in what Perry Butler called a somewhat 'cultivated obscurity', John Keble had been vicar since 1836.[8] Keble was something of a legend in his own lifetime, his ministry at Hursley being understood as the high point of the Tractarian pastoral paradigm.[9] By all accounts he was well

---

[6] On Huntington, see John Wallace Suter, *Life and Letters of William Reed Huntington: A Champion of Unity* (New York: The Century Co., 1925) (hereafter, *Life and Letters*); Lesley A. Northup, 'William Reed Huntington: First Presbyter of the Late 19th Century', *Anglican and Episcopal History* 62 (1993), pp. 303–5; *Memories of William Reed Huntington Doctor of Divinity by One of His Staff of Clergy* (Hartford, Conn: Church Missions Publishing Company, 1929); John F. Woolverton, 'William Reed Huntington and Church Unity: The Historical and Theological Background of the Chicago-Lambeth Quadrilateral', Columbia University PhD 1963; George William Douglas, *Essays in Appreciation* (New York: Longmans, 1912), pp. 55–68; Clyde Griffen, 'An Urban Church in Ferment: the Episcopal Church in New York City, 1880–1900', PhD Columbia University, 1960, pp. 199–218. On Huntington and Church Union, see Charles J. Minifie, 'William Reed Huntington and Church Unity', *Historical Magazine of the Protestant Episcopal Church* 35 (1966), pp. 155–66. More generally, see Robert Prichard, *A History of the Episcopal Church* (Harrisburg, PA: Morehouse, 1999), pp. 188–90. On the origins of the national church idea, see Paul T. Phillips, 'The Concept of a National Church in Late Nineteenth-century England and America', *Journal of Religious History* 14 (1986), pp. 26–37, especially pp. 31–2.

[7] Huntington's difficulties with the Articles are noted in several letters from 1861 See *Life and Letters*, pp. 46–8, 54.

[8] Perry Butler, 'Keble, John (1792–1866)', *Oxford Dictionary of National Biography* (Oxford: Oxford University Press, 2004), online edn, January 2006: http://ezproxy.ouls.ox.ac.uk:2117/view/article/15231 (accessed 23 February 2017).

[9] S. A. Skinner, *Tractarians and the 'Condition of England': The Social and Political thought of the Oxford Movement* (Oxford: Oxford University Press, 2004).

acquainted with the needs of the poor, establishing allotments and a savings bank,[10] but he was also frequently ill from his work among the sick. In a later report of his visit, and apparently forgetting that he was a layman at the time, Huntington recounted that at Hursley it 'was my great good fortune, when a young man, just in orders, to have an hour or two with Keble in his beautiful home at Hursley. He seemed as shy and bashful as a girl, and though it was easy to believe that I was in the presence of a saint, it was difficult to believe that the saint was also one of the best known men in England.'[11] On Huntington's return to the United States Bishop Eastburn relented and he was ordained on 1 October 1861. After his ordination as a priest in December 1862 he was appointed rector of All Saints', Worcester where he stayed until 1883. Having declined the nomination as Bishop of Iowa and several other prominent positions,[12] he became rector of Grace Church, New York from 1883 until his death.

Huntington's trip to England seems to have made a huge impression on how he perceived Anglicanism. This can be clearly observed in a sermon he preached at Trinity Church, Boston in the spring of 1865 to the Church Union of Massachusetts which bore the striking title, 'American Catholicity'. He began by reminding his audience that following the conclusion of the Civil War, the nation was entering a period of 'reconstruction in the State; God grant that it may also be a period of reconstruction in the Church'. He continued by noting that in 'venturing to approach the problem of American Catholicity, I am not blind to the profound difficulties that encompass it'. Nevertheless he felt that Church reconstruction was an imperative: 'Let every one who feels deeply in the matter, be he young or old, do what he can by speaking out his thought honestly and plainly, and the fruit will ripen in due time.'[13] Huntington then goes on to define 'the three conditions of American Catholicity: a simple creed; a varied worship; a generous polity'.[14] This did not mean that the 'American Church ought to reflect all American traits, be

---

[10] Georgina Battiscombe, *John Keble: A Study in Limitations* (London: Constable, 1963), pp. 178, 162.

[11] Huntington, letter to Catherine Meredith, 4 June 1879, in *Life and Letters*, p. 189.

[12] Huntington, *Life and Letters*, p. 107.

[13] Huntington, *American Catholicity: A Sermon, preached before the Church Union of the Diocese of Massachusetts in Trinity Church, Boston, Tuesday, May 16, 1865* (Boston: Printed for the Church Union, 1865), p. 6.

[14] Huntington, *American Catholicity*, p. 8.

they good or bad', but rather 'that it will not do to import an ecclesiastical system, in its totality, from a foreign country and expect it to answer all our purposes without change or adjustment'. On the one hand, Huntington held, 'since we are mainly English in our origin, use the English tongue, and inherit most of the traditions of English life and manners', it was not unreasonable that the 'National Church [should] bear a strong *resemblance* to the English Church'. On the other hand, however, he felt that it was fatal for 'the Church of America [to] embody pure Anglicanism'. This was a blunder that could prove fatal: there was no possibility that American Anglicanism could ever acquire the form of uniformity or conformity that was secured by the English establishment.

At the same time, and with more than a hint of irony, Huntington pointed to the enticements of what he later called 'Church of Englandism', perhaps echoing Jeremy Bentham's critique of the English establishment.[15] He found it 'quite easy to understand worthy people becoming so enamored of Anglicanism, in its more favorable aspects'. However, he felt that this blinded them to the need to modify it in order to meet what he called its 'cis-Atlantic requirements'. He went on with a degree of sophisticated hilarity in a passage which is worth citing in full:

> Let us imagine, for instance, a zealous young candidate for orders making a pilgrimage to that paradise of English Churchmen, the quiet little village in Hampshire where John Keble works and prays and sings. He arrives of a sweet morning in June. The Church bell is calling in the villagers to daily prayer as a preparation for their homely toil. All is as calmly beautiful as a poem in the Christian Year. Presently the service is over. The children of the parish school patter down the paved aisle, and go to their places in the school-room. Our pilgrim, after studying awhile the well-designed symbolism of the building, the inscriptions and the blazoned windows, goes out too, and finds his way, through a maze of shrubbery bursting into bloom, and vocal with the music of singing birds, to the deeply shaded vicarage. Here he is hospitably welcomed, and has an hour of delightful

---

[15] *Churchman*, 26 October 1895, cited in Woolverton, 'William Reed Huntington', p. 101. See Jeremy Bentham, *The Collected Works of Jeremy Bentham: Church-of-Englandism and its Catechism Examined*, edited by James E Crimmins, the late Catherine Fuller, and Philip Schofield (Oxford: Oxford University Press, 2011).

communion with one of the best of men and holiest of priests. With the memory of all this fresh in his mind, the young man returns to his American home and is ordained. He is appointed, we will suppose, to missionary work in a Massachusetts, or New Hampshire town, where some violent sectarian quarrel has made a timely opening for the Prayer Book. 'Now', he says to himself, 'is my opportunity. I will show these Yankees the beauty of holiness. I will make this place a Hursley. I will have real ivy and choral worship and a parish school. I am the Rector; here are the peasantry', And so with the best possible intentions, but, at the same time, with a lamentable lack of common sense, he goes to work to compass – an impossibility. It is an Anglo-, not an Anglified, Americanism we are to seek.[16]

Huntington's visit to England convinced him that a distinctive form of American Catholicity was required: he felt that Anglicanism did not require what he referred to in one of his favourite metaphors as the ivy of the English country church. Instead, American Anglicanism was to be located in a revitalized Catholicity grounded in the primitive church. Its 'visible unity' was to be upheld by the 'unity of government' which was established 'under that system which is both old and new, conservative and progressive, catholic and reformed, the system of republican episcopacy'. This telling final phrase implies a kind of constitutionalism which placed what Huntington called 'a weighty responsibility' on 'churchmen to take the initiative in the work of Christian reunion'.[17] He concluded by noting that a constitutional church bridged the gap between the primitive church and that of today:

> It is idle to prate about the Church of the future, unless you can find for it some point of historical attachment to the Church of the past. Just this 'missing link' the Protestant-Episcopal Church in the United States supplies, a Church that traces its lineage all the way back to the first century, which, at the same time, she is, in her constitution, perfectly conformed to the structure of civil government under which we live.[18]

Shortly before his sermon on American Catholicity Huntington had spoken on the theme of Church unity in an address delivered to the American Bible Society on 11 May 1865 where he observed that all who were gathered were

---

[16] Huntington, *American Catholicity*, pp. 15–16.
[17] Ibid., p. 12.
[18] Huntington, *American Catholicity*, p. 12.

'also members of one holy catholic Church'. He noted a 'strong desire growing up, all over Christendom, for reunion, for visible reunion'.[19] Throughout his life Huntington continued his quest for American Catholicity in a number of books, in numerous sermons and addresses, as well as through his work in General Convention.[20] Despite this prolific output, however, his ideas underwent remarkably little development. Shortly before his death, he delivered an address at the Boston Church Congress in May 1909. Looking back at his 1865 sermon, he affirmed that for the three principles of 'a simple creed, a varied worship, a generous polity' he had 'during the four and forty years, through evil report and through good report, contended; and by them I stand, strengthened by the ancient watchword, Hope on, hope ever'.[21]

The conception of 'Republican Episcopacy' and 'American Catholicity' coalesced a few years later in a sermon Huntington preached at Worcester on 30 January 1870 on I Cor. 12.4-6 as the third of a series on the 'Church of the Reconciliation'.[22] He felt that the Church should be something like the YMCA, functioning as a kind of clearing ground for the future Church of the Reconciliation. Preaching against any sense of pride in denominationalism, and reminding his congregation that the 'pearly gates swing not on their hinges either to a proud or to an unloving soul',[23] he called for the humility to search out what was essential in the Christian Church from what was merely cultural. Indeed, he considered this quest for essentials to be the particular vocation of Anglicanism in promoting Christian unity:

> Firmly convinced that in the Anglican principle lies the only reasonable
> hope of Christian unity in these latter days, I have made it my endeavor to
> disentangle the principle from all accidental and unessential to it; to strip it
> of the wrappings in which the various circumstances of time and country
> have enfolded it, and to set it before you in simplicity. In a word, it has been
> to the strict anatomy of the subject and to nothing else that I have turned
> your thoughts.

---

[19] Unpublished manuscript, cited in Minifie, 'William Reed Huntington', p. 159.
[20] See Huntington, *Life and Letters*, p. 467.
[21] 'The Four Theories of Visible Church Unity', address at the Boston Church Congress, 1909, in *Papers, Addresses and Discussions of the Twenty-Seventh Church Congress in the USA* (New York: Thomas Whittaker, 1909), pp. 159–63. See also Woolverton, 'William Reed Huntington', pp. 84–5.
[22] Huntington, *Life and Letters*, p. 162.
[23] Ibid., pp. 162–63.

After removing the cultural accretions, Huntington felt he had reached the essential core of what he called the 'Anglican Principle'. He had whittled down 'the points which that principle could not possibly surrender without self-destruction' to four. They were as follows:

1. The Holy Scriptures, as the Word of God.
2. The Primitive Creeds as the Rule of Faith.
3. The two Sacraments ordained by Christ Himself.
4. The Episcopate as the center or keystone of governmental unity.

These four points, like the four famous fortresses of Lombardy, make the Quadrilateral of Anglicism [*sic*]. With them the Church of the Reconciliation stands secure.

For Huntington, American Catholicity was expressed in four simple points. The military metaphor would probably have been familiar to his congregation, since the seemingly impenetrable Austrian Quadrilateral fortresses of Mantua, Verona, Peschiera and Legnano had been much in the news during the Austro-Prussian war a few years previously.[24] The choice of metaphor, however, was perhaps somewhat unfortunate: although Italy had been defeated during the course of the war, and the fortresses had held out, by the end of the year Austria had lost control of all four to the relatively new Italian state through the terms of the Austrian Armistice with France and Prussia. Nevertheless, the term 'Quadrilateral' stuck as a description of American Catholicity. It seemed to offer a way forward for the Episcopal Church which required neither the English ivy, nor the imperial Crown.

Huntington's trilogy

In addressing the theme of American Catholicity, Huntington published an expanded version of his 'Church-Idea' sermon in a book of the same title in 1870. This was followed by two further volumes, *The Peace of the Church* in 1891,[25] based on the Bohlen lectures given at Holy Trinity, Philadelphia, and *A*

---

[24] The term 'Quadrilateral' had been used in the *Saturday Review of Politics, Literature, Science and Art* 22 (21 July 1866), p. 65.
[25] *The Peace of the Church* (New York: Charles Scribner's Sons, 1891).

National Church in 1899, based on lectures given at Kenyon College in 1897.[26] While each of these books elaborated – often somewhat repetitively – on the theme of American Catholicity, together they constituted what Huntington called in a letter to a friend in 1907 'a sort of trilogy, and have really only one theme variously treated'. He noted that the final volume was the clearest 'justification of the national Church principle, which has not, so far as I know, been elsewhere made out on the same lines'.[27] Another friend, Phillips Brooks, was particularly impressed by *The Peace of the Church*, which, he felt, was 'full of sober richness of thought, that spirit of justice and truth which we have all delighted to find in these many years'.[28] Alongside the trilogy Huntington also addresses the theme of American Catholicity in a wide range of sermons and addresses.

In *The Church-Idea*, which became his most well-known book and which is the main focus of this chapter, Huntington develops the themes of his sermon at much greater length, and is far more explicit about the divisions in his own nation. As in the sermon he promoted what he called the Church of the Reconciliation where unity was to be established on the basis of the 'Anglican principle', which would allow the church to become what he called 'the reconciler of a divided household'.[29] He thus begins *The Church-Idea* by describing the division in the churches and also reminding his readers of the Vatican Council and its declaration of infallibility. Such division, he wrote, 'best expresses the state of mind in which Christendom finds itself to-day. ... Unrest is everywhere. The party of the Curia and the party of the Reformation, the party of orthodoxy and the party of liberalism, are all alike agitated by the consciousness that a spirit of change is in the air.'[30] In his later books he follows a similar pattern using several metaphors to describe the different parties in the church, which, he felt, were either far too fluid in their boundaries or far too prescriptive. Although he was an apologist for a degree of comprehensiveness, Huntington saw this as upheld by a common shared minimum of faith embodied in the Quadrilateral, rather than as something maintained by

---

[26] *A National Church* (New York: Charles Scribner's Sons, 1899).
[27] Huntington, letter to Judge Charles Andrews, 10 December 1907, *Life and Letters*, p. 492.
[28] Letter from Phillips Brooks, 23 May 1891, in Woolverton, 'William Reed Huntington', p. 70.
[29] William Reed Huntington, *The Church-Idea: An Essay Towards Unity* (New York: E. P. Dutton, 1870; fourth edition, Charles Scribner's Sons, 1899), p. 169.
[30] *Church-Idea*, p. 1.

establishment, as A. P. Stanley, Dean of Westminster, had argued.[31] Throughout his life, Huntington continued to maintain the importance of a diversity of practice rooted in a common faith. The problem with the English church was its failure to recognize such diversity and to seek to impose uniformity.

In his understanding of the church, Huntington was something of a theological original, and somewhat eclectic in his influences: he knew the work of the German historian August Neander and had read both Charles Kingsley and Thomas Carlyle, as well as A. P. Stanley, with whom he later enjoyed a correspondence, on the Eastern Church.[32] Among Americans he knew the works of William Porcher DuBose, who in turn greatly admired his writings.[33] Huntington also seems to have been clearly influenced by Edward A. Washburn, who had lectured at Berkeley Divinity School between 1854 and 1863 while rector of St John's, Hartford, Connecticut.[34] Attacking the partisan nature of Anglicanism, he claimed in his chapter on 'The Church of the Future' that 'Anglicanism has its solid kernel of truth in demand for unity above all special Protestant confessions; it only fails because it identifies the Church with a divinely ordered Episcopate. It is yet far from a harmonious solution.'[35]

At the same time, while there is a degree of superficial similarity between Huntington and some of the English apologists for the national church from earlier in the nineteenth century, including Stanley's mentor, Thomas Arnold, as well as Samuel Taylor Coleridge and F. D. Maurice, Huntington's method was quite different. He was far less philosophical and far more a historicist in his understanding of the church: his Anglican principle was clearly located in the past rather than in the Platonist ether. In a letter to his friend Catherine Meredith in 1879 he confessed 'to not feeling the same indebtedness to Maurice as a "Master" which many of the clergymen with whom I most associate acknowledge.'[36] Although he once called the Broad Churchman B. F. Westcott 'my favourite among contemporary theologians,'[37] he refused to align himself with any of the church parties. English church parties were so

---

[31] 'The Talisman of Unity' (New York: Thomas Whittaker, 1899), p. 18; *The Peace of the Church*, p. 228.
[32] Huntington, *Life and Letters*, p. 182.
[33] DuBose to Huntington, 18 January 1892, in Woolverton, 'William Reed Huntington', p. viii.
[34] Minifie, 'William Reed Huntington', pp. 158–59.
[35] Edward Abiel Washburn, *Epochs of Church History*, edited by C. C. Tiffany (New York: E. P. Dutton & Co., 1883), p. 197.
[36] Letter to Catherine Meredith, 30 December 1879, in *Life and Letters*, pp. 127–8.
[37] Letter to Catherine Meredith, 26 April 1888, in *Life and Letters*, p. 132.

clearly related to the distinctive English constitutional settlement that it was difficult to apply them outside their original context. Writing to a friend in 1874, he was particularly clear that he did not regard himself either as a Broad Churchman, or a liberal inclusivist:

> If you map out four distinct parties, and name them ritualistic, high, low, and broad, I am a good deal in doubt where I properly belong, and therefore I question whether … I could properly stand as an advocate of any one of the four divisions. Whatever I may have been called by others, I have never called myself a Broad Churchman, pure and simple, for the reason that there are several features of what is commonly known as Broad church theology, e.g. the contempt for dogmatic principles and the unconcern for visible unity in the Church, with which I have no sympathy whatever.[38]

Given his emphasis on the primitive church, however, it is probably best to categorize Huntington as a catholic, but of a distinctively American kind.

First principles

It was on the basis of his vision of the past that Huntington sought to locate the common principles of Christianity that would provide the basis for Christian unity. In *The Church-Idea*, he was clear that the solution to the problems of party and divisions in the Church rested in a return to the first principles of the primitive church, particularly its early creeds.[39] These, he felt, contained a sufficient statement of doctrine.[40]

> Clearly we have come upon a time for the study of first principles, a time to go down and look after the foundations upon which our customary beliefs are built. The more searching the analysis, the more lasting will the synthesis be sure to be.[41]

As in his sermon, so in *The Church-Idea*, Huntington developed the theme of the 'Anglican principle' as a means of moving beyond centralism, sectarianism or liberalism. Using another military metaphor, he claimed that 'Anglicanism

---

[38] Letter to R. H. Newton, 28 August 1874, in *Life and Letters*, p. 126.
[39] See Woolverton, 'William Reed Huntington', p. 199.
[40] *Church-Idea*, p. 170.
[41] Ibid., p. 2.

stands, as Wellington's squares of infantry stood at Waterloo, firm, patient, dogged, if we must call it so, but true, – true as steel'.[42] Thus he asked, 'What are the essential, the absolutely essential features of the Anglican position?' His answers were both radical and provocative. In a famous passage, he develops an understanding of Anglicanism removed of the sort of romantic provincialism and Englishness he had experienced at Hursley:

> When it is proposed to make Anglicanism the basis of a Church of the Reconciliation, it is above all things necessary to determine what Anglicanism pure and simple is. The word brings up before the eyes of some a flutter of surplices, a vision of village spires and cathedral towers, a somewhat stiff and stately company of deans, prebendaries, and choristers, and that is about all. But we greatly mistake if we imagine that the Anglican principle has no substantial existence apart from these accessories. Indeed, it is only when we have stripped Anglicanism of the picturesque costume which English life has thrown around it, that we can fairly study its anatomy, or understand its possibilities of power and adaptation.
>
> The Anglican principle and the Anglican system are two very different things. The writer does not favor attempting to foist the whole Anglican system upon America; while yet he believes that the Anglican principle is America's best hope. At no time since the Reformation has the Church of England been in actual fact the spiritual home of the nation. A majority of the people of Great Britain are to-day without her pale. Could a system which has failed to secure comprehensiveness on its native soil, hope for any larger measure of success in a strange land?[43]

The growing awareness of the special vocation of the Anglican church as an expression of American Catholicity was to be established by removing its Englishness. While this attack on Englishness bears more than a passing resemblance to some of the anti-Britishness of the founding myths of the American republic, it also denies the centrality of the English constitutional settlement as the guarantor of catholicity, which continued to be maintained even by those who moved closest in the direction of the criterion of primitiveness.

Having stripped Anglicanism of its ivy-clad English accretions, Huntington next moves on to describe what he calls the 'true Anglican position', which, he

---

[42] Ibid., p. 124.
[43] Ibid., pp. 124–5.

claims, 'like the City of God in the Apocalypse, may be said to lie foursquare'. Once again he describes the fundamental principles of the Quadrilateral in almost identical words to those he had used in his sermon. The only difference was that the word 'center' was removed to describe the role of the Episcopate, which meant it became solely the 'keystone of governmental unity'. These four points, he continued, formed 'pure Anglicanism':

> Within them the Church of the Reconciliation may stand secure. Because the English State–Church has muffled these first principles in a cloud of non-essentials, and has said to the people of the land, 'Take all this or nothing', she mourns to-day the loss of half her children. Only by avoiding the like fatal error can the American branch of the Anglican Church hope to save herself from becoming in effect, whatever she may be in name, a sect. Only by a wise discrimination between what can and what cannot be conceded for the sake of unity, is unity attainable.[44]

A non-English Anglicanism fit for the American republic was the basis for the Church of the Reconciliation. This had been the intention of at least one of the founders of the American church as he later claimed from the floor of the House of Deputies: 'The reason why we have made such progress as we have in the United States of America is because we have modified Church of Englandism. Oh, for an hour of the wisdom of William White! Oh, for an hour of his courage!'[45]

Of the four points of the Quadrilateral, it was the assertion of the centrality of the episcopate that provoked most discussion. Huntington was keen from the outset to ensure that he was not understood as demanding the absolutist theory of bishops promoted by the Oxford Movement and its heirs and successors. Instead he sought a 'primitive episcopacy' as a sign of both unity and continuity, but which could be interpreted in very different ways. It was hard, he claimed, 'to associate absolutism, or any offensive features of royalty with so inoffensive a symbol as a shepherd's crook'.[46] Instead of a monarchical episcopate he simply sought what he called a 'harmonious and self-consistent method of administering the word and the sacraments' which 'suggests

---

[44] Ibid., pp. 125–6.
[45] *Churchman*, 26 October 1895, cited in Woolverton, 'William Reed Huntington', p. 101. On White, see W. H. Stowe (ed.), *The Life and Letters of Bishop William White* (New York: Morehouse, 1937).
[46] *The Peace of the Church*, p. 189.

that a system of oversight safe-guarded by carefulness in the transmission of authority'.[47] He worked hard to promote his views on episcopacy among members of different churches through establishing the League of Catholic Unity,[48] under the presidency of the Princeton Presbyterian Charles W. Shields who wrote *The Historic Episcopate* [49] and *The United Church of the United States*.[50] Shields defended episcopacy as 'a universal institution, common to Eastern and Western Christendom and not confined to the American House of Bishops'.[51] In *The Peace of the Church*, Huntington was clear that he had carefully avoided the phrase 'Apostolical Succession', which would have 'committed them hopelessly to a particular philosophy of the ministry'. The words used 'express a fact without at all insisting on any theory of the fact'.[52] Jesus Christ established the basis for the 'historic episcopate' 'by washing his disciples' feet'.[53] At the end of his life Huntington was even more adamant about the need to be flexible on the nature of episcopacy. The alternative was to risk becoming irrelevant:

> We go on insisting that those who are willing to recognize the episcopate as the centre of governmental unity shall also accept it as the sole depository of divine grace ... we may indeed continue to maintain our corporate existence, even as the Nonjurors of Scotland and the Jansenists of Holland maintained theirs, but our hope of ever becoming for America the Church of the Reconciliation will have been blasted.[54]

A non-English Anglicanism

Throughout his career, and frequently with more than a touch of humour, Huntington made broadsides against the identification of Englishness and

---

[47] Ibid., p. 205.
[48] For a statement of the League's aims, see Woolverton, 'William Reed Huntington', Appendix II, pp. 411–2.
[49] Charles Woodruff Shields, *The Historic Episcopate: An Essay on the Four Articles of Church Unity Proposed by the American House of Bishops and the Lambeth Conference* (New York: Charles Scribner's Sons, 1894).
[50] Shields, *The United Church of the United States* (New York: Charles Scribner's Sons, 1895).
[51] Shields, *The Historic Episcopate*, p. 26.
[52] *The Peace of the Church*, p. 204.
[53] Ibid., p. 176.
[54] 'The Four Theories of Visible Church Unity', p. 162.

Anglicanism. For instance, in *A National Church* he makes use of one of his favoured botanical analogies:

> The English ivy is a beautiful plant, and nothing is one-half so becoming to church walls; but unfortunately the English ivy does not flourish in all climates, and to insist that it shall be 'Ivy or nothing' in a land where the woodbine and other fairly presentable vines are indigenous is a mistake.[55]

While the churches of America obviously owed a great deal to England, Huntington urged his audience not to be drawn to 'the fools' paradise of those who fancy that American Christianity in its entirety can be Anglified'.[56] Instead, such Christianity should be as diverse as American society.

Perhaps remembering his early days when he experienced difficulties with the Thirty-Nine Articles, he criticized such formularies for frustrating the simplicity of the creeds. Since so much was concerned with maintaining the authority of the monarch, circumstances had rendered them redundant. In *The Peace of the Church* he claimed that 'ever since their transfer from English to American soil' the Articles had 'a provisional and transitory look. ... Surely it can never have been imagined that of such a sort would be the permanent dogmatic constitution of a great Church. ... The Thirty-Nine articles were originally drawn up by the English Church as a defence against the Rome of the sixteenth century.' The changed circumstances of the Roman Church after 1870, however, had completely transformed their apologetic target. Thus, drawing on another military metaphor, he asked, 'Rome having deliberately changed her base in the year of our Lord 1870, does not our elaborate battery look to the critical eye of present-day strategists, a little out of range?'[57] He felt that trying to supplement the Creeds was detrimental to the future of the church: 'The thing that makes the Episcopal Church seem narrow with respect to doctrine is the exceeding tenacity with which it clings to certain articles of the faith which it accounts, whether rightly or wrongly, to be the foundation stones of the Christian religion.'[58]

In an article in the *Hibbert Journal*, Huntington wrote what he called Tract XCI which he felt explained the Thirty-Nine Articles from an American point

---

[55] *A National Church*, p. 51.
[56] Ibid., p. 52.
[57] *Peace of the Church*, p. 234.
[58] *Popular Misconceptions of the Episcopal Church* (New York: Thomas Whittaker, 1891), pp. 46–7.

of view.[59] Commenting on Newman's Tract XC, which he felt 'launched a torpedo destined to blow the Thirty-Nine Articles, in their supposed character of a protestant irenic, to shivers,'[60] he claimed that the Articles had proved an open failure since Newman. Indeed, he suggested, Newman gave them a 'fatal stab from which they have practically bled to death'.[61] From an American point of view, he asked, 'What is their legal *status*? What, under twentieth century conditions, is their theological value?'[62] Since so many of the Articles were contextual to England, such as Article 21 that General Councils were to be convened by princes, Huntington felt that there was need for radical revision.[63] There was so much confusion and lack of clarity in the Articles that 'no-clear cut, frank, direct answer is to be had to the question, To what do I commit myself doctrinally if I enter the ministry of the Church?' His solution was to reassert the Lambeth Quadrilateral with its minimal definition of the faith: 'The Lambeth Platform, to be sure, has an answer to this question, as clear as a bell. "The Nicene Creed, it declares," is "the sufficient statement of the Christian Faith".'[64] The only addendum to the creed was, he felt, the worship of the church.[65] He consequently felt that the Articles should be given a dignified retirement alongside Henry's *Primer* and Jewel's *Apology*:

> The Confessions have their day and cease to be; the Creeds live on – all the days are theirs, The Creeds are like Stonehenge and the Pyramids; – to go at them with hammer and chisel, under the pretext of reparation, were little short of sacrilege. The Thirty-Nine Articles are a sixteenth century Episcopal residence of many rooms, some of them out of repair. ... What a handsome set of Archives they would make, and how happily the Thirty-Nine Articles would fit in! *Bibliotheca Anglicana* we will call it, and it shall have glass doors to protect the honoured pages from an otherwise inevitable dust.[66]

For Huntington, the fundamental denominational identity of the Episcopal Church was to be found in the primitive Catholic Church as it related to the

---

[59] William Reed Huntington, 'Tract No. XCI. The Articles of Religion from an American Point of View', *Hibbert Journal* 20 (1907), pp. 808–20.

[60] Huntington, 'Tract No. XCI', p. 810.

[61] *Life and Letters*, p. 479.

[62] Huntington, 'Tract No. XCI', p. 811.

[63] Ibid., p. 813.

[64] Ibid., p. 814.

[65] Ibid., p. 819.

[66] Huntington, 'Tract No. XCI', p. 820.

American context. Pure Anglicanism expressed a *national* ideal as it sought to embrace all those Christians prepared to adopt the minimal definition of what constituted the Church contained in the four points of the Quadrilateral. Towards the end of *The Church-Idea* Huntington spoke candidly of the danger of Episcopalianism becoming little more than a respectable sect denying all claim to catholicity. To counter all such tendencies, Huntington held up a very different vision of the Church:

> If we aim at something nobler than this, if we would have our Communion become national in very truth ... then let us press our reasonable claims to be the reconciler of a divided household, not in a spirit of arrogance (which ill befits those whose best possessions have come to them by inheritance), but with affectionate earnestness and an intelligent zeal.[67]

The Chicago–Lambeth Quadrilateral

Such was Huntington's influence that his four points were taken up by the House of Bishops at the General Convention of the American Episcopal Church held at Chicago in 1886.[68] They were presented as part of the Report of the Committee on Christian Unity, which had been established at the General Convention of 1880 and which was composed of five bishops under the leadership of A. N. Littlejohn of Long Island. The report was not formally enacted by the House of Deputies but it was instead incorporated as part of a general plan for study and action by a new Joint Commission for Christian Reunion.[69] The aim of the

---

[67] *The Church Idea*, p. 169.

[68] See William T. Manning, *Be Strong in the Lord: Sermons and Addresses on Various Occasions* (New York: Morehouse-Gorham Co., 1947), pp. 110–11.

[69] Text and note in *The Book of Common Prayer* (New York: Church Hymnal Corporation, 1979), p. 877. It was, however, accepted in the General Convention of 1892 and 1895 to provide the Commission for Christian Unity to restore unity 'on the basis of those things declared essential' in 1886: *Journal of the Proceedings of the Bishops, Clergy, and Laity of the Protestant Episcopal Church in the USA, Baltimore, 1892* (Printed for the Convention, 1893), pp. 87, 148, 150. The full report and motion is at pp. 545–6. This resolution was reiterated in 1895, with the addition of the reaffirmation of the Quadrilateral at Lambeth in 1888: *Journal of the Proceedings of the Bishops, Clergy, and Laity of the Protestant Episcopal Church in the USA, Minneapolis, 1895* (Printed for the Convention, 1896), pp. 144–5, 155, 157. The Report is at pp. 596–7. Both the 1886 and 1888 versions of the Quadrilateral are included among the 'Historical Documents' in the 1979 *Book of Common Prayer* of the American Episcopal Church (pp. 876–8).

declaration was to promote national unity and reconciliation.[70] The scattered denominations were invited to participate in the unity of the primitive church as represented by Anglicanism. The declaration was thus addressed 'especially to our fellow-Christians of the different Communions in this land, who, in their several spheres, have contended for the religion of Christ'.[71] The most important amendment to Huntington's original expression of the Quadrilateral was the insertion of the word 'historic' before 'episcopate', which appeared to restrict Huntington's original intention of seeing the Episcopate as a sign first and foremost of continuity and primitiveness rather than a guarantee of validity. At the same time, the entry requirement into the church was simply baptism, while in 'all things of human ordering or human choice, relating to modes of worship and discipline, or to traditional customs, this Church is ready in the spirit of love and humility to forego all preferences of her own'. Unity was expressed in terms of continuity with

> the principles of unity exemplified by the undivided Catholic Church during the first ages of its existence; which principles we believe to be the substantial deposit of Christian Faith and Order committed by Christ and his Apostles to the Church unto the end of the world, and therefore incapable of compromise or surrender by those who have been ordained to be its stewards and trustees for the common and equal benefit of all men.

These principles were regarded as 'essential to the restoration of unity among the divided branches of Christendom'. The bishops went on to 'declare our desire and readiness, so soon as there shall be any authorized response to this Declaration, to enter into brotherly conference' with other Christians in the hope of reaching organic unity.[72]

---

[70] For a strongly worded account, see S. D. McConnell, *History of the American Episcopal Church* (Milwaukee: Morehouse, 1934), pp. 422–7. See also James Thayer Addison, *The Episcopal Church in the United States: 1789-1931* (New York: Charles Scribner's Sons, 1951), chapter 19; William Mancross, *A History of the American Episcopal Church* (New York: Morehouse-Gorham Co., 1959), pp. 313–8.

[71] Resolution of the General Convention 1886: *Journal of the Proceedings of the Bishops, Clergy, and Laity of the Protestant Episcopal Church in the USA, Chicago, 1886* (Printed for the Convention, 1887), pp. 78–80. The motion was passed on 20 October.

[72] The Quadrilateral passed at Chicago read as follows: '1. The Holy Scriptures of the Old and New Testaments as the revealed Word of God. 2. The Nicene Creed as the sufficient statement of the Christian Faith. 3. The two Sacraments – Baptism and the Supper of the Lord – ministered with unfailing use of Christ's words of institution and of the elements ordained by Him. 4. The Historic Episcopate, locally adapted in the methods of its administration to the varying needs of the nations and peoples called of God into the unity of His Church.'

Two years later a version of American Catholicity was accepted by the bishops gathered from across the Anglican Communion at the Third Lambeth Conference.[73] The bishops adopted a slightly revised version of the Chicago quadrilateral as the basis 'on which approach may be by God's blessing made towards Home Reunion'.[74] A crucial difference, however, was that instead of simply seeing the four points as the basis for home reunion, the Lambeth Resolution[75] regarded the four points as 'Articles'. Subsequent application of the Lambeth Quadrilateral reveals that they have been understood as constitutive of the identity of the *Anglican* Communion rather than simply as principles for reunion.[76] Once again the question of precisely what was meant by 'the Historic Episcopate, locally adapted in the methods of its administration to the varying needs of the nations and peoples called of God into the Unity of His Church' provoked a significant discussion at the 1888 Conference.[77]

Gradually Huntington's 'Anglican Principle' became less a description of the requirements for reconciliation at home and more an outline of what was

---

[73] *Conference of Bishops of the Anglican Communion holden at Lambeth Palace, in July 1888. Encyclical Letter from The Bishops, with the Resolutions And Reports* (London: SPCK, 1888). The Report of the Home Reunion Committee explains the importance of the 1886 General Convention (pp. 83–4). The encyclical letter (pp. 15–16) spoke of the bishops 'after anxious discussion' laying down their four 'Articles'.

[74] Resolution 11 of the Lambeth Conference of 1888 read as follows:'That, in the opinion of this Conference, the following Articles supply a basis on which approach may be by God's blessing made towards home reunion:The Holy Scriptures of the Old and New Testaments, as "containing all things necessary to salvation," and as being the rule and ultimate standard of faith. The Apostles' Creed, as the baptismal symbol; and the Nicene Creed, as the sufficient statement of the Christian faith. The two sacraments ordained by Christ himself – Baptism and the Supper of the Lord – ministered with unfailing use of Christ's words of institution, and of the elements ordained by him. The historic episcopate, locally adapted in the methods of its administration to the varying needs of the nations and peoples called of God into the unity of his Church': *Conference of Bishops*, pp. 25–6; also at Roger Coleman, *Resolutions of the Twelve Lambeth Conferences* (Toronto: Anglican Book Centre, 1992), p. 13.

[75] On the circumstances surrounding the resolution, see Alan M. G. Stephenson, *Anglicanism and The Lambeth Conferences* (London: SPCK, 1978), chapter 6; H. G. G. Herklots, 'The Origins of the Lambeth Quadrilateral', *Church Quarterly Review* (January to March, 1968), pp. 61–8; Louis A. Haselmeyer, *Lambeth and Unity* (London: Dacre Press for the American Church Union, 1948), part one.

[76] Gillian R. Evans, 'Permanence in the Revealed Truth and Continuous Exploration of its Meaning', in J. Robert Wright (ed.), *Quadrilateral at One Hundred* (London: Mowbray, 1998), pp. 111–25, especially pp. 114–15.

[77] See Mark Chapman, *Anglican Theology* (London and New York: T&T Clark, 2012), pp. 195–6. See, for example, William Croswell Doane, 'The Historic Episcopate', in *The Church Review* 59 (1890), pp. 158–64; William Stevens Perry, 'Church Reunion Discussed on the Basis of the Lambeth Propositions of 1888', *The Church Review* 59 (1890), pp. 165–73; Arthur Cleveland Coxe, *The History and Teachings of the Early Church as a Basis for the Re-union of Christendom*, Lectures delivered in 1888, under the auspices of the Church Club (Third edn, New York: E. and J. B. Young, 1892); William Stevens Perry, Bishop of Iowa, *The Third Lambeth Conference, A Personal Narrative*, Privately printed, 1891 (available at Project Canterbury).

required for membership of the Anglican Communion.[78] The wider use of the Lambeth Quadrilateral was most obvious at the 1920 Lambeth Conference which issued its famous *Appeal* influenced by A. C. Headlam's Bampton Lectures, *The Doctrine of the Church and Christian Reunion.*[79] Thus there emerged a definition of Anglicanism in which anything distinctively English, including the Prayer Book or any doctrinal formulary was conspicuously absent. Although Huntington's own understanding of the episcopate was broad and could have accommodated a number of different expressions, the inclusion of the 'historic episcopate' into the Quadrilateral elevated one distinctive version of the doctrine of episcopacy into part of the definition of worldwide Anglicanism which has frequently served to make ecumenical reconciliation at the very least highly complex.[80] Equally important in relation to the contemporary internal issues facing Anglicanism, was anything equivalent to the Royal Supremacy: there was no legal structure or Constitution to put the Quadrilateral into effect at an inter-church or international level. It had little to say about structures and relationships at the global level. In his own development of the Quadrilateral, however, Huntington increasingly recognized the need for a further dimension of ecclesial authority which might become a non-English functional constitutional equivalent of the Royal Supremacy.

A Constitutional Church

Huntington's understanding of American Catholicity increasingly moved towards a form of constitutionalism, which he saw as closely connected with

[78] See Stephenson, *Anglicanism and The Lambeth Conferences*, p. 132. See Charlotte Methuen, 'Lambeth 1920: the appeal to All Christian People, an account by G.K.A. Bell and the redactions of the appeal' in M. Barber, G. Sewell and S. Taylor (eds.), *From the Reformation to the Permissive Society: a Miscellany in Celebration of the 400th Anniversary of Lambeth Palace Library*. Series: Church of England Record Society (18) (Woodbridge: Boydell & Brewer, 2010), pp. 521–64.

[79] A. C. Headlam, *The Doctrine of the Church and Christian Renunion* (London: John Murray, 1920). The move towards a principle of home reunion towards a minimum definition of Anglicanism was noted in Ruth Rouse and Stephen Neill (eds), *A History of the Ecumenical Movement* (London: SPCK, 1954), p. 265. See Stephenson, *Anglicanism and The Lambeth Conferences*, p. 132. See Charlotte Methuen, 'Lambeth 1920: the appeal to All Christian People, an account by G.K.A. Bell and the redactions of the appeal', in M. Barber, G. Sewell and S. Taylor (eds), *From the Reformation to the Permissive Society: a Miscellany in Celebration of the 400th Anniversary of Lambeth Palace Library*. Series: Church of England Record Society (18) (Woodbridge: Boydell & Brewer, 2010), pp. 521–64.

[80] See my essay, 'The Politics of Episcopacy', in Ingolf U. Dalferth (ed.), *Einheit bezeugen/Witnessing to Unity* (Frankfurt am Main: Verlag Otto Lembeck, 2004), pp. 150–69.

what he once described as the 'theocratic republic' in which he worked.[81] The grounds for such constitutionalism were straightforward. While the primitiveness of scripture and the creeds might function as criteria for discerning the Anglican principle, there was no mechanism to ensure that they would be treated as foundational in the Church. He consequently spent a great deal of energy in trying to introduce the Quadrilateral into the Episcopal Church's Constitution. Indeed, he felt that it was particularly important that the Anglican religion, which was in theory 'hospitable and inclusive', would be able to realize this vision of unity so that 'when the Constitution does finally emerge from the fires of reconstruction a finished thing, it may prove of such sort as shall further the uplifting of a United Church of the United States'.[82]

For Huntington, such constitutionalism was straightforward: 'Would not the embodiment in the first Article of our Constitution of what the Bishops at Lambeth laid down with respect to the Scriptures and the Creeds completely meet our needs?'[83] Unity would be expressed not by a uniformity but by the sort of unity 'as unites the States themselves, namely, a unity so real that it can show indisputable tokens like the flag'.[84] Like the state, the church's boundaries would be broad, but they would never be able to embrace the ecclesiastical equivalent of the outlaw, or those who did not wish to be comprehended.[85] According to Huntington, the Episcopal Church was thus to be 'the most comprehensive Church in Christendom, loyal to the Scriptures of both Testaments, loyal to the early Creeds, loyal to the Sacraments of Christ, loyal to Holy Order – a spiritual house large enough for a nation'.[86]

Constitutionalism, Huntington held, would provide a serious alternative to the other forms of unity, which he labelled imperial, liberal and federal.[87] What was required was a 'merger' not a 'limited partnership', which, like the American Constitution would be 'an indissoluble union of indestructible states',[88] 'in which the rights of all parties are conserved. It means unity by contribution,

---

[81] *The Theocratic Republic, A Sermon Preached before the Twenty-fifth National Conference of Charities and Correction in Grace Church, NY, Sunday, May 22, 1898* (no further details given), p. 6.
[82] *Whole Church: A Plea for the Four Temperaments*, p. 10.
[83] *The Peace of the Church*, p. 234.
[84] 'The Talisman of Unity', p. 7.
[85] Ibid., p. 8.
[86] Ibid., p. 18.
[87] 'Four Theories', p. 162.
[88] *'Inter-Church' or Intra-Church, Which? A Sermon about Federation*, 19 November 1905 (New York: no publisher, 1905), pp. 14–15.

not unity by subtraction'.[89] Such constitutionalism would function by elevating the key principles enshrined in the Quadrilateral into what Huntington called 'the permanent bases or cornerstones of ecclesiastical unity'. These would be counted 'constitutional', and all else would be 'statutory and changeable'.[90]

American Catholicity and the International Church

Huntington's impact on the development of Anglicanism cannot be underestimated. Yet his vision of American Catholicity has never been seriously explored. Although his Quadrilateral, with its elevation of a non-English version of the Anglican principle established on primitiveness, has shaped the theology of the Anglican Communion from 1888, and has deeply influenced the recent efforts to produce a somewhat more extended version of Anglican basics in the Anglican Communion Covenant, the idea of constitutionalism remains undeveloped in Anglican theology. The creation of a form of constitutional legal governance which might provide a functional equivalent to the royal supremacy, which was so crucial for Anglican identity in its English years, has not been tested. Indeed, what is conspicuously absent in recent documents is a transnational system of legitimate constitutional authority. The assumption is that the current Instruments of Communion can simply be made to work.

American Constitutionalism, however, with its highly complex system of relationships between the states and the government guaranteed by a constitution, might offer a way forward. Whatever the virtues of the Covenant, it is clearly failing to gain the support of the majority of the churches of the Anglican Communion, including the Church of England, chiefly on the grounds of the legitimacy of those who would have to implement it. The key issue is not so much the summary of Anglican basics, but the final section with its mechanism for what it calls 'dispute resolution'. In some parts of the Communion, the so-called Instruments of Communion have yet to win the legitimacy that might once have been accorded to the monarch in the traditional English Anglican settlement. To gain the trust of all churches, extra-provincial authority requires a form of constitutionalism acknowledged across the

---

[89] 'Four Theories', p. 161.
[90] Ibid., p. 161.

Communion. American Catholicity was one such model, grounded as it was in the primitive church but legitimized (or contained) by its relationship to a constitutional settlement based on what Huntington called 'fair representation'. What this might look like at a worldwide level is obviously not clear, but it is hard to see the current Instruments of Communion as legitimized by their representative or constitutional character. The quest for legitimate consensus-building structures which do not simply promote conversation, but which build reunion in and between the seriously divided churches of the Anglican Communion, seems urgent. This seems to require some sort of constitution, some sort of representation, some sort of legitimized structures, and some sort of conciliar meeting. The future thus seems to need a kind of constitutional conciliarism, which, as Paul Valliere suggests, is 'an instrument of the centre'.[91] Constitutionalism requires both a constitution, which may well look something like the Covenant, but for it to move into the form of international catholicity demanded by a global communion, it also requires at the same time representative and legitimate structures both within and between the national churches. One might perhaps hope that a Pan-Anglican Council of Reunion conducted on Huntington's principles might be on agenda for the 2020 Lambeth Conference.

---

[91] Paul Valliere, *Conciliarism: A History of Decision-Making in the Church* (Cambridge: Cambridge University Press, 2012), p. 244.

5

The Making of 'An Appeal to All Christian People' at the 1920 Lambeth Conference

Charlotte Methuen

Introduction

In 1920 the Lambeth Conference issued 'An Appeal to All Christian People', a clarion call to ecumenical endeavour and church unity. It grew out of and reflected the post-First-World-War sense that churches must urgently find a way of acting together in order to prevent future hostilities on the scale of that war. The *Appeal* was issued in a period of intense political and ecumenical activity.[1] Responses to the 1919 Versailles Treaty were not only changing the political shape of Europe, but also affecting theological and intellectual standpoints, and with them ecumenical relations. The 1920 Lambeth Conference's *Appeal* followed closely on the Encyclical issued by the Ecumenical Patriarch in January 1920, 'Unto the Churches of Christ Everywhere' which, 'in view of the hopeful establishment of the League of Nations' called for 'rapprochement between the various Christian churches and fellowship among them', proposing a series of practical measures to bring this about.[2]

---

[1]   See, for instance, and directly relating to the context of the *Appeal*, J. G. Lockhart, *Cosmo Gordon Lang* (London: Hodder and Stoughton, 1949), pp. 266–7. For relationships between German and English theologians during and immediately after the First World War, see Mark D. Chapman, *Theology at War and Peace: English Theology and Germany in the First World War* (London: Routledge, 2016), pp. 106–55; Catherine Ann Cline, 'Ecumenism and Appeasement: The Bishops of the Church of England and the Treaty of Versailles', *The Journal of Modern History*, 61 (1989), pp. 683–703; Charlotte Methuen, '"Fulfilling Christ's own wish that we should be one": The early ecumenical work of George Bell as Chaplain to the Archbishop of Canterbury and Dean of Canterbury (1914–1929)', in *Kirchliche Zeitgeschichte*, 21 (2008), pp. 222–45 especially 226–8; reprinted in Andrew Chandler (ed.), *The Church and Humanity: The Life and Work of George Bell, 1883–1958* (Aldershot: Ashgate, 2012), pp. 25–46.

[2]   These included agreement on the date of Easter, exchanges between professors and students of theology and the organization of pan-Christian conferences. The text can be found at https://

Even before the First World War, international ecumenical initiatives had led to the establishing of the World Conference on Faith and Order which, after a preparatory meeting in Geneva in 1920, held its first full meeting in Lausanne in 1927.[3] The World Alliance for Promoting International Friendship through the churches had initiated visits between England and Germany in 1908 and 1909 and was meeting in Germany when war broke out.[4] Initiatives taken at the Alliance's first post-war meeting, held in 1919 at Oud Wassenaar, near The Hague, gave rise to the Life and Work movement.[5] Anglicans were closely involved in both: the Faith and Order Continuation Committee was chaired initially by Charles Brent, Episcopal (Anglican) Bishop of Western New York, and after Brent's death in 1929 by the newly appointed Archbishop of York, William Temple; from 1932 until 1934, George Bell, Bishop of Chichester, was President of Life and Work.

In the Church of England, the *Appeal* marked the beginning of nearly two decades of unprecedented ecumenical activity, which resulted in agreements of what was then known as intercommunion between Anglicans and the Lutheran Church of Sweden, the Old Catholic churches of the Utrecht Union and the Finnish, Latvian and Estonian Lutheran churches.[6] In addition, the

---

incommunion.org/2004/10/24/unto-the-churches-of-christ-everywhere/ (accessed 13 May 2017). Bell continued to cite the practical measures suggested in the encyclical in his work with the World Council of Churches (WCC). See Bell to the Central Committee of the WCC, 9 December 1950, in Gerhard Besier, 'Intimately associated for many years': George A. K. Bell's and Willem A. Visser't Hooft's common life-work in the service of the church universal, mirrored in their correspondence, Part Two, 1950-1958 (Newcastle upon Tyne: Cambridge Scholars Publishing, 2015), p. 694. For a discussion of the significance of the encyclical for Anglican–Orthodox relations, see soon Jonathan Gough, 'Ecumenical Relationships between the See of Canterbury and the Churches of the East 1900-1940', PhD thesis in progress, University of Glasgow.

[3]   See Tissington Tatlow, 'The World Conference on Faith and Order', in Ruth Rouse and Stephen Charles Neill (eds), *A History of the Ecumenical Movement 1517-1948* (2nd edition, London: SPCK, 1967), pp. 403–41. Compare also Günther Gassmann, *Konzeptionen der Einheit in der Bewegung für Glauben und Kirchenverfassung, 1910-1937* (Göttingen: Vandenhoeck & Ruprecht, 1979).

[4]   For the Friendship Movement, see Keith W. Clements, *Ecumenical Dynamic: Living in more than one place at once* (Geneva: World Council of Churches, 2013), pp. 57–76; Barbara Fink, *Der Weg zur Bewegung für praktisches Christentum ('Life and Work'): der Hintergrund der deutschen Beteiligung von der 'Freundschaft' bis zur Konferenz in Stockholm 1925* (Bern: Peter Lang, 1985), especially pp. 97–165; Julian Jenkins, 'A Forgotten Challenge to German Nationalism: The World Alliance for International Friendship through the Churches', *Australian Journal of Politics & History*, 37 (1991), pp. 286–301.

[5]   See Wolfram Weisse, *Praktisches Christentum und Reich Gottes: Die ökumenische Bewegung Life und Work, 1919-1937. Kirche und Konfession* (*Veröffentlichungen des Konfessionskundlichen Instituts des Evangelischen Bundes*, 31; Göttingen: Vandenhoeck und Ruprecht, 1991).

[6]   Discussions between the Anglican Communion and the Church of Sweden recommended mutual eucharistic hospitality, invitations to preach and participation of bishops in episcopal consecrations; this was approved at the 1920 Lambeth Conference, Resolutions 24 and 25. Church of England conversations with the Finnish church (1933-4) and with the churches of Latvia and Estonia (1936 and 1938) led to similar agreements. The agreement with Finland was also affirmed by the 1948

1920s saw a series of conversations between the Church of England and the Federation of Free churches; they saw the recognition of Anglican Orders by some Orthodox churches, and the Malines Conversations with the Romans Catholics. In a report composed for the 1930 Lambeth Conference, George Bell commented on the importance of the *Appeal*:

> Since its issue in August 1920, the 'Appeal to all Christian People' has received marked attention in many Christian Communions and in many parts of the world. It has been translated into a variety of languages – Latin, Modern Greek, French, German, Italian, Russian, Portuguese, Spanish and Esperanto. It has indeed given a momentum of its own to the whole Reunion Movement.[7]

The modern Anglican Ecumenical Movement still views the *Appeal*, together with the Lambeth Quadrilateral, as informing its work.[8] This chapter examines the context from which the *Appeal* emerged before considering what is revealed about its intentions by accounts of the discussions of the Committee on Church Reunion at the 1920 Lambeth Conference. Central to understanding the *Appeal* are its concept of unity and its approach to episcopacy.

Bell's 1930 account of the fruits of the *Appeal* is notable for its English focus. However, the context of the 1920 *Appeal* was entirely international, arising from attempts across the Communion to come to closer agreement with other churches. 'Reunion' – which would now be described as ecumenical relations – had been on the agenda of every previous Lambeth Conference from 1867 to 1908, and from the first it played an important role in the programme planned for the sixth Lambeth Conference. The Conference, originally scheduled to take place in 1918, had been postponed on account of the First World War. As plans took shape after the Armistice, it was clear that the question of relations between the churches had become even more important in a world shaken and debilitated by four years of war. Many church

---

Lambeth Conference, Resolution 70. Those with Latvia and Estonia were also received at Lambeth 1948, Resolution 71, but it was recognized that they had been overtaken by political events; the British Government's Foreign Office was cautious about plans inviting Latvian and Estonian bishops to take part in the 1948 Lambeth Conference although it recommended that the Church of England should continue to attempt to maintain direct contact. Lambeth Palace Library (LPL), CFR correspondence, Lutheran and Reformed Churches, file 21 (Estonia), letters of 12 December 1946 and 31 December 1946.

[7] 'Reunion: A Report on replies to the Appeal to all Christian People', issued by the Lambeth Conference, 1920 (LPL, Lambeth Conference Papers [LC] 1930 Agenda III), p. 1.

[8] For the Lambeth Quadrilateral, see Mark Chapman, 'William Reed Huntington, American Catholicity and the Lambeth Quadrilateral' in this volume, pp. 84–106.

leaders – especially Protestants – felt a particular responsibility to work to ensure that such a conflict would never again arise; finding ways to overcome their own differences was one aspect of this. Reunion was set to become a major focus of the 1920 Lambeth Conference.

The Reunion Committee was easily the largest committee of the conference, attracting more than sixty members under the chairmanship of the Archbishop of York, Cosmo Gordon Lang.[9] It was divided into subcommittees, one focusing on Reunion with Episcopal churches, and the much larger Sub-Committee for Reunion with non-episcopal churches, which was also chaired by Lang. In preparation for the Committee's work, a questionnaire was circulated which asked for information about existing agreements and relations with non-episcopal churches, both in terms of 'action … which involves Churches *in their corporate capacity*' – that is, plans for federation, association or union with other churches – and 'action which mainly affects individuals' – occasional admission to communion, preaching by ministers of non-episcopal churches, joint services of prayer, shared facilities for training and education, or other examples of cooperation.[10] The results were collected in *Documents bearing on the Problem of Christian Unity and Fellowship 1916-1920*, prepared at the instigation of the Archbishop of Canterbury, Randall Davidson, by George Bell, who had been his Chaplain since 1914.[11]

The context of the Appeal to all Christian People

The documents included in this collection reflected a range of relationships and plans for reunion across the Anglican Communion, including the first

---

[9]   This figure is based on Lang's account, corroborated by counting the bishops mentioned in George Bell's account of the making of the *Appeal*. For the text of this account and notes on the bishops involved, see Charlotte Methuen, 'Lambeth 1920: The Appeal To All Christian People (editions of an account by George Bell and the redactions of the Appeal with an introduction)', in Melanie Barber, Gabriel Sewell and Stephen Taylor (eds), *From the Reformation to the Permissive Society: A Miscellany in Celebration of the 400th Anniversary of Lambeth Palace Library* (Woodbridge: Boydell & Brewer, 2010), pp. 521–64, at 534–549.

[10] LPL, Lambeth 1920, Official Papers &c, document 14.

[11] G. K. A. Bell (ed.), *Documents bearing on the problem of Christian unity and fellowship, 1916-1920* London: SPCK, 1920). A more detailed discussion of these documents can be found in Charlotte Methuen, 'The Kikuyu proposals in their contemporary ecumenical perspective', in Jeremy Bonner and Mark C. Chapman (eds), *Costly Communion: Ecumenical Initiative and Sacramental Strife in the Anglican Communion* (forthcoming). For Bell's ecumenical involvement during this period, see Methuen, '"Fulfilling Christ's own wish that we should be one"'.

two interim reports of the English Committee for the World Council on Faith and Order, published in 1916 and 1918; the proposed concordat between the Protestant Episcopal Church of America and the Congregationalist Churches in the United States (1919);[12] proposals for Church Union between the Anglican Church, the South India United Church and the Syrian Mar Thoma Church (1919);[13] the Constitution of Alliance of Missionary Societies in British East Africa (drawn up at Kikuyu 1918), and the Bishop of Zanzibar's counter-proposals;[14] and a range of reports on discussions and conferences involving the Church of England, Wesleyan Methodists, the Federal Free Church Council and the YMCA.[15]

Unsurprisingly, episcopacy was a key theme. The Second Interim Faith and Order Report of the English churches suggested of relations between episcopal and non-episcopal churches: 'What we desire to see is not grudging confession, but a willing acceptance for the common enrichment of the united church of the wealth distinctive of each.' With regard to the episcopate, the report suggests, this should mean 'that continuity with the historic Episcopate should effectively be preserved', that 'the Episcopate should re-assume a constitutional form, both as regards the method of the election of the bishop as by clergy and people, and the method of government after the election'; and 'that effect acceptance of the fact of Episcopacy and not any theory as to its character should be all that is asked for'.[16] It commented further:

> The acceptance of Episcopacy on these terms should not involve any Christian community in the necessity of disowning its past. ... We hope and desire that each of these Christian communions would bring its own

---

[12] *Documents 1916-1920*, pp. 9–15. For plans for a United Churches of Christ in America, drawn up between 1918 and 1920, and rejected by the Presbyterian Church in the United States in 1920, see Stephen Charles Neill, 'Plans of Union and Reunion 1910-1948', in Rouse and Neill (eds), *A History of the Ecumenical Movement*, pp. 443–505, at 445–6.

[13] *Documents 1916-1920*, 15–24. For the Church of South India proposals, see Neill, 'Plans of Union and Reunion', pp. 473–6, and, in great detail, idem, 'Church Union in South India', in J. J. Willis et al., *Towards a United Church 1913-1947* (London: Edinburgh House Press, 1947), pp. 77–148.

[14] *Documents 1916-1920*, pp. 37–48. The proposals had emerged from a consultation between Anglican, Methodist, Baptist, Presbyterian and other missionaries considering how Christians might best respond to Islam, which had ended with the extension of communion to the non-Anglicans. The Bishop of Zanzibar had protested, particularly at the offering of eucharistic hospitality to members of non-episcopal churches by the Bishops of Uganda and Mombassa, who had presided at the Eucharist. For the Kikuyu proposals, see J. J. Willis, 'The Kikuyu Conference' in Willis et al., *Towards a United Church 1913-1947*, pp. 15–51, and J. W. Arthur, 'After "Kikuyu"', in ibid., pp. 52–74.

[15] *Documents 1916-1920*, pp. 48–54 (relations with Wesleyan Methodists), 54–7, 59–62, 62–5, 65–8, 68–72, 73–7 (relations with Free churches), 72–3 (resolutions on intercommunion).

[16] *Documents 1916-1920*, p. 13.

distinctive contribution ... and that all that is true in the experience and testimony of the uniting Communions would be conserved to the Church.[17]

The language and tone of this report would found a place in the *Appeal*, in its hope that 'the office of a bishop should be everywhere exercised in a representative and constitutional manner', its affirmation that 'it is not that we call in question for a moment the spiritual reality of the ministries of those Communions which do not possess the episcopate', and in its conviction that a reunited church would be enriched by 'much that has long been distinctive in [the] methods of worship and service' of the uniting churches.[18]

These theological discussions found practical shape in some of the other documents included in the collection. The Bishop of London offered the intriguing suggestion that from henceforth all Church of England and Wesleyan Methodist ordinations should simply be joint ordinations: 'If you can get a date after which all ordinations will be considered valid by both bodies, you have ... arrived at a point after which eventually and automatically the division between the two bodies will cease.'[19] The far more formal concordat between the Episcopal and the Congregationalist Churches of the United States made provision for congregational ministers who wished to exercise their ministry in an episcopal context to be ordained in order to do so. The South India proposals noted the need to integrate 'three Scriptural elements': congregational – emphasizing 'the development of the whole body'; Presbyterian – the 'delegated, organised element'; and the episcopal – the 'representative, executive' element.[20] It suggested the consecration of bishops from within the South India United Church, by at least three Anglican bishops, leading immediately to intercommunion in the context of which a deeper, structural unity would develop.[21]

The mission societies involved in the Kikuyu proposals argued for a geographical division of East Africa along confessional lines and recommended that 'the administration of the Sacraments shall normally be by recognised

---

[17] Ibid., p. 13.
[18] Lambeth Conference 1920, Resolution 9 (Appeal), IV and VII. The bishops also commended the Faith and Order work, recording that they had 'heard with sympathetic and hopeful interest of the preliminary meeting of the proposed World Conference on Faith and Order about to be held at Geneva' (Lambeth 1920, Resolution 16).
[19] *Documents 1916-1920*, p. 48.
[20] Ibid., p. 25.
[21] Ibid., p. 26.

ministers of the branch of the Church of Christ occupying the district' – the word 'normally' was intended to allow missionaries to minister to churches of their own denomination in other areas[22] – and noted: 'While earnestly desiring such a measure of unity that full intercommunion between the members of the Allied Mission may become possible, the Allied Missions recognise that in existing conditions, such intercommunion between Episcopal and Non-Episcopal Missions is not yet possible.'[23] This latter provision was a revision of the Alliance's earlier position, for at their first conference all delegates had controversially been invited to receive communion at a 'United Communion Service', at which the Anglican Bishops of Uganda and Mombassa presided. As the *New York Times* reported:

> It was the admission of the Methodists, Baptists, Presbyterians and others to the communion administered by Anglican Bishops according to the order of the Anglican prayer book which excited the fierce disapproval of a portion of the Church. The Bishop of Zanzibar openly accused the Bishops of Mombassa and Uganda of heresy.[24]

As a result of the Bishop of Zanzibar's intervention, and after 'exhaustive enquiries and consultation with the Consultative Body of the Lambeth Conference', the Archbishop of Canterbury had issued an 'Opinion', ruling that this kind of 'full intercommunion' was, for the present at least, impossible:

> Members of non-episcopal Churches might and would be welcomed at the Holy Communion in Anglican Churches, when temporarily isolated from their own. Bishops could not, however, bid their own Church members, similarly isolated, seek the Holy Communion at the hands of Ministers not episcopally ordained. Such ministers might be invited to preach on occasion in Anglican Churches.[25]

The Bishop of Zanzibar had subsequently offered proposals for a United Church in East Africa.[26] In matters of ministry, he maintained that the foundation of a united church must include 'the acceptance of the fact that

---

[22] Ibid., pp. 38–39.
[23] Ibid., p. 43.
[24] *New York Times*, 4 January 1914.
[25] *Documents 1916-1920*, p. 45.
[26] Ibid., pp. 46–8.

Episcopacy has always existed and is today in the possession of the far greater part of Christendom'. However, Zanzibar also suggested that

> episcopacy must not involve us in a monarchical diocesan episcopate. Many Bishops may serve one local church. The Bishops should be freely elected, and should rule with the clergy and laity. ... Non-episcopal bodies accepting episcopacy would remain in full exercise of their own constitutions, working parallel with the present episcopal churches.[27]

Moreover, at a conference in 1918, the Bishop of Zanzibar affirmed that 'if the non-Episcopal bodies would ... consent to some Episcopal Consecration and ordination so as to enable them to minister, by invitation, in episcopal churches', then 'he for his part would gladly come before any of their congregations and accept any form of popular recognition' required by the non-episcopal churches.[28] This affirmation also found its way into the *Appeal*, which affirmed its confidence that 'terms of union having been otherwise satisfactorily adjusted, bishops and clergy of our Communion would willingly accept from these authorities a form of commission or recognition which would commend our ministry to their congregations, as having its place in the one family life'.[29]

Proposals for more immediate measures resulted from the discussions between Anglicans and Free Churchmen held at Mansfield College Oxford in 1919. These called for 'interchange of pulpits, under proper authority', joint study and prayer, local conferences, missions and 'inter-denominational Committees' as 'immediate practical means of furthering this movement towards Unity'.[30] In response, a group of Anglo-Catholic clergy meeting at Pusey House, Oxford, petitioned the Archbishop of Canterbury and the Bishops of the Convocation of Canterbury, stating that, 'while it is not inconsistent with our principles to join with members of non-episcopal Christian bodies for public discussions with introductory prayer', and that prayer, discussion and study with members of non-episcopal churches 'are not necessarily inconsistent with our principles, and may be lawfully attended in certain special cases', nonetheless

> It is not possible for us in any circumstances to preach or minister in the places of worship belonging to non-episcopal bodies, at any of their services,

---

[27] Ibid., p. 46.
[28] Ibid., p. 47.
[29] Lambeth 1920, Resolution 9 (Appeal), VIII.
[30] *Documents 1916–1920*, p. 55.

although we may, at their invitation, expound our beliefs to them subject to the consent of the bishop and the parish priest. ... There are no circumstances in which we can invite members of non-episcopal bodies to minister or preach in our Churches. ... It is not permissible to admit members of non-episcopal bodies to Communion, except in the case of a dying person who has expressed a desire for reconciliation with the Church.[31]

The practical measures recommended by the *Appeal* would fall between these two poles. While the Lambeth Conference agreed that 'it cannot approve of general schemes of intercommunion or exchange of pulpits' or of 'the celebration in Anglican churches of the Holy Communion for members of the Anglican Church by ministers who have not been episcopally ordained',[32] it allowed a bishop to issue 'occasional authorisation to ministers, not episcopally ordained, who in his judgement are working towards an ideal of union such as is described in our Appeal', to preach in Anglican churches, or to the diocesan clergy to preach in these ministers' churches.[33] Moreover, the bishops agreed, in a decision that over sixty years later would shape the Meissen Agreement, that during negotiations for a specific scheme of Reunion, the 'baptized but unconfirmed communicants of the non-episcopal congregations concerned' might be admitted to communion in Anglican churches.[34]

It is apparent, then, that there was considerable disagreement in the Church of England and in some parts of the Anglican Communion as to the proper basis for working towards Reunion. The Bishop of Zanzibar's caution was quite restrained in comparison with some of his Anglo-Catholic colleagues, but others in the Church of England were keen to move towards closer relationships more quickly, and not only in the foreign mission field. In 1918, for instance, Hensley Henson, then Dean of Durham, had accepted an invitation to preach at Carr's Lane Congregational Church, Birmingham, and had caused some scandal first by honouring this invitation even after his appointment as Bishop of Hereford, and later by preaching at other Free churches.[35] Henson was in favour of the recognition of all Protestant orders.

---

[31] Ibid., p. 60.
[32] Lambeth 1920, Resolution 12, B.
[33] Lambeth 1920, Resolution 12, A.i.
[34] Lambeth 1920, Resolution 12, A.ii. Confirmation here presumably refers to episcopal confirmation, since many "non-episcopal" churches retained confirmation.
[35] Herbert Hensley Henson, *Retrospect of an Unimportant Life* (Oxford: Oxford University Press, 1942), vol. 1, pp. 281–4, 288.

When, in the spring of 1920, he received an invitation to attend and assist at the consecration of a Bishop in the Church of Sweden, he immediately accepted it, only subsequently informing the Archbishop of Canterbury, who 'at first expressed satisfaction, then incertitude', not least because of a concern that the 1920 Lambeth Conference might decline to recognize the Church of Sweden's orders.[36]

It was against the backdrop of this wide range of attitudes towards both the idea of 'Reunion' and the schemes that had been proposed to further it that the Lambeth Conference of 1920 embarked on its deliberations. The Archbishop of Canterbury was keen that the Lambeth Conference should seek both to inspire and to guide the process of reunion. Lang, as Chair of the Reunion Committee, was not confident. Soon after the conference opened, he wrote to his old friend Wilfrid Parker of the challenges facing him:

> I have a Committee of more than 60 Bishops to deal with, containing every variety of opinion, from Zanzibar and Nassau to Durham, and my heart fails when I think of the difficulties. But we must trust that through the help of the Holy Spirit we may get some kind of common mind and be able to do something better than merely repeat platitudes of pious aspiration. It is one of the most difficult things I have ever had to do, and I wish I were more sanguine as to the result.[37]

The making of the *Appeal*

The 'Appeal to All Christian People' and its associated resolutions form Resolutions 9–13 of the 1920 Lambeth Conference Report.[38] Textual hints in this final version suggest that it was the result of some discussion, not least in its language about ministry and episcopacy, which does not simply

---

[36] Henson, *Retrospect of an Unimportant Life*, vol. 1, pp. 319–20. Henson replied with 'a short letter indicating my surprise at his suggestion of difficulties with the Lambeth Conference, and stating that I would not acknowledge any authority in a body avowedly gathered for purely advisory purposes to control me in the exercise of my undoubted liberty' [ibid, p. 321]. The Lambeth Conference did take the decision to enter into 'intercommunion' with the Church of Sweden, on the basis of agreement about 'the succession of bishops of the Church of Sweden' and 'the conception of the priesthood': Lambeth 1920, Resolution 24.

[37] LPL MS 2883, Lang to Wilfrid Parker, 9 July 1920, fol. 245.

[38] The Resolutions of Lambeth 1920 can be found at http://www.anglicancommunion.org/resources/document-library.aspx?author=Lambeth+Conference&year=1920.

reproduce the Lambeth Quadrilateral. That the *Appeal* was indeed the result of complex discussions can in fact be seen, both from a series of redactions which demonstrate the development of the actual text,[39] and from the detailed notes of the discussions taken by Bell, who attended most of the sessions, and Cosmo Gordon Lang, Archbishop of York, who chaired the Reunion Committee.[40] Bell's diary gives a useful overview of the proceedings.[41] Finally, both Bell and the Archbishop of Canterbury wrote brief reflections on the Lambeth Conference; in Bell's case detailing the process which led to the *Appeal*.[42]

After an opening reception in Canterbury Cathedral on 3 July and an opening service at Westminster Abbey the following day, the 1920 Lambeth Conference met from 5 July to 7 August. The first week was devoted to a presentation of the themes of the different committees on the basis of plenary lectures by the respective chairs; for the Reunion committee this was the task of the Archbishop of York. Bell noted in his diary of this opening session:

> Ebor[43] leads off in admirable speech, as to temper and attitude, but I thought that second half of speech rather shut the door gently which the first half appeared to throw wide open. ... Debate did not get a move on until after lunch when Bombay[44] prophesied and exploded, both. Much was said about principles, but principles must, as Armagh[45] said, be right principles and must also not be in the air! A lot about the Catholic Church – moving and impressive. Zanzibar[46] spoke, a curious and eloquent man. Henson[47] was

[39] Redactions of the *Appeal* (in order of drafting) can be found in the following volumes held at LPL: Douglas Papers, vol. 1, fol. 356-7; LPL LC 115 fol. 18-21; LC 117, fol. 14-18; Douglas Papers, vol. 1, fol. 354-355r; Douglas Papers, vol. 1, fol. 366-370; LC 115, fol. 24v-28 (§§ 1-6) and fol. 31-33 (§§ 7-9). Drafts of the accompanying resolutions are found in Douglas Papers, vol. 1, fol. 358 (and cf. LC 117, fol. 21-22); Douglas Papers, vol. 1, fol. 361-362 (and cf. Bell 255, fol. 50v-51r); Douglas Papers, vol. 1, fol. 363. Drafts of the *Appeal* with Resolutions with corrections discussed in the final plenary session are in Douglas Papers, vol. 1, fol. 409-412. An edition showing the main phases of redaction and reproducing Bell's account of the process can be found in Methuen, 'Lambeth 1920', pp. 521–64.

[40] LPL Bell Papers, vols 253 and 255; Lang Papers, vols 208 and 209. This article will draw mainly on Bell's notes which, although not easy to read, are considerably more legible than Lang's.

[41] Bell Papers, vol. 251 (Diary 1920), fols 61r-75r.

[42] LPL Davidson Papers, vol. 14, 'Memorandum of Lambeth 1920', fol. 40-60; Bell Papers, vol. 251 (Diary 1920), fols 75v-86r. For the latter, cf. also Methuen, 'Lambeth 1920', pp. 534–49, which includes biographical notes of the Bishops mentioned by Bell.

[43] That is, Cosmo Gordon Lang, Archbishop of York 1908–28.

[44] Edwin James Palmer, Bishop of Bombay 1908–29.

[45] Charles Frederick D'Arcy, Archbishop of Armagh 1920–38.

[46] Frank Weston, Bishop of Zanzibar 1908–24.

[47] Herbert Hensley Henson, Bishop of Hereford 1918–20; Bishop of Durham from 1920. Although referred to in Bell's diary as 'Durham', at the time of the Lambeth Conference he was technically Bishop of Durham elect, having been appointed after the death of his predecessor in May, but not yet installed. To his annoyance, he appeared as Bishop of Hereford on the list of Bishops attending; see Bell Papers, vol. 251 (Diary 1920), fol. 75v-86r (Methuen, 'Lambeth 1920', p. 540).

very powerful and I thought moderate in simply asking for recognition of Presbyterian orders in first instance. He also went out of his way to repeat and insist upon his belief in the Divinity of our Lord.[48]

Lang argued that it was necessary to start with principles:

What is our conception of the Church? Foolish to profess such things as interchange of pulpits, intercommunion, without principles set forth. We desire a visible unity. What are terms upon which a truly Catholic Church can be recovered?[49]

These, he suggested, must include 'Common Faith [expressed in the] Nicene Creed; … Common Sacraments; Common Ministry which stands for whole Church'. The latter point implied that, on the one hand, 'episcopacy must be decided not [only] tolerated', but at the same time, Lang thought, 'we [cannot] insist on a Tractarian view of apostolic succession'. 'What of then asserting it not [to] repudiate their ministry but add the valid mark?' Lang asked. This would imply 'acknowledg[ing the] place of non-episcopal churches in the great Church … we are all in a state of schism – no profit in speaking of others in schism. May we not pronounce positively on value of other ministries in God's sight?'[50] Ultimately, Lang suggested, in seeking reunion, 'We don't contemplate a new church but a union of churches.'[51]

Lang's address and the responses to it set the scene for the work of the Reunion Committee which met from 12 to 24 July. The committee began by discussing the possible ideal of unity, concluding that full unity would require a process by which it could be established, and that diversity would be characteristic of a reunited church. The role of episcopacy in such united church remained a central point. Early in the proceedings, Henson put in a plea for redrafting the final section of the Lambeth Quadrilateral, arguing that although the Lambeth Quadrilateral was 'adequate' with regard to faith and doctrine, the fourth article on the episcopate should be redrafted:

'Episcopate' needs rewriting … My issue is that presbyterate is essential & episcopate is a dimension of that. Congregationalism sets ministers open to

[48] Bell Papers, vol. 251, fol. 63v-64r.
[49] Notes taken on Lang's address, 'Relation to and Reunion with other Churches', Bell Papers vol. 253, fol. 17.
[50] Ibid.
[51] Ibid.

injury. Wishes recognition of presbyterian orders, retaining episcopate for domestic order.[52]

Henson's aim was the recognition of Presbyterian orders. Inevitably, not all his episcopal colleagues agreed, either with his proposal or his aim.

The committee moved on to hear presentations by expert witnesses, including leading non-conformists such as Tissington Tatlow and Bertie Shakespeare, but also retired Anglican bishops including Charles Gore. The first draft of the *Appeal* was presented two days later. Bell recorded on the afternoon of the second day of sessions, 'H Knight,[53] Ebor, Bombay & Bristol[54] concoct (for 4 hours) a statement or "Prologomena" on unity,'[55] which was presented the next morning.[56] After noting the duty of all Christians to strive towards unity, that unity was defined:

> Our aim, therefore, is not merely or mainly that some of the Churches, into which the one Church has been split up, should be united with ours, but that all should co-operate in manifesting in one visible body the fullness of the diverse gifts of the Spirit.
>
> Thus our ideal is neither the absorption of these churches into one uniform system, nor their alliance in a loose federation, but a living fellowship in which the various gifts and graces bestowed by God upon each shall be no longer kept in separateness, but used and enjoyed for the enrichment of the whole body.[57]

The key aspects of recognizing that unity followed that defined in the Lambeth Quadrilateral:

> We believe that the visible unity of the Church will be found to involve at least (a) the acceptance of the canonical scriptures of the old and new Testaments as containing all things necessary to salvation, and the Nicene Creed as the sufficient statement of the Christian faith, (b) the acceptance of the two Sacraments of Baptism and the Supper of the Lord, as ordained by Christ Himself, and (c) a common Ministry which possesses the commission

---

[52] Notes from the reunion committee: Bell Papers, vol. 255, fol. 17v.
[53] Henry Joseph Corbett Knight, Bishop of Gibraltar 1911–20.
[54] George Nixon, Bishop of Bristol 1914–33.
[55] Bell Papers vol. 251, fol. 65v.
[56] The text of this first draft is found in LC 115, fol. 18-21. This is Text A in Methuen, 'Lambeth 1920', pp. 550–9.
[57] Methuen, 'Lambeth 1920', p. 553.

of Christ and the authority of the whole Body. This Common Ministry, we believe, can only be secured through episcopal ordination.[58]

This last statement was amended in discussion to read: 'A Ministry which will be accepted by every part of the Church, as possessing the commission of Christ and the authority of the whole Body. In view of the position of episcopacy in the past history and present life of the Church, we believe that this common ministry is to be secured through episcopal ordinations.'[59] The wish both to affirm the ministry of non-episcopal churches while maintaining the central importance of episcopacy was emphasized in the final paragraphs:

> While expressing this belief with regard to the authority necessary for the Ministry of the whole Church, we yet gladly acknowledge, that God has been pleased to confer gifts of His Holy Spirit upon the Ministry of Churches which have not accepted Episcopal ordination, and to use the Sacraments administered in them as effectual means of grace.
>
> We believe that the acceptance of the Historic Episcopate would not only secure for the whole Church a common Ministry, but also prove in the future, as in the past, to be a powerful means of maintaining the Unity and continuity of the Church.[60]

The committee accepted this first draft, although the final paragraph resulted in four abstentions.

Although it was accepted, the draft received a somewhat lukewarm reception. In their speeches that afternoon, Bishop Charles Gore, Bishop Ryle (Dean of Westminster) and the Dean of Wells all emphasized the need not to compromise on episcopacy.[61] In a statement typical of the three speeches, Ryle commented that episcopacy was necessary both because it was 'far older than divisions of Xnty' and 'for practical gov[ernmen]t'; he added: 'We w[oul]d not unchurch the Noncon[formist]s,' but claimed, 'In their hearts Noncon[formist] leaders probably believe episcopacy to be the basis.'[62]

However, Lang's first draft was also felt not to go far enough. It 'got one very little further than the old Lambeth Quadrilateral', reflected Bell.[63] 'It's devilish,'

---

[58] Ibid., p. 554.
[59] The amendments to the first draft are found in Douglas Papers, vol. 1, fol. 356–7. This is Text A2; changes are shown in italics in Methuen, 'Lambeth 1920', here p. 554.
[60] Methuen, 'Lambeth 1920', pp. 555–6.
[61] Bell Papers, vol. 255, fol. 23r–24v.
[62] Bell Papers, vol. 255, fol. 24r.
[63] Bell Papers, vol. 251, fol. 65r.

Neville Talbot, Bishop of Pretoria, commented to Hettie Bell.[64] In response, Bell suggested to the Archbishop of Canterbury

a possibility of Zanzibar, Talbot & Brent (and one or two others!) getting together to articulate Zanzibar's proposals of a Great Church in which the denominations of Noncon[formist] origin sh[oul]d be groups. He agreed that there may be something in it and told me to set NST[albot] at Zanzibar.[65]

Discussion of the second proposal began on 16 July (no meeting of the committee took place that day since a number of Bishops were receiving honorary degrees at Cambridge). Bell recorded: 'Neville, Brent, Pennsylvania, Bombay, Winton,[66] Peterboro',[67] Chichester,[68] Zanzibar all meet as group in Lollards [Tower] to thrash out Zanzibar scheme. It seems like [it has] been satisfactory.'[69] After this meeting, the Bishops of Pretoria, Peterborough, Zanzibar and Pennsylvania drafted a further text; Bell 'saw it & made one or two slight suggestions. The draft was revised in [the] evening and given to Ebor.'[70]

This second draft[71] drew on the first, but was more explicit both in its affirmation 'that GOD wills fellowship',[72] and in its recognition that all churches participate in and prolong the sin of division: 'This condition of broken fellowship we acknowledge to be sinful, and we desire frankly to confess our share in the guilt of thus crippling the Society of Christ and hindering the activity of His Spirit.'[73] The separation of churches results in 'each one keeping to itself gifts that rightly belong to the whole fellowship'.[74] In order to overcome the division:

The time has come, we believe, for the separated groups of Christians to join together in forgetting the things which are behind, and reaching out towards the goal of a reunited Catholic Church. We have a vision of many groups

---

[64] Ibid.
[65] Bell Papers, vol. 251, fol. 65r-v.
[66] Edward Stuart Talbot, Bishop of Winchester 1911-1923 (Neville Talbot's father).
[67] Frank Woods, Bishop of Peterborough 1916–23.
[68] Winfrid Oldfield Burrows, Bishop of Chichester 1919–29.
[69] Bell Papers, vol. 251, fol. 66v.
[70] Ibid.
[71] The second draft is found in LC 117, 14–18. A subsequent revision is found in Douglas Papers, vol. 1, 354-5a. These are drafts B and B2 in Methuen, 'Lambeth 1920', pp. 550–9.
[72] Methuen, 'Lambeth 1920', p. 551.
[73] Ibid., p. 552.
[74] Ibid., p. 551.

retaining their own systems while combined in one organic fellowship, in which all the treasures of faith and order, possessed at present separately, may find full scope and be available for the whole body.

This means an adventure of goodwill, and to this adventure we are now called.[75]

The restatement of the Lambeth Quadrilateral was retained, but the subsequent comments on the episcopate were expanded:

We confidently claim a place by the side of the ancient episcopal communions of East and West, awaiting hopefully such mutual re-union as will again unite us in completeness of fellowship.

We believe that in the future as in the past, the Episcopate will prove to be the most effective means of maintaining the unity and continuity of the Church. But we greatly desire that the office of the Bishop should be increasingly exercised in a representative and constitutional manner in accordance with the ideals of the early and undivided Church.

We want this Ministry to be available for the whole Fellowship. On the other hand, we desire to share in the inheritances of Grace held in trust by the other groups; and should the authorities of these groups so desire we are persuaded that Bishops and Clergy of our Communion would be willing to accept formally from them some suitable recognition or commission which would commend our ministry as having its place in one family life.[76]

The second draft thus explicitly articulated both the wish to recognize non-Episcopal churches and the gifts that they offered, while claiming the Anglican Communion's place as one of the 'ancient episcopal communions'.

The Archbishop of York presented the revised text on 19 July, commenting, Bell recorded, that it expressed 'an extraordinary diversity of situations, in India, USA, China, etc and still again in England and Scotland'. The challenge, he suggested, was to speak into this diversity: 'How can this C[ommit]tee, & the Conference, attempt to lay down rules or any other questions addressing situations so diverse in different parts of world?'[77] Lang went on:

In view of all this [I] feel we are being led to see that our problem [is] rather to make a new beginning in problems of Reunion, the putting aside of misunderstandings, and to put out plan for reuniting in one church in all parts

[75] Ibid., pp. 553–4.
[76] Ibid., pp. 555–7.
[77] Bell Papers, vol. 255, fol. 44r.

of world. [The] best step for L[ambeth] C[onference] to take now w[oul]d be not to publish a long series of resolutions but to send forth earnest appeal to all Xtian churches to consider again and cooperate with us in search for one Catholic Church and to indicate lines along which we thought a basis could be found: then to shew Conference decision that Churches of Anglican Communion sh[oul]d enter formally into communication with authorities of other churches, also non-episcopal; thirdly to let the provinces deal in their own way with their problems.[78]

Despite some caveats, it was agreed that the new text should form the basis of the committee's further work, and that after revision it should be issued as an *Appeal* to all the Christian churches, not only the non-episcopal churches, with accompanying resolutions intended to offer a guide to how it might be put into practice.

The discussion of this second text was characterized by a real sense of urgency. Some had a strong sense that it was a step towards doing something new:

Winchester – Statement commends itself to me. Two things have come home to us (1) Impression that time has by no means stood still has led to acute difference but a new Spirit abroad in Conference. I've not before felt the truth that Reunion is for whole Body of Christians. ... (2) The old agonising alternative of leaving the Protestant world or sacrifice some authentic things.[79]

The Bishop of Pretoria, as one of the drafting group, suggested that the *Appeal* for reunion

corresponds to mind of [the] younger generation. Younger men and women don't look upon themselves as Baptists, Wesleyans etc, but have something bigger in view. This Appeal [is] true to spiritual experience of the younger generation.[80]

Moreover, he suggested, 'If Episcopacy is simply the mark of a denomination, for God's sake let us throw it down.'[81] The *Appeal*, as conceived by its drafters, was intended to make it possible to move towards a different understanding of what reunion might mean.

---

[78] Bell Papers, vol. 255, fol. 44r.
[79] Bell Papers, vol. 255, fol. 45r.
[80] Bell Papers, vol. 255, fol. 47v-48r.
[81] Bell Papers, vol. 255, fol. 48r.

On the other hand, some Bishops, especially those in the mission field, felt that what had been proposed did not go far enough and was not explicit enough. The Bishop of Uganda commented:

> [He] does not want to add to difficulties but we missionaries would go back really disappointed if this appeal was the only thing which went out from this conference. Certain clear issues (1) recognition (2) communion have been raised. … Free churches will ask 'on what terms' esp. of recognition and intercommunion. Must on these two points make up our mind. 'Up to this point we do recognise this ministry' that is what we ought to say. Poor reception from e.g. General Assembly of [the] Ch[urch] of Scotland inevitable.[82]

His concerns were echoed by the Bishop of Madras:

> statement unsatisfactory as drawn up before we know what our position is. This document would be a bitter disappointment to me, to Non-Con[formist]s, to South India. Time has come when we ought to make up our minds on the g[rea]t questions common to all local situations. If the Ang[lican] Comm[union] is divided on such questions as the recognition of non-episcopal orders and intercommunion, let us say so: and that different views on these points can legitimately [be] held, and that no one opinion is to dominate the situation.[83]

The Bishop of Dornakul also felt that the second draft was a retrograde step: 'We have gone back in this document on the one agreed last week,' he said while the Bishop of Montreal commented that the second draft was 'not very definite – is new on first reading. But on re-reading it seems to combine much.'[84] As the bishops debated, a consensus developed that more explicit practical guidance was needed as well as a theological call to reunion.

Lang set about drafting a set of Resolutions designed to offer guidance in specific situations; these were proposed on 19 July.[85] Like the *Appeal*, the Resolutions 'acknowledge[d] the Ministry of Non-Episcopal Churches as a Ministry possessing the gifts of the Spirit, and the Sacraments administered by them as effectual means of grace', while stating categorically that 'future Ordinations in any united Church of which we can be a part must be Episcopal'.[86]

---

[82] Bell Papers, vol. 255, fol. 45v.
[83] Bell Papers, vol. 255, fol. 46v-47r.
[84] Bell Papers, vol. 255, fol. 48r.
[85] These are found in LPL LC 117, fol. 21-22, with a further copy in Douglas Papers, 1, fol. 358. This is text F in Methuen, 'Lambeth 1920', 560-2.
[86] Methuen, 'Lambeth 1920', p. 560.

In an important step, the first draft of the Resolutions allowed invitations to preach to be extended to 'Ministers, who have not been Episcopally ordained but are taking a definite part in the work of re-uniting the Church'.[87] Regarding admission to the Eucharist, the resolutions suggested:

> 7. During negotiations looking towards corporate Re-union Communicant members of Churches involved, although unconfirmed may be admitted by Priests of our Church of Communion when they have no opportunity of receiving Holy Communion from their own Ministers.
>
> 8. After a Province has completed an Act of Union those who were at the time of the Act of Union Communicant Members of Churches which have united, may be admitted to Holy Communion by Ministers episcopally ordained if otherwise admissible even though they be not confirmed.
>
> 9. Apart from negotiations for Re-union we do not think that Communion should be refused by Priests of our Church to devout Communicant members of non-Episcopal bodies who are temporarily deprived of the opportunity of receiving the Holy Communion from their own Ministers.[88]

These were not provisions for intercommunion with other churches, but they did constitute a step towards it.

This was, however, a step too far for some. The Bishop of Zanzibar responded to Lang's draft with his own, rather more restrictively worded proposals, which, although they made possible much of what Lang had suggested, also imposed limitations.[89] These were discussed and amended (the version quoted here shows the amendments arising from the discussion in underlined italics and deletions in curly brackets):

> [The Conference] cannot {countenance} *approve within the Churches of the Anglican [Communion], celebration of the Holy Communion by Non-Episcopal Ministers* {the ministrations of Non-Episcopal ministers at Anglican altars}, nor can it with a united voice approve *save in quite exceptional circumstances* the reception by Anglican Communicants of the Lord's Supper administered by such ministers in their own Churches, or the invitation of separated Christians to communion at Anglican altars, or the interchange of pulpits.

---

[87] Ibid.

[88] Ibid., pp. 561–2.

[89] Handwritten versions are found in Bell Papers 255, fol. 50v-51r and in Douglas Papers, vol. 1, fol. 359–60; a typed version with *amendments* [G1] in Douglas Papers, vol. 1, fol. 361–62. This is the first part of text G in Methuen, 'Lambeth 1920', pp. 560–1.

Nevertheless, the Bishops are unanimously agreed: -

(a) THAT no Priest has canonical authority to refuse Communion to any{one kneeling at the altar} *baptized person kneeling before the Holy Table*, unless he be excommunicate by name, or, in the canonical sense of the term, a cause of scandal to the faithful,

(b) THAT a Bishop is justified in {admitting to his pulpits occasionally for good reason}, *authorizing an occasional interchange of pulpits between his own clergy and* ministers of separated bodies who have publicly and formally assented *openly assented* to and are whole-heartedly working for the proposals put forth above [i.e. the Appeal].[90]

What would become Resolution 12 represented a reworked version of these two drafts, with an additional note on Communion proposed in an unlikely but very welcome alliance between the Bishop of Zanzibar and the Bishop of Durham.[91] This affirmed:

The Bishops are unanimously agreed: —

(a) That no Priest has canonical authority to refuse Communion to any baptized person kneeling before the Lord's Table, unless he be excommunicate by name, or, in the Canonical sense of the term, a cause of scandal to the faithful

(b) That a Bishop is justified in giving occasional authorization to ministers, not episcopally ordained, who in his judgement are working towards an ideal of union such as us defined in our Appeal, to preach in Churches within his Diocese and to clergy of his Diocese to preach in the Churches of such Ministers.

(c) They will not question the action of any Bishop who in the few years, during which a definite scheme of union is maturing, shall countenance the irregularity of admitting to Communion the baptized but unconfirmed communicants of the non-episcopal congregations concerned in that scheme.

(d) That they confidently commit to the various suitable *illegible*, Provinces, Synods, etc of the Anglican Communion the task of effecting union with other Christian Communions on lines that are in general harmony with these proposals and resolutions.

That in accordance with the principles of Church Order and faith in the Preface to the Book of Common Prayer, the Conference cannot approve

---

[90] Methuen, 'Lambeth 1920', pp. 560–1.
[91] LC 117, fol. 23.

of the celebration of in Anglican Churches of the Holy Communion for members of the Anglican Churches by Ministers who have not been episcopally ordained.[92]

Although the final form of Resolutions did not go as far as some of the bishops no doubt wished – especially Durham and some of the bishops engaged with plans for reunion – it did allow for more flexibility of practice than had hitherto been the case.

The *Appeal* and Resolutions were very much a joint effort by bishops from across the Communion, and the work inspired some surprising alliances. Bell noted in his diary:

> Zanzibar proposes a long Resolution of his own in place of the 'Official' Resolutions drawn up by York & Co. Zanzibar's accepted as basis – he proves most conciliatory. Interesting to see Durham & Zanzibar hobnob. Today the crucial day – an extraordinary spirit of fraternity & conciliation displayed. Zanzibar the chief.[93]

But many others were involved. Hettie Bell recounted coming across a group late one night in Lollards Tower working on texts: 'Jimmy Bombay sitting cross-legged on the floor like an Indian Buddha, Neville Talbot draped along the mantelpiece, cups of tea everywhere, and George, pen and notebook in hand, correlating all the words of wisdom.'[94] Bell thought that 'the chief work of all – the Appeal – was itself due to a little self-appointed C[ommit]tee meeting in Lollard's Tower on Friday m[ornin]g July 16 when the full C[ommit]tee did not meet'.[95] Archbishop Davidson remembered another crucial meeting:

> On the middle Sunday of the Conference, during the Committee fortnight, a little group sat all afternoon, under the tree on the lawn. It consisted of the two Archbishops, Bishop Rhinelander of Pennsylvania, Bishop Brent, the Bishop of Peterborough – Edith was also with us. We went through the various drafts, resolutions etc. which had been suggested, but on the whole decided to turn it into an Appeal of a consecutive sort. The Bishop of Peterborough wrote a draft beginning with the words 'God wills fellowship etc.' This draft was

---

[92] LC 117, fol 23-24. Slightly reordered, this constitutes the second part of Text G, Methuen, 'Lambeth 1920', pp. 561–2.

[93] Bell Papers, vol. 251, fol. 67v.

[94] R. C. D. Jasper, *George Bell, Bishop of Chichester* (London: Oxford University Press, 1967), p. 57.

[95] Bell papers 251, fol. 78v; Methuen, 'Lambeth 1920', p. 539.

manipulated considerably afterwards by the Archbishop of York and much improved. It was, however, the outcome of that afternoon's conversation.[96]

Conclusions

The 'Appeal to All Christian People' was felt by many to be the high point of the 1920 Lambeth Conference, offering a new vision of Christian unity and opening a new age of ecumenical endeavour. Lang's biographer commended the 1920 Lambeth Conference for having 'attempt[ed] the apparently impossible task of securing a wide measure of agreement on some action which would transport the whole question from the realm of distant ideals into that of practical politics'.[97] Weston later expressed concerns about the Appeal, because he was concerned that the Conference had gone too far; Henson because he believed that it had not gone far enough. For Bell, in contrast, the *Appeal* became the guiding principle of his ecumenical work over the next two decades. Looking back on the Conference, Lang felt that it had been truly inspired:

> I was afraid that the remaining 200 Bishops, who had not worked together as we had for a fortnight of ceaseless toil, would cut the thing to bits. Instead of that, when I presented the Report it seemed to be taken out of my hands and what Neville called 'a rushing mighty wind' seemed to sweep away difficulties and criticism, and instead of days of anxious discussion the appeal and its accompanying resolutions were adopted in less than one day with only a handful of Bishops objecting. I think most of us who were present will not forget that day, for it was difficult – to me impossible – to think that this wind was other than the wind of the Spirit: anyhow, I must believe that somehow God has a purpose in a thing which came with so much unanimity from 200 Bishops who really prayed and asked for guidance at a critical time.[98]

The resonance from elsewhere had also been good:

> Here is dear old Halifax writing that few things in his life have given him more pleasure [than the *Appeal*]: That he thinks that it will do untold good. And on the other hand here is Scott Lidgett saying that [it] is the most remarkable thing since the Reformation. Shakespeare, saying that it is the

---

[96] Davidson Papers, vol. 14, fol. 49.
[97] Lockhart, *Cosmo Gordon Lang*, p. 267.
[98] LPL MS 2883, Lang to Wilfrid Parker, 10 August 1920, fol. 248-249.

Finger of God. Horton that it creates a new epoch. And Zanzibar pleading with all his fellow Catholics that they will make it their guiding vision for years to come. How can one doubt with all this in mind, that there is some purpose of God in this thing?[99]

Lambeth's 'Appeal to All Christian People' had caught the spirit of the times.

Davidson too was relieved, not least because he had feared that the whole Lambeth Conference might go badly wrong:

> I was by no means easy in my mind for we had to deal for the first time, as I frequently pointed out in conversation, with the probability that we should find a minority in the Conference who would not be content to be an acquiescent minority, but might march out denouncing us, or raise cohorts outside.[100]

His strategy had been to provide well-selected reading material in advance, and he felt that this had paid off. With prescience, Lang commented of the whole Conference: 'There was a really admirable spirit of fellowship; this is important, as it is only in this sense of brotherhood among the bishops which keeps all these independent churches which now form the Anglican Communion together.'[101] The *Appeal* was an expression of that 'sense of brotherhood'.

Moreover, although the *Appeal* did not go as far as some had hoped, it inspired Anglican relations with other churches for the next decade and beyond. In 1921 the *Appeal* and its accompanying resolutions were confirmed by the Convocations of Canterbury and York,[102] and gave a real impetus to the ecumenical work of the Church of England for the next decade. It inspired the

---

[99] LPL MS 2883, Lang to Wilfrid Parker, 21 August 1920, fol. 250r-v. Charles Lindley Wood, 2nd Viscount Halifax (1839–1934), a notable ecumenist and long-term president of the English Church Union (1868–1919 and 1927–34), was the Anglican initiator of the Malines Conversations. John Scott Lidgett was a leading Methodist theologian who helped to found the Federal Council of the Evangelical Free churches and served as its moderator from 1923 to 1925. John Howard Shakespeare was a Baptist minister who was president of the Free Church Council from 1919 until 1925. Robert Forman Horton, a Congregationalist Minister, helped to found Mansfield College, Oxford, and served as president of the Congregational Union of England and Wales (elected 1903), and president of the National Free Church Council (elected 1905). See, for all these, the *Oxford Dictionary of National Biography*: http://www.oxforddnb.com/ (accessed 24 March 2017).

[100] Davidson 14, fol. 40.

[101] LPL MS 2883, Lang to Wilfrid Parker, 10 August 1920, fol. 247.

[102] A Resolution was passed in the Upper House of the Convocation of Canterbury on 27 April 1921; in the Lower House on 6 July 1921 (with a rider asking for the restriction of permission to non-episcopally ordained people to preach 'to occasions other than, and apart from, the regular services of the Church'). Resolutions were carried by both Houses of the Convocation of York on 23 February 1921. In 1922, however, the Convocation of York expressly restricted the invitation to those not episcopally ordained to events which were 'not part of regular services': passed in the Upper House on 15 February 1922; Lower House on 16 February 1922.

Malines Conversations, unofficial discussions between Anglicans and Roman Catholics, which took place from 1921–6 at the initiative of Viscount Halifax and the French Catholic Fernand Portal under the auspices of Cardinal Mercier, Archbishop of Malines, and from 1923 with the sanction of both the Archbishop of Canterbury and, it seems, the pope. These conversations were, however, implicitly condemned by Pope Pius XI in his 1928 encyclical *Mortalium Animos*.[103]

Another immediate response to the *Appeal* was the initiation of discussions between the Church of England and the Free churches. These ran from 1921 to 1925, with Bell as the Anglican secretary, reaching a significant level of agreement, but foundering on the Anglican requirement of episcopal ordination in a united Church.[104] The *Appeal* also bore fruit in the establishing of the Church of England's Council on Foreign Relations, which had its origins in resolutions passed by the Church Assembly in 1927 and 1932 and was tasked with 'the survey[ing] and promotion of the Relations of the Church of England with Foreign Churches'.[105] Under the Chairmanship of the Bishop of Gloucester, Arthur Cayley Headlam, it worked on relations with a range of churches, including overseeing discussions which resulted in agreements for intercommunion with Old Catholic churches and the Lutheran churches of Finland, Latvia and Estonia.

For the Church of England, the approach advocated by the *Appeal*, that of recognizing and affirming the gifts offered by other churches, and of allowing pulpit exchange and mutual Eucharistic hospitality in the context

---

[103] For the conversations, see Bernard Barlow OSM, 'A brother knocking at the door': The Malines Conversations 1921-1925 (Norwich: Canterbury Press, 1996); A. Denaux and J. Dick (eds), From Malines to ARCIC: The Malines Conversations Commemorated (Bibliotheca Ephemeridum Theologicarum Lovaniensium, 130; Leuven: Leuven University Press/Peeters, 1997); John A. Dick, The Malines Conversations Revisited (Bibliotheca Ephemeridum Theologicarum Lovaniensium, 85; Louvain: Leuven University Press/Peeters, 1989); R. J. Lahey, 'The Origins and Approval of the Malines Conversations,' Church History 43 (1974), pp. 366–84.

[104] See 'Memorandum on the Status of the Existing Free Church Ministry', Documents on Christian Unity, pp. 52–9, especially pp. 54–5, and the resolutions adopted by the Federal Council in response, pp. 60–5. The full reports and resolutions relating to the conversations, including the decision to suspend them, are included in the full report: The Church of England and the Free Churches: proceedings of joint conferences held at Lambeth Palace, 1921-25, ed. G. K. A. Bell and W. L. Robertson (London: Oxford University Press, 1925). The conversations resumed in 1931 in response to Resolution 44 of the 1930 Lambeth Conference, and Bell was appointed to the Joint Subcommittee which guided its work. For the appointment, see Bell Papers, 170, fols 100, 102, 103. The process is discussed briefly in Methuen, '"Fulfilling Christ's own wish"', pp. 232–3.

[105] See the introduction to the Council at http://www.lambethpalacelibrary.org/content/council-foreign-relations.

of explorations of deeper unity, underlies the Meissen, Reuilly and Fetter Lane Agreements with the German Protestant Church, the French Lutheran and reformed churches and the Moravian Brethren, respectively, and the Anglican Methodist Covenant, all signed between 1991 and 2003.[106] In the inter-War period, the *Appeal* continued to shape the approach of Bell and other Anglican Bishops to ecumenical matters, not only at home but abroad, especially through their engagement in the Life and Work and Faith and Order movements.[107] Arguably, therefore, the *Appeal* had a role to play in the decision in 1937 to bring together these movements and to establish a World Council of Churches, which finally became reality in 1948. A century later, the 'Appeal to All Christian People' of the 1920 Lambeth Conference continues to set a marker for Anglican ecumenical relations.

---

[106] For a discussion of these and other relationships in the context of the *Appeal*, see Charlotte Methuen, 'Anglicans and Ecumenism', in *The Oxford Handbook of Anglican Studies*, ed. Mark Chapman, Sathianathan Clarke, Ian Douglas and Martyn Percy (Oxford: Oxford University Press, 2015), pp. 464–78. These agreements were also strongly influenced by the work of the World Council of Churches, especially "Baptism - Eucharist - Ministry" (1982) and bilateral Anglican-Lutheran and Anglican-Reformed dialogues.

[107] For Bell's use of the *Appeal*, see Methuen, "'Fulfilling Christ's own wish'", pp. 233–41.

6

Christian Mission and the Lambeth Conferences

Ephraim Radner

The Lambeth Conferences were originally an expression of Christian mission, understood in the basic terms of nineteenth-century 'Great Commission' language: proclamation, conversion, catechesis and discipling. The Conferences came into being as a result of Anglican missionary energies, and until the First World War, the Conferences sought to provide helpful ordering for the difficult and often extraordinary missionary work being done by its member dioceses and churches, while quite openly leaving that work to its locally organized members. By the 1920 Conference, however, the idea of missionary support merged with an idea of communion that made the latter itself a form of mission. The Conferences, as it were, *became* 'mission', at least ideally: the mission of unity. On the one hand, this change was quite conscious and explicit, as well as theologically focused; it emerged, furthermore, from quite concrete historical pressures. But on the other hand, the vision of 'communion as mission' failed to gain articulate traction among member churches. Instead, the Conference as an agent of this mission of unity, expressive and in service of a broader missionary vocation of its member churches, slowly took on this broader vocation itself. The 1920 Conference's attempted balance between missionary expression and communion agency failed to cohere. The latter part of the twentieth century saw an evolution fraught with tensions that ultimately destabilized the Conferences' original goals of missionary facilitation for its members. Rather than existing in a balance, communion and mission have, by the twenty-first century, become vying elements among Anglicans, and as a result the Conferences have lost credibility in relation to both aspects of Anglican life. In our own day, however, these elements' effective decoupling may indicate a new direction for the

Conferences' own rationale, one in which a particular missionary role has now been laid upon the Conferences themselves: Anglican reconciliation.

In this chapter, I will try to trace the story just summarized, by using mostly the formal documents of the Lambeth Conferences, in their resolutions and reports. These constitute traces of the Conferences' own movement from missionary expression to missionary agent, an agency aimed today most pointedly, though only potentially, at reconciliation.

I Missionary origins of 'communion' self-identity

The reality of something called the Anglican 'Communion', simply as a concept, was primarily missionary in its origins and meaning. The idea of an 'Anglican Church' with a peculiar 'communion' originated in the seventeenth century and then took shape through the self-conscious missionary movement of the Church of England into America, and later elsewhere. By the early nineteenth century, the notion of 'Anglican church*es*' in the plural – not just the Church of England – was well founded; in the early 1840s, the legal permission to set up missionary bishoprics outside of Britain was in place, and a significant Colonial Bishops' Fund was established for their support, seeing thirty-three such bishops in place by 1860.[1] Finally, by the mid-nineteenth century, the actual phrase 'Anglican Communion' emerged from a very specific missionary context: the Jubilee Anniversary of the Society for the Propagation of the Gospel (SPG), which had been a leader, despite all its foibles, in the Anglican spread of the Gospel. There *is* a communion of Anglican churches, observers noted, precisely as it is the embodied expression of the missionary thrust of Anglican*s* to plant the Gospel in all places.[2]

Everything about a 'communion' derived from this missionary thrust, as did the original idea of an episcopal gathering representative of this communion. Again, it was the organization of the SPG's silver jubilee in 1851 that occasioned the Archbishop of Canterbury's first suggestion that 'every

---

[1] Steven S. Maughan, *Mighty England Do Good: Culture, Faith, Empire, and World in the Foreign Mission of the Church of England, 1850-1915* (Grand Rapids, MI: Eerdmans, 2014), p. 69.

[2] Ephraim Radner, 'The Anglican Communion and Anglicanism', Jeremy Morris (ed.), *The Oxford History of Anglicanism, Volume IV: Global Western Anglicanism, c. 1910-present* (Oxford: Oxford University Press, 2017).

one of [the English and American] dioceses ... take part in commemorating the foundation of the oldest Missionary Society of the Reformed Church'. The American Presiding Bishop, John Hopkins of Vermont, responded with a robust suggestion for 'communion in the primitive style, by meeting together in the good old fashion of Synodical action' in a 'Council of all the Bishops in communion' with Canterbury.[3]

To be sure, Hopkins and others who took up the call shortly afterwards (e.g. Francis Fulford, the Bishop of Montreal) were concerned about the 'bold and false assumption of Rome' on the world stage, and thought that an Anglican synod of bishops could provide a 'moral' ballast to Roman pretensions. But the very possibility of such a worldwide Anglican profile was given in the missionary life of the newly recognized communion's churches. Order and cooperation were envisioned as sustaining and protecting this life in the face of perceived adversarial threats, whether ecclesial or doctrinal. Once the formal Lambeth Conferences took hold, then, they devoted themselves mainly to missionary concerns from the side of stability and coherence, hardly from that of theology and evangelistic principle or strategy. The Lambeth Conferences were expressive of mission in this sense, and very quickly saw their role as engaging in the supportive aspects of the Communion's churches in their evangelistic witness, for which ecclesial life formed the basis and container. The first Pan-Anglican Conference, of 1908, was put together by the Mission Boards of York and Canterbury. The Lambeth Conference of that year, and later Conferences, worked synergistically and often through overlapping personnel with the long string of world missionary conferences that began in the late nineteenth century: London's Anglican missionary conference in 1894, Edinburgh in 1910, Jerusalem in 1928 and Tambaram in 1938. At every step of the Communion's life, it was the world missionary impetus that upheld it, justified it, called it forward.

It is important to see the informing direction here, wherein the missionary realities of Anglicans pressed for a reconsideration of episcopacy and gathering, rather than the other way around. We tend to read the history of Anglicanism over the past 160 years as one of increasing structural coordination, and, in a catholic narrative, of increasing ecclesiastical rootedness: councils, episcopacy,

---

[3] *Reports* of the Society for the Propagation of the Gospel in Foreign Parts, 1849-1851, Vol. XIII, pp. lxxxiv-v, xcii–iii, quoted in William Redmond Curtis, *The Lambeth Conference: The Solution for Pan-Anglican Organization* (New York: Columbia University Press, 1942), pp. 79–80.

ecumenical responsibility. All this is true in one way. But it was only the more primary *missionary* invigoration of Anglicanism, in the nineteenth century especially, that led to the reinvigoration of both the Anglican episcopacy and its press to synodality, a fact of enormous historical and theological significance. The advent of the explicitly missionary bishop outside England, which was a nineteenth-century phenomenon, was directly tied to the recapturing of a vision of pastoral self-expenditure (not that it was ever wholly lacking in Britain), the enlarging of synodal reach, and, in the United States and Britain both, the reestablishment of synodal life more structurally. From the late eighteenth century on, in North America and then in Africa, India and Asia, the missionary reordering of the pastorate had the effect of revitalizing a scriptural notion of episcopacy, in a way that fed back into some of the other theological and pastoral movements that spread throughout the church in the nineteenth century. The grasping after new forms of provincial synodality (as well as developing notions of subsidiarity that provincial councils provided) was only, then, the *first stage* of modern Anglicanism's missionary influence. Its initial ecclesiastical fruit by 1867 in the first Lambeth Conference, and then – as we will see – in the last 'Decade of Evangelism' in the twentieth century, its celebration of the modern 'missionary bishop' of, for example, Nigeria, discloses the ongoing power of mission in shaping Anglican structures. The fact that these structures are today in visible need of reordering takes nothing away from their originating missionary source; it is the mission itself that is taking on a new character.

II Interpreting the origins of the first Lambeth Conference

The story of how the first Lambeth Conference came about is usually framed in terms of the nascent Communion's increasing complexity and conflictive disorder. William Redmond Curtis' 1942 discussion, still so valuable in many ways, laid out this story in a classic manner: worries over Roman Catholic aggressiveness and doctrinal overreach (e.g. the Marian dogmas), the 'unsettling' effect of the *Essays and Reviews* controversy, spilling over to South Africa's division over John Colenso's writings and episcopacy, and tensions between evangelical and catholic parties that, in Canada, finally pressed for the formal request for a Conference.[4] Steven Maughan's wide-ranging recent study of the inner struggles among and within Britain's nineteenth-century missionary societies – the SPG and the Church Missionary Society (CMS) – does little to change this larger picture, although it now provides a wealth of detail as to the inner workings and social pressures attending the debates in Britain itself.[5] Debates over theology, missionary control and ecclesial power, Maughan shows, both made the search for a wider Communion discussion necessary and drove the manner in which it finally came about in the Lambeth gathering. Intercommunion was as much a strategic necessity as it was a Christian desire. These divisions, furthermore, persisted into the 1870s and beyond, providing key flashpoints of discussion and presaging later conflict along a more explicit set of doctrinal lines.

The first Lambeth Conference's formal 'Address to the Faithful' by the attending bishops reflects some of this story. The Address provides a general exhortation, in New Testament resonance, to common love, and to keeping 'whole and undefiled the faith once delivered to the saints'. But the main body of this short letter is a reassertion of Scriptural authority, an attack on the 'growing superstitions' and 'pretension' of the 'See of Rome', a plea for continued sacramental intercommunion (explicitly spoken of in Resolutions I and II), and a warning against internal Anglican party 'divisions'.[6] The declaration is energetic, but there is a hovering concern about doctrinal and ecclesial retrenchment, indicating an episcopal conference oriented to self-discipline more than anything.

Nonetheless, underneath this muscular call to order are the notes of the Anglican churches' expanding mission as a presupposition, sounded in the terms of spreading the Gospel. The bishops founded their address on the fact that 'the knowledge of Christ ... through you hath been spread abroad among the most vigorous races of the earth'. They encouraged Anglicans around the world to 'show forth before all men by your faith, self-denial, purity, and godly conversation, as by your labours for the people amongst whom GOD hath so widely spread you ... that ye are indeed the servants of Him who died for

---

[4] Curtis, *The Lambeth Conference*, pp. 127–8.

[5] See Note 1.

[6] *The Six Lambeth Conferences, 1867–1920* (London: SPCK, 1920/1929), pp. 49–50. Resolutions and reports will be taken from this edition. The 1920 Conference material provided in this book, it should be noted, begins at a new Page 1.

us'. Despite the overwhelming concern of the Conference's resolutions with matters of organization and ecclesiastical structure, what always informs this discussion is the acknowledged fact that (Anglican) churches have now multiplied around the world. It is not just the problematic areas of Natal that are noted, but the many 'Churches of our Colonial Empire and the Missionary Churches beyond them'.[7] Indeed, the Resolutions taken as a whole (see below) were geared to the practicalities and challenges of a missionary church, no more and no less.

Maughan's picture of political, doctrinal and factional struggle behind the scenes of the emerging Communion makes sense only in the context of a great missionary ferment, something he does not deny. As the nineteenth century wore on, the CMS and SPG privatized their funding, raised enormous sums, sent out missionaries in the hundreds, worked with and sometimes against overseas bishops, and themselves splintered into newly energized smaller missionary groups. 'Missionary fairs' were regularly held in dioceses, local counties and even seminaries like Cuddesdon, bringing news and knowledge of wider international work, inspiring support and vocations and raising monies.[8]

The vigour of this process and its centrifugal currents of ramified missionary engagement, however, are easily missed if one remains rooted in the details of local machinations among the societies and bishops in England. In fact, studies like Maughan's, which have little to say about life in the mission field and focus instead on inner-British realities, are, in a sense, analysing the shadows cast by this larger reality, not the substance itself. Looking at the attendees at the first Lambeth Conference, who are mostly British and North American diocesan leaders, one nonetheless finds a wide geographical representation, behind which lie the difficult labours of hundreds of missionaries and, more importantly, of indigenous catechists and clergy: Harding of Bombay, Williams of China and Japan, Beckles of Sierra Leone, Tozer of Central Africa, Jackson of Antigua, Selwyn of New Zealand, Anderson of Rupert's Land and others. Burrowing into their sermons, journals and other work-related material, we get a glimpse of the central purposes behind the more formally debated structural struggles, as well as the actual expenditure of spiritual capital within

---

[7] Resolution 8.
[8] Cf. *Cuddesdon College, 1854-1904: A Record and a Memorial* (London: Longmans, Green, and Co., 1904), pp. 73–91.

the difficult contexts in which these individuals worked. These volumes, published and read by the public within the sending churches, constructed a shared vision of the Church as oriented towards a basic missionary task, which can be defined in simple terms: conversionary evangelism and the formation of faithful Christian disciples bound by a shared ecclesial life and order.[9] Compared to these tasks, the new 'Anglican Communion' was but the visage, not even the organizer, of breathtaking apostolic expenditure. A popular work like H. W. Tucker's *Under His Banner* (1872) which went through numerous editions – perhaps the first real story of the Communion ever written – is a narrative of explicit and exclusive missionary service, carried out by a host of larger and smaller societies and individuals. The Anglican Communion and Lambeth Conference are mentioned in its hundreds of pages only a few times, and positively, but as a kind of place-holder for a panoply of extended labours expressing the Gospel of a Catholic Church, not as a cohesive ecclesial entity.[10]

Shortly after the first Lambeth Conference, the bishops of India sent a public letter to the Convocations of York and Canterbury, which ended with the following peroration, summing up the underlying sense of vocation that informed the initial emergence of Anglican Communion 'structures'. The 'work' of the age was not simply laying such structural groundwork, but fulfilling the demand of discipling in a way that was nation changing. The letter is filled with the language of 'empire' that may today disturb readers. Yet the writers in fact detail with some sensitivity the cultural peculiarities of India, in its social and religious diversity, itself undergoing a process of profound reconfiguration. The question was how to transform 'millions' of the 'human family' whose lives were rooted in the absorbing particularities of a specific set of cultures. This Christian work is the hard task, not structural grounding:

> On the Colonial World – in America, in Africa, in Australia, in the Islands of the Pacific – you have bestowed during the life of one generation, the Church of God, in the fulness of its order and the completeness of its gifts; building it on the foundation of the Apostles, and of CHRIST its corner-

---

[9] This definition is obviously limited, and mission is properly defined in a variety of ways that go beyond conversionary evangelism and discipleship. Still, these elements stand as historically fundamental to the Anglican context. More broadly, though, see Kevin Ward, 'Mission in the Anglican Communion', in Mark Chapman, Sathianathan Clarke, Martyn Percy (eds), *The Oxford Handbook of Anglican Studies* (Oxford: Oxford University Press, 2015), pp. 60–76.

[10] H. W. Tucker, *Under His Banner: Papers on the Missionary Work of Modern Times* (London: SPCK, 1872).

stone. A work, vaster, and far more difficult, is now before you; and it is not we, but GOD Himself, and JESUS CHRIST His Son, Who calls you to it. It may be the work of the age, the work which, when the history of this and of the twentieth century is written, will shine conspicuous above all which art and science (in this great era) have accomplished. Consider it with that breadth of mind and largeness of heart which it demands from you. And may the Father, the Son, and the Holy Spirit be with you, to guide your counsels and to shape your ends.[11]

If some commentators on the first Lambeth Conference focus on the shift in self-descriptive language from 'synod', in the preparatory stages, to that language's rejection as the Conference took shape, one should not allow this ecclesiastical debate to overshadow the Conference's missionary well-spring.[12] In the Conference's actual reports and resolutions, the focus was now squarely placed on 'colonial' churches' needs, and on the articulated larger communion that their life now reflected as representatives of distinct peoples, nations and cultures. The Conference, in the Archbishop's invitation, was aimed at 'all avowedly in communion with our church', with the goal of 'advancing kingdom of God, union in missionary work, intercommunion'. The Conference's common acts of worship, discussion and practical agreements were to take place through what was called 'brotherly consultation'[13] – elements that came to define, however constrictedly, subsequent Conferences. Their purpose was to engage, in the end, fundamental matters deriving from the Communion's missionary life: dealing with unstable relations, holding dispersed churches together, responding to the now colliding worries among local churches as they reverberated in other parts of the globalizing Christian culture of Anglo-American mission.

Because of the peculiar character of Anglican ecclesiology itself, born of national Reformation, globalizing mission meant navigating the claims of national particularity. The American church was already the embodiment of such a particularity, ecclesially ordered. But the general vocation of the Church,

---

[11] Letter from Indian bishops to York and Canterbury convocations, 27 November, 1873, in *The Colonial Church Chronicle, and Missionary Journal*, July 1847 to December 1874, p. 255.

[12] Early proponents, Abp. Longley included, had used the language of 'synod' and 'general council' to describe what they had in mind with respect to the first Lambeth Conference; but these terms were later dropped in the face of worries regarding an international synod's relation to the British Crown, and other local concerns. The final invitation to the Conference was clear: dealing with matters of doctrine would be beyond the gathering's 'competence'. See Curtis, *The Lambeth Conference*, pp. 125–34.

[13] The phrase, in the original invitation, proved a key one to the Conference's self-description.

as Anglicans saw it, included taking seriously the integrity of 'nations'. One of the most tricky elements the first Conference dealt with, and which continued to challenge the Communion, was the matter of parallel or overlapping jurisdictions, whereby bishops for expatriate colonials and for native peoples sometimes coexisted in the same geographical area.[14] The abstract ecclesial challenge has, ironically, reappeared as an Anglican issue in the twenty-first century. Arguably, however, and despite very different originating contexts, both nineteenth-century and twenty-first-century problems of overlapping episcopal jurisdictions are basically mission derived, according to the elemental definition of mission used above. At issue is how the Christian Church can find its missionary embodiment in a way that rightly serves and reflects the distinctiveness of particular 'nations' and cultures for whom the Gospel is offered, even while maintaining unity within a single ecclesial body. The missionary proliferation of churches around the world that began in earnest among Anglicans in the nineteenth century had fulfilled hopes few had expected to see accomplished so quickly, providing the reality of a 'communion' that even fewer had anticipated as an ecclesial reality. Just within this dynamic had emerged the demands of national distinctiveness that were seen, by thinkers as influential as the historian John Robert Seeley, as properly respected by Anglican mission, but also as a model for global international relations.[15] By

---

[14] On this important topic, see the following: C. Peter Williams, *The Idea of the Self-Governing Church: A Study in Victorian Missionary Strategy* (Leiden: E. J. Brill, 1990) provides detail into the complexities here. Cf. his discussion of South India, pp. 57–89; 203–14. See also Williams' essay, "'Too Peculiarly Anglican: The Role of the Established Church in Ireland as a Negative Model in the Development of the Church Missionary Society's Commitment to Independent Native Churches, 1856–72', in W. J. Sheils and Diana Wood (eds), *Churches, Ireland and the Irish: Papers Read at the 1987 Summer Meeting and the 1988 Winter Meeting of the Ecclesiastical History Society* (Oxford: Basil Blackwell, 1989), pp. 299–310; Cecil John Grimes, *Towards An Indian Church : The Growth of the Church of India in Constitution and Life* (London: SPCK, 1946); Kenneth John Trace Farrimond, 'The Policy of the Church Missionary Society Concerning the Development of Self-Governing Indigenous Churches 1900-1942', PhD dissertation, University of Leeds, 2003.

[15] Seeley's ideas were influential on outlooks carried through in the late-nineteenth-century Anglican Congresses. On Seeley, see Duncan S. A. Bell, 'Unity and Difference: John Robert Seeley and the Political Theology of International Relations', in *Review of International Studies*, 31 (2005), pp. 559–79; and David Armitage, *Ideological Origins of the British Empire* (Cambridge: Cambridge University Press, 2000), pp. 16–24. See earlier, R. T. Shannon, 'John Robert Seeley and the Idea of a National Church', in R. Robson (ed.), *Ideas and Institutions of Victorian Britain: Essays in Honour of George Kitson Clark* (London: Bell, 1967). Seeley's notion of a federated set of independent national states, upheld by Christian religious principles such as Anglicanism would provide, was one that pressed him towards a certain view of Anglican 'communion' that was actually less chauvinistic than his more American-oriented antagonist E. A. Freeman, whose ideas regarding Anglo-Saxon character were actually more in tune with American imperialist sentiments. Seeley is quoted at the opening of the 1897 Lambeth Report 10 on 'Duties of the Churches to the Colonies', asserting religious ties as fundamental to the national network that formed British interests around the world. See R.

the time the great 1920 Lambeth Conference provided its towering enunciation of the Communion's vocation, this convergence of missionary demand and articulated national expression had become foundational to Anglican self-definition.[16]

III Specific concerns with mission in the early Conferences

Until the later twentieth century, then, the work of the Lambeth Conferences emerges *out of* the reality of Anglican missionary life. This expressive function provides glimpses, as it were, behind the curtain of these episcopal gatherings, at the apostolic life sustaining the Communion.

We have noted above the way that the first Conference aimed to hold together the now multiplied elements of Anglican ecclesial life that had grown up around the world. Some of the resolutions and reports therefore address the careful (and constantly threatened) balance of voluntary and ecclesial–episcopal ordering of mission, whereby the work of the missionary societies was seen as requiring integration within the wider structural framework of diocesan life. Much of the Conference was devoted to regularizing now standard elements of Anglican life, founded on the diocesan principle, and involving synods, provinces, metropolitans, the movement of clergy between areas and the like. Eliciting these concerns were, of course, the very multiplication of missionary bishoprics, the sometimes overlapping regions of jurisdiction that had arisen,[17] and the reality on the ground of missionaries and clergy whose originating responsibilities had derived from their supporting missionary societies. The wording of the Reports reflected caution in stepping on these many toes: along with the 'should' regarding structural policy,[18] there were many 'it is desirable', 'as far as possible', 'peculiar cases may occur', 'generally', 'as a general rule' expressions when it came to actual missionary practice and authority, including even the seemingly obvious anomaly of overlapping jurisdiction. The CMS was not a part of the first two Lambeth Conferences,

Davidson (ed.), *The Six Lambeth Conferences, 1867-1920* (London: SPCK, 1920), p. 276. The citation is from his *The Expansion of England: Two Courses of Lectures* (London: Macmillan, 1883), p. 11.

[16] 1920 'Encyclical Letter', section 'International Relations', *Six Lambeth Conferences*, p. 19.

[17] See Report G.

[18] Cf. Report F on Provinces.

but its broad work was represented by many bishops and participants, and the society's more flexible attitudes towards ecclesial structures informed the Conference's ever-cautious attitude towards simple prescription.[19]

The 1878 Conference's discussions did not step out from this carefully considered business of structural missionary support. Diversity of worship had become a question,[20] and the ongoing tensions between missionary clergy from a given society and local bishops continued to be felt.[21] By this point, however, it is clear that the Communion's missionary organization lay primarily in either English or American hands, and the Conference simply acknowledged this fact as a means of deferring authority to those actually supporting missionary endeavours. As mission work by England and America geographically overlapped in places (e.g. China), and as individual missionaries from this or that society found themselves working in areas organized in new ways by these churches, we discover in this Conference the first explicit acknowledgement that mission itself need not and surely will not find its originating energies in these two churches only: mission is something that will be done locally, in ways that will step outside the direct control of England or America in more confusing ways, and will therefore demand the coordination of multiple localities. The Conference therefore recommended a communion board of representatives from the two larger churches who might oversee developing responses to the missionary needs of such new churches, for example, new prayer books.[22] The challenge of national influence and ecclesiastical power, as it affected local missionary life became an increasingly troubling issue in the course of the next century. But it was already recognized even at this second Lambeth Conference.

The 1888 Conference was relatively devoid of explicit interest in the Church's mission. Most of the Conference was devoted to social and ethical matters, as well as ecumenical issues – a new seed that will flower in coming Conferences. Along with this were the usual questions of maintaining some order within the rapidly ramifying churches of the Communion. Mission itself, however, was barely mentioned. One might wonder at this, given that during this period

---

[19] Farrimond, 'The Policy of the Church Missionary Society', p. 72.
[20] Report 1.VI.
[21] Report 3:III.
[22] Report 3.

essential missionary energies were in full swing around the world. Perhaps it was just this well-understood *obligato* of ministry that made overt discussion less necessary. One window onto this ongoing reality, however, was the specific attention given to the question of polygamy (and even polyandry) and baptism.[23] Most of the bishops involved in the discussion worked in Africa, and their conclusions – which take a strong line against the baptism of male polygamists (but not necessarily of their wives), even as they encouraged their welcome into the catechumenate – were couched in a way that was driven by a standard conception of Christian marriage. Still, there were repeated acknowledgements of the need for local latitude on precise rules.[24] The attempt to integrate particular missionary challenges with universal norms of doctrine and practice will become one of the ongoing interests of the Conferences. It is notable that the famous Quadrilateral,[25] aimed at 'Home Reunion', was not long afterwards taken up by mission-minded Anglicans, like the CMS, as a means of integrating divided *Anglicans* on intrinsically Anglican principles. That is, ecumenical vision was appropriated to mission, even as mission itself spurred ecumenical vision.[26]

The 1897 Conference, in any case, returned to earlier issues of missionary support in a way that simply demonstrates their ongoing pertinence over the previous two decades. A series of resolutions (14–27) were explicitly devoted to mission, grouped together under the rubric of the Great Commission 'to evangelise all nations' that the Conference insists must never be obscured as a 'necessary and constant element in the spiritual life of the Body'.[27] The Report on Foreign Missions[28] is one of the most extensive mission reports in the history of the Conferences, and was explicitly commended in the Resolutions. It touched broadly and hortatively upon mission among Eastern religions, Jews and Muslims, as well as turning to the particular structural concerns of

---

[23] Report 4, Resolution 5, and a section of the Encyclical.
[24] See Timothy Willem Jones, 'The Missionaries' Position: Polygamy and Divorce in the Anglican Communion, 1888-1988', *Journal of Religious History* 35:3 (September 2011), 393–408, for comparative historical discussions, though without much theological engagement.
[25] Resolution 11.
[26] On the 1888 Anglican Quadrilateral as a basis for CMS-originated native dioceses, so that local 'reunion' could be done always on the basis of Anglican rather than separatist principles, see Farrimond, 'The Policy of the Church Missionary Society', p. 69, which references a 1901 CMS memorandum.
[27] Resolution 14.
[28] Report 4, in *The Six Lambeth Conferences*, pp. 222–39.

missionary order typical of the early Conferences.[29] Vocational recruitment and support were laid out as an essential responsibility of the Communion, and the Report spoke of the ideal of the Church as a whole to be a 'great Missionary Society of the world'.[30] Outside of the Conferences, in fact, Anglicans were expressing admiration for the American church's ecclesial self-designation as a single 'missionary society', and some of this discussion has now filtered up to the Lambeth bishops.[31] One senses a note of tension now with the particular concerns of individual missionary societies, often struggling among themselves and, as in the past (and future) trying to find some integration with local diocesan bishops and provinces. But the Conference was nonetheless adamant that these smaller organized societies have been necessary and 'providential'.[32]

Three further points stand out from the 1897 Conference. First, there is an explicit, if cautiously realistic, press for enabling the independence and particularity of local 'native' churches, in a way that reflects the long-standing (if often stymied) strategic goals of the societies themselves, especially the CMS. 'Native' is indeed the key phrase, and is contrasted with the notion of a 'foreign' missionary body.[33] Second, however, the Conference is keen to underscore the integrated unity and universality of the Church, as something that includes and rises above the particularities of locality. Not only is there only one integral 'Catholic Faith' to be inculcated in the form of 'Apostolic

---

[29] The continued question of overlapping jurisdiction arises (Res. 24 and Report), now framed in terms mostly of the competing originating churches, and less in terms of cultural diversity and pragmatism. Conflict on these matters, in China in particular, between American and British churches, had re-emerged in 1897–8. But it went back, as noted above, to the 1850s, and the American General Convention of 1853 had already addressed the matter. See *Journal of the Proceedings … of the Protestant Episcopal Church … Assembled in General Convention … 1853* (Philadelphia: King & Baird, 1854), p. 308 and the *Journal of the Proceedings … 1856* (Philadelphia: King & Baird, 1857), p. 138. G. F. Moule, the English Bishop of mid-China since 1880, had responded (12 April 1898) to the American desire for integration with an interesting argument: it's complicated, he wrote to the American Bishop Frederick Graves, and the various Anglican churches have commitments to their own members (colonists), and one day, in any case, there will be a Chinese church that will be independent of both. For now, 'May I venture to add that in my opinion, in the absence of any inter-ecclesiastical Tribunal clothed with the requisite knowledge and authority to decree a precise delimitation of sphere or area, the status quo is not without its redeeming features, and has in it nothing that need alarm loyal members of either the English or American Branches of the Church.' *Letters, Documents, &c. in the Matter of Episcopal Jurisdiction in China* (N.p., n.p. c. 1904), pp. 31–5. The interchange and issues continue to have relevance in the Communion today.

[30] *The Six Lambeth Conferences*, p. 238.

[31] The 1894 Missionary Conference (see below) discussed this matter: see George A. Spottiswoode (ed.), *The Official Report of the Missionary Conference of the Anglican Communion On May 28, 29, 30, 31 and Jun 1 1894* (London: SPCK, 1894), pp. 512–45. It was already on the table, however – and with some caution – in Tucker's *Under His Banner*, pp. 431–7.

[32] *The Six Lambeth Conferences*, p. 238.

[33] Cf. Resolutions 18–20.

unity', but the practical recognition of and adjustment to diversity in a given church must not 'obscure the fact that the many races form but one Church'. Here, the office of a local bishop is identified as just that symbolic focus of unity.[34] The ecclesiological implications are not insignificant. Finally, the Conference for the first time linked missionary work with the larger call to ecumenical unity,[35] not only in terms of means, but also in terms of actual cooperative recognition of non-Anglican missionaries in the 'unity of the Spirit'. This theme was taken up again at the 1908 Conference and finally formed a great centrepiece of the 1920 Conference's magisterial appeal to the larger Christian Church.

The 1908 Conference offered little new on matters of mission, repeating many of the themes already enunciated at earlier conferences, including the notion that separate and 'independent' churches, 'racially' defined and living 'side by side' are simply 'inconsistent' with the reality of Christian 'unity', wherein peoples are 'welded together as one Body'. Its reference, in Resolution 26, to the missionary importance of the 1908 Pan-Anglican Conference, however, points to the ongoing vitality of Anglican missionary practice outside the immediate articulations of the Conference's documents. In fact, during all the decades of the late nineteenth century leading to the Great War, missionary energies drove the public discussions of the church, not only through print communication,[36] but through gatherings of missionary conferences that began, for Anglicans, with the large Missionary Conference of 1894 in London that was sponsored by the Mission Boards of York and Canterbury.[37] The 1894 Conference engaged topics, at length and with gusto,

---

[34] Resolution 21. Cf. Thomas Valpy French's episcopal sermon on the new cathedral in Lahore (1887), where he dwelt powerfully on the need for the cathedral to be a meeting place of all races, a 'house of prayer for all nations' where all are brought together, including the 'sons of the stranger', and none excluded. Herbert Birks, *The Life and Correspondence of Thomas Valpy French, First Bishop of Lahore* (London: John Murray, 1895), vol. II, pp. 107–8.

[35] Resolution 27.

[36] The most notable medium was *The Colonial Church Chronicle and Missionary Journal*, 1847–74. The *Church Quarterly Review*, an organ of the SPCK, took up some of these interests more broadly in 1875. Individual societies had their own publications, which numbered in the dozens. All of these were the main location for vigorous discussions of Communion life, directly or indirectly. Lambeth set up The Advisory Council on Missionary Strategy in 1878 but it does not appear that it ever met; it is reset in 1948. See W. M. Jacob, *The Making of the Anglican Church Worldwide* (London: SPCK, 1997), p. 264.

[37] On the larger Protestant missionary conferences of the era, within whose broader concerns the Anglican conferences should be located, see Wolfgang Günther and Guillermo Cook, 'World Missionary Conferences', *Dictionary of Mission: Theology, History, Perspectives*, Karl Müller et al., eds (Maryknoll, NY: Orbis, 1997); W. R. Hogg, *Ecumenical Foundations: A History of the*

that were to prove key areas of concern for the Lambeth Conferences over the next century. But running underneath all the discussions of societies, dioceses, cultural and national distinctives, Communion synodality and doctrinal or liturgical commonality was the common sense that evangelism and the Gospel were to drive all these practical decisions in ways that demanded imaginative and structural flexibility.

This first Pan-Anglican Congress was a remarkable confluence of these elements.[38] Years in preparation, and sponsored by various mission boards and societies, it was designed to take place in London shortly before the 1908 Lambeth Conference. Every diocese of the Communion was invited to send six delegates, regardless of rank, office or sex, to a Congress 'dealing with missionary and other questions affecting the extension of the Redeemer's Kingdom throughout the world'. With formal guests, correspondents, visitors and peripheral gatherings around the edges of the week-long gathering, venues like the Royal Albert Hall were required, involving up to 13,000 persons at one time. There were various sectional themes, divided into subgroupings, that mirrored many of the topics taken up by the Lambeth Conferences, from social concerns to ministry to the education of the young, all framed by deeply missionary attitudes of evangelism, outreach and international demands. Two of the most spirited groups dealt with socialism (many of the English representatives proving themselves surprisingly clear in their socialist commitments) and the potential need for a centralized Anglican Communion authority, a matter that drew intense debate and provided no consensus. Yet it was less the substance of the debates than the overall impression

---

International Missionary Council and Its Nineteenth-Century Background (New York: Harper, 1952). On the 1894 Anglican Missionary Conference, see Maughan, pp. 46–7; 295–6. More fully, see George A. Spottiswoode (ed.), *The Official Report of the Missionary Conference of the Anglican Communion On May 28, 29, 30, 31 and Jun 1 1894* (London: SPCK, 1894). The figure of Alfred Barry (Bishop of Sydney, 1884–9) looms large here and through the next fifteen years. His Hulsean Lectures, *The Ecclesiastical Expansion of England in the Growth of the Anglican Communion* (London: Macmillan, 1895) was a landmark essay, and showed how relatively liberal Broad Church leaders still fell squarely within the traditional missionary framework of the Communion.

[38] See the remarkable preparatory book *Mankind and the Church: Being an Attempt to Estimate the Contribution of Great Races to the Fulness of the Church of God, by Seven Bishops* (London: Longmans, Green and Co., 1907), which, for all the racial stereotyping and condescension involved, presses towards a non-ethnocentric view of the Church, an issue that was such a source of struggle in Anglicanism. See also the pre-Conference essay by the Dean of Durham, J. E. C. Welldon, 'An "Imperial Conference" of the Church and Its Significance', *The Living Age*, July 4, 1908. See also R. S. Bosher, 'The Pan-Anglican Congress of 1908', *Historical Magazine of the Protestant Episcopal Church* (June, 1954), pp. 126–42.

of the Conference that perhaps proved its most potent significance. One correspondent described the final gathering:

My pen trembles at its utter inability to convey any adequate idea of the scene when 8,000 worshippers were gathered within the walls of the cathedral – a thousand delegates, members of many races and colors, being massed together. Nor of the sound, when the swelling and falling tones of the organ were suddenly hushed as the faint echo of the Litany sounded from afar. The procession has never been equalled, even in St. Paul's majestic history, nor has the effect of the choristers' insistent reiteration, 'We beseech Thee to hear us, good Lord', ever been surpassed. Nor can that piercing note of the single trumpet, breaking into the meditations of the waiting multitude, with Mendelssohn's triumphant air – 'All that has life and breath, sing to the Lord' – ever be forgotten. Some thirty minutes were spent in placing on the altar the slips of parchment upon which were written the sums collected for the offering of Thanksgiving. Perhaps the most thrilling moment of the occasion was when the Primates, metropolitans, and Presiding bishops knelt, 'one solid mass of scarlet', on the steps of the altar, as the Archbishop of Canterbury pronounced the benediction from the highest step. The glorious *Te Deum* was in every sense a fitting conclusion. In the opinion of those who were present no official service held in the cathedral in the memory of man approached in magnificence and impressiveness this great public act of thanksgiving.[39]

The advent and experience of the Great War undercut this emotionally swelling hope. The war eviscerated the Church of England's own internal confidence and national credibility, as well as simply depriving it of a whole generation of educated leadership.[40] The full extent of the war's transformative power on the British church would take years, and another war, to become clear. But the profound revelation of human depravity and ecclesial powerlessness in its face was clear from the start, and the 1920 Lambeth Conference gathered, prayed together over five weeks and voiced its sense of God's calling in a conscious

---

[39] Bosher, 'The Pan-Anglican Congress of 1908', pp. 139–40.

[40] Albert Marrin, *The Last Crusade: The Church of England in the First World War* (Durham, N.C.: Duke University Press, 1974); Alan Wilkinson, *The Church of England and the First World War* (Cambridge: Lutterworth, 2014); id., *Dissent or Conform?: War, Peace, and the English Churches, 1900-1945* (London: SCM, 1986). For a more positive take, at least in terms of wartime experience, see Robert Beaken, *The Church of England and the Home Front, 1914-1918: Civilians, Soldiers, and Religion in Wartime Colchester* (Woodbridge, Suffolk, UK/Rochester, NY: Boydell Press, 2015).

posture of repentance and reordered vision.[41] That vision was given within the sharp and almost exclusive perspective of 'unity'.

The 1920 Conference's remarkable letter by the bishops outlined this perspective relentlessly, and indeed the idea of 'fellowship' that the letter addresses is the thread running through all the conference, not just in the famous 'Appeal To All Christian People' for the 'Reunion of Christendom' of Resolution 9. The *Appeal* is rightly seen as a watershed in Anglican and in more broadly Christian ecumenism, and its opening claim that 'God wills fellowship', given the term's sixteenth-century use as a translation of the New Testament's *koinonia*, is rightly seen as one of the first great enunciations of what today we call 'communion ecclesiology'.[42] But the opening letter sets the *Appeal*, driven in the shadow of the Great War and its horrors, in a broader missionary context of divine purpose that has often been overlooked. Having stated upfront that the 'one idea [that] runs through all our work in this Conference' is 'the idea of Fellowship' – again, what today we translate as 'communion' – the letter goes on to sketch the way that the war had brought into clear view the need for and the transformative power of human fellowship, even as it had assaulted human hope for its attainment. Then came the key text by which 'fellowship' was given its essential missionary meaning:

> Men to-day are tempted to despair of the world and to blame its design. But this at least we can say: the life of men upon earth was designed to give opportunities for love and nothing has defeated that design. Those things which most perplex us, suffering and sin, have been the occasion of the most conspicuous triumphs of love. This design is the clue to the labyrinth of life. We lose our way in the maze whenever we let go this clue. Men lost the clue and they are always losing it, for they will not keep God in their knowledge, nor love in their hearts. It is ours to recall men to God and to His revealed purposes and His acts which reveal them. It is ours to bid them pause in the hurry and stress of life, in the midst of its trivialities and its tragedy, and contemplate anew the ways of God. He made men for love, that they might love Him and love one another. They rejected His purpose, but He did not

---

[41] On some background, including George Bell's work behind the scenes, see Charlotte Methuen, "'Fulfilling Christ's own wish that we should be one": The early ecumenical work of George Bell as Chaplain to the Archbishop of Canterbury and Dean of Canterbury (1914-1929)', *Kirchliche Zeitgeschichte*, 21:2 (2008), pp. 221–45.

[42] Lorelei F. Fuchs, *Koinonia and the Quest for an Ecumenical Ecclesiology: From Foundations Through Dialogue to Symbolic Competence for Communionality* (Grand Rapids, MI: Eerdmans, 2008), pp. 87–8.

abandon it. He chose a nation, and made it in a special sense His own, that within it love of God and men might be cultivated, and that thus it might enlighten the world. Into that nation He sent forth His Son, both to reconcile the world to Himself and to reconcile men one to another. And His Son formed a new and greater Israel, which we call the Church, to carry on His own mission of reconciling men to God and men to men. The foundation and ground of all fellowship is the undeflected will of God, renewing again and again its patient effort to possess, without destroying, the wills of men. And so He has called into being a fellowship of men, His Church, and sent His Holy Spirit to abide therein, that by the prevailing attraction of that one Spirit, He, the one God and Father of all, may win over the whole human family to that fellowship in Himself, by which alone it can attain to the fulness of life. This then is the object of the Church.[43]

This sketch of the divine purpose deftly integrated what had long been the Anglican missionary goal of Great Commission discipling, with a history of national in-gathering, an almost Irenaean vision of humanity's full retrieval into communion with God through Israel's vocation, Christ's life and his Church's service. Unity is not only 'for' mission, but the mission of the Church is in fact the unity of humankind drawn together in Christ. To further communion and to be in communion *are* the divine 'mission' given to the Christian Church.

The effects of this claim are interesting. They do not, for instance, subvert the long-standing commitment of the Conferences to engage the particularities of nation and culture, whose integrity nonetheless had, as we have seen, raised questions about the unity of Catholic teaching. In 1920, however, 'fellowship' is presented as the base of, and is expressed by, national identities: 'The ideal of the one Church should never be obscured,'[44] even if localities remain the key centre of missionary endeavour and Christian life. 'Discipling' the nations does not involve obliterating nationality, but purifying it, and lifting it up in its many diversities. Hence, in the resolutions on mission (which are not numerous) we see an interest in the way that the Communion might encourage, sustain and protect national particularities and free local indigenous ministries (a clear challenge) for the sake of and in the Gospel. Nonetheless, as the letter writes in more broadly ecumenical terms, a 'vital connexion with the Head' provides the 'positive value in the differentiation of the members'. According to the

---

[43] *The Six Lambeth Conferences*, 1920, pp. 10–11.
[44] Resolution 35.

letter's fundamental ecclesiological claim, 'the one body exists; it needs not to be made, nor to be remade, but to become organic and visible. ... We have only to discover it, and to set free its activities'.[45] With this understood and embraced, the freedom of the Communion's local mission, shaped by each's particular location, need cause no anxiety.

If the mission of the Catholic Church is communion, and communion itself orders the particularities of mission more traditionally understood, then the Anglican Communion, according the 1920 Conference, can be more clearly understood as a missionary enterprise taken as a whole. This is perhaps the most novel and striking claim of the letter, at least in Anglican terms. It is often alluded to in twenty-first-century Anglican discussion, only because the claim has failed to achieve practical purchase on Communion life. Rather than being only the result of mission, and the responsible ordering of mission, the 1920 Conference insisted that the Anglican Communion was a *microcosm* of communion for the Catholic Church, and the world. Only on this basis did the famous *Appeal* make sense: Anglicans were engaged in communion uncovering, and doing so in the midst of a world riven by the dark side of national particularities. As a now global phenomenon, driven by missionary outreach, Anglicans 'must clear ourselves of local, sectional, and temporary prepossessions, and cultivate a sense of what is universal and genuinely Catholic, in truth and life'.[46] They must do so, not under compulsion but freely (the non-legislative nature of the Conference is stressed), with a Christian 'independence' that 'recognizes the restraints of truth and of love'. Anglican churches are 'not free to deny the truth; they are not free to ignore the fellowship'.[47] This responsible freedom, given over to the truth and love that mark true communion, is precisely the vocation of all Christians in the universal Church. Hence, Anglicans have a witness to perform and gifts to be given over to others. 'The fact that the Anglican Communion has become world-wide forces upon it some of the problems which must always beset the unity of the Catholic Church itself. Perhaps, as we ourselves are dealing with these problems, the way will appear in which the future reunited Church must deal with them'.[48]

---

[45] *The Six Lambeth Conferences*, 1920, p. 12
[46] Ibid., p. 13.
[47] Ibid.
[48] Ibid.

The 1920 Conference represents a turning point in the long-standing tension between the more particular organizing energies of the private missionary societies, and the more general diocesan and now increasingly provincial structures of Anglican churches. The pertinent resolutions were listed, tellingly, under the heading of 'Missionary Problems', and although the societies were given their usual praise, the goal of integral independent churches is underlined, as well as the ideal of a 'whole Church' as the primary missionary agent in any particular locality.[49] In fact, and for the first time, the 1920 Conference included two indigenous bishops, Azariah, Bishop of Dornakal, and Oluwole, Assistant Bishop of Western Equatorial Africa. While modest, this marked the beginning of a major shift in representation that indicated the increased rooting of mission in local communities rather than in foreign-originated leadership. Having said that, CMS-related bishops at the 1920 Conference were numerous, and demonstrated how the societies' work was moving more seamlessly along the lines the Conference had in mind than is sometimes acknowledged.[50] In 1921 a Missionary Council was established for Anglicans that aimed at subordinating the societies, who were present only as 'members', to broader coordinating needs. By this time, furthermore, the societies began shifting their missionary emphasis to 'institutional' work, such as women and schools.[51] Finally, by moving towards greater inclusion in the structured ecclesial life of the Anglican churches, the societies fell under pressure for inclusion of more 'liberal' views in their midst (e.g. on Scripture, in the case of CMS), and local demands, as in India where society-related churches were being handed over for direct diocesan control. Not everyone was happy with these trends, and splits within the societies ensued, such as the formation in 1922 of the more conservative Bible Churchmen's Missionary Society.[52] The weakening of the societies, in this manner, went apace with the growth of local ecclesial institutions, and the Conference's support of these moves.

To what degree any of this actually furthered traditional missionary endeavours is unclear. Lambeth 1920s reorientation did not take place in a

---

[49] Resolutions 33–4.

[50] For example, the Bishops of Chekiang, Fukien, Honan, Kwangsi, Lagos, North China, Persia, Tinnevelly and Western China. See Farrimond, 'The Policy of the Church Missionary Society', p. 134.

[51] Farrimond, 'The Policy of the Church Missionary Society', chapters 5 and 6 generally.

[52] Cf. the new CMS 'General Principles' in 1924 for transfer of churches, in Farrimond, 'The Policy of the Church Missionary Society', pp. 161–8.

vacuum. As with other Lambeth Conferences, the specifically missionary undercurrents of Christian work outside of the coordinating institutional life of the Anglican churches were pressuring the terms of the bishops' discussion. Already before the war, the great 1910 Edinburgh conference had begun to couple mission and Christian unity in a new way.[53] Arguably, the war rattled confidence in the Western centre of mission, and inspired newly emerging Christian churches to enter the mission field themselves. Subsequent world missionary conferences, like Jerusalem (1928) and Tambaram (1938), in which Anglicans participated, express some of this. Retrospective evaluations of Christian mission after the war point out, however, that whatever the ecumenical concerns Edinburgh and Lambeth may have laid on the table, actual Christian growth was primarily driven by indigenous, and less institutionally tethered, labours.

> The most effective instrument of that transfiguration would not be western mission agencies or institutions of any kind, but rather a great and sometimes unorthodox miscellany of indigenous pastors, prophets, catechists, and evangelists, men and women who had little or no access to the metropolitan mission headquarters and the wealth of dollars and pounds which kept the missionary society machinery turning; they professed instead to rely on the simple transforming power of the Spirit and the Word.[54]

Certainly the shift towards local ecclesial control that began in 1920 would, once it was complete by the 1960s and 1970s, correlate with unprecedented evangelistic expansion, including ecclesial growth.[55] But how deeply connected this was with specifically institutional relocations of power, or simply with a general loosening of control more broadly, is less obvious.

It may be, then, that Lambeth 1920, in its stress upon mission-as-communion, was thus charting a position that would prove somewhat at odds with the actual movement of evangelism in the world more broadly. Despite the Conference's commitment to 'spiritual' oneness rather than legislative unity, its concern for institutional stability and control – for example, its desire for a 'central

---

[53] Brian Stanley, *The World Missionary Conference, Edinburgh 1920* (Grand Rapids, MI: Eerdmans, 2009), pp. 277–81.

[54] See Joshua Kalapati, 'Edinburgh to Tambaram: A Paradigm Shift in Missions, or the horizon of Missions broadened?', in *Dharma Deepika: A South Asian Journal of Missiological Research*, January, 2010, np.

[55] A key discussion of this is Lamin Sanneh, *Whose Religion Is Christianity? The Gospel Beyond the West* (Grand Rapids, MI: Eerdmands, 2003).

consultative body' that would be the interim agent for the Conference between meetings – expressed a tension that has remained intrinsic to Communion life.

The Lambeth Conference 1930 shows little evolution beyond this initially given tension, and indeed seems mostly to reflect it. We see the ongoing push towards independent churches, now located in dioceses as the 'fundamental unit' of the church.[56] From this sprang the Conference's concerns about local input on diocesan elections in Resolution 57. The 1930 Conference is notable for its clear, if theologically anodyne, definition of the Anglican Communion;[57] but when it comes to a Communion ecclesiology, it falls back from the 1920 vision of mission-as-communion to a more general sense of the Church itself as a 'cooperative' means to mission.[58] Indeed, the Edinburgh vision seems to have taken root – whatever its growing irrelevance to on-the-ground evangelization – and the 1930 Conference's concern with ecumenical mission can be directly tied now to the work that was beginning to take place for Indian reunion that was finally to give rise to the Church of South India after the Second World War.[59]

As it turned out, mission societies like the CMS ended up being major supporters of reunion in India. The project was already taking shape after the First World War. It was the CMS's less institutionally oriented missionary concern, perhaps, that allowed them the latitude to consider positively the reordering of ministry that would make reunion in India possible. This went so far as insisting on the freedom of duly constituted 'Anglican' churches to leave the Communion for the sake of some greater unity. Canterbury's encouragement of the whole scheme proved crucial to its final achievement. But it is important to note a missionary society's key facilitation of Lambeth 1920's larger communion vision, over and against many more 'catholic' Anglican objections in this case, since it complicates the standard notion of communion, including visible *reunion*, at least in Anglican terms, as

---

[56] Report and Resolution 49.

[57] Resolution 49.

[58] The CMS's then Secretary, W. Wilson Cash's report from 1928 Jerusalem Missionary Conference stressed that mission is not about 'church'; but rather Church is about cooperative unity in mission. 'The Jerusalem Meeting of the International Missionary Council', *The Churchman*, 42:4 (October 1928), p. 277. (This was Cash's own message at the Conference itself; cf. Reports, III, 'The Relation between the Younger and the Older churches', *Report of the Jerusalem Meeting of the International Missionary Council, March 24-April 8, 1928* [Oxford University Press, 1928], vol. 3, pp. 165-7.) 'Cooperation' as a more primary organizing concept for 'unity', than 'fellowship' or 'communion', is an interesting note that is struck. On Cash more broadly, see also Farrimond, 'The Policy of the Church Missionary Society', pp. 183–259.

[59] Bengt Sundkler, *Church of South India: The Movement Towards Reunion, 1900-1947* (London: Lutterworth Press, 1954).

something governed by strict institutional rules. Furthermore, the subsequent challenges that the Church of South India has faced in terms of evangelistic mission poses yet new complications in the way we might perceive communion itself as a liberative mission. Freedom *for* communion, which a group like the CMS upheld, and freedom *in* communion, which might have resulted in a missionary blossoming, were not linked in an obvious way.

IV The turn of mid-century: National churches as reality, not ideal

After the Second World War, cultural and political diversity was pressing on the consciousness and decision-making demands of governments, and the term 'inter-national' had taken on a new and burdensome meaning. Anglicanism had for a long time, after all, stressed the integrity of national cultures and polities. We should note that this was now clearly *seen*. At Lambeth 1948 there were, by my own count, 9 non-Western bishops, only one of whom was African. At the Minneapolis Anglican Congress in 1954 there were 12 native bishops, and now, from Africa, Islam was discussed with some concern. In Toronto, at the 1963 Anglican Congress, there were over 25 non-Western indigenous bishops, and over 161 non-Western delegates. It was a striking and accelerating shift, and one whose outcome we all know today: at the 1998 Lambeth Conference 364 non-Anglo-American bishops came to Lambeth, almost half the total number. Yet the 1948 Lambeth Conference contains repeated notes of tension between the need to acknowledge and uphold this diversity and the now dangerous demands of newly independent and vying nations, among whom, somehow, the Church was to press for the one Gospel.[60] Since 1948 the Communion seems to have mirrored the development of this fear into reality, as regional and cultural–economic differences have become dominant in our conflicts.

The politically refashioned landscape after the Second World War furthered ecclesial change that had already been taking place, in a now rapid and obviously dislocating fashion. Lambeth Conferences had already been advocating local

---

[60] Unless otherwise noted, resolutions for the subsequent Conferences are cited from the Anglican Communion website, http://www.anglicancommunion.org/structures/instruments-of-communion/lambeth-conference.aspx.

autonomy, indigenization of leadership and cultural sensitivity. The war provided two new realities: a sense of missionary urgency (for the salvation of Christian civilization itself) and a willingness to let go of institutional supports in a sudden and major way – money, personnel, leadership – and to rely on improvised local missionary energies.[61] Max Warren, the new CMS head, for example, showed a remarkable willingness to engage positively the emerging forces of nationalism in the post-war context.[62] With nationalism, however, came new regimes (perhaps most spectacularly, for Anglicans, in India), indigenously controlled, but also quickly aligned with the emerging Cold War axes in sometimes unexpected ways. Christians and their churches were often minority groups in these newly independent nations, and both institutional and traditional mission had to adapt to these realities in which, in a post-colonial order, not just financial resources but social supports were suddenly withdrawn in many places. Missionary societies tended to be more nimble in response, but also more easily appropriated to local political currents. Institutionalized churches simply moved towards indigenous leadership in a sudden leap, leaving these new leaders the difficult job of navigating their churches within rapidly changed and politically charged national contexts in which they had little power.

A period of institutional precariousness took hold – in Asia after the war, and in Africa, after independencies took over – as churches and their increasingly autonomous missionary leaders sought to figure out their roles, assess their possibilities and restructure their resources. Growth was constrained, and in the face of rapid economic change as well – urbanization, educational expansion and the dissemination of ideological struggle – it seemed as if larger forces of religious opposition were weighing against the Church's global vocation: communism, revivals in other religions like Islam or Hinduism, and, now stated clearly, something called 'secularism'.[63] The 1952 Willingen

---

[61] Andrew Porter, 'War, Colonialism and the British Experience: The Redefinition of Christian Missionary Policy', in *Kirchliche Zeitgeschichte*, 5:2 (1992), pp. 269–88.

[62] This was not a new orientation. See the remarks of the then CMS Secretary, William Cash, made at the 1928 Jerusalem Conference, in *Report of the Jerusalem Meeting of the International Missionary Council*, p. 274.

[63] The issue was, obviously, not a new one; but it had taken time to raise its head so publicly as a supposedly international issue. See, for earlier, Jeffrey Cox, *The English Churches in a Secular Society: Lambeth, 1870-1930* (New York: Oxford University Press, 1982), who offers a more subtle description of some of the forces undercutting the Church's central place in British society during this period, with a focus on nonconformity as a major lens.

International Missionary Conference took place amid 'profound uneasiness'.[64] Anglican discussions at Lambeth, in 1948 and 1958, were also tinged with anxiety and worry, and these spilled out to the revived Anglican Congresses of 1954 in Minneapolis and 1963 in Toronto.

The 1948 Lambeth Conference is almost wholly devoid of any discussion of mission. It is as if a new world has dawned after the war, in which all the concerns of the past had mostly disappeared, with unexpected ones now firmly in their place. The key reality is something called 'The Modern World', defined in terms of the debris left by National Socialism and the war that defeated it, and the threats of communism. The opening resolutions on 'The Christian Doctrine of Man' briefly laid the foundation for the intrinsic value of the human person before and with God, upon which were built the dozens of resolutions that followed: on war, nuclear arms, human rights, the state, education, the place of women and labour. In place of the older categories of 'mission', the Conference now attended to the 'Church Militant' and the 'Christian Way of Life', which tended to collapse social and evangelical concerns into a single Kingdom-building 'witness'.[65]

Unity formed a central concern as well, but it was almost wholly pragmatic and structural. Mentioning the 1920 *Appeal*, concerns were couched in terms of practical planning: South India especially, North India and other specific engagements were now discussed in terms of the way that ministries might be recognized across a host of ecclesial lines. A shift to this broader ecumenical context is signalled by the first mention of the World Council of Churches.[66] Only one resolution was directly related to mission: Resolution 80, recommending a Joint Advisory Council on Mission Strategy for the Communion. It was out of this – a group whose actual work never quite coalesced – that the appointment of a 'Communion' officer, Stephen Bayne, arose; and from his work, the Toronto Congress of 1953, and then, in 1968, the establishment of the new permanent structures for the Communion's ongoing ministries that ordered common life alongside the Lambeth Conference. This today includes not only the Communion Office and secretariat, but the Anglican Consultative Council (ACC) and (later) the Primates' Meeting, along

---

[64] Porter, 'War, Colonialism and the British Experience' p. 288.
[65] Cf. Resolutions 39–42.
[66] Resolution 76.

with the many commissions that have proliferated in their wake. It should be noted, however, that although hardly anything was said directly about this in the 1948 resolutions, the actual Report on the Communion, chaired by Bishop Carrington of Quebec, had pointedly raised worries about the dissolution of common life in the Communion due to the growing diversity of liturgy, training and theological purpose.[67] It was to prove a prescient warning regarding fragmentation and was raised again more explicitly in the 1963 Toronto Congress, and then dominated late-twentieth-century Conferences. The responses to this threat proposed by Carrington's group, under the guise of 'reciprocal' and 'mutual' relations and values – taken up, again, in Toronto – proved theologically, and hence ecclesiologically, inadequate to the actual threat, at least if measured by subsequent events.[68]

The 1958 Conference exuded a sense of greater equilibrium. Despite a central set of resolutions, built around its 'Missionary Appeal', the real issues that touched upon mission were now fully located in coordinative 'strategy' among self-initiating entities. The whole church, the Conference affirmed, was called to mission,[69] but the issue was how to order the many now clearly independent and mostly indigenously rooted churches of the Communion in some practical way. The 'Missionary Appeal' was brief, and 'strategy' predominated. For the first time, a 'full time secretary' to the Advisory Council on Missionary Strategy was called for,[70] a position filled by Bayne and which led to the formation, in the 1960s, of a Communion 'office'. There was much talk about sharing resources. Yet for 1958 other matters predominated: the Bible, in the opening set of resolutions, was addressed in the context of obvious concern with 'scientific' study of its contents, and the need was now clearly seen to demand culturally relevant sensitivities in its presentation, at least in terms of the Anglo-European Modernist worries. The lack of development, to this point, of indigenous intellectual leaders within most Anglican churches

---

[67] The 'Report on the Anglican Communion' (IV) in *the Lambeth Conferences (1867-1948): The Reports of the 1920, 1930, and 1948 Conferences, with Selected Resolutions from the Conferences of 1867, 1878, 1888, 1897, and 1908* (London: SPCK, 1948), pp. 81–94.

[68] 'Report on the Anglican Communion', p. 86. The Communion was, at this time, offered a specific missionary 'character' of mutuality, termed 'giving and receiving' in the build-up to the Lambeth Conference. See E. R. Morgan and Roger Lloyd (eds), *The Mission of the Anglican Communion* (London: SPCK, 1948), Pt. II, pp. 133–209, one of the more notable attempts to articulate a 'communion missiology' in the twentieth century.

[69] Resolution 58.

[70] Resolution 62.

within decolonizing nations made this a mostly Western discussion. Most of the social concerns of the Conference were packed into a set of resolutions dealing with 'resolving conflict within and among nations' and were carried on in another long set of resolutions regarding 'the family in contemporary society'. The driving worries here, again mostly Western ones, were uncovered in Resolution 122, which described these matters as critical given the pressures of the 'crushing impact of secularism'. Concerns about population now emerged, informing the notorious resolution on 'family planning'.[71] The many resolutions on unity eschewed theological discussion, and were focused solely on practical matters with and among churches.

The 1963 Toronto Congress, called for in 1958,[72] was devoted to 'The World-Wide Mission of the Church' and proved of deep significance in orienting the structural development of the Communion.[73] In a way, the Congress embodied a hinge-moment between the vital missionary character of the Communion's origins and formation, and, in the midst of the pivoting of the Communion to a set of autonomously institutionalized churches, the new character of cultured beleagueredness that the post-Second-World-War era had produced. The threat of external forces – communism, other religions and secularism – hovered over reports and sermons, even as the strains of diversity upon the sense of commonality were now being openly discussed.[74] Anxiety and urgency both coloured the Congress, even while participants – led by Bayne – sensed a need to rationalize cooperation in new institutional ways. The moniker of 'Mutual Responsibility and Interdependence' (MRI)[75] nimbly described the feel for this new rationalized cooperative venture, but it lacked both the ecclesiological depth and missiological demand of Lambeth 1920s notion of missionary communion.

In fact, a de facto segregation had taken hold of the Communion. Even as a range of cooperative structures were put into place in the 1960s, Western and non-Western churches, now ensconced in their autonomous spheres

---

[71] Resolution 115.

[72] Resolution 68.

[73] Radner, 'Supranational Ecclesiology', *The Living Church*, 11 October 2013; http://www.livingchurch. org/supranational-ecclesiology (accessed 20 January 2017). A good bit of the structural history can be found in various chapters in Stephen Fielding Bayne, Jr., *An Anglican Turning Point: Documents and Interpretations* (Austin, TX: The Church Historical Society, 1964), with a chronological documentary overview on pp. 3–97.

[74] R. Fairweather (ed.), *Anglican Congress 1963: Report of Proceedings* (Toronto: Anglican Book Centre/London: SPCK, 1963).

[75] See Stephen Fielding Bayne, Jr., *An Anglican Turning Point*, pp. 80–1. See also his details on pp. 6–7.

of self-determination, could simply move according to their own rhythms and concerns.[76] In theory, this allowed for truly pursuing mission in local ways. The post-war pause, oriented to the demands of post-colonial political independence and revolution, of nation building and ideological struggle, finally gave way to a veritable resurgence of Christian evangelizing growth in non-Western countries, in Africa especially.[77] Much of this was unstructured and unstrategized, at least in terms of institutional intention, as revival, itinerant catechesis and unchoreographed conversion took over. While much of this spilled out into non-ecclesial contexts, Anglican churches were able to hold some of it within their structured bounds, and by the 1970s, tremendous growth was seen in many areas of Eastern and Western Africa in particular. It was not, however, a *Communion* phenomenon, and its meaning never penetrated the Lambeth Conferences, at least not until the Conferences had lost a sense of common mission sufficient to include these new realities. At that point, mission had become a destabilizing force for the coherence of the Communion, rather than unifying.

Instead, the 1968 Lambeth Conference cast all of its missionary concerns in terms of Western secularization, worrying over the contributions of modern 'psychology' and leisure, 'contemporary' morality and confusions over God-language. There were, in 1968, resolutions dealing with 'experimentation' and adaptations, 're-stating' old truths in new ways, and the rest.[78] In retrospect, the disconnect between these kinds of interests and the realities of contemporaneous African evangelism could not appear more stark. The national make-up of Lambeth bishops still strongly favoured Western participation. But that was

---

[76] Bayne single-handedly represented 'mission' in the Anglican Communion from the late 1950s through to the end of the next decade. The traditional missionary societies, while still important as resources, had begun to lose their directive powers, especially as their personnel shrunk. Following the establishment of the ACC, which first met in 1971, a string of formal 'commissions' devoted to mission in the Communion, under an array of bewildering acronyms, have met. See the brief overview in *Living Communion: The Official Report of the 13th Meeting of the Anglican Consultative Council, Nottingham, 2005* (London: Anglican Communion Office, 2006), pp. 333–7. All these groups engaged in important discussions, but tended, like most such gatherings, to be reflective of concerns internal to the groups, couching topics in language and concepts of increasing jargon.

[77] For an accessible documentary survey, which captures some of the public profile of this long period, see Todd Shepard, *Voices of Decolonization: A Brief History With Documents* (Boston, MA: Bedford/ St. Martin's, 2015).

[78] See the Conference's 'Renewal in Faith: Report', or Resolution 2, as it celebrates '(b) the prospect of human control of the natural environment, (c) the searching enquiries of the theologians, calls the Church to a faith in the living God which is adventurous, expectant, calm, and confident, and to faith in the standards of Christ, who was, and is, and is to come, as the criterion of what is to be welcomed and what is to be resisted in contemporary society'.

soon to change, and when it did, the sudden realization that the Communion's missionary vocation, in its traditional sense, had been wholly taken over by the younger non-Western churches rattled Lambeth out of its slumber and into an awkward facing of its devolved incapacities: neither expressive of mission nor able to grasp its own missionary identity as a communion, the Lambeth Conference decided to reinvent itself as its own missionary agency. It proved a short-lived experiment.

V Contemporary challenge

The language of novelty and suddenness is probably too strong to apply to the period after the 1960s, though it reflects the lack of preparedness that the Communion evidenced in the face of Western religious confusion and non-Western ecclesial growth. The transformation and shrinkage of the private missionary societies had been set in motion since the 1920s and then especially after the Second World War. The growing Lambeth call for mission to be seen as a vocation of 'the whole church', once linked to de-colonizing and granting of independence to non-Western churches, demanded an inevitable shift in missionary focus and ordering away from any common originating locus. The Lambeth Conferences naturally settled into their role as 'support' at best. But because mission was now diversely directed and enacted, and because the churches where it was engaged had grown in their diversity, centrifugal forces obscured the compelling character of a common mission, let alone the belief in mission-as-communion, and had instead rendered that mission's apprehension impossible.

Attempts at defining church and mission were made in various official ecumenical dialogues beginning in the 1970s. But nothing bubbled to the surface at that decade's Lambeth Conference as a result. The 1978 Conference was a desultory affair. Resolutions 1 and 2, cast in the mode of a common appeal, provided a relatively long statement aimed at responding to the obvious need to guard the 'well-being' of the earth and of humanity as a whole, on the basis of the dangers of economic injustice and technological degradation. If this was meant to recapture some of the sonorous moral high-ground of earlier Lambeth Conference 'statements', it fell flat. Most of the remaining resolutions, surprisingly limited in view of previous Conferences, were a hodgepodge of various concerns, with little coherence.

Resolutions 7–8 offered a positive, if muted, response to the charismatic movement. We see as well the first inklings of the sexuality debate sniffing about.[79] The long Resolution 15, on Partners in Mission, spelt out aspects of a rejigged MRI perspective, now organized into a common structure. There were, of course, several resolutions regarding women in ministry, given the ordinations that had taken place two years earlier in the United States and changes afoot in other churches on that score. Resolution 21 noted, in passing, that Anglican 'diversity' in matters of 'doctrine and practice' (in this case, with respect to women's ordination) may be of concern to other ecumenical partners, but the bishops seemed to think that this reality was simply something to be taken at face value. By contrast, an ominous note was sounded in Resolution 11, which had earlier acknowledged the destructive character of autonomous action by member churches, and recommended a study on 'authority' in the Communion. And, of course, there were the usual ecumenical concerns, none of which, including those commending agreed statements in dialogue, engaged in any ecclesiological reflection. As a whole, the Conference seems, in comparison with earlier gatherings and given what we now see to be the enormous stakes involved in some of the issues addressed, unfocused and lethargic in its vision.

The 1970s saw some major shifts in the Communion's ecclesiastical culture finally emerge into visibility, in particular the fading of the Anglo-Catholic impetus within the larger Church. This had been a long process. In missiological terms, a major element in this devolution had been the failure of Anglo-Catholic missionary areas to encourage indigenous church leadership, something all mission groups struggled with, but that, by the mid-twentieth century had clearly afflicted Anglo-Catholics more than others. The fact that this difficulty in promoting native clergy especially was linked to an often far greater openness by Anglo-Catholics to local cultural expressions within the church's life is a paradox many have noted.[80] Yet it is a fact that, after the Second World War, evangelical

---

[79] Resolution 10.

[80] Maughan's volume covers the earlier interaction and comparative outlooks of the Evangelicals and High Church/Anglo-Catholic missionary societies; Rowan Strong offers a window on some early missiological ideals in 'Origins of Anglo-Catholic Missions: Fr Richard Benson and the Initial Missions of the Society of St John the Evangelist, 1869-1882', *Journal of Ecclesiastical History*, 66:1

churches of the Communion grew far more rapidly than did their Anglo-Catholic counterparts – Africa being a prime example. The structural flexibility, which was more amenable to lay and indigenous leadership, as well as growing evangelistic, and in some cases openly revivalistic, energies of evangelical Anglicanism, proved more adaptable to the rapidly changing and often-turbulent social contexts of the post-war era.[81] By the 1970s, Anglo-Catholicism was an evidently declining force in the Communion. Within Anglo-American contexts, the decision to move forward with women's ordination proved deeply divisive, and drove hundreds of catholic clergy, and many laypeople, out of the established Anglican churches altogether, some forming new splinter churches, others joining existing Roman and Orthodox churches.[82] Joined to the already weakening missionary profile of Anglo-Catholicism, the 1970s saw the movement as a whole virtually collapse.[83] In its place arose the burgeoning evangelical 'Global South', whose energies and numerical heft would alter the tenor of the Communion's increasingly confused missionary vision.

Only at Lambeth 1988 does the realization arise that something has profoundly changed, perhaps driven by the recognition of the Communion's own transformation in membership in favour of Majority-World churches. Over a third of the bishops attending in 1988 were non-Westerners, and the number of African bishops had doubled since 1978.[84] The simple visual

---

(January 2015), pp. 90–115. On the 'paradox' itself, see Andrew Porter, 'The Universities' Mission to Central Africa: Anglo-Catholicism and the Twentieth-Century Colonial Encounter', in Brian Stanley, *Missions, Nationalism, and the End of Empire* (Grand Rapids, MI: Eerdmans, 2003), pp. 79–107; Maimbo Mndolwa, both confirms and nuances Porter in 'In Two Minds? African Experience and Preferment in UMCA and the Journey to Independence in Tanganyika', *Mission Studies*, 33 (2016), pp. 327–51; but his discussion does show how political adaptation went hand in hand with the loosening of Anglo-Catholic theology more broadly.

[81] There are both complications and counterfactuals to this general picture. On South Africa, see the rich biography by Piers McGrandle, *Trevor Huddleston: A Turbulent Priest* (London/New York: Continuum, 2004). Melanesia has usually been viewed as a thriving area of Anglo-Catholic missionary origins. Understanding how church growth and theology interact in such areas – as anywhere – is difficult, however. See David Wetherell, 'Whatever Happened in Torres Strait? Interpreting the Anglican split of 1998', *The Journal of Pacific History*, 36:2 (September 2001), pp. 201–14.

[82] Douglas Bess, *Divided We Stand: A History of the Continuing Anglican Movement* (Berkeley, CA: Apocryphile Press, 2006).

[83] A broad overview can be found in W. S. F. Pickering, *Anglo-Catholicism: A Study in Religious Ambiguity* (London: Routledge, 1989); for a somewhat partisan description of the American scene through the end of the twentieth century, see Thomas C. Reeves, 'The Light that Failed: Reflections on Anglo-Catholicism in the Episcopal Church', *Anglican and Episcopal History*, 68:2 (June, 1999), pp. 215–30.

[84] For an extended discussion of the dynamics behind and in consequence of this change, see Vinay Samuel and Christopher Sugden, *Lambeth: A View from the Two Thirds World* (Harrisburg, PA: Morehouse, 1989).

impression of this change – made even more dramatic in the 1998 Conference – was astonishing to many, and the practical challenges of engaging in a conference where so many participants did not speak English as a first language were noticeable. In an almost passing acknowledgement of what had been going on elsewhere in the world, the Conference, with little fanfare, resolved to declare a 'Decade of Evangelism' for the Communion:

> This Conference, recognising that evangelism is the primary task given to the Church, asks each province and diocese of the Anglican Communion, in co-operation with other Christians, to make the closing years of this millennium a 'Decade of Evangelism' with a renewed and united emphasis on making Christ known to the people of his world.[85]

The Report in question had been chock-full of discussions aimed at renewing a Communion commitment to primary evangelism in the traditional sense. Hence, immediately following, Resolution 44 stated that

> This Conference:
> 1. calls for a shift to a dynamic missionary emphasis going beyond care and nurture to proclamation and service; and therefore
> 2. accepts the challenge this presents to diocesan and local church structures and patterns of worship and ministry, and looks to God for a fresh movement of the Spirit in prayer, outgoing love and evangelism in obedience to our Lord's command.[86]

Other resolutions followed on equipping all people for mission, on the ministry of bishops in mission, on liturgical 'freedom' for the sake of local relevance, ministry to 'youth' in the context of evangelism. These mission-oriented notes appear in the centre of a set of resolutions that, like those of Lambeth 1978, are otherwise a mishmash of other social, structural and ecumenical concerns. Driven mostly by the members of the Mission and Ministry Report group, the evangelism resolutions represented concerns of the now ascendant African bishops, and were laid upon the Lambeth gathering almost as a surprise. It was one that was accepted, but also received, as it turned out, with difficulty.

Certainly, the announced 'Decade of Evangelism' gained a quick public profile, and it was energetically supported by Archbishop of Canterbury

---

[85] Resolution 43; see further paras. 14–23 of the report on 'Mission and Ministry'.
[86] See further paras. 10–13 of the report on 'Mission and Ministry'.

George Carey, who became archbishop in 1991. The Communion's offices organized materials and a mid-decade conference that was filled with buzzing excitement, while individual provinces made efforts, in different ways, to engage the challenge. Booklets were written, gatherings were held sharing experiences, and reports issued. The decade was initially embraced with much excitement, even if – or perhaps because – its initiating impulses were largely African. It was as if a non-Western centre of gravity had finally emerged in a practical way, itself proof of Anglican missionary achievement. First reactions stressed the richness and biblical ordering of this ongoing work.[87] A 1995 'mid-point' evaluation of the decade, held at Kanuga, North Carolina, proved one of the largest Anglican missionary conferences in several decades, and was filled with enormous energy.[88] By the end of the decade, there was much to celebrate, but by now the substance had subsided to a somewhat predictable pastiche of anecdotal 'stories' from around the world that emphasized diversity rather than common vocation.[89] Meanwhile, the American church historian John Booty gave a somewhat ironic twist to the decade early on, in a lengthy set of essays that not only hinted at the cultured Western scepticism towards such an evangelistic project, but also offered a subtle warning against its rapidly charging incoherence, which seemed to have little rooting in traditional Anglican forms of catechesis and commitment.[90]

Whatever the outcome, the announced Decade of Evangelism had suddenly turned the Conference into a missionary vehicle, at least in terms of ordering and supporting a basic evangelistic project. It is hard to know what 'might' have happened to this energy had other communion-disrupting dynamics not intruded. But it was clear, when the 1998 Lambeth Conference convened ten years later, that the decade's work had somehow been marginalized in the intervening years. The Conference's Report on mission was one of the longest of the gathering, though oddly it said nothing about the decade itself. Within the Report, the largest single section was devoted to relations with other

[87] Cf. Christopher Wright and Christopher Sugden (eds), *One Gospel – Many Clothes: Anglicans and the Decade of Evangelism* (Oxford: Regnum Books, 1990).

[88] See Cyril C. Okorocha (ed.), *The Cutting Edge of Mission: A Report of the Mid-Point Review of the Decade of Evangelism* (London: Anglican Communion Publications, 1996).

[89] Eleanor Johnson and John Clark (eds), *Anglicans In Mission: A Transforming Journey. Report of MISSIO, the Mission Commission of the Anglican Communion, to the Anglican Consultative Council, meeting in Edinburgh, Scotland, September 1999* (London: SPCK, 2000).

[90] John Booty, 'Wisdom In All Her Ways: The Sixteenth Century Informs the Decade of Evangelism', *Sewanee Theological Review*, 34 (September 1991), pp. 11–72.

faiths – which, joined to another complete report on the theme, made interfaith relations the most extended topic treated by the Conference overall. Since the 1897 Conference, this theme had been standard for the Lambeth gatherings, but, as we have seen, the approach over the previous century had moved from evangelism to antagonistic anxieties. Now, in line with new values of cultural internationalism the focus had moved to understanding and engagement. As for the traditional concerns with conversionary and discipling mission, the Report said little that was new. Instead, the Report's opening set the context of its discussion in the current of a distinct, though conceptually novel, idea: 'globalisation' and its challenging and descriptively negative dynamics. These included urbanization, anomie, unrooted younger generations, unordered cultural fragmentations, submersion of the Gospel in market economics and the failure of the Good News to positively touch many in the Majority World. There was, not unlike the Toronto Congress's orientation, a sombre tone being sounded here, with a diffuse timbre that coloured the tenor of the Church's own life.

Resolution II.6 of the Conference provided a succinct and focused commendation of traditional missionary tasks, including a specific mention of the need to evangelize unreached peoples. The Decade of Evangelism was here (unlike in the Report) mentioned in a sentence. But framework was given in terms of broader economic aspects (e.g. 'Jubilee' sharing of money among churches). Indeed, the other resolution in which the decade was mentioned,[91] devoted to 'Transformation and Renewal', began by noting, obliquely, the inadequacy of the decade's work in addressing the deeper realities of social ills: 'While Lambeth 1988 called for a Decade of Evangelism during which we have witnessed welcome changes in the world and enhanced efforts to share the Gospel of Christ, many other injustices still disfigure our world and challenge our commitment to share the love of God.' These injustices were then listed: they involved economic disparities and a long catalogue of 'transformation' challenges among youth, cultures, interfaith relations and ethnic divides. The reach of this enumeration is notable, as is its abstracted character.

That abstraction pointed to deeper uncertainties. The only missionary resolution that had the force of a practical directive to come from the Conference expressed a desire to have a communion 'secretary' for mission and evangelism,

---

[91] Resolution V.4.

that would contribute to greater central coordination.[92] This recommendation, if only briefly, pointed to the difficulty that had now arisen in the Communion, and that was seen as reflecting the larger world scene: diversity. Diversity was, in fact, the major theme of the 1998 Conference as a whole: religious, cultural, economic, national and finally theological.[93] Mission matters, in the Report and resolutions, stood as free-floating concerns, decoupled from the other reports, where structural issues for the Communion were explicitly tied into the issue of 'diversity and unity', and moved into elaborated discussions of 'order' and the tensions of 'authority'. The Communion itself had become a diversity issue, with its potential conflictual elements (cf. the deference shown to the Eames Commission's recommendations regarding women's ordination), along with ecumenism and interfaith questions. Resolution I.10 on sexuality became notorious in its clear proscription of homosexual relations on the basis of Scripture. But the resolution also made little sense outside the much larger worries over diversity and its cracks, even its threatening chasms (so it seems now in retrospect). The 'Jubilee' notes, mentioned above, picked up a common liberationist thread from several decades of mission reflection. Whatever deep commitments they actually expressed, however, these were publicly overshadowed by a broader sense of turmoil and mutual antagonism on public display.[94] Those writing about the Communion at the time could not escape a sense of entropy setting in.

The 1998 Conference was the last common Lambeth Conference. The 2008 gathering was boycotted by a broad range of Global South bishops (including around 60 per cent of the African bishops) and consequently decided to forego decisional resolutions altogether, focusing instead on common listening groups and feedback on the proposed Anglican Covenant.[95] In the intervening decade, the divisions over especially sexuality matters effectively broke the Communion apart into competing factions: the Anglican Mission in America,

[92] Resolution II.2.

[93] John L. Kater, Jr., 'Faithful Church, Plural World: Diversity at Lambeth 1998', *Anglican Theological Review*, 81:2 (April, 1999), pp. 235–60.

[94] The much-publicized attempt by an African church leader to exorcize the leader of a gay-inclusion group reflected, however extravagantly, the depth of those currents of disagreement running through the Conference. See Stephen Bates, *A Church at War: Anglicans and Homosexuality* (London: I. B. Tauris, 2004), p. 137. Miranda K. Hassett provides a wide analysis in *Anglican Communion In Crisis: How Episcopal Dissidents and Their African Allies Are Reshaping Anglicanism* (Princeton, NJ: Princeton University Press, 2007), especially chapter 3, pp. 106–49.

[95] The expected 2018 Conference was suspended, and rescheduled for 2020.

which partnered Rwandan and South-East Asian churches with conservative American Anglicans (AMiA) was formed in 2000, the Convocation of Anglicans in North America (CANA), a Nigerian–American alliance, in 2005, and the Anglican Church in North America (ACNA), a mostly American but then later umbrella group including some of the others, officially in 2009.[96] These North American-centred movements, whose American members mostly had left either the Episcopal Church or the Anglican Church of Canada, see themselves as structurally independent Anglican churches, though bound in communion with their supporters from among African and Asian Anglican churches. A broader coalition of some Global South churches in 2008 formed a confessional movement (the Global Anglican Future Conference or GAFCON), that openly set itself up in opposition to the effective leadership of Canterbury for the Communion, and has generally cast suspicion on the value of the Lambeth Conferences overall.[97] At the same time, these groups, along with some other Global South and conservative Western dioceses, sought to order their own missionary life and enthusiasm. A major missionary conference sponsored by Global South Anglicans was held in Bangkok in 2012, and the work of traditional evangelism and discipling has been pursued in places like East Asia, on local terms unattached to the Communion structures – its offices, commissions and societies – that had increasingly sought to coordinate matters since the later twentieth century. Formal Communion efforts at staking out a missionary vision in the wake of this cascading division have, instead, seemed inadequate both theologically and ecclesially, given the fracturing of the Communion's membership.[98]

---

[96] Basic data with some references can be found in George Thomas Kurian and Mark A. Lampart (eds), *Encyclopedia of Christianity in the United States* (Lanham, MD: Rowman & Littlefield, 2016), vol. 5, pp. 92–6. The best examination of the division in the American church from a local perspective is Christopher Brittain, *A Plague On Both Their Houses: Liberal vs. Conservative Christians and the Divorce of the Episcopal Church USA* (New York: Bloomsbury T&T Clark, 2015).

[97] Mark Thompson, 'The Global Anglican Future Conference (GAFCON)', in J. Barney Hawkins IV, Ian S. Markham et al. (eds), *The Wiley-Blackwell Companion to the Anglican Communion* (Hoboken, NJ: Wiley & Sons, 2013), pp. 739–49.

[98] The 'Covenant For Communion in Mission' (2005) was put together after the major ruptures caused by The Episcopal Church (USA)'s election and consecration of a partnered gay bishop in 2003. Presented to the 2005 ACC by the Inter Anglican Standing Commission on Mission and Evangelism (IASCOME), it was an explicit response to the Lambeth Commission's Windsor Report on the Communion's strained coherence, and sought both some common ground in mission and proposing that such a ground would actually form the basis of communion. In a sense, these goals were built on long-standing intuitions that the Lambeth Conferences had articulated over and over. In this case, however, the actual articles of the 'covenant' – which never got traction in the Communion – were vague and framed in abbreviated jargon (e.g. 'celebrate our strengths and

Looking back to the Decade of Evangelism proclaimed by the 1988 Conference, and despite the initial enthusiasms, one can now see how theological drift and differentiation, with its growing sense of antagonism, had restrained the initiative's pursuit.[99] The decline in membership among Western Anglican churches over the past few decades has been dramatic; even as non-Western churches, despite rapid growth in some areas, have had their struggles.[100] Western churches were caught up in concerns over and within the dynamics of secularization, while many non-Western churches were still governed by traditional notions of mission, but felt hampered by a lack of resources and support from richer parts of the Communion.[101] Resentments and differences over what constituted mission and the actual message of the Gospel in its Scriptural form grew, and mission itself became politicized within the Communion, gathering its various construals around antagonistic alliances or 'compacts', as Sathianathan Clarke calls them.[102] By 2014, the president of The Episcopal Church's House of Deputies, Gay Jennings, insisted that African Anglicans were homophobic specifically because of the missionary instruction they received in 'biblical literalism', conceived as a crude, abusive and anti-intellectualist bequest of earlier missionaries.[103] GAFCON, on the other hand,

---

mourn our failures', 'live into the promise of God's reconciliation for ourselves and for the world'). As the fragmenting antagonisms grew, rather than lessened, the 'covenant' appeared more as a final sigh than a call to renewal. See *Communion in Mission: Travelling Together in God's Mission: Report of the Inter Anglican Standing Commission on Mission and Evangelism 2001-2005, to the 13th Meeting of the Anglican Consultative Council in Nottingham* (London: Anglican Communion Office, 2006), pp. 21–4 (followed by Spanish, Portuguese, French and Kiswahili translations).

[99] On the relative failure of the decade in the Church of England, numerically speaking, see Leslie J. Francis and Carol Roberts, 'Growth or Decline in the Church of England during the Decade of Evangelism: Did the Churchmanship of the Bishop Matter?', in *Journal of Contemporary Religion*, 24:1 (January 2009), pp. 67–81. Critiquing the Nigerian model of diocesan 'expansionism' associated with the decade, see Stephen Ayodeji A. Fagbemi, 'Territorial Expansionism or Passion for the Lost? A Reflection on 21st-Century Mission with Reference to the Anglican Church of Nigeria', in *Transformation: An International Journal of Holistic Mission Studies*, 31:2 (2014), pp. 69–78.

[100] Recent figures have been collected and analysed in David Goodhew (ed.), *Growth and Decline in the Anglican Communion: 1980 to the Present* (New York: Routledge, 2016).

[101] One can see a notable split between the West and elsewhere in the way that 'mission' is understood to take place and what its goals are, in the array of anecdotes and narratives in Eleanor Johnson and John Clark (eds), *Anglicans in Mission: A Transforming Journey* (London: SPCK, 2000).

[102] Sathianathan Clarke, 'Ecumenism and Post-Anglicanism, Transnational Anglican Compactism, and Cosmo-transAnglicanism', in Mark Chapman, Sathianathan Clarke, Martyn Percy (eds), *The Oxford Handbook of Anglican Studies*, pp. 341–55. See the various stories and applications of the concept of 'mission' in *Communion in Mission: Report of the Inter-Anglican Commission on Mission and Evangelism, 2001-2005, to the 13th Meeting of the Anglican Consultative Council in Nottingham* (London: Anglican Communion Office, 2006). 'Mission' itself had become both the common term of value among most competing factions, and a wax nose with respect to its actual meaning.

[103] Gay Clark Jennings, 'How Homophobia In African Churches Threatens LGBT Individuals', *The Huffington Post*, 27 January 2014. http://www.huffingtonpost.com/2014/01/27/homophobia-christian-africa_n_4675618.html.

judged Western Anglican witness as promoting a 'false Gospel'.[104] Some Global South Primates in 2011 had already stated that the Communion's instruments of unity (i.e. Canterbury, Lambeth, the ACC and the Primates' Meeting) were incapacitated, had 'become dysfunctional' and had lost 'the ecclesial and moral authority to hold the Communion together'.[105] Three years later, the instruments were pronounced 'utterly failed' by one GAFCON leader.[106] The gap between unity and mission became obvious, and discord over the reasons for this fuelled yet further attempts to proclaim missionary commitment in more and more places and forms. The ever-widening scope of 'mission' that Lambeth and other Communion commissions articulated, that seemed to take in more and more aspects of contested ministry and politics, reflected confusion, not renewed focus. Once everything had become 'mission', as Bishop Stephen Neill had earlier warned, the term would lose its purchase. In the Communion's case, this loss was in part because there was little sense that anything integral remained of an Anglican common life that might render the concept definable.[107]

It is true that the great exhortations to unity 'for the sake of mission', made in the various early twentieth-century world missionary conferences, had proven practically overblown: ecclesial division had *not* held back the great post-war explosion of Christian growth outside the West. But matters may have changed in the twenty-first century. The slowing of growth, in many non-Western areas, and the overwhelming powers of a smothering secular global culture have unmasked the weaknesses of broken communion. The earlier line of formative movement within Anglicanism had been clear: it was a current of mission, through private societies and then local missionary dioceses and their final indigenous order, driving towards communion and seeking support. In the early twenty-first century, however, two new elements were now in play: first, missionary confusion in the sense of incoherent versions of the missionary vocation, and, at least in terms of numerical measures in many places in the West especially, missionary failure; second, for others, there was now a feeling

[104] Archbishop Nicholas Okoh, 3 November 3, 2016, https://www.gafcon.org/news/chairmans-october-2016-letter

[105] 14 September 2011 Communiqué of the Global South Primates meeting in China, http://www.globalsouthanglican.org/index.php/blog/comments/communique_of_the_global_south_primates_during_their_visit_to_china_in_sept.

[106] Phil Ashey, 3 October 2014, 'Observations from the Anglican Front Lines', https://americananglican.org/current-news/observations-anglican-front-lines/.

[107] 'When everything is mission, nothing is mission': Stephen Neill, *Creative Tension: The Duff Lectures, 1958* (London: Edinburgh House Press, 1959), p. 81.

that the Communion's structures were themselves constraining mission.[108] The Lambeth Conference seemed to have failed in locating evangelistic freedom within the ordering of communion.

VI Conclusion

One might simply judge the Communion's missionary life as an episode drawing to an end. On the one hand, the political dynamics and forms that had supported the great nineteenth-century Anglican missionary movement, including colonialism, have mostly dissolved, and been replaced by new, and yet uncertain, political orderings, in which the churches generally play a role of vastly reduced authority. On the other hand, the actual context of conversionary mission has been altered by the unexpected expansion of Christianity itself, and its central location in the midst of many formerly non-Christian areas. We see the Lambeth Conferences reflecting these changes, bit by bit, over the last century. From a Christian perspective, however, it is unlikely that these developments could ever signal the 'end' to traditional mission, simply because its Scriptural mandate (e.g. in Matthew 28 or Acts 1) remains embedded in the essential character of the Church herself, such that one could not, until '*the*' end, avoid it. Anglicanism itself, with its particular Scriptural centre, is unlikely to shake this mandate unless, as a vital tradition, Anglicanism itself withers. Changed historical circumstances have not yet indicated a lessening of this reality. If anything, Western secularization and global religious turmoil point to the mandate's renewed urgency, if in a transformed key.

So it is also possible that the historical moment of Anglican mission has only concluded its first phase, and is now being translated into its next ordering. The 1920 Lambeth Conference had intriguingly suggested that the Anglican Communion was a kind of microcosm of the larger Church's engagement with the world. One could today perceive this microcosmic reflection as mirroring global struggles more negatively, as the Communion herself embodies the agonized search for local identities, and the failure to provide these identities with stable existences within the often violent pull of jumbled global demands.

---

[108] See Peter Jensen, former Archbishop of Sydney and GAFCON organizer, in 'The Heart of GAFCON', 3 November 2016, https://www.gafcon.org/blog/the-heart-of-gafcon.

Such a negative reflection would perhaps then manifest the need to reengage the 1920 Conference's more positive exhortation to ecclesial reconciliation, recognizing more fully that 'gathering' itself is a form of missionary movement, and not simply the instrument of such a movement's functioning. The 1920 Conference's exhortation, however, rested on a very clear evangelical claim regarding the story of Israel and the Church, centred in Christ. Even a Lambeth sceptic, like Archbishop Peter Jensen of Sydney, has understood that the missionary enterprise is furthered by communion, and by the Anglican Communion in particular, and such mission depends upon such communion in a central way, which itself represents the fruit of a missionary heart.[109]

The 1920 Lambeth Conference, however, insisted that communion was, in a sense, a 'given', that it 'already' exists. The goal of this claim was to emphasize divine grace and initiative in ecclesiological unity. The emphasis on the 'already', however, perhaps ended up by masking the dissolving powers of Christian disunity and the destroying consequences of divine judgement upon such disunity. The ease with which too many Anglicans, by the later twentieth century, moved from 'given' communion to an acceptance of antagonistic diversity demonstrates a misunderstanding of the brutalizing context and concrete fears from which the 1920 *Appeal* arose. Later Anglican–Roman Catholic discussions of communion,[110] especially framed by the obvious impasse to which Anglican division has led the dialogues, was perhaps more helpfully pointed: the Church's communion is itself a *mission*, and not a static essence or characteristic of the Church that she holds by virtue of existing in the first place. Certainly, understood according to the Scriptural vision of ecclesial vocation outlined by Lambeth 1920, communion is a mission in terms of being a historical task that must define the shape of our conversion in that it embodies the form in which and the degree to which we have answered the call of Jesus and been taken up by his transforming Spirit within the preaching

---

[109] Jensen, 'The Heart of GAFCON'.

[110] See the 2006 Agreed Statement of the International Anglican-Roman Catholic Commission for Unity and Mission (IARCCUM), which sought to provide an overview of forty years of dialogue, but had to face the fact that Anglican disunity and diverse decisions to change teaching and practice in matters of sexual life and ordination had raised tremendous obstacles in the dialogue (paras. 5–6). Still, IARCCUM's sobered evaluation of Anglican–Roman Catholic relations was not a judgement against the vocation of communion itself (cf. paras. 15–25). Rather, it underlined the fact that, as had already been stated in earlier agreements, communion and mission were integral aspects of the same life in Christ that is the Churches'. See *Growing Together In Unity and Mission*, https://iarccum.org/archive/IARCCUM/2007_iarccum_growing_together_en.pdf.

of the Gospel to the Nations. Christian communion's own apprehension in time is an instrument of all of the other aspects of evangelical witness through which the conversion of the world takes place.

It is true that the 1920 Conference's framing of communion in terms of national distinctions today seems too neat, and in fact perhaps even politically and morally risky. But the Conference's sensitivities to peoples, cultures and local needs remain not only very Anglican but a still-forceful imperative for engaging the task of reconciliation in a world in which cultural and national particulars cannot be dissolved by *fiat*. Furthermore, as the basis for a missionary vision, 'reconciled diversity' (and for all its unfulfilled promise as an ecumenical programme)[111] is an inescapable framework for any microcosmic witness among Anglicans. Earlier Lambeth Conferences were able to balance such witness, perhaps unconsciously, upon the back of flexible structures, including sometimes overlapping jurisdictions and parallel missionary enterprises. It might be worth revisiting some of these elements as capable of fruitful adaption to our present context.[112] The Lambeth Conference is, in all events, at a crossroads. In one direction lies a path trodden in the last fifty years, a dynamic of conflicted distraction that has lost a common missionary vision, and hence has lost the trust of many of the Conference's ecclesial members. In the other lies a new kind of conciliar missionary identity, where bishops gather, but only as those committed to a basic evangelistic vision that can work itself out diversely in the world. That may well require newly flexible diocesan and provincial structures. But taking counsel for just such a purpose would embody the reconciling gifts to mission that the Conferences have sought after from their origins.

---

[111] For a brief survey of the ecumenical theme of 'reconciled diversity', which was first articulated in the 1970s, see David Carter, 'Unity in reconciled diversity: Cop-out or rainbow Church?', in *Theology*, 113:876 (Nov./Dec. 2010), pp. 411–20.

[112] This realization has been made, albeit in constricted and often antagonistic ways, by those struggling with the divisions among North American Anglicans. Those who have left the Episcopal Church and the Anglican Church of Canada have needed to rethink 'provinciality' itself. Cf. Bishop Jack Iker's comments about the new ACNA 'province': 'This new provincial reality will mean the recognition of overlapping jurisdictions, under one College of Bishops, with affinity based networks, clusters and dioceses.' Jack Iker, 'Global Anglicanism: Beyond the Elizabethan Settlement towards the New Anglican Conciliarism', a lecture delivered on 18 January 2009, in Charleston, SC; see http://www.fwepiscopal.org/bishop/mereanglicanism2009.html.

7

Episcopal Leadership in Anglicanism, 1800 to the Present: Changing form, Function and Collegiality[1]

Jeremy Morris

[The Church of England's] steady refusal to canonise … is at least a pledge and a symbol of its profound belief in the effectiveness of Christian meekness. Its repudiation of what has come to be called the Leadership Principle is often a cause of bewilderment among its own children and wrath among many onlookers, both of whom, in times of crisis, are heard constantly crying, 'Give us a lead.' But they are asking in effect for an extension of the papal system to the Anglican Church. Whether they are right to ask for this is not here argued or decided. What is certain is that so far they have asked in vain.[2]

Analysing leadership: The nature of the problem

Roger Lloyd's endorsement of Christian meekness probably has a hollow sound today. When 'leadership' courses abound in Church of England and other Anglican circles, and reflection on leadership styles is an obligatory part of ordination training, it is no wonder that preoccupation with church leadership seems to be at an all-time high. Yet what kind of leadership do bishops actually exercise today? That is a deceptively simple question, to which

---

[1] An earlier and shorter version of this chapter was published in L. Alexander and M. Higton (eds), *Faithful Improvisation? Theological Reflections on Church Leadership* (London: Church House Publishing, 2016), pp. 148–65; I am grateful to Church House Publishing for permission to use material from that version.

[2] R. Lloyd, *The Church of England in the Twentieth Century*, vol. I (London: Longmans, 1946), p. 4.

no clear and unchallengeable answer has yet been forthcoming. Controversy over the 'Green' report, the report on 'Talent management for future leaders and leadership development for bishops and deans' produced in September 2014 by a Church of England working group chaired by Lord Stephen Green, highlighted the lack of common agreement across the Church. Reception of the report was marked by a seeming polarization between those who endorsed its recommendations as sound and sensible for a Church struggling to overcome the challenge of continuing decline and shrinking resources, and those who bewailed its lack of theological rigour and its apparent capitulation to management theory.[3] The present chapter, which works particularly with material from the Church of England but also aims to make some broader, Communion-wide connections, seeks to transcend this polarization, neither denying the significance of the theology of ministry and endorsing an alternate norm in secular management theory, nor rejecting the idea that there are things to be learnt from 'non-theological' factors. Instead it argues that the question of leadership – studied as a problem of Christian history – goes beyond the common terms of doctrine and theological discussion, to include matters of social, political and cultural context which are crucial influences on the form and shape of Christian ministry.[4]

The justification for including such an analysis in a book dedicated to considering the place of the Lambeth Conference in Anglicanism is that the Conference is first and foremost a gathering of bishops, and therefore behind the history of the Conference lies a broader and yet more 'invisible' history, namely that of the changing shape and character of the leadership exercised by bishops in Anglicanism. Only by taking that broader history into account, can we really understand why the Conference has come to play such a leading role in the Anglican Communion. Much can be said about the formal constitution, scope and authority of the Conference itself. But it is always necessary to bear in mind too what the situation was before the first Lambeth Conference met in 1867, and just what kind of authority bishops were assumed to exercise at the time. And this is far from an easy or familiar task for the modern church historian.

---

[3] Cf. M. Percy, 'Are these the leaders we really want?', *Church Times*, 12 December 2014.
[4] Cf. for a theological survey of the theme, P. Avis, *Becoming a Bishop: A Theological Handbook of Episcopal Ministry* (London & New York: Bloomsbury T&T Clark, 2015).

A history of episcopal leadership in Anglicanism cannot be written simply on the back of the classic texts of Anglican ecclesiology. That much may be obvious, but it raises a considerable challenge to the mode in which the history of ministry has conventionally been written. The limitations of the conventional approach are evident, once comparison is made between the ecclesial situation of the present, and that of two hundred years ago. Anyone looking for a comprehensive theoretical discussion on the sources, nature and shape of episcopal leadership will find little useful material, until mechanisms existed in the twentieth century (paid church 'civil servants', church commissions, synodical process, commissioned reports and such like) which initiated and steered lines of enquiry into what these mechanisms themselves identified as a problem. There was, of course, running controversy on the nature of the ordained ministry, and that included significant discussion on episcopal authority, and in particular on its relation to Christ's foundation of the Church. A proper attention to the theology of episcopacy would therefore look particularly to Sumner on the *Apostolic Preaching*, to Newman on the *Ministerial Commission* (*Tracts For the Times* 1), to Palmer on the *Church of Christ*, to Hatch, Lightfoot, Moberly and Gore on the apostolic ministry, and in the twentieth century, inter alia, to the Kirk v Carey exchange, and perhaps (as influences) Küng and Schillebeeckx.[5] These at least are some of the more obvious reference points. It might also, coming up to date, include Church of England documents such as *Apostolicity and Succession* and *Bishops in Communion*, as well as the 'Lima' document, *Baptism, Eucharist and Ministry*.[6]

These familiar *loci* could provide a clear narrative of change and development in the Anglican doctrine of ministry over the last two hundred

[5] J. B. Sumner, *Apostolical Preaching considered in an Examination of St Paul's Epistles* (London: Hatchard, 1815); J. H. Newman, *Thoughts on the Ministerial Commission, respectfully addressed to the clergy* (Oxford: Rivingtons, 1833, 1840 edition); W. Palmer, *A Treatise on the Church of Christ* (London: Rivington, 1838); J. B. Lightfoot, *St Paul's Epistle to the Galatians* (London: Macmillan, 1876); E. Hatch, *The Growth of Church Institutions* (London: Hodder & Stoughton, 1887); R. C. Moberly, *Ministerial Priesthood: Chapters (preliminary to a study of the Ordinal) on the rationale of ministry and the meaning of Christian priesthood* (London: SPCK, 1897); C. Gore, *The Church and the Ministry: A review of the Rev. E. Hatch's Bampton Lectures* (London: Rivingtons, 1882); K. Kirk (ed.), *The Apostolic Ministry* (London: Hodder & Stoughton, 1946); K. Carey (ed.), *The Historic Episcopate in the Fullness of the Church* (London: Dacre Press, 1954); H. Küng, *Why Priests?* (London: Collins, 1972); E. Schillebeeckx, *The Church with a Human Face* (London: SCM, 1985).

[6] Faith & Order, *Baptism, Eucharist and Ministry* (Geneva: World Council of Churches, 1982); House of Bishops, *Apostolicity and Succession* (London: Church House Publishing, 1994); House of Bishops, *Bishops in Communion* (London: Church House Publishing, 2000).

years, though a comprehensive scholarly treatment has yet to be written.[7] Such a narrative would surely recognize that the early-nineteenth-century understanding of episcopacy emphasized as much the legal authority of rightly commissioned ministers, and especially bishops, as it did the intrinsic spiritual authority derived from apostolic succession; it was a Tractarian innovation to emphasize the latter at the expense of the former.[8] Under the influence of Tractarianism and then of Anglo-Catholicism more widely, the 'supercharged' doctrine of apostolic succession risked unchurching Lutheran and Reformed churches, steered the ecumenical interest of many Anglicans towards the Roman Catholic and Orthodox churches as fellow 'branches' of the Christian Church, renewed interest in patristic models of ministry, reinvigorated certain strands of sacramental theology and encouraged the development of various sacramental and ritual practices. Though provoking theological division and internal 'church party' development (not least through the determined Evangelical defence of what were perceived to be the historic Reformation roots of Anglican arguments on church order), nevertheless Anglo-Catholicism arguably shifted the balance of Anglican views of ministry overall, so that even moderate proposals for church reunion – such as that which eventually became known as the Lambeth Quadrilateral – carried something of the imprint of the renewed emphasis on episcopacy and succession.[9] Yet all this happened at a time when the historical claims on which the Tractarian view of the ministry rested were becoming more contested, and as a result alternative readings – such as the 'representative' view supported by, inter alia, F. D. Maurice and J. B. Lightfoot – were also articulated.[10] To cut a long story short, in the late nineteenth and the twentieth centuries the sharper edges of Anglo-Catholic

---

[7] The most comprehensive survey remains that of Paul Avis, *Anglicanism and the Christian Church: Theological Resources in Historical Perspective* (London: T&T Clark, new edn., 2002); but Mark Chapman has also provided a useful, brief alternative reading in *By What Authority? Authority, Ministry and the Catholic Church* (London: Darton, Longman & Todd, 1997).

[8] P. B. Nockles, *The Oxford Movement in Context: Anglican High Churchmanship 1760-1857* (Cambridge: Cambridge University Press, 1994), especially chapter 3: 'Ecclesiology: the apostolic paradigm', pp. 146–83.

[9] See the essays in J. Robert Wright (ed.), *Quadrilateral at One Hundred* (Oxford: Mowbray, 1988). On Evangelical opposition to Tractarianism, see P. Toon, *Evangelical Theology 1833-1856: A Response to Tractarianism* (London: Marshall, Morgan & Scott, 1979) and M. Wellings, *Evangelicals Embattled: Responses of Evangelicals in the Church of England to Ritualism, Darwinism and Theological Liberalism 1890-1930* (Milton Keynes: Paternoster Press, 2003).

[10] F. D. Maurice's views on the threefold ministry, and particularly episcopacy, are to be found in *The Kingdom of Christ*, vol. 2 (London: Macmillan, 4th edn., 1891), pp. 171–5; there is a summary in J. N. Morris, *F. D. Maurice and the Crisis of Christian Authority* (Oxford: Oxford University Press, 2005), pp. 85–6.

arguments on ministry were taken off by the concessions that theologians such as Gore and Moberley made to the representative view (that is, the idea that the authority of the ministry derived first and foremost from the whole body of the Church, rather than from the historical succession of ministers traced back to the apostles). Later still, under the influence of ongoing patristic scholarship, elements of continental Catholicism and developing ecumenical relations, a certain reimagining of ministerial authority could take place, re-emphasizing the apostolicity of the whole Church and the location of the apostolicity of the ministry *within* it, and reconnecting the authority of the ministry with that of the whole people of God.[11]

Doubtless there are many *lacunae* in this all-too-brief summary of main lines of Anglican argument on the authority of the ministry over the last two hundred years – Evangelical arguments, trends in biblical interpretation, and revisionism in Patristics, inter alia. But there is a bigger 'miss' still. Consideration of the points above might tell us much about the evolution of the theological *meaning* of the episcopate, but not of its actual exercise of authority, nor of the half-concealed and rarely articulated operative norms through which this putative meaning was expressed. The theology of ministry in any one time and place sits inside a matrix of ideas and values which help to constrain and define the way it is deployed in practice, so that to ask the question, 'What was the nature of episcopal leadership in the last two centuries in the Church of England?', is to require an answer passing beyond the conventional boundaries of theological analysis into the complexity of social history.

But this suggests, furthermore, that the question also cannot be answered simply by detailed attention to practice – if, that is, we mean by it the data amenable to quantification, such as diocesan geography, population size of diocese, length of residency, frequency of visitation, creation of representative institutions and so on. These are certainly important indices of changing conceptions of episcopacy, and the stuff of a number of very important monographs (Best and Chandler on the Church Commissioners, and Burns on the diocesan revival, for example), but merely marrying them to theological developments will also miss much of the understanding of the ethos and evolution of episcopal leadership

---

[11] On this trajectory, the arguments of Robin Greenwood probably represent an extreme development of the representative view, to the point at which no substantive argument can be made for the authority of the ministry, or indeed its specific functions, other than one located entirely in the interaction of the whole body of the faithful: see his *Transforming Priesthood* (London: SPCK, 1994).

in the last two centuries.[12] It is obvious enough that changes in practice rarely follow or precede changes in theory in a straightforward way, not least because any such 'simple' relation would seem to presuppose only two sets of relevant variables. If we want to get at what 'episcopal leadership' in Anglicanism in the last two hundred years really involved, and how it changed, we certainly cannot do that merely by placing doctrine alongside pastoral practice.

The changing language of leadership

A useful index of the complications involved can be found in the history of language, since a concept such as 'leadership' obviously has its own history, and its own register, in a changing social and cultural context. Analysis of the history of the term, then, can help to elucidate something of the complexity of the phenomenon it expresses. Here, the work of the historian has been eased tremendously by the creation of searchable digital databases, which enable a concept or cluster of concepts to be pursued through the press and other ephemeral literature in a way inconceivable just a decade ago. Foremost among these are the Times Digital Archive (covering the years 1785–1985), the 17th-18th Century Burney Collection of Newspapers (British Library, covering some 1,270 newspapers, chap books and journals) and the 19th Century British Library Newspapers (covering currently 48 national and local titles, with over 2.2 million pages from 1800 to 1900, and listed in two parts). This material must be used with caution: the results of a word or phrase search are not the same thing as the assembly of a comprehensive battery of evidence; rather they represent an indication, a symptom, of change. But they are telling, nonetheless. Take the phrase 'episcopal leadership', a seemingly straightforward term. No citations appear at all in the seventeenth and eighteenth centuries, nor are there any for 'bishop's leadership'. Turning to *The Times*, we can find just 10 citations for 'episcopal leadership', the earliest of them occurring in 1968 in a report on criticism of Archbishop Michael Ramsey in the Church

---

[12] G. F. A. Best, *Temporal Pillars: Queen Anne's Bounty, the Ecclesiastical Commissioners and the Church of England* (Cambridge: Cambridge University Press, 1964); R. A. Burns, *The Diocesan Revival in the Church of England c.1800-1870* (Oxford: Oxford University Press, 1999); A. Chandler, *The Church of England in the Twentieth Century: The Church Commissioners and the Politics of Reform, 1948-1998* (Woodbridge: Boydell & Brewer, 2005).

Assembly.[13] Changing the search term to 'bishop's leadership' yields just one reference, in 1985, and that was to Bishop Muzorewa's leadership of the United Methodist Church in Zimbabwe.[14] Turning to the database of *19th Century British Library Newspapers*, the phrase 'episcopal leadership' here yields some nineteenth-century uses – but just 6 in all. The first was in the *Morning Post* in 1852, in an article on church reform which attributed revival not to 'episcopal leadership', but to the bottom-up 'rekindling of dying embers'.[15] But there were *no* results at all to match the term 'bishop's leadership'.

The problem is clearly the connection of the term 'leadership' with 'episcopal' or 'bishop's', since a search on the word 'episcopal' on its own yields over 18,000 citations in *The Times* alone, and on 'leadership' 4,750 citations before 1900. If neither 'episcopal leadership' nor 'bishop's leadership' were commonly nineteenth-century terms, what might have been the common equivalent term, or at least the word most used in connection with 'episcopal' or 'bishop's'? It was, probably, 'rule'. A search of the database of *19th Century British Library Newspapers* on the term 'episcopal rule' yields 318 results between 1800 and 1900, and a search on 'bishop's rule' a further 120. A search of the *Times* Digital Archive using the term 'episcopal rule' yields 24 citations, 19 of which occurred between 1834 and 1899, with the latest twentieth-century citation in 1935 (in an obituary of Cardinal Bourne).[16] Searching the same resource using 'bishop's rule' yields 6 citations, with the latest in 1938. These figures perhaps do not sound particularly impressive, but they are a far cry from the near-silence on episcopal 'leadership'. *The Times'* report on Archbishop Lang's tribute to Bishop Winnington-Ingram of London can serve as a useful indicator of the sense in which 'rule' was commonly used: 'Thirty-three years ago the Bishop summoned him to be a comrade and a successor as Bishop of Stepney, and he spent eight happy years under the Bishop's rule.'[17] But note that the *17th–18th Century Burney Collection of Newspapers* yields *no citations at all* for 'episcopal rule' and 'bishop's rule' between 1600 and 1800 – in other words, no uses at all of the term before the nineteenth century. That is surely prima facie somewhat surprising.

---

[13] *The Times*, 15 February 1968.
[14] *The Times*, 13 November 1985.
[15] *The Morning Post*, 7 January 1852.
[16] *The Times*, 1 January 1935.
[17] *The Times*, 11 July 1934.

This admittedly crude yardstick of database searches suggests at least an outline trajectory. The term 'leadership', as coupled with 'episcopal' and 'bishop', is largely a late-twentieth-century usage. It was hardly used at all in the nineteenth century, and never before then. Instead, in the nineteenth century the much more common term was 'rule'. This might be thought to have been a 'survival' from some pre-modern idea of hierarchy and divine right, but not so, as there were no pre-nineteenth-century instances in the databases cited above. The concept of 'rule' was essentially a nineteenth-century innovation, possibly influenced by Tractarian or High Church conceptions of the threefold office of Christ and of the ministry, possibly also expressing a renewed or revived emphasis on the intrinsic spiritual authority of the episcopate, possibly also capturing something of the fantasy of Gothic or Medieval revivalism, but also possibly expressing a renewed confidence in the episcopal office as one of civic influence and governance (more on that shortly). We find Henry Liddon, for example, using the language of rule and government in his sermon 'A Father in Christ': 'Not only does a father teach; he governs .... As the father of his diocese, the Bishop is its ruler. His right to rule is derived, not from a body of electors ... but from the character which he inherits from the Apostles.'[18] Bishop George Ridding (d. 1904, and not by any means a High Churchman, but a conservative Broad Churchman), first Bishop of Southwell, carried on his tomb the simple inscription 'Bishop – Pastor – *Ruler*'.[19] Likewise Bishop Ernest Wilberforce (d. 1907) of Chichester had on his tomb the description that he was 'for twenty-five years a bishop in the Church of God, during nearly twelve of which he ruled over the See of Chichester'. There are doubtless other examples.

Why did this language disappear in the twentieth century? It would be a mistake to assume that it simply represented a hierarchical reaction, a 'throwback' engineered by the alleged social conservatism of the Tractarians and others.[20] After all, many of those self-same bishops who were content to use the language of 'ruler' and 'rule' were also pioneers of representative church government and of the voice of the laity in church affairs. George Ridding, for example, was almost certainly one of the few pre-1914 bishops to adopt the

---

[18] H. P. Liddon, *Clerical Life and Work* (London: Longmans, 1895), p. 302.

[19] Author's emphasis. Cf. J. N. Morris, 'George Ridding and the Diocese of Southwell: a Study in the National Church Ideal', in *The Journal of Ecclesiastical History*, 61 (2010), pp. 125–42.

[20] Simon Skinner's monograph on *The Tractarians and the Condition of England* (Oxford: Oxford University Press, 2004) in any case qualifies the over-simplistic view of Tractarianism as reactionary.

use of the wider and more 'democratic' baptismal franchise for the Southwell Diocesan Conference – wider, that is, than the more restricted (but much more common) communicants' franchise.[21] In other ways Ridding was but one example of the widespread phenomenon of late-nineteenth-century reforming bishops, busily overseeing almost every aspect of the operations, administration and governance of their dioceses. 'Rule' did not necessarily imply autocracy, but rather responsible administration, albeit with a paternalistic face. That perhaps is a pointer to its decline in the 1920s and 1930s. 'Leadership', on the other hand, is a characteristically contemporary ascription, rarely found before the 1960s, which just happened to be – something confirmed belatedly by recent developments in the historiography of secularization – the decade in which churchgoing underwent a sharp, steep contraction.[22]

Thus consideration of the 'problem' of leadership – whether that means the problem of formulating it clearly, or the problem of discouraging inappropriate or inefficient forms – over a period of two hundred years requires elucidation of the cultural and ideological forms under which the particular individuals who were and are bishops, and who have themselves expected and experienced episcopal leadership, interpreted their theological task. Taking *that* as a prospectus yields a complex and sometimes surprising reading of what episcopacy has meant in the Church of England and other Anglican churches over the last two centuries or so, and this brief essay cannot do more than suggest an outline of key trends and factors, taking its lead particularly from the Church of England.

The early nineteenth century: Bishops, nobility and the confessional State

Early-nineteenth-century episcopacy, including the Irish episcopate as well as the English and Welsh (an exception perhaps being the Scottish), assumed an intimate relationship to the court and to Westminster, and to the social

---

[21] Morris, 'George Ridding', p. 140.
[22] C. G. Brown, *The Death of Christian Britain: Understanding Secularisation 1800-2000* (London: Routledge, 2001); Hugh McLeod, *The Religious Crisis of the 1960s* (Oxford: Oxford University Press, 2007); Nigel Yates, *Love Now, Pay Later? Sex and religion in the fifties and sixties* (London: SPCK, 2010). But note F. R Barry's *Church and Leadership* (London: SCM, 1945).

rhythms of the élites who constituted the 'political nation' in the pre-Reform (pre-1832) era. There were no suffragan or area bishops, and diocesan geography was essentially unchanged from the sixteenth century. Transport was often difficult, and winter was usually passed in London during the parliamentary season. Episcopal income varied wildly, from the fortunes of Durham, London, Canterbury and Winchester, to the relative poverty of St Asaph and Llandaff; but most bishops were aristocrats or gentry, with significant private income. This can hardly be surprising to those familiar with the novels of Jane Austen and, later, Anthony Trollope. But we should be wary of reading back that assumption into an earlier age. The dominance of the episcopate by the nobility and wealthy gentry was a relatively recent development. No less than eighteen of the seventy-three bishops who held office in the Church of England at some point under Charles II, for example, had been of 'plebeian' origin, compared with only five from the nobility.[23] By the second half of George III's reign the proportion was reversed, with just one out of thirty-two who served between 1790 and 1820 coming from plebeian origins, compared with nine from the nobility. Of course, it was consistently true that the majority of bishops were from gentry or, broadly, 'genteel' backgrounds; nevertheless the virtual disappearance of humble origins, and the growing prominence of aristocratic origins ('an aristocratic resurgence in the procurement of bishoprics', as Ravitch called it), are very striking.[24] By the end of the eighteenth century, the social composition of the English, Welsh and Irish episcopate had moved much closer to that of the French Church.

Why had this change taken place? Whatever else they were, bishops were a crucial element of the governance of pre-Reform Britain. But in the turbulent years of the sixteenth and seventeenth centuries, nobles generally sought other means than the Church for exercising power and influence, and the usefulness of bishops as servants of the Crown was underscored by the prominence of able but humble clergy who, through the grammar schools and Oxford and Cambridge, were able to acquire an education appropriate to their role. By the middle of the eighteenth century in two respects the ministry in general, and the episcopate in particular, had become of greater interest once again

---

[23] N. Ravitch, 'The Social Origins of French and English Bishops in the Eighteenth Century', *Historical Journal*, 8 (1965), pp. 309–25 at p. 319.

[24] Ravitch, 'Social Origins', p. 319.

to the nobility and wealthy gentry. First, in an economy marked by a steady rise in agricultural income the attractiveness of church livings (dependent particularly on income from glebe and tithe) as a rich field of patronage was markedly increased, and the ability of clergy in this period to hold livings in plurality if anything increased the attraction, even as in theory it made it possible for relatively poor clergy to 'roll up' income from several positions at once. For example, the great Joseph Butler (1692–1752), philosopher–Bishop and author of the *Analogy of Religion* (1736), held a prebendal stall at Rochester simultaneously with being rector of Stanhope in County Durham, and later bishop successively of Bristol and then Durham, and was Dean of St Paul's.[25] But, second, the emergence of cabinet government in the eighteenth century, and especially under the long premiership of Robert Walpole, underlined the usefulness of the bishops to successive ministries. This was the period of a commonly presumed division between a Whig episcopate and a Tory lower clergy; it is likely that things were never quite so simple, but it is certainly true that, after the death of Queen Anne, monarchs rapidly lost personal influence in the selection of bishops. According to Ravitch, thereafter the 'needs of the ruling ministry took precedence over the personal wishes of the monarch'.[26]

Appointment to the episcopate was thus exceptionally vulnerable to external or non-ecclesiastical influences. As the historian William Gibson has pointed out, in practice the eighteenth and early nineteenth centuries were subject to an almost unprecedented degree of lay influence: 'From patronage of a living to nomination to a see, laity dominated the Church.'[27] In the pre-Reform political system, the rhythms of episcopal life inevitably had to be accommodated to those of political life. In the late seventeenth and the eighteenth centuries, some 43 per cent of bishops held London parishes 'in plurality' with their sees; the effect of the Ecclesiastical Commissioners' reforms in the 1840s was to see this figure fall rapidly to around 20 per cent by the middle of the nineteenth century.[28] In the pre-Reform era, the widespread and mostly acceptable operation of clientage and patronage saw some – by modern standards – unusual routes to the episcopate. Thomas Burgess, later

---

[25] 'Joseph Butler', *ODNB*.
[26] Ravitch, 'Social Origins', p. 316.
[27] W. Gibson, 'The Professionalization of an Elite: the Nineteenth Century Episcopate', *Albion*, 23 (1991), pp. 459–82 at p. 460.
[28] Gibson, 'The Professionalization of an Elite', p. 471.

Bishop of Salisbury, was appointed to the See of St David by Prime Minister Addington, 'with whom he had been to school, but from whom he had not heard for almost thirty years'.[29] Burgess had only once been to Wales in his life.[30] Yet he proved an energetic and reforming bishop there. His later translation to Salisbury was almost certainly influenced by the fact that he had been domestic chaplain to Shute Barrington, Bishop of Salisbury, his patron and mentor; when Shute Barrington was translated to Durham, Burgess had followed him there and taken a lucrative prebend in the cathedral, a position he held until he could afford to relinquish it when appointed himself to Salisbury at the age of sixty-eight.[31]

Examples such as this indicate why a later generation of Evangelicals and Tractarians could depict the pre-Reform bishops as worldly, Whiggish and craven, but there is plenty of evidence to suggest that the Anglican episcopate pre-Reform was probably at best conservative Whig or even Tory in sympathy, and often High Church in doctrine.[32] It was also marked by significant examples of zealous, devout, reforming pastors, such as Burgess himself; whatever we think of the social world in which they lived, it did not prevent the emergence of able and energetic church leadership.[33] Posterity has cast the bishops who voted against the Great Reform Bill in 1831 as 'out of touch', but arguably their resistance to reform merely expressed the perfectly rational response of those whose conception of pastoral care included a significant element of moral censure and social order. In a controversial intervention in British social and political history, Jonathan Clark argued that the pre-reformed British constitution, far from being characterized by a somewhat cynical 'alliance' of Church and state as conceived by William Warburton in his 1736 pamphlet, in fact was predicated on a close and widely assumed connection between Trinitarian belief and social order, and that the established Church in particular provided the essential rationale for the particular form of political settlement (sometimes characterized as a 'confessional State') that had

---

[29] Ibid., p. 468.

[30] 'Thomas Burgess', *ODNB*.

[31] Ibid.

[32] Cf. R. Mackley, 'The Bishops and the Church of England in the Reign of George II: High Churchmanship and Orthodoxy', unpublished PhD thesis, University of Cambridge, 2016.

[33] Philip Tovey's recent study of confirmation in the Church of England in the eighteenth century has argued forcefully against the common supposition that the Georgian bishops were careless about catechizing and confirming: *Anglican Confirmation 1662-1820* (Farnham: Ashgate, 2014).

achieved almost a century of domestic peace.[34] One does not have to accept in its entirety Clark's reconfiguration of the stability and order of Britain's 'Ancient Regime' to acknowledge that the late Georgian bishops, whatever their social origins, were not simply obtuse or selfish defenders of the *status quo*, but believed profoundly that the Anglican settlement was intrinsic to domestic peace and human flourishing.[35] For them, episcopal office – still not at this stage commonly characterized with the word 'rule', a much more expansive concept – essentially involved the competent management of routine episcopal duties, the conscientious exercise of patronage and political influence, and evident loyalty to the monarchy and the constitutional settlement. This was precisely why Radical critics of the established Church in the early nineteenth century were so hostile to the bishops.[36]

Nineteenth-century transitions: Reform and renewal

By the mid-nineteenth century, the social and political world of the episcopate in Britain was being transformed by a variety of different pressures, driven not least by rapid economic and social change, and by the rapid growth of overseas Anglican churches through the process of colonial expansion. The Tractarian 'supercharging' of the concept of apostolic succession is what has attracted the attention of theologians. But far more momentous was the programme of Church reform initiated by the state in the wake of the Reform crisis (and with the collapse of Anglican hegemony), accompanied by the programme of diocesan reform so well delineated by Arthur Burns.[37] Contrary to the sweeping statements sometimes made by 'modernising' Anglicans today about Anglicanism before the late twentieth century, the Victorian clergy

---

[34] J. C. D. Clark, *English Society 1688-1832* (Cambridge: Cambridge University Press, 1985). For a re-reading of Warburton which downplays later, quasi-Utilitarian readings of his theory, see S. Taylor, 'William Warburton and the Alliance of Church and State', *Journal of Ecclesiastical History*, 43 (1992), pp. 271–86.

[35] It is interesting to note that this is, after all, precisely the theme of S. T. Coleridge's *On the Constitution of the Church and State* (1830), though it would hardly be credible to think that this was widely read by the Anglican hierarchy.

[36] For a subtle re-reading of the myth of the 'Greek-play bishop' as a Radical satire which has passed into the historical conventions, see R. A. Burns and C. Stray, 'The Greek-play bishop: polemic, prosopography, and nineteenth-century prelates', *Historical Journal*, 54 (2011), pp. 1013–38.

[37] Burns, *Diocesan Revival*.

were dynamic change-makers who engineered an extraordinary revival in the fortunes of the Church of England.[38] Reform saw the emergence of a more elevated and interventionist understanding of episcopal leadership. Reform of diocesan geography presupposed bishops who sought actively to control and manage their dioceses in person. Diocesan administration was rationalized and extended through the revival of the office of rural dean, the equalization of see income and the removal or diminution of interests (cathedral chapters, prebends, collegiate churches, non-resident clergy, lay patronage and sale of advowsons) which had previously acted as a check on the exercise of episcopal power.

The crucial turning point was the sequence of parliamentary acts which preluded church reform and transformed the Church of England from a sole partner of the state (at least in England, Wales and Ireland) into one among a number of denominations, albeit one still in an unusually close relationship to the state. The abolition of discriminatory legislation against Dissenters and Roman Catholics in 1828–9 (which enabled their entry formally into Parliament and also ended any pretence that Parliament could act as the 'lay synod' of the Church of England), the Reform Act of 1832, the Irish Church Temporalities Act of 1833, the Municipal Reform Act of 1834, and the Marriage and Registration Acts of 1836 (which established the civil registration of births, deaths and marriages), all these pieces of legislation taken together represented a constitutional revolution. Radical and Dissenting pressure for Disestablishment was given a fillip, and moved seriously on to the political agenda, being achieved in Ireland in 1869 and eventually in Wales in 1912 (enacted 1920), but never finally in England. The dismantling of key elements of the 'confessional State' largely ended the significance of the bishops as constitutional and court leaders, and ushered in a period of intense internal division in the Church of England, not least because of the fierce criticism unleashed by the Tractarian movement in opposition to Whig/Liberal reform of the Church and in favour of a stronger concept of the Church's intrinsic spiritual authority and autonomy.

---

[38] See, for example, T. Beeson, looking back on his time at Westminster Abbey and claiming that 'the changes that have taken place since [1951] have been enormous – perhaps greater than at any time since the sixteenth century, when the Abbey ceased to be a Benedictine monastery': *Window on Westminster* (London: SCM, 1998), p. 283.

In this context, reform of the Church of England had a paradoxical effect. The state interference bewailed by the Tractarians appeared to highlight the fragility of the Church, so that their clarion call to arms – 'magnify your office', as Newman urged the clerical readers of Tract 1, 'On the Ministerial Commission' – could be interpreted as a sign of anxiety that the Church was on the verge of being lost to hostile secular forces.[39] But in fact its effect was unquestionably to strengthen the Church, removing obvious abuses, renewing its power of independent action, and enhancing its historic disciplinary and regulatory mechanisms.[40] Arguments have abounded about the motivation of church reformers. Edward Norman, sharing some of the contempt of the Tractarians for 'modern-minded' bishops, has depicted them as shifting seamlessly through the common prejudices of the age, just as today it is alleged that bishops have capitulated to management theory.[41] Certainly some, like Bishop Blomfield of London, spoke the Utilitarian language of efficiency; most, however (and Blomfield himself in other moods) interpreted the diocesan revival as traditional renewal, drawing conveniently on Tractarian *ressourcement* when it suited them.[42] Lay patronage was a particularly significant index of changing sensibilities. Of the 10,693 benefices in England and Wales in 1821, some 6,619 were in the hands of private patrons, and just 1,301 in the hands of the bishops.[43] Running criticism of the patronage system concentrated mostly on the abuse of patronage sale, and not on the principle of private patronage per se, for private patronage – whether in the hands of individuals, or of trusts or corporate bodies such as colleges – was too useful a mechanism for placing family members in suitable livings (particularly in the early part of the century), or for ensuring that clergymen of the 'right' doctrinal persuasion were placed in parishes (as with, for example, the operation of the Evangelical Simeon Trust) to be abandoned altogether. However it was

---

[39] Newman, Tract 1, *On the Ministerial Commission.*

[40] One of the best studies of this process, based ultimately on detailed research in the diocese of Lincoln, is F. Knight, *The Nineteenth-Century Church and English Society* (Cambridge: Cambridge University Press, 1995).

[41] Cf. E. R. Norman, *Church and Society in England 1770-1970: A Historical Study* (Oxford: Clarendon, 1976); also, M. Percy, *The Future Shapes of Anglicanism: Currents, Contours, Charts* (London and New York: Routledge, 2017).

[42] Cf. R. A. Burns, '"Standing in the old ways": Historical legitimation of Church reform in the Church of England, c.1825-65', in R. N. Swanson (ed.), *The Church Retrospective: Studies in Church History*, 33 (Woodbridge: Boydell, 1997), pp. 407–22.

[43] M. J. D. Roberts, 'Private Patronage and the Church of England, 1800-1900', *Journal of Ecclesiastical History*, 32 (1981), pp. 199–223 at p. 202.

also a particularly useful tool for ensuring episcopal control of newly created benefices in urban areas. By the end of the century, even before the impact of major reform of patronage (ending their sale) in 1898, episcopal patronage had more than doubled.[44] Church reform enhanced the power of diocesan bishops, and ultimately began to curtail the influence of lay patrons. Here there was, then, an interesting – if fainter – echo of the centralizing power of the nineteenth-century papacy over episcopal and clerical appointments in the Catholic Church.[45]

And yet the authority of the diocesan bishops in the nineteenth century did not rest solely on the reform of ecclesiastical machinery, but in some measure on their social prestige, and on the paternalism that flowed through social relations in this period. Walter Bagehot famously observed that deference was the oil which ensured that the British constitutional machine ran smoothly, but the same argument could be applied to the Church: the bishop, unconsciously or not, accrued to himself an assumption of social influence which more than compensated for any post-1832 loss of income and actual political power.[46] This was as true in the churches in the overseas colonies as it was in Britain itself, for the colonial episcopate, small as it was for much of the nineteenth century, was almost entirely drawn from the Church of England, and from the same social echelons as were bishops in Britain. This was the period in which the language of 'rule' came to the fore. Bishops were municipal and civic leaders, and their local prominence depended in no small measure on their office, rather than on their birth and 'gentlemanly' qualities. By the late nineteenth century, the numbers of aristocracy entering the episcopate were in decline; they were being replaced by the middle classes. As Gibson has argued, this transition helped to ensure a fresh intake of capable and energetic bishops, for 'potential bishops had increasingly to prove their abilities in a way that was unnecessary when the bench of bishops was dominated by the aristocracy'.[47] Indeed it could even be argued that a certain 'professionalization' was under way, with the establishment of a common route to episcopal preferment through the career trajectory of Oxbridge Fellow to headmaster of a public

---

[44] Roberts, 'Private Patronage'.
[45] Cf. N. Atkin & F. Tallett, *Priests, Prelates and People: A History of European Catholicism since 1750* (Oxford: Oxford University Press, 2003), especially pp. 129–94.
[46] W. Bagehot, *The English Constitution* (London: Chapman & Hall, 1867).
[47] Gibson, 'The Professionalization of an Elite', p. 461.

school to bishop. Both Temples were excellent examples, Frederick (1821–1902; Fellow of Balliol College, Oxford; Headmaster of Rugby school, 1857–69; Archbishop of Canterbury 1896–1902) and William (1881–1944; Fellow of Queen's College, Oxford; Headmaster of Repton school, 1901–14; Archbishop of Canterbury 1942–4). The prevailing assumption here was presumably that a combination of proven intellectual ability and administrative competence was not a function of birth and background (Frederick Temple's birth was relatively humble, though of course one can hardly make the same claim about his son), as much as of experience in running corporate bodies, and especially educational ones. Another common 'track' was from fellowship to cathedral position, to bishopric. Gibson noted that the emergence of these more clearly defined career paths had the effect of raising significantly the average age of appointees to the bench, from the upper forties in the early nineteenth century to the mid-fifties by the end of the century.[48] Bishops were still also commonly regarded as national intellectual leaders, a phenomenon probably on the wane by the early twentieth century, though masked by the prominence of men such as Charles Gore and William Temple. According to Gibson, almost a third of the nineteenth-century episcopate was drawn from men whose first post after ordination was either a college fellowship or a teaching position.[49] That figure would rise significantly if subsequent posts before episcopal appointment were taken into account.

Reform and its effects cemented the episcopate's involvement in local and county affairs. Particularly in the mid- and late nineteenth century, before the construction of the Welfare State, the prominence of philanthropy and the ideology of voluntarism ensured that churches were actively engaged in large-scale and widespread programmes designed to ameliorate homelessness, ill-health, destitution and lack of education. The patronage and leadership ('rule') of the bishop were objects much sought after by Anglican charities, as well as by parishes promoting 'church extension' (the contemporary term for building new churches and creating new parishes). That is why the location of the cathedral in the newly created sees was often a source of much debate, with a

---

[48] Ibid., p. 476.
[49] Ibid., p. 469.

strong current of opinion in favour of choosing the county town.[50] It is also the reason why episcopal appointment continued to be a prized aspect of Crown and prime ministerial patronage, even as the bishops' political usefulness to particular administrations began to decline with political reform and the widening parliamentary franchise.[51] The list of qualities that Gladstone desired in a bishop is testimony to the importance of the work he considered they had to perform: they included 'piety, learning, eloquence, administrative strength, energy, tact, allegiance to the Church, equitable spirit, knowledge of the world, accomplishment, ability to work with other bishops, legal understanding, circumspection, courage, maturity, and [significantly] "Liberal" sentiments'.[52] Prime ministers could get it wrong, all the same, if they were not attentive to church matters: Palmerston apparently appointed Robert Bickersteth in error to the see of Ripon in place of his father, and was then surprised to discover that Robert was just forty years of age, unusually young in a period when appointments to the bench of men in their sixties and even seventies were not uncommon.[53]

Historians may have used the term 'professionalization' to describe changes in the ordained ministry in the nineteenth century, pointing to the foundation of the new theological colleges and the reform of theological education, to the reform of the administration of clerical discipline, and to new and distinct concepts of pastoral work as exemplified in the increasing number of manuals devoted to parish and pastoral work.[54] But one has to be sceptical about how far this can be pushed. 'Professionalization' is a wonderfully plastic term that can be applied to developments in the ministry in almost any period.

---

[50] P. S. Morrish, 'County and urban dioceses: Nineteenth-century discussion on ecclesiastical geography', *Journal of Ecclesiastical History*, 26 (1975), pp. 279–300; id., 'Parish-church cathedrals, 1836-1931: Some problems and their solutions', *Journal of Ecclesiastical History*, 49 (1998), pp. 434–64.

[51] There are a number of detailed studies of the exercise of ecclesiastical patronage in the nineteenth century: see N. Scotland, *'Good and proper men': Lord Palmerston and the bench of bishops* (Cambridge: James Clarke, 2000); W. Gibson, 'Disraeli's church patronage', *Anglican and Episcopal History*, 61 (1992), pp. 197–210; W. Gibson, '"A Great Excitement": Gladstone and Church Patronage 1868-1890', in J. Loades (ed.), *Gladstone* (Bangor, 1992).

[52] Gibson, 'The Professionalization of an Elite', p. 478, citing his own article, '"A Great Excitement": Gladstone and Church Patronage 1868-1890', in J. Loades (ed.), *Gladstone* (Bangor, 1992).

[53] Gibson, 'The Professionalization of an Elite', p. 476; however, either Gibson's source is in error here, or Palmerston's mistake was even more egregious, since Bickersteth's father had actually died a year earlier: 'Robert Bickersteth', *ODNB*.

[54] Cf. the discussion in A. Russell, *The Clerical Profession* (London: SPCK, 1980); also, R. O'Day, 'The men from the ministry', in G. Parsons (ed.), *Religion in Victorian Britain, vol. 2: Controversies* (Manchester: Open University, 1988), pp. 258–79.

Definite changes did take place in the nineteenth century in the assumptions underpinning the measurement of episcopal suitability, however. By the mid-nineteenth century, the gradual dismantling of the system of clientage and patronage which had underpinned the operation not only of the Church, but also of the armed forces and the law, now meant that clergy who were ambitious were encouraged to work hard to prove themselves. Gibson again cites, as a case in point, Edward Bickersteth's bombardment of Gladstone with pamphlets, books, tracts and sermons to secure his attention.[55] Another example is William Boyd Carpenter's relentless preaching around: some 70 times in one year in pulpits other than his own (though 125 times in his own).[56]

By the end of the century, the epitome of the diocesan bishop was a figure such as the relentlessly energetic George Ridding. Apart from his amateur interests in philology and archaeology, and his frequent travel on the continent and in the Middle East, Ridding showed an active concern in practically every possible aspect of his diocese's church life. 'Church work', he said, 'is the spread of temperance, and purity, and honesty, and kindness. I should like to know the agencies in each parish, to promote mental, moral and social advance.'[57] He spent much of his own considerable private fortune on church extension in the new diocese of Southwell, and patronized charitable agencies across Nottinghamshire. According to his wife, he was proud of his attempts to intervene in industrial disputes in the county, including the great coal lock-out of 1893, the 'Coal War'.[58] This was a far cry from the courtly, noble bishops of the previous century.

Conciliarity and collegiality: bishops and the representative system

So far, much of what I have described applies principally to the relationship of bishops to their dioceses. But if we want to broaden out the scope of this analysis, and look ultimately at the particular development in episcopal

---

[55] Gibson, 'The Professionalization of an Elite', p. 467.
[56] Gibson, 'The Professionalization of an Elite', p. 471.
[57] G. Ridding, *The Church and Commonwealth: The Visitation Charges* (London: Edward Arnold, 1906), p. 14.
[58] L. Ridding, *George Ridding, Schoolmaster and Bishop* (London: Edward Arnold, 1908), pp. 265–8.

authority represented by the Lambeth Conference, we have to consider questions of collegiality and conciliarity (bishops working in collaboration with other bishops, and with other clergy and laity). Anglican episcopal ministry in the early nineteenth century was exercised in a way that would seem autocratic, independent and even individualistic today. The bishops of the Church of England (still at this period including Wales) certainly met each other socially and in the House of Lords, corresponded with each other from time to time, and generally, coming mostly as they did from similar social backgrounds, shared a wide range of attitudes and presuppositions. Indeed, with the bishops of the Church of Ireland they were commonly described by others – including critics as well as supporters – in terms that suggested a common identity. Bishops were expected to attend court functions as bishops, and not just as prominent individuals. The *Morning Post*, for example, reported the bishops of Chester, Exeter, Winchester, London, Lincoln, Clogher and Bangor as attending the King's levee – a morning reception at which ambassadors, nobles, senior officers of the armed forces, among others were presented to the King – at Carlton House in January 1821; there was nothing unusual or exceptional about their attendance, and reports such as this were routine in the newspapers of the time.[59] So there were clear social expectations of the bishops. Yet there were no active mechanisms by which the episcopate could act in concert to consider church business, to formulate policy, or to respond to criticism or challenge. The common means by which bishops made their views known to the clergy and laity of their dioceses was the episcopal 'charge', a pastoral letter read aloud at the beginning of a formal visitation (that is, an inspection of parishes and diocesan organizations) and frequently published afterwards. But the 'charge' was personal and individual. Only when various episcopal 'charges' were compared was it possible to tell if anything like a 'common mind' existed on any one issue. Perhaps the most famous example from the period was the series of episcopal charges that condemned John Henry Newman's attempt in 1841 to argue, in the ninetieth of the *Tracts for the Times*, that it was possible to reconcile Roman Catholic doctrine with the Thirty-Nine Articles of Religion.

This incapacity to determine anything collectively was increasingly exposed as a profound weakness by the process of church reform that governments

---

[59] *The Morning Post*, 27 January 1821.

initiated through the Ecclesiastical Commissioners in the 1830s, and carried through Parliament thereafter. Bishops needed to consult each other and their clergy, formally; in time they began to see that they also needed to consult the laity. In the Church of England, the first step towards the emergence of a representative system was the reconvening of Convocation of the Province of Canterbury, the clerical assembly suspended since the early eighteenth century, in 1852. Additionally, developments in the wider Anglican world had their influence. Colonial bishops such as William Broughton of Australia and George Selwyn of New Zealand realized that the cluster of assumptions, customs and institutions that enabled the Church of England to function as it did simply could not carry the same force in the colonial context, and the Church–state link likewise simply could not apply: the new churches of Australia and New Zealand, and eventually elsewhere too, required their own form of governance, and their own assemblies. As a result, diocesan 'synods', or assemblies, were formed, echoing the clerical synods of the early Church, but with a modern twist – the representation of laity too, with quasi-parliamentary systems of voting and representation. By the early twentieth century, something like the modern representative church system had come into being, consisting of levels of council or synod, from parish up through rural (or 'area') deanery, and archdeaconry, to diocese and Province.

In the long run, this representative system undoubtedly eroded the ability of bishops to conceive of themselves as 'rulers' of their dioceses. It had always been true of course that a bishop depended on the willingness of his clergy and people to carry out his policy. In practice, for most bishops – not only in the British Anglican churches, but further afield too – this had meant that it was very difficult to carry through a consistent policy in every detail. The more charismatic and energetic bishops could hope to effect real change, if they judged astutely the mood of their people; but bishops were never the equivalent of a modern CEO (nor are they now), with power to hire and fire at will. In the sixteenth and seventeenth centuries, the Church's own courts could exert some discipline, fining people or imposing other penalties for various offences, but the church courts were falling into disuse in Britain by the mid-eighteenth century, and were rarely summoned in the nineteenth. The sheer challenge of raising the vast sums of money and manpower required to power church growth in Britain and in the colonies in the nineteenth century obliged bishops to work collaboratively with rich and influential laity, and with other institutions as well as politicians, and ultimately to reflect as much as to command the values of ordinary churchgoers. But the actual effects of the growth of synodical power were masked at first, arguably, by the deference that pervaded British society well into the twentieth century, both 'at home' and overseas: since bishops were, as we have seen, drawn predominantly from the upper middle and upper classes, and often (like George Ridding) independently wealthy, they continued to command social influence accordingly. Nonetheless, synods and assemblies inevitably became the dominant means through which episcopal authority was actually exercised.

By the early twentieth century, the growth of this representative system throughout the Anglican Communion had begun to encourage a much more collegial, collective notion of church administration and governance. Issues of importance for a church were brought forward for consultation and discussion. Bishops were – understandably – increasingly reluctant to act unilaterally. Through the synodical system, they could draw on wider lay and clerical support, fund specialized bureaucracies, and if need be summon specialized commissions to advise on particular problems, or to formulate policy. A straw in the wind was the summoning of the first Doctrine Commission in the Church of England by Archbishop Randall Davidson, which was chaired by William Temple, and reported after some fifteen years of deliberation in 1938. But developments such as this were not restricted to the Church of England. In Australia, it was through a committee appointed by General Synod that the Australian Church studied social welfare and the political contest of the 1930s, reporting on *Christian Revolution and Social Welfare* in 1934.[60] By this means, it was possible to test and develop something like a 'common mind' on issues of importance for the episcopate, and for the Church at large.

On the widest stage of all, the worldwide Anglican Communion, the crucial development had occurred earlier, nonetheless, in the summoning of the first Lambeth Conference in 1867, largely in response to a division in the Church of South Africa over the 'liberal' biblical interpretation of J. W. Colenso.[61]

---

[60] I. Breward, 'Anglicanism in Australia and New Zealand', in J. Morris (ed.), *The Oxford History of Anglicanism. IV: Global Western Anglicanism, c.1910-present* (Oxford: Oxford University Press, 2017), p. 341.
[61] Cf. A. M. G. Stephenson, *The First Lambeth Conference* (London: SPCK, 1967); also id., *Anglicanism and the Lambeth Conferences* (London: SPCK, 1978).

Archbishop Longley famously resisted the pressure of some bishops to turn the conference into an executive synod that could formally censure Colenso; it was to be a means of consultation, a conference, only. And so it has remained. Bishops assemble for the Lambeth Conference approximately every ten years and it would be wrong to think that because the Lambeth Conference is not an executive or legislative body, it has little authority. As an expression of the mind of the assembled bishops of the Communion, it has considerable moral authority, as well as whatever authority its resolutions may be given within each participating church. In the twentieth century, the collegiality the Lambeth Conference represents has been underlined by the formation of the Anglican Consultative Council (ACC), and the occasional meetings of the Primates of the provinces of the Anglican Communion.[62] Perhaps the most important point – for the purposes of this chapter – is that the Lambeth Conferences, like the general development of representative assemblies in Anglicanism, have underlined the growing importance of consultation and collegiality for bishops' ministry and leadership. Beginning in the mid-nineteenth century, this growing emphasis on *conciliarity* – the principle according to which authority in the Church is exercised first and foremost through collective, conciliar means of organization – in Anglicanism has subtly modified bishops' understanding of what exactly their authority and leadership actually entails, persuading them of the importance of acting in concert, not alone.

Asserting that the authority of the Lambeth Conference is essentially a moral authority does not by any means imply that it is somehow light or easily ignored – far from it. The Anglican churches, after all, are voluntary bodies. Even the Church of England, maintaining as it does an 'established' status, and therefore a degree of legal or statutory authority unique in the Anglican Communion, can give its bishops little actual power to *compel* their clergy to carry out diocesan policy to the letter; much depends on creating and maintaining trust between bishop, clergy and people. If the resolutions of the Lambeth Conferences carry no legislative weight as such in the Communion – and after all, the Communion is not a centralized, 'command' structure, but a federation of autonomous churches – nonetheless the fact that

---

[62] On the development of these instruments of unity and communion, see C. Podmore, 'The Development of the Instruments of Communion', in Morris, *Oxford History of Anglicanism. IV*, pp. 271–302.

the bishops of the Communion can meet, discuss and formulate a common mind on particular issues gives their views immense influence within the Communion as well as their own churches. And the same principle holds good for provincial and diocesan synods. Thus there is a correlation between the growing trends towards conciliar modes of consultation and action in Anglicanism, and the decline of the kind of social and political influence – the 'rule' – wielded by bishops at the beginning of the nineteenth century. In summary, moral authority came to fill the gap left by declining civic and social authority. But this in turn raises the question as to how, in the twentieth century, bishops came to understand and articulate this new situation?

The twentieth century: Democracy, equality, decline

If George Ridding of Southwell is testimony to a powerful model of socially engaged episcopacy, educationally privileged and sustained in influence by strong if invisible threads of social deference, in turn the social world which underpinned this mode of exercising episcopacy was changing. In Britain, the rise of the Labour movement, reform of local government and welfare, above all the democratization of parliamentary government – all this in time forced a dramatic change in the scope of a bishop's authority and in the degree of influence he could exercise. The participation of many of the English and Welsh bishops in the Christian Social Union, a body formed in 1889 for the study of contemporary social and industrial problems, and much mocked by Edward Norman ('central, respectable, and vague'), was a sign of their growing awareness of how fast the world was changing around them.[63] It was precisely because of his realization that the arrival of mass democracy required the Church to transform its governance that William Temple, the leading figure in the reform-minded 'Life and Liberty' movement during the First World War, pressed for the Church of England to adopt a baptismal franchise (i.e. the widest possible franchise compatible with professed Trinitarian belief) for the new system of church governance formalized by the Enabling Act of 1919, in preference to the confirmation franchise urged by Anglo-Catholics.

---

[63] Norman, *Church and Society*, p. 180.

The Church Assembly that was subsequently created in fact never fulfilled Temple's hope for mass working-class participation in the Church of England. Nevertheless, even as they seemingly endorsed the principles of the new mass democracy within the Church itself, in a wider sphere the bishops were gradually losing significant political influence. This was perhaps acutely symbolized by the failure of the Prayer Book revision proposals in Parliament in 1927 and 1928, coming as it did in the wake of almost a generation's hard work developing and refining liturgical revision.

Much has been made – rightly so – of the continuing power of Christianity between the wars to shape and articulate the aspirations and identities of the nation, both in Britain itself, and also in Australasia and Canada.[64] This is particularly evident in the concept of 'Christian civilisation' which would help to express growing distaste for fascism, and especially Nazism, up to and into the Second World War, and which featured so tellingly in Churchill's wartime speeches. This persisting influence – characterized by Callum Brown as the 'salvation economy' – can be traced even in the new suburbs of London, where churchgoing remained a significant feature of local life.[65] It coexisted, however, with troubling evidence of a gradual decline in active church membership in most of the mainstream denominations, including Anglicanism, a decline echoed elsewhere in Western Anglicanism, albeit with local variation.[66] It also helped to conceal a diminution of the social and political standing of the bishops. Nothing illustrates this better, perhaps, than the mostly ill-fated efforts of bishops to intervene in industrial disputes. Famously, Bishop Westcott had 'broken the impasse' in the Durham miners' strike of 1892 by inviting both sides to his house – an incident commemorated in the stained glass of All Saints' Church, next to Westcott House in Cambridge.[67] The efforts of William Temple – then Bishop of Manchester – and others to mediate in the General Strike in 1926 were controversial and came to nothing. But even

---

[64] Cf. M. Grimley, *Citizenship, Community, and the Church of England: Liberal Anglican Theories of the State between the Wars* (Oxford: Oxford University Press, 2004).

[65] R. A. Walford, *The Growth of 'New London' in Suburban Middlesex (1918-1945) and the Response of the Church of England* (New York: Edwin Mellen, 2007).

[66] C. D. Field, 'Gradualist or Revolutionary Secularization? A Case Study of Religious Belonging in Inter-War Britain 1918-1939', *Church History and Religious Culture*, 93 (2013), pp. 57–93; cf. also Breward, 'Anglicanism in Australia and New Zealand', and S. A. Kujawa-Holbrook, 'North American Anglicanism: Competing Factions, Creative Tensions, and the Liberal-Conservative Impasse', in Morris, *Oxford History of Anglicanism, IV*.

[67] O. Chadwick, *The Victorian Church, Part Two: 1860-1901* (2nd edn, London: SCM, 1972), p. 285.

more tellingly, the previous year, during the national coalminers' strike, the Durham miners, mistaking the Dean of Durham, James Welldon, for the Bishop, Hensley Henson, nearly threw him into the River Wear.[68] Above all, it was perhaps the perceived role of Archbishop Lang in the abdication crisis of 1936, and in particular his apparent criticism of the abdicating king for abandoning his duty, which ended for a couple of generations the capacity of bishops to intervene decisively in national affairs.[69]

Notwithstanding their gradual marginalization from social and political life (and it *was* gradual, but by no means smooth), the bishops remained, like most political leaders (bar the new Labour Party) predominantly a private school and Oxbridge-educated elite well into the middle or even late-twentieth century. Yet a shared social background and education did not necessarily produce passivity or obsequiousness in the face of the state. Early- and mid-twentieth-century bishops viewed themselves as leaders of Christian conscience, a point underscored by Matthew Grimley's study of Anglican theories of the state, and by Andrew Chandler's discussion of the bishops and saturation bombing.[70] As Chandler notes, 'However influenced by the attitudes of their social class the bishops may have been, and however many landed connections they might enjoy, they remained conscious that as Christians they must justify themselves by principle, at every turn, and not by the opportunity of the moment or the advantage of party.'[71] That was why many of them perceived the anti-Jewish policies of the Nazis to be 'evil', and they were likely to come to aristocratic parties to which Ribbentrop had been invited only if they could 'remonstrate that the anti-Jewish policies of the German government were wicked'.[72]

The sociologist David Morgan, in a study which to some extent complements that by William Gibson covering the nineteenth century, has sketched three main phases in the development of the modern episcopate.[73] Up to around the middle of the nineteenth century, according to Morgan, the bishop was very

---

[68] O. Chadwick, *Hensley Henson: A Study in the Friction between Church and State* (2nd edn., Norwich: Canterbury Press, 1994), pp. 166–7.

[69] Cf. R. Beaken, *Cosmo Lang: Archbishop in War and Crisis* (London: Tauris, 2012).

[70] Grimley, *Citizenship, Community, and the Church of England*; A. Chandler, 'The Church of England and the Obliteration Bombing of Germany in the Second World War', *English Historical Review*, 108 (1993), pp. 920–46.

[71] Chandler, 'The Church of England and the Obliteration Bombing', p. 923.

[72] Ibid.

[73] D. H. J. Morgan, 'The Social and Educational Background of Anglican Bishops – Continuities and Changes', *The British Journal of Sociology*, 20 (1969), pp. 295–310.

much the member 'of a broad upper class elite, expected to spend much of his time in London and perhaps to devote some attention to classical scholarship. There was a relatively loose, minimal definition of the formal aspects of his episcopal role.'[74] On this last point – even noting the persistence of the 'Greek play' myth in Morgan's account – Morgan was admittedly too negative: the recent tide of historical revisionism has sharply refocused attention on the way in which eighteenth- and early-nineteenth-century bishops sought to fulfil conscientiously the inherited conception of responsibilities, which were by no means minimal or loose. However, as Morgan noted, and as I demonstrated above, a shift did take place in the Victorian era, in which 'we see the rise of the "busy bishop", one who was active in the affairs and the administration of the Church yet one who was still attached to "gentlemanly" values.'[75] 'Gentlemanly values' here is plainly shorthand for that world of deference and patrician responsibility or 'rule' described above. According to Morgan, a further shift took place in the course of the twentieth century, by which 'we see the growth of the "professional" bishop, required to spend much time in diocesan administration, sitting on committees and participating in commissions, attentive to the concerns of the Church and her mission rather than to any external considerations.'[76] This is a particularly weak characterization of the process of change, for these three phases blended into each other, and were by no means mutually exclusive.

But Morgan nonetheless had a point. Some bishops continued to operate along 'older' lines even as the world around them was changing. A surprising example, perhaps, was George Bell (1883–1958; Bishop of Chichester 1929–1958) who, for all his upbringing in the reign of Victoria, is more conventionally considered in the light of his ecumenical commitments, his friendship with Dietrich Bonhoeffer and his opposition to saturation bombing, all causes which have tended to position him as one of the most prominent of twentieth-century 'modern' bishops in the Church of England. Andrew Chandler has claimed that Bell's humanitarian interests to some extent put him at odds with the 'growing tendency [of bishops] in the church to concentrate primarily

---

[74] Morgan, 'The Social and Educational Background', p. 307.
[75] Ibid., p. 308.
[76] Morgan, 'The Social and Educational Background', p. 308.

on its own affairs and to organize its structures more efficiently'.[77] Yet Bell's characteristic habits of mind, and his modes of administration, were typically those of the late nineteenth and early twentieth century. John Moorman (1905–1989; Bishop of Ripon 1959–1975), reading Ronald Jasper's life of Bell, made a wondering marginal note about Bell's constant habit of writing round to a large number of people before taking any decision: 'Note GB's passion for writing round for advice. Before making any major decision he took soundings from all sorts of busy people. Did he learn this from R Davidson? Why did he do it? Was it because once he had made a decision he never went back on it? Or because he wasn't really sure of himself? No one behaves like this nowadays.'[78] Episcopal leadership – which had always been in some sense consensual (see Bell's habit) – was losing the platform of social deference and paternalism on which bishops had relied in the past; habits of consultation had to change accordingly.

Also changing were the social background and status of the bishops and of other senior clergy. Morgan, again, notes some striking trends, which may be reinforced by more familiar books by Towler and Coxon, and Russell.[79] The falling attractiveness of the Church as a horizon of ambition for the gentry and aristocracy accompanied accelerating educational opportunities for the lower-middle and working classes from mid-century. Whereas some 33 per cent of the bench were sons of aristocracy and gentry in 1860, this figure had fallen to just 2 per cent by 1960; by contrast, the proportion of those with professional fathers had risen from 61 per cent in 1860 to 70 per cent a hundred years later, with the increase in sons of clergy particularly noticeable, from 18 to 54 per cent.[80] Even in 1960, however, Morgan could find no bishop whose father could definitely be described as a manual worker.[81] His conclusion bears quotation here: 'Speaking generally, we may characterize the change in the backgrounds of bishops as depicting a shift from a situation where the episcopacy was part of a broader social elite to one where it is a more narrowly

[77] 'George Bell', *ODNB*.
[78] Notes in Moorman's copy of R. C. D. Jasper, *George Bell, Bishop of Chichester* (London: Oxford University Press, 1967), in author's possession.
[79] R. Towler and A. P. M. Coxon, *The Fate of the Anglican Clergy* (London: Macmillan, 1979); Russell, *The Clerical Profession*.
[80] Morgan, 'The Social and Educational Background', p. 297.
[81] Ibid., p. 298.

defined ecclesiastical elite.'[82] In the 1860s, according to Morgan, six bishops had been educated at Eton; by 1960, just one had been.[83] The trend Morgan described has not been reflected in ongoing change, arguably, though statistics about social background are not easy to come by. In 2014, in the wake of the appointment of Justin Welby as Archbishop of Canterbury, the *Church Times* carried out a brief survey of the educational background of the bench of bishops, finding that nearly 50 per cent had been educated privately, with just 13 per cent having attended a comprehensive school.[84] Nevertheless, even this was a noteworthy shift away from the situation a hundred years earlier.

It may often seem today as if the Church of England – and I suspect that this could be extended to Anglicanism in some other parts of the Communion – functions as a traditional, hierarchical institution, conservative in outlook and led mostly by people drawn from a relatively small social and educational elite. But in fact anyone occupying a position of responsibility in the Church, whether lay or ordained, whether senior or junior, has to operate in a context in which authority is being constantly challenged and therefore constantly negotiated. Bishops are no longer significant shapers of public opinion; they are just one source of opinion among a bewildering variety of voices. Until the rapid cultural changes which began in the 1960s and 1970s, bishops were generally among the foremost guardians of public morality (hence the outrage at Bishop John Robinson's stance in the *Lady Chatterley's Lover* trial, when he defended D. H. Lawrence's allegedly 'pornographic' novel on the grounds that the love it portrayed was beautiful, and even holy). But that is no longer the case – and after all, what *is* 'public morality' today? What bishops are able to say with authority, and especially the question of who will listen to them with sympathy when they do speak out, has been immensely complicated by the inexorable rise of the 'rights' agenda. If the arguments over gay marriage show anything, it is the near-impossibility nowadays of the Church of England shaping public opinion on a question widely perceived to be one of equality before the law. Nor are bishops automatically perceived to be authoritative teachers of religious truth: the transformation in the life of universities since the Robbins report (1963), and the rise of religious studies

---

[82] Ibid., p. 299.
[83] Ibid., p. 299.
[84] *Church Times*, 5 September 2014.

and 'secular' theology departments, have significantly shifted the focus of critical, constructive theology away from ecclesial preoccupations.

Of course, what I am describing here are trends and normative influences, rather than sharp and easily identifiable changes. Much of what constitutes episcopal ministry today would be recognizable to the nineteenth-century episcopate. Morgan, again, attributed elements of continuity in the episcopal elite to the nature and understanding of episcopal authority as defined for example by the Ordinal and by the authorized liturgy of the Church of England, whereas change in the sense that he was describing he attributed to changing roles.[85] But this distinction of role and ideas is questionable. Morgan's article was a product of its time, and arguably read a quasi-Marxist 'base' and 'superstructure' model into the history of the episcopate. The roles *have* changed, as we have seen, but so have the ideas: the Church of England has seen ongoing efforts since the 1960s to reconceive, reform and redirect its understanding of what formally constitutes episcopal ministry. One could begin to look at that, for example, by considering the torrent of reports on ministry – including episcopal ministry – since the 1960s, triggered partly by arguments over the ordination of women, and partly by the exigencies of ecumenical dialogue and ecumenical relations. The Paul report on *The Deployment and Payment of the Clergy* (1964), which perhaps began this long process of ongoing reflection, hinted at the challenges that the Church of England would face in the process of reconceiving ministry in the years to come when it acknowledged that the ministry was indeed a profession: 'Whatever else the ordained ministry is, it is also a profession. Like other free professions, it has the means of controlling entry into its ranks, of regulating ethical practices, of determining standards and pressing for their maintenance.'[86]

What underlay the declining social and political prominence of bishops in England was the rapidly changing context of Christianity in Britain since the war. Classic theories of secularization have come under heavy attack in recent decades, and it is no longer possible to talk with any confidence about a consensus view. In summary, the 'classical' theory of secularization, illustrated, for example, in Bryan Wilson's *Religion in Secular Society* (1966) and which assumed an intrinsic link between modernization and religious decline, was

---

[85] Morgan, 'The Social and Educational Background', p. 305.
[86] Leslie Paul, *The Deployment and Payment of the Clergy* (Church Information Office, 1964), p. 89.

increasingly questioned from the 1980s on, when its statistical fragility was pointed out: churchgoing rose in Britain for much of the nineteenth century, stabilized in the early twentieth century, and did not fall significantly until the 1960s.[87] Argument continues about the trajectory of churchgoing in Britain in the twentieth century, and in particular about how to interpret the observable trends.[88] While historians have noted the persisting ability of bishops, among other religious leaders, to challenge government policy on a range of issues from the 1980s (the decade of *Faith in the City*) to the present, they have also noted the thinning-out of knowledge of key tenets of Christian faith and morality in the population at large, at the same time registering the growing presence of other communities of faith.

Conclusion

Whether consciously or not, the sheer fact that the Church of England now operates in a much more religiously pluralist context than was the case two or three generations back has conditioned the growing adoption of the language of the market to describe the mission of the Church. Similar changes could be observed in other Anglican churches of the 'global north', especially in Australasia. It is true that the conditions and challenges of the churches of the 'global south' are quite different, both because of their context as churches that have moved out of colonial government, and because their experience in the late twentieth century has been characterized not by decline, but by growth. Until the mid-twentieth century, the colonial episcopate was almost exclusively British in upbringing and education, but that has ceased to be the case in the 'Global South'. Some at least of what I have described is relevant even here, nonetheless, and particularly the impact of Anglicanism conciliarism. In that sense, an assessment of the impact of the Lambeth Conference on Anglicanism must reckon with the effect that Anglican conciliarism has had

---

[87] B. R. Wilson, *Religion in Secular Society: A Sociological Comment* (London: Watts, 1966). For a critical overview of the literature on secularization theory, see J. N. Morris, 'Secularization and Religious Experience: Arguments in the Historiography of Modern British Religion', *Historical Journal*, 55 (2012), pp. 195–219.

[88] Cf. Brown, *Death of Christian Britain*; also S. J. D. Green, *The Passing of Protestant England: Secularisation and Social Change, c.1920-1960* (Cambridge: Cambridge University Press, 2010).

on the ways in which bishops have been obliged to exercise their ministry even within their own dioceses, let alone in concert with other bishops. Yet this is a sorely neglected matter. In the Anglican West, arguments about church leadership mostly reflect both a conviction that mission might be facilitated by the selective adoption of business models, and an anxiety that those models are an inappropriate or ineffective basis for the exercise of episcopacy. What this chapter has sought to demonstrate is that close study of the history of the episcopate helps us to see not only the evolution of its exercise of authority through several perceptible stages over the last two hundred years, but also the pervasive influence of a vast range (and this piece has no more than scratched the surface) of factors that have arisen from the embedding of the institutions of the Church in the social history of the nation. Bishops may have lost much of the social prestige which once sustained their practical exercise of authority, just as the intricate patterns of social relationship which constituted British – and aspects of colonial – society have mutated and diversified bewilderingly over the last two centuries, but their task of pastoring, encouraging and challenging the Christian community continues to be shaped, as it always was, by a delicate fusion of traditional, liturgical, Scriptural and yet also social and political norms, and a distinct role in its own right.

All in all, the evolution of episcopal leadership has been the result of a complex matrix of factors which include many things hidden from the usual theological discussion, not least as they bear on the social, political and economic conditions in which episcopacy has to be exercised. If this points to anything concrete, it is the capacity to respond to the sheer complexity and diversity demanded of senior clergy by the world in which we live. A single or preferred model of episcopal leadership is unlikely to gain much traction.

8

Before and After Lambeth I.10:
The Lambeth Conference on
Sex and Marriage

Andrew Goddard

Debates over marriage and sexuality, more specifically the proper response to homosexual people and behaviour and to those in same-sex unions, have bitterly divided much of the Anglican Communion for nearly twenty years.[1] In contrast to most other Anglican debates, a specific resolution of the Lambeth Conference – Resolution 1.10 of the 1998 Lambeth Conference and its reception, and particularly non-reception, in parts of the Communion – has played a central role in these conflicts.[2] Although 1998 was only the third Lambeth Conference to make direct reference to homosexuality, wider issues and debates about marriage and sexuality have been discussed and pronounced upon in almost all Lambeth Conferences. This chapter seeks to set recent debates in that wider context. From the late nineteenth century and throughout the twentieth century the pattern is one of dialogue and development as an existing understanding of marriage and right sexual conduct faces the challenges of social developments which reject or undermine that understanding. In the face of these challenges, the bishops at the Lambeth Conference wrestle with how to respond and, in particular, whether (and, if so, how) the church's practice should adapt to and accommodate new social realities, and whether the church should reformulate its teaching. After a

---

[1] The language of 'sexuality' is used in this chapter very generally to refer to all matters relating to humans as sexual beings (e.g. their sexual desires and behaviour) as a matter distinct from but related to the institution of marriage as a particular form of sexual relationship.

[2] For a discussion, see Andrew Goddard, 'Sexuality and Communion', in Mark D. Chapman, Sathianathan Clarke and Martyn Percy (eds), *Oxford Handbook of Anglican Studies* (Oxford: Oxford University Press, 2015), pp. 413–26.

chronological overview which steps back and summarizes Lambeth discussions over the fourteen conferences, the core, consistent elements of Conference teaching are outlined. The Conferences' work in relation to three recurring challenges – polygamy, divorce and contraception – is then examined before returning to the current controversy over homosexuality and considering it in the light of these other areas.

I Lambeth Conferences on marriage and sexuality – 1867–2008

The Lambeth Conferences are best known for their resolutions. Those referring to marriage and sexuality are the focus here but need to be read and interpreted in the light of the more detailed reports produced by a specific committee of bishops within the conference. These add theological depth and context to the resolutions' brief wording. In addition, most conferences have issued an encyclical letter and its treatment of subjects is also often illuminating. Finally, there are wider debates both within and beyond the Conference. The table in the Appendix traces the naming, positioning, focus and relative importance of matters relating to marriage and sexuality across the fourteen Conferences.

Despite Bishop Colenso's more accommodating stance towards baptizing polygamists being an element in the controversy behind the first Conference,[3] this and other matters relating to marriage did not gain detailed attention until the third conference, in 1888, when the focus was on purity, divorce and polygamy.[4] The report on purity was reissued in 1897. From the start of the twentieth century until 1968 these and other subjects were a significant part of the next five conferences. In 1908 – addressing the subject through

---

[3] Bishop Colenso had in 1855 first aroused controversy by arguing that 'the method, at present adopted by the Missionaries, of requiring a man, who had more than one wife, to put away all but one, before he could be received to Christian Baptism, was ... unwarranted by Scripture, opposed to the practice of the Apostles, condemned by common reason, and altogether unjustifiable': John Colenso, *Remarks on the Proper Treatment of Cases of Polygamy* (Pietermaritzburg: Ray & Davis, 1855); available online: http://anglicanhistory.org/africa/colenso/polygamy1855.html (accessed 16 January 2017).

[4] The 1878 encyclical had stated that 'steps should be taken by each branch of the Church, according to its own discretion, to maintain the sanctity of marriage, agreeably to the principles set forth in the Word of God, as the Church of Christ hath hitherto received the same': Randall Davidson, *The Five Lambeth Conferences* (London: SPCK, 1920), p. 96.

the lens of 'marriage problems' – there was a particular focus on divorce and, for the first time, 'artificial restriction of the family' with a firmly conservative stance on both. Twelve years later there remained a sense of combating moral decline and addressing problems. While there was no substantive change, the tone moderated with a recognition of the need to set out the church's teaching rather than assume it and react to problems.

The 1930 Conference is famous for its revisionist attitude to contraception but perhaps as important a shift occurred in no longer approaching 'problems' but considering the 'life and witness of the Christian community'. After the war, the major concern was divorce in terms of 'The Church's Discipline in Marriage' while in 1958 there was the fullest ever discussion of marriage and sexuality by a Lambeth Conference. A group chaired by the American Bishop Stephen Bayne (Diocese of Olympia), who was shortly afterwards appointed the first Anglican Executive Officer, explored 'The Family in Contemporary Society', a title lifted from a Church of England report prepared for the Conference. The Conference report was widely praised: 'The most far-reaching and important report,'[5] 'perhaps no Lambeth Conference has ever reached a more sustained and positive note,'[6] 'one of the finest treatises available on the ideals of Christian family life.'[7] It offered both a 'theology of sexuality and the family' (the first use of 'sexuality', a category which would become increasingly prominent) and a study of 'the family in an industrialized society' while further developing the Conference's response to contraception.

The 1968 Conference contrasts with all others of the twentieth century and marks a transition. It was structured around three areas (faith, ministry and unity) comprising thirty-three committees looking at specific areas. None of these were on marriage or any aspect of sexuality despite the radical cultural changes we associate with the 1960s, many of which were already evident even if their significance was not as obvious at the time.[8] The publication by the Vatican of *Humanae Vitae* (reaffirming traditional opposition to contraception)

---

[5]   Alan M. G. Stephenson, *Anglicanism and the Lambeth Conferences* (London: SPCK, 1978), p. 208.
[6]   Dewi Morgan, editorial secretary of the SPG, quoted in ibid., p. 209.
[7]   James B. Simpson and Edward M. Story, *The Long Shadows of Lambeth X* (New York: McGraw-Hill, 1969), p. 316.
[8]   The previous year had seen the decriminalization of male homosexual behaviour in England and Wales after much heated debate over many years and the year before that the Church of England had published a controversial report on divorce – *Putting Asunder* – which shaped the 1969 Divorce Reform Act.

on the day the Conference opened meant that that subject had to be addressed again and indeed dominated the first few days, resulting in a resolution largely restating the 1958 decision. The next three conferences all returned to the earlier pattern and gave specific attention to areas around marriage and sex although these subjects were much less prominent. Attention focused less on marriage and more on the family and sexuality, contraception ceased to be a concern, as largely did divorce, while in 1988 the refusal to baptize polygamists was reversed. From 1978 issues of homosexuality increasingly became a focus and cause of tension, culminating in resolution I.10 in 1998. The 2008 Conference discussions were closely tied to consideration of the nature of life in communion, given the major stresses which divisions on these subjects were clearly causing between and within provinces.

II Lambeth on marriage and sexuality – continuities

Before tracing the development of Lambeth teaching and debates and tensions in relation to contraception, divorce, polygamy and homosexuality, it is helpful to set out five consistent underlying features of the conferences.

First, there is a belief that the church has received divine revelation about the nature, and importance, of marriage and the family in God's purposes for human flourishing. Although this revelation is rarely expounded in detail, its biblical basis is frequently summed up by reference to Jesus' teaching (referring to Genesis). Thus, while 'the family is not a peculiarly Christian institution … through Holy Scripture, and supremely through Christ's teaching, God has led his Church to uniquely deep insights into the nature of the family and its necessities and possibilities'.[9] Similarly, appeals are made to 'the Scriptural norm' and 'in view of the teaching of Scripture'.[10] In the fullest treatment, in 1958, the bishops were clear that Christian teaching in this area must be thoroughly theological:

> The Conference records its profound conviction that the idea of the human
> family is rooted in the Godhead and that consequently all problems of sex

---

[9] 'The Family in Contemporary Society' in *The Lambeth Conference 1958* (London: SPCK, 1958), Part 2, p. 142.
[10] 1978 Conference, Resolution 10; 1998 Conference, Resolution I.10 (b).

relations, the procreation of children, and the organisation of family life must be related, consciously and directly, to the creative, redemptive, and sanctifying power of God.[11]

Marriage, defined as 'sacred, instituted by God and blessed by our Lord Jesus Christ',[12] is at the heart of this teaching. In 1988, the report stated that

> the definition of marriage set forth in the canons of the Scottish Episcopal Church is representative of all the Provinces of the Communion: 'The doctrine of this Church is that marriage is a physical, spiritual and mystical union of one man and one woman created by their mutual consent of heart and mind and will thereto and is a holy and lifelong estate instituted by God.' This union signifies to us the mystery of the union between Christ and his Church.[13]

There is also a strong emphasis on the importance of this teaching for wider society's flourishing and on the church's calling to uphold marriage and the family. The 1888 encyclical describes the sanctity of marriage as 'the centre of social morality'[14] and a century later the pastoral letter opens with a quotation from 1930 – 'The beauty of the family is one of God's most precious gifts, and its preservation is a paramount responsibility of the Church'.[15] As a result, a repeated concern of conferences is the importance of the church teaching about sex and marriage, preparing couples for marriage, and all work to support marriage.[16]

Second, as is most obvious in the earlier conferences' emphasis on 'purity', behaviour in relation to sex and marriage is an important area in Christian holiness. The 1888 encyclical, echoing even stronger language in the report, highlighted the theological basis of this in speaking of 'a crusade against that sin

---

[11] 1958 Conference, Resolution 112.

[12] *The Official Report of the Lambeth Conference 1998* (Harrisburg, PA: Morehouse Publishing, 1999), p. 93, referring to resolutions in 1978 and 1988.

[13] *The Truth Shall Make You Free: The Lambeth Conference 1988* (London: Church House Publishing, 1988), p. 182, para 128. The Scottish Episcopal Church revised this canon in 2017 to permit same-sex marriage. The 1998 subsection report similarly stated: 'Holy Matrimony is, by intention and divine purpose, to be a life-long, monogamous and unconditional commitment between a woman and a man' (*The Official Report of the Lambeth Conference 1998*, p. 93).

[14] Davidson, *The Five Lambeth Conferences*, p. 108.

[15] Pastoral Letter, 'The Family as a Gift from God', in *The Truth Shall Make You Free: The Lambeth Conference 1988*, p. 318.

[16] Examples here include 1920 Conference, Resolution 71; 1930 Conference, Resolution 12; 1948 Conference, Resolution 93; 1958 Conference, Resolutions 114, 116 and 117; 1978 Conference, Resolution 10.

which is before all others a defilement of the body of Christ and a desecration of the temple of the Holy Spirit'.[17] In 1978, taking a more positive tone, the bishops focused on cultivating virtues not combating vices: 'The Conference gladly affirms the Christian ideals of faithfulness and chastity both within and outside marriage, and calls Christians everywhere to seek the grace of Christ to live lives of holiness, discipline, and service in the world'.[18]

The 1920 Conference, in line with previous Conferences, clearly articulated what such holiness involved:

> Recognising that to live a pure and chaste life before and after marriage is, for both sexes, the unchangeable Christian standard, attainable and attained through the help of the Holy Spirit by men and women in every age, the Conference desires to proclaim the universal obligation of this standard, and its vital importance as an essential condition of human happiness.[19]

This was reaffirmed in 1930: 'Sexual intercourse between persons who are not legally married is a grievous sin'.[20] More recent conferences have restated this fundamental ethic as in the 1988 call for bishops to develop diocesan strategies 'to reaffirm the traditional biblical teaching that sexual intercourse is an act of total commitment which belongs properly within a permanent married relationship'.[21]

Third, there is a recurring strong sense that Christian teaching and the goods of marriage and family are under pressure and that individual Christians and the church corporately are in danger of failing to bear faithful witness to God's purposes. The particular focus of this shifts and has not been quite as

[17] Davidson, *The Five Lambeth Conferences*, pp. 107–8.
[18] 1978 Conference, Resolution 10.
[19] 1920 Conference, Resolution 67. The report behind this was particularly strong on the importance of holiness: 'The Christian Church has a code of morals as imperious in its claims as the rule of faith given in the Creeds. The Clergy are commissioned to teach the Christian Religion, which is to guide and hallow men's lives. To bear witness to the Divine Will, and to work for the fulfilment of that Will in the elevation and perfection of human life, is the very purpose of the Church's existence in the world. If the Church is to leaven human society, it must faithfully uphold this standard at any cost, both by its teaching and by the exercise of discipline, refusing the privileges of the Church to those who transgress the divine commandment. This witness is the duty not only of Bishops and Priests, or of the Church collectively in synod or convention, but of individual Christian people. Laws to be enforced, whether ecclesiastical or civil, must have a background of public opinion. Hence the great importance of being rightly informed as to the Christian law in this as in other matters, as well as of faithfulness and courage in bearing witness to it': *Conference of Bishops of the Anglican Communion Holden at Lambeth Palace, July 5 to August 7, 1920* (London: SPCK, 1920), p. 108.
[20] 1930 Conference, Resolution 18.
[21] 1988 Conference, Resolution 29, also Resolution 34. See also 1998 Conference, Resolution I.10 (b).

prominent recently but the strong sense of threats and problems is remarkably consistent.

For example, the first reference to marriage, in 1878, refers to 'difficulties' due to changes in secular law[22] while the 1888 report warns of sins of impurity being 'a grave public scandal ... festering beneath the surface, and eating into the life of multitudes in all classes and in all lands'.[23] As already noted, the 1908 and 1920 conferences viewed the subject in terms of 'problems' and Resolution 10 in 1930 presented Christ's teaching as 'the solution of the problems with which we are faced'.[24] The classic report of 1958 opens with the sentence, 'Everywhere in the world there is restless concern for the well-being of the family as a basic institution in society',[25] while Resolution 122 refers to 'the crushing impact of secularism on family life'. Even in the relative silence of 1968 a short section on 'the sickness of the contemporary world' refers to a 'permissive' society',[26] while the 1978 report warned of 'enormous strains on that basic unit of our society'[27] and referred to homosexual behaviour being 'a problem'.[28] A decade later, reports from across the Anglican Communion were noted as demonstrating that 'in every Province marriages are experiencing many stresses'.[29]

Fourth, the bishops seek both to bear faithful witness to God's will and to encourage the Church to support those under pressure and those who fall short. The emphasis between these two elements varies across time (with the trajectory being more towards the latter) and subject matter. The rationale for this dual task was most clearly set out in the 1948 report in relation to marriage discipline. It spoke of 'the two-fold responsibility of the Church in the exercise of its pastoral ministry':

---

[22] Davidson, *The Five Lambeth Conferences*, p. 96.

[23] Ibid., p. 130.

[24] The encyclical was clear that 'Christ's community has been commissioned to set a standard of life which is not that of the world. Too often has the standard of Christians been assimilated to that of the surrounding society or of the spirit of the age': *The Lambeth Conference 1930* (London: SPCK, 1930), p. 21.

[25] 'The Family in Contemporary Society', in *The Lambeth Conference 1958* (London: SPCK, 1958), Part 2, p. 142.

[26] *The Lambeth Conference 1968: Resolutions and Reports* (London: SPCK, 1968), p. 72.

[27] *The Report of the Lambeth Conference 1978* (London: Church Information Society, 1978), p. 62.

[28] Ibid., p. 64.

[29] *The Truth Shall Make You Free: The Lambeth Conference 1988*, p. 183, paras 132, 133.

1. a duty to the community at large to uphold Christ's principle and standard of marriage as a lifelong union so that 'we cannot condone what our Lord condemns', and

2. 'the duty of shepherding those who have failed to live up to this standard' so that 'in the divine light of our Saviour's tender compassion, we cannot turn our eyes away from those men and women in deep distress and sore need who are looking to the Church for sympathy and help'.[30]

Reflecting this, after a strong resolution on no remarriage during the lifetime of a former spouse, resolution 95, illustrating that pastoral responses bear on the issue of provincial autonomy and diversity, reads, 'Mindful of the needs of those who are in deep distress and claim the Church's sympathy, the Conference urges that provincial and regional Churches should consider how best their pastoral responsibility towards those who do not conform to our Lord's standard can be discharged.' A similar balance is found in 1998 Resolution I.10 by combining a refusal to commend same-sex blessings with a call to 'listen to the experience of homosexual persons' and 'minister pastorally and sensitively to all'.

Fifth, the history of the Conference consistently shows the need to revisit previous statements and reaffirm, reword or significantly revise and adapt its teaching and practice. Before looking at these in detail it is worth noting the broad sweep.

While continuing to uphold 'monogamy as God's plan and as the ideal relationship of love between husband and wife',[31] the regularly reaffirmed judgement that 'persons living in polygamy be not admitted to baptism'[32] was replaced after a century with 'a polygamist who responds to the Gospel and wishes to join the Anglican Church may be baptised and confirmed with his believing wives and children' on certain conditions.[33]

While continuing to describe marriage as a 'lifelong union',[34] the Conference has moved from recognizing divorce only for fornication or adultery and refusing to 'give any sanction to the marriage of any person who has been

---

[30] *Lambeth Conference 1948* (London: SPCK, 1948), Part II, p. 100.

[31] 1988 Conference, Resolution 26.

[32] 1888 Conference, Resolution 5.

[33] 1988 Conference, Resolution 26.

[34] 1998 Conference, Resolution 1.10.

divorced contrary to this law, during the life of the other party'.[35] It has reached a situation where for many conferences it has largely avoided statements on the issue and left provinces to develop their own responses to marriage breakdown and remarriage.

While continuing to emphasize the importance of children and the connection between marriage and family,[36] the Conference moved from the total condemnation of contraception (1908 and 1920) to a slightly more permissive stance, allowing freedom of conscience under certain conditions (1930). Later conferences commended birth control (1958 and 1968), but failed to follow this up with adequate reflection on the proper relationship between sex, marriage and children, and there is no sense that contraception was a morally significant issue.

The developments in these three areas merit further discussion and analysis.

III Lambeth on polygamy

Prior to the first Lambeth Conference there was already debate about how the church's consistent teaching on marriage as monogamous[37] applied when the Gospel entered polygamous cultures. The third conference (1888), which apart from Bishop Crowther, present for the first time, heard from no other native African voices, addressed 'polygamy of heathen converts'. The committee was unanimous that this was 'condemned by the law of Christ' but there was not full agreement on how to respond. While leaving minor points to local discretion, the Conference laid down a clear sacramental discipline, despite some objections (83 for, 21 against). Resolution 5 read: 'Persons living in polygamy be not admitted to baptism, but ... be accepted as candidates and kept under Christian instruction until such time as they shall be in a position to accept the law of Christ.' A more accommodating approach was allowed for polygamists' wives who could 'be admitted in some cases to baptism, but

---

[35] 1888 Conference, Resolution 4.

[36] 'The family is closely related to the institution of marriage and partakes of its sacredness': Pastoral Letter, 'The Family as a Gift from God', in *The Truth Shall Make You Free: The Lambeth Conference 1988*, p. 318, para. 2.

[37] On this tradition, particularly in reference to law in the Christian West, see John Witte, *The Western Case for Monogamy Over Polygamy* (Cambridge: Cambridge University Press, 2015).

... it must be left to the local authorities of the Church to decide under what circumstances they may be baptized' (a vote of 54-34).

Bishop Mylne of Bombay explained: 'Not a word, I think, was said in favour of compulsory Divorce; not a voice raised in favour of injustice; of throwing helpless women on the world, or of granting them maintenance alone without a husband's care, unless they elected for that alternative,'[38] but these and other major problems arose with refusal to baptize. This was recognized in 1920 when the committee on 'Missionary Problems', commended in Resolution 39, reaffirmed the 1888 resolution against baptizing polygamists. The committee stressed that 'if a polygamist wishes to separate from his wives and be baptized, care must be taken that he make proper arrangements for the separated wives before he can be accepted'.[39] It also explored other areas of marriage discipline such as marrying a non-Christian in non-Christian rites and distinguished Christian marriage from marriage generally. Making clear that polygamy was not the only problem, it rejected baptism of 'a person married as a non-Christian to a person whose relationship to him or her is within the degrees prohibited by the Christian Church unless they separate after due arrangement made for the future of the wife'.[40] In 1948, though focusing on divorce, the committee exploring the church's discipline in marriage again returned to mixed marriages[41] but simply noted that African polygamy required 'special consideration' and was 'largely dealt with' in 1920.

By 1958, while reaffirming monogamy as 'the divine will, testified by the teaching of Christ himself, and therefore true for every race of men', the Conference admitted that the church had not yet solved the problems of introducing it into polygamous societies where it brought 'a social and economic revolution'. It called for further study and prayer 'that God may lead his Church to know the manner of its witness and discipline in this issue'.[42] The report acknowledged that 'discipline in this matter may sometimes differ in various provinces of the Church, according to what is thought to be wise', but

---

[38] Quoted in Stephenson, *Anglicanism and the Lambeth Conferences*, p. 88.

[39] *Conference of Bishops of the Anglican Communion Holden at Lambeth Palace, July 5 to August 7, 1920*, p. 89.

[40] Ibid.

[41] It thought in relation to the marriage of a Christian to a non-Christian that 'each province must be left to work out the details of its discipline, but this Committee agrees that these mixed marriages should be forbidden, except in cases approved by the bishop of the diocese': *Lambeth Conference 1948*, Part II, p. 103).

[42] 1958 Conference, Resolution 120.

was emphatic that 'the proclamation of the truth and responsible willingness to face the cost of it are alike inescapable obligations laid upon the Church'.[43]

A decade later, resolution 23 made little change despite the hopes of some for more guidance. Recognizing that 'polygamy poses one of the sharpest conflicts between the faith and particular cultures', it asked 'each province to re-examine its discipline in such problems in full consideration with other provinces in a similar situation'. This Conference revealed division among African Anglicans – an earlier draft sought to state that 'polygamy is a fact in some countries and that the abrupt termination of polygamous marriages may cause great suffering and great disruption to many', but African evangelicals led by Archbishop Sabiti of Uganda, Rwanda and Burundi got this removed.[44]

Despite that call for provincial reflection, and attention being given to the subject by the new Anglican Consultative Council (ACC),[45] there were no resolutions on this topic at Lambeth 1978. It was only in 1988, as the African churches became more prominent, and following a concerted effort supported by the ACC in 1984,[46] that the Conference reconsidered and marked the centenary of its original decision by not simply revising but reversing its discipline.[47] It upheld 'monogamy as God's plan, and as the ideal relationship of love between husband and wife', but now permitted the baptism and confirmation of converted polygamists on three conditions: a promise 'not to marry again as long as any of his wives at the time of his conversion are alive'; the consent of the local Anglican community to receiving such a polygamist; and the refusal to compel the putting away any of the wives which would

[43] 'The Family in Contemporary Society', in *The Lambeth Conference 1958*, Part 2, p. 154.

[44] Simpson and Story, *The Long Shadows of Lambeth X*, pp. 142–3.

[45] At its first meeting in 1971 the ACC responded to the South Pacific Anglican Council request that under certain circumstances polygamists should be baptized, noting that 'there are places where polygamists are already being baptized and that it is for the diocesan to make the decision', but the ACC was 'unable to give any general advice' as 'there is at present lack of a common mind on this subject' (Resolution 29). In 1973, recommending a study by Adrian Hastings commissioned by African Archbishops (*Christian Marriage in Africa* (London: SPCK, 1973)) the ACC recommended that 'in the case of the conversion of a pagan polygamist, he should be received into the Church with his believing wives and children, provided that this should only be done in suitable cases with the willing consent of the local Christian community, and only within a context where the Church's teaching on monogamy is strictly recognized' (Resolution 25).

[46] ACC (1984) Resolution 18: 'Be it resolved that this ACC-6 requests the Council for Anglican Provinces in Africa (CAPA) to study the issue of polygamy and the Christian family further in both its theological and pastoral dimensions and asks CAPA to co-ordinate the studies and to make available its findings to the Lambeth Conference of 1988.'

[47] A key contribution to this debate was from the Kenyan Bishop, later Archbishop, David Gitari, 'The Church and Polygamy', *Transformation*, 1.1 (1984), pp. 3–10.

lead to their social deprivation. Recognizing that some became polygamists after conversion, it also called on provinces to share 'their pastoral approach to Christians who become polygamists so that the most appropriate way of disciplining and pastoring them can be found'.[48]

IV Lambeth on divorce and further marriage

Prior to the 1968 Conference, one West African Bishop described Western practice as permitting 'consecutive polygamy'.[49] Up to that time, Lambeth Conferences regularly wrestled with the challenge that divorce and further marriage present to a Christian understanding of marriage's permanence and in particular to Christ's teaching in Mark 10 and Matthew 19. Only ten years before the first Lambeth Conference, the Matrimonial Causes Act transferred divorce from ecclesiastical to civil courts in England and allowed divorce with the right to remarry (only for adultery) through the courts rather than a special Act of Parliament.[50]

The 1888 encyclical protested against easier divorce and spoke of 'our duty to reaffirm emphatically the precept of Christ'.[51] Drawing on the Matthean exception, Resolution 4 declared

> inasmuch as our Lord's words expressly forbid divorce, except in the case
> of fornication or adultery, the Christian Church cannot recognise divorce
> in any other than the excepted case, or give any sanction to the marriage of
> any person who has been divorced contrary to this law, during the life of the
> other party.

It was clear that a guilty party could 'under no circumstances' receive 'the blessing of the Church' on marriage during the lifetime of the innocent party but recognized differing views on remarriage of the innocent party. The resolution recommended for the innocent party 'that the clergy should not be

---

[48] 1988 Conference, Resolution 26.

[49] Simpson and Story, *The Long Shadows of Lambeth X*, pp. 142–3. Witte's study of monogamy is clear that remarriage after divorce is often seen in Christian tradition as an equivalent denial of Christian monogamy: successive polygamy (Witte, *The Western Case for Monogamy*, pp. 31–2).

[50] On this and subsequent changes in English law, see Stephen Cretney, *Family Law in the Twentieth Century: A History* (Oxford: Oxford University Press, 2005), chapters 5 and 6.

[51] Davidson, *The Five Lambeth Conferences*, p. 108.

instructed to refuse the sacraments or other privileges of the Church to those who, under civil sanction, are thus married'.

The 1908 report stated that one of the church's roles was 'to guard the sanctity of the marriage bond so long as they both shall live'[52] and the bishops declared that they 'felt it to be our duty to re-affirm the principles on the subject of divorce which were laid down by the Lambeth Conference twenty years ago, and to assert our conviction that no view less strict than this is admissible in the Church of Christ'.[53] Resolution 39 restated the 1888 resolution and by a very narrow margin (87 to 84) the following resolution went further, agreeing with the majority on the committee that 'when an innocent person has, by means of a court of law, divorced a spouse for adultery, and desires to enter into another contract of marriage, it is undesirable that such a contract should receive the blessing of the Church'. The committee was also horrified by legal changes, particularly in the United States. It argued that 'there is at most but one cause for which a marriage rightly performed and also consummated ought ever to be broken by a court of law' and called on Anglicans 'never to rest until they have purified the law of divorce by the excision of all causes save the one' and to refuse social relations with those guilty of adultery.[54]

A significant new phase in Lambeth resolutions arose in 1920 with the introduction in resolution 67 of the language of marriage as indissoluble (despite objections from some such as Bishop Hensley Henson of Durham):[55]

> The Conference affirms as our Lord's principle and standard of marriage a life-long and indissoluble union, for better or worse, of one man with one woman, to the exclusion of all others on either side, and calls on all Christian people to maintain and bear witness to this standard.

This reflected changing judgements on the Matthean exception although, as affirmed in that resolution, the committee did 'admit the right of a National Church to deal with the excepted case recorded in St. Matthew under such safeguards and disciplinary provisions as such Church may lay down'.

---

[52] Ibid., p. 396.
[53] Ibid., p. 309.
[54] Ibid., pp. 396–7. The committee also addressed the question of prohibited degrees, concluding that it was 'within the competence of a local Church to make its own conditions with regard to prohibited degrees, so that they be not repugnant to the law of God' (p. 399).
[55] Stephenson, *Anglicanism and the Lambeth Conferences*, p. 149.

Nonetheless, the Matthean exception defined the absolute limit of acceptable change.[56]

The 1930 Conference reaffirmed this language and discipline but also made clear that it was 'passing no judgement on the practice of regional or national Churches within our Communion'. It also held that 'where an innocent person has remarried under civil sanction and desires to receive the Holy Communion, it recommends that the case should be referred for consideration to the bishop, subject to provincial regulations'.[57]

By the 1948 Conference there had been significant changes in English law (A. P. Herbert's 1937 Act giving more grounds for divorce in the face of church opposition), the effect of war on marriages,[58] and new canons in the American church allowing the church to annul certain marriages. The Conference, concerned about 'the great increase in the number of broken marriages and the tragedy of children deprived of true home life' (Resolution 92), gave detailed attention to the subject, although the report's positive vision of marriage was not set out fully in any resolution. Resolution 92 recalled the previous two Conferences' statements but removed the language of indissolubility in recognition of different views as to whether marriage's permanence was a matter of fact or obligation: 'This Conference desires again to affirm that marriage always entails a life-long union and obligation.' Resolution 94 reaffirmed the stance of 1930 (adopted by the Convocations of Canterbury and York in 1938)[59] though with an important qualification. This arose out of the American church's canonical changes in 1946 allowing a Bishop to judge that no marriage bond exists in certain cases:

---

[56] The committee on 'missionary problems' drew a sharp distinction between Christian marriage (involving two Christians) and marriage (which is 'potentially dissoluble'). It held that the latter is 'not raised to the level of Christian marriage by the baptism of one party' and, with reference to 1 Corinthians 7, claimed desertion by the non-Christian meant that 'the Christian partner is free under the "privilegium Paulinum" to regard the existing marriage as dissolved and to marry again with any baptized Christian'. They held, however, that this did not apply when a Christian married a non-Christian and the Bishop ruled the marriage as valid and 'consequently indissoluble on the side of the Christian' (*Conference of Bishops of the Anglican Communion Holden at Lambeth Palace, July 5 to August 7, 1920*, pp. 88–91 on 'Holy Matrimony').

[57] 1930 Conference, Resolution 11.

[58] Clare Hanghamer, *The English in Love: The Intimate Story of An Emotional Revolution* (Oxford: Oxford University Press, 2013), p. 5, notes that '1946 was a peak year for divorce petitions with two-thirds of these initiated by husbands: the number of divorces granted in 1947 was not surpassed until 1972'.

[59] The report described this as 'the key-stone in all that we envisage toward building up a sound and instructed public opinion on the meaning of marriage' (*Lambeth Conference 1948*, Part II, p. 100).

The Conference affirms that the marriage of one whose former partner is still living may not be celebrated according to the rites of the Church, *unless it has been established that there exists no marriage bond recognised by the Church.*[60]

In the words of the encyclical this meant: 'The Church will not marry anyone who has been previously married save where no marriage bond as recognized by the Church still exists.'[61]

Following an emphasis on pastoral concern (Resolution 95), the Conference returned to the issue of admission to Communion. The report was unhappy with the historic distinction between guilty and innocent parties but was clear that 'if the Church is to be true to its doctrine and to re-establish its discipline with regard to marriage, it must make it plain that its members who enter upon marriage not recognized by the Church forfeit by so doing their right of admission to Holy Communion'.[62] Their proposal granting episcopal discretion to admit remarried divorcees was set out in Resolution 96 while other resolutions challenged easy divorce, warned against marriage under Roman Catholic canon law and, rather ironically given developments in the West over the following decades, stressed 'the importance of building up a sound Christian tradition of family life in the younger Churches of the Anglican Communion, and therefore urges their members to observe loyally the marriage canons and rules of their provinces or dioceses' (Resolution 99).

Despite giving detailed attention to marriage, the 1958 Conference did not modify discipline. It was marked by emphasizing the need for forgiveness, reconciliation and marriage guidance (Resolutions 116 and 117). Recognizing the changing legal context, it continued to encourage consideration of annulment (Resolution 118). Previous resolutions, although not explicitly reaffirmed by the Conference (although they were by the committee),[63] were described as 'of great value as witnessing to Christ's teaching about the life-long nature of marriage', and the bishops urged 'that these Resolutions,

---

[60] Italics added. This approach effectively replaced the previous distinction between innocent and guilty parties in earlier Conference resolutions.

[61] *Lambeth Conference 1948*, Part I, p. 25.

[62] Ibid., Part II, p. 101.

[63] The report added the 1948 resolutions as an appendix and was clear that the committee 'fully and wholeheartedly makes its own the conclusions of their study ... we cannot challenge our world with any lesser standard than the one our Lord gave us' ('The Family in Contemporary Society', in *The Lambeth Conference 1958*, Part 2, p. 153).

and their implications, should continue to be studied in every province' (Resolution 119). The encyclical letter reaffirmed 'the permanence of the marriage bond'.[64]

By 1968, earlier Conference resolutions had been effectively ignored in relation to both the church's response to changes in secular law (notably the Church of England's 1966 report *Putting Asunder*) and, more significantly, the relaxation of church discipline on remarriage (with an increasingly broad understanding of annulment in the United States and new 1967 canons in Canada). Resolution 23 on 'Marriage Discipline' focused on polygamy but by referring to the 'lifelong' nature of marriage implicitly included divorce and remarriage. Rather than reaffirming past statements the Conference simply asked 'each province to re-examine its discipline in such problems in full consideration with other provinces in a similar situation', a strong emphasis on provincial autonomy. Archbishop Ramsey supported this in answering a question from a member of the Mothers' Union (which did not admit divorcees) on whether Lambeth would give further direction on the Church's stand on divorce: 'The Churches [of the Anglican Communion] have their own rules about marriage ... and those rules are partially influenced by the Lambeth Conference.'[65]

This handing over to provinces of marriage discipline in relation to response to divorce and remarriage explains the actions of subsequent Conferences. These saw bishops who worked on statements about marriage expressing alarm and concern about rising divorce but, in marked contrast to previous Conferences, no longer proposing how churches should respond in terms of their marriage discipline. For example, although 1998 Resolution I.10 reaffirmed marriage as a 'lifelong union' (neither that language nor 'permanence' had appeared in 1978 or 1988 resolutions) it said nothing about marriage breakdown.

The story of successive Lambeth Conferences is therefore of a move from rejecting divorce and remarriage except for the biblically based exception of adultery to a more rigorist doctrine of indissolubility (with stricter Eucharistic discipline). This was then loosened and there was an exploration of annulment before the Conferences fell silent, effectively allowing provinces to make their

---

[64] Ibid., Part 1, p. 22.
[65] Simpson and Story, *The Long Shadows of Lambeth X*, p. 163 n6.

own judgements without explicit guidance, thereby enabling greater diversity and liberalization of policies.

V Lambeth on contraception

A further evil with which we have had to deal is of such a kind that it cannot be spoken of without repugnance. No one who values the purity of home life can contemplate without grave misgiving the existence of an evil which jeopardises that purity; no one who treasures the Christian ideal of marriage can condone the existence of habits which subvert some of the essential elements of that ideal.[66]

These words in the encyclical letter of 1908 referred to 'a widespread prevalence amongst our peoples of the practice of resorting to artificial means for the avoidance or prevention of childbearing' and appealed 'to the members of our own Churches to exert the whole force of their Christian character in condemnation of them'.[67] This was summed up in Resolution 41: 'The Conference regards with alarm the growing practice of the artificial restriction of the family, and earnestly calls upon all Christian people to discountenance the use of all artificial means of restriction as demoralising to character and hostile to national welfare.'[68]

The resolution arose from a committee's consideration of 'restriction on population'.[69] This gave significant attention to falling birth rates which were, 'most marked among the English-speaking people, once the most fertile of races'. The cause was viewed by the committee as 'the loss of the sense of responsibility to God for the fruits of marriage' and it warned that 'the deliberate intention of defeating one of the chief ends of marriage is to deprave the ideal of marriage'. Appeal was also made to 'the verdict of Nature ... moral instinct' and (drawing parallels with 'self-abuse') negative health effects ('serious local ailments ... nervous enfeeblement ... mental and moral vigour may become

---

[66] Davidson, *The Five Lambeth Conferences*, p. 310.
[67] Ibid., pp. 310–11.
[68] Resolution 42 was even stronger in relation to abortion: 'Deliberate tampering with nascent life is repugnant to Christian morality,' while Resolution 43 supported 'medical men who have borne courageous testimony against the injurious practices spoken of'.
[69] Davidson, *The Five Lambeth Conferences*, pp. 399–402.

impaired, and the question has been asked whether the increase of insanity may not be closely connected with these habits of restriction'). There were concerns that divorce would rise and a call for bans and prosecutions was supported with the shocking argument:

> There is the danger of deterioration whenever the race is recruited from the inferior and not from the superior stocks. There is the world-danger that the great English-speaking peoples, diminished in number and weakened in moral force, should commit the crowning infamy of race-suicide, and so fail to fulfil that high destiny to which in the Providence of God they have been manifestly called.[70]

The discussion was more measured in 1920 when there were already signs of dissent. The Committee, recognizing that it could not deal with strictly medical matters and that 'the physical union of husband and wife has a sacramental value by which is expressed and strengthened the love that the one ought to have for the other' nevertheless urged 'the paramount importance in married life of deliberate and thoughtful self-control'.[71] In Resolution 68, the Conference, 'while declining to lay down rules which will meet the needs of every abnormal case', warned 'against the use of unnatural means for the avoidance of conception'[72] and of 'the grave dangers – physical, moral and religious – thereby incurred, and against the evils with which the extension of such use threatens the race'. The problem was identified as encouraging 'married people in the deliberate cultivation of sexual union as an end in itself', whereas among the governing considerations of Christian marriage are 'the primary purpose for which marriage exists, namely the continuation of the race through the gift and heritage of children; the other is the paramount importance in married life of deliberate and thoughtful self-control'.

By 1930 the Conference was providing a much more nuanced account and reversed its prohibitionist stance on what was still viewed as 'one of the most

---

[70] Ibid., p. 402.

[71] *Conference of Bishops of the Anglican Communion Holden at Lambeth Palace, July 5 to August 7, 1920*, p. 112.

[72] Henson, presumably alluding to homosexual practice (on which see the 1920 reference noted below), objected, 'I could not be a party to what branded as "unnatural" the methods which modern science provided, and, considering the associations of the word, I thought its use offensive' (Stephenson, *Anglicanism and the Lambeth Conferences*, p. 150).

urgent and perplexing problems of our day'.[73] Resolution 13, while noting that 'intercourse between husband and wife as the consummation of marriage has a value of its own within that sacrament, and that thereby married love is enhanced and its character strengthened', nevertheless affirmed that 'the primary purpose for which marriage exists is the procreation of children' and that this purpose and 'the paramount importance in married life of deliberate and thoughtful self-control' should be the governing considerations. Resolution 14 affirmed 'the duty of parenthood as the glory of married life', 'the benefit of a family as a joy in itself, as a vital contribution to the nation's welfare, and as a means of character-building for both parents and children', and 'the privilege of discipline and sacrifice to this end'. Having thus clearly stated the importance of procreation, Resolution 15, by a vote of 193 to 67, reversed past statements, leading at least one bishop to walk out:

> Where there is clearly felt moral obligation to limit or avoid parenthood, the method must be decided on Christian principles. The primary and obvious method is complete abstinence from intercourse (as far as may be necessary) in a life of discipline and self-control lived in the power of the Holy Spirit. Nevertheless in those cases where there is such a clearly felt moral obligation to limit or avoid parenthood, and where there is a morally sound reason for avoiding complete abstinence, the Conference agrees that other methods may be used, provided that this is done in the light of the same Christian principles. The Conference records its strong condemnation of the use of any methods of conception control from motives of selfishness, luxury, or mere convenience.

The committee report (revising an earlier more controversial draft)[74] set out the reasoning.[75] It begins with *why* Anglicans were free to reject the finality of 'a very strong tradition that the use of preventive methods is in

---

[73] The debates were not simply about the ethics of contraception but were influenced by various other debates about the scientific evidence and, in particular, the different reactions to the widespread support for eugenics. The fullest discussions are found in two unpublished dissertations: Theresa Notare, '"A Revolution in Christian Morals": Lambeth 1930 – Resolution #15 History and Reception' (The Catholic University of America, 2008), which offers a Roman Catholic perspective; and Anna Louise Poulson, 'An examination of the ethics of contraception with reference to recent Protestant and Roman Catholic thought' (Kings College London, 2006), which is from an Anglican perspective.

[74] See Stephenson, *Anglicanism and the Lambeth Conferences*, p. 170.

[75] The report appears at *The Lambeth Conference 1930*, pp. 85–95. The quotations below come from pp. 90–1. The fullest account of the Conference deliberations is Notare, op. cit., chapters 4 and 5 (pp. 310–462).

all cases unlawful for a Christian'. First, 'it is not founded on any direction given in the New Testament' and second, 'it has not behind it the authority of any Ecumenical Council of the Church'. Furthermore, there are 'facts and conditions which were not present in the past, but which are due to modern civilisation'. Appealing to a consensus that 'there are circumstances in married life which justify, and even demand, the limitation of the family by *some* means', it issued some clear prohibitions: 'It is axiomatic that parenthood is for married people the foremost duty; to evade or disregard that duty must always be wrong' and 'it can never be right to make pleasure or self-indulgence the motive for determining to limit or refuse parenthood'. However, it would also be wrong to have intercourse which might lead to conception in certain situations (such as grave danger to health). Although total abstinence is 'the primary and most obvious' response, if 'there is good moral reason why the way of abstinence should not be followed' then 'we cannot condemn the use of scientific methods to prevent conception, which are thoughtfully and conscientiously adopted'. Crucially the bishops concluded, 'Each couple must decide for themselves, as in the sight of God, after the most careful and conscientious thought, and, if perplexed in mind, after taking competent advice, both medical and spiritual'.[76]

Despite Pope Pius XI's strong restatement of the traditional stance in response (in the encyclical *Casti Conubii*, December 1930), it was not until 1958 that the Conference revisited the subject, drawing on the recent Church of England report to positively commend family planning in Resolution 115 in three main points. First, that 'the responsibility for deciding upon the number and frequency of children has been laid by God upon the consciences of parents everywhere'. Second, that 'this planning, in such ways as are mutually acceptable to husband and wife in Christian conscience, is a right and important factor in Christian family life and should be the result of positive choice before God'. Third, that 'such responsible parenthood, built on obedience to all the duties of marriage, requires a wise stewardship of the resources and abilities

---

[76] Resolution 16 made clear that this more nuanced approach to contraception did not extend to life after conception by reiterating previous resolutions against abortion ('The Conference further records its abhorrence of the sinful practice of abortion') while other resolutions were clear that contraception was not a way of responding to poor economic and social conditions (Resolution 17). Concerns about legitimating premarital sex led to calls for 'legislation forbidding the exposure for sale and the unrestricted advertisement of contraceptives, and placing definite restrictions upon their purchase' (Resolution 18).

of the family as well as a thoughtful consideration of the varying population needs and problems of society and the claims of future generations'.

It is noteworthy that this resolution says nothing specific about which *means* are legitimate, leading *The Living Church* to claim that the resolutions 'could be subscribed by the Pope himself without changing a word'.[77] The report did, however, address this aspect, largely following the 1930 reasoning and its own account of marriage's purposes. Warning against selfishness and concern for one's own comfort it said that having children earlier in marriage was generally better and, emphasizing that sexual intercourse was about the expression of mutual love, was emphatic that 'it is utterly wrong to urge that, unless children are specifically desired, sexual intercourse is of the nature of sin. It is also wrong to say that such intercourse ought not to be engaged in except with the willing intention to procreate children'.[78] The means used were considered 'largely matters of clinical and aesthetic choice' but 'subject to the requirement that they be admissible to the Christian conscience'.[79] Praising continence, self-control and chastity within marriage and 'the beauty and strength of abstinence mutually accepted', the report named a number of unacceptable means of family planning and expressed concerns about sterilization. The general principle was that the 'duty to bear children' and 'duty to each other' need to be kept in balance. In the words of the conference encyclical:

> Because the two great purposes of Christian marriage illumine each other and form the focal points of constructive home life, we believe that family planning, in such ways as are mutually acceptable to a husband and wife in Christian conscience, and secure from the corruption of sensuality and selfishness, is a right and important factor in Christian family life (1.22).[80]

Ten years later, faced with the Vatican restating traditional prohibitions in *Humanae Vitae* (despite the majority in its own advisory group proposing something similar to the Anglican approach), the 1968 Conference, in the last

---

[77] 'Lambeth and Abraham', *The Living Church*, Editorial, 7 September 1958, p. 19.
[78] 'The Family in Contemporary Society', in *The Lambeth Conference 1958*, Part 2, p. 147.
[79] Ibid.
[80] *The Lambeth Conference 1958*, Part 1, p. 22. Later the encyclical, concerned about the impact of population rises in some parts of the world and their impact on 'the survival of young and old', went further and stated that 'in such countries population control has become a necessity' and 'methods of control, medically endorsed and morally acceptable, may help the people of these lands' (*The Lambeth Conference 1958*, Part 1, p. 23).

formal statement on the subject, reaffirmed the three resolutions of 1958 in Resolution 22 on 'Responsible Parenthood'.

In summary, contraception, from being a cause of moral outrage and disgust to be wholly rejected, later became something permissible after careful moral thought, but still problematic. Now, for half a century, Anglican bishops have, like other Protestant churches (as it has been put), 'in allowing the use of contraceptives … failed to accompany this permission with effective catechesis and discipline with respect to the purposes of sex and marriage'.[81]

VI The Lambeth Conference on homosexuality

There is no direct reference to homosexuality until 1978, following a period when England and many other countries saw homosexual practice decriminalized and the subject of whether homosexual relationships may be legitimate began to be discussed among Christians. However, two previous Lambeth Conference reports allude to it. In their report on purity in 1888 the bishops refrained from being specific about the sexual behaviour they condemned, noting that 'we dare not utter all that we know' and 'we are not blind to the danger of dealing publicly with the subject of impurity. We dread the effect, especially upon the young, of any increased familiarity with the details of sin. Notwithstanding we hold that the time has come when the Church must speak with no uncertain voice'.[82] Part of the context within England was the 1885 Criminal Law Amendment Act which, after public scandals, addressed prostitution, especially child prostitution, and, through the infamous Labouchere Amendment, private acts of 'gross indecency' between males.[83] This, plus the echo of Romans 1 in the bishops' warning that 'the wrath of God, alike in Holy Scripture and in the history of the world, has been revealed against the nations which have transgressed the law of purity; and we

---

[81] Gilbert Meilaender and Philip Turner, 'Contraception: A Symposium', *First Things*, December 1998. Available online: https://www.firstthings.com/article/1998/12/contraception-a-symposium (accessed 16 January 2017).

[82] Davidson, *The Five Lambeth Conferences*, p. 130.

[83] On the amendment see Jeffrey Weeks' work, especially *Coming Out: Homosexual Politics in Britain, from the Nineteenth Century to the Present* (London: Quartet Books, 1977) and the recent critique of his highly influential reading by Graham Baxendale in 'The Discursive Production of Homosexual Regulation' (unpublished PhD, Southampton University, 2013); available online: http://eprints.soton.ac.uk/354370/1/Post-viva%20thesis.pdf (accessed 16 January 2017).

solemnly record our conviction that, wherever marriage is dishonoured and sins of the flesh are lightly regarded, the home-life will be destroyed, and the nation itself will, sooner or later, decay and perish',[84] suggest that homosexual behaviour was likely part of their concern about impurity.

The committee report in 1920 was more direct in referring to same-sex sexual behaviour and relating it to the protection of young men:

> The aid of men of good and disciplined character is needed for the help of boys and young men, and in combating horrible temptations to which they are often exposed from elders of their own sex. The Committee is compelled to notice the prevalence in some quarters of unnatural vice. The strengthening of general sentiment in abhorrence of such practices is of the greatest importance. We fear that the public conscience is not sufficiently alive to this terrible mischief.[85]

In contrast, by 1978 a group specifically addressing homosexuality noted that it 'has rarely received understanding either in Church or in society'.[86] Set in the context of not expecting everyone to conform to a norm but rejoicing in variety, it called on church and society to 'approach the subject compassionately and without prejudice', especially given requests by homosexuals (which it said most Christians would not accept) to recognize 'that their homosexual relationship can express mutual love, as appropriately for the persons concerned as a heterosexual relationship might for others'. Noting the complexity of questions, which some provinces were beginning to study, the group highlighted cultural differences ('places (e.g. in the Church of Africa) where homosexual behaviour has not emerged as a problem') and the need for biblical study of texts 'such as Romans 1.18-32 which depicts homosexual behaviour as one of the manifestations of the fragmentation of life in a fallen world'. They called on 'every local Church' to become Christ's 'accepting community' for all. Resolution 10 of the Conference then reaffirmed 'heterosexuality as the scriptural norm' but called for 'deep and dispassionate study of the question of homosexuality, which would take seriously both the teaching of Scripture and the results of scientific and medical research' and 'recognising the need for pastoral concern for those who are homosexual, encourages dialogue with them'.

---

[84] Davidson, *The Five Lambeth Conferences*, p. 131.
[85] *Conference of Bishops of the Anglican Communion Holden at Lambeth Palace, July 5 to August 7, 1920*, p. 114.
[86] *The Report of the Lambeth Conference 1978*, pp. 64–5.

By 1988, the issues were being approached in terms of sexual orientation in the group's report.[87] This noted that 'many Provinces have traditionally maintained that homosexuality is a sin whilst others are responding differently to the issue'. Because 'sexuality is an aspect of life which goes to the very heart of human identity and society' and 'this issue remains unresolved', it was viewed as 'a pastorally sensitive issue which requires further study and reflection by Church leadership' (noting science, Scripture and sociocultural factors). The report continued to encourage 'dialogue with, and pastoral concern for, persons of homosexual orientation within the Family of Christ'. Resolution 64 addressed these concerns. Headed 'Human Rights for Those of Homosexual Orientation' it originated with the American Bishop Paul Moore, who was later revealed to have had a number of gay affairs while married.[88] He hoped for a more positive statement but was met with strong opposition, particularly from Africa. The final wording reaffirmed the 1978 statement, particularly the continuing need for study, highlighted the factors noted above 'that lead to the different attitudes in the provinces of our Communion' and called on 'each province to reassess, in the light of such study and because of our concern for human rights, its care for and attitude towards persons of homosexual orientation'.

It was clear that this would become a major issue in 1998 as the gulf between provinces, noted in earlier resolutions, widened. The American church was ordaining same-sex partnered clergy (a practice accepted by the Righter Trial of 1996) and those opposed to this were increasingly connected with Anglicans in the Global South who, in 1997, issued the Kuala Lumpur Statement on Human Sexuality.[89] The conference subgroup on human sexuality, after fractious meetings, eventually agreed a statement.[90] This described some expressions of sexuality as 'inherently contrary to the Christian way and ... sinful', but confessed 'we are not of one mind about homosexuality' and set out a range of four understandings present. It stated that 'a majority of bishops is not prepared to bless same sex unions or to

---

[87] *The Truth Shall Make You Free: The Lambeth Conference 1988*, p. 187.

[88] Jordan Hylden, 'The contradictions of Paul Moore'; available online: http://livingchurch.org/covenant/2014/11/19/bishop-paul-moore-of-new-york/ (accessed 13 February 2017).

[89] On this, see Miranda Hassett, *Anglican Communion in Crisis: How Episcopal Dissidents and Their African Allies Are Reshaping Anglicanism* (Princeton: Princeton University Press, 2007) and Goddard, 'Sexuality and Communion'.

[90] *The Official Report of the Lambeth Conference 1998*, pp. 93–5.

ordain active homosexuals' and noted that many wanted a moratorium on such actions, before calling for more study while working to maintain unity. The group also agreed a resolution which then faced numerous amendments in a full Conference debate.

The final resolution, agreed by 526 votes to 70 with 40 abstentions, commended the group report and then covered three broad areas. In relation to teaching it restated traditional teaching ('in view of the teaching of Scripture, upholds faithfulness in marriage between a man and a woman in lifelong union, and believes that abstinence is right for those who are not called to marriage') and, in a crucial amendment carried by 389 votes to 190, explicitly rejected 'homosexual practice as incompatible with Scripture'. In relation to church practice it said that the Conference 'cannot advise the legitimising or blessing of same sex unions nor ordaining those involved in same gender unions'. Pastorally, it recognized 'that there are among us persons who experience themselves as having a homosexual orientation' who 'are seeking the pastoral care, moral direction of the Church, and God's transforming power for the living of their lives and the ordering of relationships'. In another important amendment the bishops committed themselves 'to listen to the experience of homosexual persons' and assured them 'that they are loved by God and that all baptised, believing and faithful persons, regardless of sexual orientation, are full members of the Body of Christ'. They also called 'on all our people to minister pastorally and sensitively to all irrespective of sexual orientation and to condemn irrational fear of homosexuals, violence within marriage and any trivialisation and commercialisation of sex'. While not repeating earlier calls for further study, the resolution requested 'the Primates and the ACC [Anglican Consultative Council] to establish a means of monitoring the work done on the subject of human sexuality in the Communion and to share statements and resources among us'.

An early sign that the resolution was going to be questioned came in the following weeks when 185 bishops from fourteen provinces (76 from the United States), including nine Primates and some future Primates such as Rowan Williams, signalled their support for 'A Pastoral Statement to Lesbian and Gay Anglicans'. Five years later, the approval of a liturgy for blessing same-sex unions in Canada's New Westminster diocese and the election of Gene Robinson as Bishop of New Hampshire created greater polarization and led to many bishops staying away from Lambeth 2008 whose Indaba processes wrestled with the ecclesiological fallout of the reactions to the 1998 decision.

VII Conclusion

Given the current divisions among Anglicans over homosexuality, the history described above raises the question whether there is precedent in Lambeth Conference resolutions on marriage and sex that could justify a future Lambeth Conference rethinking the 1998 decision and moving to a less rigorist position. In relation to polygamy, the shift took a century and was only in relation to exclusion from baptism. No Lambeth Conference or Anglican Province has commended polygamy or approved ordaining polygamists and no Lambeth Conference has urged that those in same-sex relationships be denied baptism.[91] In relation to contraception, there was a shift from absolute condemnation of 'unnatural' behaviour to greater freedom of conscience, a shift which could be paralleled in relation to moral evaluation of homosexual behaviour. This shift, however, explicitly appealed to the lack of biblical teaching in this area and concerned a matter of personal and private moral judgement, not authorization of public ecclesial acts of blessing or ordination. The parallel is therefore again weak.

The strongest parallels are with the response to divorce. Here the Conferences faced a major social change in relation to marriage. Early Lambeth statements appealed to the teaching of Scripture (indeed to Christ himself) and its necessary and restrictive implications for church practice, just as Lambeth resolutions on homosexuality have done. There followed a recognition of the need to respond to pastoral realities in many provinces and debate about how one best described marriage as permanent in the face of its breakdown (the indissolubility and annulment questions). This ultimately led – perhaps not intentionally and certainly without the formal explicit reversal by a Conference seen in the other two cases – to greater diversity, silence from

---

[91] For a discussion of polygamy in relation to homosexuality, see George Sumner, "'Patience Leads to Character": The Polygamy-Homosexuality Analogy in Contemporary Debate', in Catherine Sider Hamilton (ed.), *The Homosexuality Debate: Faith Seeking Understanding* (Toronto: Anglican Book Centre, 2003), pp. 216–26.

Lambeth Conferences, and an acceptance that provinces could develop their own varied responses even if these were less rigorous than the teaching and practice of earlier Lambeth Conference resolutions. A similar evolution to this could, theoretically, take place in relation to homosexuality. However, the continued insistence that marriage should be permanent and must be entered as a lifelong union, and that divorce was a sign of sin and failure, all provided continuity with the past and coherence across diversity. Particularly with debate increasingly focused on same-sex marriage, it is difficult to discern what would be parallel continuities in the doctrine of marriage in relation to possible developments in response to homosexuality.

Ultimately, whether or not a similar trajectory *does* occur (and if so at what speed) depends in large part on political realities. These, with the rise of the Global South and the deep divisions of recent years, are quite different from arguments earlier in the twentieth century about divorce. Whether or not developments *should* occur depends on two main judgements: first, the biblical and theological arguments specific to homosexuality; secondly, whether the evolution in relation to divorce offers a positive model in terms of ecclesiology and moral and pastoral theology, or whether it represents a failure of nerve and theological rigour on the part of the Lambeth Conferences in relation to its witness on marriage and sexuality.

Appendix – Lambeth Conferences on marriage and sex[92]

Date	Committee	Resolutions	Prominence	Significance
1867	None	None		
1878	None	None	Encyclical ('Local peculiarities regarding the Laws of Marriage', pp. 94, 96).	Decision on not baptizing polygamists.
1888	Committees on Purity (pp. 130–2), Divorce (pp. 132–3) and Polygamy (pp. 133–5)	3–5	3 of 19 resolutions. 3 of 12 committees. Encyclical ('Purity', 'Sanctity of Marriage' and 'Polygamy', pp. 107-9).	
1897	None	None	Encyclical ('Purity' and 'Sanctity of Marriage', pp. 183–4). 1888 Purity Report reissued.	
1908	'Marriage Problems' (pp. 395–408)	25, 37–43, 67	9 of 78 resolutions. 1 of 11 committees. Encyclical ('Marriage Problems', pp. 309–11). 'Marriage' in committee on 'Foreign Missions' (pp. 374–75).	Focus on divorce and birth control (first discussion)
1920	'Problems of Marriage and Sexual Morality' (pp. 107–15)	39, 66–72	8 of 80 resolutions. 1 of 8 committees. Encyclical ('Marriage and the Family', pp. 17–18).	First use of 'indissoluble' for marriage. Resolutions on 'Missionary Problems' and 'Problems of Marriage and Sexual Morality' cover divorce, contraception, impurity and polygamy.
1930	'Marriage' and 'Sex' (pp. 85–95)	9–21	12 of 75 resolutions. 2 of 5 subjects covered within 'Life and Witness of the Christian community' (1 of the 5 committees). Encyclical ('Marriage and Sex', pp. 21–3).	Significant change on contraception. Resolutions on 'The Life and Witness of the Christian Community - Marriage and Sex.'

Year	Report	Resolutions	Details	Description
1948	'The Church's Discipline in Marriage' (2.96-105)	92–99	8 of 118 resolutions. 1 of 6 committees. Encyclical (1.24-25).	Resolutions focus on divorce and remarriage.
1958	'The Family in Contemporary Society' (2.141-171)	112–24	13 of 131 resolutions. 1 of 5 committees. Encyclical ('Reconciliation in Society', 1.21–23).	Fullest ever consideration of marriage, sexuality and family planning. Resolutions on marriage, polygamy and the family.
1968	None	22 and 23	2 of 68 resolutions. None of 33 groups.	Resolutions on 'Responsible Parenthood' (response to *Humanae Vitae*) and 'Marriage Discipline'.
1978	'Sexuality and the Family' reported on 'The Family', 'Sexuality – Masculinity and Femininity' and 'Homosexuality' (pp. 62-5)	10 and 34	2 of 37 resolutions. 1 of 11 groups within 'What is the Church For?' (1 of 3 sections).	First explicit discussion of homosexuality. Resolutions on 'Human Relationships and Sexuality' and 'Anglican-Roman Catholic marriages'.
1988	'Living Together in Families' covering 'Marriage', 'The Family', 'Sexual Orientation' and 'Sexual Abuse' (paras 127-60, pp. 182–8)	26, 28, 29, 34 and 64	5 of 73 resolutions. 1 of 4 groups within 'Christianity and the Social Order' (1 of 4 sections). Pastoral Letter – 'The Family As A Gift from God' (pp. 318–20).	Resolutions on 'Church and Polygamy', 'Sexual Abuse', 'AIDS', 'Marriage and Family' and 'Human Rights for Those of Homosexual Orientation'.
1998	'Human Sexuality' (pp. 93–5)	I.10	1 resolution, incorporating elements of many proposed resolutions. 1 of 6 subgroups within 'Called to Full Humanity' (1 of 4 sections).	Resolution which led to major disagreements over homosexuality within the Communion, especially after 2003.
2008	Indaba discussions	Indaba	'Human Sexuality' (paras. 105-120, pp. 31–34) under 'Strengthening our Anglican Identity' in Reflections document.	

[92] The page references are to Davidson, *The Five Lambeth Conferences* up to 1908 and then from 1920 onwards to the reports of each individual conference as cited above.

9

The Windsor Process and the Anglican Covenant

Gregory K. Cameron

The institutional Anglican Communion was born out of controversy. The issue at the forefront in the 1860s was sexual mores: more specifically polygamy, since conservative voices in Canada objected to the liberal line taken by the colonial Bishop John Colenso of Natal. For some, the Lambeth Conference's *raison d'être* was to be a remedy for potential Church-dividing conflict, although others objected strongly to the idea of a Pan-Anglican Synod and felt that the context of mutual consultation on mission should take priority. Two distinct threads have nevertheless been closely intertwined in the history of the Lambeth Conferences: controversy itself, and the transcending issue of how to resolve such controversy. The Communion has needed to engage in a dual dialogue, articulating not only its answers to controversial questions, but also to give an account of the processes and authority by which it resolves controversy.

Although the first Lambeth Conference eschewed any synodical authority, it did in fact confer upon the Communion a legitimacy and a unity which has sustained its life as a worldwide Christian Communion for the last one hundred and fifty years.[1]

This vocation to articulate the boundaries of Anglicanism remained with the Lambeth Conference in its successive incarnations: for example, in 1888 when the Conference refined the Chicago/Lambeth Quadrilateral;[2] in 1920

---

[1] See G. K. Cameron, 'Locating the Anglican Communion in the History of Anglicanism', in Ian Markham et al. (eds), *The Wiley-Blackwell Companion to the Anglican Communion* (Chichester: Wiley-Blackwell, 2013), pp. 3–14.

[2] Resolution 11, *The Lambeth Conference*, 1888.

when it articulated the nature of the Communion;[3] and in 1930 when it again gave voice to the nature of the relationship between the Churches of the Communion.[4]

In the later part of the twentieth century, however, in an age of accessible international air travel, the baton of defining Anglicanism has tended to pass to specially empowered Commissions. It was the Eames Commission that discerned the way ahead on the ordination of women,[5] the Virginia Report of the Inter-Anglican Theological and Doctrinal Commission[6] which attempted to rearticulate the mechanisms of the Communion in time for the 1998 Lambeth Conference,[7] and more latterly the Inter-Anglican Standing Commission for Unity, Faith and Order which has sought to interpret the structures of the Communion in two papers presented to the fifteenth and sixteenth meetings of the Anglican Consultative Council (ACC).[8]

The origins and authority of the Windsor Process

'The Windsor Process' encompasses a number of related threads in the life of the Anglican Communion set in motion by the Instruments of Communion during the archiepiscopate of Rowan Williams (Archbishop of Canterbury, 2002–12) as responses to the recommendations of the *Windsor Report* of 2004. The *Windsor Report* had also been conceived in crisis, as the Anglican Communion sought to contain tensions over new attitudes towards human sexuality which had been pushing persistently to the fore in Anglican life, and indeed in all Christian World Communions, in the second half of the twentieth century.

In October 2003 Archbishop Williams had summoned an extraordinary meeting of the Primates and Moderators of the Anglican Communion at Lambeth Palace to address a specific flashpoint when the 74th General

---

[3] Encyclical Letter, *The Lambeth Conference* 1920.
[4] Encyclical Letter, The Lambeth Conference, 1930; see especially the section reproduced as document 400 on p. 389 of *The Anglican Tradition*, ed. G. R. Evans and J. Robert Wright (London: SPCK, 1991).
[5] *The Eames Commission: The Official Reports* (Toronto: Anglican Book Centre, 1994).
[6] The *Virginia Report* (London: Anglican Consultative Council, 1997).
[7] Ibid.
[8] 'Towards a Symphony of Instruments', presented within the IASCUFO Report to ACC-15, Auckland, New Zealand, 2013, and 'Instruments of Communion: Gifts, Signs and Stewardship', presented within the IASCUFO Report to ACC-16, Lusaka, Kenya, 2016.

Convention of the Episcopal Church, meeting a few months earlier in late July and early August, had confirmed the election of a bishop who was a divorced man living in an acknowledged same-sex relationship. The Primates had agreed that the Archbishop should establish a commission to explore the theological and legal resources by which the resulting tensions might be addressed.[9]

The *Windsor Report*, which was published a year later, did not address the issue of sexuality directly as a topic and accepted the position adopted by the Primates in their communique of the 2003 Lambeth meeting, which reaffirmed the much referenced 1998 Lambeth Resolution 1.10 as the position of the Communion.[10] Rather, the report focused upon the second thread of dialogue: how the Anglican Communion operated in a time of crisis as a family of Churches. The report reflected on the nature of Christian discernment, and the mechanisms by which the different Provinces could respond together to the theological and ecclesiological challenges of new developments.[11]

Although it was not named explicitly in the report, at the heart of the analysis of the *Windsor Report* was the conviction that there was what can be termed as an 'ecclesial deficit' in the life of the Communion: that is, that despite the existence of a number of mechanisms for consultation, there was

[9] 'We have noted that the Lambeth Conference 1998 requested the Archbishop of Canterbury to establish a commission to consider his own role in maintaining communion within and between provinces when grave difficulties arise. We ask him now to establish such a commission, but that its remit be extended to include urgent and deep theological and legal reflection on the way in which the dangers we have identified at this meeting will have to be addressed. We request that such a commission complete its work, at least in relation to the issues raised at this meeting, within twelve months.' *Primates' Communique,* http://www.anglicannews.org/news/2003/10/a-statement-by-the-primates-of-the-anglican-communion-meeting-in-lambeth-palace.aspx (accessed September 2016).

[10] 'We also re-affirm the resolutions made by the bishops of the Anglican Communion gathered at the Lambeth Conference in 1998 on issues of human sexuality as having moral force and commanding the respect of the Communion as its present position on these issues.' Ibid.

[11] The nomenclature of the Anglican Communion could be a paper in itself. The Churches of the Anglican Communion are called Provinces, reflecting the fact that the Church of England itself consists of two provinces, Canterbury and York. Bishops were listed this way in the earliest lists of attendances at the Lambeth Conferences, which were intended to emphasize the overall unity of the Communion, and the existence of a single episcopal college. There was a problem, however, in that the Church of England was not alone in having internal subdivisions within the single national Church. The Church of Ireland likewise had two provinces, Armagh and Dublin, and, as they developed, the Anglican Church of Canada and the Episcopal Church of the USA moved to a similar form of internal subdivision. The convention observed therefore in Anglican documentation is that 'a province' refers to internal provinces, while in the term 'a Province', when it refers to a whole Church as a member of the Anglican Communion, is shown with the 'P' capitalized.

no clear process which was capable of authoritatively resolving disputes over doctrine and discipline and maintaining the unity of the Church.

The *Windsor Report* acknowledged that the Archbishop of Canterbury had a limited role as a voice for the views of the Communion,[12] but without the authority to enforce it, and that the other three (conciliar) Instruments of Communion – the Lambeth Conference, the ACC and the Primates' Meeting – all exercised a moral rather than a juridical authority.[13] Resolutions of the Lambeth Conference can express the thinking of the bishops, but they cannot bind the Churches,[14] while the ACC is exactly that: consultative. The fourth instrument, the Primates' Meeting, despite calls for it to be given an enhanced status,[15] could not carry more authority that each Primate brought to the table; that is, that they could not bind their Provinces collectively since no individual Primate possesses that authority in his or her Province. The strength of any resolution passed by any of the Instruments of Communion therefore depends entirely on its ability to command respect. Such an approach may not be entirely and distinctively Anglican of course, since it is itself one expression of the operation of an ancient canonical principle which refers to the *sensus fidelium* as the final authority in Christian discernment.

The process by which the recommendations of the *Windsor Report* commanded consideration in the Communion was initiated by the Primates' Meeting which took place in spring 2005 after the publication of the report in the previous November. The report, being just one in a long line, could not have any intrinsic authority in itself, and its significance in the life of the Communion is founded upon its acceptance by all four Instruments of Communion.[16] It is their commendation of it to the Provinces that confers on the report's recommendations the right to be considered.

Before progressing the recommendations of the report, the instruments did not act without reference to the wider Communion. Between the publication of the report and the consultation of the Primates at Dromantine, the Archbishop of Canterbury set up a small Reception Reference Group, which

[12] *The Windsor Report 2004* (London: Anglican Consultative Council, 2004), paragraph 109.
[13] *The Windsor Report*, paragraph 110.
[14] Ibid.,102.
[15] Cf. Resolution 18.2(a) of the 1988 Lambeth Conference.
[16] For discussion of the report's reception by the four Instruments of Communion, see below.

canvassed opinion both across the Anglican Communion and from Anglican ecumenical partners to the proposals of the report. Alongside a presentation on the report by Archbishop Robin Eames as the Chair of the Lambeth Commission, the Reception Reference Group reported to the Primates at Dromantine, having received 332 responses from across the Communion in a process of consultation.[17] This pattern of working – of publication followed by consultation and then recommendation – was repeatedly used throughout the early years of the Windsor Process.

In his report to the Primates at Dromantine, Primus Bruce Cameron,[18] the second Chair of the Reception Reference Group, reported that roughly a third of respondents had welcomed the recommendations of the report, and that a third resisted them. A crucial final third had been positive towards aspects of the recommendations, but had also expressed caution about them. Evaluation of the responses had been nuanced. How much weight could be put on a response from a national synod, say, as compared to a response from an individual? It seems straightforward to give more weight to the synod, until it is added that the synod composed its response in a fifteen-minute debate at the end of an overrunning three-day meeting, while the individual was a Professor of Anglican ecclesiology. The overall balance of responses as reported was received by the Primates as giving broad support across the Communion for the recommendations of the report and encouragement to proceed, and on this basis, the Primates at Dromantine felt able to take several of the recommendations forward.

The Primates' recommendations in the Communique of the Dromantine meeting initiated what has come to be known as the Windsor Process, encompassing three major threads:

1. A request for moratoria on those actions which exacerbated the problem and increased strain on life in communion.
2. A consideration of the issue of homosexuality itself.
3. Reflection on the common life of the Anglican churches, and how they might respond in a collegial way to the challenges facing them.

---

[17] *Communique of the Primates Meeting in Dromantine*, 2005, paragraph 5.
[18] Primus of the Scottish Episcopal Church 2001–6.

Discussion about the Windsor Process has tended to concentrate on the last theme of these three, largely because the *Windsor Report* recommended a reorientation and real empowerment of the Instruments of Communion. However, each of the three threads should not really be taken or considered apart from the others, because they all together constituted the strategy promoted by the *Windsor Report*, and were intended to buttress one another in responding to the crisis through which the Anglican Communion has been travelling.

The Primates and the Windsor Process

The delicate nature of the relationship between the Instruments of Communion, and the contested nature of authority within the Communion, have been revealed by repeated questioning of the competency of the Primates' Meeting to be the instrument which effectively took the driving seat in the process.[19] The uncertain authority wielded by the Primates' Meeting has been an ongoing complication in the life of the Communion, and the decisions of the Primates and the authority that they command have often been the focus of discontent and dispute. The simple truth in October 2003 was that the Primates' Meeting was both the easiest and least expensive of the instruments to convene at short notice, and which brought many of the key players responding to events in the United States into the same room. By and large, however, the Primates appear to have been conscious of the limits of their authority and the delicate balance between the Instruments of Communion, so that care has usually been taken to defer to and consult the other instruments, and to seek their affirmation and agreement to any proposals put forward as soon as a scheduled meeting of that instrument takes place.

---

[19] Cf. Paragraph 151 of *The Reflections of the Lambeth Conference 2008*: 'There is much discomfort about the role that the Primates' Meeting now finds itself exercising. Many fear that it is trying to exercise too much authority. Others believe that the Primates are the only ones who can bear the weight of our current challenges. Perhaps their key role is in supporting the Archbishop of Canterbury. The primates should not exercise collectively any more authority than they have in their Provinces.' Accessed August 2016 at http://www.anglicancommunion.org/media/72554/reflections_document_-final-.pdf.

From the first, the Primates' Meeting in Dromantine acted to affirm and encourage the acceptance of the report's recommendations,[20] taking key decisions to advance recommendations made in the report. The decisions at Dromantine were explicitly referred to the ACC taking place in Nottingham in June 2005,[21] and formally discussed and affirmed there.[22]

---

[20] *Communique of the Primates' Meeting held in Dromantine*, paragraphs 7–17, accessed January 2017 at http://www.anglicancommunion.org/media/68387/communique-_english.pdf.

[21] Cf. Paragraphs 16 and 17 of the *Communique of the Primates Meeting at Dromantine*, accessed at http://www.anglicancommunion.org/media/68387/communique-_english.pdf (accessed August 2016).

[22] Resolution 10: Response to the Primates' Statement at Dromantine
The Anglican Consultative Council:
   a takes note of the decisions taken by the Primates at their recent meeting in Dromantine, Northern Ireland, in connection with the recommendations of the *Windsor Report* 2004
   b notes further that the Primates there reaffirmed 'the standard of Christian teaching on matters of human sexuality expressed in the 1998 Lambeth Resolution 1.10, which should command respect as the position overwhelmingly adopted by the bishops of the Anglican Communion'
   c endorses and affirms those decisions
   d consequently endorses the Primates' request that 'in order to recognise the integrity of all parties, the Episcopal Church (USA) and the Anglican Church of Canada voluntarily withdraw their members from the Anglican Consultative Council, for the period leading up to the next Lambeth Conference'
   e interprets reference to the Anglican Consultative Council to include its Standing Committee and the Inter-Anglican Finance and Administration Committee.

Resolution 11: Supplementary Resolution of Thanks
The Anglican Consultative Council:
   a notes with appreciation the response of the Episcopal Church (USA) and the Anglican Church of Canada to the request of the Primates' Dromantine Statement
   b expresses its thanks for the presentations made on Tuesday, 21st June; and requests the observers from those Provinces to convey those thanks back to their Provinces
   c reminds all parties to have regard for the admonitions in paragraphs 156 and 157 of the *Windsor Report*.
The *Windsor Report*, paragraphs 156 and 157
156. We call upon all parties to the current dispute to seek ways of reconciliation, and to heal our divisions. We have already indicated (paragraphs 134 and 144) some ways in which the Episcopal Church (USA) and the Diocese of New Westminster could begin to speak with the Communion in a way which would foster reconciliation. We have appealed to those intervening in Provinces and dioceses similarly to act with renewed respect. We would expect all Provinces to respond with generosity and charity to any such actions. It may well be that there need to be formal discussions about the path to reconciliation, and a symbolic Act of Reconciliation, which would mark a new beginning for the Communion, and a common commitment to proclaim the Gospel of Christ to a broken and needy world.
157. There remains a very real danger that we will not choose to walk together. Should the call to halt and find ways of continuing in our present communion not be heeded, then we shall have to begin to learn to walk apart. We would much rather not speculate on actions that might need to be taken if, after acceptance by the primates, our recommendations are not implemented. However, we note that there are, in any human dispute, courses that may be followed: processes of mediation and arbitration; non-invitation to relevant representative bodies and meetings; invitation, but to observer status only; and, as an absolute last resort, withdrawal from membership. We earnestly hope that none of these will prove necessary. Our aim throughout has been to work not for division but for healing and restoration. The real challenge of the gospel is whether we live deeply enough in the love of Christ, and care sufficiently for our joint work to bring that love to the world, that we will 'make every effort to maintain the unity of the Spirit in the bond of peace' (Eph. 4.3). As the primates stated in 2000, 'to turn from one another would be to turn away from the Cross', and indeed from serving the world which God loves and for which Jesus Christ died.

The Windsor Process was accommodated as a subject within the programme of the Lambeth Conference of 2008,[23] and specific hearings were scheduled to allow the bishops to discuss and respond to the outworking of the proposals being carried forward. Although the 2008 Conference eschewed the making of any resolutions, there was a significant attempt to encapsulate the thinking of the bishops arising out of Indaba in the Reflections Document, and that included a description of the views expressed in the Conference on the Windsor Process.[24] The Windsor Process has therefore reiterated the repeated cycle of consultation, consolidation, report and then recommendation in the life of the Communion.

Proponents of the view that the Primates should regulate the life of the Communion point to successive resolutions of the Lambeth Conference urging the Primates to assume more authority to uphold the doctrinal standards of the Communion.[25] However, any such assertions run up against the fact noted above that resolutions of the Lambeth Conference are themselves only advisory, and do not command juridical authority in the Churches of the Anglican Communion unless given that authority by adoption in national synods. The authority of the Primates' Meeting remains therefore highly circumscribed. As noted above, if a Primate cannot speak juridically within his or her jurisdiction and authoritatively bind his or her own Province, there is no reason why the Primates together should have an authority that they do not hold individually.

In the end therefore, what authority is carried by the Windsor Process in the life of the Communion? It carries the moral weight of the commendations which it receives from the Instruments of Communion. All four Instruments of Communion are on record as having commended the Windsor Process, but none of these act with legislative authority to impose the recommendations of the process in the Communion. The Windsor Process relies entirely upon its ability to win the approval of the churches which make up the membership of

---

Accessed August 2016 at http://www.anglicancommunion.org/structures/instruments-of-communion/acc/acc-13/resolutions.aspx#s10.

[23] Two Hearings were organized for an hour and a half on 23 and 28 July, while the Windsor Process was the theme of the Indaba session on 2 August.

[24] Sections J & K of the *Reflections* Document of the 2008 Lambeth Conference, accessed January 2017 at http://www.anglicancommunion.org/resources/document-library.aspx?author=Lambeth+Conference.

[25] For example, Lambeth Conference 1988, Resolution 18.2(a), and Lambeth Conference 1998, Resolution III.6.

the Communion. More cynically and pragmatically, the recommendations of the *Windsor Report* can only be effective to the extent that they are made to stick, and that Provinces and Anglicans generally show themselves willing to abide by them. As of late 2016, there is little sign that they will.

The Major Themes of the Windsor Process

1 The Moratoria

The intention of the Windsor Report was to recommend a process by which the common life of the Anglican Communion could be reasserted even in the face of deep and divisive theological difference. The strategy that the report proposed was a halt to those interventions which were aggravating the situation, in order to allow the Communion time for a dispassionate articulation of the common heritage that held the Provinces together, and the development of mechanisms that would be acceptable to allow them to face new challenges to unity and diversity. The report identified three areas which were exacerbating the current situation:

1. The election of openly gay and lesbian clergy to episcopal ministry and Christian leadership,
2. Innovation with respect to the ministry offered by the church to people of a homosexual orientation,
3. The growth of interventions from other Provinces in North America at the invitation of dissenting minorities within the Anglican Churches.

The report therefore invited all those involved in any of these actions to express regret, and to exercise restraint from repeating actions which would cause offence.[26] It would be fair to say however that, in the twelve years since the publication of the *Windsor Report*, the three moratoria have been more noticeable for being disregarded in the life of the Communion rather than being observed. This has created a situation which has increasingly fuelled further conflict and undermined trust. Furthermore, the fact that the Anglican Communion has not given itself any breathing space has meant that other

---

[26] The *Windsor Report 2004*, paragraphs 134, 144 and 155. The exactly parallel language used in these three paragraphs should be noted as intentional, indicating that the Commission wanted all three areas to be handled in a similar fashion.

initiatives, such as the Anglican Communion Covenant, which was intended to fix ground rules for future re-engagement, have themselves been adopted as weapons in the battle over sexuality.

It is not possible to identify an order of priority within the moratoria recommended in the *Windsor Report*, and things started well – the Episcopal House of Bishops took the distinctive step of offering what was requested – regret – for the decisions taken in their Church with respect to the consecration of an openly homosexual bishop,[27] and going further, to express repentance at the failure to consult properly.

This rather surprising act of restraint offered by the leadership of the Episcopal Church was not reciprocated by the Provinces offering support to dissidents within its life. In the first place, several critical voices argued that regret did not equate to repentance – even if this went far beyond the recommendation and request of the *Windsor Report*. There was no attempt at all to discontinue support for emergent ecclesial bodies in North America which took a strident stance against the innovations of the Episcopal Church, and indeed several African Anglican provinces increased their interventions in North America rather than drawing back.

The interventions by the African Provinces were fostered by some of the theologically conservative Anglican constituencies of North America, who became intent in identifying themselves against the Episcopal Church. For such groups, separation from an increasingly liberal Church and finding an Anglican identity apart from the Episcopal Church became their deliberate agenda. They argued that in moving to accommodate new sexual mores, the Episcopal Church was also moving away from the historic basis of Christianity grounded in its obedience to the Holy Scriptures. Despite a clear and consistent line being taken against the interventions by the Primates' Meetings,[28] the

---

[27] http://www.anglicannews.org/news/2005/03/house-of-bishops-adopts-covenant-statement.aspx (accessed January 2017).

[28] There have been statements in the communiques of every Primates' Meeting between 2000 and 2009 that the development of alternative parallel structures of Anglican life was not appropriate. The Singapore consecrations of 2000 were noted with serious concern, and the Primates endorsed the Archbishop of Canterbury's statement that he was not in communion with the bishops so consecrated (Oporto 2000), and asked that further steps of a similar kind would not be taken (Oporto 2000, Kanuga 2001). There should be respect for the integrity of other Provinces (Gramado 2003, Lambeth 2003, Dar es Salaam 2007). A panel of reference might act as a broker of pastoral care for dissidents (Dromantine 2005), which had some limited moderating effect (Dar es Salaam 2007). Interventions were exacerbating the situation and the integrity of Provinces ought to be respected

churches of Uganda and Nigeria in particular stated very clearly that they would not abandon their friends, and that they did not believe that the issues of obedience to the traditional reading of Scripture could be accorded equal significance to issues of ecclesiastical boundaries and jurisdiction.[29]

Nevertheless, there can be little doubt that the offence caused by these interventions in the Episcopal Church and the hostile rhetoric employed often personally against the Presiding Bishop, hardened opinion within the liberal wing of the Episcopal Church, and early conciliatory statements were replaced by an attitude that appeasement was not worthwhile. All three moratoria recommended in the *Windsor Report* have been effectively inoperative.

Although conservatives rejected the moratorium requested on intervention, the Windsor Process did have one significant effect. It concentrated minds on the evolution of the Anglican Church of North America (ACNA) as an emerging Province of the Anglican Communion so that the conservative presence in North America might at least have a mantle of respectability.

At first, even fairly conservative voices such as Archbishop Drexel Gomez of the West Indies and Archbishop John Chew of Singapore distanced themselves from the ongoing interventions and sought to be faithful to a wider Anglican Communion process of discernment. This was reflected in particular by the criticism offered of the interventions in the work of the Windsor Continuation Group. The Windsor Continuation Group was another of the working parties convened to carry forward the work of the Windsor Process. It functioned between February 2008 and February 2009 to monitor and reflect on progress in the Windsor Process and reported to the Primates' Meeting in Alexandria in 2009. It was trenchant in its criticism of the emerging Anglican Church of North America for its lack of ecclesiological density.[30] Slowly but surely however, the Anglican Church of North America, which was originally a confederation of seven dissenting movements, has sought to integrate and to codify its life as a single Church, and to achieve recognition as an Anglican Province.

(Dar es Salaam 2007). The emergence of parallel jurisdictions had to be treated with a high degree of caution (Alexandria 2009).

[29] Cf. *Statement of the Global South Primates Meeting* in Nairobi in January 2005, paragraph 10, accessed January 2017 at http://www.globalsouthanglican.org/index.php/blog/comments/a%20 href=/P960.

[30] *Report of the Windsor Continuation Group*, 2009, paragraphs 92-101, accessed January 2017 at http://www.anglicancommunion.org/media/100354/The-Windsor-Continuation-Group.pdf.

It has now reached the stage where the Anglican Church of North America has been given some form of recognition, albeit without clarity. Although the ACC is the only body in the Anglican Communion with the constitutional mechanisms to alter a schedule of provinces of the Anglican Communion, and a clear process for accession, the (105th) Archbishop of Canterbury, Justin Welby, took the decision to invite the Primate of the ACNA to Canterbury in February of 2016. The GAFCON Provinces had made it clear that their Primates would not attend without the presence of the Primate of ACNA, so a procedural device was adopted whereby Archbishop Foley Beach was present for a Primates' *Gathering* for three and a half days at the beginning of the week, and a Primates' *Meeting* appears to have been constituted only after he had departed on the Thursday.

How this matter will evolve for the Primates' Meeting of 2017, or its consequences for the Lambeth Conference in 2020, is held only in the mind of the Archbishop of Canterbury for the time being. The *Windsor Report* had made it clear that invitations were solely at the discretion of the Archbishop of Canterbury,[31] a principle that had been applied for the 2008 Lambeth Conference, and accepted by the bishops then, as indicated by their presence or absence.[32]

2 The listening process

The *Windsor Report* had been clear that although it did not address the substantive issue of Christian teaching towards homosexuality, it was something which should be a priority for the Communion.[33] Accordingly, the Primates' Meeting in Dromantine decided that although the Episcopal Church delegates should not attend ACC-13 in Nottingham, UK, representatives should be invited to give a presentation of why they believed gay and lesbian inclusion should be a matter to be advanced in the life of the Communion, and how this related to existing Christian teaching. The Standing Committee

---

[31] The *Windsor Report*, paragraph 110.
[32] Namely, no one refused to attend because three bishops were not invited; and some Provinces refused to attend because another had been, but no one argued that the Archbishop did not have the right to do as he had done. The three bishops not invited were the Bishop of New Hampshire, the Bishop of Harare and a Bishop of the Church of South India.
[33] The *Windsor Report*, paragraph 26.

of the ACC endorsed this proposal and a presentation was consequently made. The ACC then commissioned an ongoing process of engagement on the topic of sexuality known as the listening process, or 'Indaba'. It is far beyond the scope of this chapter to record the progress of the listening process, which has developed a sprawling and vibrant life of its own. It is important to note, however, that it was the listening process that was requested by the Instruments of Communion to bear the weight of actually addressing head-on the issues of disagreement over teaching on human sexuality.

3 The Anglican Covenant

The *Windsor Report* envisaged a situation in which the moratoria would create a space for two things to happen: first, for there to be the listening process – a substantive discussion on sexuality, which, if successful, might uncover some new consensus, or at least a modus vivendi on the matter; and second, for there to be a new articulation of the ground rules of the Anglican Communion, so that a clear framework for authoritative discernment and the resolution of disagreement might be established.

At the third and final meeting of the Lambeth Commission in Windsor Castle in September 2004 consideration was given to the mechanisms by which the different Provinces of the Communion might 'walk together'.[34] One of the members of the Commission, Professor Norman Doe, had an interest in the development of International Law, and it was he who first voiced the idea that perhaps some sort of common Anglican Communion law might be recommended. Professor Doe had given a paper in the 2001 Primates' Meeting in Kanuga, at the invitation of Archbishop George Carey, in which he had offered a juridical analysis of the Communion, and explored both the 'centrifugal' and the 'centripetal' forces in the Communion.[35] These ideas had been developed at the Primates' Meeting in Canterbury in 2002, which had sanctioned the creation of a Legal Adviser's Network, and a project to discern common Anglican Communion canon law.[36] In the discussion of the commission preparing the

[34] This section is partly based on personal recollection of the meetings described.
[35] Norman Doe, 'Canon Law and Communion', *Ecclesiastical Law Journal*, 6 (2002), pp. 241–63.
[36] The fruition of this project was published as *The Principles of Canon Law Common to the Churches of the Anglican Communion* (London: Anglican Consultative Council, 2008) and presented at the 2008 Lambeth Conference.

Windsor Report, the commission asked Professor Doe and other members to draft something which might give the commission an idea about how such a law might look; the draft was published as Appendix 2 of the report.

Designed by a professor of law, this first articulation of what an Anglican Communion process for dispute resolution might look like looks and feels juridical. Ultimately the Commission took the decision that a law-based approach of this kind would require such a detailed and diverse series of legislative processes in the national synods of the Provinces that it was unlikely to be steered to a successful conclusion – perhaps a premonition in fact of what was to come.

Noting the successful adoption of 'covenants' in ecumenical Church relations,[37] one of the central ideas of the Windsor Process was born: the possibility of an Anglican Covenant, which would be a solemn commitment between the Provinces setting out the basics of the common inheritance of Anglicans across the world, and formulating ways in which the Instruments of Communion could work together to maintain coherence, integrity and communion. The Commission felt that the case for a covenant was strong, even if it was not entirely convinced that Appendix 2 was the right expression of the idea.[38]

Once again, it was the Primates' Meeting in Dromantine that formally set the Covenant process in train.[39] An early group produced a scoping exercise,[40] and by late 2006 a Covenant Design Group was appointed, under the chairmanship of Drexel Gomez, Archbishop of the West Indies, and remarkably quickly the basics of a Covenant draft were established.

From the first, the feeling was that any Covenant should not seek to impose innovation on the Communion. It should attempt to be a document which

---

[37] In an unpublished paper presented to a seminar at the General Theological Seminary, New York, in 2008, I argued that there were several instances where the concept of 'covenant' had been successfully implemented in Anglican polity and ecumenical relations. These included the Welsh ecumenical covenant of 1975, *Called to Common Mission* of the Episcopal Church and the Evangelical Lutheran Church in America, and the five existing intra-Anglican covenants between the Episcopal Church and their former dependent missionary churches.

[38] The arguments of the Lambeth Commission for an Anglican Covenant are presented in paragraph 119 of the *Windsor Report*.

[39] The *Primates' Communique from the Dromantine Meeting in 2005*, paragraph 9.

[40] 'Towards an Anglican Covenant: A report on the Covenant Proposal of the Windsor Report, presented to the Joint Standing Committee, March 2006', available at http://www.anglicancommunion.org/media/100663/Towards-an-Anglican-Covenant.pdf.

drew the Communion together on the basis of what already was the case.[41] When the group convened in Nassau in January 2007 the Covenant Design Group surprised itself by how easy it was to develop the architecture of a covenant text, and to write a summary of Anglican faith and ecclesiology, drawing on existing documents. The draft was already strongly advanced by the end of the first meeting: the so-called Nassau Text.[42] The text drew heavily on the Church of England Declaration of Assent, and set out a number of affirmations intended to describe the Anglican inheritance of faith, together with commitments to preserve these dynamics.

The text which this first meeting produced was presented to the Joint Standing Committee for comment at Dar es Salaam prior to the Primates' Meeting,[43] and then to the Primates and received significant support. Up to this point, the narrative was clear, the Covenant was an honest attempt to define what united Anglicans, and was broadly welcomed.

Following the Dar es Salaam Primates' Meeting however, the two members of the Episcopal Church who were part of the Covenant Design Group, Dr Ephraim Radner and Dr Katherine Grieb, were invited to speak on the work of the group to the Episcopal House of Bishops. While the paper of Dr Radner was conservative but broadly supportive, the paper of Dr Katherine Grieb offered a new analysis: the Covenant was vulnerable to becoming a tool by which the conservative Primates of Africa would forge the exclusion of the Episcopal Church from the Communion, and replace it with a new breakaway Province.[44]

Dr Grieb's paper introduced the possibility of a narrative in the debate around the Covenant that had previously not been articulated. Now, there was a strong take up of the idea that the Covenant was not about providing neutral ground around which the Anglican Communion could unite and then address a process of discernment with respect to sexuality. Rather it began

---

[41] The *Windsor Report*, paragraphs 118, 120.

[42] Each of the drafts was named after the location at which the Covenant Design Group was working at the time: hence Nassau in 2007, St Andrew's House in London, the home of the Anglican Communion Office, in 2008, and Ridley Hall theological college in Cambridge in 2009.

[43] The Joint Standing Committee was a meeting of the Standing Committee of the ACC and the Executive Committee of the Primates' Meeting, a more ad hoc body, which included a representative Primate from each continent.

[44] Katherine Grieb, 'Interpreting the Proposed Anglican Covenant through the Communiqué', accessed November 2016 at http://anglicansablaze.blogspot.co.uk/2007/03/katherine-grieb-interpreting-proposed.html.

to be regarded as a device to assert traditional teaching and to provide the necessary constitutional mechanisms to expel the Episcopal Church from the Communion. This narrative was to prove highly corrosive to the whole Covenant project, because from this point on, judgements were not made on the content of the Covenant text itself, but on the perceived effects that any text would have on the sexuality debate. Broadly speaking, therefore, those who were liberal and inclusive on the sexuality agenda saw the Covenant as reasserting traditional teaching and inimical to change, accompanied moreover by a centralization of authority.

In the meantime, the Covenant design process proceeded unimpeded. The Nassau and subsequent St Andrew's drafts of the Covenant text were sent out for consultation in the Provinces, and both garnered some substantial agreement, so much so that the Ridley Cambridge draft, a third recension which was produced at a meeting in Ridley Hall, Cambridge, at the end of March 2009, was put to the Fourteenth Meeting of the ACC in Jamaica as a possible definitive text to be sent out for the approval of the Provinces of the Communion.

Having evolved over three texts (two of which had been sent out across the Communion for consultation), the structure of the Covenant text presented at Jamaica had an introduction followed by four major sections, with each section falling into two parts. In each case, the first part of a section was descriptive of those matters which the Churches of the Anglican Communion were believed already to affirm, followed by a section written in the light of the first, in the form of a number of commitments which each Province would carry forward into the future. The four sections covered 1. 'Our Inheritance of Faith', 2. 'The Life that we share: Our Anglican Vocation', 3. 'Our Unity and Common Life' and 4. 'Our Covenanted Life Together'.

At the meeting in Jamaica, the first three sections proved to be relatively uncontroversial. Section One (Our Inheritance of Faith) went little further than a restatement of the Chicago/Lambeth Quadrilateral, with commitments to the shared study of Scripture. Section Two (The Life we share with others) offered a digest of the history of mission in the Anglican Communion, with a commitment to the Five Marks of Mission, a well-established formula in the life of the Communion.[45] Section Three offered a description of the four

---

[45] http://www.anglicancommunion.org/identity/marks-of-mission.aspx (accessed January 2017).

Instruments of Communion and a call to mutual engagement and listening. It is not surprising, given the relatively cautious text, that feedback on the sections had been good, and the Council responded favourably.[46] The fly in the ointment was always going to be provincial autonomy.

Provincial autonomy and the Covenant

It has been noted that the very first Lambeth Conference had been called when the conservative churches of North America took exception to the liberal teaching of the colonial bishops of Africa – specifically, John William Colenso, first Bishop of Natal. Colenso had incurred considerable wrath by his publication of critical studies of the Old Testament; when he began advocating support for polygamy as a way of ensuring that second and third wives would not be ruined by renunciation upon the husband's conversion, there was enough anger to trigger a lobby of the Archbishop of Canterbury to call an international synod of all Anglican bishops. From the first, however, there was resistance to any idea that such a synod could be held to call Provinces or bishops to account. A third of the invited bishops, led by the Archbishop of York, refused to attend, and the attendance of the majority was only secured by a clear renunciation of any pretence that the Conference would have synodical powers. Thus a fundamental principle of the Anglican Communion – that each Province enjoys autonomy – was asserted, and a pattern was set for the future of international Anglicanism which it has been both chafed against and celebrated at different times.

Down through the decades, there have been several attempts to attribute greater authority to the Lambeth Conference: the most recent is the virtual canonization of the 1998 Lambeth Resolution 1.10. To this point in the Communion's history, all of these attempts have been rebuffed, while trying to articulate some formula of words which maintained the fellowship of the Provinces. One of the most significant attempt was quoted by the *Windsor*

---

[46] Resolution 11 of ACC-14: 'The Anglican Consultative Council ... thanks the Covenant Design Group for their faithfulness and responsiveness in producing drafts for an Anglican Communion Covenant and, in particular, for the Ridley Cambridge Draft submitted to this meeting ... [it] recognizes that an Anglican Communion Covenant may provide an effective means to strengthen and promote our common life as a Communion'.

Report itself.[47] One of the latest initiatives to urge greater integration was the Virginia Report, a precursor to Windsor, and chaired by the same person, Archbishop Robert Eames of Armagh.[48]

In the Windsor Process, it fell to the Covenant Design Group to seek to encapsulate a difficult history which would do justice to both the autonomy and the interdependence of the Provinces in one short text. In the Nassau draft the intention had been to be descriptive rather than prescriptive, and the Covenant Design Group sought to describe the processes that they had actually witnessed at work in the Communion. It was therefore the Primates' Meeting, as a small easily convened body in which each Province was represented that was offered as the broker of the mind of the Communion, mirroring the role that it had in fact played in the immediate past. In the commitments of Section Six of the Nassau draft, it was acknowledged that 'the Instruments of Communion have no juridical or executive authority in our Provinces' although they should be recognized 'as those bodies by which our common life in Christ is articulated and sustained, and which therefore carry a moral authority which commands our respect'.[49] Churches were asked, however, to commit themselves 'to seek the guidance of the Instruments of Communion, where there are matters in serious dispute among churches that cannot be resolved by mutual admonition and counsel … by submitting the matter to the Primates Meeting'. After consultation, it would thereafter fall to the Primates' Meeting to offer 'guidance and direction'.

Not surprisingly, this draft seemed to run directly into all the criticism and fear that the Primates had generated by being the whip hand of the Windsor Process, and fed into the spectres raised following the Grieb paper. In the second recension, the St Andrew's text (in a section now numbered four due to a substantial reordering of the text), the Covenant Design Group therefore moved in the opposite direction, offering a more generalized appeal to the guidance of all four Instruments of Communion, without specifying specific responsibilities or powers. This was, however, criticized as being vague in the

---

[47] The *Windsor Report*, paragraph 86, quoting from page 14 of the *Evangelical Letter* of the 1920 Lambeth Conference.

[48] http://www.anglicancommunion.org/media/150889/report-1.pdf (accessed January 2017).

[49] http://www.anglicancommunion.org/media/100711/nassau_draft_20070504.pdf (accessed November 2016).

extreme and without substance: if the Nassau Text had been too directive, the St Andrew's text fudged the issue.

The Ridley Cambridge text produced in 2009 therefore proposed a model in which decisions on Communion matters were processed by the Joint Standing Committee, the executive body to which the Standing Committee of the ACC and the Primates sent members. This body had a claim to be effectively an executive in which all four Instruments of Communion had a stake. Could the Joint Standing Committee act as a clearing house for dispute resolution?

Yet again, this failed to find favour, however, and received a less than enthusiastic reception from the ACC in Jamaica. There were far too many fears that the autonomy of Provinces was under threat. In the light of the fact that there was no consensus over Section Four, discussion among officers at Jamaica centred upon whether it would have been better at this stage to sever the fourth section of the Covenant and to put the first three sections to the Council for ratification, so that at least those parts of the Covenant which had broad support could be adopted, but the Archbishop of Canterbury (Rowan Williams) was against this idea, and felt that the whole covenant text stood or fell together. The ACC therefore asked a small working group to look at the matter again, and after some revision, a final version was brought to the Joint Standing Committee at their meeting in December 2009.

The final text sought to emphasize the principle of provincial autonomy. The Joint Standing Committee was obliged to consult with the other Instruments of Communion, but could make a declaration that certain actions were 'incompatible with the Covenant' and suggest what relational consequences might follow.[50] Recommendations of the Joint Standing Committee would be sent back to the Provinces for their decision, however – the Instruments of Communion would not be a final arbiter at all, but could only make recommendations to the autonomous Provinces.[51]

The balance was set as finely as it possibly could be between coordinated custodianship of the direction of Anglicanism at Communion level through the Instruments of Communion and the fact that provinces of the Anglican

---

[50] *The Anglican Communion Covenant*, draft sections 4.2.4 to 4.2.7, accessed January 2017 at http://www.anglicancommunion.org/media/99905/The_Anglican_Covenant.pdf.
[51] *The Anglican Communion Covenant*, section 4.2.7.

Communion were regarded as autonomous and were the final locus of authority within the Communion.

The reception of the Anglican Covenant

In December 2009, therefore, the Anglican Covenant was sent out to the Provinces for their consideration. First reactions, although slow, were positive: The Church of the Province of Southern Africa adopted the covenant in October 2010 and other Provinces early on commended the Covenant to dioceses for reflection and comment.[52] In January 2011 the Anglican Communion News Service was reporting that three further Provinces had adopted the Covenant.[53] By May of that year, the Church of Ireland had subscribed to the Covenant and it was received by the Church of the Province of South East Asia; in November 2011, the Anglican Church of the Southern Cone of America adopted the Covenant, and in December the Church of Papua New Guinea followed suit.

However, the narrative that the Covenant was in fact a mechanism for the imposition of a traditional orthodoxy on sexuality was also gaining ground and this meant that the whole concept of covenant elicited some scathing attacks. Almost every attack that could be offered was offered. The very concept of a covenant was alien to Anglicanism, and was an abuse of a biblical concept of covenant, in which covenants were always between God and his people, and never between the various groupings of the people of God.[54] The Covenant was too strong, and sought to create a single universal jurisdiction, which was alien to the ecclesiology of the Anglican Communion.[55] It would create fear in the heart of every priest in his or her pulpit, as the Joint Standing Committee took on the role of a new inquisition.[56] The Covenant was too weak, it was 'a chocolate

---

[52] Australia, England and Canada.

[53] http://www.anglicannews.org/news/2011/01/west-indies-adopts-the-anglican-communion-covenant.aspx (accessed November 2016).

[54] John Barton, 'Covenant in the Bible and Today', in Mark Chapman (ed.), *The Anglican Covenant* (London: Mowbray, 2008), pp. 193–203.

[55] Who steers the Ship? Paul Bagshaw, accessed January 2017 at http://modernchurch.org.uk/index.php/downloads/finish/14-forewords/36-who-steers-the-ship-the-poverty-of-the-draft-anglican-covenant/.

[56] Advertisement taken out by the 'Modern Church' and 'Inclusive Church' associations in the *Church Times*, Friday, 29 October 2010.

teapot', that could not deliver the enforcement of solutions to disputes.[57] The one thing that united all those who authored such criticisms is that they came from the liberal wing of the Church. The very diversity of the criticism suggests that it was not the Covenant as such to which objection was being made; it was the end to which the Covenant might be used that attracted the ire of such commentators. The Covenant had to be written off for fear that a mechanism of enforcement might be used against inclusive attitudes on sexuality.

At the same time, the Global South started to withdraw its support for the Anglican Covenant. As more liberal Provinces were beginning to withdraw support for the Anglican Covenant because they feared that it would be used as an instrument to enforce conformity, the Provinces of the Global South began to withdraw support as they feared that the Covenant was not strong enough, and that it simply could not be used in that way.

The movement of the Global South within Anglicanism goes back some decades, when leaders within the Anglican Communion sought to unite Provinces in the undeveloped world in mission. Very quickly, however, friendships between the more conservative leadership of the African Provinces and the more conservative voices within the Episcopal Church meant that the two groups began to recognize certain commonalities of interest and to work together under the one umbrella to reassert a strongly conservative approach.

As the Episcopal Church moved to embrace further liberal agendas, particularly on questions of sexuality, the more traditional sections of the Episcopal Church started to look for allies in Africa. Their pleas for help did not fall on unresponsive ears, and one early initiative was the consecration of two of the leading American conservative voices as bishops by the episcopal leadership in Rwanda and South East Asia.[58] These consecrations threatened to disturb the unity of the Communion, and George Carey, the then Archbishop of Canterbury, moved quickly to distance himself from them.[59] At the same time, however, ordination as bishops gave some legitimacy to the forming groups and very quickly other conservative Episcopal leaders were looking to

---

[57] Alan Wilson, 'Anglican Covenant: Teapot on the hob?': http://bishopalan.blogspot.co.uk/2012/03/anglican-covenant-teapot-on-hob.html, (accessed January 2017).

[58] Charles Murphy and John Rodgers were consecrated bishops on 29 January 2000 by the Primates of South East Asia, Moses Tay, and Rwanda, Emmanuel Kolini.

[59] Press reports at http://anglicansonline.org/archive/news/articles/2000/000214a.html (accessed November 2016, original links removed).

be consecrated as a way of reinforcing their ministry and recruiting support from their friends and allies in African Provinces. Martyn Minns, the Rector of an Episcopal Church in the diocese of Washington, was consecrated Bishop in June 2006 by the hierarchy of the Church of Nigeria for 'the Convocation of Anglicans in North America' (a nifty renaming of a structure originally intended to be 'the Convocation of Anglican Nigerians in America')[60] and this was very quickly followed by the consecrations of a number of other Americans by different African Primates.

The multiplicity of such groups, and the way in which their leadership was consecrated into a series of little more than personal prelatures, was hardly going to be a process which would find Communion-wide support, however – and indeed, was plainly in contravention of the moratoria recommended by the *Windsor Report*. This gave impetus for several dissenting groups to come together to form an entity which would have some ecclesial density: the Anglican Church of North America (ACNA). This body was originally little more than a coalition of eight disparate bodies, but it has used time wisely and shaped itself into an increasingly coherent body, which has been recognized by the churches of the Global South as the legitimate body representing Anglicanism in North America. In January 2016, a coveted place at the table with the Primates of the Anglican Communion was gained for its second Archbishop, Foley Beach, even if his presence was at the Primates' Gathering, and not for the Primates' Meeting into which it elided.

In parallel with the creation of the Anglican Church of North America, a bolder plan was conceived by the leadership of the Global South: nothing less than the reformation of the Anglican Communion around their vision of orthodoxy. In the same year that Archbishop Rowan Williams was inviting the bishops of the Anglican Communion to Canterbury for the 2008 Lambeth Conference, the leadership of the Provinces which repudiated his invitation invited themselves to a gathering in Jerusalem to be known as the Global Anglican Future Conference. There they proceeded to write their own statement of Anglican orthodoxy, the Jerusalem Declaration. Why support a compromise Anglican Covenant, when they now had their own definitive statement of orthodoxy?

---

[60] Reported in a private conversation with Archbishop Drexel Gomez.

By now, the Covenant process was looking beleaguered. Liberal leaders saw the whole exercise as a tool for conservative centrism; the conservatives had their own much stronger articulation of the kind of Anglican Communion that they wanted to see established. The Covenant was not without its advocates among those who saw Anglicanism as an altogether more moderate and uniting force. The original vision that the Covenant might address the ecclesial deficit of the Communion and offer a robust articulation of what holds Anglicanism together was not lost on several commentators.[61] However, it may be said that the voice of reason seeking to build up the centre by articulating the case for the Anglican Covenant had been outflanked on both sides.

At this point, the reception process in the Church of England itself came into focus. The Anglican Covenant appeared as an item in the business of the General Synod in November 2010, where a draft Act of Synod adopting the Anglican Covenant was passed. Since the draft act was deemed to introduce a change in the relationship between the Church of England and the other Churches of the Anglican Communion, it was required by the Constitution of General Synod to be referred for ratification by the dioceses. This process meant however that the text of the Anglican Communion Covenant became immured in a series of diocesan wrangles. Left to a myriad of different interpretations, each diocese made of the Covenant text what they could, often with the diocesan Bishop taking a strong pro or anti stance, which could either lead a diocese, or cause a revolt. In the event, the majority of dioceses decided not to back the Covenant, and this meant that the synod itself, meeting in February 2012 and receiving the report on the responses of the dioceses, could not give force to the definitive form of an Act of Synod adopting the Covenant. The Church of England had not received the Covenant.

The outcome of this process, and England's failure to embrace the Covenant, effectively halted the reception process in its tracks. If the 'mother Church' of the Communion did not back the Covenant, was there any chance of it being accepted in the Communion at large? This was certainly the stance taken by the Church in Wales, whose governing body met shortly after the meeting of the General Synod in the Church of England. The Welsh Governing Body, in a

---

[61] For which, for example, see Benjamin M. Guyer (ed.), *Pro Communione: Theological Essays on the Anglican Covenant* (Eugene, OR: Pickwick, 2012) and Paul Avis, *The Vocation of Anglicanism* (Bloomsbury: T&T Clark, 2016), chapter 4, 'A Covenantal Vocation'.

revised resolution, neither endorsed nor rejected the Covenant, but requested the ACC to give guidance on the status of the reception process in the light of the Church of England's decision.[62]

The answer requested by the Church in Wales never came. By the time that the ACC met in Auckland, New Zealand, there was a new Archbishop of Canterbury (Justin Welby) with a very different sense of priorities, and a very different approach to reconciliation. The Anglican Covenant never even made it to the main agenda of the fifteenth meeting of the ACC, and has been in stasis ever since.

Full circle

The Windsor Process arising out of the 2004 *Windsor Report* has never been officially abandoned and its place in the life and history of the Anglican Communion in the early twenty-first century is unlikely to receive definitive evaluation so close to the events which precipitated the *Windsor Report* and while the tensions roused by questions of sexuality remain unresolved. In 2016 the difficulties spawned by differences over teaching on sexuality still remain high on the radar of intra-Communion relations, but the debate has moved on. Gene Robinson has been consecrated, enthroned, has exercised his episcopal ministry and has retired as Bishop of New Hampshire. Other Episcopal bishops now carry forward the mantle of gay and lesbian inclusion, and bishops living in same-sex relationships have been considered and appointed in other Provinces of the Communion. But their existence has retreated into the shadow cast by the debate over same-sex marriage, for the issue confronting the Church is now not whether it will recognize or bless same-sex partnerships, but whether it can move with the secular recognition of equal marriage in an increasing number of states across the globe.

In 2020 the Lambeth Conference will meet for the fifteenth time, and in a surprising way, as the Design Group begins its work, the agenda does not seem to have moved very far from that set by Archbishop Charles Longley in 1867:

---

[62] The resolution of the Governing Body of the Church in Wales in April 2012 may be found at http://www.anglicancommunion.org/media/39753/provincial-reception-of-the-anglican-covenant-for-acc-rev.pdf (accessed January 2017).

in a time when the missional context is again pressing, controversy about sexual mores remains distracting (although now it is North America which has become liberal, and indigenous African bishops who tend to represent the forces of conservatism). Therefore, a crucial question is whether the Anglican Communion has the mechanisms to resolve deep theological controversy and move beyond it to consider its presentation of the Gospel to a needy world?

The fact that sexual mores in society have moved so far so fast, at least in the Western world (and captured by the arresting headline on one news website 'From prison to the altar in under 60 years')[63] has left the Church wrong-footed. Should it kowtow to secular opinion, as the conservative narrative would have it, or repent of its past intolerance and persecution, as the liberal agenda describes it? Fundamentally, however, there remains an unfinished dialogue which the Lambeth Conference will have to address if it is to make progress: How do Anglicans make decisions on what they discern to be the will of God? Is there a common Anglican heritage which commends a distinctive theological method and approach and which can unite Christians from the differing cultures of the globe?

Without predicating the answer to the particular moral question of sexuality, the Anglican Covenant had argued that Anglicanism did have a coherent inheritance and a coherent theological method by which it approached the moral and doctrinal issues posed to it by a rapidly changing world. If the potentially warring liberal and conservative bishops who gather in Canterbury in 2020 can look beyond their divisions on the issue of sexuality to seek to articulate the unity they have in the Anglican tradition, then the text and arguments of the Anglican Covenant may yet have their day.

---

[63] 'From prison to the altar in under 60 years', News 24, 22 December 2012. http://www.news24.com/MyNews24/From-prison-to-the-altar-in-under-60-years-20121222 (accessed November 2016).

10

The Resolutions of the Lambeth Conference and the Laws of Anglican Churches

Norman Doe and Richard Deadman

This chapter considers the nature of the correlation between Lambeth Conference resolutions and the laws of particular Anglican churches. The first conference in 1867 was called to address a specific issue and the report of its resolutions was brief (a mere thirteen resolutions). Since then, successive Conferences have seen their business burgeon, so that a comprehensive consideration of our subject would take several volumes. As well as topics that are of immediately obvious common concern (e.g. baptism preparation)[1] in the context of 'brotherly counsel and encouragement',[2] everything becomes local. Thus polygamy may not have been of pressing concern to bishops of countries rooted in the Western world, but it has been a periodic subject of conversation at the Conferences;[3] although none of the Western-rooted provinces has adapted their law as a result of the deliberations. So what follows considers the reciprocal influences of the Lambeth Conferences and the Laws of particular churches, focusing on three phenomena: the nature and relationship of the Anglican Communion and its member churches, with particular reference to the legal status of resolutions of the Lambeth Conference; the historic formularies; and the rights of the laity.

---

[1] LC (Lambeth Conference) 1897, Resolutions 48f.
[2] The stated purpose of the Lambeth Conference of 1867, as expressed by Archbishop Longley who had convoked the conference in the face of opposition from some of the English bishops. See N. Doe, *Canon Law in the Anglican Communion* (Oxford: Clarendon Press, 1998), p. 346, n32.
[3] LC 1888 res 5; LC 1958 res 120; LC 1968 res 23; LC 1988 res 26.

The relationship between the Anglican Communion and the provinces

Analysing the relationship between the Lambeth Conferences and the laws of individual provincial churches is, to some extent, a speculative exercise.[4] While it is true that there is significant overlap between Conference resolutions and the laws of churches, particularly when they are viewed as a whole, establishing a clear line of cause and effect is not easy.[5] First, the mere fact that a topic was on the agenda would suggest that at least some bishops were minded to act on the matter, whether or not the Conference produced a relevant resolution; and, as we shall observe below, provinces might act, but not always as the resolution urged. Secondly, laws are made by a synodical process. It would be very difficult to prove that a majority of those voting at home on a particular issue decided one way or another because a Lambeth Conference had spoken. Yet, there is an enduring sense that Conference resolutions are more than an ephemeral expression of the corporate episcopal mind.[6]

The common view is that a resolution of the Lambeth Conference does not have the status of law *proprio vigore*: so the Conference has no competence or coercive jurisdiction to legislate for each of the churches of the Communion. In other words, the main obstacle to seeing its resolutions as law is that, as the Lambeth Conference states several times, every Province is an autonomous entity.[7] Indeed, this has led some to deny any legal force to Conference resolutions.[8] Moreover, there is no formal agreement between the churches that its acts should have binding force; again, Resolutions from time to time reject moves towards some such centralization.[9] The travails of the Anglican Communion Covenant, beset as it is by fears of incipient

---

[4] 'Provincial' is used as a convenient term to embrace the variety of different identities of the autonomous church units, which comprise the Anglican Communion; see Doe, *Canon Law in the Anglican Communion*, pp. 9f.
[5] There are very few examples of an explicit allusion to any particular Conference resolution in provincial laws.
[6] See Doe, *Canon Law in the Anglican Communion*, p. 340.
[7] See, for example, LC 1930 res 48.
[8] See Doe, *Canon Law in the Anglican Communion*, pp 346ff.
[9] A proposal to create an appellate body for the whole Anglican Communion was rejected on the ground of the autonomy of the constituent provinces; see LC 1930 res 51.

papalism, illustrate the point.[10] Nevertheless, in 1897 the Conference resolved:

> That, recognising the advantages which have accrued to the Church from the meetings of the Lambeth Conferences, we are of opinion that it is of great importance to the wellbeing of the Church that there should be from time to time meetings of the bishops of the whole Anglican Communion for the consideration of questions that may arise affecting the Church of Christ.[11]

And: 'That the Resolutions adopted by such Conferences should be formally communicated to ... the Anglican Communion for their consideration, and for such action as may seem to them desirable'.[12] It would seem, therefore, that in those days the bishops envisaged that their resolutions would have morally compelling force – in the sense of requiring serious consideration by the provinces.[13] This may be the meaning of the designation of Conference resolutions as 'quasi-legislation': normative material but with no legally binding or enforceable character.[14]

However, there is more to such an aspiration than mere optimism. The gatherings of bishops for the Lambeth Conference look quite similar to the sequence of councils that punctuated the life of the early Church and it would not be unreasonable to assign to them a comparable role in the life of the Anglican Communion today. Yet a significant difference between then and now is the synodical constraint on the prerogatives of Anglican bishops today;[15] and it is, perhaps, unlikely that the priests and laypeople who have not participated in the 'brotherly counsel and encouragement' of a Lambeth Conference would feel the same moral compulsion as those who were there. Nevertheless, as we shall see, there are significant connections between the Lambeth Conference resolutions and provincial Law, such that it is possible to say that the legal character of the provinces is reflected to some extent in the resolutions.

One might have expected that the definition of what it is to be an Anglican Church would have demonstrated the greatest strand of exchange

---

[10] See, for example, S. Noll, 'Sea-change in the Anglican Communion' (2013): http://www.anglican. ink/article/sea-change-anglican-communion.

[11] Res 1.

[12] Res 3.

[13] As might be inferred from LC 1987 res 24.

[14] See Doe, *Canon Law in the Anglican Communion*, p. 347.

[15] The legislative role being exercised within the context of synods.

between the Lambeth Conferences and constituent provinces of the Anglican Communion. However, the evidence is patchy. The substance of an Anglican identity as laid out by successive Lambeth Conferences was developed in the wake of the Oxford Movement,[16] the promulgation of *Apostolicae Curae* condemning Anglican Orders,[17] the subsequent response of the Archbishops of Canterbury and York,[18] and the continuing discussions with the Orthodox churches about some degree of rapprochement.[19] The Conferences may well have reflected a process of self-analysis in the light of these events, one that disturbed the unspoken assumptions on which the Church of England had rested for centuries. It is helpful, therefore, to explore these understandings of the Anglican Communion, its Instruments of Communion, the churches within it and their relationships, as they appear in the principles of canon law and the provincial laws underlying them. A recent comparison of these laws led to the launch at the Lambeth Conference 2008 of a document entitled *The Principles of Canon Law Common to the Churches of the Anglican Communion* (hereinafter PCLCCAC). This document is not a system of international canon law but a statement of principles of canon law which articulate the common ground between the legal systems of each of the churches of the global Communion; the principles are induced from the profound similarities that are shared by these laws.[20]

Long before that, in 1930, the Lambeth Conference attempted to define Anglicanism, stating that 'the true constitution of the Catholic Church involves the principle of the autonomy of particular Churches based upon a common faith and order'.[21] Moreover, the following resolution (Res 49) finds almost comprehensive resonance in *PCLCCAC*:

> The Anglican Communion is a fellowship, within the one Holy Catholic and Apostolic Church, of those duly constituted dioceses, provinces or

---

[16] An approximate date of 1833 might be assigned to the inception of the Oxford Movement. See S. Sykes and J. Booty, *The Study of Anglicanism* (London: SPCK, 1988), pp. 34ff.

[17] Pope Leo XIII, *Apostolicae Curae* (1896).

[18] *Saepius Officio* (1897).

[19] See, for example, LC 1897 res 36; LC 1930 res 33.

[20] *The Principles of Canon Law Common to the Churches of the Anglican Communion* [PCLCCAC] (London: Anglican Communion Office, 2008); the work of the Anglican Communion Legal Advisers Network; launched at the Lambeth Conference 2008; for background to the project, see p. 97: N. Doe, 'The contribution of common principles of canon law to ecclesial communion in Anglicanism'.

[21] Res 48.

regional Churches in communion with the See of Canterbury, which have the following characteristics in common:[22]

a. they uphold and propagate the Catholic and Apostolic faith and order as they are generally set forth in the Book of Common Prayer as authorised in their several Churches;[23]

b. they are particular or national Churches, and, as such, promote within each of their territories a national expression of Christian faith, life and worship;[24]

c. they are bound together not by a central legislative and executive authority,[25] but by mutual loyalty sustained through the common counsel of the bishops in conference.

The Communion, therefore, has no formal body of law applicable globally to its member churches, each church being autonomous with its own legal system. The Communion is held together by 'bonds of affection':[26] shared loyalty to scripture, creeds, baptism, Eucharist, historic episcopate,[27] and its four institutional Instruments of Communion.[28]

The Lambeth Conference

The 1897 Conference acknowledged 'the advantages which have accrued to the Church from the meetings of the Lambeth Conferences' and urged that, for 'the wellbeing of the Church ... there should be from time to time meetings of the bishops of the whole Anglican Communion for the consideration of questions that may arise affecting the Church of Christ'.[29] Something similar was said in 1978[30] and again ten years later.[31] In 1998, it was 'suggested' that the Lambeth Conference 'be recognised as a significant consultative body which gives a sense of unity and direction to the whole Communion, by receiving

---

[22] PCLCCAC, Principle 10.1. See also Thirty Nine Articles of Religion, Art. 19: 'The visible Church of Christ is a congregation of faithful men, in the which the ... Word of God is preached, and ... the Sacraments ... ministered according to Christ's ordinance.'

[23] PCLCCAC, principle 10.2.

[24] PCLCCAC, principle 15. 1–5.

[25] PCLCCAC, principle 12.

[26] PCLCCAC, p. 97.

[27] See below.

[28] See LC 1998 sII.2b.

[29] Res 1.

[30] Res 13.

[31] Res 18.3.

and reviewing reports of significant activities carried out as part of the work of the Communion.[32] This last point rather implies at least a feeling that the Conference was not fulfilling this purpose very well. These were febrile times and in 2008 some churches were not represented at the Conference, which produced no resolutions, but simply a narrative of discussions.[33]

Although PCLCCAC cites the Lambeth Conference as one of the Instruments of Communion,[34] it features very little in the formal law of the churches. Its vigour, such as it is, inheres in the very fact of its happening. This is, perhaps, unsurprising, given the constant disclaimers that the Conference does not create law. Were churches to incorporate the Anglican Communion Covenant into their law, they would thereby include references to the Lambeth Conference.[35]

The Archbishop of Canterbury

The Archbishop of Canterbury was the de facto president of the Lambeth Conference from the outset and there are passing references to this in the resolutions.[36] However, it is not until 1998 that the role of the Archbishop, as one of the Instruments of Communion, is stated.[37] Later in the text, the Archbishop is described as 'a personal sign of our unity',[38] and later still it is stated that being in communion with the See of Canterbury is a feature of Anglican identity.[39] In 1968 the Conference referred to the fact that a principal executive role of the Archbishop's presidency is issuing invitations to the Lambeth Conference.[40] It is the Archbishop of Canterbury who decides which bishops should represent a particular Anglican church at each Lambeth Conference.

Being in communion with the See of Canterbury is listed as a characteristic of Anglican identity in PCLCCAC,[41] though this is slightly mitigated by a reference to the Archbishop's role as the focus of unity.[42] There is some

---

[32] Res II.2(f).
[33] See *Lambeth Indaba* (2008) sA3.
[34] Principle 11(4).
[35] s3.1.4(I and II).
[36] For example, 1948 res 68 (b); 1978 res 12.
[37] Res II.2(b).
[38] Res III.6(e).
[39] Res IV.6(a).
[40] Res 65(a).
[41] Principle 10(1).
[42] Principle 11(4).

material to buttress this view in the Laws of Anglican churches, speaking of the Archbishop enjoying 'first place' among Anglican Metropolitans,[43] and in the requirement for newly consecrated bishops to pay deference.[44] In many ways, the significance of the Archbishop's role is highlighted by the removal of references to him in 2005 from the constitution of the Church in Nigeria, following differences of opinion.[45]

The Primates' Meeting

The Primates' Meeting has its roots in a resolution of 1920 to establish a consultative body, which functioned as 'a continuation committee', as it were, to join up the dots between conferences, and which 'neither possesses nor claims any executive or administrative power'.[46] In 1958 it was decided that the membership of this body should comprise all the Primates of the Communion.[47] In 1978, this group appears in the resolutions as the 'Primates Committee'[48] and there is a sense that the Archbishop of Canterbury should exercise his presidency in a more collegial manner within the context of this Primates' Committee.[49] In 1988 the Primates' Committee became the Primates' Meeting and there are many subsequent references to its activities. The desire for the Archbishop of Canterbury to act collegially with the Primates is restated, so enhancing the role of the Primates' Meeting.[50] In considering the Instruments of the Anglican Communion in 1998, the developing collegial role is mentioned again.[51] Later in the text there is a suggestion that 'the exercise of ... responsibilities by the Primates' Meeting should carry moral authority calling for ready acceptance throughout the Communion'.[52] Thus the mooted moral authority enjoyed by the Lambeth Conference is now being refracted through the Primates' Meeting. References to the Primates' Meeting are ubiquitous in

---

[43] Sudan Const Art 2; Central Africa Fundamental Declarations II.
[44] West Indies Can 8.
[45] See M. N. Sison, 'Who's Anglican and Who's Not', *Anglican Journal* (1 January 2006): http://www. anglicanjournal.com/articles/whos-anglican-and-whos-not-3081.
[46] LC 1920, res 44; LC 1930 res 50(a).
[47] Res 61(b).
[48] For example, res 11.
[49] For example, res13f.
[50] Res 18.2(a); Res 18.6(a).
[51] Res III.6(a).
[52] Res III.6(c).

the resolutions:[53] those who are concerned about the centralizing influences of the Anglican Communion Covenant may be watching the wrong show.

PCLCCAC simply lists the Primates' Meeting as one of the instruments.[54] Otherwise and tellingly, the other references to the Primates' Meeting are contained in the commentary, mainly in the account of how the document came into being. Norman Doe's study of Canon Law in the Anglican Communion of 1998 makes only passing reference to the Primates' Meeting and does not mention participation in the Primates' Meeting in the account of the primatial role.[55] This reflects the absence of references to the Primates' Meeting in national laws. One might infer that the influence of the Primates' Meeting stems from the pooling of authority represented by the gathering of Primates. In other words, its power is rooted in the individual legal systems, from which the Archbishops and other Primates come. However, as we observed, bishops' prerogatives with regard to deciding anything for their churches is constrained by the synodical process; and this is even more the case for an individual Bishop – the Primate. The rejection of the Anglican Communion Covenant (promoted by the Primates) by some national synods illustrates the point.[56]

The Anglican Consultative Council

The Anglican Consultative Council (ACC) developed in conjunction with the Primates' Meeting. The consultative body that was reconstructed in 1920 comprised only bishops.[57] At the 1968 Conference the participants endorsed a proposal to establish a separate body: the ACC.[58] Unlike the other instruments, the ACC is governed by a written constitution, which was submitted for

---

[53] Some thirty-seven direct references spread across nearly all the issues considered at the conference.
[54] Principle 11.4.
[55] Doe, *Canon Law in the Anglican Communion*, pp.104f.
[56] Though, of course, others (eleven at the time of writing) have voted to adopt it: http://www.anglicannews.org/news/2016/04/a-report-from-the-anglican-communions-secretary-general.aspx. Under the terms of the Covenant (s4.2), the instruments, particularly the ACC and the Primates' Meeting, would have roles in addressing breaches of the Covenant by member churches and in making recommendations to member churches with regard to impaired communion (s4.2.7) consequential upon such a breach. It is up to individual Instruments of the Communion and churches to decide how to respond to these recommendations. It does not say whether any churches that refuse to accept the recommendations might themselves be investigated for breach of the Covenant.
[57] Res 54(a).
[58] Res 69.

approval to all the national churches.[59] Its membership comprises episcopal, clerical and lay representatives of all the churches.[60] While the meetings are infrequent, there is a standing committee, which moves forward the business between meetings.[61] Although the ACC has no formal legislative competence, its role in providing guidance and forming policies makes it a source of 'quasi-legislation'.[62] As with the Primates' Meeting, references to the ACC burgeon in subsequent Conference resolutions, often indicating cooperation between the two institutions.[63]

PCLCCAC lists the ACC as one of the Instruments of Communion,[64] but as with the Primates' Meeting, all other references are in the commentary. There are a couple of references to the ACC in national laws,[65] requiring some sort of conformity with the decisions of the ACC, but Chile captures the formal position that the ACC is 'an organisation with no legislative character which is obligatory for the provinces [of the Communion]'.[66]

It is therefore the case that, for the most part, the institutions of the Anglican Communion are not rooted in national laws; their functions within the life of the Communion are more a matter of developing convention. However, their increasing involvement with an ever-wider range of issues (particularly in the case of the Primates' Meeting and the ACC) at policy-forming and administrative levels has almost inevitably increased the influence that the instruments exert over Anglican Communion affairs.[67] A salient instance occurred in 2016: a communiqué from the Primates' Meeting stated that 'consequences follow for The Episcopal Church in relation to the Anglican Communion following its recent change of marriage doctrine'. The statement continued:

> It is our unanimous desire to walk together. However given the seriousness of these matters we formally acknowledge this distance by requiring that

---

[59] Res 69.
[60] Res 69 Constitution Membership.
[61] Res 69(7) – once every two years. Res 69(8).
[62] Res 69. See, Doe, *Canon Law in the Anglican Communion*, p. 350.
[63] See, for example, LC 1988 res 18.5.
[64] Principle 11.4.
[65] For example, Tanzania Const IV.15; Kenya Can II; Canada BXVIII.10.
[66] Can A7; and see PCLCCAC, Principle 11.2: 'The churches ... are bound together, not juridically by a central legislative, executive or judicial authority, but by mutual loyalty sustained through the instruments of Anglican unity'; 11.5: the latter 'enjoy such binding authority within a church as may be prescribed by the law of that church'.
[67] The role of the ACC in advising on the creation of new provinces and their constitutions is a conspicuous example of the potential of the Council to shape Anglican identity (Constitution s5.3).

for a period of three years The Episcopal Church no longer represent us on ecumenical and interfaith bodies, should not be appointed or elected to an internal standing committee and that while participating in the internal bodies of the Anglican Communion, they will not take part in decision making on any issues pertaining to doctrine or polity.[68]

While this represents an informal agreement in which TEC acquiesced, its substance reflects the provisions of the beleaguered Anglican Communion Covenant,[69] which, if adopted, would represent a small step towards a centralized judicial, if not law-making, authority.[70]

While the trends outlined above are demonstrable, we should not overstate the case. The Primates' Meeting and the ACC are creations of the Lambeth Conference and the position of the Archbishop of Canterbury has been formally incorporated into the resolutions of the Conference (and, to an extent, circumscribed by them); their authority is delegated to them by the Conference. Were their roles to be further extended or their powers enhanced, it is difficult to think of another forum where this cause could be promoted. Equally, of course, the Lambeth Conference does not have the prerogative to impose the decisions of its creatures on the individual provinces. As we see with the Anglican Communion Covenant, this has to be done severally at the provincial level.

Synodical government of the provinces

Although in 1930 it was said that 'the minimum organisation essential to provincial life is a college or synod of bishops which will act corporately in dealing with questions concerning the faith, order and discipline of the Church,'[71] ten years earlier the Conference had stated that, in the establishment of new dioceses, 'it is important to the cause of reunion that every branch of

---

[68] http://www.anglicannews.org/features/2016/01/communique-from-the-primates-meeting-2016. aspx.

[69] The Anglican Communion Covenant S4.2; http://www.anglicancommunion.org/media/99905/ The_Anglican_Covenant.pdf.

[70] For an interesting reflection on this, see M. D. Chapman, 'The Dull Bits of History: Cautionary Tales for Anglicanism', in idem, ed., *The Anglican Communion Covenant* (London: Mowbray, 2008), pp. 81ff.

[71] Res 53b.

the Anglican Communion should develop the constitutional government of the Church and should make a fuller use of the capacities of its members for service.'[72] It continued:

> A newly constituted synod of bishops shall proceed as soon as possible to associate with itself in some official way the clergy and laity of the province, provided that in the case of provinces including missionary dioceses this procedure shall be subordinate to local circumstances. It is understood that each national and regional Church will determine its own constitutional and canonical enactments[73].

From these sparse pieces of exhortation has developed one of the consciously characteristic features of an Anglican church: synodical government, usually including houses of bishops, (lower) clergy and laity. The representative participation of the laity in these institutions of Anglican governance at all levels is a key feature of them.[74] These synods constitute autonomous source(s) of law (typically provincial law created by a synod or other assembly representative of bishops, clergy and laity) and laws made at more localized levels (e.g. diocesan law created by the diocesan synod of Bishop, clergy and laity).[75] These laws exist in 'a variety of formal sources', such as constitutions, canons, rules, regulations and other instruments.[76] Quasi-legislation is also a feature of Anglican governance.

Interestingly, the process of law making receives no attention in the Lambeth Conference resolutions. However, the many references to the formation of provinces, particularly in the documents relating to earlier conferences imply

---

[72] Res 14.

[73] Res 43f.

[74] There are a few examples of bicameral synods, in which cases, as it were, the houses and clergy are combined: for example, TEC Art I ss1-4; Ireland Constitution Pt1 s2. PCLCCAC, Principle 16.1; see also 15.6: 'Each church, province, and diocese has an assembly, namely a synod, council or other body, the function of which is to govern'; 18: 'Representative government is fundamental to church polity, and in matters which touch all, all should have a voice'; 22: 'Lay people are entitled to participate in the governance of a church', subject to conditions as to eligibility and selection. See: Doe, *Canon Law in the Anglican Communion*, p. 43.

[75] LC 1930 recognized that 'the balance between provincial authority and diocesan autonomy may vary from province to province according to the constitutions agreed upon in each case': Res 53(d). PCLCCAC, Definitions: 'The expression "general law of a church" means the law of that body which has competent jurisdiction over that church, as distinct from laws of unity within a church such as a diocese.'

[76] PCLCCAC, Principle 4.1-3: 'Scripture, tradition and reason are fundamental authoritative sources of law'; 4.5. 'Laws should be short, clear and simple to the extent ... consistent with their purpose, meaning', etc.

an understanding that the primary locus of legislative competence and coercive jurisdiction in Anglicanism is the Province, typically national and with a metropolitan or archbishop.[77] Each Province has a central assembly (General Synod or Council) representative of bishops, clergy and laity, competent to legislate, and assisted by various administrative bodies.[78] In turn, the diocese is governed by an assembly (Diocesan Synod or Council) composed of the Bishop and clerical and lay representatives; it is competent to legislate for the diocese and is assisted by various administrative bodies.[79] A diocese is divided into parishes each with a priest and with a council representing the laity, with predominantly administrative functions.[80] Each church also has a system of courts at provincial and diocesan levels but not at parochial level.[81] The 'exercise of ecclesiastical governance should be characterised by the Christian virtues, transparency, and the rule of law applied with justice and equity', and laws should set out clearly the composition and functions of institutions and the relationship between them.[82]

The historic formularies

The Lambeth Conferences were born into the question of where the limits of Anglicanism lie. Archbishop Longley had been pressed to address the perceived theological aberrations of Bishop Colenso of Natal.[83] However, it is often said that Anglicanism is not part of the confessional tradition: there is no definitive statement of what doctrines are required of a person or of a church (nor doctrines required to be eschewed) in order to be counted as Anglican.[84] Equally, given the assertion of provincial autonomy, there had to be some definition of what would constitute an Anglican church. In 1888, the Lambeth

---

[77] PCLCCAC, Principle 15; see above Chapter 1.

[78] PCLCCAC, Principle 18.2-4 and 19: the central assembly is organized in 'houses, orders or other cameral systems' (with persons elected/admitted to it); 19: it may legislate for the whole of the church.

[79] PCLCCAC, Principle 20.

[80] PCLCCAC, Principle 21.

[81] PCLCCAC, Principle 24: see post Chapter 4.

[82] PCLCCAC, Principle 15.12-14; 17: administrative practices must be lawful, competent and courteous, and for example, consultation and cooperation are key elements of good ecclesiastical administration.

[83] See LC 1867 especially ress 6f.

[84] See Doe, *Canon Law in the Anglican Communion*, p. 197.

Conference had a first go at formulating the Faith and Order of Anglicanism; it resolved:

> That, in the opinion of this Conference, the following articles supply a basis on which approach may be by God's blessing made towards home reunion:
> a. The Holy Scriptures of the Old and New Testaments, as 'containing all things necessary to salvation', and as being the rule and ultimate standard of faith.
> b. The Apostles' Creed, as the baptismal symbol; and the Nicene Creed, as the sufficient statement of the Christian faith.
> c. The two sacraments ordained by Christ himself – Baptism and the Supper of the Lord – ministered with unfailing use of Christ's words of institution, and of the elements ordained by him.
> d. The historic episcopate, locally adapted in the methods of its administration to the varying needs of the nations and peoples called of God into the unity of his Church.[85]

This resolution reproduces more or less precisely the Chicago quadrilateral – a notion of the core identity of Anglicanism as outlined by an American Episcopalian priest, William Reed Huntington.[86] He, in turn, was able to infer this framework from the *historic formularies* of the Church of England.[87] However, during successive Lambeth Conferences, the prominence and significance of those historic formularies have somewhat waned.

As early as 1888, the Conference decreed that aspirant members of the Communion should 'hold substantially the same doctrine as our own, and that their clergy subscribe articles in accordance with the express statements of our own standards of doctrine and worship', that did not require them 'to accept in their entirety the Thirty-Nine Articles of Religion'.[88] In 1968, the Conference stated:

> The Conference accepts the main conclusion of the Report of the Archbishops' Commission on Christian Doctrine entitled 'Subscription

---

[85] Res 11.
[86] See P. Butler, 'From the Early Eighteenth Century to the Present Day', in Sykes and Booty (eds), *The Study of Anglicanism*, p. 40; and see LC 1998 res IV.2 (a).
[87] These are the Thirty-Nine Articles of Religion, the Book of Common Prayer (1662) and the Ordinal appended to the BCP; they are termed the *historic formularies* in the Church of England *Declaration of Assent* (Canon C15).
[88] Res 19.

and Assent to the Thirty-nine Articles' (1968) and in furtherance of its recommendation:

(a) suggests that each Church of our Communion consider whether the Articles need be bound up with its Prayer Book;

(b) suggests to the Churches of the Anglican Communion that assent to the Thirty-nine Articles be no longer required of ordinands;

(c) suggests that, when subscription is required to the Articles or other elements in the Anglican tradition, it should be required, and given, only in the context of a statement which gives the full range of our inheritance of faith and sets the Articles in their historical context.[89]

The Thirty-Nine Articles of Religion are not mentioned again. While they may be consonant with the Word of God, they are no longer, for all churches of the Anglican Communion, the 'Standard of Faith' that they were said to be for the Church of England in 1849.[90] In 1857 New Zealand incorporated into its Law that the Anglican Church there 'doth hold and maintain the Doctrine and Sacraments of CHRIST ... as the United Church of England and Ireland hath received and explained the same ... and in the Thirty-nine Articles of Religion'.[91] However, without repealing that provision, in 1928 the Province was given the autonomous authority to 'to alter, add to, or diminish the Formularies, or any one or more of them, or any part or parts thereof'.[92] The impetus to such a change could not be inferred from the 1888 resolutions, since the Anglican Church in New Zealand is deliberately and consciously a continuation of the Church of England.[93] At the same time it anticipated the 1968 resolution by forty years.

Other provinces include references to the Articles in their Law.[94] The Province of Southern Africa appends the Articles to its constitution without any reference to the Articles in the text of the constitution itself.[95] In Melanesia, the law reflects closely the 1968 Conference resolution: the Church of Melanesia accepts:

1. the Thirty-nine Articles of Religion as the historic statement of the Anglican position in faith and practice at the time of the Reformation, without thereby subscribing to every statement contained therein;

---

[89] Res 43.

[90] Gorham v Bp of Exeter (1849) 2 Rob Ecc 1 at 55 per Sir Jenner Fust (Ct of Arches).

[91] Fundamental Provisions 1. The means of changing this authority involves the innovation of 'the [now separated] unified Church of England and Ireland' (Fundamental Provisions 2).

[92] Pursuant to the provisions of the Church of England Empowering Act (1928) s3 (New Zealand).

[93] See Fundamental Provisions 4.

[94] *Zaire Const Art 3(3); Uganda Const Art 2(c); West Africa Const Art 2(a).*

[95] See Doe, *Canon Law in the Anglican Communion*, p. 197.

2. that clergy are not required to subscribe to the Thirty-nine Articles of Religion;

3. that the Thirty-nine Articles of Religion be not printed with the official liturgy.[96]

The church in Kenya permits individual dioceses to include references to the Articles in their diocesan constitutions without according them any legal significance in its own text.[97] Other churches just do not mention the Articles at all in their systems of provincial law.[98] Ireland is rare in specifying that any person who is a candidate for Ordination must 'be able to yield an account of such person's faith according to the Articles of Religion'.[99] The Church of England has a canonical requirement that a candidate for ordination must have 'sufficient knowledge of Holy Scripture and of the doctrine, discipline, and worship of the Church of England as set forth in the Thirty-nine Articles of Religion'.[100] However, the authority of the Articles as a doctrinal standard is somewhat undermined by the Delphic requirement to assent to them as 'historic formularies', which have borne witness to 'the faith which is revealed in the Holy Scriptures and set forth in the catholic creeds', a faith that 'the Church is called upon to proclaim afresh in each generation'.[101]

'Proclaiming afresh' and doctrinal development have, in one way or another, preoccupied the Lambeth Conferences from the outset. In 1867 the first Lambeth Conference stated that

in order to the binding of the Churches of our colonial empire and the missionary Churches beyond them in the closest union with the Mother-Church, it is necessary that they receive and maintain without alteration the standards of faith and doctrine as now in use in that Church.[102]

By 1930, however, perceptions had changed:

We believe that, in view of the enlarged knowledge gained in modern times of God's ordering of the world and the clearer apprehension of the creative process by which he prepared the way for the coming of Jesus Christ,

---

[96] Standing Resolution 10.
[97] Const Art 2 (i).
[98] For example, the Episcopal Church.
[99] Const IX 21 (3) (c).
[100] Canon C7; see also TEC art 8.
[101] The Declaration of Assent (Canon C15).
[102] Res 8.

there is urgent need in the face of many erroneous conceptions for a fresh presentation of the Christian doctrine of God.[103]

The risk of autonomous provinces setting off on individual odysseys of doctrinal inquiry was immediately obvious; and a framework was provided:

> We affirm the supreme and unshaken authority of the Holy Scriptures as presenting the truth concerning God and the spiritual life in its historical setting and in its progressive revelation, both throughout the Old Testament and in the New ... . The doctrine of God is the centre of its teaching, set forth in its books 'by divers portions and in divers manners'. As Jesus Christ is the crown, so also is he the criterion of all revelation. We would impress upon Christian people the necessity of banishing from their minds the ideas concerning the character of God which are inconsistent with the character of Jesus Christ. We believe that the work of our Lord Jesus Christ is continued by the Holy Spirit, who not only interpreted him to the Apostles, but has in every generation inspired and guided those who seek truth.[104]

The primacy of Holy Scripture in the determining of doctrine echoes Article VI of the Thirty-Nine: 'Holy Scripture containeth all things necessary to salvation: so that whatsoever is not read therein, nor may be proved thereby ... should not be believed as an article of Faith'.

This axiom finds expression in some of the laws of Anglican provinces. The Church in Australia, for example, 'receives all the canonical scriptures of the Old and New Testaments as being the ultimate rule and standard of faith given by inspiration of God and containing all things necessary for salvation'.[105] However, the laws of other churches make no such reference in relation to the doctrine and discipline of their provinces.[106]

Alternatively, some laws locate the authority for doctrine in the tradition of the Church; in the first place, the Catholic Creeds.[107] In 1888 the Apostles' and Nicene Creeds were specified as sources of doctrinal authority for Anglicans.[108] In 1908, the Conference 'place[d] on record its conviction that the historical

---

[103] Res 2.
[104] Res 3.
[105] Const pt1, ch1, 2; cf. Scotland can 17.2; Southern Cone Const Art 1.
[106] For example, Jerusalem and the Middle East Const Art 4 (iii).
[107] As the Church of England terms the Nicene Creed, the Apostles' Creed and the Athanasian Creed, though many laws do not include the last of these.
[108] See above.

facts stated in the Creeds are an essential part of the faith of the Church'.[109] Similar statements are repeated at regular intervals.[110] This frequent citing of the two creeds does reflect the fact that they are the most commonly cited sources of doctrinal authority throughout the Anglican Communion.[111]

A further development of this tendency is the adoption of the early Councils of the Church as sources of authority;[112] though the laws rarely specify which Councils are intended.[113] The early Councils are never mentioned in this (or any other) connexion in the Conference resolutions and, significantly, such an approach does not sit completely comfortably with Article XXI of the Thirty-Nine:

> General Councils ... forasmuch as they be an assembly of men, whereof all be not governed with the Spirit and word of God, they may err and sometime have erred, even in things pertaining to God. Wherefore things ordained by them as necessary to salvation have neither strength nor authority, unless it may be declared that they be taken out of Holy Scripture.

An interesting addendum to this issue is the encouragement given by the 1978 Conference to remove the *Filioque* clause from the Nicene Creed in pursuit of ecumenical advantage.[114] Only the Episcopal Church has made any move towards this step,[115] and the further initiative at the 1988 Conference was theirs.[116] However, they have not subsequently revised their liturgical books – though it is not clear what could stand in the way of that intention.

---

[109] Res 2.

[110] LC 1920 res 9 (vi); LC 1958 res 74 (a); LC 1968 res 46; LC 1988 res 18 (6) (a); LC 1998 res II.1 (b) (i) res III.8 (d); and even in the discursive document describing the fractious conference of 2008: para 125.

[111] Though never on their own. See, for example, Southeast Asia Fundamental Declarations 1; Jerusalem and the Middle East Const Art 4 (i), etc.

[112] For example, Spain Fundamental Declarations I; Portugal Cans Preamble.

[113] The West Indies (Declaration of Fundamental Principles (a–c)) speaks of the 'undisputed' councils and Kenya (cited in Doe, *Canon Law in the Anglican Communion*, p. 199) identifies them as the 'First four Councils'. The first four councils being, presumably, Nicea (AD 325), Constantinople (AD 381); Ephesus (AD 431); Chalcedon (AD 451).

[114] Res 35 (3); and reiterated in LC 1988 res 6 (5).

[115] Dependent on ratification of the move at the 1988 LC (see n 51); and so reaffirmed: 'Resolved, the House of Deputies concurring, That this 71st General Convention, following the resolution of the 68th General Convention, and responding to Resolution 19 of the joint meeting of the Primates of the Anglican Communion and the Anglican Consultative Council (Capetown 1993), hereby reaffirm its intention to remove the words "and the Son" from the third paragraph of the Nicene Creed at the next revision of the Book of Common Prayer.' See *Journal of the General Convention of … The Episcopal Church, Indianapolis, 1994* (New York: General Convention, 1995), p. 759.

[116] See Episcopal Press and News Service 1962 - 2006 19 ix 1985 no 85176: http://www.episcopalarchives.org/cgi-bin/ENS/ENSpress_release.pl?pr_number=85176.

It could be argued that those provinces that invoke the general councils as sources of doctrinal authority should have been more enthusiastic since the *Filioque* clause does not form part of their decrees.[117] The Church in New Zealand takes the credal basis of doctrine one stage further by providing in its constitution a brief commentary on the Four Marks of the Church, linking the doctrine to the daily life of the Church,[118] almost expounding the Conference resolution of 1930.[119]

Notwithstanding the 1930 resolution, some provinces state that doctrine cannot change,[120] but others state that their right is to explain the norms of Faith.[121] Once you move from the letter of a doctrinal formulation to explaining and expounding it, the prospect of development is never far away. The church in Kenya is explicit in stating its autonomous right 'to draw up its own formularies of faith and to set forth in terms that it considers suitable to the present day and to the needs of the people of this Province, the Faith which this church holds'.[122]

Those provinces that make structural provision for doctrinal development approach the matter in one or both of two ways. First, there are doctrinal commissions.[123] These are deliberative, rather than decision-making, bodies, feeding information and reflection into the legislative process.[124] Secondly, provinces that make provision for doctrinal development invariably reserve this function to the highest legislative level,[125] often requiring the bishops' approval in addition to a synodical majority.[126]

---

[117] See D. Knowles, *The Middle Ages (604 – 1330)* in H. Cunliffe-Jones (ed.), *A History of Christian Doctrine* (Edinburgh: T&T Clark, 1980), p. 244. It has been the practice at enthronements of Archbishops of Canterbury, as an ecumenical courtesy, to omit the clause: the only real warrant for this would seem to be the Conference resolution.

[118] Const Art 2.

[119] Res 49.

[120] Australia (Const XI.66); Canada (Declaration of Principles 6 (i)); Burundi (Const art 3.3) – though even here there is the possibility of modifications, which conform to Holy Scripture, and the standards of Faith of the Anglican Communion throughout the world. West Indies (Dec of Fundamental Principles (d) and (e)) disclaims the right to change standards of Faith, but can accept alterations permitted by the governing bodies of the Church of England.

[121] Zaire (Const art 3.3); North India (Const I.I.III).

[122] Const Art II (c).

[123] See, for example, Australia General Synod Commissions Canons 1998 – 2007, part V; West Indies Can 33.1.A; England GS 1782; Scotland Can 52.23.

[124] See Doe, *Canon Law in the Anglican Communion*, p. 204.

[125] New Zealand Church of England Empowering Act (1928), Sch I, Fundamental Provisions A2, Const B5f.

[126] Wales Const II: 34 – 43; North India Const I.III; England Synodical Government Measure (1969), Sch 2 art 7, Worship and Doctrine Measure (1974) s5 (1).

A few churches provide in their laws for the prerogative to adopt doctrinal developments that have occurred in the Church of England or other Anglican provinces.[127] For instance, the Church of the West Indies asserts 'the right of accepting any alterations in the Formularies of the Church which may be allowed by any General Synod, Council, Congress or other Assembly of the Churches of the Anglican Communion'.[128] In 1978 the Lambeth Conference established what might be viewed as an embryonic body of just this type. The Conference endorsed a proposal 'to set up an inter-Anglican theological and doctrinal advisory commission', and asked the Standing Committee of the ACC to establish the commission with the advice of the Primates, and mandated the Primates and provinces, 'by whatever means they feel best, to review its work after a period of not more than five years'.[129] However, thus far the Commission has not achieved the kind of authority that would presumably be necessary to satisfy the conditions of the Church in the West Indies; and it would until recently have seemed unlikely that it ever would, since the Lambeth Conference of 1878 disclaimed for the Communion any such central appellate role.[130] However, the proposals for an Anglican Communion Covenant might have taken steps in this direction, albeit in a persuasive rather than coercive form.[131]

The laws of most provinces provide for resolution of doctrinal questions; and a few specify that intractable issues should be referred outside the Province. In Central Africa, there is 'a right of appeal to a Final Court consisting of the Archbishop of Canterbury and two bishops of the Province of Canterbury or the Province of York'.[132] This might very directly reflect the resolutions of 1878 – indeed go further than the recommendation – which, having dismissed the idea of an Anglican Communion central appellate body, went on to say:

> If any province is desirous that its tribunal of appeal should have power to obtain, in matters of doctrine, or of discipline involving a question of doctrine, the opinion of some council of reference before pronouncing sentence, your Committee consider that the conditions of such reference

---

[127] Uganda Const Art 2 (e).
[128] Declaration of Fundamental Principles (e).
[129] Res 25; see also LC 1988 res 18.
[130] Rec 8 (a); see also LC 1930 res 51.
[131] The Anglican Communion Covenant S4.2: http://www.anglicancommunion.org/media/99905/The_Anglican_Covenant.pdf.
[132] Can 26.

must be determined by the province itself; but that the opinion of the council should be given on a consideration of the facts of the case, sent to it in writing by the tribunal of appeal, and not merely on an abstract question of doctrine.[133]

Few provinces have followed the lead of Central Africa in this regard.[134]

Formal structures are all very well; but every week, many thousands of bishops, priests, deacons and others preach and teach the Faith. As has been said, in 1968 the Lambeth Conference made it clear that it did not expect candidates for Ordination to subscribe to the Thirty-Nine Articles of Religion.[135] Nevertheless, all provinces require deference to the doctrine of the Church to be sworn by candidates for Ordination,[136] as well as by holders of some other offices.[137] They also provide for tribunals and processes whereby the doctrinally errant clergy may be disciplined.[138] Yet, in practice, formal judicial process against clergy for doctrinal offences is rare; it has been said that in England (in common with at least some other provinces) demonstrating a doctrinal offence to the satisfaction of a court would be challenging.[139] That said, there have been a few trials for doctrinal offences.[140]

A parallel story charts the changing position in the life of the Anglican Communion of the Book of Common Prayer (BCP) and the Ordinal.[141] While technically the BCP and the Ordinal are separate documents,[142] for our purposes they are considered together under the reference of the BCP; also, liturgical books are not of themselves law, but their contents, particularly the rubrics and the doctrine implied by their texts, can be given legal authority and as such are enforceable when they are specified in Law.[143]

---

[133] Rec 8 (b).

[134] Though Southern Africa: Declaration of Fundamental Principles 1870.

[135] Res 43 (c).

[136] Australia Can 7 1973; New Zealand Can A. I - II; Scotland Canons App 11; England Can C15; TEC Const Art VIII.

[137] For example, Readers in England Can E5 (4) and layworkers E8 (4); Readers in Scotland Canons App 19 Form B.

[138] A few provinces include laypeople within the scope of this provision: Wales Const XI.1 (c) (i); North India Const II.V.VI.1; Canada can XVIII.8 (g). EC: Canons Title IV; England: Ecclesiastical Jurisdiction Measure (1963) pts 4f.

[139] P. Forster, 'The Significance of the Declaration of Assent', *EccLJ* 8 (2005), pp. 162ff.

[140] For example, in 1995 of Bishop Walter Righter of the Episcopal Church.

[141] 1662. There had been a number of editions prior to that year; but this edition was prescribed by The Act of Uniformity (1662) (14 Car 2 c 4), which provision of the act remains in force.

[142] Cf. Church of England (Worship and Doctrine) Measure (1974) s5(1).

[143] See Doe, *The Legal Framework of the Church of England*, pp. 284ff.

At the first Lambeth Conference, it was stated that

> each province should have the right to make such adaptations and additions
> to the services of the Church as its peculiar circumstances may require.
> Provided, that no change or addition be made inconsistent with the spirit
> and principles of the Book of Common Prayer, and that all such changes be
> liable to revision by any synod of the Anglican Communion in which the
> said province shall be represented.[144]

In 1878, if anything, the insistence on the Book of Common Prayer was
stronger:

> Your Committee, believing that, next to oneness in 'the faith once delivered
> to the saints', communion in worship is the link which most firmly binds
> together bodies of Christian men, and remembering that the Book of
> Common Prayer, retained as it is, with some modifications, by all our
> Churches, has been one principal bond of union among them, desire to call
> attention to the fact that such communion in worship may be endangered by
> excessive diversities of ritual.[145]

And:

> It is expedient that Books of Common Prayer, suitable to the needs of native
> congregations in heathen countries, should be framed; that the principles
> embodied in such books should be identical with the principles embodied
> in the Book of Common Prayer; and that the deviations from the Book of
> Common Prayer in point of form should only be such as are required by the
> circumstances of particular Churches.[146]

By 1888, the pressure for reform is clear in the resolution

> That, inasmuch as the Book of Common Prayer is not the possession of
> one diocese or province, but of all, and that a revision in one portion of the
> Anglican Communion must therefore be extensively felt, this Conference is
> of the opinion that no particular portion of the Church should undertake
> revision without seriously considering the possible effect of such action on
> other branches of the Church.[147]

---

[144] LC 1867 res 8.
[145] Rec 7.
[146] Rec 10.
[147] Res 10.

Eleven years later the Conference yielded to that pressure,[148] and again in 1908,[149] until in 1920 it stated:

> While maintaining the authority of the Book of Common Prayer as the Anglican standard of doctrine and practice, we consider that liturgical uniformity should not be regarded as a necessity throughout the Churches of the Anglican Communion. The conditions of the Church in many parts of the mission field render inapplicable the retention of that Book as the one fixed liturgical model.[150]

In 1948, revision is taken for granted:

> The Conference holds that the Book of Common Prayer has been, and is, so strong a bond of unity throughout the whole Anglican Communion that great care must be taken to ensure that revisions of the Book shall be in accordance with the doctrine and accepted liturgical worship of the Anglican Communion.[151]

In 1958, there were three resolutions specifically about the revision of the BCP.[152] In these the focus is shifting away from the BCP towards international (ecumenical)[153] principles of liturgical reform, not least the recovery of ancient forms of worship.[154] The BCP is not mentioned again, though there are references to liturgy and its revision:

> This Conference resolves that each province should be free, subject to essential universal Anglican norms of worship, and to a valuing of traditional liturgical materials, to seek that expression of worship which is appropriate to its Christian people in their cultural context.[155]

We see, therefore, a move away from the liturgical gold-standard of the BCP to a more nebulous idea of an Anglican liturgical tradition. While this may be a difficult phenomenon to pin down with any certainty, liturgical scholars

---

[148] Res 46.
[149] Res 24.
[150] Res 36.
[151] Res 78 (a).
[152] Ress 73–75.
[153] See res 73.
[154] Res 74 (c).
[155] For example, LC 1988 res 47.

sometimes claim to detect its boundaries.[156] Indeed, it is hardly challenging to appreciate why Provinces of the Communion would find the BCP problematic – it is a very English book,[157] and one born of a particular era of English history. Even in the land of its inspiration, from a time very soon after the first Lambeth Resolution in 1867, it was recognized that some revision was necessary.[158]

The question, therefore, is not so much the fact of revision, but the extent to which the 'spirit and principles of the Book of Common Prayer'[159] are safeguarded in provincial laws. In England, the General Synod must ensure that 'the forms of service contained in the Book of Common Prayer continue to be available for use in the Church of England'.[160] However,

> Any Canon making any such provision as is mentioned in subsection (1) of this section, and any regulations made under any such Canon, shall have effect notwithstanding anything inconsistent therewith contained in any of the rubrics in the Book of Common Prayer.[161]

Furthermore, Canon A 3 states:

1. The doctrine contained in The Book of Common Prayer and Administration of the Sacraments and other Rites and Ceremonies of the Church according to the Use of the Church of England is agreeable to the Word of God.
2. The form of God's worship contained in the said Book, forasmuch as it is not repugnant to the Word of God, may be used by all members of the Church of England with a good conscience.

In other words, the BCP contains an acceptable form of worship, but it is not claimed to be the pattern by which all else is measured. Canon B 3 on the approval of forms of worship makes no reference to the spirit and principles of the BCP. The BCP is not a dead duck in England; it is still in use, both in its own

---

[156] See, for example, A. McGowan, *Eucharistic Eplicleses, Ancient and Modern* (London: SPCK, 2014), pp. 223ff.
[157] The use of Tudor English would be little different to praying in Latin for some provinces; there are also the frequent references to the sovereign, let alone what amounts to little more than a liturgical presentation of the British Constitution in the Litany. More subtly, the prose, while undeniably beautiful to English ears, might not resonate so harmoniously in countries of different styles of expression; and, equally, the impliedly restrained character of celebration might also fail to engage people of every culture.
[158] See R. C. D. Jasper, *The Development of the Anglican Liturgy* (London: SPCK, 1989), pp. 54ff.
[159] LC 1867 res 8.
[160] Worship and Doctrine Measure (1974) s1 (1).
[161] s1(2).

right and also in versions interpolated into the volumes of *Common Worship*, but it is hardly a 'principal bond of union'.[162] This perception is reinforced once we turn our attention to the Anglican Communion as a whole.

The Melanesian Canons do not mention the BCP at all; in Scotland the English Book of Common Prayer (1662) ceased to be one of the normative standards for worship in the Scottish Episcopal Church in 1867;[163] and in the United States the Book of Common Prayer is not the version of 1662, but the provision published by ECUSA (now TEC) in 1979[164] (the version of 1662 is not mentioned). By way of contrast, the law of the Anglican Church in Australia mirrors quite closely the English situation.[165] However, the BCP seems to retain a stronger claim: 'No alteration in or permitted variations from the services or Articles therein contained shall contravene any principle of doctrine or worship laid down in such standard.'[166] And, 'The authorisation of A Prayer Book for Australia in no way diminishes the authority of the Book of Common Prayer ... as the authorised standard of worship and doctrine of the Church as declared in the Constitution.'[167]

In Canada, the Book of Common Prayer is mentioned only once in the law of the Church: 'We are determined by the help of God to hold and maintain the Doctrine, Sacraments and Discipline of Christ as the Lord hath commanded in His Holy Word, and as the Church of England hath received and set forth the same in "The Book of Common Prayer".'[168] In the Principles of the Canadian church (part of its constitutional order), there is reference to the General Synod's competence to produce *a* BCP without any reference to the volume of 1662.[169] In fact, it is not as a liturgical model per se, but as a source of doctrine that the BCP retains its place; and as we have seen, various provinces explicitly and all, in practice, have felt free to contextualize this historical body of doctrinal material.

This pattern rather reflects the disappearance of references to the BCP in Lambeth Conference resolutions. Although it has been stated that the BCP

---

[162] LC 1867 res 8.
[163] Preamble s8.4.
[164] Title II, Canon 3.1.
[165] Part I, ch2.4.
[166] Part I, ch2.4.
[167] Canon 13(4).
[168] Declaration of Principles 1 (Solemn Declaration).
[169] Declaration of Principles 6 (j).

is still a standard of Anglican liturgy,[170] this is not universally the case even in theory. In practice, it would take a nuanced account of present liturgical provision across the Communion to demonstrate that it is simply a revision of the BCP; indeed, as we noted from the Conference of 1958, the guiding principles are much more ecumenical than those emanating from the fruits of scholarly inquiry. Nonetheless, there are limits to where these impulses can take the churches. In the Anglican Church of Southern Africa, liturgical revision must be consistent with the spirit and teaching of the BCP;[171] and in Korea it must be consonant with the Anglican Faith.[172]

In 1897, the Lambeth Conference had recognized 'the exclusive right of each bishop to put forth or sanction additional services for use within his jurisdiction, subject to such limitations as may be imposed by the provincial or other lawful authority'. And had also recognized 'in each bishop within his jurisdiction the exclusive right of adapting the services in the Book of Common Prayer to local circumstances, and also of directing or sanctioning the use of additional prayers, subject to such limitations as may be imposed by provincial or other lawful authority, provided also that any such adaptation shall not affect the doctrinal teaching or value of the service or passage thus adapted'.[173] These provisions, such as they may be, are a relic of the *Jus Liturgicum*, which identified the Bishop, being the principal liturgical minister, as having authority to compose and authorize liturgies. It is unlikely that bishops of the Church of England had enjoyed such a function for many centuries and, if they had it was abolished in 1974.[174]

In Australia, however, the Bishop's prerogative is preserved more fully: 'A bishop of a diocese may, at his discretion, permit such deviations from the existing order of service, not contravening any principle of doctrine or worship.'[175] Similarly, in Scotland:

A bishop may in the exercise of the powers traditionally vested in the episcopal office permit the use of services other than those specifically

---

[170] *The Principles of Canon Law common to the Churches of the Anglican Communion* 54 (1).

[171] Declaration of Fundamental Principles and Constitution Art X; see also Central Africa Art 12; SE Asia Fundamental Declarations 1.

[172] Constitutional Article 12.

[173] Ress 45f.

[174] R. H. Bursell, *Liturgy, Order and the Law* (Oxford: Clarendon Press, 1996), pp. 279, 4.

[175] Constitution ch2 para 4; this is primarily the power to respond to a request from a parish, see Rule VI.

authorised under this Canon if that Bishop deems such use to be pastorally appropriate. The Episcopal Synod may, however, restrain such exercise of these powers or impose conditions thereon and may do so either generally or with reference to particular localities, cases or circumstances.[176]

The principal safeguard here would seem to be (as mandated by the Lambeth Resolution of 1948) that the outcomes of revision should be 'in accordance with the doctrine and accepted liturgical worship of the Anglican Communion.'[177] In Melanesia, the diocesan Bishop's prerogative extends only to approving translations of the texts approved by General Synod,[178] in pursuance of the aim that 'the Church of this Province is to have one liturgical pattern for the whole Province as far as possible'.[179]

Provincial laws often allow bishops limited scope to innovate where there is a gap in the liturgical provision, as Resolution 46 suggests,[180] but the references to 'limitations as may be imposed by provincial or other lawful authority' are much more fully reflected in the laws. The 'great care' in revising the liturgy, as mandated by the resolution in 1948, is generally achieved by reserving the competence for approval[181] to the highest level of church government,[182] often with enhanced requirements for the revision to be authorized.[183] As well as the scrutiny of a General Synod or parallel body, most provinces have some sort of liturgical commission that is involved in the process of revision.[184] Some of these bodies are simply advisory,[185] while others have a formal part in the process of revision.[186] The result is a huge variety of liturgical provision across the Anglican Communion; and while many provinces retain the BCP as one possible (and maybe revered) option, its role in the distinctive identity of modern Anglicanism is hard to pin down. Its fate is intertwined with the

---

[176] Canon 22 (4).

[177] For example, Korea Const Art XII.

[178] Title B C1 (c); see also TEC Title II C4.

[179] Const Art 5 (a).

[180] See Ireland Canons Part I (5), England CB4 (3). See also *The Principles of Canon Law common to the Churches of the Anglican Communion* 54 (8). This is not really the exercise of any *Jus Liturgicum*, since it a prerogative of positive law.

[181] Though some limited role is sometimes accorded to bishops at the stage of experimentation: see Melanesia Title B C1 (g).

[182] Australia Const s28 (1).

[183] For example, TEC Const Art X; England CB2 (2).

[184] *The Principles of Canon Law common to the Churches of the Anglican Communion* 54 (3).

[185] Australia Canon 19 (1998) pt4 s11; and for England, see Doe, *Canon Law in the Anglican Communion*, p. 287.

[186] Melanesia Canons Title B 1 (a).

history of the Articles of Religion; and one would expect nothing else, since, as Prosper of Aquitaine famously observed, doctrine and worship are inextricably linked.[187] The gradual retreat and then disappearance of both liturgy and doctrine from the Lambeth Resolutions is reflected in the provincial laws that provide for more flexible regulation of both.

The rights and duties of the Laity

The Lambeth Conferences do not provide a set of distinct rights and duties for the laity; rather, they have articulated a set of responsibilities common to all the faithful, laity and clergy alike. In 1948, the Conference produced a codified list of what these included.[188] The churches have not generally reproduced this list;[189] but as PCLCCAC indicates,[190] most bodies of law contain the substance of the resolution scattered throughout their laws and included with the sections on the subjects to which they apply. The Conference urged all Church people

> to look upon their membership of Christ in the Church as the central fact in their lives. They should regard themselves as individually sharing responsibility for the corporate life and witness of the Church in the places where they live. They should discharge this responsibility and give a distinctive witness
>
> (a) by the regularity of their attendance at public worship and especially at the Holy Communion;[191]
> (b) by the practice of private prayer, Bible reading, and self-discipline;[192]
> (c) by bringing the teaching and example of Christ into their everyday lives;[193]
> (d) by the boldness of their spoken witness to their faith in Christ;[194]

---

[187] Liber praete ritorum sedis apostolicae episcoporum auctoritates de gratia de iet libero voluntati sarbitrio VIII, PL 51:209–210; though whether the maxim was originally his, is open to doubt.

[188] LC 1948 res 37.

[189] But see Chile: Cans. A2: Mexico Can 10.

[190] PCLCCAC, Principle 26.6; for 'duties of church membership';

[191] See, for example, England Canon B15(1); Australia Canon P4 1992 2; TEC can II.1; S Africa can 3.3.5.

[192] LC 1948 res 112 specified that embracing these responsibilities should be a fruit of confirmation preparation; most churches have requirements for confirmation preparation; for example Melanesia Can A3; Scotland Can 30.2(3); Chile Can F4.

[193] This, too, is wrapped up in Confirmation preparation.

[194] For example, Chile Can A2.

(e) by personal service to Church and community;[195]

(f) by the offering of money, according to their means, for the support of the work of the Church, at home and overseas.

'Thus', it concluded, 'there will be in every locality a living centre of Christian faith, witness, and fellowship.'

From the earliest Conference, the bishops were at pains to emphasize that the role of the laity in Anglican churches was not simply to be the chorus line to a company of clerical stars. In 1867, as the Lambeth Conference resolved to replace the errant Bishop of Natal, among the stipulations, it resolved that 'a godly and well-learned man should be chosen by the clergy, *with the assent of the lay communicants of the Church*'.[196] This foreshadowed a constant and incremental concern in Lambeth Conference resolutions that the laity should be included in the governance and administration of Anglican churches. This is made explicit in 1908: 'The ministry of the laity requires to be more widely recognised, side by side with the ministry of the clergy, in the work, the administration, and the discipline of the Church.'[197] This was further examined in Resolution 94:

> The Conference, believing that the laity, as baptized members of the Body of Christ, share in the priestly ministry of the Church and in responsibility for its work, calls upon Anglican men and women throughout the world to realise their Christian vocation both by taking their full part in the Church's life and by Christian witness and dedication in seeking to serve God's purpose in the world.

In 1968, the Conference recommended that 'no major issue in the life of the Church should be decided without the full participation of the laity in discussion and in decision.'[198]

Ten years later, this concern was underlined by a call 'for the training of lay and pastoral leadership in urban mission ... that greater use be made of the specialist skills of our lay members to inform the Church's decision-making on social, economic, and technological issues.'[199]

---

[195] Korea cans 42f; S India Const VI.2; again see LC 1948 res 112(c).
[196] Res 7; italics added.
[197] Res 46; see also Res 77.
[198] Res 24.
[199] Res 2(2); and see Res 42.

Running in tandem with this emphasis was a desire to enhance the understanding that the laity included both men and women. In 1920, the Conference stated: 'Women should be admitted to those councils of the Church to which laymen are admitted, and on equal terms. Diocesan, provincial, or national synods may decide when or how this principle is to be brought into effect.'[200] And in 1930 the Conference 'insisted on'

> the great importance of offering to women of ability and education, who have received adequate special training, posts which provide full scope for their powers and bring to them real partnership with those who direct the work of the Church, and genuine responsibility for their share of it, whether in parish or diocese; so that such women may find in the Church's service a sphere for the exercise of their capacity.[201]

Further resolutions followed developing the theme.[202] There are few, if any, examples of these resolutions being included in church laws for the simple reason that the laws had not explicitly stated that the laity only included men. However, the practice of churches has increasingly reflected the substance of these resolutions and as we shall see below, some churches have incorporated provisions into their laws prohibiting any discrimination against women. As we have seen, the most salient example of this promoting of lay participation in the life of the churches is the system of synodical government, which characterizes all Anglicanism. Obviously, laypeople are engaged in all areas of the churches' work: as judges, administrators and advisors. These rights and responsibilities are often termed 'acquired rights', since they accrue to the laity by virtue of their membership of the Church.

There is another strand of rights: what are often called 'inherent rights' or 'human rights', those rights that we have simply by virtue of being human. In 1920 the Conference received a 'Report on Missionary Problems', which stated, inter alia, that 'the Church would be failing in her work if the acceptance of the truths did not awaken in her converts a higher sense of their dignity as human beings, of their rights as well as their duties.'[203] In 1948, as the United

---

[200] Res 46.
[201] Res 66.
[202] For example, LC 1958 res 93.
[203] See res 41.

Nations Declaration on Human Rights was on the point of being adopted,[204] the Lambeth Conference threw itself behind the initiative.[205] On the basis that, like charity, respect for human rights should begin at home,[206] some churches have incorporated the duty into their laws.[207]

Churches have followed suit in setting these rights in a theological context: 'All persons, equal in dignity before God, have inherent rights and duties inseparable from their dignity as human beings created in the image and likeness of God and called to salvation through Jesus Christ; however, baptism is the foundation of Christian rights and duties, and a church should respect both sets of rights and duties.'[208] Furthermore,

> All the faithful, ordained and lay, enjoy their rights acquired by Baptism, the duties of others, 'and the law of that church' (rights to government, ministry, teaching, worship, sacraments, rites, and property) within the context of the inherent (human) rights intrinsic to their human dignity; indeed, in a church there is to be no unlawful denial of equal rights, status or access to the life, membership, government, ministry, worship, rites and property of that church on grounds of race, colour, ethnic, tribal or national origin, marital status, sex, sexual orientation, disability or age.[209]

In 1948, the Conference articulated these rights within a theological context:

> The Conference declares that all men, irrespective of race or colour, are equally the objects of God's love and are called to love and serve him. All men are made in his image; for all Christ died; and to all there is made the offer of eternal life. Every individual is therefore bound by duties towards God and towards other men, and has certain rights without the enjoyment of which

---

[204] See LC 1948 res 8.

[205] Ress 6–8; see also LC 1978 res 3.

[206] Cf. LC 1988 res 64(3).

[207] See, for example, Papua New Guinea: Const., Art. 3: 'all persons are of equal value in the sight of God';

[208] PCLCCAC, Principle 26.1-3; 4: a church should respect rights and duties founded on the dignity of the human person and on baptism and those afforded by ecclesiastical authority; 5: the church is concerned with the welfare of people in all its aspects, physical, mental and spiritual, and should as far as possible respond to the needs of all. Melanesia: Const., Art. 4: the church 'will take care to provide for the needs of all people committed to its charge'.

[209] PCLCCAC, Principle 26.7-8. See for example Indian Ocean: Const., Art. 3 and TEC: Cans. I.17.5: non-discrimination. PCLCCAC: 26.10: 'All the faithful should recognise the unique status and needs of children and young people ... and a church should make such provision ... to ensure their special protection. Mistreatment of children, especially their sexual abuse, offends their humanity and the teaching of Christ.'

he cannot freely perform those duties. These rights should be declared by the Church, recognised by the state, and safeguarded by international law.[210]

In other words, human rights are set within the context of divine and natural law, since they create the necessary conditions for humankind to develop its relationship with God, to ensure that 'the divine dignity of every human being is respected and … justice is pursued.'[211] As such, they are of 'capital and fundamental importance' for human dignity.[212] PCLCCAC also infers from the laws that 'all persons are equal in dignity before God' and that 'all persons have inherent rights and duties inseparable from their dignity as human beings created in the image and likeness of God and called to salvation through Jesus Christ.'[213]

The issue of human rights has featured frequently on the agenda of Lambeth Conferences and, as a topic, is too broad for more than cursory treatment here.[214] In brief, it calls upon 'all the Churches to press upon governments and communities their duty to promote fundamental human rights and freedoms among all their peoples.'[215] The Conference commonly attacks breaches of human rights on the basis that such breaches are contrary to 'the teaching of Christ.'[216] It classifies human rights in terms of political rights, which include 'a fair and just share' for people in government, and economic rights, in so far as 'human rights must include economic fairness and equity, and enable local economies to gain greater control over their own affairs.'[217] Since all humans are created in the image of God,[218] 'the Christian must … judge every social system by its effect on human personality.'[219] Consequently, Anglican churches are 'to speak out' against breaches of human rights, 'support all who are working for [the] implementation of human rights instruments'[220] and 'urge compliance

---

[210] Res 6, which follows five resolutions on 'the Doctrine of Man'.
[211] *The Official Report of the Lambeth Conference 1998* (Harrisburg, PA: Morehouse Publishing, 1999), p. 77.
[212] See, for example, LC 1998, Res. 1.1.
[213] PCLCCAC, Principle 26.1 and 2.
[214] See N. Doe, 'Canonical approaches to human rights in Anglican churches', in M. Hill (ed.), *Religious Liberty and Human Rights* (Cardiff: University of Wales Press, 1998), pp. 185-205.
[215] LC 1968, Res. 16.
[216] LC 1978, Res. 3.
[217] LC 1920, Res. 75; LC 1920, Res. 78; 1958, Res. 110; *Called to Full Humanity*, LC 1998, *Official Report*, p. 79.
[218] LC 1958, Res. 110; and LC 1968, Res. 16.
[219] LC 1948, Res. 5.
[220] LC 1988, Res. 33.

with the United Nations Declaration of Human Rights by the nations in which our various member Churches are located, and [by] all others over whom we may exercise any influence'.[221]

The Lambeth Conference call to the individual members of Anglican churches to promote human rights usually finds no direct echo in the actual laws of most churches. The constitution of the church in South India is, therefore, exceptional; it requires its members to

> contribute to the total ministry of the Church ... by responsible participation in secular organizations, legislative bodies ... and in other areas of public life, [so that] the decisions which are made in these areas may be controlled by the mind of Christ and the structures of society transformed according to His will.[222]

However, the general absence of such regulation in the laws does not indicate insouciance on the part of the churches towards this facet of Christian mission. There is a common understanding that there is an obligation on the churches 'to press upon governments and communities their duty to promote fundamental human rights and freedoms among all their peoples'[223] and that each autonomous church exists to 'promote within each of their territories a national expression of Christian faith, life and worship' and that both clergy and the laity are under a duty 'to take part in the mission of the Church'.[224]

The laws of churches of the Anglican Communion promote human rights in civil society through the establishment and work of institutions of the church such as in the Philippines where the church has a National Commission on Social Justice and Human Rights or in the West Indies where the Provincial Synod has a Standing Commission on Social Justice and Human Rights.[225] At the same time, catechetical material encourages individuals to contribute to the promotion of human rights in their work for 'justice and reconciliation' in civil society.[226]

---

[221] LC 1998, Res. 1.1(a).
[222] For example, South India: Const., VI.2.
[223] LC 1968 res 16.
[224] LC 1930, Res. 48 and 49; LC 1958, Res. 58.
[225] For example, Philippines: *Social Concerns Resolutions and Statements of the Philippine Episcopal Church* (1988); West Indies, Can. 33.1.C.
[226] For example, Southern Africa: Prayer Book 1989, 434.

The regulatory instruments of Anglicanism also generate interaction between church and society. This is the case at all ecclesial levels and in relation to all sorts of activities. In turn, the laws of churches sometimes spell out the mission of the church in wider society; these may include the duty to contribute to the 'moral and spiritual' welfare of society,[227] to promote justice in the world,[228] 'to transform unjust structures of society, caring for God's creation, and establishing the values of the Kingdom',[229] and to engage in 'educational, medical, social, agricultural and other service'.[230] Consequently, social service is a key function which provincial laws and other regulatory instruments assign to the assemblies of the church.[231] Typically, the governing body of each parish must 'promote the whole mission of the church, pastoral, evangelistic, social and ecumenical'.[232] Similarly, diocesan assemblies (synod, councils and conferences) stimulate service.[233] Indeed, in its treatment of mission, the Anglican Communion Covenant commits the churches 'to respond to human need by loving service', 'to seek to transform unjust structures of society', and 'to strive to safeguard the integrity of creation and to sustain and renew the life of the earth'.[234]

The Lambeth Conference and Anglican Communion Church Law

The foregoing presents us with a complex picture of the relationship between the Lambeth Conference and the laws of individual Anglican provinces. It might be said that the Conference's principal impact has been achieved through creating a common framework in which sometimes complicated subjects can

---

[227] Venezuela: Const., II.

[228] See, for example, Philippines: Const., Art. 1.1; Canons 1.2.2(d): one of the functions of the Provincial Synod's Commission on Social Concerns is 'to study the nature and root causes of poverty and underdevelopment in the country and review the participation of the Church in the development process'.

[229] New Zealand: Const., Preamble.

[230] North India: Const., II.I.II; see also Chile: Statutes, Art. 2.

[231] For a comparative study of national mission, see N. Doe, 'The notion of a national church: a juridical framework', *Law and Justice* 149 (2002), p. 77.

[232] PCLCCAC, Principle 21.6.

[233] See, for example, New Zealand: Cans. B.XXII: the duties of the inter-diocesan synod.

[234] TACC, 2.2.2; the Anglican Communion has various networks and other bodies to assist in these tasks.

be considered and discussed by churches that represent very different cultural situations. The influence of this on individual provinces has been gradual and perhaps subtle, leading them to clarify in their own canonical provisions the matters that have received attention at the Lambeth Conference. At the same time, of course, the influence has not flowed in only one direction. Over time the Lambeth Conference has created not law, but norms of Anglican identity; not least as initially tentative resolutions are reiterated at subsequent gatherings after a period of reflection around the world. However, just as often, provinces have returned to the Conference with their own (not always supportive) response to those resolutions.

At one end of a spectrum, there is the focus on human rights. While the emphasis on this subject did not erupt ex nihilo at the conferences, it would seem fair to say that it was in this context that ideas were clarified and articulated in a way that provided momentum for the individual churches to address the issue – sometimes in their laws and almost invariably in their practice.

In the area of doctrinal development, the Conference's role was less proactive. In these cases, the real pressure came from increasing ecumenical contact with other Christian denominations, the social contexts of the provinces and continuing theological inquiry resulting in a range of principled revisions. As the position of the 'historic formularies' was questioned, the individual churches hummed the tune (indeed, a number of tunes) and the conferences found some words to fit them. However, this led to a problem.

The historic formularies were replaced by a set of broad principles for the development of doctrine and worship, which permitted a thousand doctrinal flowers to bloom; and almost all of the provinces have, for different reasons, become increasingly dissatisfied with the look of the resulting meadow. The Conference found itself in an increasingly frantic effort to keep up with developments.[235] In 2008 events simply overwhelmed the Conference and a different form was adopted to absorb the tensions.[236] The Conference that might have been expected in 2018 will now happen in 2020. While the influence of the Conference seems to have been declining, that of the Instruments of the Anglican Communion seems to be rising, particularly that of the Primates' Meeting and the ACC. The challenge for them is twofold.

---

[235] See, for example, R. Deadman, *Women in Anglican Communion Laws*, in Daimon 9 (2009), pp. 73ff.
[236] There were no resolutions, just 'conversations and reflections'. See the Lambeth Indaba 2008.

In the first place, they need to guide the Anglican Communion towards an understanding of what Anglican identity is. The Lambeth Conferences had successfully established structural characteristics (most notably synodical government with lay representation; and, more recently, the work culminating in PCLCCAC demonstrating a significant commonality in the legal frameworks of Anglican provinces); but it has not been as easy to assert the doctrinal boundaries. Several provinces have now travelled a long way down the roads that other provinces believe to lead to unacceptable destinations. Conference resolutions alone will not resolve these fissures.

So, secondly, these instruments, creations of Lambeth Conferences, are attracting to themselves executive influence in an attempt to solve the problems; but here the development runs into a quandary. For decades Lambeth Conferences foreswore the very centralizing powers of Pan-Anglican institutions, which these instruments might acquire; and they have no purchase in the laws of individual churches. The rejection by some provinces of the Anglican Communion Covenant reflects an enduring suspicion in these churches of such a development. There is currently an informal acceptance of a role for these instruments during a period of crisis management; but that cannot last forever. A resolution of this situation may need to see a paradigm shift in the formal relationship of the Lambeth Conference and its institutions, on the one hand, and the laws of the individual churches of the Anglican Communion, on the other. Whether and, if so, how this rebalancing might be achieved remains to be seen.

Part Two

Personal, Pastoral and Political Perspectives

11

'Such Unfolding of the Truth of the Gospel': Post-colonial Reflections on the Missiological Dimension of the Lambeth Conference

Cathy Ross

Introduction

It was July 1988. We had landed – young, nervous, full of anticipation. We had finally arrived in Lubumbashi, Zaire (Democratic Republic of Congo) to begin our missionary service with and in the Diocese of Shaba. However, we were disappointed to learn that the Bishop was not there – he was in England attending the Lambeth Conference (hereafter, LC). Several weeks later he returned bearing greetings and a video of the closing service at Canterbury Cathedral. This was our first encounter with the Lambeth Conference. I still remember the dissonance of watching this lavish service in the vast, magnificent Canterbury Cathedral sitting in the simple living room of the Bishop with dozens of other people crammed in around the tiny TV set. I also remember their visible excitement, joy and pleasure at watching this service. This was their church; this is our church; this is family. This experience was our introduction to the Anglican Communion and to what it meant for Anglicans in the francophone Province of Zaire.

It meant that they are not alone. They belonged to something bigger which lifted them beyond the daily struggle of existence. They had brothers and sisters who were praying for them, who cared about them all over the world. We experienced the power of the 'bonds of affection' and the reality of conciliarity. This was not just another conference far away in a foreign language; it was a gathering that involved us all as the whole body which 'shares the responsibility and comes together in a representative way to take counsel'.[1] This was also our first inkling of the missiological dimension of the LC. Here was a gathering that was taken seriously by francophone Anglicans who wanted to serve Jesus and be part of the wider Anglican Communion. As a young New Zealander who had sat rather loosely to all things Anglican, it was a challenge to begin to understand the structures of the church of which we were a part and to appreciate the potential for mission within it.

Unexpectedly, I have enjoyed reading the Lambeth Resolutions produced since 1867. They are wide-ranging, eclectic and fascinating. Naturally, they reflect on and capture some of the wider dimensions of society at the time, so they present us with a snapshot of the world at that moment. Sometimes there are too many resolutions; as the LC entered the digital age, the number of resolutions and the quantity of verbiage increased hugely. Who reads these resolutions and what difference do they make? I wondered as I trawled through them. However, I was chastened by reading the following two responses to my unspoken question. Professor Owen Chadwick claimed that resolutions on justice, peace and humanitarian concerns are a way of 'making sure that prayers were directed where they were needed'. Archbishop Desmond Tutu endorsed this by declaring, 'They help create a particular climate, help shape public opinion, help victims of oppression. It is important for us at Lambeth not to be seen as just a talk shop.'[2] So the resolutions, ideas, themes and reports are important for Anglican life together and for mission.

There have been various understandings and definitions of mission since the first LC in 1867. Archbishop Longley's invitation letter of 22 February, 1867 invites his brother Bishops 'to consider together many practical questions, the settlement of which would tend to the advancement of the kingdom of our Lord and Master Jesus Christ, and to the maintenance of greater union in our missionary work and to increased intercommunion among ourselves'.[3] So mission was there from the beginning. The understanding of mission that

---

[1]   Paul Avis, 'Anglican Conciliarism: The Lambeth Conference as an Instrument of Communion', in M. Chapman, S. Clarke and M. Percy (eds), *The Oxford Handbook of Anglican Studies* (Oxford: Oxford University Press, 2015), p. 50.

[2]   Quoted in Michael Marshall, *Church at the Crossroads: Lambeth 1988* (London: Collins, 1988), pp. 149–50.

[3]   Letter to Bishops, 18 February, 1867: http://www.archive.org/stream/a589564000lambuoft/a589564000lambuoft_djvu.txt (accessed 7 May 2016).

was offered in the LC of 2008 was expressed in ways that picked up some more recent discussions in missiology and ecclesiology, such as holistic mission and *missio Dei*:

> Mission belongs to God and we are called to engage in this mission so that God's will of salvation for all may be fulfilled. In this sense, mission is not primarily an activity of the church, but an attribute of God. The Church exists as an instrument for that mission. There is church because there is mission, and not vice versa. To participate in mission is to participate in the movement of God's love toward people, since God is the fountain of sending love.[4]

In order to consider the missiological dimension of the LC, I would like to focus on four themes that pervade and are embedded in the Conferences from the first LC in 1867. These are contextualization and culture, world Christianity, creativity and the importance of addressing contemporary issues.

Contextualization and culture

Traditionally contextualization simply meant the process of making the Gospel understood; the process 'whereby Christians adapt the forms, content and praxis of the Christian faith so as to communicate it to the minds and hearts of people with other cultural backgrounds'.[5] The scriptural message is constant, but its presentation depends on culture. So contextualization has been typically regarded as a task which concerns the application and communication of timeless truths.

However, there are a few problems with this view. First, as Lesslie Newbigin, Steve Bevans and Andrew Walls have reminded us, there is no such thing as a pure Gospel; there is only a Gospel enfleshed in culture and context. The Gospel is always embodied in a cultural context. Moreover, contextualization touches on how we do theology, so that our cultural context actually shapes the message. We assume that we know the Gospel and that all we have to do is

---

[4] *Lambeth Indaba, Capturing Conversations and Reflections from the Lambeth Conference, 2008,* p. 9: http://www.anglicancommunion.org/media/72554/reflections_document_-final-.pdf (accessed 7 May 2016).
[5] Moreau quoted in Jackson Wu, *One Gospel for All Nations: A Practical Approach to Biblical Contextualization* (Pasadena, CA: William Carey Library, 2015), p. 5.

to package it in the appropriate way for the receiving context, but that is naïve. It is a more complex process than that and in fact contextualization works both ways: as we attempt to engage in contextualization, we become recipients of contextualization. It seems that the seventy-six Bishops who attended the first LC in 1867 were largely sympathetic to this perspective when they issued Resolution 8:

> That, in order to the binding of the Churches of our colonial empire and the missionary Churches beyond them in the closest union with the Mother-Church, it is necessary that they receive and maintain without alteration the standards of faith and doctrine as now in use in that Church. *That, nevertheless, each province should have the right to make such adaptations and additions to the services of the Church as its peculiar circumstances may require.* Provided, that no change or addition be made inconsistent with the spirit and principles of the Book of Common Prayer, and that all such changes be liable to revision by any synod of the Anglican Communion in which the said province shall be represented. (italics added)

This emphasis is found throughout the LC from the beginning. There is clear encouragement that 'native Churches' should understand that 'the church is their own and not a foreign Church'[6] and that 'the Church should be adapted to local circumstances'.[7] By LC 1908, they were discussing the necessity of self-government and self-support and encouraging national churches 'to adopt native forms of marriage and consecrate them to Christian use'.[8] By 1948, just after the end of the Second World War and the founding of the World Council of Churches and the United Nations, there were 43 resolutions (out of a total of 118) that addressed 'The Church in the Modern World', reflecting the spirit of the age and exhorting 'the Church to think out afresh the Christian gospel of work in terms relevant to modern working conditions' and governments 'to ensure to these peoples their economic rights and the best elements of the spiritual and cultural heritage of their own lands'.[9]

---

[6] LC 1897, Resolution 18: http://www.anglicancommunion.org/structures/instruments-of-communion/lambeth-conference.aspx (accessed 6 May 2016). All subsequently quoted Resolutions may be found at this website.

[7] LC, 1897, Resolution 19.

[8] LC, 1908, Resolutions 21 and 25.

[9] LC, 1948, Resolutions 21 and 24.

So what is culture and why does cultural heritage matter? There are many definitions of culture ranging from the more technical to the more practical. Perhaps a simple definition will be the most serviceable for our purposes: 'Culture is simply the way we do things around here.'[10] These days cultures are no longer thought of as static nor fixed entities but rather as dynamic and fluid. They may entail multiple meanings and ways of viewing the world. These patterns of meanings and perspectives can be contested and carry deep assumptions about who we are, how we behave and live in the world. Anthropologist Gerald Arbuckle reminds us that 'who we are is primarily to be found in the way we live day by day in a particular context or environment'.[11] In our postmodern world both personal and cultural identities are formed in this matrix of negotiating the interplay of history, culture and power. Bishop John V. Taylor, in his prescient book, *The Primal Vision*, reminds us of the importance of separating out the gift of the Gospel from Western culture so that contextualization can take place. 'The Church, unfortunately, has too often retreated from the bold position of the Council of Jerusalem and demanded of its converts some cultural equivalent of circumcision.'[12]

Thirty years later, in 1978, we find the LC issuing a strong statement on cultural identity which acknowledges the growth of the Anglican Communion and endorses contextualization:

> The Conference recognises with thanksgiving to God the growth of the Church across the world and encourages every particular Church to strengthen its own identity in Christ and its involvement with the community of which it is part, expressing its faith through the traditions and culture of its own society except where they are in conflict with the essentials of the Gospel.[13]

The LC 1978 produced some very interesting preparatory information for the Bishops. David Barrett, the respected founder and editor of the *World Christian Encyclopedia* and the *World Christian Database*, prepared thirty-eight pages of tables and commentaries entitled 'The Anglican World in

---

[10] Attributed to Archbishop Derek Worlock.

[11] G. Arbuckle, *Culture, Inculturation, and Theologians: A Postmodern Critique* (Collegeville, MN: Liturgical Press, 2010), p. 66.

[12] John V. Taylor, *The Primal Vision: Christian Presence Amid African Religion* (London: SCM, 1963), p. 106.

[13] LC, 1978, Resolution 36.

Figures'. In the introduction he claimed that this is 'the most thorough and accurate survey of the Anglican world undertaken to date'.[14] The tables include the number of Anglicans in each country in the Anglican Communion, the numbers of baptized and communicant members, birth and death rates in the Anglican family, ratios of clergy and laity, numbers of 'Anglicans engaged in mission abroad', finances and more. For our purposes, I found the table entitled 'Anglican Increase per Year, 1977' and its accompanying commentary the most enlightening and challenging, when read from the vantage point of the early twenty-first century. Barrett explained that fourteen of our thirty-one churches showed an annual net gain of converts, while the other seventeen showed an annual net loss. Where were the new converts coming from? Central Africa, Kenya, Papua New Guinea, Sudan, Tanzania, Uganda – in other words the Majority World or the Global South. They mostly came from traditional tribal religions and were former animists. Where were the losses? They were taking place in the older churches of the West – Australia, Canada, England, Ireland, New Zealand, Scotland, the United States, Wales. Barrett claimed that most were not leaving to join other churches. These losses represented people who, in public-opinion polls in 1976, stated that they were 'Anglican', 'Episcopalian', 'Church of England', etc., but one year later (1977) answered, 'I have no religion'. In other words, they were people who, in a single year had abandoned altogether any profession of Christianity, let alone of Anglicanism. Defections of this order of magnitude are common also to all the other major Roman Catholic and Protestant churches of the Western world.[15] The 1978 Conference resolutions did not follow up either the growth in the Majority World churches or the worrying trend of 'defections' in the churches of the West. Astonishingly, it seems that these trends were ignored.[16]

For the Church of England, it took another sixteen years for some of these insights and challenges to emerge in a more systematic and structural way. In 1994 *Breaking New Ground: Church Planting in the Church of England* was published. It was the first formal document to 'own planting as a missionary

---

[14] *The Lambeth Conference 1978, Preparatory Information, Statistics: Documentation: Addresses: Maps,* (Oxford: Bocardo and Church Army Press, 1978), p. 2.

[15] Ibid., p. 19.

[16] See now David Goodhew (ed.), *Growth and Decline in the Anglican Communion, 1980 to the Present* (London: Routledge, 2017).

strategy'.[17] Ten years later, in 2004, the *Mission Shaped Church (MSC)* report was published to enable reflection on 'our ongoing and shared calling to embody and inculturate the gospel in the evolving cultures and contexts of our society'.[18] This report has sold over 27,000 copies – an unprecedented number for a Church of England report. The Fresh Expressions of Church movement was launched in 2005, shortly after the publication of *MSC*. Jonny Baker, Director of Mission Education at the Church Mission Society (CMS) claims that it was youth workers in the 1980s who were the main activists in mission in the British context. They were learning to inhabit a new culture by letting go of traditional approaches – a kind of letting go of the Gospel for the sake of the Gospel. He writes:

> I have noticed for years now that youth ministry is the backdoor for renewing the Church. What you see in youth ministry you tend to see the Church picking up on ten years later. So it is highly influential, subversive and strategic to be in youth ministry. You can trace the Church's current resurgence of interest in mission, pioneering and a cross-cultural approach directly to the practice being developed in youth ministry back then.[19]

Gill Poole, in a report written for CMS, refers to 'edgeworkers' as those people 'who are working on the edges, often purely in faithful response to God and without any formal or institutional support'.[20] Presumably, it was some of these initiatives and experiments on the ground that began to foster some new thinking around mission and comprised the beginnings of a response to the worrying trends uncovered by Barrett. The Five Marks of Mission was also an important influence on the *MSC* report.

Perhaps part of the response was also found in the Lambeth Conference 1988 where a call was issued for a Decade of Evangelism for the last decade of the millennium.[21] The conference made a plea for relevant and contemporary communication of the Gospel:

---

[17] *Mission Shaped Church: Church Planting and Fresh Expressions of Church in a Changing Context* (London: Church House Publishing, 2004), p. xi.

[18] Ibid., p. xii.

[19] Jonny Baker, 'Pioneer Youth Ministry – Part 1', *Youthwork* (Premier Christian Media), Vol. 2, Issue 33, September 2013. See https://www.youthandchildrens.work/Youthwork-past-issues/2013/September-2013/Pioneer-Youth-Ministry-Part-One (accessed 26 May 2016).

[20] Gill Poole, 'The Church in Britain & World Mission: An Enquiry', Internal Report, July 2002; p. 4.

[21] LC, 1988, Resolution 43.

This Conference:

(a) Recognises that culture is the context in which people find their identity.
(b) Affirms that God's love extends to people of every culture and that the Gospel judges every culture according to the Gospel's own criteria of truth, challenging some aspects of culture while endorsing and transforming others for the benefit of the Church and society.
(c) Urges the Church everywhere to work at expressing the unchanging Gospel of Christ in words, actions, names, customs, liturgies, which communicate relevantly in each contemporary society.[22]

This theme is further elaborated on in the Conference Reports where there are reflections on where Christianity 'has come in harness with a colonial power'[23] and a clear acknowledgement of the missionary role of the Anglican churches in the Majority World. 'In this way the younger churches of Asia, African and Latin America have often become evangelists of the Churches of the northern hemisphere.'[24]

The official report of the 1998 LC runs to 534 pages, of which there are 63 pages of resolutions. In its second section report entitled 'Called to Live and Proclaim the Good News', it endorsed that the Five Marks of Mission have proved a serviceable and robust framework for mission for the Anglican Communion. In 1998 these were:

• To proclaim the Good News of the Kingdom
• To teach, baptise and nurture new believers
• To respond to human need by loving service
• To seek to transform the unjust structures of society
• To strive to safeguard the integrity of creation, and sustain and renew the life of the earth.[25]

However, the Five Marks of Mission are not a static document but part of a dynamic process. There was a request by the Anglican Church of Canada at the 2009 'Mutual Responsibility and Mission Consultation' in Costa Rica to add a sixth mark of mission relating to peace, conflict transformation and

---

[22] LC, 1988, Resolution 22.
[23] 'Dogmatic and Pastoral Concerns', in *The Truth Shall Make You Free, The Lambeth Conference 1988: The Reports, Resolutions and Pastoral Letters from the Bishops* (London: Church House Publishing, 1988), paragraph 28, p. 88.
[24] Ibid., paragraph 38, p. 91.
[25] *The Official Report of the Lambeth Conference 1998* (Harrisburg, PA: Morehouse, 1998), p. 150.

reconciliation. The initiative for this suggestion came from Canada with their attempts at reconciliation with indigenous peoples, and was strongly supported by Burundi, a country heavily involved in post-conflict reconciliation. In response to this request, at ACC-15 in Auckland, Aotearoa/New Zealand in 2012 the Council unanimously agreed to adjust the wording of the current fourth mark of mission to read: 'To seek to transform unjust structures of society, to challenge violence of every kind and to pursue peace and reconciliation'. The 1998 LC also had two strong Resolutions on the theological foundations of mission (Resolution II.1) and on future priorities in Mission (II.6).

After the many Resolutions and worthy reports of the 1998 LC, the different approach of the LC 2008 comes as a relief. The Conference themes were 'Equipping Bishops for God's Mission' and 'Strengthening Anglican Identity' – themes which very much reflect the *zeitgeist* of the era with mission seen as a vital component of Anglican life and sadness over the emergence of Global Anglican Future Conference (GAFCON) in 2008. Some see GAFCON as an alternative to the Lambeth Conference and the beginning of a realignment of Anglicanism worldwide. GAFCON described itself on its website in 2016:

> The GAFCON journey began in 2008 when moral compromise, doctrinal error and the collapse of biblical witness in parts of the Anglican Communion had reached such a level that the leaders of the majority of the world's Anglicans felt it was necessary to take a united stand for truth. A crowd of more than one thousand witnesses, including Primates, Archbishops, Bishops, clergy and lay leaders gathered in Jerusalem for the Global Anglican Future Conference (GAFCON).[26]

The LC 2008 adopted a more modest approach. Archbishop Rowan Williams borrowed a model from another part of the Communion as a way of framing this conference. Indaba was adopted from South Africa as a way of encouraging respectful listening and ensuring that all voices were heard and respected. 'This process generated honest interchange and mutual understanding and assisted bishops to respond to the concerns and mission imperatives of their colleagues.'[27] This focus on conversation, and listening to one another's stories is a pastoral practice that recognizes the importance of storytelling as a fundamental part of

---

[26] http://gafcon.org/about/ (accessed 7 May 2016; page no longer extant).
[27] 'A Summary of Lambeth Indaba: Capturing Conversations and Reflections': http://www.anglicancommunion.org/media/72635/executive_summary.pdf (accessed 7 May 2016).

our human experience. Likewise we have all experienced the power of intentional listening – a practice that validates and honours another's experience. 'With careful listening can come the gifts of being heard, known and understood.'[28]

Again, culture and contextualization are highlighted as crucial for mission with a more nuanced understanding of contextual witness:

> We affirm that the Church is called to be faithful in the exercise of its mission in the context within which it is located with due regard to culture. We acknowledge that in its understanding of the exercise of this responsibility what may be positive, acceptable and fitting in one culture, may be negative, harmful and may affect the witness and proclamation of the gospel in other parts of the Communion due to cultural differences. The Bible must be taken as [sic] authoritative guiding principle in our proclamation of the gospel.[29]

Each of the section summaries of the LC 2008 is mission focused. The section titles are Mission and Evangelism, Human and Social Justice, Environment, Ecumenism, Relations with Other World Religions, Anglican Bishops and Anglican Identity, Human Sexuality, The Scriptures, The Anglican Covenant, The Windsor Process and Statements of Solidarity. Some of the sections deal with internal processes and housekeeping but most of the content of the sections has a lively interest and concern to engage with God's world with 'bold humility' (to pick up a phrase used of one of the foremost missiologists of the twenty-first century, South African, David Bosch).[30] By modelling the Indaba process, the LC is beginning to show a greater awareness of and appreciation for other members of our Anglican Communion.

World Christianity

Anglicans are, of course, members of a world family. The Anglican Communion has a membership of approximately eighty-five million. We know that most Christians in the world now do not live in the West but rather

---

[28] Mary Clark Moschella, *Ethnography as a Pastoral Practice* (Cleveland, OH: Pilgrim Press, 2008), p. 254.

[29] LC 2008, 'Lambeth Indaba, Capturing Conversations and Reflections from the Lambeth Conference 2008', Section B: Mission and Evangelism, paragraph 31: http://www.anglicancommunion.org/resources/document-library/lambeth-conference/2008/section-b-mission-and-evangelism?author=Lambeth+Conference&year=2008 (accessed 7 May 2016).

[30] See W. Saayman and K. Kritzinger (eds), *Mission in Bold Humility: David Bosch's Work Considered* (Maryknoll, NY: Orbis, 1997).

in the Majority World. In 2014, a significant milestone in world Christianity went unnoticed. For the first time ever, Latin America surpassed Europe as the continent with the most Christians. We note that in 1900 Europe had six times as many Christians as Latin America. Looking ahead to 2025, we see that Latin America is likely to be surpassed by Africa, with 628 million in the former and more than 700 million in the latter. We can also project that by 2050, Asia will surpass Europe in the number of Christians. Each of the three continents in the Global South could outnumber Europe, together accounting for nearly 80 per cent of all Christians (an increase from just over 20 per cent in 1900).[31]

How aware are we of these trends in global Anglicanism? In England, it certainly seems as though the Church of England is the default setting for Anglicanism, without much appreciation of the wider Anglican Communion and its different perspectives. Many are amazed to hear that the average Anglican is 'an African woman with a very strong post-colonial Christian agenda'.[32] Not only that – she is also likely to be young, Bible believing and extremely poor. This is the Anglican family. How do we play our part as members of this family? How might this reality shape our theological understandings, our discipleship, our engagement in mission?

The West African theologian Tite Tiénou claims that many around the world still 'perceive Christianity as a Western religion'.[33] This is surprising as we have known for many years of the shift in the centre of gravity, namely that representative Christianity is now to be found in the Majority World. Scottish missiologist and historian Andrew Walls wrote over twenty years ago that 'the future of the Christian faith, its shape in the twenty-first and twenty-second centuries, is being decided by events which are now taking place in Africa, Asia and Latin America, or which will do so in the near future'.[34] Ten years later he was still reminding us that Christianity is primarily a non-Western religion, that our twenty-first century faith will require robust scholarship from the soil of Africa, Asia and Latin America and that the 'most urgent reason for the

---

[31] Todd M. Johnson, Gina A. Zurlo, Albert W. Hickman and Peter F. Crossing, 'Christianity 2016: Latin America and Projecting Religions to 2050', *International Bulletin of Missionary Research*, January 2016, Vol. 40(1), p. 23.

[32] David Moxon, 'The Anglican Communion and its Future: A Synopsis': http://www.anglicancentreinrome.org/Publisher/File.aspx?ID=149667 (accessed 7 May 2015).

[33] T. Tiénou, 'Christian Theology in an Era of World Christianity', in C. Ott and H. Netland (eds), *Globalising Theology: Belief and Practice in an Era of World Christianity* (Nottingham: Apollos, 2007), p. 42.

[34] A. Walls, quoted in Tienou, 'Christian Theology', p. 44.

study of the religious traditions of Africa and Asia, of the Amerindian and the Pacific peoples, is their significance for Christian theology; they are the substratum of the Christian faith and life for the greater number of Christians in the world'.[35] Twenty years on from this statement (published in 1997), are we any closer to this reality? Have we in the West really taken on board what it means to be world Christians or are we still operating under the paradigm of colonial Christianity? Are we still, as Kenyan professor John Mbiti asserted in 1976, kerygmatically universal but theologically provincial?[36] In other words, do we still believe in and proclaim a universal Gospel but allow our theology to remain limited and constrained by our own provincial horizons? The LC was aware of this challenge in 1930! I quote Resolution 4, 'The Christian Doctrine of God', in full to emphasize how prescient and prophetic our forebears were:

> The revelation of Christ was presented to the world under the forms of Jewish life and thought. It has found fuller expression, not without some admixture of misunderstanding, through the thought of Greece and Rome, and the sentiment of the Teutonic and Slavonic races. We anticipate that when this same revelation possesses their minds, the nations of Asia and Africa will still further enrich the Church of Christ by characteristic statements of the permanent Gospel, and by characteristic examples of Christian virtue and types of Christian worship. We welcome such unfolding of the truth of the Gospel as one of the ways by which the nations may bring their riches into the service of Christ and his Church.[37]

The LC 1968 reminds us of the vital need for the Christian faith to cross borders in order to flourish and grow. 'When the Christian faith becomes completely identified with any particular culture the result is stagnation: the faith dies with the culture. Only by God's grace and in a new culture will it be renewed.'[38] Christianity thrives on the borderlands where cultures overlap and encounter one another. Christianity is nurtured in cultural encounters and then develops and nurtures cultures. For example, it was when the Chinese took in Jesus

---

[35] A. Walls, 'Old Athens and New Jerusalem: Some Signposts for Christian Scholarship in the Early History of Mission Studies', *International Bulletin of Missionary Research*, 21:4 (October 1997), p. 153.

[36] J. Mbiti, quoted in Tienou, 'Christian Theology', p. 45.

[37] http://www.anglicancommunion.org/resources/document-library/lambeth-conference/1930/resolution-4-the-christian-doctrine-of-god?author=Lambeth+Conference&year=1930 (accessed 7 May 2016).

[38] *The Lambeth Conference 1968, Resolutions and Reports* (London: SPCK, 1968), pp. 75–6.

Christ and nurtured and understood him in their own Confucian ways that he became Chinese enough to be understood and appropriated by Chinese people. This border crossing and encounter with other cultures is absolutely essential for the growth and vitality of Christianity. Moreover, Christianity atrophies if it is not missionary in nature. When the faith is crossing boundaries, it is most alive – whatever these borders may be: geographic, linguistic, cultural, sociological, economic. If, as churches, we remain only in Christian environments or institutions, our faith wanes and becomes static; it becomes most alive in border-crossing encounters. We can make the same observation concerning our own personal faith and discipleship as well.

We know that a majority of Christians are no longer to be found in the West or associated with centres of power. Christianity is increasingly becoming a religion practised as a minority faith without 'Christian' government support. 'There is a larger *percentage* of the general population worshipping weekly in Brunei, Singapore, Egypt and Lebanon (not to mention Ghana, Nigeria and Uganda) than in any country in Western Europe.'[39] Those countries do not enjoy the 'Christendom' comfort and power that Western Christians had in the past. The old model of Christianity flourishing under Christian rulers is at an end. It is now rather a worldwide faith of the poor and the little ones – from the barrios and the neighbourhoods rather than from palaces, institutions and centres of power. Therefore this inevitably means (or will eventually mean) a shift away from Western power and control, Western hegemony. World Christianity – and this is true for the Anglican Communion, though we in the West are struggling to accept it – does not conform to Western practices, liturgies and theologies. Recent events in the Anglican Communion have made that very clear – but we continue to practise a 'dialogue of the deaf'[40] and prefer not to listen. In the twentieth century Christianity has broken out of its Western Christendom captivity and has ploughed a new furrow. Whether that will lead to a new form of captivity is yet to be seen. I am hopeful that it will not, precisely because it is moving away from the centres of power, because it is owned by the little ones and because it is constantly on the move, being reshaped and re-envisioned.

---

[39] Scott Sunquist, *The Unexpected Christian Century: The Renewal and Transformation of Global Christianity, 1900-2000* (Grand Rapids, MI: Baker Academic, 2015), p. 150.
[40] T. Tienou, 'Christian Theology', pp. 37–51.

Christianity engages with local cultures both in continuity and in discontinuity with the culture. How might the Gospel best be expressed and flourish in this new soil? And how might this new soil enhance the understanding and depth of the Gospel? One of the key principles that was learnt from the reception of Christianity in Africa, for example, is that it was not what Western missionaries said that mattered in the long term but rather how local or African Christians appropriated Christ in ways that made sense to them, utilizing African spiritual maps of the universe. This is a lesson for us here and now when we consider mission. Are we able to engage in ways that are truly contextual allowing faith communities to flourish in local soil using local spiritual maps? And, conversely, do we, in the Anglican Communion, find our own understanding and appropriation of the faith challenged, enhanced and transformed by deep listening to the varying contexts in the Communion? Christianity must have a local flavour. This is something that we understand in Anglicanism – the principle of subsidiarity was clearly affirmed at the LC 1998. But how does this play out on the ground in the various parts of our Communion? Many of our sisters and brothers know that the transformative power of Christianity is not to be found in worldly power and they know the daily reality of suffering as part of the DNA of being a Christian. Christianity is growing from below and is locally based without political protection. Today Christianity is still the largest world religion, but much of its growth is from the edges, the margins, the fringes and this will bring new agendas, new thought forms and new creative challenges to our life.

Creativity and imagination

Creativity and imagination is not one of the most prominent themes of the LC statements, but it is certainly present. The 1958 LC made an appeal for the use of creativity and imagination in presenting the biblical message:

> The Conference believes that the presentation of the message of the Bible to the world requires great sensitiveness to the outlook of the people of today, and urges that imaginative use be made of all the resources of literature, art, music and drama, and of new techniques appealing to the eye as well as to the ear.[41]

---

[41] LC 1958, Resolution 10.

The accompanying report affirmed that the message of the Bible 'is addressed to the eye and the imagination. Art and drama, no less than music and poetry, can be powerful means of serving the truth; and so can the techniques of television and radio.'[42] Ten years later in 1968, the LC was encouraging a more courageous use of local art and culture:

The church must always be sensitive to the arts and other cultural forms of the community in which it is placed, and must make discerning use of them so that they may appropriately express the Christian faith to that community. In particular there is need for bolder experiment in adapting local and familiar art-forms and prayer-forms, as well as modern forms of expression, in the development of the Church's teaching and liturgy. We should not hesitate to give expression to exuberance and joy.[43]

We have to wait until the LC 2008 to find a similar statement. There young people are exhorted to bring their 'idealism, enthusiasm and creativity' to the church.[44]

The Pioneer Leadership Training at CMS has taught me a great deal about creativity, imagination and 'bolder experiments'. Walter Brueggemann's idea of prophetic imagination has been a constant theme among the students. Brueggemann writes about grief and amazement – grief at where we have become stuck and numb – perhaps overwhelmed by the task before us or unable to see a way out. Amazement enables us to postulate that a new world is possible. Brueggemann reminds us that a prophetic imagination can be dangerous and subversive and requires a break from the dominant imagination. This is the challenge presented to us by the shift in the centre of gravity of world Christianity. We require an alternative imagination as to what it means to be a Christian and an Anglican in our world today. In our post-Christian Western contexts, in our increasingly Christian and also marginally Christian Majority World contexts, we desperately need this alternative imagination in order to live out the Christian faith in those places. We need imagination and creativity which can nurture a posture and a vision where alternative approaches are possible. We need to have what John V. Taylor called, an 'adventure of the imagination'.[45]

---

[42] *The Lambeth Conference 1958, The Encyclical Letter from the Bishops together with the Resolutions and Reports* (London: SPCK, 1958), 'The Holy Bible: Its Authority and Message', Section 2.17.

[43] *The Lambeth Conference 1968, Resolutions and Reports* (London: SPCK, 1968), p. 76.

[44] LC 2008, 'Lambeth Indaba: Capturing Conversations and Reflections from the Lambeth Conference 2008, Section B: Mission and Evangelism', paragraph 26.

[45] John V. Taylor, *The Primal Vision*, p. 41.

Local language, local theology and local artistic expression are all needed to engage in this adventure. The LC 1958 endorsed the production of literature 'in every language area' for the benefit of the whole church and 'not least for the commending of Christianity to those outside the church'.[46] We will all be enriched by listening to and learning from local theologies. Recently I heard an excellent example of this approach from Kenyan professor John Mbiti who is collecting African names for Jesus. So far he has 310. These are names that place Jesus squarely in an African setting and depict 'a spirit of endearment and loving attachment to Jesus'. There are more familiar names such as 'ancestor, healer, king, path', and then there are ones which may surprise and delight from an African context such as 'untiring porter, great forest canopy, string of priceless beads, elephant hunter' – names which show Africans at home with Jesus.

> This is not an ecclesiastically formulated Christology of any institutional church. It is a spontaneous Christology, a collective Christology, a mass Christology, a lay person's Christology, a Christology in the fields, in the streets, in the villages, in the Christian homes, in the shops and schools. It is a lived and living Christology of African Christianity, infectious and self-propagating![47]

Here we see imaginative use being made of local resources to make Christianity come alive for the contemporary context.

Contemporary issues

The LC has always demonstrated a keen interest in contemporary issues. It has been a strength of the LC that it has intentionally engaged with society and reflected theologically on it. As early as the second LC in 1878 the Bishops considered 'modern forms of infidelity and the best means of dealing with them'.[48] Over the decades since, the LC has addressed issues of poverty, debt,

---

[46] LC 1958, Resolution 71.
[47] From a lecture given to *Missio Africanus* at CMS Oxford, 27 June 2015. See http://missioafricanus. org/tnew/videos/.
[48] Archbishop's Letter of Invitation, 10 July 1877: http://www.archive.org/stream/a589564000lambuoft/ a589564000lambuoft_djvu.txt (accessed 30 May 2016).

racism, the use of power, environmental issues, market forces, economics, wealth, sexual abuse, militarism, justice and peace, other faiths, land rights for indigenous peoples, land mines, creation care, technology, trade, refugees and migrants and more. Some may think that this sounds like a list more appropriate for the United Nations than the LC. However, it is vital for Anglican Bishops to understand these issues and to be resourced to face them theologically.

The LC 1948 endorsed the Covenant on Human Rights that was being debated at the United Nations. It also urged the governments of all countries represented at the LC to admit as many migrants as possible who had been made refugees after the Second World War. This theme emerged again in 1958, 1988 and 1998. In 1998 the LC stated presciently, 'The Church needs to be watchful of the migration policies of governments.'[49] Exodus, exile and diaspora are biblical themes. Care for the alien and the stranger, the widow and the orphan is an ancient Christian virtue. Recognizing the alien, the stranger and the migrant as not merely a recipient but also a Gospel-bearer is embedded in our Scriptural tradition – we think of Ruth, the Syro-Phoenician woman in the Gospels and the injunction of Hebrews 13:2. Hospitality towards the migrant is a fundamental part of the mission of the church in her attempts to welcome the stranger and to promote human dignity and flourishing. The LC 2008 continued the pattern of engaging with the contemporary world; it addressed issues of human and social justice, the environment, relations with other world religions and human sexuality. Resources were offered in all of these areas to help Anglicans to engage theologically and thoughtfully.

Conclusion: 'Such Unfolding of the Truth of the Gospel'

In studying the Lambeth Conference, I have come to appreciate that it has always had a missiological dimension. Ever since Archbishop Longley's first letter, where he invited the Bishops to 'tend to the advancement of the kingdom of our Lord and Master Jesus Christ and to the maintenance of greater union in our missionary work', there has been a focus on mission without as well as an exhortation to greater communion within ('and to increased intercommunion

---

[49] LC 1998, Section B, paragraph 28.

among ourselves').[50] Contextualization of the Gospel has been encouraged and supported; the Anglican place in world Christianity has been increasingly understood; appeals for a posture of creativity and imagination have been made; and contemporary issues have been addressed. At its best, the LC has modelled double listening (to the world and to the Scriptures), taking and receiving counsel, consultation, hospitality and the fostering of deeper relationships. The Indaba approach was an attempt to model something different in the way that the LC does its business, enabling it to appropriate treasures from across the Communion.

My sadness is that these missiological dimensions are not well known and that we have lost some of the treasures discovered and explored along the way. The LC does indeed risk becoming just a 'talk shop' if we cannot communicate these riches. The challenge for the LC of the future is to communicate the riches of our Anglican Communion with all its diversity and difference. If we could do this, then we would indeed be offering a treasure to the world. Perhaps lengthy meetings and worthy resolutions are not the way forward. Perhaps contextualization needs to start at the heart of the LC itself. But contextualization is risky. It is a challenge and risk to allow contextualization to be done or carried out by the local communities. It might mean letting go of the Gospel for the sake of the Gospel. It is a lengthy, difficult and delicate task. 'This is because it engages in the risky business of balancing reverence for local contexts and local wisdom with faithful presentation of Christian truth and connection with the wider church.'[51] Have we become too safe and domesticated as we have tried to witness to Jesus?

World Christianity is part of our DNA as Christians. We belong to a border-crossing faith, a faith that delights in journeys and a faith that makes a home anywhere and everywhere. This is an important and powerful message for our day where ethnicities are becoming more defined and notions of national sovereignty are attractive to many. Of course, we want to celebrate the local – local identity is important – but so also is our citizenship of the world and the responsibility that it brings as members of a world family. An understanding

[50] Letter to Bishops, 18 February, 1867: http://www.archive.org/stream/a589564000lambuoft/a589564000lambuoft_djvu.txt (accessed 7 May 2016).
[51] S. Bevans and R. Schroeder, 'Letting Go and Speaking Out, Prophetic Dialogue and the Spirituality of Inculturation', in *Prophetic Dialogue: Reflections on Christian Mission Today* (Maryknoll, NY: Orbis, 2011), p. 88.

and appreciation of contextualization and World Christianity bring the local and the global together in a helpful way. Creativity and imagination, the use of the arts of many cultures, are sorely needed in our churches today if we are to communicate the Gospel effectively – as is deep theological reflection on contemporary issues in the world God loves.

I have discovered treasures buried in the LC documents. I wish that some of these treasures had been unearthed and communicated more clearly and plainly for our instruction. Perhaps this is the challenge: to disseminate these insights and treasures more effectively and simply throughout the Anglican Communion so that we may all benefit and learn from them. There are indeed deep and rich missiological dimensions in the LC which are instructive for all of us in our task of the 'unfolding of the truth of the Gospel'.[52]

---

[52] http://www.anglicancommunion.org/resources/document-library/lambeth-conference/1930/resolution-4-the-christian-doctrine-of-god?author=Lambeth+Conference&year=1930 (accessed 7 May 2016).

12

The Household of Faith: Anglican Obliquity and the Lambeth Conference

Martyn Percy

The American cultural analyst Theodore Roszak, in his classic *The Making of a Counter-Culture*, suggests that the agenda before those who seek to transform society is not centred on organizing, managing or repairing. It is, rather, about asking, 'How shall we live?' 'The primary aim of counter-culture', Roszak writes, 'is to proclaim a new heaven and a new earth ... so marvellous, so wonderful, that the claims of technical expertise must of necessity withdraw to a subordinate and marginal status.'[1] The implications of Roszak's point for Anglican polity – its identity, mission and ministry – in the twenty-first century are potentially profound. Here, I make some opening observations. Churches are meant to be households of faith, providing shelter and inclusion for all. And deep within the 'DNA' of Anglican polity and identity, wherever it is encountered in the world, there is a disposition towards comprehensiveness, breadth and inclusion. The Anglican vision of the church is first and foremost, a blueprint for the ordering of human community. Anglican polity is a social vision that has ecclesial consequences. It is not (merely) an ecclesiastical polity with accidental social consequences.[2]

This clearly matters for the Lambeth Conference as an institution. Anglicans invariably converge at these gatherings with many concerns that relate to their internal ecclesial life. However, the real agenda is not so much about the world joining the church (concerns over recruitment and membership of parishes and congregations, for example), but rather about how Anglicans take their

---

[1] Theodore Roszak, *The Making of a Counter-Culture* (London: Faber, 2000), p. 166.
[2] On the nature of polity, see Paul Avis, 'Polity and Polemics: The Function of Ecclesiastical Polity in Theology and Practice', *Ecclesiastical Law Journal*, 18 (2016), pp. 2–13.

place in the world. The Lambeth Conference, as an enduring institution in its own right, has a role in guarding unity, but also in affirming the diversity of the Communion, in the countries and cultures that its churches serve. The Lambeth Conference affords a special opportunity to look outwards, as it frequently connects thickly to other Christian World Communions, especially through study of ecumenical texts and the presence of ecumenical observers, as well as to wider spheres of social life.

One question that Anglicanism faces today is, 'Who is Anglican?' Any investment in an overly narrow specification of membership will have profound consequences for the identity and organizational shape of Anglican ecclesiology, including performative–liturgical arenas such as Christian initiation. The sociocultural expectations that are invested in baptism by those outside the worshipping congregation require constant local, pastoral negotiation between churches, clergy and the communities they serve. The socio-theological vision of Anglican polity therefore needs to understand its theological roots more deeply. Theology and the supernatural authority of the church, which she is called to embody and proclaim, cannot simply allow its ethos, identity and practice to be replaced with what I have consistently termed 'consecrated pragmatism'.[3] This is particularly the case in relation to the question of how people become part of a social and spiritual body, like the church, that is fundamentally inclusive in nature and character.

The current turn towards organization and management, with which this essay is partly concerned, focuses particular attention on how people become part of the church.[4] Specifically, it presses the question as to whether the global expressions of Anglican polity are distinctive, bounded and overtly member-based organizations in character, seeking clarity of identity; or whether they are broader social and sacramental institutions to which a much wider public relates in a variety of ways. I am mindful that most ecclesial ecologies will contain both of these elements and will be a blend of those who feel a sense of strong attachment (often expressed as 'membership'), and those whose basically affirmative relationship to the church involves a more variegated

---

[3] For my earliest discussion of this, see Martyn Percy, 'Consecrated Pragmatism', *Anvil*, 14.1 (1997), pp. 18–28.

[4] The background to the distinction between organization and institution lies in the writings of Philip Selznick. For a discussion of his work in this field, see Martin Krygier, *Philip Selznick: Ideals in the World* (Stanford, CA: Stanford University Law Books, 2012).

form of commitment. Moreover, I propose that such patterns of personal engagement can be treated as significant examples of obliquity. My concern is with the concept of belonging in Anglican polity as a whole.[5]

In order to explore this agenda, the chapter, like much of my work, is shaped and influenced by social-scientific disciplines such as sociology and anthropology. I am mindful that theologians such as John Milbank have argued that the social sciences have little to contribute to our understanding of theology. Milbank has suggested that sociology or anthropology attempt to 'police the sublime'. While I have consistently argued that social sciences and theology are rich in their complementarity, I am deeply concerned that the management sciences are now shaping the ecclesiology in Anglican polity – 'policing the sublime' in a slightly different way to the one envisaged by John Milbank.[6] Certainly, the combination of managerialism and organizational praxis across the Anglican Communion is appearing to rein-in in more creative and radical theological traditions, as well as patrolling Anglican praxis in relation to pastoralia, and arguably also taming theological creativity. Wisdom can all too easily be pushed to the edges; organizational thinking, often masquerading as 'vision', dominates our institutional life.[7] In contrast, I wish to suggest that the very *indirectness* of Anglican polity and its pastoral practice is one of its great charisms, and also a gift to the wider world.

So this chapter, like others in this book, seeks to situate itself as a contribution to the next Lambeth Conference, and affirms its strategic importance as an enduring institution within the life of the Anglican Communion. And it seeks to aid the revival of Anglican ecclesiology, theology and self-understanding, by resetting contemporary Anglican thought and practice within a broader social and intellectual framework. I take my cue from Richard Hooker, Samuel

---

[5] On this topic, see Paul Avis (ed.), *The Journey of Christian Initiation: Theological and Pastoral Perspectives* (London: Church House Publishing, 2011). See also M. Percy, *Shaping the Church: The Promise of Implicit Theology* (Farnham: Ashgate, 2010) for a detailed discussion of baptism as a broader cultural practice, which enables the child, having been 'blessed' and 'christened', to be received back into a local community as a recognized and publicly affirmed member of that society. For a closer ethnographic study of this phenomenon, rooted in the fishing village of Staithes on the NE coast of England, see David Clark, *Between Pulpit and Pew* (Cambridge: Cambridge University Press, 1982).

[6] See J. Milbank, *Theology and Social Theory: Beyond Secular Reason* (Oxford: Blackwell, 1993).

[7] On this, see M. Percy, *The Future Shapes of Anglicanism: Currents, Contours, Charts* (London: Routledge, 2017); and for alternative perspectives, see Ellen K. Wondra, 'The Shape of an Eschatological Ecclesiology: *More than Communion* by Scott MacDougall', *Anglican Theological Review*, 99. 1 (2017), pp. 111–6.

Taylor Coleridge, T. S. Eliot, Daniel W. Hardy and others, who in their different ways, have asserted that Anglicanism is, first and foremost, a social vision. It is about the shaping of true sociality, rather than imagining a domestic ecclesiastical polity.

More specifically, I wish to argue that virtuous dispositions and practices, such as kindness, hospitality, moderation, generosity, sympathy and courtesy, are gifts that help to shape the wider world, as well as being among the 'protected characteristics' that one can encounter within most expressions of global Anglican polity. Moreover, I suggest that in a world increasingly polarized by religious and political extremism, this gentle, open 'middle-way' of faith and practice might be a profound, even prophetic gift to the wider world in this twenty-first century. I argue that the gift of Anglican ecclesiology to the wider world is under threat from within, with too much of the current emphasis on evangelism (as distinct from the broader concept of 'mission') leading to an unhelpful over-investment in mechanistic and organizational frameworks, where insufficient attention is paid to the pastoral and institutional. Put in another way, moderate, temperate religion, that works through its dilemmas without resorting to violence or permanent polarization, might be of inestimable *public* value.

Such boldness, I must add, with due ecumenical humility, is hardly confined to Anglican polity. One need only scan the headline of one report from the World Council of Churches in 1966, to read that 'the world is the agenda, not the church'. As Walter Hollenweger noted in his editorial of the report, 'When the Church takes seriously the agenda of the world, this does not mean the Church is ready for compromise.'[8] Rather, suggested Hollenweger, if one began with a serious theology of the Kingdom of God, rooted in the life and ministry of Jesus, then challenging and changing the injustices of the world would be the first task the church turned towards. If we are not about deep social transformation, we are not about anything. If the church is consumed with its own managerial and organizational goals, including increasing its own numerical growth and 'discipling' its members, it will have lost its soul. And herein, I hold, we find another element of global Anglican polity: it posits an inclusive church; a non-member-based institution that seeks to serve society

---

[8]   W. Hollenweger (ed.), *The Church for Others: Two Reports on the Missionary Structure of the Congregation* (Geneva: World Council of Churches, 1967), pp. 3–4.

as a whole, rather than a member-based organization that primarily exists for its committed subscribers.

Defining the context

In her prescient book, *The Precarious Organisation*,[9] the Dutch ecclesiologist Mady Thung suggests that national churches in Northern Europe have come under increasing pressure in the post-war years to become self-consciously 'organisations', marked by 'nervous activity and hectic programmes ... constantly try[ing] to engage' their members in an attempt to reach 'non-members'. She contrasts the 'organisational' model and its frenetic activism with the 'institutional' model of the church – the latter offering, instead, contemplative, aesthetic and liturgical models that take longer to grow and are often latent for significant periods of time, but which may be more culturally resilient and conducive than those of the activist–organizational model. Thung concludes her book by suggesting that the model being adopted by many national churches – a kind of missional 'organisation–activist' approach – is what drives the population away. It leads, logically, to a sectarian mindset.

Karl Barth observed that the true growth of the church should be understood in mainly intensive, rather than extensive terms. Barth argued that the vertical (or intensive) growth of the church – its height and depth in relation to God – does not necessarily lead to extensive numerical growth. He added that 'we cannot, therefore, strive for vertical renewal merely to produce a wider audience'. Barth concluded that if the church's mission were to be directed merely at extensive growth, its inner life would lose its meaning and power: 'The church can be fulfilled only for its own sake, and then – unplanned and unarranged – it will bear its own fruits.'[10] Many parish clergy, and those working in sector ministries, already know this to be true. The church does not exist to grow exponentially. Mission is deeper than that. The church exists to be the Body of Christ in the world.

---

[9] Mady Thung, *The Precarious Organisation: Sociological Explorations of the Church's Mission and Structure* (The Hague: Mouton & Co., 1976).

[10] K. Barth, *Church Dogmatics*, ed. G. W. Bromiley and T. F. Torrance (Edinburgh: T & T Clark, 1958), IV. ii. 15 (p. 648).

Church going in Anglican polity has generally been a matter of relating to and inhabiting a complex institution, where the idea of 'membership' of a subscriber-based organization is seen as a more 'Congregationalist' kind of ecclesiology. I mean no disrespect to Non-Conformist chapels and congregations in saying this. I simply draw attention to the fact that a parish church exists for the spiritual well-being of the whole surrounding community, and it seeks to serve that community independently of any subscription or support that the people in the community might provide. This is by no means a unique characteristic of Anglicanism. It is the form of ministry exercised by ecumenical chaplains in prisons, hospitals, schools and colleges, the armed services and other arenas, where the ministers elect to serve the whole body, not merely the committed minority. And amid the general anxiety about apparently declining numbers of attendees at regular Sunday worship in the Church of England, at least one group of churches has bucked the trend: the cathedrals. The numbers worshipping in English Anglican cathedrals have been consistently resilient, apparently immune to the decline seen elsewhere. Indeed, many cathedrals report an increase in the number of worshippers. But what do these numbers actually show?

As with much statistical analysis, it is the story behind the numbers that tells us how to interpret the bare arithmetic. To understand the growth of worshippers in cathedrals, one needs to have some grasp of the nuanced ecology of English church going. Social exchange theory can help with such interpretation. Classic cathedral worship is typically a 'low threshold' pursuit – that is to say, anyone can come, without any need or pressure to join a rota, group, class or any other supplementary activity. However, 'low threshold' is most likely combined with 'high reward': the music will invariably be superb, the preaching of a consistently high calibre and the liturgy predictable and elegant. In contrast, the dominant preferred ecclesial model in the Church of England today is 'high threshold and high reward'. The justification for this formula is usually the priority of 'discipleship', which is preferred to anything that smacks of vicarious religion, or a lack of clarity in matters of belief. 'High-threshold/ high-reward' churches will offer attendees a rich menu and a variety of groups and activities that they will be expected to join. The committed can be identified easily enough – by the range and scale of their involvement in groups and activities. Those who are less involved will be deemed to be, by the same token, less committed. Thresholds for joining and participating are therefore set deliberately high, and this often manifests itself in areas such as restrictive practices in respect of baptisms and marriages, and can even extend, occasionally, to restricting funerals to 'members'.[11]

The problem with the 'High-Threshold-High-Reward' churches is that, while there is a stress on discipleship and commitment, the model of church being offered is unavoidably narrow. Moreover, the concentration of resources and monies in these ecclesial paradigms means that other churches – I do not include cathedrals here – can quickly develop into 'High-Threshold-Low-Reward' churches. By that, I mean that the instinct of affirming the church as being for everyone in the community, while laudable, comes at a cost that falls only on a few. The quality and quantity of worship, pastoral ministry and more besides, can only operate if a few will fund this for the many. This is by no means certain.

There is a further complication to be mindful of here. The emerging millennial generation increasingly characterizes itself as 'spiritual but not religious', and when asked to describe its nascent religious or denominational roots or 'home', chooses to say 'none'. The rise of the 'Nones' is a significant challenge to all forms of ecclesial polity and the theology that underlies them. Despite being, as a generation, more sensitive to faiths than previous eras, 'Nones' are often characterized as insouciant and indifferent towards the church, an interpretation that plays into the hands of those who want to turn all church attendees into explicit 'disciples' – preferring the 'High-Threshold-High-Reward' pattern of polity. This takes the church further way from public life, and tends towards sectarianism. Slow, 'low-threshold' churches that might appeal to the young as epiphanies of spirituality and transcendent encounter are at risk here, as their engagement with 'Nones' does not quickly seek to convert them – but does offer a viable base and resource from which to continue to be 'spiritual-but-not-religious'.[12] Emerging concepts of membership and belonging in relation to churches are now patently more complex.

---

[11] This is a more subtle cultural–theological issue than space permits us to explore here, but for further discussion, see John Shelton Reed, *Glorious Battle: The Cultural politics of Victorian Anglo-Catholicism* (Nashville, TN: Vanderbilt University Press, 1996) and W. S. F. Pickering, *Anglo-Catholicism: A Study in Religious Ambiguity* (London: SPCK, 1989).

[12] See Kenda Creasy Dean, *Almost Christian: What the Faith of Our Teenagers is Telling Us about the American Church* (New York: Oxford University Press, 2010).

That said, the neo-conservative revolution of the last fifty years within Anglicanism has seen both the High and Low wings entirely out-narrate the middle ground (i.e. Broad Church), and then move on to rebrand the moderate-middle as 'liberal'. In turn, the very term 'liberal' was swiftly allotted a consistently negative value in ecclesial climes. For Catholic Anglican conservatives, and some conservative Anglican Evangelicals, this arguably began with 'Gender Wars' (i.e. the debate on the ordination of women). The vast majority of clergy and laity who desired (and eventually voted for) women priests found themselves re-positioned as 'liberals'. On sexuality, a gradual acceptance of lesbian, gay and bisexual Christians, and an eventual (still-growing) acceptance of same-sex marriages has also led to the Broad Church and middle ground being labelled, once again, negatively, as 'liberal'.

What is intriguing in all of this is that the Broad Church element within Anglicanism normally holds sensible, moderate and accommodating views on gender, and progressive (note, not radical or liberal) views on sexuality.[13] The Broad Church, such as it is, tends to be entirely orthodox on creeds, doctrines (e.g. the physical resurrection of Jesus), articles of faith, liturgical proclivities, ecclesiastical polity, Christian practice and canon law. It practises what many see as 'generous orthodoxy'. The Broad Church elements within Anglicanism tend to be, if anything, theologically conservative. And they view the high and low elements of the church as rather more sectarian – and inclined towards 'membership-speak' – than the more inclusive, 'public' ministry that they would seek to embody and practice.

In terms of belonging vis-à-vis the church, the post-war story of English Anglicanism has witnessed the slow accretion of greater density towards the wings: a density, moreover, consisting not merely of numbers, but also of theological and ecclesiological intensity. Both wings – whether one refers to them as high and low, evangelical and catholic – have tended to be more prescriptive about what constitutes 'membership' (not only of their own respective groups and societies, but also wider membership of the church)

---

[13] For some further discussion of this, see M. Percy, *The Future Shapes of Anglicanism*. For more historical perspectives, see W. J. Conybeare, 'Church Parties' (1853), included in *Essays Ecclesiastical and Social* (London: Longman, Brown, Green, 1855) and C. R. Sanders, *Coleridge and the Broad Church Movement* (Durham, NC: Duke University Press, 1942). On church parties, readers are also referred to the relevant chapters of M. Chapman, S. Clarke and M. Percy (eds), *The Oxford Handbook of Anglican Studies* (Oxford: Oxford University Press, 2015).

and accordingly have been zealous on areas such as liturgical reform and other divisive debates, such as those on sexuality and gender. In this, 'baptism' as a means of incorporation within the church, and symbolically too in being named to wider society, has become a rite that has attracted wider ecclesial collateral. Specifically, is 'Christening' a shared social-sacramental covenant between church and world, and God and people? Or, rather, as the high and low, or evangelical and catholic wings tend to claim, an essentially private rite, albeit performed in public, that inducts individuals into something more obviously bounded, organizational and contained? In addressing this issue, we remain mindful of studies that speak of baptism differently, namely as the rite performed by and in the church that confers a name and a status in the community on the child in question. So through baptism and naming, the child becomes not only a member of the church mystical, but also a member of the visible social community.[14]

Mady Thung concludes her work with something of a prophetic warning to churches, and here I include global Anglicanism. She accepts the inevitability of churches needing to become more organized, and more like organizations, replete with plans for numerical growth and measurable impact. But Thung also sounds a note of caution, namely that every step churches take *towards* the tighter and clearer forms of organization, coupled to overt, intentional mission and evangelism, targeted at the surrounding society, is one further step *away* from the public at large, which, she claims, is looking for more open forms of institutional life, ones marked more by obliquity than clarity. So it is to a discussion of obliquity, therefore, that we now turn.

Introducing obliquity

According to John Kay, the concept of obliquity describes a simple process: that of achieving complex objectives indirectly.[15] One thinks immediately of Emily Dickinson's poetic invocation to tell the truth, but only in such a

---

[14] For a closer ethnographic study of this phenomenon, see David Clark, *Between Pulpit and Pew* (Cambridge: Cambridge University Press, 1982).
[15] John Kay, *Obliquity* (London: Profile Books, 2011).

manner that it is slanted, lest the light dazzle and blind us all.[16] Or of Polonius' speech in Hamlet, where he suggests we reach our wisdom and goals through indirect means.[17] Kay discusses the verdict of Charles Jencks, the architectural commentator, who opined that Modernism ended at 3.32 pm on 15 July 1972. That is the date when contractors detonated fuses that blew up a housing development in St Louis. Only two decades earlier, such housing – high rise tower blocks, most notably – had been feted by Le Corbusier, who famously claimed that such buildings were the supreme expression of Modernism, and that a house was (merely) 'a machine for living in'. But as Kay points out, the Modernists knew less than they thought. A house is not simply a machine to live in. Indeed, there is a difference between a *house* and a *home*. The utility of property and its actual functionality is only one element in design. The spaces that we inhabit are formational. They say things about individuals and groups. They arrange social living. Buildings have aesthetics that can promote subtle qualities and values. Some prompt alienation and individualism. Others, in contrast, can foster civic sociability, generosity and mutual flourishing.

Because churches are essentially 'households of faith', in that telling biblical phrase (Gal. 6.10) adopted by James Hopewell,[18] the very shaping of their spatial environment matters more than most ministers, denominations, congregations and theologians will usually allow for. Hopewell writes of how churches – and especially churches' missiological or ecclesiological constructions – tend to see themselves in either mechanistic or contextual or symbolic or organic terms. And as we shall suggest, this has implications for how people might enter the (Anglican) household of faith.

Kay's concept of obliquity is more fertile than it may at first appear, and especially in relation to missiological or ecclesiological constructions of ecclesial polity. To take church growth as an example: Is this best achieved by clear aims and objectives, and with clarity about programmes and activities? Or, is growth better achieved through oblique means? To some extent, the answer will depend on what is meant by 'growth'. If measurable numerical growth is the primary goal, and is rooted in a concept of member-based

---

[16] Emily Dickinson, from 'Tell All the Truth, But Tell it Slant', *The Collected Poems of Emily Dickinson*, ed. Harold Bloom (New York: Chelsea House Publications, 1985), p. 18.

[17] William Shakespeare, *Hamlet*, Act 2, Scene 1: Polonius' speech (London: Signet Classic edition, 1998).

[18] James Hopewell, *Congregation: Stories and Strictures* (London: SCM Press, 1987).

organization, then yes, straight, direct and forthright programmes will be cherished and valued. The missional activity will have manifest intent, and a clarity to its aims, objectives and outcomes that is often 'measurable'.

In contrast, an approach to missiological or ecclesiological endeavour that is rooted in the concept of obliquity might be more circumspect. Pastoral care, programmes of theological or spiritual exploration, an investment in aesthetics (e.g. art, architecture, music, etc.), an emphasis on the wider neighbourhood, and programmes fostering social well-being and renewal will more likely be to the fore. These will not necessarily build manifestly bigger congregations. But the latency of such an approach to mission and ministry will produce, and ultimately harness, a work of deep fusion between church and society. The size and intensity of the congregation may not grow numerically, in a manner comparable to a measurable organization, at least initially. But the extensity of the church – rooted in obliquity – does grow, as the capacity of the church extends to being a broad institution, in which many participate, perhaps cherishing the values of the church, without necessarily becoming identifiable members.

Three brief illustrations and reflections that highlight some aspects of ecclesial obliquity may suffice here. Jane Platt's study of Anglican parish magazines from the mid-Victorian period until the end of the Edwardian era shows that the epidemic of publications that emerged at that time pointed in three distinct directions.[19] First, it pointed to the homespun way in which cheap printing and production costs afforded many churches the opportunity to communicate directly with their parishes and the communities within them, independent of patterns of local church attendance. Second, with the production of inserts by numerous evangelical and catholic societies, these wings of the church (evangelical and catholic, and later, liberal and traditionalist) could communicate cheaply and effectively with local communities, if the local clergy were minded to or could be persuaded to adopt the inserts. So parish magazines gained higher levels of production, incorporating well-printed and mass-produced covers and inserts. This medium enabled the consolidation of emerging ecclesial identities in local parishes: remote congregations could now feel a sense of 'belonging' to a national movement. Thirdly, parish

---

[19] Jane Platt, *Subscribing to Faith? The Anglican Parish Magazine 1859-1929* (London: Palgrave, 2015).

magazines were local, and they actively encouraged neighbourhood and community activity. And therein lay the obliquity of early parish magazines, in effect. They built 'thicker' local community cohesion and stronger bonds between congregation and parish, but this was done indirectly, due to the agenda of the national church societies. Homespun parish magazines were made more visually appealing through the highly attractive covers and inserts provided free by the national societies, who were using local parish magazines as vehicles for their own agendas.

The second example is Abby Day's prescient study of 'Generation A' within the Anglican Communion. It charts a kind of 'farewell' to those laywomen who, born in the 1920s and 1930s, have provided the backbone to organizations such as the Mother's Union.[20] Day's analysis picks up on the function of these laywomen in churches who are often found providing support through 'soft' forms of pastoral care and, in particular, through catering. Day shows how activities such as communal baking – which are technically uneconomic – nonetheless provide an environment that promotes mutual care, flourishing, prayer and pastoral well-being. The obliquity lies in the gap between the manifest and latent function of the activities that Day so richly describes. The manifest intention of the communal baking is to provide a supportive catering service to the church and community. The latent intent that emerges is the thick pastoral care that the gatherings engender, which also produce deeper and richer spiritual lives.

For my third example, I take the fact that every denomination is, to some extent, and to borrow a phrase from John Caputo, an attempt to express the 'mood of God'.[21] Ecclesial life is, inevitably, the social reification of any group's theological priorities and spiritual proclivities. It follows from this that the actual mood or feel of a congregation has a more direct bearing on the wider sociality than it may know. To be sure, the average Anglican's 'mental map' of the Church has witnessed a remarkable change through the temporary

---

[20] Abby Day, 'Farewell to Generation A', in Abby Day (ed.), *Contemporary Issues in the Worldwide Anglican Communion: Powers and Pieties* (London: Ashgate, 2016), pp. 3–20. See also Abby Day, *The Religious Lives of Older Laywomen: The Last Active Anglican Generation* (Oxford: Oxford University Press, 2017).

[21] See Gary Gutting, 'Deconstructing God', *The New York Times*, March 9, 2014: http://opinionator.blogs.nytimes.com/2014/03/09/deconstructing-god/?_r=0, in an interview with John Caputo discussing his book, *The Prayers and Tears of Jacques Derrida: Religion without Religion* (Bloomington, IN: Indiana University Press, 1997).

triumph of neo-conservative Anglicanism. It used to be a simple triptych: high, middle or low. The High Church party had a distinctive theology, vocabulary, liturgical aesthetic – and even, for clergy, modes of dress. The Low Church party was just as easy to identify, yet quite different. And in the middle was the Broad Church – neither high nor low, and capable of blending and infusing the best elements of either wing, passionately committed to holding the centre ground.

The Broad Church was, at its best, the primary vehicle of generous, orthodox, inclusive Anglicanism. It was not Laodicean – a tepid compromise of warm, balmy Catholicism (or hotter Pentecostalism in other parts of the Anglican Communion) with the more chilly climes of Calvinism. The Broad Church was, quite simply, temperate and measured – reflective, cool and capacious. It was an embodiment of the faith of the church as an open, non-membership-based institution. It eschewed sectarianism, and sought, above all, to serve the whole of society. It was clement and mild, and so perfectly suited to the pastoral climates it served – at least in England. To some extent, there are parallels between Broad Church and broad-casting. Michael Sadgrove put it eloquently in a recent short essay, and quotes a 'convert' (I use the word advisedly) to BBC Radio Three's *Choral Evensong*. The listener writes:

> I turned on *Choral Evensong* by accident one afternoon a year or so ago and I've been listening ever since. The music is beautiful, but the special quality of Evensong lies in other places too, in the paradoxical contrast between the sinewy intricacy of sixteenth-century language, and the simplicity of the thoughts it expresses: prayers for courage, for grace, for protection from the dark, for a good death. These are things to which our minds have particularly lately turned in the aftermath of recent terrible events, but they were there all the time in the psalms and collects of Evensong. For almost 500 years the same words have been repeated by people in times of trouble or of triumph. The presence of that cloud of unseen witnesses lends an intangible quality to Choral Evensong. You could call it calm or spiritualty. You could call it holiness. But it's very precious.[22]

This outcome is arguably not the manifest intention of the broadcaster, but it is the outcome for this listener. Obliquity, then, is an important concept for

---

[22] Michael Sadgrove, 'Choral Evensong', *Prayer Book Society Magazine*, Lent 2017, pp. 11–12.

comprehending the deeper ways in which churches and denominations – here Anglicanism – might shape society. So where does the mission and ministry of the church belong in such a world, and perhaps especially in contemporary English culture? Clearly, it lies in keeping space for the sacred and pastoral both possible and open, as well as alive and engaged. In offering faith both to and for institutions, churches and clergy have a unique role in calling individuals and bodies to the horizons that lie beyond the scope of immediate priorities. The role might be said to consist of pastoral care in the present (of course); but pointing beyond the temporal and pragmatic to the world of the spiritual, the domain of values, and to the social transcendent. Indeed, churches continue to occupy and bridge the gap between created and redeemed sociality. The church holds the world before God. It is the social-sacramental skin for the community. It is not an enclave for the redeemed, but rather a resource for all those seeking meaning and truth in a world that longs for hope.

Anglican obliquity and identity

Augustus Pugin's architectural aesthetics in the nineteenth century, and whose designs for new churches emerged out of his profound sense of anxiety in relation to the spiritual decay of national life, left a marked impact on the Church of England. Pugin believed himself to be living in degenerate times, and he therefore sought to create sacred spaces that restored the renaissance – and a romanticized notion of the Middle Ages – in order to rescue society from its moral implosion. Pugin, in effect, attempted to return architecture to a 'natural' age, and away from the brutalism of industrialization. In so doing, he simply leant on a romantic myth – albeit one with some substance – that beauty, art and architecture could raise national and spiritual morale amid 'those dark satanic mills' that William Blake and other romantics had also set their faces against. So Pugin's architecture was rooted in his flawed, but understandable implicit theology. Pugin saw modernity as alien, brutalizing and evil, and believed it had to be driven out by art and beauty. The principles of his architecture were governed by his theological assumptions, which in turn became the means whereby new worlds were ordered for others. Pugin's worldview shaped his architecture. His architecture, in turn, shaped the new generation of the romantic renaissance in the church which quickly found expression in Anglo-Catholicism.[23]

It could be argued that Pugin is an explicit exponent and advocate of Anglican aesthetics. Certainly, his 'ecclesial intelligence' and sensibilities shaped his architectural horizons. But equally, it could be argued that Pugin could not have foreseen how his buildings, as households of faith, would then be used and how they would go on to shape pastoral, liturgical and ecclesial practice. The concept of obliquity is a helpful lens through which to understand the complexity and breadth of Anglican polity at precisely this point. The genius of Anglicanism, wherever it is encountered across the Communion, lies in its blendedness and breadth. It is a faith marked by hybridity: high, low, broad; Catholic and reformed; liberal and conservative; modern and traditional – and more besides. Its own inner ecclesial intelligence somehow knows that the blend also depends on directness and indirectness. Or to paraphrase Emily Dickinson, it 'tells the truth but tells it slant', and does so through art, music, architecture, poetry and other aesthetic media. But it also does this through patterns of behaviour, including the indirect mediation of virtues, which create an accommodating culture of civility and kindness and a distinctively mild polity. Few who study Anglican polity grasp the significance of its ecclesial obliquity, and its implications for mission, ministry and identity. But as the following three illustrations demonstrate, the balance between obliquity and clarity in Anglican polity is a crucial field of enquiry if one is to comprehend the deeper codes embedded in its identity.

The first illustration concerns an apparent superficiality, since it can appear to certain observers and commentators that some congregations talk about God all the time, while others never do. An Australian commentator, Caroline Miley, offers an apparently damning description of what constitutes Anglican polity at congregational level:

> A considerable source of surprise for newcomers to the Church is that Christians do not like talking about Christianity. Not only do they not talk about it willingly and enthusiastically but they have a tendency to become alarmed or resentful if the topic is openly addressed or pursued. This applies to both clergy and laity. This is very odd as in every other interest-based

---

[23] See Rosemary Hill, *God's Architect: Pugin and the Building of Romantic Britain* (New Haven CT: Yale University Press, 2009), pp. 114ff and 243–7.

organisation, discussion of the interest is universal, even mandatory. Hang-gliding clubs are full of people who discuss hang-gliding. Rotarians discuss rotary; football fans bore others to death with discussion of their fancy. Christians, however, do not discuss Christianity. To do so after church on Sunday morning is to be made aware that one has committed a frightful faux pas.[24]

But this account ignores three vital things. First, the deeply coded ways in which people talk and act about God. 'I'll be thinking of you this week' is usually indirect speech that actually means 'I'll be remembering you in prayer.' 'I'll drop by with some scones' means 'I will pay you a bereavement visit, to console and comfort you in your aching loss.' These are not instances of spiritual evasion, but modes of subtle and intimate religious communication. Secondly, that religious language is carried in the emotion, timbre and cadence of worship – which for Anglicans is often cool, reflective and apparently detached (when compared to the 'warmer' and more intimate language of, say, charismatics or Pentecostals). Thirdly, that deeply coded language is not a strategy for avoiding explicit theological language. Rather, it carries and conveys a range of rich implicit theological concepts that engage people at a variety of missiological and ecclesiological levels, including intellectually and relationally. But it refracts such directness through a lens of obliquity, rendering it indirect: truth and love 'told slant'.

The second illustration concerns the more direct ways in which contextual theologians have sought to understand Anglican polity and practice. Writing almost half a century ago, Stephen Bayne observed that 'the Church of England, alone among the churches of the Anglican Communion, has its unity given to it. That unity is given from the outside. It is given by the establishment of the church, by the formal identity of the church and the nation.' Bayne continued:

> The Church of England does not need to be held together by the voluntary loyalty of its members ... it has succeeded in giving to the Church of England – and in turn, to all the rest of the churches of our Communion – an extraordinary liberality of spirit and gentleness of mind, which tolerates wide differences of opinion and variations in theological outlook, within the working unity of the Catholic church of the land ... this is one of the most

---

[24] Caroline Miley, *The Suicidal Church: Can Anglicanism Be Saved?* (Sydney, NSW: Pluto Press, 2002), p. 7.

precious gifts. And I rejoice to find it transplanted … to North America, to Japan, to Central Africa, to Brazil, to any other part of the world you can mention. It was given to the Church of England, because of its hopes and necessities as a national church, to discover a profound secret of unity – that the unity of the church does not consist of people thinking alike but in people acting together.[25]

In the light of Bayne's comments, we may note three profound changes in recent times. The first is that the Church of England is moving rapidly towards a culture where it is 'held together by the voluntary loyalty of its members'. Secondly, and linked to this, like-mindedness becomes a more important characteristic in such institutions, which paves the way for narrower and more sectarian modes of ecclesial existence. Thirdly, we note again the appeal to 'soft' virtues and behaviours, with Bayne citing specifically 'extraordinary liberality of spirit and gentleness of mind, which tolerates wide differences of opinion and variations in theological outlook'. One might say that our Anglican ecclesiology is to be seen not only in terms of shared and agreed propositions, but also as a shared range of virtues, acquired skills and practices. We are formed not only by what we say, but by the manner and modes of our expression.[26]

The third illustration comes from a British journalist, who attended her mother's parish church on Mothering Sunday some years ago. As Christina Patterson confessed, she had her own children to keep under control, and she only really went to church to please her own mother, who accompanied them. Nor is she especially religious. So she was rather dreading the morning. But as Patterson goes on to say, the encounter that took place in the parish church spoke to her more deeply, and obliquely, than she could have anticipated. She expresses this encounter powerfully and movingly (here paraphrased by me from her article in *The Independent* in 2009), in the following terms:

I love the Church of England because it is patient. It does not expect the world to change in an instant, or to be bludgeoned into belief, because it knows that certain things take centuries. I love it because it is kind. It is kind enough to welcome strangers, whatever their beliefs, and shake their

---

[25] S. Bayne, *An Anglican Turning Point* (Austin TX: Church Historical Society, 1964), p. 181.
[26] On breadth and patience in Anglican polity, see Stephen Pickard, 'Innovation and Undecidability: Some Implications for the *Koinonia* of the Anglican Church', *Journal of Anglican Studies*, 2.2 (2004), pp. 87–105.

hands, and offer them a coffee after church. I like the fact that it is neither envious (of more flamboyant, more attention-seeking and more successful-at-proselytising religions), nor boastful. I like the fact that it is not normally arrogant or rude. I like the fact that it does not insist on its own way, but is genuinely tolerant of other religious beliefs – and none. I like the fact that it does not rejoice in wrongdoing, but quietly presents an ethical framework of kindness. I like the fact that it believes in the values of the New Testament, and of St Paul's description of love, which I've just paraphrased, but also believes that it is more important to embody them than to quote them.[27]

Patterson continues her meditation, affirming that she values a church that doesn't speak like a child, think like a child, or reason like a child. She affirms the fact that it is mature enough to value faithful doubt. She affirms the fact that Anglicanism is mostly calm. She likes the fact that it recognizes that the religious impulse is here to stay, and that the more you try to crush it, the stronger it will become. And that all human beings, irrespective of their beliefs, have yearnings for the transcendent. And she likes the fact that although secured in Scripture, tradition and reason, it is not afraid to seek and find God in our wider culture – in art, literature, nature and in society. [28]

But can it be helpful to read Anglican polity, as that of a global Communion, replete with local expressions and specific contextual particularities, in this way? In articulating Anglican identity, I have argued before that the Anglican Communion can be visualized analogically as a vast mansion, replete with newer evangelical and catholic wings, added in the nineteenth century.[29] It remains a large stately home. Albeit one in which the vast rooms are now becoming sealed off and made into self-contained flats. Everyone still has the same official address and shares the imposing exterior and frontage: but different internal relations within the 'storied dwelling' mean the union is not as it once was. As we noted earlier in relation to baptismal practice, the high and low or catholic and evangelical wings of this mansion tend to be more prescriptive in what is required for membership and belonging in general, and Christian initiation in particular.

[27] C. Patterson, 'Thank God for the Church of England', *The Independent*, July 25 2009, p. 12.

[28] See also M. Percy, *Anglicanism: Confidence, Commitment and Communion* (Farnham, Surrey and Burlington, VT: Ashgate, 2013).

[29] M. Percy, 'Reluctant Communion', in J. Jobling and I. Markham (eds), *Theological Liberalism : Creative and Critical* (London: SPCK, 2000), pp. 114–25.

The mansion analogy fits the current state of Anglicanism. Yet the Anglican Communion can also evoke what Benedict Anderson describes as an 'imagined community'.[30] Most of the 'members' of the Communion have never met one another, and never will. Yet members will readily acknowledge a deep, horizontal comradeship of belonging. The Communion is bound together by an ethos, codes, memories and aspirations that allow it to cohere in the minds of its members, but without that coherence necessarily being practised at either a deep or extensive level. Most of the modes of activity that enable the life of the Communion rest in the blend of clarity and obliquity, of directness and indirectness. It is arguably the case that in a mature polity that enjoys significant historical and cultural grounding, an ethos rooted in diplomatic and well-mannered modes of behaviour will have come to strongly condition the pervading culture. In this respect, we can regard the Anglican Communion as a kind of filial network of understanding, in which certain types of belief and certain modes of behaviour are cherished.

Anglican polity and pastoral practice

There can be no question that Anglicanism contains elements of coherence, and a notion of a shared life and identity, bound together through a common sense of purpose, history and teleology. But what exactly are the elements that are particular to Anglican identity? Authors such as Sykes, Avis, Booty and Wright may be able to nominate particular theological priorities. From a more sociological perspective, we can point to Pickering's work that identifies ambiguity and aesthetics as being culturally significant. More generally, however, and to return to the concept of obliquity, the phenomenologist Thomas Tweed frames the importance of values and behaviour in faith communities when he writes that religions, at their best, are 'confluences of organic-cultural flows that intensify joy and confront suffering by drawing on human and supra-human (i.e. divine) forces to make homes and cross boundaries'.[31] This definition of religion suggests that grounded pastoral faith

---

[30] B. Anderson, *Imagined Communities: Reflections on the Origin and Spread of Nationalism* (London: Verso, 1991), pp. 6–7 and 15–16.
[31] Thomas Tweed, *Crossing and Dwelling* (Harvard: Harvard University Press, 2006), p.12.

performs four important functions that will be familiar to most Anglican churches. First, practised faith intensifies joy. It takes the ordinary and makes it extraordinary. It knows how to celebrate lives, love and transitions. It blesses what is good, and raises hope, thanks and expectation in prayer and praise. It lifts an institution and individuals to a new plane of existence – one of the blessing and thankfulness for what is and can be. And it not only moves, but also intensifies. Just as a birth becomes even more in a baptism, so in ministry does a ceremony become more with prayer and celebration. Second, suffering is confronted. Working with pain, bereavement, counselling and consolation will be familiar to all clergy and congregations, providing the safe space and expertise that holds and slowly resolves the suffering that individuals and institutions carry inside them. Third, the making of homes is a profound analogical – and literal – reference to the function of faith. Making safe spaces of nourishment, well-being, maturity, diversity and individuation; our 'faith homes' are places both of open hospitality and security. Fourth, faith helps us to cross boundaries, to move forward and over the challenges of life to new places. It can be crossing deserts to find promised lands or passing from darkness to light. Religion never keeps us in one place; even within our homes, it moves us on.

I also want to suggest that the manner or mood in which Anglican clergy and congregations engage with their communities is just as important as the actual programmes and events that might be offered. Sometimes, it is the way of being and the character of individual ministry that carries more weight and resonance than those things that seem concrete and planned. This is not surprising, since faith communities often make contributions to social capital that are not easily calculated or calibrated. Because they foster and focus distinctive values that provide leaven in complex contexts, faith communities often find themselves promoting forms of goodness that secular and utilitarian organizations might miss. Bruce Reed explains how religion partly functions through obliquity, by drawing on an analogy from nature:

> If bees could talk, and we came across them busy in a flower garden and enquired what they were doing, their reply might be: 'Gathering nectar to make honey.' But if we asked the gardener, he would most certainly answer: 'They are cross pollinating my flowers.' In carrying out their manifest

function to make food, the bees were performing a latent function of fertilising flowers. The mutual dependence of bees and flowers is an analogue of churches and society.[32]

Through the simple, apparently oblique ministry of 'deep hanging out',[33] attentiveness, hospitality, care and celebration, clergy can often do more good for a local institution or community than they can usually know. Churches and church leaders may simply offer regular lunches, or open house for tea and coffee at any time – and these are manifest intentions, of course. But the potency of the gesture and practice lies more in their latency, and is significant. Indeed, the latency and obliquity of the ministry being offered are more striking in their effect than any manifest clarity.

Most clergy will know all about the deep value of local community work, or about the art of making oneself available to a widespread network of neighbourhoods. These practices say something about the possibilities for different kinds of spaces in communities and institutions – social, pastoral, intellectual, spiritual. They open up a different side of the humanity of the institution to those individuals within it. In being there with programmes and events, as well as in being purposefully hospitable, churches and congregations frequently enable communities and neighbourhoods to begin transcending themselves. As we noted earlier, Anglicanism is, first and foremost, a social vision – a vision of true human community and communion – with ecclesial consequences, and not an ecclesiology with social consequences, though the two are closely interrelated.

James Hopewell's contextual theological analysis of churches – in effect, a kind of 'cultural reading' within the field of ecclesiology – can be of further help in our understanding of obliquity and identity in Anglican polity. Hopewell points out how some who are looking to join a church – choosing a household of faith – behave like 'house hunters'. Some 'buyers' focus on the *contextual* nature of the dwelling: 'Viewed in this way, a dwelling is a texture whose weaving reveals the strands that originate in the larger context of the neighbourhood'. Alternatively, some focus on *mechanisms*, 'and how well the house does its job'. Typical features of 'mechanistic' approaches to church

---

[32] Bruce Reed, *The Dynamics of Religion* (London: Darton, Longman & Todd, 1978), p. 139.

[33] A phrase appropriated from the writings of Clifford Geertz; see his *The Interpretation of Cultures* (New York: Basic Books, 1973).

life and education focus on aims, outcomes, programme effectiveness and demonstrable success. Hopewell likens mechanistic approaches to church life to engineering. Now this approach is in stark contrast to those who value churches as *organisms*, where the interior and exterior of the house are primarily assessed on their aesthetics, and the ability of the building to 'fit' with the natural biography of the house hunters. Hopewell equates this approach to church life to architecture. The *symbolic* approach explores how the building conveys and reifies meanings, and what it communicates to its wider context. Symbolic concerns typically focus not on effectiveness, but on reception and meaning within a wider community. In each of these approaches, knowledge, reflection, mission and pastoral care are handled and valued in different ways by individuals and communities. Apparently trivial reflections (e.g. how does our church *look*?) take on a whole new significance.

Becoming a member of the household of faith

The nature of the household of faith will be a blended negotiation across the grid of the four approaches identified by Hopewell. No one church will be merely mechanistic, or entirely organic. But the leading edge of each negotiation – organic, contextual, symbolic or mechanistic – will have profound implications for those seeking entry to the household of faith. For example, a mechanistic approach to the household will invariably be carried across to confessional vetting procedures for potential members who wish to join the house. Likewise, a household stressing the symbolic is likely to invest in liturgies of baptism that reflect the nature of the household the child or adult will be baptized within and into.

Wade Clark Roof notes in *Community and Commitment* (1985) that the beliefs of churches cannot be construed entirely in terms of their professed theological foundations, as they depend on wider factors, such as those identified by Hopewell: 'Theological doctrines are always filtered through people's social and cultural experiences. What emerges in a given situation is "operant religion" [which] will differ considerably from the "formal religion" of the historic creeds, and more concern with the former is essential to understanding how belief systems function in people's daily lives.'[34] Roof's 'operant religion' is a term that approximates to the use of the expression 'vernacular religion', 'common spirituality', 'implicit religion' or 'ecclesial obliquity'. Studies that pay attention to concepts such as obliquity or vernacular spirituality can be especially important when considering baptismal practice. For here one can see that such practices are rarely driven by explicit theology or by commonly owned (let alone understood) confessional formulae. For example, in a church that is geared more towards a mechanistic-organizational paradigm, there may be considerable suspicion about 'open' baptism policies. The practice of the church will be restrictive, making sure that all who apply for baptism are subjected to appropriate interviews and courses that establish a level of understanding about what the nature of the rite is, and what it confers. Other households of faith may be more 'open', but their policy will simply speak obliquely of the power of symbols.

Stark and Bainbridge use sociological exchange theory to construct their models of church. They balance the *tension* that a group desires or tolerates with the *rewards* (sometimes called *compensators*, if rewards cannot be actualized) that its members seek. The tension signifies the relationship with the world and the internal structure of the group. Rewards are the spiritual benefits of belonging. The degree of 'exchange' or the 'success' of the congregation is determined, to an extent, by the amount of power that the congregation appears to have, or can call upon, and can exercise. The more powerful a congregation is, the greater the (apparent) rewards on offer.[35] A 'successful' church may offer a ministry principally concerned with individual salvation. In a 'high-tension' relationship with the world, it assumes certain sectarian and communitarian properties, and is likely to eschew 'open' baptismal policies. However, a neighbouring congregation with fewer members may well offer a more 'open' baptismal policy, not only for theological reasons, but also because it neither gains nor loses by offering lower thresholds of entry for membership. Put another way, whereas one church can offer a tightly defined type of membership, another may seek a looser form of connectedness that is expressed both in its polity and its baptismal praxis. Both models are valid

---

[34] W. Clark Roof, *Community and Commitment* (New York: Elsevier, 1978), pp. 178–9.
[35] See R. Stark and W. Bainbridge, 'Typologies of Church, Sect & Cult', in *A Theory of Religion* (Peter Lang: New York, 1987).

attempts to construct a theological conversation with the world, which in turn will lead to the conferring of membership. Both models also tend to imply their theological position through praxis, rather than through explicitly stated formulae.

One should also recognize that practices shape beliefs and beliefs shape practice. In any ecclesiology (perhaps especially when focused on rituals such as Christian initiation), the infusion of religion within culture (and vice versa) must be given its due. Kathryn Tanner notes that religious beliefs are 'a form of culture, inextricably implicated in the material practices of daily social living on the part of those who hold them. ... In the concrete circumstances in which beliefs are lived ... actions, attitudes, and interests are likely to be as much infiltrated and informed by the beliefs one holds as beliefs are to be influenced by actions, attitudes and interests.'[36] In other words, doctrines practise us; practices are not just things that Christians do in the light of doctrine: 'Practices are what we become as we are set in motion in the space of doctrine.'[37] Theology is performative, and it 'gains power and meaning insofar as it is embodied in the total gestalt of community life and action.'[38] But there is an irony here for the theologian, and for the church. For in gaining an understanding of how the worlds of belief and practice begin to cohere, one immediately sees that they, in fact, do not necessarily do so easily. For every example of clarity and directness, there is one of obliquity and indirectness. As Tanner says,

> Christian practices do not in fact require (1) much explicit understanding of beliefs that inform and explain their performance, (2) agreement upon such matters among the participants, (3) strict delimitation of codes for action, (4) systematic consistency among beliefs or actions, or (5) attention to their significance that isolates them from a whole host of non-Christian commitments. More often than not, Christian practices are instead quite open-ended in the sense of being undefined in their exact ideational dimensions and in the sense of being always in the process of re-formation in response to new circumstances.[39]

[36] K. Tanner, *Theories of Culture* (Minneapolis, MN: Fortress Press, 1992), p. 9.
[37] M. Volf and D. Bass (eds), *Practicing Theology* (Grand Rapids, MI: Eerdmans, 2002), p. 75.
[38] G. Lindbeck, *The Nature of Doctrine* (Philadelphia: Westminster Press, 1984), p. 36.
[39] K. Tanner, 'Theological Reflection and Christian Practices' in Volf and Bass (ed.), *Practicing Theology*, p. 229.

Conclusion

The purpose of the chapter is to challenge a current trajectory in Anglican polity and to invite a deeper pondering of Anglican identity. Is an ecclesiology that veers towards mechanistic and organizational models likely to lead to more compressed and contracted forms of polity, that operate at a greater distance from the public they are trying to reach and engage? And if so, the time is now surely right to re-inhabit and celebrate a model of the church that is more institutional, accommodating and pervasively pastoral, in order for Anglicanism to recover its vocation as an open, public entity. Anglicanism, wherever it is encountered and inhabits the world, needs to be faithful to the paradigm of incarnation – it needs to be engaged in public theology, not private church-speak.

Anglican polity offers a rich blend of clarity and obliquity within its ecclesial framework: therein its 'success in circuit lies'. Successive Lambeth Conferences have tended to busy themselves too much with church-related matters. But the primary agenda is the world, not the church. Moreover, the Lambeth Conference may now have a special role – even a prophetic calling – in moving the Communion beyond its tired and divisive binaries to inhabit more confidently the place that Christ came to live and die for, namely the world. Ultimately, Anglicanism – its pastoral practice, mission and ministry – does not have its identity rooted in being an eclectic and selective member-based organization, requiring detailed confessional subscription from believers. Anglicanism is, rather, far broader: an institutional body that has many kinds of support and supporters, though with room still for those who want to regard themselves as insider-subscribers. Anglicanism offers itself to the world on these terms, and in so doing, is an oblique foretaste of the inclusive Kingdom of God, embodied in Jesus Christ.

13

The Lambeth Conference: Has it succeeded? Can it survive?

Mark D. Thompson

The Lambeth Conference began as an exercise in global fellowship in the face of a perceived crisis faced by Anglicans in one part of the world. The synod of the Canadian Province expressed its concern that developments in Britain – namely decisions of the Judicial Committee of the Privy Council in the case of Bishop John Colenso of Natal, effectively overturning his deposition for heresy by the Bishop of Cape Town, and the reactivation of the Convocations of Canterbury and York in 1852 and 1861 – might 'leave us governed by canons different from those in force in England and Ireland, and thus cause us to drift into the status of an independent branch of the Catholic Church'.[1] The Canadians proposed a 'national synod of the bishops of the Anglican Church at home and abroad' that would ensure a common canonical regime applicable to Anglicans around the world.

However, when this idea was taken up by the Archbishop of Canterbury, it was significantly modified. Archbishop Longley's address to the Upper House of the Convocation of Canterbury on 15 February 1867 insisted that 'it should be distinctly understood that at this meeting no declaration of faith shall be made, and no decision come to which shall effect generally the interests of the Church, but that we shall meet together for brotherly counsel and encouragement. ... I should refuse to convene any assembly which pretended to enact any canons, or affected to make any decisions binding on the Church'.[2] The opening address at the first Lambeth Conference,

---

[1] R. T. Davidson (ed.), *The Lambeth Conferences of 1867, 1878, 1888* (London: SPCK, 1896), p. 3.
[2] Chronicle of Convocation, 15 February 1867, p. 807 cited in Davidson, *The Lambeth Conferences*, pp. 10–11.

delivered on 24 September 1867, repeated this determination: 'It has never been contemplated that we should assume the functions of a general synod of all the churches in full communion with the Church of England, and take upon ourselves to enact canons that should be binding upon those here represented. We merely propose to discuss matters of practical interest, and pronounce what we deem expedient in resolutions which may serve as safe guides to future action.'[3]

Why was the Archbishop so emphatic in his denial that the conference he had convened should bind the churches represented? A few days prior to the first of these speeches, Archbishop Longley told the Upper House of Convocation, 'I repudiate all idea of convening any assembly that can be justly called "a Synod", or that can enact canons or attempt to do acts which be *in direct opposition to the authority of the Crown*, which forbids taking any such step.'[4] Ben Guyer's chapter in this book presents a persuasive case that Longley was concerned about the lack of a royal mandate for such a gathering, something that might be considered necessary according to Article 21 of the Thirty-Nine Articles: 'General Councils may not be gathered together without the commandment and will of Princes.' We might say that Longley, like Samuel Wilberforce (Bishop of Oxford), was particularly sensitive to the question of the royal supremacy, as indicated by the italicized words above. That would hardly be unexpected in mid-Victorian Britain. However, there is no reason why other factors might not have played a part in this as well.

One such factor is an arguably more fundamental aspect of Anglican polity that stems from the earliest years of the English Reformation. A presenting issue in the breach with Rome under Henry VIII had been ecclesiastical interference across national boundaries. The pope had no jurisdiction in England, Henry and his parliament argued, since the church was part of an integrated commonwealth under the rule of the monarch.[5] The clergy, those charged with pastoral care in a particular jurisdiction, should, in concert with the prince or state, direct the affairs of the church in that jurisdiction. For this we might

---

[3] Opening Address, 24 September 1867, cited in Davidson, *The Lambeth Conferences*, p. 14.

[4] *Chronicle of Convocation*, Upper House: Tuesday, 12 February, 1867, pp. 646–7. I am indebted to Ben Guyer for this reference.

[5] See the programmatic statement in the Preamble to the Ecclesiastical Appeals Act 1532 (24 Hen 8 c 12), cited in J. R. Tanner, *Tudor Constitutional Documents, A.D. 1485–1603* (Cambridge: Cambridge University Press, 1922), p. 41.

appeal to Article 37 of the Thirty-Nine Articles: 'The King's Majesty hath the chief power in this Realm of England, and other his Dominions, unto whom the chief Government of all Estates of this Realm, whether they be Ecclesiastical or Civil, in all causes doth appertain, and is not, nor ought to be, subject to any foreign jurisdiction.' Compare the bold statement in Article 34: 'Every particular or national Church hath authority to ordain, change, and abolish, ceremonies or rites of the Church ordained only by man's authority, so that all things be done to edifying.' Interference of the church in one part of the world with what was going on in another part of the world was a deeply troubling issue in the English Reformation, picking up resentments built up over centuries due to papal excommunications, interdicts and the like. Each national Church should order its own affairs, the English reformers insisted, but only in matters ordained by man's authority, as Article 20 witnesses: 'The Church hath power to decree Rites or Ceremonies, and authority in Controversies of Faith: And yet it is not lawful for the Church to ordain any thing that is contrary to God's Word written, neither may it so expound one place of Scripture, that it be repugnant to another.' Anglican polity has always been uncomfortable with the notion of a 'universal primacy' and any infringement on the rights and responsibilities of national churches. Persuasion, rather than coercion, is the principle of Christian ministry generally: it is all the more to the fore when it comes to the relationship between Christian congregations and national churches.

Yet this should not be understood as a licence to refashion the Christian faith in each jurisdiction. A universal allegiance to Christ, and recognition of the authority of God's word to direct Christian life and thought, was not limited to national boundaries. Hence the claim that 'it is not lawful for the Church to ordain any thing that is contrary to God's word written'. The national responsibility for governance and the determination of appropriate 'Rites or Ceremonies' was one thing. The universal responsibility of fidelity to the word of God in teaching and practice was quite another. Cranmer and his colleagues did not consider that in the doctrinal sections of the Articles of Religion they were expounding a distinctly 'Anglican' faith. After all, just prior to the publication of the 42 Articles in 1553, Cranmer was pursuing a pan-continental Protestant confession.[6] Cranmer believed instead that he was

---

[6]   D. MacCulloch, *Thomas Cranmer: A Life* (New Haven: Yale University Press, 1996), p. 503.

faithfully expounding the one Catholic faith and its practical application to the national (and in particular political) realities of England.

Of course, the idea of an Anglican Communion was hardly in view when Cranmer, and later Parker, worked on the Articles of Religion. The Anglican Communion came into being through a complex of factors, including an interplay of colonization, flight from religious coercion or persecution, and the missionary movement.[7] Many of those involved in what today might be described as pioneer church planting work were office holders within the Church of England. So, for instance, the chaplain sent with the First Fleet to New South Wales in 1787 was the Rev Richard Johnson, ordained by the Bishop of Oxford in 1784. As churches grew in such colonial contexts, they tended to see themselves as organically connected to the Church of England, with a real and yet ill-defined relationship to the office of the Archbishop of Canterbury. Bishops were appointed for these churches, first from among the clergy of the Church of England, and in time from their own ranks, ultimately chosen by processes developed in each new jurisdiction. The churches retained much English liturgical practice, adopted English ecclesiastical dress and looked for guidance and direction – in varying degrees – to the leadership of the Church of England. In Canada, military chaplains, settlers and missionaries from England established congregations in the English settlements. In 1787 the Diocese of Nova Scotia was created by letters patent from the Crown and an Irish clergyman who had spent time in colonial America was consecrated as its first Bishop by the Archbishop of Canterbury, John Moore, in Lambeth Palace. The emerging dioceses across Canada would take the name 'The Church of England in the Dominion of Canada'.[8]

Colonial and post-revolutionary America was a special case. At first, Anglican ministry in the British colonies was conducted within the jurisdiction of the Bishop of London, exercising his ministry by means of commissaries. The character of the Church of England as the 'established' church in England

---

[7] Groups within the Church of England were critical in spreading Anglicanism alongside the growth of the empire. Such groups included the Society for Promoting Christian Knowledge (founded 1698), the Society for the Propagation of the Gospel in Foreign Parts (founded 1701), The Church Missionary Society (founded 1799) and the British and Foreign Bible Society (founded 1804). Available online: http://www.anglicancommunion.org/identity/about.aspx (accessed 17 January 2017).

[8] This was changed to 'The Anglican Church of Canada' in 1955. For more detail on the early years of Anglicanism in Canada, see C. W. Vernon, *The Old Church in the New Dominion* (Toronto: SPCK, 1929) and P. Carrington, *The Anglican Church in Canada: A History* (Toronto: Collins, 1963).

was an impediment to the spread of Episcopalian ministry in some parts of colonial America. After all, many of the first English colonists had fled England in the wake of various attempts to enforce doctrinal and liturgical uniformity. Another impediment was Article 37, which made unqualified assent to the Thirty-Nine Articles a prerequisite for consecration as a Bishop in England; difficult, to say the least, following the revolution. However, this did not dampen the desire to express Anglican doctrine, polity and liturgical forms in congregations across America.[9] So, in 1784, Samuel Seabury of Connecticut travelled to Scotland to secure consecration at the hands of the nonjuring bishops there. In 1787, following legislation in the British parliament to allow it, William White of Pennsylvania and Samuel Provoost of New York were consecrated as bishops by the Archbishop of Canterbury without the ordinary oaths of allegiance.

It is significant that the first calls for an international gathering of Anglican bishops should come from the United States and then from Canada, rather than England. As a result, this was not initiated as an exercise of jurisdiction by the English church but rather as a call from outside of England for fellowship and guidance. It is even more significant that bishops from America should come to Lambeth in 1867 and keep coming to subsequent Lambeth Conferences. The fierce American commitment to political autonomy did not eliminate a sense of intimate ecclesiastical connection and, in some measure, accountability to a wider fellowship.

This tension between a recognition of each national church's freedom and right to order its own affairs on the one hand, and a strong sense of connection and indeed a responsibility to each other on the other, is a critical background to the history of the fourteen Lambeth Conferences up to this point in time. The bishops who attend expect the collective mind of the delegates to be taken with the utmost seriousness. Likewise, they resist any attempt to bind them or coerce them into decisions and practices of which, on grounds of conscience informed by Scripture, they disapprove. A conference with no legislative power that nevertheless expresses the mind of Anglican leaders from around the globe can succeed only when there is a common mind and a shared faith.

---

[9] For more detail on this early history of American Episcopalianism, see R. W. Pritchard, *A History of the Episcopal Church* (rev. edn; New York: Morehouse, 1999).

Where this is called into question, whatever authority it might have begins to unravel. It is this sad reality which has played itself out in the past twenty years.

One hundred and forty years after the first conference, in the lead up to the fourteenth Lambeth Conference in 2008, Archbishop Rowan Williams, faced with the claim from the Primates of the Global South that 'the fabric of the Communion has been torn at the deepest level', attempted his own explanation of what the Lambeth Conference had become in an advent letter to 'the Primates of the Anglican Communion & Moderators of the United Churches', dated 14 December 2007: 'It is not a canonical tribunal, but neither is it merely a general consultation. It is a meeting of the chief pastors and teachers of the Communion, seeking an authoritative common voice. It is also a meeting designed to strengthen and deepen the sense of what the episcopal vocation is.'[10] This stated search for 'an authoritative common voice' is intriguing because it tacitly concedes that no such authoritative common voice has yet been found. Just as intriguing is the apparent hope that one might be found at the end of this search. The Archbishop was simply stating facts when he remarked that the Episcopal Church had decided 'to act against the strong, reiterated and consistent advice of the Instruments of Communion', which thus includes Resolution 1.10 of the 1998 Lambeth Conference. Archbishop Williams also stated the facts when he observed that 'argument continues about exactly how much force is possessed by a Resolution of the Lambeth Conference.'[11] However, he was doing something more than just stating the facts when he suggested that the unity of the Anglican Communion 'depends not on a canon law that can be enforced but on the ability of each part of the family to recognise that other local churches have received the same faith from the apostles and are faithfully holding to it in loyalty to the One Lord incarnate who speaks in Scripture and bestows his grace in the sacraments.'[12] It was precisely that recognition that was being questioned at that time (and since) and which explains the unravelling of the Anglican Communion.

The success of the Lambeth Conference depends on more than mere good will on the part of those invited, though it certainly cannot succeed without

---

[10] R. Williams, 'Letter sent to Primates of the Anglican Communion & Moderators of the United Churches, 14 December 2007', p. 3. Available online: http://rowanwilliams.archbishopofcanterbury.org/articles.php/631/the-archbishops-advent-letter-to-primates-2007 (accessed 11 July 2016).

[11] Williams, 'Letter', p. 2.

[12] Williams, 'Letter', p. 1.

that. It depends on the recognition that each church represented has not only received the faith of the apostles but continues in a resolute determination to hold to that faith. It depends on a common willingness to be disciplined by the teaching of Scripture and to repent where our doctrine or practice has wandered from this norm. Just as there is one body and one Spirit, one hope, one Lord, one faith, one baptism and one God and Father of all, so the unity which we seek to maintain is not an institutional unity first and foremost but 'the unity of the Spirit in the bond of peace' – and that Spirit is 'the Spirit of truth' (Eph. 4.4-5; Jon. 14.17; 15.26; 16.13). Yet when it becomes obvious by synod resolutions, by enacted canons and by public teaching and action that a member church has forsaken the teaching of Scripture, and refuses to be called back to that teaching by other member churches, then this unity has been fractured. It is vitally important on such occasions that responsibility for that fracture is properly attributed. Who moved? Who shifted from the consensus of the churches over the past 2000 years? In every case the onus of proof lies with the innovators, not with those who are teaching and doing what the churches have always taught and done, to demonstrate that they have not departed from 'the faith once for all delivered to the saints' (Jude 3).

Lambeth 2008 saw a very significant body of bishops, representing by far the majority of attending Anglicans worldwide, decline the invitation to the Conference and stay away. Many of those gathered instead with clergy and other Christian workers in Jerusalem weeks before, to confirm their commitment to the worldwide mission of the Gospel and their determination to uphold the teaching of Scripture in the face of liberal revisionism. This Global Anglican Future Conference (GAFCON) established the Fellowship of Confessing Anglicans (FCA).[13] The warnings, that the fabric of the Communion would be torn at the deepest level if, in defiance of the international outcry, the innovators acted on their declared intentions to consecrate a practising homosexual person or to bless same-sex unions, had gone unheeded. Lambeth 2008 itself would provide abundant proof that this had indeed happened: the fabric of the Communion was indeed torn. In reality, the trajectory that ended in this public breach of fellowship had been set decades before in those provinces,

---

[13] See M. D. Thompson, 'The Global Anglican Future Conference (GAFCON)' in I. S. Markham, J. B. Hawkins IV, J. Terry, and L. N. Steffensen (eds), *The Wiley-Blackwell Companion to the Anglican Communion* (Chichester: Wiley-Blackwell, 2013), pp. 739–49.

with an abandonment of the truthfulness and authority of Scripture on a range of issues. However, it was in 2008 that the scale of the catastrophe began to be seen by many for the first time.

1 Has the Lambeth Conference succeeded?

Has the Lambeth Conference succeeded as 'an instrument of unity'? Given that this is how the Lambeth Conference is currently described, this should be the first criterion by which it is judged. In light of the events of 2008 the answer must sadly but definitely be 'no'. The emergence of GAFCON/FCA and the public statements of the Global South Primates were prima facie evidence that the Communion had indeed begun to unravel. The urging of the Archbishop of Canterbury, successive Primates' Meetings,[14] and indeed an overwhelming majority in the 1998 Lambeth Conference for Resolution 1.10 on human sexuality (526 votes for, 70 votes against, 40 abstentions) had not been enough to maintain unity. The Canadian and American provinces had refused to listen. Astonishingly, in the face of the size of the majority which supported Resolution 1.10, the Episcopal Church, at the next meeting of its General Assembly, resolved that 'the issues of human sexuality are not yet resolved'.[15]

---

[14] Oporto, Portugal (22–29 March 2000): 'Clear and public repudiation of those sections of the Resolution [Lambeth 1.10] related to the public blessing of same-sex unions and the ordination of declared non-celibate homosexuals, and the declared intention of some dioceses to proceed with such actions, have come to threaten the unity of the communion in a profound way.' The full text of the communiqué can be found online at http://www.anglicannews.org/news/2000/03/a-communique-from-the-primates-of-the-anglican-communion.aspx (accessed 15 March 2017). When the Primates met in Kanuga, North Carolina (2–9 March 2001), they recognized 'the difficulties of those who are estranged from others because of changes in theology and practice – especially with regard to the acceptance of homosexual activity and the ordination of practicing homosexuals – that they believe to be unfaithful to the gospel of Christ'. The full text of the pastoral letter issued by the meeting can be found online at http://www.touchstonemag.com/archives/article.php?id=14-05-054-r (accessed 15 March 2017). The Primates' Meeting at Lambeth Palace (16 October 2003) responded to the decision to consecrate Gene Robinson: 'If his consecration proceeds, we recognise that we have reached a crucial and critical point in the life of the Anglican Communion and we have had to conclude that the future of the Communion itself will be put into jeopardy. In this case, the ministry of this one bishop will not be recognised by most of the Anglican world, and many provinces are likely to consider themselves out of Communion with the Episcopal Church (USA). This will tear the fabric of our Communion at its deepest level, and may lead to further division on this and further issues as provinces have to decide in consequence whether they can remain in communion with provinces that choose not to break communion with the Episcopal Church (USA).' The full text of the communiqué can be found online at http://www.globalsouthanglican.org/index.php/blog/comments/a_statement_by_the_primates_of_the_anglican_communion_meeting_in_lambeth_pa (accessed 14 March 2017).

[15] Resolution 2000-D039.

Both the American provinces (the Episcopal Church and the Anglican Church of Canada) proceeded to create 'facts on the ground' which they expected would force a rethink on the part of those who had insisted their stated trajectories would split the Anglican Communion. The Synod of the Diocese of New Westminster in the Anglican Church of Canada voted to authorize a rite for the blessing of same-sex unions in June 2002 and other Canadian dioceses soon followed suit. In November 2003 the Episcopal Church consecrated a non-celibate homosexual man as Coadjutor Bishop of New Hampshire and in May 2010 a non-celibate lesbian woman was consecrated as Suffragan Bishop of Los Angeles. In the light of these moves, other provinces responded by setting up structures to protect the vulnerable and disenfranchised who continued to hold to 'the faith once for all delivered to the saints' and who, in the years since, have been subject to pernicious litigation.

It is no wonder then that when American and Canadian bishops were invited to the Lambeth Conference in 2008, some orthodox bishops around the world found it difficult to attend.[16] Instead, they met in Jerusalem to pray and encourage each other in the apostolic mission of evangelism and Christian witness. The Global Anglican Future Conference was not billed as an alternative to Lambeth but rather as an opportunity to refocus on biblical truth and faithful discipleship and to encourage others who were persevering in these while under intense pressure from the revisionists. Some of the GAFCON bishops did attend the Lambeth Conference as well, hopeful that they would have an opportunity to be heard in their plea for repentance and a return to the clear teaching of Scripture.[17] This was to prove a forlorn hope.

Those who parted ways in the first decade of the twenty-first century have not been able to come to a common mind. The American and Canadian provinces remained unrepentant. After the 2008 Lambeth Conference, the Bishop of Tasmania, John Harrower, reported that instead of openly engaging with the other bishops, the American bishops participated in the Indaba process by reading from pre-written 'sample narratives' and a 'Messaging

---

[16] Bishop Gene Robinson of New Hampshire was not invited but refused to stay away and was very visible at the conference venue.

[17] On the clarity of Scripture in the face of contemporary challenges, see M. D. Thompson, *A Clear and Present Word: The Clarity of Scripture* (Nottingham: IVP, 2006).

Strategy'. Having witnessed this behaviour, Bishop Harrower described it as 'one of the saddest moments of the Conference'; he further explained that because the Americans had predetermined the content of their interactions, 'any idea of transparency and trust through Indaba had been tragically thrown in our face'.[18] During the 2008 Conference, Bishop Mouneer Anis of Egypt spoke of 'a great wall being put up by revisionists against those orthodox who believe in the authority of Scripture … I am shocked to say that we are finding it very hard to come together on even the essentials of the faith we once received from the Apostles'.[19] Indeed, ever since the Lambeth Conference of 1998, those who have protested against revisionist teaching about human sexuality, on the basis of Scripture, were caricatured and ridiculed. Bishop Richard Holloway of Edinburgh described the fundamentalism displayed at the Conference as 'attractive in the same way that fascism was attractive'. Bishop John Spong of Newark commented, 'If they feel patronised that's too bad. I'm not going to cease to be a twentieth century person for fear of offending someone in the Third World'.[20] It is entirely understandable that large swathes of the Communion have concluded in the wake of all this that those who have embraced these innovations are no longer faithfully holding to the apostolic faith. The litigious persecution of orthodox Anglicans by the hierarchy of the Episcopal Church, intensified since Lambeth 2008, has been viewed with horror by Christians around the world. It is abundantly clear that the Lambeth Conference has not been able to express nor strengthen the unity of the churches which make up the Anglican Communion.

However, given that the concept of 'an instrument of unity' is a relatively recent one, we could, and perhaps should, rephrase the question in terms of the original vision articulated by Archbishop Longley. This may prove to be a more appropriate criterion by which to judge the success of the Lambeth Conference as an 'institution'. Has the Lambeth Conference been able to

---

[18] See the report of the Bishop of Tasmania at http://www.anglicantas.org.au/lambeth/ (accessed 13 January 2017).

[19] 'Primate of the Middle East Mouneer Anis' Comments at Today's Press Conference' at http://www.globalsouthanglican.org/index.php/comments/primate_of_the_middle_east_mouneer_anis_comments_at_todays_press_conference/ (accessed 13 January 2017).

[20] For Bishop Richard Holloway, see the BBC article 'UK Lambeth 1998: Unity at a Price'. Available online: http://news.bbc.co.uk/1/hi/uk/147678.stm (accessed 13 January 2017); for Bishop John Spong, see Andrew Carey, 'African Christians? They're just a step up from witchcraft: What Bishop Spong had to say about his fellow Christians'. Available online: http://www.starcourse.org/spong/interview.html (accessed 13 January 2017).

provide 'safe guides to future action' in the current circumstances? Sadly, the answer must again be an emphatic 'no'. Such are the vested interests in the structures of the Communion, such is the pressure applied by those with financial muscle, such is the determination of the Episcopal Church and the Anglican Church of Canada to go ahead with their innovations no matter what the cost and with cavalier disregard for the concerns of others, that 'safe' is not an adjective that can be contemplated when describing what has followed the last two Lambeth Conferences. The 'conversations' attempted at the 2008 Conference were compromised from the start by the tactics of the revisionists. Conservative voices have been either ridiculed or silenced and strong public statements have been necessary in response. It can be fairly said that any attempt at 'brotherly counsel and encouragement' has been overshadowed by pain and hurt on both sides of the divide. Again, when measured against Archbishop Williams' search for 'an authoritative common voice', the hope of strengthening and deepening 'the sense of what the episcopal vocation is', and 'the ability of each part of the family to recognise that other local churches have received the same faith from the apostles and are faithfully holding on to it', the Lambeth Conference must again be judged to have failed.

Nevertheless, the real failure, it must be admitted, is not that of the Lambeth Conference per se. In 1998 it put biblical fidelity above cultural consensus, gently but firmly reiterating the incompatibility of homosexual practice with the teaching of Scripture.[21] The failure lies more in an inflated view of what the Lambeth Conference can accomplish when general agreement on the nature of the Gospel and the authority of Scripture over cultural preferences and agendas is no longer a reality. Lambeth cannot create a unity among churches if it does not already exist through a shared commitment to the crucified and risen Saviour and the authority of his word. An overwhelming vote in support of a resolution (88 per cent) was not able to secure or maintain a common

---

[21] Resolution 1.10: 'This conference ... b. in view of the teaching of Scripture, upholds faithfulness in marriage between a man and a woman in lifelong union, and believes that abstinence is right for those who are not called to marriage ... d. while rejecting homosexual practice as incompatible with Scripture, calls on all our people to minister pastorally and sensitively to all irrespective of sexual orientation and to condemn irrational fear of homosexuals, violence within marriage and any trivialization and commercialization of sex.' Available online: http://www.anglicancommunion.org/resources/document-library/lambeth-conference/1998/section-i-called-to-full-humanity/section-i10-human-sexuality?author=Lambeth+Conference&year=1998 (accessed 13 January 2017).

mind, as the events following Lambeth 1998 made clear. No amount of Indaba can restore it given the precedent of unilateral repudiation in the actions of the Episcopal Church and the Anglican Church of Canada.

2 Does the current crisis represent an opportunity?

It might be natural to see this inability to reinforce a particular type of unity – whether that is viewed as unity in orthodox Christian faith and practice or merely institutional unity – as a failure. It is understandable that some would view the disintegration of the Anglican Communion as a tragedy that should be avoided at all costs. Schism remains a devastating corporate sin. Yet it would be more dangerous, both in the short term and in terms of eternity, if an illusory institutional unity were preferred to tackling seriously the departure from the faith that has caused the current crisis. The truly schismatic act of the last twenty years was the decision to defy the urgings of 1998 Lambeth Conference, subsequent Primates' Meetings, and even the Archbishop of Canterbury and determinedly pursue the revisionist agenda. Everything that has happened since then is consequential upon this decision to go it alone.

The Apostle Paul, faced with party spirit in the church in Corinth, wrote of how 'there must be factions among you in order that those who are genuine among you may be recognized' (1 Cor. 11.19). He was not encouraging division. After all, he began the same letter saying, 'I appeal to you, brothers, by the name of our Lord Jesus Christ, that all of you agree, and that there be no divisions among you, but that you be united in the same mind and the same judgment' (1 Cor. 1.10). He did not want to see divisions among them, but he recognized that a certain type of division is necessary. This is not, as some suggest, a necessity brought about by the nature of the church in Corinth or the eschatological time of testing.[22] Rather, Paul himself explains the necessity 'that those who are genuine among you may be recognized [lit. 'made manifest']'. Division of a certain kind, not division on the basis of party association or institutional allegiance, but division where the truth of the Gospel of grace is augmented, compromised or denied, is not necessarily a

---

[22] G. Fee, *The First Epistle to the Corinthians* (NICNT; Grand Rapids: Eerdmans, 1987), pp. 538–9.

loss or failure.[23] Such division is necessary so that those who are willing to live humble, repentant, obedient lives, holding fast to the Gospel of forgiveness and faith and new life in Christ, might be recognized and strengthened to the glory of God. Furthermore, doctrinal or ethical disagreement between Christian brothers and sisters need not be destructive and divisive, provided each side is willing to sit under the word of God, humbly accepting any challenge to genuine repentance of the mind and of the heart that arises from the Scriptures themselves. In such cases, difference and disagreement might indeed be something that results in greater clarity and faithfulness in teaching and in life.

The church is a creature of the word of God (*creatura verbi dei*), brought into existence by the Gospel of salvation embraced in repentance and faith. As Anglican theologian John Webster put it, 'The church is the form of common human life and action which is generated by the gospel to bear witness to the perfect word and work of the triune God ... [it] will be characterized in all its speaking by a deference to Holy Scripture.'[24] Such a deference is most clearly seen in repentance and faith, as the word confronts our compromise with the world which refuses God's lordship and summons us to radical difference even if it means we will be despised. In that light, global Anglicans are presented with a moment of opportunity.

The current crisis will reveal who is really willing to be 'humble and contrite in heart' and tremble at God's word (Isa. 66.2). It will make manifest who is willing to stand against the trends of culture and intellectual presumption to walk the narrow road of Christian discipleship despite the cost (Matt. 7.13; 16.24). It will lay bare 'those who are genuine among you' (1 Cor. 11.19). Few enjoy a crisis. Few would deliberately choose the hard road of suffering and loss and disappointment. Few want to be separated and at odds with others who identify themselves as Christians. Yet betrayal and self-righteousness do cause real harm. False teaching and hypocrisy are always dangerous, wherever they are found. Immorality, no matter what sophisticated justification we are

---

[23] Heinrich Schlier, 'haereomai', in G. Kittel (ed.), *Theological Dictionary of the New Testament*, trans. G. Bromiley; 12 vols (Grand Rapids Eerdmans, 1964), I: pp. 182–3, suggests that the contemporary understanding of *heresy* was not so much 'heresy', but the rather more neutral meaning of school. However, influenced by later Christian use, he suggests *heresy* is the very opposite of *ekklesia* in 1 Corinthians and carries 'an eschatological magnitude'.

[24] J. Webster, '"The Visible Attests the Invisible"', in M. Husbands and D. J. Treier (eds), *The Community of the Word: Toward an Evangelical Ecclesiology* (Downers Grove: IVP, 2005), pp. 96–113, at 96, 111.

able to provide for it, eats away at faith in Christ and unless we who indulge in it repent, we can expect the judgement of God. Nevertheless, the God who brought light out of darkness and order out of chaos is not thwarted by our weakness or perversity. He will prevail. His word will stand forever. His rule and his ultimate purpose is not the slightest bit disturbed by our failures. Difficult periods like those the Anglican Communion has gone through in recent days give us the opportunity to ask the hard questions of ourselves: Will we seek God's righteousness above our own, his word rather than the most sophisticated arguments of our time? Will we live out our character as a fellowship of disciples taught, shaped and directed by the word of our Master? Will we build our house upon the rock or upon the sand of our own pretentions?

3 A future for the Lambeth Conferences?

The Lambeth Conferences have a future if they will not overreach and seek to acquire an authority that rightly only belongs to the word of God. They will have a future if they move beyond endless discussion and political manoeuvrings to speak the truth to each other – clearly, directly and lovingly. But speaking the truth also means dispelling error. That, after all, is a central role of the Bishop as defined in the Ordinal of 1662: 'With all faithful diligence, to banish and drive away all erroneous and strange doctrine contrary to God's Word'. Only if the fellowship of bishops is willing to call out those who have departed from 'the faith once for all delivered to the saints' rather than pretend episcopal collegiality is more important than holding to the faith of the apostles 'in loyalty to the One Lord incarnate who speaks in Scripture and bestows his grace in the sacraments', will it be worth calling another Lambeth Conference. Only if our Gospel not only proclaims the kingdom but calls for both repentance and faith in the light of it is there any future at all for Anglicanism.

The Lambeth Conference began as a meeting for brotherly counsel and encouragement, though it was dogged with controversy right at the start. Some English bishops refused to attend the first Lambeth Conference due to concerns about its legality.[25] Even the famed Lambeth Quadrilateral, plucked

---

[25] Davidson, *The Lambeth Conferences*, p. 13.

from its original use and given more prominence than was ever intended, is challenged and questioned in certain circles.[26] Indeed, most of the Lambeth Conference resolutions have faded into history without much of a trace. Yet the practice of Anglican bishops from across the world meeting to stir one another to love and good works (Heb. 10.24) still has value. The urgent question that remains is whether genuine repentance or a hardness of heart will follow in the wake of the events of the past twenty years. We cannot afford to pretend that if we just go on doing it as we have done it before, it will all settle down eventually. After all, everything that we do, even something like this, is done in the presence of the living God.

The Lambeth Conference is no longer the only international gathering of Anglican bishops. The Global South encounters began in 1994 when twenty-three Anglican provinces were represented at a meeting of bishops, clergy and people. This gathering was not conceived as a reaction to developments in the West but rather as an opportunity to discuss the Gospel mission and its context in the churches of the Global South. Life in the Global South presents its own peculiar challenges for those who wish to advance the mission of Christ and mutual encouragement and support is particularly valuable. However, as these 'South to South' encounters have continued, it has proven impossible to ignore the contemporary crisis over revisionist approaches to human sexuality, and homosexual practice in particular. The communiqué or 'trumpet' from the third of these encounters (Cairo, 25–30 October 2005) responded to the developments we have described in America and Canada: 'Apart from the world condition, our own Anglican Communion sadly continues to be weakened by unchecked revisionist teaching and practices which undermine the divine authority of Holy Scripture. The Anglican Communion is severely wounded by the witness of errant principles of faith and practice which in many parts of our Communion have adversely affected our efforts to take the Gospel to those in need of God's redeeming and saving love.'[27] This was even more explicit in the fourth encounter (Singapore, 19–23 April 2010): 'We continue to grieve over the

---

[26] D. B. Knox, 'Lambeth and Reunion' in P. G. Bolt, M. D. Thompson and R. Tong (eds), *The Faith Once For All Delivered: An Australian Evangelical Response to the Windsor Report* (Sydney: Anglican Church Record/Anglican Church League, 2005), pp. 81–6.

[27] 'Third Trumpet: Communiqué from 3rd South to South Encounter'. Available online: http://www.globalsouthanglican.org/index.php/blog/comments/third_trumpet_communique_from_3rd_south_to_south_encounter (accessed 20 January 2017).

life of The Episcopal Church USA (TEC) and the Anglican Church of Canada and all those churches that have rejected the Way of the Lord as expressed in Holy Scripture'.[28] In October 2016 the sixth Global South to South encounter was held in Cairo and a joint statement was issued with the GAFCON Primates which, following a positive statement about the Bible's teaching on the nature and purpose of marriage as created by God, included the warning that 'any pastoral provision by a church for a same-sex couple (such as a liturgy or a service to bless their sexual union) that obviates the need for repentance and a commitment to pursue a change of conduct enabled by the power of the Holy Spirit, would contravene the orthodox and historic teaching of the Anglican Communion on marriage and sexuality'.[29]

The Global South provinces and those associated with GAFCON/FCA have sought and found the encouragement in mission and faithful living that was not possible at Lambeth 2008. The Global South Encounters and the GAFCON Conferences (Jerusalem 2008, Nairobi 2013) have proven to be genuine exercises of global fellowship, united by a humble submission to the word of God and focused not on their opposition to revisionist teaching and practice but rather on their commitment to proclaiming Christ and living as disciples who take his word seriously. In this they provide a model of what the Lambeth Conference could become if those who convene and organize it are willing to leave behind the patterns of the past which have been unable to deliver a clarity of purpose and direction for the Anglican Communion. Yet even if the Lambeth Conference were to take on a new lease of life as a conference that promotes and protects doctrinal orthodoxy and faithful ecclesial practice, there would still be a place for both GAFCON and the Global South gatherings. They are, in and of themselves, reminders that the centre of gravity in global Anglicanism has moved from the northern hemisphere to the South. They are also challenges to put the Gospel of grace and forgiveness with its summons to repentance and faith at the centre of our Communion and to leave room for

---

[28] 'Fourth Trumpet from the Fourth Anglican Global South to South Encounter'. Available online: http://www.globalsouthanglican.org/index.php/blog/comments/fourth_trumpet_from_the_fourth_anglican_global_south_to_south_encounter (accessed 20 January 2017).

[29] 'Statement from the Global South Primates and GAFCON Primates Council Concerning Same-sex Unions'. Available online: http://www.globalsouthanglican.org/index.php/blog/comments/statement_from_the_global_south_primates_and_gafcon_primates_council_concer (accessed 20 January 2017).

the Scriptures to do their work of teaching, correcting, rebuking and training in righteousness (2 Tim. 3.17).

Archbishop Longley wanted Anglican leaders from around the world to gather for 'brotherly counsel and encouragement'. He longed for resolutions that would be 'safe guides for future action'. Factors within and outside of the actual meetings have, especially in more recent times, conspired to keep the Lambeth Conferences from reaching this ideal. Nevertheless, not least as a result of the example of these newer international gatherings of bishops and others (GAFCON, the Global South), we may dare hope for something closer to it in the future.

14

The Ecumenical Dimension of the Lambeth Conference

Mary Tanner

The First Lambeth Conference 1867 establishes the ecumenical dimension for future Conferences

When the Bishop of Montreal urged Archbishop Longley to call the bishops of the Anglican Communion together, against considerable opposition, he suggested that 'there was one function for which a conference would be indispensable: the question of reunion between Anglicans and other Churches'.[1] In his letter of invitation to the conference, Archbishop Longley asked for suggestions of subjects that ought to be raised. Eight bishops suggested reunion. One hoped that the longed-for reunion between East and West would be promoted; another focused attention on methods of bringing about intercommunion with both Scandinavian and Greek churches, naming in particular relations with Swedish Lutherans; another was hopeful for reunion with Continental Protestants. From the first there was concern for the unity of the Church and for what would later be described as Anglican 'all round' ecumenical commitment.

The encyclical letter sent from the conference claimed that the best hope for reunion was in drawing each of the churches closer to their common Lord and in giving themselves to much prayer and intercession, something that was to be urged in every subsequent conference. Even if the first conference had been called primarily for reasons of internal Anglican unity, it turned out also to be

---

[1] Owen Chadwick, Introduction in Roger Coleman (ed.), *Resolutions of the Twelve Lambeth Conferences 1867-1988 (Toronto:* Anglican Book Centre, 1992), p. xi.

committed to the reunion of divided churches. There was a mutual relationship of Anglicanism, as a growing self-conscious entity, with the developing self-consciousness of the movement to relate separated Christian bodies to each other in the one Body of Christ.

Archbishop Michael Ramsey, reflecting on the first conference, suggested that while that conference 'didn't handle the intellectual crisis of the time with distinction … it wrought better things in the realm of Christian unity where it affirmed the Anglican appeal to a primitive Catholicity and prepared the way for the Chicago/Lambeth Quadrilateral of 1888'.[2]

1888: The Quadrilateral a basis for home reunion and for the ecumenical agenda

The second conference was concerned almost entirely with Anglican unity, but by 1888 the ecumenical dimension of conferences was firmly established. Seven of the nineteen resolutions concerned relations with other churches. One requested the various branches of the Anglican Communion to make it known that 'they hold themselves in readiness to enter into brotherly conference … with the representatives of other Christian communions … to consider what steps can be taken, either towards corporate reunion, or towards such relations as may prepare the way for fuller organic unity hereafter'.[3] Another encouraged efforts to be made to establish more friendly relations with Scandinavian churches; and that approaches of the Swedish Church 'be most gladly welcomed, in order to the ultimate establishment, if possible, of intercommunion on sound principles of ecclesiastical polity'.[4]

The Conference affirmed the Quadrilateral, which had been adopted by the House of Bishops and the General Convention of the Protestant Episcopal Church of the United States in 1886. In the opinion of the conference this was

---

[2] Michael Ramsey, Preface in Alan M. G. Stephenson (ed.), *The First Lambeth Conference, 1867* (London: SPCK, 1967).
[3] Resolution 12, 1888.
[4] Resolution 14, 1888.

to serve as 'a basis on which approach may be by God's blessing made towards home reunion'. The Quadrilateral offered four requirements for unity:

> (a) The Holy Scriptures of the Old and New Testaments, as 'containing all things necessary to salvation', and as being the rule and ultimate standard of faith. (b) The Apostles' Creed, as the baptismal symbol; and the Nicene Creed, as the sufficient statement of the faith. (c) The two sacraments ordained by Christ himself – Baptism and the Supper of the Lord ... (d) The historic episcopate, locally adapted in the methods of its administration to the varying needs of the nations and peoples called of God into the unity of his Church.[5]

From 1888 on the Quadrilateral became foundational, not only for Anglican unity but also as describing the requirements necessary for visible unity with other Christian bodies. Henry Chadwick described it as offering an 'iron ration' ecclesiology and unity at a 'bargain basement price'! In the years that followed there was an interplay between the developing understanding of what constitutes Anglican identity and unity and the requirements for the unity of churches in the one Body of Christ.

The Encyclical sent from the Conference spoke of the conditions on which intercommunion was possible, saying that Anglicans could not desert their position on faith or discipline nor be blind to the blessings of other Christian bodies.[6]

1897: Issues of episcopacy and succession crucial for ecumenical advance

The longing for Christian unity remained, with the bishops in 1897 resolving 'that every opportunity be taken to emphasise the divine purpose of visible unity amongst Christians as a fact of revelation'.[7] The Conference reaffirmed the Quadrilateral, believing that 'the Anglican Church' had a vocation to exemplify Christian unity in its own life. Relations with Episcopal churches remained important. The Conference asked for a high-level committee of the

---

[5] Resolution 11, 1888.
[6] Oliver Tomkins, 'The Chicago-Lambeth Quadrilateral and the Ecumenical Movement', in Jonathan Draper (ed.), *Communion and Episcopacy* (Oxford: Ripon College Cuddesdon Publications, 1988), p. 6.
[7] Resolution 34, 1897.

Archbishops of Canterbury and York to confer and to correspond with the Eastern Patriarchs, the Holy Governing Synod of the Church of Russia, and with the authorities of the Eastern churches, to foster ever closer relations between the Churches of the East and the Anglican Communion. It looked for the setting up of a committee to collect more information about Moravian orders in the hope of establishing closer relations and another to inquire into the question of the validity of the orders of the Swedish Church and report back to the next Conference. It had become even clearer that issues of episcopacy and succession were vital for deepening relations with Episcopal churches not deemed to be in the historic succession. The bishops repeated the 1888 expressions of sympathy 'with the brave and earnest men of France, Italy, Spain and Portugal who have been driven to free themselves from the burden of unlawful terms of communion imposed by the Church of Rome; and continue to watch these movements with deep and anxious interest'.[8] Relations with the Roman Catholic Church had to wait until after Vatican II before they featured prominently on Lambeth Conference agendas. Responsibility for monitoring ecumenical relations between conferences was entrusted to the Archbishop of Canterbury. The conference also asked the Archbishop of Canterbury to create a consultative body to which national churches, Provinces, and extra-Provincial Dioceses could go for advice between conferences, another sign of the growing sense of being a world communion. Ecumenical matters were sometimes on the agenda of the Consultative Committee.

A further development in 1897 was concern for relationships with other Christian churches in their local setting. Bishops were urged to appoint local committees to watch for opportunities for united prayer and mutual conference and to report progress to the next conference. Here was a growing Anglican concern for deepening ecumenical relations at the local, national and global levels.

1908: The inextricable link between unity and mission emphasized

Unity remained central in 1908 with bishops reaffirming what previous conferences had resolved: 'Every opportunity should be taken to emphasize

---

[8]   Resolution 32, 1897.

the divine purpose of visible unity among Christians as a fact of revelation' and 'in all partial projects of reunion and intercommunion the final attainment of the divine purpose should be kept in view ... and care should be taken to do what will advance the reunion of the whole of Christendom, and to abstain from doing anything that will retard or prevent it.'[9] Though having no juridical authority, the Lambeth Conference assumed a crucial role in reviewing the progress of relationships with different ecumenical partners, at both the global and regional levels, showing concern for coherence and consistency.

Relations with the churches of the Orthodox East remained high on the agenda with agreement to baptize children of any Church of the Orthodox Communion in cases of emergency and to admit them to communicate when deprived of the ministrations of their own churches.[10] Moves were made with the ancient separate churches of the East. There was concern to strengthen friendly relations with Old Catholics and four resolutions focused on the relationship with Moravians, recommending that any official invitation to take part in the consecration of Moravian bishops should be accepted, provided that three Anglican bishops participated in both the saying of the prayer of consecration and the laying on of hands, and that Synods of the *Unitas* adopt a rule about the administration of confirmation more akin to Anglican practice. The Archbishop of Canterbury was requested to set up a committee with representatives of the *Unitas Fratrum* and another to develop relations with the Church of Sweden.[11]

The Lambeth Conference 1908 was concerned not only with advancing relationships with episcopally ordered churches but also with any Presbyterian or other non-episcopal churches, suggesting that any approach to reunion might be on the basis of consecrations to the episcopate on the lines of precedent of 1610 when the episcopate was temporarily restored in the Church of Scotland through the agency of three bishops consecrated in England.[12] With this more inclusive concern, not surprisingly, issues of episcopacy and succession gained even more importance. In spite of the concern for all-round ecumenical partnerships, there remained a Roman Catholic-shaped hole in the ecumenical dimension of the Lambeth Conferences. Indeed, Resolution 67 warned against

---

[9]   Resolution 58, 1908.
[10] Resolution 62, 1908.
[11] Resolutions 74–5, 1908.
[12] Resolution 75, 1908.

'members of our Communion contracting marriages with Roman Catholics under the conditions imposed by modern Roman canon law'.[13]

There was an important new emphasis in the resolutions of 1908. The bishops stressed that every opportunity should be welcomed to cooperate with members of different Communions in all matters of social and moral welfare of people, with a reminder that building friendly relations, theological exploration and action belong together in a single ecumenical agenda.[14]

Although St John's Gospel, chapter 17, provided the divine image of unity, what was hardly stressed in early Conferences was the inextricable link between the unity and mission of the Church. That became imperative for the bishops in 1908. They commended the suggestion of the Committee on Foreign Missions, for 'correlation and co-operation between missions of the Anglican Communion and those of other Christian bodies'.[15] The waste of effort in the mission field called for unity.[16] This emphasis was not surprising. Lambeth 1908 took place as the Missionary Conference in Edinburgh 1910, usually hailed as the beginning of the modern Ecumenical Movement, was being prepared. Anglican bishops were among its leaders. Edinburgh was to express a growing realization that the division of the churches in the mission field contradicted the Gospel message of unity. Another development at Edinburgh was to affect the ecumenical dimension of future Lambeth Conferences. Bishop Charles Brent, a missionary Bishop of the (then named) Protestant Episcopal Church of the USA (PECUSA), believing that the implications of John 17 demanded a unity deeper than mere cooperation, called for a conference to look at issues that had been the original cause of separation and continued to keep churches apart. A world war intervened and it was not until 1927 that a World Conference on Faith and Order met in Lausanne, Switzerland. The thinking of the Lambeth Conferences on unity, particularly the Quadrilateral's requirements for visible unity, influenced the multilateral faith and order agenda from Lausanne onwards; at the same time, the faith and order discussions in the multilateral world conferences challenged and enriched Anglican thinking on unity. In a similar way, Anglican ecumenical insights would influence the agendas of the Assemblies of the World Council

---

[13] Resolution 67, 1908.
[14] Resolution 76, 1908
[15] Resolution 23, 1908.
[16] *Six Lambeth Conferences, 1867-1920* (London: SPCK, 1929), pp. 313–14.

of Churches, which in turn would themselves be influenced by the reflections of those assemblies from the first assembly in Amsterdam from 1948 onwards.

The ecumenical dimension of the first five Lambeth Conferences

A number of features emerged in the ecumenical dimension of the first five Lambeth Conferences: an unshakeable commitment to unity, with the goal described as 'visible unity' or 'organic union' and 'intercommunion' as a step on the way; the items of the Quadrilateral being foundational, not least issues of episcopacy and succession, with the puzzle of how to recognize and reconcile ministries. Certain partnerships, with the churches of the East, the Lutheran Church of Sweden, the Old Catholic churches and the Moravians remained important. It was deemed appropriate that bishops, charged with a special ministry of unity, should pursue that ministry collegially and that episcopal committees should oversee deepening relations between conferences with the Archbishop of Canterbury holding a responsibility for overseeing the work. Every Conference urged the need for constant prayer for unity.

1920: *The Appeal to all Christian people*

Two Lambeth Conferences stand out for their ecumenical insight and commitment: those of 1920 and 1988. The lengthy Encyclical of 1920 begins with a moving description of the overwhelming sense of fellowship that had pervaded the Conference, all the more powerful in the aftermath of the Great War, convincing the bishops that the Church must be an example of the power of fellowship in its own life to attract the world to fellowship. It was not only Anglicans that sensed the need for Christian unity. The Encyclical refers to 'men in all communions' who are beginning to think of reunion 'not as a laudable ambition or a beautiful dream but as an imperative necessity'.[17] The 1920 conference also took place in the wake of the Missionary Conference in Edinburgh 1910, and with preparations progressing for both a World

---

[17] *Lambeth Conferences (1867-1930)* (London: SPCK, 1948), p. 24.

Conference on Faith and Order and a Conference on Life and Work. Anglican bishops were enthusiastically involved in the different aspects of the emerging Ecumenical Movement.

The 1920 Encyclical speaks first of the reunion of Christendom. The twenty-two resolutions on reunion begin with *An Appeal To All Christian People*.[18] The bishops had grasped the urgency of reunion: 'The times call us to a new outlook and new measures … . The time has come … for all the separated groups of Christians to agree in forgetting the things which are behind and reaching out towards the goal of a reunited Catholic Church.' The vision that impelled them was

> a Church, genuinely Catholic, loyal to all Truth, and gathering into its fellowship 'all who profess and call themselves Christians', within whose visible unity all the treasures of faith and order, bequeathed as a heritage by the past to the present, shall be possessed in common, and made serviceable to the whole Body of Christ. Within this unity Christian Communions now separated from one another would retain much that has long been distinctive in their methods of worship and service. It is through a rich diversity of life and devotion that the unity of the whole fellowship will be fulfilled.[19]

The bishops again say that the visible unity of the Church will be found to involve the wholehearted acceptance of the items of the Quadrilateral. After the last item concerning a ministry acknowledged by every part of the Church, they ask, 'May we not reasonably claim that the episcopate is the one means of providing such a ministry?' They do not question the spiritual reality of the ministries of those communions which do not possess an episcopate, whose ministries have been manifestly blessed, but they envisage sharing the apostolic rite of the laying on of hands expressing themselves willing to accept from others 'a form of commission or recognition'. Their suggestion is offered 'in all sincerity as a token of our longing that all ministries of grace, theirs and ours, shall be available for the service of our Lord in a united Church'.

The Appeal ends: 'We do not ask that any one Communion should consent to be absorbed in another. We do ask that all should unite in a new and great endeavour to recover and to manifest to the world the unity of the Body of Christ for which he prayed.'

---

[18] Resolution 9, 1920.
[19] Resolution 1, 1920.

While the bishops expressed a deep longing for unity, they also wanted greater clarity about the goal. Talk of reunion had thrown up different models: mutual recognition, organic union, federation, absorption, submission. The bishops were clear that unity could never mean uniformity or vague federation. For the fullness of Christian life, different traditions needed to be maintained but united in the fellowship of one visible society whose members are bound together by ties of a common faith, common sacraments and common ministry.

The resolutions on reunion reaffirm a continuing all-round ecumenical commitment with the following features: an expression of deep sympathy for the Church of Russia suffering terrible persecution; a welcome for setting up an Eastern Churches' Committee to help forward reunion with the Orthodox Church; an expression of sympathy for the persecuted Armenian, Assyrian and Syrian Jacobite Christians; and a welcome for the progress made with the churches of the East, believing that errors attributed to them over Christology may have been resolved. The bishops welcomed proposals for relations between the Church of England and the Church of Sweden: that members of the Church of Sweden be admitted to Holy Communion; permission be granted to Swedish ecclesiastics to give addresses in Anglican churches; and invitations to Anglican bishops to take part in Swedish consecrations be accepted. Friendly relations with the Old Catholics were encouraged, but concern was expressed over the administration of confirmation and the celebration of Communion by deacons in the Moravian Church. Proposals for the reunion of the Church of England and the Reformed Episcopal Church in England were not accepted.[20] Other resolutions stressed the importance of pursuing Christian unity at the various national, regional or provincial levels along the lines of the principles set out in *The Appeal* and every member of the Communion was encouraged to be prepared to take part in the universal fellowship of the reunited Church.[21]

A feature of the 1920 conference was the presence of representatives of other churches, so grounding the reflective work in personal relationships. The Ecumenical Patriarch of Constantinople sent the Metropolitan of Demotica and others to confer with members of the reunion section and the report of

---

[20] Resolutions 17–29, 1920.
[21] Resolutions 13 and 15, 1920.

the Conference acknowledged the help given by the Orthodox delegation. Optimism and vision pervaded the ecumenical dimension of Lambeth 1920.

1930: Ecumenical advances in spite of little follow-up of 1920

Although there were advances in the ecumenical dimension of Lambeth 1930, William Temple, then Archbishop of York, is said to have expressed disappointment with the follow up to the 1920 *Appeal* and the failure to live up to its promise.[22]

The Encyclical of 1930 began by recalling the theme of fellowship that had been 'dominant' in 1920.[23] However, in this conference the bishops claimed they had something even greater to chronicle: 'If holy aspirations are great, God-guided actions are greater.' There had been movements towards unity since 1920: advances with the Orthodox churches of the East and the Old Catholic churches and the scheme for reunion of churches in South India which, begun in 1919, had now reached an advanced stage. The South India scheme involved the reunion of Anglicans, Wesleyan Methodists and a united Church of Presbyterians and Congregationalists, looking to come together possessing the traditional framework of faith and order. The plan was for gradual union in which the things of God in each tradition would be preserved and enriched by 'happy combination', though there would be anomalies and irregularities about which some would have misgivings. Nevertheless, 'these are overweighed by hope and trust that God will perfect His work of reconciliation'. There was rejoicing that a part of the Church was ready to make a pioneering move for a corporate union with certain non-episcopal churches. The Church of South India would not be an Anglican Church but a distinct Province of the universal Church. There would be real intercommunion with the Anglican Communion, but those in the united Church who were not episcopally ordained would not have the right to minister in Churches of the Anglican Communion. This was a sacrifice they would make cheerfully in the hope of achieving union between

---

[22] Nicholas Lossky et al. (eds), *Dictionary of the Ecumenical Movement* (Geneva: WCC Publications, 1991), p. 977.
[23] *The Report of the Lambeth Conference 1930* (London: SPCK, 1931), pp. 19ff.

Episcopal and non-episcopal churches, towards the building up of a real living Church in India which would never be deserted by the Anglican Communion.

A further significant dimension at 1930 came in an appreciatory resolution on the Malines Conversations initiated by Cardinal Mercier and Lord Halifax. These were not official conversations and only lasted from 1921–5, nevertheless they were a sign of promise to come. The bishops regretted that after the death of the Cardinal, conversations had been forbidden by the Roman Catholic Church.[24]

There were resolutions reflecting the ongoing relations with the separated Eastern churches and another expressing sympathy with the Russian Church under persecution. Other resolutions encouraged relations with the Swedish and Finnish Lutheran churches and the Moravians and a further resolution again urged the Archbishop of Canterbury to set up bilateral commissions to nurture these relationships. Tension over intercommunion was to be left for the discretion and guidance of local bishops.

The presence of ecumenical visitors was now an established feature of the Lambeth Conference. The Ecumenical Patriarch sent a delegation headed by the Patriarch of Alexandria and an Old Catholic delegation was led by the Archbishop of Utrecht. The encyclical letter from the bishops explains that these visitors had come to tell Anglican bishops that they desired 'definite and practical steps to be taken for the restoration of communion between their churches and ours, a notable advance, crowning a long period of increasing friendliness'.[25] To the Orthodox and Old Catholic delegations were added those from the Moravians and the Church of Sweden. It was important for Anglicans that relations based on theological agreements should be grounded in and nurtured by deepening friendships.

1948: The influence of the Ecumenical Movement on Anglicans

A second world war meant that the next conference met after an interval of eighteen years. The experience of war had again strengthened a longing for unity. It was not only Anglicans who felt this. It was expressed in the First

---

[24] Resolution 32, 1930.
[25] *Report of the Lambeth Conference, 1930* (London: SPCK, 1931), p. 25.

Assembly of the WCC which was to meet later that year in Amsterdam and declare that 'we intend to stay together'. The bishops recognized the Ecumenical Movement as 'one of the principal factors in the Christian life of our times'. The first resolution on unity began by appealing to 'Christians in all Communions, whatever the differences which separate them in Church order and doctrine, to join in Christian action in all parts of the world irrespective of political party for the application of the principles of the Christian religion to all departments of national and international life'.[26]

The bishops continued their commitment to 'all round' relations expressed in recommendations on Old Catholics, Nordic and Baltic Lutheran churches, the Lusitanian and Spanish Reformed churches, and in a resolve to continue nurturing relations with Orthodox churches. Again the bishops called on the Archbishop of Canterbury to set up committees to strengthen many of these relationships before the next conference and repeated a call for a consultation of a 'wider than Anglican episcopal fellowship, advisory in character for brotherly counsel and encouragement'.[27]

Much time in 1948 was devoted to the Church of South India. While 1930 had welcomed moves in South India, the basis of the scheme had been opposed in 1942 by the Bishop of Colombo who rallied the Anglo-Catholic cause against it. Archbishop William Temple had reminded those opposed that the move to form a church in South India was not an act of schism and that 1930 had been clear that such a scheme would require Anglicans to go out of the Anglican Communion and South Indian bishops would not be invited to Lambeth Conferences. The scheme was based on an understanding that there would be no re-ordination of existing ministers and that for an interim period there would be a dual ministry. At the 1948 Conference a minority of bishops voted that all ministers should be accepted irrespective of whether they had been episcopally ordained or not, but a majority either voted against or abstained. In spite of opposition, the opening resolution on the Church of South India gave thanks for the measure of unity achieved locally and looked forward to the time when there would be full communion between the Church of South India and the Churches of the Anglican Communion.[28]

---

[26] Resolution 1, 1948.
[27] Resolution 74, 1948.
[28] Resolution 52, 1948.

There were other regional moves, in the United States, Canada, Australia and the British Isles; some for organic union, others for a mutually recognized ministry. Reflecting on the implications of such local moves for the Communion, the Encyclical suggested that

> reunion of any part of our Communion with other denominations in its own area must make the resulting Church no longer simply Anglican, but something more comprehensive. There would be, in every country where there now exist the Anglican Church and others separated from it, a united Church, Catholic and Evangelical, but no longer in the limiting sense of the word Anglican. The Anglican Communion would be merged in a much larger Communion of National or Regional Churches, in full communion with one another, united in all the terms of what is known as the Lambeth Quadrilateral.[29]

In spite of division over the Church of South India and implications of such local moves for the Communion, the bishops, echoing the 1920 *Appeal*, called on all Anglican Churches to seek earnestly by prayer and by conference the fulfilment 'of a vision of a Church, genuinely Catholic, loyal to all truth, and gathering into its fellowship "all who profess and call themselves Christians", within whose visible unity all the treasures of faith and order, bequeathed as a heritage by the past to the present, shall be possessed in common and made serviceable to the whole Body of Christ'.[30]

The bishops were clear that it is the will of Christ that they should seek to overcome separation and find a unity in Christ. The Quadrilateral remained the basis for unity, giving coherence to moves in different regions of the world. The bishops struggled to understand the effect that a move to unity in one region would have for the Anglican Communion, becoming convinced of 'a much larger Communion of National or Regional Churches in full communion'. This understanding was reached in the aftermath of the Second World War and in the context of an enthusiastic Ecumenical Movement. In a moving resolution they recognized the importance of personal friendships and urged the cultivation of such friendships.[31]

---

[29] *The Lambeth Conference 1948* (London: SPCK, 1948), p. 22.
[30] Resolution 56, 1948.
[31] Resolution 77, 1948.

1958: Regional and national union schemes and some clarification about the goal

Again the fellowship experienced at 1958 gave bishops the experience of belonging to a worldwide Communion and a conviction about the ministry of reconciliation to which they were called, reconciliation of divided churches and of divisions in society. Since the last conference the Church of South India had progressed and new unity schemes were before the bishops for advice, including the schemes of union for North India, Ceylon and Pakistan and the unity schemes with the Methodist Churches in England and in America. The Lambeth Conference had become a place to seek advice on regional schemes of union. The bishops were convinced that as Anglicans worked for Christian unity they needed to strengthen their own life of communion so that the fullness of Anglican traditions might be brought to the universal Church.

The Lambeth Conference 1958 maintained the commitment to all-round ecumenical relations: 'We know that we must pray and work with a new sense of urgency for unity with non-episcopal Churches; for harmony of spirit and agreement in doctrine with Eastern Orthodox Churches and other Ancient Churches, and for the healing of the breach between ourselves and the Church of Rome.'[32]

One significant contribution of 1958 was its statement of vision, together with the clarification of terminology about the goal of unity. The 1920 *Appeal* was reaffirmed and episcopacy was emphasized as 'given by Divine Providence' for the unity of the Church, though not in any precise form. Indeed those without the historic episcopate may have proved more faithful than the Churches of the Anglican Communion. Unity entails sufficient agreement in faith and order, expressed in the interchange of ministries and full sacramental communion marked by the bond of the historic episcopate and with active partnership of clergy and laity in the mission and government of the Church and a zeal for evangelism.

Because of inconsistency in the terminology used in regional schemes, the bishops clarified their understanding of 'full communion' and

---

[32] *The Lambeth Conference 1958* (London: SPCK and New York: Seabury Press, 1958), p. 1.27.

'intercommunion', suggesting that 'where between two Churches not of the same denominational or confessional family, there is unrestricted *communio in sacris* including mutual recognition and acceptance of ministries, the appropriate term to use is "full communion", and that where varying degrees of relation other than "full communion" are established … the appropriate term is "inter-communion"'.[33] Again, the Archbishop of Canterbury was urged to call a conference of the wider episcopal fellowship.[34] Episcopal conferences appeared to be gaining in importance to nurture unity. Lambeth 1958 held together approval of regional moves to full communion or mutual recognition with the call to visible unity in one worldwide communion, based on the requirements of the Quadrilateral, including the historic episcopate, a unity embracing the richness of diverse traditions.

The report on unity had much to say about the WCC, recognizing that 'it keeps us mindful of the universal dimension of Christian fellowship and mission, encourages conversations on faith and order, mission and evangelism, the vocation of the laity, offers training for theological students in the centre at Bossey and is a channel of Christian Aid'. But the report was equally clear that 'the WCC is not, and never must become a super Church'. Every bishop was urged to promote its work in his diocese.[35]

1968: The influence of Vatican II and a vision of the unity of the Church and the unity of the world

There were 75 'Official Observers' at Lambeth 1968, symbolizing visually a more inclusive ecumenical commitment. To observers from Orthodox churches, Old Catholic churches, the Church of Sweden and the Mar Thoma Church of India, there were those from the Assemblies of God, the Churches of Christ, the Salvation Army, the Society of Friends, as well as twelve Roman Catholic observers, including Cardinal Willebrands, a sign of Rome's ecumenical commitment after Vatican II. The Church of South India was numbered

---

[33] Resolution 14, 1958.
[34] For a discussion of the proposal for a meeting of the 'wider episcopal fellowship', see Stephen Bayne, *An Anglican Turning Point* (Austin, TX: The Church Historical Society, 1961), pp. 291–9.
[35] Ibid., pp. 257–9.

among the 'Official Observers', as were those with whom discussions of union continued, including Methodists and Lutherans.

Archbishop Michael Ramsey's opening sermon must have spoken particularly to the Ecumenical Observers.[36] In the context of a rapidly changing world with technology, secularity, contrast between rich and poor, destructive weapons of war, he reflected that 'unity comes not by combining this Church with that Church much as they are now, but by the radical altering of Churches in reformation and renewal. It is here that the Vatican Council has had influence far beyond the boundaries of the Roman Catholic Church'. He went on to speak of relations in the worldwide Anglican family and its role within Christendom:

> We shall love our own Anglican family not as something ultimate but because in it and through it we and others have our place in the one Church of Christ. Now, as the work of unity advances there will come into existence United Churches not describably Anglican but in a communion with us and sharing with us what we hold to be the unshaken essence of Catholicity. …
> Perhaps the Anglican role in Christendom may come to be less like a separate encampment and more like a colour in the spectrum of a rainbow, a colour bright and unselfconscious.

These words seem to recall the struggles of earlier Conferences to understand the Church of South India and, perhaps, the Archbishop's own desire for Anglican-Methodist reunion in England. He summed up the vision of unity and the way to unity expressed in earlier Conferences, a unity beyond Anglicanism.

The resolutions that were intended to guide the ecumenical work of the Communion in the decade ahead encouraged bishops to consider the principle enunciated at the Lund World Conference on Faith and Order of 1952, 'that we do together everything which conscience does not compel us to do separately'. The bishops suggested that prior attention in ecumenical living should be directed to the local, the national and the regional. One resolution recommended the entry into full communion with the Church of North India and the Church of Sri Lanka, where a scheme of unity that differed from South India on the integration of ministries had taken place leading to a fully

---

[36] Michael Ramsey, sermon for the opening of the 1968 Lambeth Conference, 25 July 1968, Lambeth Palace Archives.

interchangeable ministry. Another welcomed the unity scheme proposed between Anglicans and Methodists in England, believing it was 'theologically adequate to achieve its declared intentions of reconciling the two Churches and integrating their ministries'.[37] A number of resolutions covered the admission to communion and the grounds for Anglicans receiving communion in other churches.

The Conference took place in the wake of Vatican II which had opened the way for the Roman Catholic Church to become an active participant in the Ecumenical Movement, bringing a greater emphasis on the search for theological agreement in faith. This resulted in the creation of many international bilateral conversations, including what became the Anglican–Roman Catholic International Commission (ARCIC). There was no longer a Roman Catholic-shaped hole at the centre of the ecumenical dimension of Lambeth Conferences.

Influenced by the work of the WCC, the perspectives of church and world and unity and renewal became important: 'It is not a fitting together of damaged parts into a makeshift whole that we seek for the Church but a renewal and purification of each part so that the whole may reach towards the One New Man promised in Holy Scripture.'[38] The bishops recognized that the world's divisions gave a changed perspective to the understanding of Church unity and that the laity had contributions to make to this agenda. They admitted that lay participation would have given balance to their work. The bishops quote in full the Statement on Unity made at the New Delhi Assembly of the WCC in 1961, accepting its call 'to advance, in growing union with our fellow Christians towards God's high destiny for mankind renewed in Christ.'[39]

Lambeth 1968 affirmed the setting up of the Anglican Consultative Council (ACC), a meeting of bishops, clergy and laity to meet at two-yearly intervals between conferences. It was to assume some responsibility for monitoring the ecumenical agenda. At its first meeting in Limuru, Kenya, in 1971, the ordination of women to the priesthood was on the agenda. The 1968 Conference had agreed that 'the theological arguments at present presented for and against ... are inconclusive' and had asked national or regional churches

---

[37] Resolutions 49–51, 1968.
[38] *The Lambeth Conference 1968* (London: SPCK and New York: Seabury Press, 1968), pp. 119–25.
[39] Ibid., p. 125.

or Provinces to study the question and report their findings to the ACC, and, recognizing the ecumenical implications, asked for consultations with other churches before any final decision. The council at its first meeting determined that if a bishop with the approval of his Province were to go ahead before the consultation process had been completed, that would be acceptable to the Council and it encouraged other member churches to remain in communion with that Province.

1978: Emerging fruits of ecumenical conversations

Lambeth 1978 was different in many respects from earlier Conferences, having moved from London to the campus of the University of Kent at Canterbury, providing opportunity for more 'person to person, mind to mind, soul to soul encounter'. It was more sensitive to the needs of the world and the cries of the poor and less focused on passing resolutions. 'Official Ecumenical Observers' took prominent roles in the Conference: Metropolitan Anthony of Sourozh gave devotional talks and the Reverend Christopher Duraisingh of the Church of South India, still not in communion with the Anglican Communion, led Bible studies. Messages were received from leaders of churches. While the Conference was in session Pope Paul VI died and the Roman Catholic observers were invited to celebrate a Requiem Mass.

The ecumenical agenda was focused on Section 3, 'The Anglican Communion in the world-wide Church', bringing together the unity of the Church and the world. Bishops referred to programmes of the World Council of Churches, noting that younger churches felt that their concerns had been heard in the Council's programmes of relief, resettlement, education, struggles for justice and the combating of racism. The section report suggests a changing emphasis in global ecumenism:

> To many western Christians, the WCC seems very radical, but what they fail to understand is that the 'centre' has shifted dramatically with the influx of new Churches. And those Anglicans who complain about the policies and actions of the WCC need to be reminded that beloved members of our own Communion in the under-privileged areas of the world are among those who seek WCC help in their efforts to make life better for their people. The

WCC is not 'they' doing something to 'us'. It is 'we' working with our own and others in ecumenical endeavours.[40]

One of four plenary sessions on Anglican relations with other churches presented the results of the ecumenical dialogues, speaking of progress and prospects. The bishops expressed anxiety about challenges ahead, but were firm in their determination that, since the disunity of the churches was the greatest anomaly in Christendom, their attempts to resolve it should continue unabated.

The resolutions on unity show advances reached in ecumenical conversations, including reports from the Anglican-Lutheran International Conversations, raising the issue of ecclesial recognition of Lutheran churches on the basis of these reports. ARCIC's work on Eucharist, ministry and authority was deemed 'a solid achievement, one in which we can recognise the faith of our Church', hoping 'that this would provide a basis for sacramental sharing between our two Communions if and when the finished statements are approved by the respective authorities of our Communion'. Expectations for reunion with Rome were high. The Anglican–Orthodox dialogue was encouraged to continue exploring fundamental questions of doctrine and the Churches of the Anglican Communion were asked to consider omitting the *Filioque* clause from the Nicene Creed. The Faith and Order Commission's recently published report, *One Baptism, One Eucharist and a Mutually Recognized Ministry* was also warmly welcomed.

Other matters before the conference impinged on the ecumenical dimension. The first was the ongoing debate about the wider episcopal fellowship, with yet another request to the Archbishop of Canterbury to convene a meeting to discuss how bishops from these churches could best play their part in future Lambeth Conferences.[41] Another matter concerned the ordination of women to the priesthood and the episcopate. Although some bishops believed that this was settled by the 1971 ACC meeting, others felt it had not been. The bishops encouraged conversations between those holding different views and recommended extending dialogue with other churches, admitting that accepting diversity in the Anglican Communion may disappoint the Roman

---

[40] Section 3, *The Report of the Lambeth Conference 1978* (London: CIO Publishing, 1978), pp. 104 and 105.
[41] Resolution 14, 1978.

Catholic, Orthodox and Old Catholic churches, but expressing the hope that dialogue between them would continue and that no decision to consecrate women bishops would be taken without further consultation.[42] A third issue, highlighted in the opening address of Archbishop Donald Coggan, concerned where authority in the Anglican Communion should lie, an issue relevant to the subject of ARCIC and other ecumenical conversations, with clear significance for any description of what visible unity might entail.

1988: 'Who wants unity?' asks the Archbishop of Canterbury

If 1920 was an outstanding Conference for ecumenical vision, 1988 was another. Archbishop Robert Runcie's moving opening address set the unity of the Church in the context of the unity of all creation, the unity of the Kingdom. He posed a sharp question: 'Do we want unity?', answering:

> I do because our Lord prayed for it on the eve of his passion. I do because neither conflicting Churches, nor competitive Churches, nor co-existing Churches will be able to embody effectively the Gospel of reconciliation while the Churches themselves remain unreconciled. Do we Anglicans really want unity? We must do if we are to be instruments of unity and communion in a divided world.[43]

The responses of four ecumenical observers: the representative of the WCC on behalf of the Reverend Dr Emilio Castro, the Reverend Father Pierre Duprey from the Vatican, the Most Reverend John Zizioulas of the Orthodox Church, and the Reformed theologian Elizabeth Templeton, were each significant for the ecumenical dimension of the Conference.

Section 3, 'Ecumenical Relations', was chaired by the Primate of Canada, Michael Peers, himself an experienced ecumenist both in his home Province and within the leadership of the WCC. I was fortunate to be one of the six Consultants appointed to the section. The section began its work with bishops from different provinces telling each other stories of ecumenical relations in their

---

[42] Resolutions 20, 21, 22, 1978.
[43] *The Truth Shall Make You Free, The Lambeth Conference 1988* (London: Church House Publishing, 1988), p. 21.

dioceses. Many testified to heartening progress since the last Conference. There were new developments and a new impetus in the search for 'full, visible unity'. The bishops noted that for the first time the united churches of Bangladesh, India and Pakistan were welcomed as full members of the Conference, the anomaly over episcopal consecration in the Church of South India having been resolved by the passing of time. The experience of the united churches testified to the strength that Christian unity brings to once divided churches. Some bishops told of their participation in national councils of churches, some of which they celebrated as being renewed by the full participation of the Roman Catholic Church. There were stories of local ecumenical projects in England, Scotland and Wales, communities of reconciliation in Ireland, shared ministries in Canada, cooperating parishes in Australia. But, side by side with these positive stories, I remember being struck by comments from some African bishops that they were unimpressed by the agreements of international conversations, saying that the West had exported divisions and the West should now work to overcome them. It was perhaps this, as well as the opening address of Archbishop Runcie, that led the section to emphasize in its report the relationship between the unity of the Church and the unity of the whole human race. The section also painted a portrait of its vision of the goal of visible unity, which was important for those beginning to ask, 'Where are we and where are we going in the ecumenical movement as we approach the end of the ecumenical century?' The Quadrilateral remained central, but its explication provided fresh insights about each item and their interrelation when embodied in a community, breathed on by the Holy Spirit in a life of fellowship in worship and service. The most challenging and perceptive reflections on the Quadrilateral came in what was said about the fourth item. The section agreed that it is not possible to reflect long on ministry without taking account of the personal, collegial and communal (synodical) dimensions of ministry, exercised at every point in the Church's life. The discussion was influenced too by the ecumenical agreed statements from conversations with the Reformed, Orthodox and Roman Catholics, as well as by the Faith and Order Document, *Baptism, Eucharist and Ministry.* Although the section report does not record it, there was much discussion of whether a fifth item might be added to the Quadrilateral concerning structures or what the Most Reverend Edmund Browning of ECUSA referred to in his closing sermon as 'bonds of grace'.

By 1988 the Faith and Order Commission's convergence document, *Baptism, Eucharist and Ministry,* the *Final Report of ARCIC* on Eucharist, ministry and authority, *God's Reign and Our Unity* from the Anglican-Reformed International Commission, and reports from conversations with Lutherans, Methodists and Orthodox, had all been published. Each Province had been invited to respond to the reports, and the responses had been collated by a group of bishops and ecumenical officers.[44] The *Emmaus Report* was to help bishops formulate a Communion-wide response to the dialogue reports and to consider the question, 'Where are we in the ecumenical movement today and where are we going?'

The Conference passed resolutions on each report, taking note of achievements and encouraging further conversation on outstanding issues. It welcomed regional advances in ecumenical relations, in Wales, the United States, New Zealand and Canada, while regretting the failure of other schemes with Methodist and Reformed churches.[45] In spite of failures, there was a real sense that the Ecumenical Movement was moving, that Christians understood better those matters that were once a cause of division and were discovering how they might be overcome or what form legitimate diversity in communion might take. The hard slog of ecumenical conversations was providing a firm foundation for changed relations in life and greater sharing in mission and service. Good practice in different regions was shared and confidence was built.

The Conference planning group had highlighted the absence of the voices of women. As a result, Archbishop Runcie invited me to speak to the bishops about women's perspectives on the themes of the conference. Instead I agreed to draw together a group of women with different expertise and from different parts of the Communion to prepare a plenary presentation which included a dialogue with two of the bishops. The report of the conference comments that 'appropriately enough, the presentation was followed by a fireworks display'. In our remarks on unity we challenged:

> Women will never be convinced by a vision of unity which looks like the sticking together of broken bits of the Church. The interweaving of the unity of the Church and the healing of the brokenness in human community

---

[44] *The Emmaus Report: A Report of the Anglican Ecumenical Consultation 1987* (London: ACC, 1987).
[45] Resolution 13, 1988.

needs to be proclaimed more convincingly in all our ecumenical agreements and then received in the transformation of our lives. Can you in your work on **Ecumenical Relations** risk embracing something of our vision of wholeness?[46]

There were other issues which had relevance for the ecumenical dimension of the Conference, not least the continuing matter of women and the episcopate. The speeches of the ecumenical participants highlighted the importance of the issue for their relations with Anglicans. It was a mark of the closeness of partnerships that both the representative of the Vatican and of the Ecumenical Patriarch spoke freely, while Elizabeth Templeton's inspirational contribution influenced the final resolution on women and the episcopate. Resolution 1 agreed that Anglican provinces should respect the decision of other provinces and that a process of reception should continue in the Anglican Communion and also in consultation with other churches.[47]

Early conferences had understood the relation between the understanding of Anglican identity and unity and the unity sought with other churches. Lambeth 1988 had on its agenda the issue of authority, the structures and processes of discernment and decision-making in communion. ARCIC's Agreed Statement on authority, the discussions around the BEM triad, 'personal, collegial and communal' forms of ministry, and the report from the Anglican–Reformed dialogue were all relevant to this internal Anglican discussion.

It is hard to overestimate the importance of the ecumenical dimension of Lambeth 1988, coming as it did at a time of ecumenical achievements in both international dialogues and regional and local initiatives. The decision taken by the bishops on the consecration of women to the episcopate, leaving it to provinces to decide, while remaining in the highest possible degree of communion with those who held different opinions, inevitably had implications not only for internal Anglican unity but also for ecumenical relations. Nevertheless, the commitment to an ongoing process of reception within the Communion and with ecumenical partners showed a concern for ecumenical partnerships already established and a firm intention to continue together in spite of different views.

---

[46] *Women Spirit Rising: Towards Wholeness*, prepared for the Lambeth Conference 1988 by a group of women from around the Communion.
[47] Resolution 1, 1988.

1998: Called to be one but new issues with implications for ecumenical relations

The Lambeth Conference 1998 was the largest gathering of Anglican bishops ever, with the first women bishops among them. There were thirty-eight 'Ecumenical Participants', including a new listing of 'Bishops from Churches in Communion', ten in all, symbolizing advances in ecumenical partnerships with shared oversight implications. These included bishops from the newly established Porvoo Communion between the British and Irish Anglican Churches and the Nordic and Baltic Lutheran churches which had reached a significant agreement on apostolicity and succession, an issue that had concerned many earlier conferences. I was again present at the conference as a member of the ecumenical staff team, working with the ecumenical section.

In his opening address, Archbishop George Carey suggested that 'Anglicanism had never regarded itself as a final form of Christianity'. He commented on the progress in the last decade in theological conversations and new agreements between Anglicans and Lutherans in Europe, the United States, Africa and Canada, with Roman Catholics and Orthodox, and with Moravians and Methodists in England, reflecting that 'much needs to be done, but no-one can deny the progress ... a mark of the power of God's Spirit at work among us'.[48]

The Archbishop described the first objective of the Conference, 'to strengthen the theological, spiritual and personal bonds of the Communion'. This made sense in light of the tension over the matter of the consecration of women as bishops but even more now over issues in human sexuality.[49] Since the last conference the reports *Women and the Episcopate* and *The Virginia Report* from the Inter-Anglican Theological and Doctrinal Commission had been circulated.[50] The latter considered how the Communion makes authoritative decisions while maintaining unity and interdependence, acknowledging that the work of ARCIC on authority had a direct bearing on this. The final

---

[48] Ibid., p. 10.
[49] *The Official Report of the Lambeth Conference 1998* (Harrisburg, PA: Morehouse Publishing, 1998), p. ix.
[50] *Report of the Archbishop of Canterbury's Commission on Communion and Women in the Episcopate, 1989* (London: ACC, 1989). *The Virginia Report: The Report of the Inter-Anglican Theological and Doctrinal Commission* (Harrisburg, PA: Morehouse Publishing, 1999).

paragraph of *The Virginia Report* noted that 'the long history of ecumenical involvement, both locally and internationally, has shown us that Anglican discernment and decision-making must take account of the insights into truth and the Spirit-led wisdom of our ecumenical partners. Moreover, any decisions we take must be offered for the discernment of the universal Church.'[51] Both reports were relevant for the ecumenical section of the conference. While *The Virginia Report* was taken note of in some section reports and referred to in a number of resolutions, it was remarked by several after the conference that a more thorough response to it would have been valuable in view of the issues before the Communion.

Ecumenical participants again made important contributions. Cardinal Cassidy, President of the Pontifical Council for Promoting Christian Unity, preached at a service of ecumenical vespers.[52] He spoke openly about the risk of lowering sights and concentrating on short-term goals, cooperation and peaceful coexistence, insisting that 'the Catholic Church continues to be irrevocably committed to the re-establishment of full, visible unity among all the baptised'. He referred to 'new and deep divisions among Christians as a result of contrasting approaches to human sexuality and referred to *The Virginia Report* with its concern for how Anglicans make authoritative decisions, welcoming the sharing of the report with other churches, a sign of trust, showing that we are joined in 'a real degree of communion' and that our churches are increasingly bound up with one another. He stressed how important it was that Anglicans should strengthen the bonds of communion for progress towards full communion with the Church of Rome. 'I want to express in Christian love the concern of the Catholic Church when new and conflicting interpretations of the Gospel result in fresh disagreements.' The fact that the Cardinal spoke so openly to Anglicans as they anguished over matters of human sexuality was a mark of the closeness which had grown between the two Communions since Vatican II. Jean Vanier of the L'Arche Community led a vigil of meditation and prayer.

Important among the twenty-two ecumenical resolutions was the first recommitting Anglicans to the full, visible unity of the Church as the goal of the Ecumenical Movement, encouraging further explication of the

---

[51] Ibid., p. 63.
[52] Ibid., p. 455.

characteristics that belong to the portrait of visible unity and noting that the process of moving towards that goal may entail temporary anomalies. The bishops welcomed the Unity Statement: *The Unity of the Church as Koinonia* which had been adopted at the Canberra Assembly of the World Council of Churches in 1991. The Quadrilateral was reaffirmed once more as a basis on which to seek the full, visible unity of the Church as well as being a statement of Anglican unity and identity. There was a request for more work on the 'role within visible unity of a common ministry of oversight exercised in personal, collegial and communal ways at every level'. This made explicit the perceived need, both in the Anglican Communion and in any description of visible unity in ecumenical conversations, for structures of communion that maintain unity. There was a resolution on the common date for Easter and other resolutions on the Assyrian Church of the East, Baptists, Lutherans, Methodists, Moravians, the Oriental Orthodox churches and the Orthodox churches. Other resolutions proposed bilateral conversations with Pentecostals and asked the Primates to monitor the development with new churches and independent church groups, thus revealing a yet more inclusive ecumenical family.[53]

Archbishop Carey wrote in the preface to the Conference report that there was much ecumenical advance. Nevertheless, the issue that hung over the entire Conference was that of human sexuality. The Archbishop of Wales, Rowan Williams, had spoken at a plenary session on making moral decisions. Resolution 1.10 was passed by a majority of bishops in spite of the fact that no one seemed clear how it had emerged or whether the leadership of the section was behind it, let alone all members of the section. It was to have consequences not only for Anglican unity but also for ecumenical relations in the future.[54] A question with implications for the ongoing discussion on human sexuality and with ecumenical implications for visible unity was how Anglicans discern, decide and receive decisions in communion. Resolution III.9 called for a decade of study of *The Virginia Report* in the provinces, including the issue of a ministry of universal primacy, referring to the Encyclical Letter of Pope John Paul II *Ut Unum Sint*.

---

[53] Resolutions IV.1-26.
[54] Resolution I.10, 1998.

2008: A different sort of Conference

The Communion had been through a turbulent time in the years following 1998, with tensions over ethics and theology becoming acute. The resolution on human sexuality, while passed at the 1998 Conference by a majority of bishops, had left a significant minority feeling disenfranchised. A significant number of bishops refused to attend the 2008 Conference. Trust had to be built and relationships restored. The differences over human sexuality also had ecumenical consequences for relations with Orthodox and Roman Catholic partners. The work of the International Anglican-Roman Catholic Commission on Unity and Mission (IARCCUM), a joint bishops' commission working on what closer relations might be built on the convergences of ARCIC, had for a time been put on hold. Nevertheless, in response to overtures by the Archbishop of Canterbury, Cardinal Walter Kasper had replied that the Roman Catholic Church would accompany Anglicans in their disputes and a small group of theologians had been tasked with looking at events in the light of both *The Virginia Report* and the work of ARCIC on the exercise of authority.

The conference Design Group believed that passing resolutions and adopting section reports risked further polarization. This clearly had implications for the ecumenical dimension of the conference, the assessment of ecumenical progress since the last conference as well as the setting of a future ecumenical agenda by bishops. However, the ecumenical dimension was carried in other ways. Building trusting relationships was fundamental not only for Anglican identity and unity but also for restoring bruised ecumenical relations. There were seventy-two ecumenical guests of the Archbishop and much thought was given to their hospitality by a strong staff team. Each guest was accompanied throughout the conference by a Bishop. They met with the Archbishop of Canterbury to reflect on the progress of the conference. I had been invited by Archbishop Rowan Williams to act as his 'ecumenical dean', with responsibility for accompanying his ecumenical guests through the conference. The ecumenical dimension of the conference was visible, personal, relational, friendly and contributory.

Ecumenical guests spoke in plenaries and their presence was invaluable in self-select sessions where they, like the bishops, were invited to choose among many subjects. This made for informed discussions, but it also meant that the ecumenical dialogues tended to be considered by those already directly involved in them and who therefore had a special interest in the subjects chosen and were not considered by all bishops.

A major contribution came from Cardinal Walter Kasper.[55] His frank reflection on the Anglican Communion began as: 'What I am about to say, I say as a friend', adding, 'the problems of our friends are our problems too.' Turning to ecclesiological issues, he focused on the episcopal office of unity within the local level and the universal Church, pointing out that what had been said in ARCIC was echoed in the Anglican *Windsor Report*.[56] In the light of a shared ecclesiology, he wondered how the work of ARCIC on episcopacy, the unity of the Church and the need for a ministry of primacy at the universal level might serve Anglicans today. On the two issues dividing Anglicans, he was clear: 'The ordination of women to the priesthood and the episcopate effectively and definitively blocks possible recognition of Anglican Orders.' While dialogue would continue, 'it now seems that full visible communion as the aim … has receded further … our dialogue will have less ultimate goals'. Honesty, combined with sadness and affection, was conspicuous in his concluding words: 'The questions and problems of our friends are also our questions and problems.'

Archbishop Rowan Williams' three addresses to the conference set the tensions of the Communion in the context of the themes of the conference: 'Equipping bishops as Leaders in God's Mission', and 'Strengthening Communion', subjects which resonated with ecumenical issues. His insights into unity and communion and the wisdom of an Anglican Covenant were profound and of lasting significance not only for Anglican identity and unity, but also for the unity of the one holy catholic and apostolic Church and thus directly relevant to the ecumenical agenda.

In two ecumenical reflections in the final plenary Metropolitan Kallistos of Diokleia echoed the thought of Cardinal Kasper: 'Your joys and sorrows are our joys and sorrows … Your questions are our questions also or if they

---

[55] Walter Kasper, 'Roman Catholic Reflections on the Anglican Communion', in *Equipping Bishops as Leaders in God's Mission: The Fourteenth Lambeth Conference of Bishops of the Anglican Communion* (London: ACC, 2015), pp. 199–213.
[56] *The Windsor Report 2004* (London: ACC, 2004).

are not at this moment ... they will be such in the future'. He had seen the bishops proclaim 'Jesus Christ as the one and only Saviour of the whole world', but was not sure that they had unambiguously upheld the 1998 Resolution 1.10 on human sexuality. This would make Anglican–Orthodox Dialogue more difficult, he said as the Co-chair of the dialogue. 'I greatly hope the Dialogue will continue.' He ended, 'May the Lord Jesus keep you in unity! But does not truth matter more than outward unity?' The representative of the World Alliance of Reformed Churches, Professor Iain Torrance, commented encouragingly on the idea of an Anglican Covenant: 'If the Communion can forge such a covenant over the next years, it will truly be a light set upon a hill.'[57] The presence and active participation of ecumenical partners witnessed to how relationships had grown, to the point that words of warning and exhortation could be given without fear of reprisal.

Final reflections

Reviewing the ecumenical dimension of fourteen Lambeth Conferences from 1867 to 2008 shows how a conference called first for Anglican unity became inseparable from the search for the unity of all Christian people in the one Body of Christ. The imperative for unity permeated every conference, with the unity of the Church being more and more seen in the context of the unity of the whole of humanity, indeed the unity of all creation, with Christian unity as a sign, instrument and foretaste of unity.

At first, relations were mainly with the churches of the East, Swedish Lutherans, Moravians and Old Catholics but later extended to embrace non-episcopal churches, the Roman Catholic Church and more recently the Pentecostals and new churches. The goal of relationships was consistently described as visible unity or full, visible unity, with the Quadrilateral setting the requirements for unity. Much thought was given to the place of an episcopal ministry in the historic succession, while never denying the fruitfulness of ministries of churches without episcopal succession. While the requirements of the Quadrilateral were reaffirmed again and again, there was a

---

[57] Lambeth Palace Archives.

developing understanding that they were not a check list to be ticked off, but an interrelated list that belonged together in a life imbued by the Holy Spirit and lived in a communion of faith, sacramental life, mission and service. As time went on and new issues in Church order and ethics confronted Anglicans, it became necessary to consider what structures were required for discernment and decision-making in communion, in the Anglican Communion and the implications of this for the unity sought with other churches.

The vision held together the local and global dimensions of the Church and the unity of the Church came to be understood within the context of the unity of the world and the eschatological vision of God's Kingdom. This developing vision was much influenced by the insights and experiences of the Ecumenical Movement, not least of all by the work of the WCC and its statements on visible unity. Increasingly the notion of receptive ecumenism, exploring the gifts Anglicans might receive from others as well as the gifts the Anglican way might offer, was spoken of. The nurturing of ecumenical relations, the work of the doctrinal conversations, the intensified sharing in service and mission both locally and globally were held together. Continuity was important from conference to conference with a role of oversight entrusted to the Archbishop of Canterbury and nurtured by structures including the ACC and the Inter Anglican Standing Commission for Unity, Faith and Order (IASCUFO).

What emerges above all from the conference reports is not simply the importance of agreements in faith, written on paper, but friendships deepened and trust built. Relationships proved strong enough to survive new divisive issues, even if the immediate goal of full, visible unity had receded into the future. The High Priestly Prayer of Jesus in John 17 was a constant inspiration and a reminder that the Ecumenical Movement itself must be grounded in prayer and intercession. It was appropriate that bishops, charged with a ministry of unity, both individually and collegially, should devote much time to the unity of all Christian people as they gathered in the Lambeth Conference.

15

The Methodologies of the Lambeth Conference 1998 and 2008: The Impact of Process on Spiritual Discernment

Alyson Barnett-Cowan

It is a great challenge for all churches and Christian World Communions, especially divided as they are, to determine how they can best structure themselves to discern the authentic guiding of the Holy Spirit as they seek to govern their life. It seems to me that churches are always in tension with the cultural ways of decision-making, and a pressing need is to try to make that a creative tension. This is especially true of global communions, but in a multicultural world it is true for so-called national churches as well. For everyone is everywhere – migration has transformed even individual parishes into microcosms of the world, and therefore whole sets of assumptions about how best to discern something together are at play, most of them remaining unexamined.

The ways of working that have been developed in the churches over the centuries are based in part on biblical principles and the traditions of church life. But they are also much informed by the surrounding culture. For example, the General Synod of the Church of England is structured in ways that are somewhat similar to the Parliament of the United Kingdom. Its five-year cycle is opened in the presence of the monarch in Church House, Westminster, following a celebration of the Eucharist in Westminster Abbey, and the monarch addresses the new Synod. It has houses of clergy and laity (think House of Commons) and a house of bishops (think House of Lords) and it works by debate, resolution and, when necessary, majority vote.

The General Convention of the Episcopal Church was initially designed by some of the same people whose thought influenced the creation of the

Congress of the United States. It also has separate houses for clergy and laity, and for bishops – in fact their system makes these houses (of Bishops and of Deputies) even more separate than they are in the Church of England, as they meet, address agenda, debate and vote in different rooms.

Recently many churches have come to realize that, in facing challenging questions such as the ordination of women as bishops and sexuality, these quasi-legislative systems do not necessarily serve them very well. A pattern of resolution and debate does not allow for deep listening. It does not allow for the emergence of consensus. And, generally speaking, it is when consensus is reached by a group that a decision holds more authority than the dominance of a majority over a minority.

The World Council of Churches, and the Canadian Council of Churches, recognizing that majority votes cannot be binding on the member churches because of their own differing ecclesiologies, now try to work by consensus. This can be a long process, and does not always suit in a world that wants instant responses to its concerns. But it might be more authentic. The Canadian Council of Churches operates by a 'forum' method. Governing Board members evolved a sophisticated and Spirit-inspired strategy for a truly inclusive and accountable model of ecumenical governance: the Canadian Council of Churches Governing Board Forum. The fruits of Forum were an immediate harvest. From a membership of eleven denominations, dominated by the big Protestant players, the Council has expanded to twenty-one members. The Forum assurance of equal voice for all at the table has brought into a renewed ecumenical body such disparate traditions as the Canadian Conference of Catholic Bishops and Mennonite Church Canada. As Dr James Christie, a Past President of the Canadian Council of Churches, said several years ago:

> We engage regularly in the risky business of self-revelation, one to another, learning as Paul taught us that the diversity of members is the essence of the Body of Christ. But mutual understanding and increasing respect has bred neither complacency nor a harmony grounded in indifference. The consensus which now governs our deliberations is often hard-won and sometimes elusive. Through hard work and a patience that is a gift of God's grace we have developed workable protocols and procedures. Compromises are often necessary, but never at the price of conviction. How could it be

otherwise, when our priorities and our very agendas spring from the witness and mission of our constituent denominations.[1]

Anglican bishops serve all over the world – in more than 165 countries, as the tagline for the Anglican Communion Office puts it. Their contexts for witness and therefore their priorities for mission vary greatly, just as, sadly, do the resources for living out that mission. How can such a diverse group, shaped by mission history but also by their own cultural, social and historical contexts, speaking a wide range of languages, come to discern the will of the Spirit for the churches of the Anglican Communion when they meet for three weeks at the Lambeth Conference roughly every ten years?

Most of the first thirteen Lambeth Conferences were conducted in the English quasi-parliamentary mode, at least when it came time for decision-making. Resolutions were put, debated, amended and voted on, and the majority won the day. As Archbishop Williams noted, this served best those who were familiar with such a system.[2] For those for whom English is a second, third or even fourth or more language, it is a struggle to follow the debate, let alone to have the courage to stand up to speak to a resolution. Yet the product of such a system is clear: a set of resolutions agreed to by the majority of bishops, reflecting, one would hope, the best thought that could be brought to the subject at that time and place.

Since its inception, the Lambeth Conference has struggled to have a clearly agreed place in Anglican ecclesiology. In fact, its development may have provided the first occasion for consideration of what Anglican ecclesiology is, once it had moved from simply being the ecclesiology of the Church of England. And since its inception, there has been no clear consensus as to what exactly it is, and what authority and status its conclusions (Resolutions) have. Writing an introduction to the Resolutions of the Twelve Lambeth Conferences 1867–1988, Owen Chadwick reflected on the tension implicit in the first Conference, of 1867:[3]

> The first [danger] was that, if the meeting was to be acceptable to some of its more moderate opponents, it seemed to be necessary to say that the

---

[1] James Christie, 'Statement on Forum': https://www.councilofchurches.ca/about-us/governing-board/statement-on-forum/(accessed July 2017).

[2] Rowan Williams, *First Presidential Address, Equipping Bishops as Leaders in God's Mission: Reports from and reflections on the fourteenth Lambeth Conference of the Bishops of The Anglican Communion, 16 July – 4 August 2008 at the University of Kent at Canterbury*, ed. David Craig (London: Anglican Consultative Council, 2015), p. 49.

[3] Owen Chadwick, 'Introduction', in Roger Coleman (ed.), *Resolutions of the Twelve Lambeth Conferences 1867-1988* (Toronto: Anglican Book Centre, 1992), pp. i–xxviii at p. viii.

meeting was only a discussion group and none of its decisions would have any authority. Archbishop Longley of Canterbury would only summon the meeting, and several bishops would only attend it, if its resolutions were declared beforehand to have no binding force. Some of the American bishops who were determined to take no orders out of England were equally strong that this meeting was 'only' for consultation.

The second danger arose from the nature of a parliament. Large parliaments on average debate badly – it is the nature of the animal – even though the result leads to a change in the law which affects the people. Large parliaments which debate a motion, when everyone knows that the debate can have no particular outcome, are asking for a still worse debate. That is, a debate which cannot produce anything is a way to invite a feeling of irresponsibility.

Is it necessarily irresponsible for a gathering of Christian leaders not to debate binding resolutions? There should be, in the midst of a meeting which begins and ends and is suffused with prayer and the study of Scripture, a sense of being guided by the Holy Spirit, and thus of being led to some authentic discernment. If that discernment is reached by consensus, it may well be acceptable to the wider church as wise and holy guidance.

Later Chadwick writes:

We have seen that the Lambeth Conference was allowed to be founded only if it had no authority. But meetings start to gather authority if they exist and are seen not to be a cloud of hot air and rhetoric. It was impossible that the leaders of the Anglican Communion should meet every ten years and not start to gather respect, and to gather respect is to gather influence, and influence is on the road to authority. It continued to have that absence of legal authority which some of its founders wanted and which of necessity was denied to them. But in most Churches some of the most important parts of authority are not based upon the law.

The first element in this was the discovery that mere meeting was after all not mere. Some people had said that if the meeting could not decide anything there was no reason for the bishops to neglect their distant dioceses. But, as they met, they discovered that there was virtue in the original Canadian desire to know better what was going on. Here they were at Lambeth, all with an apostolic commission in different parts of the globe and therefore with different social problems and environments of peoples and laws and traditions, with a common gospel and a common way of worship and

common attitudes in spirituality and much common ethical agreement.
They found that they needed to say some prayers together; that to meet for
common worship or quiet days was no minor part of the purpose of the
meeting; that they needed to know each other personally so that the name
at the foot of the letter was nor merely a signature; and that they needed to
draw inspiration from their roots in the way of pilgrimage. ... They wanted
to talk with each other and to say their prayers together and perhaps also
to recapture the long historic dimension of their faith. Some of them found
that this was what really mattered about the Lambeth Conference. For such
visiting bishops it was not important that they could not decide anything.
They needed to meet because they needed to meet, not because they needed
to determine who was the right Bishop of Natal.[4]

I have quoted Owen Chadwick at length because his words, written before
the Lambeth Conferences of 1998 and 2008, could well have been echoed by a
large number of bishops who attended these more recent meetings.

How the agenda is set

There has evolved over the years a complex relationship between the Anglican
Communion Office and Lambeth Palace. The Archbishop of Canterbury calls
the Conference, invites the bishops to it and presides at it. But the detailed
work of managing the Conference – choosing a venue, making it suitable for
the work to be done, travel logistics, dispensing bursaries for those who need
a subsidy, arranging for daily prayer and celebrations of the Eucharist, inviting
speakers, and, above all, choosing and implementing an agenda – is done by
regular staff and contract staff of the Anglican Communion Office under the
direction of the Secretary General, alongside the staff of Lambeth Palace who
serve the personal ministry of the Archbishop. Inevitably, the responsibilities
and the relationships vary depending on the characters and priorities of the
Archbishop and the Secretary General. The Joint Standing Committee (now
just 'the Standing Committee'), made up of some members of the Anglican
Consultative Council and of the Primates' Meeting, appoint a Design Group,
who work with the Archbishop and the Secretary General to plan the overall

---

[4]   Chadwick, Introduction, pp. x–xi.

shape and methodology of the Conference. They are aided by the St Augustine's Seminar, a gathering of theologians and others who deliberate about the content and prepare advance literature. The Design Group seeks input from the bishops around the world in preparation for the conference.

According to the records of the Design Group for 1998, there was some discussion about the problem of working in the English language and in English ways. It was noted in the minutes of their meeting of 26–30 March, 1995 that 'different cultures conceptualised and articulated in different ways. The Group must enable all cultures to participate in the Lambeth Conference fully. Language and use of time must be considered. It was agreed that three members of the Design Group would consider the influence of English language and culture in the dynamics of the Conference.' I looked in vain in the files of the Design Group from the Lambeth Palace archives for a report from this subgroup. In addition, at that March 1995 meeting, 'there was some discussion about voting procedures, though it was noted that a constitutional process was being discussed in relation to a body which had no constitution. This area of concern would need further reflection at a later date.' Again, I could not find any record of this further reflection, though that of course does not mean that it did not take place.[5]

The methodology of 1998

The Lambeth Conference of 1998 followed the pattern established more or less from the beginning. The bishops were divided into sections (in earlier conferences called committees), to some degree according to their expressed preference, but also with a view to balance off geography and expertise. The Design Group, with input from St Augustine's Seminar, assigned various aspects of the work of the Communion to one of the sections.[6]

The first week was given over to orientation, the opening service, the Presidential Address and particular pieces of input from guest speakers and panels of experts (although these plenaries continued to be interspersed later

---

[5] Minutes of the Lambeth Conference Design Group for the 1998 and the 2008 Conferences, from the archives of Lambeth Palace and of the Anglican Communion Office.

[6] *The Official Report of the Lambeth Conference 1998*, ed. Mark Dyer (Chair of the Editorial Team) (Harrisburg: Morehouse, 1999).

in the conference as well). Ecumenical vespers was the highlight of a day which focused on the participation of ecumenical guests. The second week had the bishops meeting in sections and in smaller working groups within those sections. This was the critical time when attention could be paid to the detail of the work and the bishops could offer their assessment of work already done and contribute ideas for the future. This work culminated in a report from each section, together with proposed resolutions for the plenary to consider. The third week was largely given over to the debate about these resolutions. It was at this point that the conflicts over assumed patterns of decision-making came into play, as not everyone was familiar with the rules of order that were followed. From groups of 20–30 having an intense discussion, the Conference moved to a parliamentary-style plenary of some 700 people, with only a few days to reach decisions on a wide range of issues. Although there was simultaneous translation into a few of the languages of the Communion, the debate was in English and according to English rules.

The Archbishop of Canterbury had expressed concern about this stage of the Conference when he addressed the Design Group at its first meeting in 1994: 'The least impressive features [of the Lambeth Conference of 1988] were the rather tedious plenary sessions going through hundreds of resolutions.' Nevertheless, the final week of 1998 did in fact debate many resolutions, if not quite a hundred.

The topics chosen for the four sections were:

1. Called to Full Humanity (human rights and human dignity, the environment, human sexuality, modern technology, euthanasia, international debt and economic justice)
2. Called to Live and Proclaim the Good News (God's call to mission, the Church as God's partner in mission, the world God loves, the missionary congregation, being a missionary bishop in a missionary church, how to support each other in mission, resources for mission)
3. Called to be a Faithful Church in a Plural World (a plural world, a faithful church, unity and diversity in the Anglican Communion, a faithful church in a plural world)
4. Called to Be One (towards a vision of the unity to which we are called, new churches and independent Christian groups, dialogues with other churches, response and reception)

While each section had an overarching theme (issues facing humanity, mission, pluralism, and ecumenism), they each had a grab bag of miscellaneous topics given to them.

The Design Group chose not to have a particular section on Anglican ecclesiology, even though unresolved issues about this emerged in all of the sections. The important report of the Inter-Anglican Theological and Doctrinal Commission on ecclesiology, the Virginia Report, was not assigned to any one section but was expected to be treated by them all. The result was that it did not receive the focused evaluation it deserved, and the fallout after the difficulties of Resolution I.10 turned, to no small degree, on there being no consensus about how and whether the Anglican Communion has an agreed-upon central locus of binding authority. The Windsor Report of 2004 and the Anglican Communion Covenant process are testaments to this ongoing and unresolved question. However, though much has been said and written about I.10, there is no doubt in my mind that, in general, the process of deliberation in smaller groups, the preparation of a report, and the drafting and debate of resolutions served the ecumenical work of the Anglican Communion well.

The methodology of 2008

Archbishop Rowan Williams set the tone and the method in his First Presidential Address to the Lambeth Conference 2008:

> [The planning group of this Conference] recognised, with the help of those members who came from outside Europe and North America, that the methods we had got used to were very much tied to Western ways – and not only Western ways, but the habits that had developed in the later twentieth century, with tight procedural rules, great quantities of paper, close timetables and yes-or-no decisions. All those still have their attractions, but, as I've said, it isn't clear that they actually help things happen any more effectively when you're dealing with a large and very varied group. What's more, this sort of method guaranteed that the voices most often heard would be the voices of people who were comfortable with this way of doing things; but what would it take to guarantee that everyone's voice has a chance of being heard?[7]

---

[7]   Williams, First Presidential Address, p. 49.

The Design Group for the 2008 Conference was indebted to the insight of Archbishop Thabo Makgoba, Primate of Southern Africa, for the term 'indaba', which proved to be the key to this Conference's approach. As he writes: 'Indaba is a Zulu word for a gathering for purposeful discussion. It is both a process and a method of engagement as we listen to one another on challenges that face our community.' He continues:

> Indaba first and foremost acknowledges that there are issues that need to be addressed effectively to foster ongoing communal living. … In Indaba, we must be aware of these challenges or issues without immediately trying to resolve them one way or another. We meet and converse, ensuring that everyone has a voice, and contributes (praying that this might be under the guidance of the Holy Spirit); and ensuring also that the issues at hand are fully defined and understood by all. … Indaba works best when participants do not go into the discussion with a hidden agenda or a prior solution. When you bring the issues, others add to them with their own voice and a greater truth is revealed. In the process people grow, learn and increase their understanding of each other as well as the issue under discussion.[8]

So the Design Group proposed, and the Archbishop of Canterbury accepted, that the basic unit of the Lambeth Conference would be an eight-member Bible study group, which would meet each morning for prayer and study. Five of these groups came together after four mornings of work together to form Indaba groups. The Indaba groups discussed with intensity the topics for the Conference. Rapporteurs in each Indaba group recorded the insights from the discussion. Listeners drawn from all of the Indaba groups prepared the Conference Reflections document.[9]

The great challenge of this method was time. While time is obviously a factor in a parliamentary model as well, the great insight of Indaba is that the wisdom is in the group as guided by the Spirit, but that this will take the time it takes for everyone to be heard and understood, and for consensus to emerge. The Lambeth Conference did not have this time. Moreover, the

---

[8] Ibid., p. 79.

[9] A detailed description of the Indaba process, written by Stephen Lyon, can be found in *Equipping Bishops as Leaders in God's Mission: Reports from and reflections on the fourteenth Lambeth Conference of the Bishops of The Anglican Communion*, pp. 81–7.

number of topics addressed meant that the conclusions were often superficial. The advantage, however, was huge, given the climate of distrust that prevailed in much of the Anglican world that had built up in the decade before. Indaba allowed participants to come to know a cross-section of their peers in an intense situation, grounded in prayer and focused on mission. Everyone had an opportunity to speak, and attention was paid to translation into other languages. The outcome of the Conference, therefore, was not so much the words, as in resolutions, but the strengthening of the 'bonds of affection' through in-depth personal relationships.

The ecumenical work of the two conferences

Both 1998 and 2008 had representatives of the Christian World Communions as full participants throughout. There were also people from other church bodies who came as the personal invitees of the Archbishop of Canterbury, such as Brother Roger from the Taizé Community in 1998 and Metropolitan Anastasios from the Orthodox Church of Albania in 2008. Ecumenical partners participated in the sections of 1998 and in the Indaba groups of 2008. They did not speak in debate in 1998, but they were fully involved in all other ways. In 2008, since there were no votes, they participated in all of the Bible study and Indaba groups. Those ecumenical partners who were bishops were invited to share in the retreat which Archbishop Williams led in Canterbury Cathedral immediately before the Conference began. In 2008 two ecumenical partners were given a prominent place in offering observations at the end of the Conference. The difference lies in the contribution that each Conference was able to make to the ongoing ecumenical work of the Anglican Communion.

Section IV of 1998 produced a substantial report which contains some of the best thinking of the ecumenical leaders of the Communion at that time. Bishops who were assigned to Section IV included most of those who had been actively involved with particular ecumenical relationships, either by participating in one of the international dialogues or by their leadership at the local or regional level. The ecumenical partners were mostly in Section IV, and leadership was given by the then Director for Ecumenical Relations at the Anglican Communion Office, Canon David Hamid, and by coopted ecumenical staff from around the Communion.

During the second week of the 1998 Conference bishops and ecumenical partners met in sections and working groups. The methodology was to review all the international and regional work which had been done with these bilateral partners since the last Conference, and to prepare both a resolution and a section of the report giving an analysis of the progress, or lack thereof, in the dialogue, an identification of problems or areas for further work and a proposal for next steps. Staff worked with bishops to write the relevant portion of the report and to draft a resolution, which was then reviewed by the whole section before going to the plenary of the Conference in the third week.

Resolutions addressed each of the ecumenical relationships of the Anglican Communion and made telling assessments of the work of each of the dialogues. Such insights, gleaned from bishops who have actual experience of relationships with particular dialogue partners, and from those who may come from quite different contexts, steer the Anglican participants in those relationships for the next decade, and give a signal to dialogue partners as to how the fruits of dialogue are being received in Anglican churches. They may provide specific agenda items for Anglicans to bring to the table, or they may send a word of caution that a dialogue may be running too far ahead of the churches. An example is the detailed consideration that the bishops of Section IV gave to the various proposals for closer relationships between Anglican churches and churches of the Lutheran World Federation. The resulting Resolution IV.16 gave a steer to each of the regional developments and encouraged continuing international consultation.

An unfortunate situation which came about during the meeting of Section IV was that the work of the Anglican-Methodist International Commission was not able to be received as had been hoped. The Commission's report, 'Sharing in the Apostolic Communion' had been unanimously endorsed by a recent World Methodist Council meeting.[10] However, some Anglican bishops in the working group objected that the report had not been studied sufficiently by the Provinces. The resolution therefore recommended further work at the regional level, to the great consternation of Methodist ecumenical observers. The fact

---

[10] *Sharing in the Apostolic Communion* 1996. Online at http://www.anglicancommunion.org/media/102809/Sharing-in-The-Apostolic-Communion.pdf

that this report was not considered to be mature enough for endorsement by a Lambeth Conference demonstrates the complicated dance that ecumenical work needs to perform in the Anglican Communion: Provinces alone ought not to make ecumenical commitments which might have serious import without consultation with the Communion, and Lambeth Conferences alone cannot 'receive' ecumenical work without there having been consultation with the Provinces.

Lambeth Section IV also established some important principles for Anglican participation in the ecumenical enterprise. Resolution IV.1, endorsed by the whole Conference, has stood Anglican ecumenists in good stead ever since:

This Conference:

1. reaffirms the Anglican commitment to the full, visible unity of the Church as the goal of the Ecumenical Movement
2. encourages the further explication of the characteristics which belong to the full, visible unity of the Church (described variously as the goal, the marks, or the portrait of visible unity); and
3. recognises that the process of moving towards full, visible unity may entail temporary anomalies, and believes that some anomalies may be bearable when there is an agreed goal of visible unity, but there should always be an impetus towards their resolution and, thus, towards the removal of the principal anomaly of disunity.

In 2008 the ecumenical participants were part of the Bible study and Indaba groups throughout, but one day of the Indaba process was given particularly to ecumenical affairs.[11] The result of those conversations was Section E of the Reflections document. This consists of a mere fourteen paragraphs, and the insights are, to say the least, superficial. The usual commitments are made: to the full visible unity of the Church, to the Lund principle, to the need for a theological foundation for the ecumenical enterprise. Mention is made of some of the ecumenical partners with whom the Anglican Communion is in dialogue, but not of all, and there is scant detail. As the overall theme of 2008 was 'Equipping Bishops as Leaders in God's Mission', the link was made

---

[11] *Equipping Bishops As Leaders in God's Mission: Reports from and Reflections on the Fourteenth Lambeth Conference of Bishops of the Anglican Communion.*

between ecumenism and mission, between faith and order, life and work, at all levels of the Church's life.

Perhaps the greater contribution to the Lambeth Conference of 2008 was the contribution made by ecumenical participants to the plenary sessions. Cardinal Walter Kasper, President of the Pontifical Council for Promoting Christian Unity, addressed the bishops with a word of warning about the challenges of the present context. Cardinal Ivan Dias, prefect of the Congregation for the Evangelization of Peoples, spoke about Christian witness in the present context, and the inextricable link between evangelization and inculturation. Surely this is the first time that a Lambeth Conference has been addressed by two Cardinals! Brian McLaren, a Protestant pastor prominent in the Emerging Church movement, gave a slide presentation on changing contexts for evangelism.

But a singular opportunity was given to two of the ecumenical participants, Metropolitan Kallistos of Diokleia of the Ecumenical Patriarchate and the Very Revd Professor Iain Torrance of the Church of Scotland, when they were invited to offer closing reflections to the Conference. Both were forthright with both their praise and their criticism. Metropolitan Kallistos, while affirming that the bishops had in their Reflections clearly proclaimed 'Jesus Christ as the one and only Saviour of the whole world', wished that they could have made 'a firm and plain affirmation of Christian marriage'. Professor Torrance noted that the central issue for the Anglican Communion at the moment might not be human sexuality, but governance, and suggested that it address 'authority, subsidiarity and adiaphora, all under God'.[12]

I attended both of these Lambeth Conferences as a coopted staff person for the ecumenical work. My experience of each was very different. In 1998 I was working with Section IV, assigned to the working group tasked with considering relations with Lutherans and Methodists. This entailed taking detailed notes and working with a team of other staff and volunteers to draft the report and resolutions for the section, often late into the night. It was the experience of being in a working community, discerning together how best to write what would both reflect the conversation of the bishops accurately and to communicate to the wider Conference and to the Anglican Communion and

---

[12] Both speeches collected online in IASCER-Resolutions-arising-from-the-2008-meeting.pdf on www.anglicancommunion.org.

its ecumenical partners what the bishops were discerning about the ecumenical vision and the best paths to it. In 2008, as staff were not participants in the Bible studies and Indaba groups, the work consisted more of hosting the ecumenical guests. In that sense I came to know the ecumenical partners better than I had in 1998, where the work was primarily with the bishops.

On a personal level, I am still left with the strong feelings that were generated in the debate in plenary on Resolution I.10 in 1998. I sensed in the debate very strong and negative feelings. There was palpable tension. There was anger. Some bishops walked out in frustration. Some were shocked when the Archbishop of Canterbury, George Carey, stood to speak in the debate. I have since learnt that it is common for the Archbishops of Canterbury and York (Joint Presidents) to speak in debates in the Church of England General Synod, but it is not a common practice in many other churches, including my own, the Anglican Church of Canada. There was an escalating sense of danger to the unity of the Communion. I was left wondering if such an atmosphere was in fact suitable for the work of discernment of the will of the Holy Spirit.

By contrast, life at the 2008 Conference was much more serene. To a great degree, this was due to the presence and intentionality of the Archbishop of Canterbury, Rowan Williams, who seemed to hold it all together in his own person. To what extent the serenity was also due to the fact that some 200 bishops, mostly from certain churches in Africa, chose not to attend, cannot be determined. The intent, from the opening retreat through the Indaba process, was to build community, and according to most reports, that did in fact happen in the discernment circles. The problem was that there was not enough time for the bishops to move beyond the building of community to the task of deep discernment that would have led them into some common actions.

The present Archbishop of Canterbury, Justin Welby, and the Design Team have the experience of two very different approaches to the Lambeth Conference to consider as they prepare for the Lambeth Conference 2020. The need to meet, and to have sufficient time to form trusting relationships, is surely a prime imperative, particularly as the tensions in the Communion have increased rather than abated. At the same time, what is the desired outcome, what will the bishops take back to their churches? Can a means be found both to meet and to meet deeply, and to have sufficient time and trust to make well-informed decisions together? How can that happen across even more languages and cultures than before? And how would teaching from a Lambeth Conference now be received by the member churches of the Anglican Communion?

From an ecumenical perspective, what can other Christian World Communions hope for from the Conference of 2020? Will they gain a deeper understanding of how the Anglican family learns to listen to the Holy Spirit? Will they see Anglican ecclesiology put into practice and Anglican polity operating at its best? Will the various agreements reached in ecumenical dialogues have a fair hearing and evaluation? Will our ecumenical partners know that Anglicans remain deeply committed to the full visible unity of the Church?

16

Critical Solidarity: Roman Catholic Perspectives on the Lambeth Conference

Donald Bolen

1 Introduction

In an essay published not many years before the calling of the Second Vatican Council, the Anglican bishop Stephen Neill assessed the very limited prospect of deepening ecumenical ties with the Roman Catholic Church:

> All the recent pronouncements of the Roman Catholic Church make it quite clear that possible terms of union would involve for all other Christian communions the repudiation of their own past history, and total acceptance in every detail of Roman Catholic dogma . . . . There seems no likelihood that the Roman Catholic Church, now or in the future, will consider the modification of the terms of union that it offers.[1]

Many would have seen it that way at the Lambeth Conference of 1958, and with some grounds for doing so. But when Pope John XXIII became pope on 28 October 1958, calling a Council less than three months into his papacy and identifying the search for the unity of Christians as one of the Council's goals, the Anglican world began to take interest. It was seen as an encouraging development by then Archbishop of Canterbury Geoffrey Fisher. He had long been committed to fostering ecumenical relations and, nearing the end of his time as Archbishop of Canterbury, he travelled to Istanbul, Geneva and Rome. On the morning of 2 December 1960, Archbishop Fisher greeted Pope John in Rome with the words, 'Your Holiness, we are making history.'

---

[1] Stephen C. Neill, 'Plans of Union and Reunion, 1910-1948', in Ruth Rouse and Stephen C. Neill (eds), *A History of the Ecumenical Movement 1517-1948* (2nd edn, London: SPCK, 1967), p. 490.

In June 1960 Pope John agreed to the idea of setting up, among the preparatory commissions for the Council, a Secretariat for Promoting Christian Unity (SPCU), responsible for fostering relations with other Christian communities. In August 1962, when the SPCU sent out official letters to other Christian World Communions inviting them to send observers to the Council, the Anglican Communion was the first family of churches to respond. The presence of the Anglican observers at each of the four sessions of the Council, between October 1962 and December 1965, meant that the events and decisions which marked each of its sessions were regularly reported back to Anglican leaders, such that through the whole period of the Council, there was an accompanying reflection and discussion about the ecumenical implications of decisions taken there.[2]

The Second Vatican Council signalled the Catholic Church's endorsement of and entry into the Ecumenical Movement. Its Decree on Ecumenism (*Unitatis Redintegratio*) noted that the Ecumenical Movement was the work of the Holy Spirit, and set forward the principles that were to guide the Catholic Church's search for reconciliation between divided Christians and divided Christian communities. It identified theological dialogue, working together in pursuit of the common good, and spiritual ecumenism as principal means by which Christian unity was to be sought. By virtue of our common baptism into Christ, Christians could already recognize each other as brothers and sisters in Christ. Following upon and in conjunction with the ecclesiological foundations set forth in the Council's Dogmatic Constitution on the Church (*Lumen Gentium*), the Decree on Ecumenism acknowledged that elements of the Church founded by Jesus Christ were present in other churches and ecclesial communities, and that a relationship of imperfect communion even now existed between them and the Catholic Church. Furthermore, the Decree on Ecumenism noted that among those communions separated from the See of Rome at the time of the Reformation 'in which Catholic traditions and institutions in part continue to exist, the Anglican Communion occupies a

---

[2]　See Bernard C. Pawley (ed.), *The Second Vatican Council: Studies by Eight Anglican Observers* (Oxford: Oxford University Press, 1967); John R. H. Moorman (Bishop of Ripon), *Vatican Observed: An Anglican Impression of* Vatican II (London: Darton, Longman & Todd, 1967); id., 'Observers and Guests at the Council', in Alberic Stacpoole (ed.), *Vatican II by Those Who Were There* (London: Geoffrey Chapman, 1986), pp. 155–69; Donald W. Norwood, 'The Impact of Non-Roman Catholic Observers at Vatican II', *Ecclesiology* 10 (2014), pp. 293–312.

special place' (*Unitatis Redintegratio* §13). While not all of the decisions of the Council would have been pleasing to Anglican observers, its final texts were seen as a basis for dialogue.

All of this created a move away from the 'return' model of ecumenism that Stephen Neill described, and set a very different context for the Lambeth Conference of 1968. From that gathering to the present, the Catholic Church has been actively engaged in Lambeth Conferences. Popes have sent messages to each successive Conference. The SPCU – which in 1989 was renamed the Pontifical Council for Promoting Christian Unity (PCPCU) – has sent its leading officials, along with a team of observers, who have been welcomed to participate in the meeting. Roman Catholics have been asked to give presentations and have been engaged in the prayer and worship life of the gathering. And in various ways the official instruments of dialogue between the Anglican Communion and the Roman Catholic Church have had their work flow into and out of the Lambeth Conference.

The first part of this chapter will touch briefly on each of the Lambeth Conferences from 1968 onwards, setting them in the framework of Roman Catholic relations at the time and indicating some key developments at each from an ecumenical perspective. The second part of this chapter will offer five reflections on the helpfulness, significance and limitations of the Lambeth Conference as an instrument of unity within the Anglican Communion from a Roman Catholic perspective. The chapter will conclude with a brief appreciation of the Lambeth Conference as a key place for deepening Anglican–Roman Catholic relations.

2 Roman Catholic involvement in Lambeth Conferences from 1968 to 2008

In terms of Anglican–Roman Catholic relations, as already indicated, the 1968 Lambeth Conference was significantly shaped by the Second Vatican Council, but also by the visit of Archbishop Michael Ramsey to Rome in March 1966. Four major events formed that visit. The first was the dedication of the Anglican Centre in Rome, which would open in October of that year, and would become the residence for the representative of the Archbishop of

Canterbury in Rome. Secondly, the meeting of Archbishop Ramsey and Pope Paul VI in the Sistine Chapel. Pope Paul addressed the Archbishop saying: 'You rebuild a bridge, which for centuries has lain fallen between the Church of Rome and the Church of Canterbury: a bridge of respect, of esteem and of charity.'[3] Archbishop Ramsey noted: 'I greet you in my office as Archbishop of Canterbury and as President of the Lambeth Conference of Bishops from every part of the Anglican Communion throughout the world.'[4] He expressed his hope for increasing dialogue between Roman Catholic and Anglican theologians and added that dialogue might also be able to address practical matters of concern. Thirdly, a service of prayer was held at the Basilica of St Paul Outside the Walls, and at the end of the service the Pope and the Archbishop signed a Common Declaration. The Common Declaration called for a dialogue 'founded on the Gospels and on the ancient common traditions'. This was a decision to begin with what the two Communions held in common, and to build on those foundations.[5] Finally, at the end of the prayer service, before bidding each other farewell, Pope Paul placed his own archiepiscopal ring from Milan on the Archbishop's hand. It was a gesture which echoed Cardinal Mercier's dying gift to Lord Halifax, linking the proposed dialogue to that of the Malines Conversations in the 1920s; symbolically it spoke of respect and of the hope which characterized the visit and the dialogue it initiated.

Following Archbishop Ramsey's visit to the Holy See, a Joint Preparatory Commission was created to set up the contours of the forthcoming dialogue. The Commission met three times within less than a year and their work culminated in the Malta Report, completed in January 1968.[6] While not yet available to the public, it was part of the preparatory material given prior to the Lambeth Conference to all participants.

A team of seven Roman Catholics were among the sixty observers invited to take part in the conference (the first time a Lambeth Conference included ecumenical observers), and they were encouraged to participate in the work of

---

[3] 'Address by Pope Paul VI to the Archbishop of Canterbury', *The Archbishop of Canterbury's Visit to Rome, March 1966* (Westminster: Church House, 1966), p. 9.

[4] 'Address by the Archbishop of Canterbury to Pope Paul VI', *The Archbishop of Canterbury's Visit to Rome*, March 1966, p. 6.

[5] 'The Common Declaration by Pope Paul VI and the Archbishop of Canterbury Dr Michael Ramsey', Rome, Saint Paul Outside the Walls, 24 March 1966, in ARCIC, *The Final Report* (London: CTS/ SPCK, 1982), p. 118; available online at https://iarccum.org/doc/?d=20.

[6] Anglican-Roman Catholic Joint Preparatory Commission, *The Malta Report*, in ARCIC, *The Final Report*, pp. 108-16; available online at https://iarccum.org/doc/?d=1.

the three sections addressing faith, ministry and unity. The unity section spent time on Anglican–Roman Catholic relations, endorsing the Malta Report and approving the establishment of a bilateral dialogue. A subcommittee addressed the topic of Episcopacy, Collegiality and Papacy, topics that would be taken up by the Anglican-Roman Catholic International Commission (ARCIC), which began its work in January 1970.

A substantial report on the Lambeth Conference appeared in the SPCU's *Information Service*, the Secretariat's journal documenting Roman Catholic ecumenical engagement on an international level. In addition to carrying Pope Paul VI's encouraging message to the Conference, it included a word of gratitude from the observers 'for the considerable courtesy and consideration with which they were treated, for the degree to which their collaboration was enlisted and appreciated, and for the remarkable regard for the Roman Catholic Church and for ecumenical relations which was constantly evident in the Conference.'[7]

The extraordinary launch into relations between the Anglican Communion and the Roman Catholic Church that characterized the years immediately following the Council bore fruit in the initial work of ARCIC that had been completed by the next Lambeth Conference in 1978. ARCIC's agreed statements *Eucharistic Doctrine* (1971) and *Ministry and Ordination* (1973) had both claimed substantial agreement ('consensus, on questions where agreement is indispensable for unity' – *Ministry*, 17). Even *Authority in the Church* (1976) had made more progress than was anticipated, particularly on the relationship between primacy and conciliarity. This text suggested that Anglicans and Roman Catholics would each be enriched by the other's understanding of authority. It went on to note that 'primacy and conciliarity are complementary elements of *episcope*' (22) and that the 'general pattern of the complementary primatial and conciliar aspects of *episcope* serving the *koinonia* of the churches needs to be realised at the universal level' (23).

The Lambeth Conference 1978 gave a strong endorsement of ARCIC's work and in Resolution 33 it recognized 'in the three Agreed Statements of this Commission a solid achievement, one in which we can recognise the faith of our Church'. It further expressed the hope 'that they will provide a basis for

---

[7] *Information Service* 6 (1968), pp. 15–20, citing p. 20.

sacramental sharing between our two Communions if and when the finished Statements are approved by the respective authorities of our Communions'. Resolution 33 concluded with an invitation for ARCIC 'to provide further explication of the Agreed Statements in consideration of responses received by them' and asked authorities in the sponsoring churches to further consider the implications of the ARCIC statements in terms of 'a closer sharing between our two Communions in life, worship, and mission' (Resolution 33, #2–4).

However, the exceedingly positive ecumenical spirit which marked the 1968 Lambeth Conference had already passed, as some Anglican provinces had proceeded to ordain women to the priesthood, provoking a strong reaction on the Roman Catholic side. Archbishop Donald Coggan and Pope Paul VI had exchanged letters on the subject in 1975 and 1976, wherein the Pope had restated the Roman Catholic position that 'it is not admissible to ordain women to the priesthood' and that this 'new course taken by the Anglican Communion in admitting women to the ordained priesthood cannot fail to introduce into this dialogue an element of grave difficulty which those involved will have to take seriously into account'.[8] Only three Roman Catholic observers attended the 1978 Conference, with one of them, Bishop Cahal Daly, in an address to the Conference, highlighting Pope Paul's strong concern, and challenging 'what seems a prevailing tendency to regard the Roman Catholic Church's position on the ordination of women to the priesthood as unclear and somehow provisional'.[9] Daly's address was at least in part taking aim at the work of an ARCIC subcommittee on the subject, published just prior to the Lambeth Conference in the *Versailles Statement*.[10] Pope Paul VI, who had sent a letter to the Conference approving the theme of the ministry of the bishop, died during the Conference. In an extraordinary gesture of respect, the Anglican bishops invited the three Roman Catholic observers to celebrate a Requiem Mass for him, which was attended by all the Anglican bishops.[11]

The tensions between what ARCIC had achieved, on the one hand, and what the Roman Catholic Church saw as a significant obstacle to relations

[8] Letter of Pope Paul VI to Archbishop of Canterbury Most Reverend Dr Donald Coggan, 30 November 1975; available online: iarccum.org/doc/?d=465.

[9] *Information Service* 39 (I-II 1979), p. 21.

[10] Anglican-Roman Catholic Consultation on the Ordination of Women, *Versailles Statement* (3 March 1978); available online: iarccum.org/doc/?d=33. The statement was distributed to the Primates on 30 June before the Conference began. *The Times* published the complete statement on 27 July.

[11] *Information Service* 39 (I-II 1979), pp. 20–1.

in the decision of some Anglican provinces to move towards the ordination of women to the priesthood and episcopate, on the other hand, continued to deepen between Lambeth 1978 and Lambeth 1988. ARCIC I's *Final Report* had been published in 1982, with great expectation that it had produced results that would significantly change the shape of Anglican–Roman Catholic relations. On both Anglican and Roman Catholic sides, a significant process of reception began. The process of authoritative reception of major bilateral statements was a learning experience for both Communions.

On the Anglican side, consultation and deliberation in the provinces led to the publication of the *Emmaus Report*, detailing the results of those deliberations.[12] The Lambeth Conference of 1988 was the context in which the agreed statements of ARCIC I were received by the Anglican Communion, as recorded in Resolution 8. It recognized the documents on Eucharist and Ministry and their Elucidations (1981) 'as consonant in substance with the faith of Anglicans' and as offering 'a sufficient basis for taking the next step forward towards the reconciliation of our Churches grounded in agreement in faith'. In turn, it welcomed the two documents on authority (the 1976 statement on authority was complemented by *Authority in the Church II*, 1981, and the *Elucidation on Authority*, 1981) 'as a firm basis for the direction and agenda of the continuing dialogue on authority'.

On the Roman Catholic side, the working out of the respective roles of the SPCU and the Congregation for the Doctrine of the Faith was one part of the learning process in the reception of a bilateral agreement. An authoritative response to ARCIC's *Final Report* had been long anticipated, but nothing had been published in time to coincide with the Lambeth Conference of 1988.

In addition to the work of ARCIC, there had been significant positive steps in Anglican–Roman Catholic relations during the years between the Lambeth Conferences of 1978 and 1988. Of note was the momentous visit of Pope John Paul II to England in 1982 – the first such visit ever – and the Common Declaration signed by the Pope and Archbishop of Canterbury Robert Runcie during that visit. Their Common Declaration commended the work of ARCIC I for study and response, and called forth a new phase of dialogue, mandated to address 'the outstanding doctrinal differences which still separate us, with

---

[12] Anglican Consultative Council, *The Emmaus Report: A Report of the Anglican Ecumenical Consultation 1987* (London: Church House Publishing, 1987).

a view towards their eventual resolution; to study all that hinders the mutual recognition of the ministries of our Communions; and to recommend what practical steps will be necessary when, on the basis of our unity in faith, we are able to proceed to the restoration of full communion'.[13]

Another step that suggested a deepening in Anglican–Roman Catholic relations came with Archbishop Runcie's participation in and response to the 1986 ecumenical and interfaith gathering in Assisi for peace. At Lambeth 1988, Runcie noted, 'Whether we like it or not, there is only one Church, and one bishop who could have effectively convoked such an ecumenical gathering. At Assisi I saw the vision of a new style of Petrine Ministry – an ARCIC primacy rather than a papal monarchy. Pope John Paul welcomed us – including other Anglican primates ... then he became in his own words "a brother among brothers"'.[14]

After Lambeth 1988 Archbishop Runcie wrote to Pope John Paul II, relating how he had asked at the Conference: 'Could not all Christians come to reconsider the kind of primacy exercised in the Early Church, a "presiding in love" for the sake of the unity of the Churches?' Pope John Paul responded, acknowledging 'the signs of openness to fuller communion with the Catholic Church which were evident at several points in the Conference', but noting that the ordination of women to the priesthood in some Anglican provinces and the Lambeth 1988 decision to recognize the right of provinces to ordain women to the episcopacy 'appears to ... effectively block the path to the mutual recognition of ministries'.[15]

The period between the Lambeth Conferences of 1988 and 1998 saw both high and low points in terms of Anglican–Roman Catholic relations, and a shift towards what interim steps were possible in those relations. In 1991 the Catholic Church's response to the *Final Report* was finally published, and for those who had hoped for major steps forward as a result of the work of ARCIC I, the response was sobering. It acknowledged 'the achievement of points of convergence and even of agreement which many would not have thought possible before the Commission began its work' and affirmed that the

---

[13] *Information Service* 49 (II/III 1982), pp. 46–7; available online at iarccum.org/doc/?d=22.

[14] *The Truth Shall Make You Free: The Lambeth Conference 1988. The Reports, Resolutions and Pastoral Letters from the Bishops* (London: Church House Publishing for the Anglican Consultative Council, 1988), p. 21.

[15] Cf. *Information Service* 70 (II 1989), pp. 59–60 for both letters.

Final Report 'constitutes a significant milestone not only in relations between the Catholic Church and the Anglican Communion but in the ecumenical movement as a whole'.[16] But its explanatory note asked for further clarity on several points. A sub-commission of ARCIC offered a response in the form of *Clarifications* in 1993, which took steps towards addressing the concerns of the 1991 response, but major breakthroughs were not in the wings.[17]

Archbishop of Canterbury George Carey paid an official visit to Pope John Paul II in 1996; the Common Declaration they signed took note of differences regarding the ordination of women as priests and bishops, then proceeded to state: 'In view of this, it may be opportune at this stage in our journey to consult further about how the relationship between the Anglican Communion and the Catholic Church is to progress.' The remainder of the Common Declaration moved towards taking the steps in common mission which are currently possible: 'Whenever they are able to give united witness to the Gospel they must do so, for our divisions obscure the Gospel message of reconciliation and hope.'[18]

Many Anglicans responded favourably to the invitation in Pope John Paul's Encyclical *Ut Unum Sint* (1995) to engage in a 'patient and fraternal dialogue' about the papacy (no. 96).[19] But there was a strongly negative response to the Congregation for the Doctrine of the Faith's use of the example of the invalidity of Anglican Orders in the Congregation's commentary on Pope John Paul's Apostolic Letter *Ad Tuendam Fidem*, clarifying various levels of authoritative teaching in the Catholic Church. The release of that text just weeks prior to Lambeth 1998 evoked considerable tension. Lambeth 1998 nonetheless welcomed Cardinal Edward Cassidy, the President of the PCPCU, to preach at their ecumenical vespers celebration, and he offered a strong message of what had been achieved over thirty years of dialogue. The goal of full visible unity began to look more like a distant horizon, as the focus shifted towards a practical living out of the degree of communion currently shared.

---

[16] *Information Service* 82 (I 1993), pp. 47–51; available online at iarccum.org/doc/?d=18.
[17] *Clarifications of Certain Aspects of the Agreed Statements on Eucharist and Ministry, A Statement by the Co-Chairmen of ARCIC, 1993;* available online at https://iarccum.org/doc/?d=19.
[18] *Information Service* 94 (I 1997), pp. 20–1; available online at iarccum.org/doc/?d=24.
[19] *May They All Be One: A Response of the House of Bishops to* Ut Unum Sint (London: Church House Publishing, 1997).

Resolution IV.23b of 1998 reflected that practical turn in welcoming a 'proposal for a high-level consultation to review Anglican-Roman Catholic relationships in the light of the agreements reached and the "real though imperfect communion" already existing between the churches of the Anglican Communion and the Roman Catholic Church'. This proposal led to a gathering in May 2000 in Mississauga, Canada, of thirteen pairs of bishops (most were Primates or Presidents of Episcopal Conferences) from regions where Anglicans and Roman Catholics lived side by side in significant numbers. The bishops studied the ARCIC corpus together – by that point including four agreed statements from ARCIC II – and at the end of their time together issued a statement entitled 'Communion in Mission', which noted 'the very impressive degree of agreement in faith that already exists', and 'that our communion together is no longer to be viewed in minimal terms' (paragraphs 4 and 5).[20] They called for the establishment of a commission of bishops who would oversee the preparation of a text that would identify all that was held in common by Anglicans and Roman Catholics, would promote the reception of ARCIC's statements, and would encourage 'strategies for translating the degree of spiritual communion that has been achieved into visible and practical outcomes'. (12)

This call led to the establishment of a new body, the International Anglican-Roman Catholic Commission for Unity and Mission (IARCCUM). By the time of Lambeth 2008, after a long and circuitous journey, IARCCUM had produced the text *Growing Together in Unity and Mission*.[21] The first part of the text identified the level of agreement reached in nine areas that had been addressed by ARCIC, while the second part of the document asked what those areas of agreement made possible in terms of joint prayer, common witness, common mission in the service of the common good and joint study. *Growing Together in Unity and Mission* was distributed to all those gathered at the Lambeth Conference 2008 and consolidated a shift in Anglican–Roman Catholic relations in the direction of the Lund Principle: to do all things together except where deep differences require that we act separately.

---

[20] *Communion in Mission* (20 May 2000); available online at iarccum.org/doc/?d=26.
[21] IARCCUM, *Growing Together in Unity and Mission: Building on 40 Years of Anglican-Roman Catholic Dialogue*, 2007, available online at https://iarccum.org/doc/?d=32.

The lead up to Lambeth 2008 was marked by tensions within the Anglican Communion over the ordination of a person living in an openly acknowledged committed same-sex relationship and the authorization of public Rites of Blessing for same-sex unions in two Anglican provinces. A situation resulted where communion between bishops and between provinces was impaired. The Anglican Communion established a process that led to the Windsor Report, a text that reflected on the Instruments of Communion within the Anglican Communion. The text was well received by the PCPCU because it adopted an ecclesiology of communion as its foundation, consistent with the ecclesiology that had been set forth in ARCIC's agreed statements. PCPCU president Cardinal Walter Kasper noted that 'the consequences which the Report draws from this ecclesiological base are also constructive', especially 'the interpretation of provincial autonomy in terms of interdependence' and Windsor's various proposals for strengthening the bonds of communion between Anglican provinces.[22]

The 2008 Lambeth Conference had two principal points of focus: strengthening Anglican identity, and equipping bishops for their role as leaders in mission. Two hundred bishops chose not to attend the Lambeth Conference, and the internal tensions within the Communion were a concern to the Roman Catholic observers. Cardinal Kasper communicated the Roman Catholic Church's hope that the Anglican Communion would stay together and that the Anglican and Roman Catholic communions could continue their journey towards unity. The Roman Catholic delegation was the largest it had ever sent to a Lambeth Conference. Kasper had noted years earlier that tensions between or within churches should not lead to a distancing of ecumenical partners, but rather, 'precisely when there are problems there is ever greater need of dialogue'.[23]

The 'indaba' process at Lambeth 2008, led by Archbishop Rowan Williams, geared the Conference not towards resolutions but towards listening, dialogue and a strengthening of relations within the Communion. It was a moving experience to be a part of the Roman Catholic delegation and to witness the

---

[22] Letter of Cardinal Walter Kasper to Archbishop of Canterbury Dr Rowan Williams, 17 December 2004; available online at iarccum.org/doc/?d=466.

[23] Kasper, as cited in Donald Bolen, 'Walking Together Amid the Difficulties' (2007); available online at http://www.vatican.va/roman_curia/pontifical_councils/chrstuni/angl-comm-docs/rc_pc_chrstuni_doc_20070130_bolen-anglicans_en.html.

effectiveness of a patient process geared towards reconciliation. It was not a moment in time when Anglican–Roman Catholic relations were going to make great leaps forward, but the attitude that governed our relations there, as in the years leading up to the Conference, was shaped by a deep and long ecumenical friendship. It was an opportunity to assess candidly the situation that we found ourselves in and to ask how we could live our real but incomplete communion as fully as possible at that moment in time.

3 Roman Catholic perspectives on the Lambeth Conference

The above sketch of the place of the Lambeth Conference in Anglican–Roman Catholic relations over the past fifty years provides a framework for asking how Roman Catholics, committed to full visible unity, might view the Lambeth Conference as an instrument of unity. What follows are five brief reflections on the strengths and limitations of the Lambeth Conference from the perspective of a Roman Catholic dialogue partner.

First, relative to the Roman Catholic Church's other dialogue partners, the structure of the Lambeth Conference is familiar; we recognize a kindred spirit here. We know that the Archbishop of Canterbury's ministry does not directly parallel that of the Bishop of Rome; that the outcomes of a Lambeth Conference differ from those of a Roman Catholic synod of bishops or ecumenical council; that Anglican provinces and Roman Catholic episcopal conferences exercise authority and make decisions differently. But in each of those instances, there are also significant similarities. The Lambeth Conference expresses the global aspect of Anglicanism, and as a gathering of bishops in an episcopally led communion of churches, the gathering does resemble an ecumenical council in many ways. The fact that the world's Anglican bishops all come together periodically, that they do so at the invitation of the Archbishop of Canterbury, that they pray together, and seek the guidance of the Holy Spirit in order to discern together, this is all familiar to Roman Catholics and makes ecclesiological sense to us. In this instance, the experience of being in real but incomplete communion has the feel of being a welcome guest at a gathering of a family of churches to whom we are closely related.

Second, participation as observers in the Lambeth Conference, just as Anglican participation in Roman Catholic synods or councils, is exceedingly worthwhile. The great welcome that Anglicans have extended to their ecumenical guests, and the generous invitation to participate in important ways in their dialogue and discernment, deepens the bonds of friendship. The presence of observers at moments of internal tension, while difficult, may be even more important. For most of our separated past, when decisions were made that deepened the gap between us, they were made in isolation. Today, Anglicans and Roman Catholics have a wide range of instruments and structures for formal and informal communication, dialogue and cooperation. Still, relations are necessarily affected by significant changes or developments in the ecclesial life or teachings of a dialogue partner. When part of that shared faith is called into question, when a dialogue partner is in the midst of a serious discernment process, when the nature of the relationship between the churches of the Communion is under discussion, then it creates major challenges for a dialogue partner. It is especially valuable to be actually present and to witness efforts to foster unity and discern God's will at such times. The fact that the Anglican Communion has on various occasions engaged the Roman Catholic Church and its other dialogue partners in their discernment process is a still greater privilege. Consultation with ecumenical dialogue partners prior to making decisions which will significantly affect our relations remains something of a long-term goal for all churches in the Ecumenical Movement, and Anglicans are leaders in that regard.

Third, and closely related to the previous point, Lambeth Conferences have a long history of giving significant attention to the Lord's prayer and will that his disciples be one. The 1908 Lambeth Conference had noted that 'there can be no fulfilment of the Divine Purpose in any scheme of reunion which does not ultimately include the great Latin Church of the West, with which our history has been so closely associated in the past, and to which we are still tied by many bonds of common faith and tradition'. The 1920 Lambeth Conference had made 'an Appeal to all Christian People' to seek unity, adding, 'Should the Church of Rome at any time desire to discuss conditions of reunion we should be ready to welcome such discussions.' With the Second Vatican Council, that Appeal of 1920 found a willing dialogue partner, and each of the Lambeth Conferences since 1968 has given strong witness – often in new and creative ways – that Anglicans have made relations with Roman Catholics (and other ecumenical partners) a priority. That has not kept the Anglican Communion or individual provinces from making decisions that significantly complicate our ecumenical relations, but it has meant that from the Anglican side the desire to remain in the conversation has been a constant.

Fourth, Anglicans have a strong tradition of rigorous, honest and robust discussion, and the Lambeth Conference epitomizes that tradition. Conflicting voices are heard, difficult situations are grappled with, structures of consultation are taken seriously, and the voices of those on the peripheries are brought into the discussion. The Lambeth Conference is a place where the diversity of the Anglican Communion finds expression, and where the gathered bishops pray together, dialogue with each other and trust that the Holy Spirit is going to find a way forward. In the process, the bonds of affection across the Anglican Communion are strengthened. Even when things get messy, the deep honesty of the Lambeth Conference is attractive.

Fifth, the Lambeth Conference often makes Roman Catholics restless, because it lacks the definitive authority to hold the centre. The assembled bishops can say, after a prolonged process of discernment amid significant tensions: 'This is where we believe the Holy Spirit is leading us,' but they cannot ensure that Anglican Churches around the world act upon what has been agreed. The value placed by Anglicans on diocesan and provincial autonomy, from the perspective of Roman Catholic dialogue partners, results at times in differences in matters of faith and morals where we believe unity to be essential, and a resulting lack of clarity concerning the bonds of ecclesial communion. The questions raised by Roman Catholics to Anglicans in §56 of ARCIC's 1999 Agreed Statement *The Gift of Authority* speak to this concisely:

> We have seen that instruments for oversight and decision making are necessary at all levels to support communion. With this in view the Anglican Communion is exploring the development of structures of authority among its provinces. Is the Communion also open to the acceptance of instruments of oversight which would allow decisions to be reached that, in certain circumstances, would bind the whole Church? When major new questions arise which, in fidelity to Scripture and Tradition, require a united response, will these structures assist Anglicans to participate in the sensus fidelium with all Christians? To what extent does unilateral action by provinces or

dioceses in matters concerning the whole Church, even after consultation has taken place, weaken *koinonia*? Anglicans have shown themselves to be willing to tolerate anomalies for the sake of maintaining communion. Yet this has led to the impairment of communion manifesting itself at the Eucharist, in the exercise of *episcope* and in the interchangeability of ministry. What consequences flow from this? Above all, how will Anglicans address the question of universal primacy as it is emerging from their life together and from ecumenical dialogue?

Roman Catholics can appreciate that Anglicans would have a parallel critique of their structures and processes and that our own desire to safeguard unity can sometimes end up closing off debate prematurely. Indeed the questions posed by Anglicans to Roman Catholics in §57 of *Gift of Authority* are aimed precisely in that direction.

4 Conclusion

Some years ago I had the opportunity to study the debates in the Lower Houses of Convocation of the Church of England concerning the possible calling of what would become the Lambeth Conference of 1867. The debate was intense, with some arguing for the need for a structure to assist with the maintaining of orthodoxy, and others cautioning strongly against 'Romish tendencies'. This tension, deeply embedded in Anglicanism, is also present in ARCIC and is a healthy and necessary one. ARCIC's *Elucidations on Authority in the Church* (1981) ends on this note: 'Anglicans sometimes fear the prospect of over-centralization, Roman Catholics the prospect of doctrinal incoherence. Faith, banishing fear, might see simply the prospect of the right balance between a primacy serving the unity and a conciliarity maintaining the just diversity of the koinonia of all the churches' (para. 8). Paragraphs 56 and 57 of *The Gift of Authority*, referenced above, deepen that discussion. Anglicans and Roman Catholics continue to speak about authority, at least in part because we have important things to learn from each other on the topic; and what we learn there may well provide important insights for the broader Ecumenical Movement.

Some of that mutual learning will only take place when we enter into a deeper relationship. ARCIC's *Authority II* put it this way: 'Contemporary discussions of conciliarity and primacy in both communions indicate that we are not dealing with positions destined to remain static. We suggest that some difficulties will not be wholly resolved until a practical initiative has been taken and our two Churches have lived together more visibly in the one *koinonia*' (*Authority II*, para. 33). Sharing the experience of each other's conciliar gatherings is a step along the way to that lived *koinonia*, and resonates with Pope Francis' recent calls for a culture of encounter. May the Lambeth Conference continue to be a helpful instrument of unity within the Anglican Communion, and continue to be a place of encounter and learning through the practice of welcoming observers, as we walk the path that we trust will one day, in the power of the Holy Spirit, draw us into full visible communion.

17

Remembering our Future at the Lambeth Conference

Victoria Matthews

St Augustine of Hippo is the ancient figure who is most accessible to the twenty-first century. His early boyhood coincided with the brief reign of the Emperor Julian the Apostate, but by the time of his adulthood and the writing of his seminal works, his world – the world of the Roman Empire in North Africa – was crashing around him. In two of his great works, *Confessions* and *The City of God*, Augustine addresses the role of memory in the Christian journey.[1] He also names anticipation as a process of 'remembering forward' so that when what we have anticipated comes to pass, if what we imagined was reasonably on target, we recognize the imagined event. It is the purpose of this short personal contribution to demonstrate how the Lambeth Conference assists and to a degree instructs the bishops of the Anglican Communion both to remember the great Christian tradition from whence they have come and to anticipate an Anglican future together.

In 1988 the Archbishop of Canterbury, Robert Runcie, asked the attending bishops to bring their dioceses with them. The bishops brought stories and assisted each other to better understand the importance of context. In 1998, the Archbishop of Canterbury, George Carey, introduced the faces of some of the suffering churches and some of the joyful churches, often one and the same, by means of stories told by selected bishops across the communion of churches.

[1] *Confessions*, Augustine's spiritual autobiography, was written between AD 397 and 400. Available translations include *Saint Augustine, Confessions*, trans with an Introduction by R. S. Pine-Coffin (Harmondsworth: Penguin, 1961) and *Saint Augustine, Confessions*, trans with an Introduction and Notes by Henry Chadwick (Oxford: Oxford University Press, 1991). *The City of God* was published in AD 426: *Augustine, City of God*, ed. David Knowles, trans. Henry Bettenson (Harmondsworth: Penguin, 1972).

Filmed by Trinity Wall Street Communications, these videos introduced the assembled bishops at Lambeth to the various dioceses across the globe and allowed the corporate episcopal memory to include the extremely challenging circumstances of bishops from various parts of the Anglican Communion. The videos were shown in the morning and evening either before or after worship in the 'St Augustine' and 'St Columba' marquees. In 2008 the Archbishop of Canterbury, Rowan Williams, asked the bishops to share their lives as bishops and also the lives of their dioceses to such an extent that bishops would begin to understand better where each other lived, proclaimed and incarnated the Gospel. The presence of members of the Melanesian Brothers and Sisters on the chaplaincy team in 2008 invoked the memory of the seven Melanesian Brothers who were martyred in 2003. These same chaplaincy team members joined in the singing the Litany at the final Eucharist in Canterbury Cathedral while carrying the names of those seven martyrs through the long Cathedral aisle to the Chapel of the Modern Martyrs. This was arguably the moment that defined the 2008 Conference and lifted the assembled bishops above their postures and fractions into the presence of the Risen and Ascended Christ. Australian Bishop, John Harrower, offered this description: 'We were transfixed in solemnity and sorrow, yet held in resurrection hope and joy as the Melanesian Brothers and Sisters processed. ... What a profound inspiration and challenge. Give us grace and strength, Lord, to follow you in everything. Amen. Amen. Amen.'[2]

These initiatives by three very different Archbishops of Canterbury, and the respective Lambeth Conference Design Groups of the three Lambeth Conferences, were of great importance to the subsequent memory of three successive Lambeth Conferences and helped shape their life. While these memories did not bear the fruit of formal resolutions, they succeeded in deepening the sense of community and identity of each of those recent Lambeth Conferences. Simply put, they enlarged and enhanced the memory of the assembled bishops. The first Lambeth Conference assembled on 24 September 1867 at 11.00 am in the Chapel of Lambeth Palace, London, for a service of the Holy Communion. Bishop Gregory Cameron states that the first Lambeth Conference 'marks the self-conscious birth of the Anglican

---

[2] Lambeth Conference 2008 Report to the Diocese of Tasmania by Bishop John and Gayelene Harrower. See http://www.anglicantas.org.au/lambeth/

Communion. Bringing together a college of bishops from around the world, the Conference was a step unprecedented outside the Roman Catholic Church in the second millennium of Christianity, as bishops of three traditions within Anglicanism were consciously gathered together in what we can now recognize as a "Christian World Communion." The seventy-six constituted just over half of the bishops who had been invited as being in communion with the See of Canterbury, and they now began to understand themselves as belonging to one family.[3]

The anamnesis of the Eucharist is the recollection of the Lord's Passion, Resurrection and Ascension which, together with the words of institution, bring the community gathered around the Communion Table into the presence of Christ in both his earthly life and at the Messianic banquet of the Kingdom. At the Lambeth Conferences the various eucharistic liturgies, used at the daily celebrations, demonstrated both the increasing enculturation of the Provincial Prayer Books and the deep unity which transcends the Provincial and diocesan differences across the continents. We were brought into the presence of the living Christ. There is no aspect of the Christian life that is not shaped by both the memory of what has been and the anticipation of what is yet to be. Each Lambeth Conference for the past 150 years has strengthened the corporate memory of the Communion while also encouraging a renewed sense of mission as the bishops and their spouses look ahead in anticipation to returning to their diocese and sharing a vision that has emerged in prayer, study and conversation over the days and weeks. The 2008 Lambeth Conference highlighted this sharing among the bishops with the introduction of daily Indaba groups in addition to the Bible studies. The Indaba groups consisted of approximately forty bishops while the Bible studies were smaller and more intimate. In both instances important lasting relationships emerged – due, in part, to the formation of common memories and a renewed sense of mission.

As the Bishop of Hippo, Augustine knew at first-hand the grief of a church facing rapid change and certain attack. His world was crumbling around him when he published *The City of God Against the Pagans* (usually called

---

[3] Gregory K. Cameron, 'Locating the Anglican Communion in the History of Anglicanism', in Ian S. Markham, J. Barry Hawkins IV, Justyn Terry, Leslie Nuñez Steffensen (eds), *The Wiley-Blackwell Companion to the Anglican Communion* (Malden, MA and Oxford, UK: Wiley-Blackwell, 2013 (Kindle e-edition)), p. 3.

simply *The City of God*) in 426. The decline and fall of the Roman Empire was progressing and Rome's failure to enforce its rule, maintain its military forces and territories, together with the challenge of disease and rapid religious change, all in the presence of invading barbarian armies, caused widespread suffering and in some quarters despair. Between 376 and 476 there was an immense decrease in the power exercised by Rome. It was into this situation that Augustine wrote as he imagined an enduring city, *The City of God*. This city was distinctly different from the challenged world in which he lived, yet related to it. Thus while Augustine is dismissive of claims that human affection for the things of this world is the same as humanity's love for God, the two loves are related because of memory.

> What do I love when I love my God? Not physical beauty, or the splendour of time; not the radiance of earthly light, so pleasant to our eyes; not the sweet melodies of harmony and song; not the fragrant smell of flowers, perfumes, and spices; not manna or honey; not limbs such as the flesh loves to embrace. These are not the things I love when I love my God. And yet when I love him, I do indeed love a certain kind of light, a voice , a fragrance, a food, an embrace; but this love takes place in my inner person, where my soul is bathed in light that is not bound in space; when it listens to sound that time never takes away; when it breathes in a fragrance which no breeze carries away; when it tastes food which no eating can diminish; when it clings to an embrace which is not broken when desire is fulfilled. This is what I love when I love my God.[4]

In the encounter with the holy, all previous and future experience is transformed. The question is how expansive or controlled we will permit the memory of this life to be, as it engages and submits to the higher encounter with the maker of heaven and earth, the eternal and undivided Trinity. Will the bishops at the Lambeth Conference seek to include or exclude the experience of others from very different parts of the Anglican Communion in their acts of remembrance? Augustine is very clear that memory is always experienced in the present. We remember and recall the past but the act of remembering is always in the present. It doesn't matter whether the memory recalls sadness, gladness, grief, suffering, fear or raging desire, the act of remembering makes

---

[4]   Augustine of Hippo, *Confessions*, Book X, 6.

the memory present and real. In the liturgy the Church proclaims: 'Christ has died; Christ is risen; Christ will come in glory,'[5] and immediately we find ourselves present to the presence of Christ in his death and resurrection. It is truly extraordinary yet also of the heart of the Gospel that bishops as well as clergy and laity from around forty-four member churches, numbering over eighty-five million souls in over one hundred and sixty-five countries, share a common memory which shapes and guides their mission and ministry. Thus it is obvious that reinforcing the episcopal corporate faith memory of the Lord Jesus Christ is foundational for anticipating a shared Christ-centred faithful future together. Augustine describes our extraordinary memory as 'a great field or spacious palace, a storehouse for countless images of all kinds'.[6] Elsewhere, in an especially rich image, Augustine calls the memory the stomach of the mind.[7] Not so much a human stomach, for our stomach is too economical, I suspect, but a bovine one that chews over memories as a cow chews its cud. It is all part of the ascent to God and when the bishops gather at Lambeth Conferences it is a shared memory which is recalled and nurtured. For Augustine memory is neither a passive chamber nor a museum. Indeed memories undergo transformation, in the process of reflection and reconsideration. Remembered objects, events, sounds and smells can be reordered and 'placed ready to hand'. How we place a memory is part of how we order our lives.

In Augustine's younger years the Christian Gospel was a negative memory from which he was determined to flee. Then, after further exploration and considerable travel, he met Bishop Ambrose of Milan who transformed his opinion of Christ. While his initial interest in listening to Bishop Ambrose was to assess and even critique the famed orator's rhetoric, Augustine gradually moved from being a Manichean to being a sceptic to becoming a Christian disciple. 'To Milan I came, to Ambrose. ... To him was I led by You, Lord, that by him I might knowingly be led to You. That man of God received me as a father ... I hung on his words attentively.'[8]

---

5   *A New Zealand Prayer Book-He Karakia Mihinare o Aotearoa* (the Anglican Church in Aotearoa, New Zealand and Polynesia, Te hahi Mininare ki Aotearoa ki Niu Tireni, Ki Nga Moutere o te Moana Nui a Kiwa: Genesis Publications, 2005 edition), p. 438.
6   Augustine, *Confessions*, X. 11.
7   Ibid., X.xiv.
8   Augustine, *Confessions*, X.xiii.

As it is the intention of this chapter to demonstrate that St. Augustine of Hippo's extraordinarily helpful insights into memory and human imagination can assist us in considering the role and intention of the Lambeth Conference, certain questions are worth pondering. Is it possible to use the act of memory as a means of healing the Anglican Communion's brokenness for our future together? Is it within the scope of the Lambeth Conferences to reorder corporate episcopal memory and in particular to so recall our identity as the Body of Christ that this calling takes precedence over Provincial and individual bishop's disagreements?

Bishops attend the Lambeth Conference with a variety of states of mind. Some arrive excited and open to whatever is presented. Others are sceptical of what will be taught and shared; and still others come looking for proof that the Anglican Communion is in her demise. Yet what actually happens at a Lambeth Conference has much to do with the leading of the Holy Spirit, the forming of relationships and the recognition of the presence of Christ in those one might have hoped to be able to dismiss. In recent years there has been considerable concern that the role of human experience has threatened to replace the authority of Scripture and tradition in much Anglican discourse. It is worth recalling that while most of Augustine's *On Christian Doctrine* was written prior to his writing of his *Confessions*, the work *On Christian Doctrine* was not completed until AD 426, after Augustine had written his *Confessions*. The juxtaposition of these two great works, *Confessions* and *On Christian Doctrine*, suggests that Augustine could not write Book IV of his doctrinal work before recalling and reflecting upon his personal faith narrative. Bishop Augustine of Hippo had to chew the cud of his own Christian journey before he could articulate Christian doctrine. In the Anglican Communion one endeavour since the 2008 Lambeth Conference has been 'continuing Indaba' where bishops from diverse Provinces are given the time and space to tell their stories and to practise listening to one another.[9] For the bishops involved, the exercise of 'Continuing Indaba' both enlarged their existing understanding of the diversity of the Anglican Communion of churches and created a new memory which could be carried forward to future Lambeth Conferences.

---

[9] 'The aim of Continuing Indaba is to enable Anglicans worldwide to live reconciliation by facing our own conflicts, celebrate our diversity and difference and so become agents of reconciliation in the world.' See https://continuingindaba.org/process/

St Cyprian, Bishop of Carthage, who was martyred in the mid-third century, was the first to write of collaborative ministry.[10] He taught (and continues to teach us) that there is one episcopate of which every bishop has a share. Thus central to the exercise of episcopal ministry is collaboration. It is part of the role of the Lambeth Conference to bring this home, and to remind the bishops of their calling. It requires three bishops to ordain, or consecrate, a bishop. This rule underlines the truth that the making of a bishop is the act of the Church and never solely an individual decision or act on the part of one bishop or even a single diocese. Provinces have different requirements and practices about how an election or appointment of a bishop is confirmed. Where there is an electoral college or an electoral synod, the other bishops of the internal Province or of the whole Province are required to vote to give consent. In some ecclesiastical Provinces the entire General Synod membership is required to vote to confirm the choice of a new bishop. What this means is that the corporate memory of the Provincial church is called upon to test the authenticity of a bishop-elect's calling. Furthermore it is important for those persons nominating or confirming, to recall what makes a good bishop, when the time comes to vote. Any diocese choosing a new bishop, after experiencing a lengthy episcopal ministry from the previous incumbent, understandably finds it difficult to think outside the memories of their own experience. In Provinces where there is gender inclusion in episcopal selection, after hundreds of years of exclusively male episcopal leadership, reimagining the episcopate is necessary to a degree, but not to the extent of throwing out all the learnings and insights of the centuries. When newly consecrated bishops reach a Lambeth Conference there is a process of recognition and acceptance. The new bishop looks at the hundreds of other bishops milling about in the registration areas and residences of the campus of the University of Kent, England, and gradually begins a process of self recognition. 'Yes, I do recognise myself in this setting and community; I am different yet the same.'

In his handbook of episcopal ministry, *Becoming a Bishop*, Paul Avis writes:

A philosophy of cooperation, collaboration and mutual assistance is intrinsic to Christianity. The gospel implies a preferential option, so to

---

[10] Cyprian, *De Lapsis* and *De Ecclesiae Catholicae Unitate*, trans. and ed. M. Bévenot, S. J. (Oxford: Clarendon Press, 1971), p. 65.

speak, for working together on the part of its ministers, a preferential option that is based, not only on collegiality in a common ministerial calling, but ultimately on our baptismal solidarity in the body of Christ. ... When bishops, who have the highest public profile of all ministers, demonstrate mutual respect among themselves, seek to benefit from one another's wisdom and act in harmony, they give warm encouragement to the faithful who look to them for an example and, at the same time, they effectively commend the faith to those looking on from outside the Church who may come to see the humility and generosity of the bishop as pointers to the character of Christ.[11]

In these words we witness once again the possibility of both strengthening and possibly reordering a memory of collaboration among bishops and, for those new to the Lambeth Conference which is always the majority of the bishops present, the creation of new memories as the insights and learnings are taken on board.

Paul Avis goes on to name and address the personal, collegial and communal aspects of episcopal ministry.[12] Every bishop, whether a member of a diocesan college of bishops, or as a diocesan bishop in a large Province who may only gather with other bishops of the Province once a year, exercises personal, collegial and communal aspects of episcopal ministry. But it is not until the bishops of the Anglican Communion gather at the Lambeth Conference that a vision of the enormity of the calling and the intimacy of the ministry is truly brought home to them. On a personal level one hears of heartache and struggle as well as of high aspirations and wide-reaching visions. On the world stage there are stories of countries torn by famines and other natural disasters, severe interfaith tension and violence and attempted genocide. And within the church there is the ever-present tension between those seeking to be agents of change and those whose priority is to uphold what is identified as the tradition of the one holy catholic and apostolic Church.

In recent years the conviction, held by some, that the speed of change in our churches has gotten out of hand, has caused certain fractures in the Communion. The sad outcome, in some locations, is the decision to refuse to recognize one another because of a Provincial stance on sexual ethics or the

---

[11] Paul Avis, *Becoming a Bishop; A Handbook of Episcopal Ministry* (London and New York: Bloomsbury T&T Clark, 2015), p. 76.
[12] Avis, *Becoming a Bishop*, pp. 79–81.

failure of certain Primates to respect diocesan and Provincial boundaries. It is hard to exaggerate the pain that this has caused. In 2008 the bishops, spouses and staff of that Lambeth Conference were saddened and impoverished by of the decision of almost 200 bishops not to attend. Those non-attendees were sorely missed and it was clear, because of memories of earlier Lambeth Conferences, that those who did gather were far less representative of the diversity of the Anglican Communion than was desirable. Bishops who had been present in 1998 naturally spent time remembering conversations and collegial ministry with those who were not in attendance in 2008, either because of their own decision or because they had been directed by their Province or Archbishop to not attend. In 1998 when bishops of the female gender first graced Lambeth Conference with their presence, there was also some angst beforehand. The generosity and graciousness of the majority of bishops, ecumenical representatives as well as Anglican bishops, assisted in easing the tension. African bishops who were yet to seriously consider ordaining women to the diaconate and priesthood, let alone the episcopate, nevertheless recognized the women 'in purple' as colleagues and addressed them unfailingly as 'Bishop'. A new reality emerged because healthy practices were being formed and fear was cast out by Christian love. 'For just as the body is one and has many members, and all the members of the body, though many, are one body, so it is with Christ. For with the one Spirit we were all baptized into one body – Jews or Greeks, slaves or free – and we were all made to drink of one Spirit' (1 Cor. 12. 12-13, NRSV).

One of the most important roles of the Lambeth Conference is for the bishops to consult with one another. It was an opportunity to consult with one another that was at the heart of the request of the Provincial Synod of the United Church of England and Ireland in Canada, meeting in Montreal in September 1865, to the Archbishop of Canterbury, Charles Thomas Longley. The Canadian bishops were unsettled by the recent decisions of Queen Victoria's Privy Council, as well as by the schismatic situation in the diocese of Natal. Their request was for 'a national synod of the bishops of the Anglican Church at home and aboard'.[13] Not all agreed that this was a good idea and some bishops, including the Archbishop of York, refused to attend

---

[13] R. T. Davidson, *The Five Lambeth Conferences* (London: SPCK, 1920), p. 3.

the 1867 Lambeth Conference. Nevertheless the invitations went out and the first Lambeth Conference was convened for the purpose of collaborative ministry and consultation. Seventy-six bishops accepted the Archbishop of Canterbury's invitation and attended. The Lambeth Conference was a newborn infant, not yet fully formed. However the importance of bishops coming together to pray, to share their hopes and concerns for their respective churches, and to pass a few resolutions meant that they were accepting of the Conference having a certain moral authority that would grow and in time be recognized further afield. 'By the time Archbishop Archibald Tait came to invite the bishops for the second Conference which was convoked in 1878, his letter of July 19, 1877 ... was confidently addressed "to the Bishops of the Anglican Communion".'[14]

By 1920 the sixth Lambeth Conference, presided over by Archbishop Randall Davidson, had 252 bishops present. There was a sufficiently confident sense of mission (related strongly to the growth of the British Empire) that the Lambeth Conference could and did issue its 'Appeal to all Christian People' which set out a vision of the Anglican Churches moving towards full visible union with churches of other traditions. Using a slightly amended version of the Chicago–Lambeth Quadrilateral, the document called on other churches to move towards 'reunion'. The four articles of the Chicago–Lambeth Quadrilateral were claimed to be a sufficient basis on which an appeal could be made for God's blessing on Home Reunion. The first three articles are remarkably clear: a) The Holy Scriptures of the Old and New Testaments, as 'containing all things necessary for salvation'; b) The Apostles' Creed as the Baptismal Symbol and the Nicene Creed, as the sufficient statement of the Christian faith; c) The two sacraments ordained by Christ Himself – Baptism and Supper of the Lord – ministered unfailing with the words of institution and of the elements ordained by Him. But the fourth article, pertaining to the historic episcopate locally adapted, is more expectant of evolution, even interpretation. Both memory and imagination are clearly required for faithful interpretation: d) 'The historic Episcopate, locally adapted in the methods of its administration to the varying needs of the nations and peoples called of God into the Unity of his Church'. In the 1920 'Appeal to all Christian People'

---

[14] Cameron, 'Locating the Anglican Communion in the History of Anglicanism', p. 14.

the episcopate was the only order of the threefold ministry of deacons, priests and bishops that was expressly mentioned.

> May we not reasonably claim that the Episcopate is the one means of providing such a [universally accepted] ministry? It is not that we call in question for a moment the spiritual reality of the ministries of those Communions which do not possess the episcopate. On the contrary, we thankfully acknowledge that these ministries have been manifestly blessed and owned by the Holy Spirit as effective means of grace.[15]

It is not surprising that this fourth Article has been the most debated with some believing that it challenges apostolic succession and others seeing the historic episcopate as a stumbling block to ecumenical relations. It did prove to be insurmountable in the discussions between the Anglican Church of Canada and the United Church of Canada which ended in 1975.[16]

It is clear, therefore, that of the four Instruments of Communion claimed and upheld by the Anglican Communion – the Archbishop of Canterbury, the Primates' Meeting, the Anglican Consultative Council and the Lambeth Conference – the Lambeth Conference is the cornerstone of the Anglican Communion. Over the 150-year history of the Conference a corporate memory has been formed, reports written, consultation undertaken and earlier decisions revisited, revised and even reversed. The Conference is where imagination meets reality and the resulting shared vision is given expression. This evaluation of the Lambeth Conference is greatly assisted by the fact that Conference resolutions are not binding unless adopted by the member churches of the Communion. It is also strengthened by the fact that, in the same way that the bishops invited to Lambeth Conferences in recent decades have been asked to bring their diocese with them, so bishops at the end of each Conference carry home a new or renewed sense of the Anglican Communion. Just as Augustine of Hippo was transformed by encountering

---

[15] http://www.Anglicancommunion.org/resources/document-library/lambethconferences, Lambeth Conference 1920, Resolution 9 – Reunion of Christendom, also known as Appeal to all Christian People.

[16] In 1943 the General Synod of the Church of England in Canada convened a union committee and initiated a conversation with all Christian churches seeking to discuss and promote reunion. In time this became a focused conversation with the United Church of Canada with discreet ecumenical observers. However, in 1975 the House of Bishops of the Anglican Church of Canada released a 'Statement of Counsel' which stated that the Plan of Union was unacceptable. The Dialogue has been re-established and continues.

the holiness and wisdom of Bishop Ambrose of Milan, bishops from the breadth of the Anglican Communion are challenged as well as encouraged by episcopal colleagues from radically different cultures and parts of the world. It is at the Lambeth Conference that the memory of the Church is reawakened and the future of the Church of God is anticipated. Thus may future Lambeth Conferences be occasions when bishops recognize that they are called both to embody memory and tradition and to anticipate and welcome the coming of Christ's reign on earth.

Index of Subjects

Note: (1) Only the more substantial discussions of the major topics are indexed because they continually recur. (2) 'Anglicanism', 'Anglican Communion', 'bishop' 'church', 'communion' (in the sense of ecclesial, sacramental communion) and 'Lambeth Conference' are not indexed because the whole book discusses these topics. (3) Neither has it proved feasible to index the Lambeth Conference(s) by date as the references to some of them are innumerable.

Index of Names

CPSIA information can be obtained
at www.ICGtesting.com
Printed in the USA
LVHW081556030122
707742LV00007B/44